Pearl S. Buck was one of the most renowned, interesting, and controversial figures ever to influence American and Chinese cultural and literary history – and yet she remains one of the least studied, honored, or remembered. Peter Conn's *Pearl S. Buck: A Cultural Biography* sets out to reconstruct Buck's life and significance, and to restore this remarkable woman to visibility.

Born into a missionary family, Pearl Buck lived the first half of her life in China and was bilingual from childhood. Although she is best known, perhaps, as the prolific author of *The Good Earth* and as a winner of the Nobel and Pulitzer prizes, Buck in fact led a career that extended well beyond her eighty works of fiction and nonfiction and deep into the public sphere. Passionately committed to the cause of social justice, she was active in the American civil rights and women's rights movements; she also founded the first international adoption agency. She was an outspoken advocate of racial understanding, vital as a cultural ambassador between the United States and China at a time when East and West were at once suspicious and deeply ignorant of each other.

In this richly illustrated and meticulously crafted narrative, Conn recounts Buck's life in absorbing detail, tracing the parallel course of American and Chinese history and politics through the nineteenth and twentieth centuries. This "cultural biography" thus offers a dual portrait: of Pearl Buck, a figure greater than history cares to remember, and of the era she helped to shape.

Pearl S. Buck

Pearl S. Buck

A CULTURAL BIOGRAPHY

Peter Conn

PUBLISHED BY THE PRESS SYNDICATE OF THE UNIVERSITY OF CAMBRIDGE
The Pitt Building, Trumpington Street, Cambridge CB2 1RP, United Kingdom

CAMBRIDGE UNIVERSITY PRESS
The Edinburgh Building, Cambridge CB2 2RU, UK   http://www.cup.cam.ac.uk
40 West 20th Street, New York, NY 10011-4211, USA   http://www.cup.org
10 Stamford Road, Oakleigh, Melbourne 3166, Australia

First published 1996
Reprinted 1996 (three times)
First paperback edition 1998
Reprinted 1998 (twice)

Typeset in Bembo

A catalogue record for this book is available from the British Library

Library of Congress Cataloguing-in-Publication Data is available

ISBN 0-521-56080-2 hardback
ISBN 0-521-63989-1 paperback

Transferred to digital printing 2002

For Jennifer Kyung
and the five thousand other Welcome House children

For David, Alison, and Steven, too

And for Terry
with gratitude
for thirty years of love and friendship, loyalty and passion

Contents

List of Illustrations   ix

Preface: Rediscovering Pearl Buck   xi

Acknowledgments   xxiii

1: Missionary Childhood   1

2: New Worlds   45

3: Winds of Change   86

4: *The Good Earth*   121

5: An Exile's Return   163

6: The Prize   208

7: Wartime   253

8: Losing Battles   297

9: Pearl Sydenstricker   334

Epilogue: Green Hills Farm   377

Notes   383

Index   451

Illustrations

1. Carie Stulting and Absalom Sydenstricker at about the time of their marriage in 1880.   10
2. Map of China in the early twentieth century.   12
3. An itinerant storyteller in a northern Chinese village.   25
4. The Sydenstricker family in about 1901.   30
5. Twelve-year-old Pearl Sydenstricker, standing behind Grace, teaches English and hygiene to a class of Chinese girls.   38
6. Carie, Grace, and Pearl Sydenstricker, shortly before Pearl's enrollment at Randolph-Macon Woman's College in 1910.   43
7. Pearl Sydenstricker, president of her class at Randolph-Macon Woman's College, stands behind the "even post" in this 1913 picture.   49
8. Pearl's graduation picture, which appeared in the 1914 edition of *Helianthus*.   52
9. Lossing Buck and Pearl Sydenstricker on their wedding day, May 30, 1917.   60
10. Farmers threshing wheat in northern China.   64
11. One of the gates in the Nanking city walls at about the time Pearl and Lossing Buck moved to the university (1919).   69
12. Pearl and her daughter Janice in Nanking, about 1930.   116
13. The Chinese people according to Robert Ripley's "Believe It or Not" (May, 1932).   130
14. A woodcut from a Chinese edition of *Shui Hu Chuan*.   138
15. Pearl Buck at the "even post" during her visit to Randolph-Macon in 1933.   156
16. Richard Walsh on his visit to China in 1933.   161
17. Pearl Buck, Margaret Sanger, and Katharine Houghton Hepburn at a dinner in Sanger's honor in 1935.   182
18. The Walshes with their new sons, Richard and John.   189

19. Pearl Buck at Green Hills farm in the mid-1930s.   190
20. Eleanor Roosevelt and Pearl Buck at Constitution Hall, April, 1936. 191
21. A scene from the MGM production of *The Good Earth* (1937).   193
22. Luise Rainer and Paul Muni in the MGM production of *The Good Earth* (1937).   195
23. Pearl Buck and Enrico Fermi during the Nobel Prize ceremonies in Stockholm, December, 1938.   213
24. Pearl Buck receiving the Nobel Prize from King Gustavus V in Stockholm, December, 1938.   214
25. Pearl Buck in a studio photograph taken shortly after she won the Nobel Prize.   218
26. Pearl Buck and Mrs. Y. H. Wei, treasurer of the Chinese Women's Relief Association (January, 1940).   228
27. Pearl Buck and Wendell Willkie launching the United China Relief campaign, March, 1941.   244
28. Pearl Buck and Senator Arthur Capper.   251
29. Pearl Buck and Channing Tobias at a Greater New York Inter-Racial Rally, June, 1942.   262
30. Pearl Buck and Jesse Jones, U.S. Secretary of Commerce, June, 1942.   267
31. Pearl Buck and a group of Chinese-American supporters during a break in her testimony before the House Committee on Immigration and Naturalization, May, 1943.   275
32. Green Hills Farm.   283
33. Carol Buck in the early 1940s.   284
34. Pearl Buck in one of the libraries she added to Green Hills Farm.   292
35. A page from Pearl Buck's FBI file.   301
36. Pearl Buck and Mrs. Vijaya Lakshmi Pandit, April, 1948.   311
37. Pearl Buck in a portrait photograph taken by Clara Sipprell in the 1940s.   321
38. Pearl Buck with Welcome House children, parents, and friends in the early 1950s.   327
39. Pearl Buck and Eleanor Roosevelt in 1956.   339
40. Pearl Buck and President John F. Kennedy at a White House dinner, April, 1962.   347
41. Harvard philosopher Ernest Hocking.   351
42. Pearl Buck and Ted Harris.   357
43. Pearl Buck and one of the Welcome House children in the late 1960s.   361
44. Pearl Buck and other honorary degree recipients at Rutgers University, June, 1969.   367

Preface: Rediscovering Pearl Buck

THIS BOOK BEGAN at a picnic.

Every year, on the first Saturday in June, hundreds of the families who have adopted children through an agency called Welcome House gather in a state park north of Philadelphia for a day of games and barbecues and annual reunions. The families look different from most. The children come from all over the world: from Asia and Eastern Europe, from Central and South America, from every region of the United States. Tinicum Park becomes, for a day, a pint-sized United Nations, exploding with children – from two weeks old to teenagers, white, black, and every color in between. It is an unforgettable sight.

My wife, Terry, and I attended our first Welcome House picnic in 1973, when we had begun to think about adopting a child. After three biological children, we had decided that we had some obligation to find room for one of the world's homeless boys or girls. We had also found much joy in the children we had, and we thought (quite accurately, as it turned out) that another child would add to our joy. We started the process, and after the usual months of waiting and anxiety, we met our new two-year-old Korean daughter, Jennifer Kyung, when her plane arrived at Kennedy Airport on February 4, 1975.

The rest, as they say, is history; or her story. But it is not the story in this book. This book is about Pearl Buck, the woman who in 1949 founded Welcome House, the first international, interracial adoption agency in the United States.

When Terry and I first approached Welcome House, I could have written everything I knew about Pearl Buck on a three-by-five index card. I knew that Buck was the author of *The Good Earth,* a book I had read in high school, though I had trouble recalling many of the details. (I dimly remembered a scene in which a peasant woman gave birth over a bucket and then went back to work.) I also knew that Buck had won the Nobel Prize for literature, though I didn't know exactly when, and I had traveled long enough in advanced literary circles to know that Buck's prize was not at all respectable. Finally, I had a vague impression that Buck was the daughter of Protestant missionaries, but I had no idea what that might actually mean.

Over the years that followed, Terry and I kept in close touch with Welcome House, working as volunteers and even serving on the board. In spite of myself, I was tempted by an increasing interest in Pearl Buck. I met a number of people who had known her, and who had obviously been changed for the better by the relationship. I discovered that Welcome House was only one of a dozen major projects Buck had initiated in support of children's welfare and interracial understanding. Frankly, Terry and I were touched by the extraordinary effort Buck had made to combine a literary life with a commitment to human service. After all, how many successful writers or intellectuals ever go beyond the occasional painless gesture, the sanctimonious petition or letter, and actually spend their time and money trying to do some social good?

Still, I kept my distance from Buck as a possible subject; she seemed too risky an investment. A smug consensus has reduced Pearl Buck to a footnote – a judgment, I hasten to add, in which I had routinely concurred. As recently as 1989, I published a 600-page history of American literature, in which I found room for everyone from the seventeenth-century Puritan preacher Urian Oakes to the twentieth-century proletarian propagandist Giacomo Patri, but I never mentioned Pearl Buck. Then, as I learned more about Buck's prodigious productivity, both as writer and humanitarian, I was less convinced by the received wisdom. Pearl Buck's disappearance from the American cultural scene was not self-explanatory.

To begin with, this was a woman who had written over seventy books, many of them best-sellers, including fifteen Book-of-the-Month Club selections. She had worked in virtually every genre of writing: novels, short stories, plays, biography, autobiography, translations (from the Chinese), children's literature, essays, journalism, poetry. However steeply she had fallen from critical favor, she had in fact won the Nobel Prize in literature (with Toni Morrison, she is one of only two American women ever to do so), and a Pulitzer, and the Howells Medal, and election to the National Academy and Institute of Arts and Letters, and a dozen honorary degrees.

Her novels continue to be read around the world, in English and in scores of translations. Buck's novels can still be found in villages and isolated farmhouses in Tanzania, New Guinea, India, Colombia. A friend of mine who served in the Peace Corps read her first Pearl Buck story, a disintegrating paperback copy of *Imperial Woman*, while she was living in a hut in Malawi.

In a word, Pearl Buck was one of the most popular novelists of the twentieth century. This in itself would be reason enough to look at her life and work more closely. Not long ago, critic Cary Nelson usefully observed: "We should take it as axiomatic that texts that were widely read or influential need to retain an active place in our sense of literary history, whether or not we happen, at present, to judge them to be of high quality."[1] Pearl Buck perfectly exemplifies a writer who once loomed large on our cultural landscape, and whose disappearance has damaged our historical understanding.

Discussing the 1930s, one of Buck's most productive decades, historian Lawrence Levine has made a similar point. Levine reminds us that a study of popular arts is necessary to any cultural history that would presume to fullness. "One does not have to believe," Levine writes, "that aesthetically Superman rivals Hamlet or that Grant Wood compares to Michelangelo to maintain that Superman and Wood potentially have much to tell us about the Great Depression, that they therefore merit the closest examination, and that they won't necessarily be simple to fathom."[2]

Ironically, if predictably, neither Cary Nelson nor Lawrence Levine, despite their enthusiasm for searching out the forgotten places of American culture, ever mentions Pearl Buck. Nonetheless, her career abundantly confirms the validity of their thesis. Whatever the aesthetic claims of Buck's novels and stories, her once-remarkable prominence makes her indispensable to any account of America's twentieth-century intellectual and imaginative life. Beyond that, however, I will argue in the following chapters that quite a lot of Buck's fiction and nonfiction is strong enough to command a fresh appraisal on its own merits. The biographies she wrote of her mother and father, for example, are unparalleled accounts of the strange and terrible vocations pursued by generations of missionaries in China. Not long before he died, I asked John Hersey, also a missionary child, for his opinion of Buck's writing. Hersey wrote me: "As a China 'mishkid,' I still, to this day, reverberate with pity and horror to the memory of some of the images" in those books.[3]

Buck's fiction broke new ground in subject matter, especially in her representations of Asia, and above all in her portraits of Asian women. In 1992, I attended a conference at which the Chinese-American writer Maxine Hong Kingston saluted Buck for making Asian voices heard, for the first time, in Western literature. By representing Chinese characters with "such empathy and compassion," Kingston said, Buck "was translating my parents to me and she was giving me our ancestry and our habitation."[4] More recently, Toni Morrison looked back on her early reading of Buck's novels and said, with affectionate irony: "she misled me . . . and made me feel that all writers wrote sympathetically, empathetically, honestly and forthrightly about other cultures."[5]

Pearl Buck was, as historian James Thomson has recently reminded us, "the most influential Westerner to write about China since thirteenth-century Marco Polo."[6] Thomson's assessment is at once indisputable, familiar, and yet, upon reflection, astonishing. Never before or since has one writer so personally shaped the imaginative terms in which America addresses a foreign culture. For two generations of Americans, Buck invented China.

AMERICANS HAVE FOUGHT three Asian wars in the last fifty years. More recently, armed combat has been followed by economic competition: since the late 1970s, half-a-dozen Asian nations have been the sites of unprecedented development in manufacturing and trade. In addition, within the United States itself, Asians make up the fastest-growing ethnic populations; Asian and Asian-American immigrants and native-born citizens now number over six million people, a doubling in ten years. Americans are beginning to realize that their future is entangled with Asia.

Nevertheless, amid pious invocations of multiculturalism, a shrinking world, and the imminent arrival of the Pacific Century, the peoples of Asia and the West continue to view each other through veils of cliché and misunderstanding. At such a moment in political and cultural history, Pearl Buck's stories should be a subject of increasing relevance and even urgency. Whatever the strengths or limits of her Asian images, she was a pioneer, introducing American readers to landscapes and people they had long ignored.

Her stories of China were based on her own experiences and observations as a missionary daughter. Her parents were an ill-matched pair of Southern Presbyterians named Absalom and Carie Sydenstricker. Pearl was born in West Virginia, while her parents were on a home leave, but she was taken to China at three months old and lived there most of the next forty years. She grew up bilingual, speaking and reading both English and Chinese. In her own favorite metaphor, she described herself as "culturally bifocal." At the same time, from her earliest days, she felt herself homeless in both her countries, an outsider among people different from herself.

Unlike almost every other American of her generation, Pearl Buck grew up knowing China as her actual, day-to-day world, while America was the place of conjecture and simplified images. Furthermore, almost uniquely among white American writers, she spent the first half of her life as a minority person, an experience that had much to do with her lifelong passion for interracial understanding.

She went to college in the United States, at Randolph-Macon Woman's College in Virginia, but returned to China immediately after graduation. Shortly after going back to China, she married her first husband, the agricultural economist J. Lossing Buck, and began a family. For several years, the couple lived in the town of Nanhsuchou (Nanxuzhou) in rural Anhwei (Anhui) province. Buck published her first stories and novels, including *The Good Earth,* while still living in China.★

In the early 1930s, with China torn by civil war, Japanese invasion, and mounting anti-foreign violence, she moved to the United States, buying a dilapidated eighteenth-century farmhouse in Bucks County, north of Philadelphia. The place was called Green Hills Farm, and it served as home and headquarters for several decades of activity. Here she continued to write, to raise the seven children she adopted, and to manage the various organizations she founded to address the problems of ethnic hatred and to help displaced and disadvantaged children.

Throughout her American years, Pearl Buck was one of the leading figures in the effort to promote cross-cultural understanding between Asia and the United States. In 1941, for example, she and her second husband, Richard Walsh, founded the East and West Association as a vehicle of educational exchange. The association became a target of McCarthyism and expired in the early 1950s. In addition, for over a decade Buck and her husband published the magazine *Asia,* which had a substantial influence on American opinion about East Asia. In the early 1940s, Buck and Walsh led the national campaign to repeal the notorious Chinese exclusion laws. Finally, throughout World War II, despite her close association with Chinese resistance to Japanese aggression, Buck was one of the few Americans who spoke out strongly against the U.S. internment of Japanese-Americans.

Both in Asia and the United States, Buck devoted much of her time and money to the welfare of children. In particular, she worked for children who were mentally or physically disabled or were disadvantaged because of their race. She founded Welcome House because existing adoption agencies considered Asian and Amerasian children to be unadoptable. In forty-five years, Welcome House has placed over five thousand of these children in American homes.

In 1950, the year after she created Welcome House, Buck published a book called *The Child Who Never Grew,* a story about her retarded daughter, Carol. The book was a landmark. Specifically, it encouraged Rose Kennedy to talk publicly about her retarded child, Rosemary. More generally, it helped to change American attitudes toward mental illness. In 1964, Buck set up a foundation in her own name, which has provided medical care and education for over twenty-five thousand Amerasian children in a dozen Asian countries.

In terms of the invidious sexual division of labor in our society, Pearl Buck's special concern for children may have been labeled as characteristically female. It was, more accurately, humane, and it was sadly prophetic. The World Health

★For a note on the spelling of Chinese proper names, see page xxi.

Organization recently estimated that ten million children under the age of five die each year – thirty thousand every day, more than one thousand every hour – from disease, violence, or hunger. What most of these children have in common is poverty: whether they are born in Somalia, Bangladesh, Brazil, or Pennsylvania. These were the lives that Pearl Buck tried to save.

Along with her efforts in children's welfare, Buck was also active throughout her adult life in the American civil rights movement. From the day she moved to the United States in 1934, she was a regular contributor to *Crisis,* the magazine of the National Association for the Advancement of Colored People, and to *Opportunity,* published by the National Urban League. Walter White, longtime executive secretary of the NAACP, said at a 1942 Madison Square Garden rally that only two white Americans understood the reality of black life, and both were women: Eleanor Roosevelt and Pearl Buck.

Buck served on the Urban League board and was an active trustee of Howard University for many years. She received an honorary degree from Howard in 1942, and responded with an important address on the complex issue of black patriotism in the early days of World War II. Throughout the 1940s, Buck associated herself with such writers as W. E. B. Du Bois in opposing British colonialism. Buck's friendships in the 1930s and 1940s included Paul and Eslanda Robeson. In 1949, Buck and Eslanda co-authored a book called *American Argument,* a dialogue on American racism. Years and even decades before most white intellectuals had even noticed racial injustice, Pearl Buck made major contributions to the American struggle for civil rights.

Buck's efforts on behalf of equality included tireless support for women's rights. She promoted modern birth control and called her friend Margaret Sanger "one of the most courageous women of our times," a person whose name "would go down in history" as a modern crusader for justice. In the 1930s and 1940s, Buck also spoke out repeatedly in support of an Equal Rights Amendment for women, at a time when opposition to it included the majority of organized women's groups.

As a highly visible proponent of international understanding and of civil rights for women and African-Americans, Pearl Buck inevitably attracted the hostile curiosity of FBI Director J. Edgar Hoover. Buck's FBI file, which was initiated as early as 1937, reaches nearly three hundred pages, of which a little over two-thirds has been declassified. (I am still appealing for release of the other material.) The paltry gossip and innuendo in these pages would be amusing if it were not outrageous, a sad reminder of the paranoia that has infected America's domestic politics for over half a century.

HOW DOES A WOMAN of this magnitude and range slip away from our national consciousness? She has not exactly disappeared. Rather, as one reader of an earlier draft of this book shrewdly put it, she has been "hidden in plain sight," obscured beneath a caricature that belies her complexity and her achievement. She has become a durable, one-woman punch line, trapped in some version or other of the old joke, "If Pearl Buck is the answer, then what is the question?"

In the years after World War II, Buck's literary reputation shrank to the vanishing point. She stood on the wrong side of virtually every line drawn by those who constructed the lists of required reading in the 1950s and 1960s. To begin with, her principal subjects were women and China, both of which were regarded as peripheral and even frivolous in the early postwar years. Furthermore, she preferred episodic plots to complex structures and had little interest in psychological analysis. In addition to all that, she was not a felicitous stylist, and she even displayed a taste for formulaic phrases. Needless to say, none of this endeared her to that vast cultural heartland stretching from the East River to the Hudson.

On the other hand, she told exciting stories, she created a gallery of memorable characters, and her vivid images of Asia in war and peace broadened the reach of American fiction. Many of her books contain narrative and descriptive passages of considerable drama, powerful scenes of work, warfare, ceremony, childbirth, and poverty that manage to transcend the often commonplace prose in which they are presented. And, whatever their literary merits and defects, her novels, short stories, and essays regularly raised unsettling questions about the racial and sexual status quo.

In the pages that follow, I will not claim that Pearl Buck was the author of unjustly suppressed masterpieces. I will argue, on the other hand, that a dozen or so of her books, mostly from the 1930s and 1940s – I am thinking of the biographies of her parents, *The Exile* and *Fighting Angel;* her autobiography, *My Several Worlds;* a number of the China books, including *The Mother, First Wife and Other Stories, Sons, Dragon Seed, Imperial Woman,* and *Kinfolk;* and one or two of the books she wrote about America, including *This Proud Heart* – ought to be valued more highly than they are. In addition, her collection of feminist essays, *Of Men and Women,* which was once compared to the work of Virginia Woolf, should be part of contemporary discussions of gender in America.

A list such as that – note that I did not mention *The Good Earth,* which is quite a special case – makes up a considerable achievement. To be sure, she wrote too much, and too quickly. Her later work, in general, is consistently less interesting. Buck has been damaged by a kind of aesthetic Gresham's law, in which her bad books have driven her entire body of work out of circulation.

She was also the victim of political hostility, attacked by the right for her active civil rights efforts, distrusted by the left because of her vocal anti-Communism. Beyond that, she undoubtedly suffered because of her gender: more often than not, it was her male rivals and critics who declared that her gigantic success only demonstrated the bad judgment of American readers – especially women readers, who have always made up the majority of Buck's audience. (In the course of gathering material for this book, I have corresponded with upwards of 150 librarians and archivists around the country. Fully a dozen of them have told me that Pearl Buck was their mother's favorite writer. Fathers are never mentioned.)

Given the influence of her writing and the sheer breadth of her accomplishments, it seems reasonably clear that some reconsideration is past due. Yet, in spite of the assorted renovations and second thoughts that have restored other writers to a measure of academic respectability and public attention, Pearl Buck remains largely neglected. This book – based in part on documents and manuscripts that have not previously been available – represents an effort to reclaim Buck's life and work.

I have called this book a cultural biography, and I should explain what that term means. I have tried to situate Pearl Buck's career in the many contexts that are needed to understand her development and her significance. This has involved a continuous act of negotiation between her life and the social and political circumstances that surrounded her. Consequently, along with Buck's biography and writing, readers will find in these pages a good deal of information about both Chinese and American history and literature.

Since she lived for so many years in China, and spoke and read Chinese, Buck had a unique vantage point as a witness to the making of the modern Chinese nation. She was caught up in the Boxer Uprising of 1900, the 1911 Revolution, and the civil wars of the 1920s and 1930s. She knew personally some of the men and women who participated in the "science and democracy" movement and the May Fourth movement. She took part in the debates over Confucianism, and was a sympathetic observer of the Chinese struggle to emancipate women. All of these subjects are described in the following pages.

Similarly, Buck's American years, from the mid-1930s to her death in 1973, can only be illuminated by reference to a further list of cultural subjects: the history of American attitudes toward China; the controversy over imperialism and the debate over immigration; the problematic status of popular culture; the American civil rights and women's rights movements; the witch-hunts of the McCarthy period.

Finally, a large cast of characters appears in this book. At one time or another in the course of her eighty years, Buck's friends and adversaries included Sinclair Lewis, Margaret Mead, James T. Farrell, Chiang Kai-shek and Mme. Chiang, Theodore Dreiser, Margaret Sanger, Edgar Snow and Helen Foster Snow, Lin

Yutang, Eleanor Roosevelt, Winston Churchill, Alaine Locke, Will Rogers, Charles Lindbergh, Hu Shih, Rose Kennedy, John Kennedy, Oscar Hammerstein, II, Indira Gandhi, James Yen, Owen Lattimore, Henry Luce, Christopher Isherwood, and Jawaharlal Nehru, among many others.

James Michener, who served on the original Welcome House board of directors, recently recalled his long association with Pearl Buck: "She was a spokesman on all sorts of issues: freedom of the press, freedom of religion, the adoptability of disadvantaged children, the future of China, especially the battle for women's rights, for education. If you followed in her trail, as I did, you were put in touch with almost every major movement in the United States – intellectual, social, and political."[7]

In writing this biography, I, too, have been following in Pearl Buck's trail. I have spent several days roaming through the Virginia and West Virginia countryside where her parents grew up and where she was born. I have talked with dozens of people who knew her, among them her younger sister, the late Grace Yaukey, several of her children, some of her neighbors in Nanking (Nanjing) in the 1920s and 1930s, a number of missionaries who worked in the China field, and a variety of Chinese and American scholars.

In the summer of 1993, my wife and I traveled to China as the guests of Nanjing University, where Buck taught in the 1920s. Terry and I visited Buck's childhood home in Chinkiang (Zhenjiang), and we made a trip into Anhwei province, to the town of Nanhsuchou, the setting of *The Good Earth*.

In Nanhsuchou, Terry and I spent an afternoon with a dozen aging Chinese Presbyterians, men and women in their seventies and eighties, all of whom were quite familiar with the name Pearl Buck. In the exchange of gifts that followed tea, one elderly woman gave us a clipping from the local newspaper. It was a story about Pearl Buck that had appeared in June, 1992, on the hundredth anniversary of Buck's birth.

On several occasions during our visit, Terry and I were told that Chinese scholars and students are exhibiting a renewed interest in Pearl Buck. When we came back from Anhwei province to Nanking, for example, we spent several evenings with Liu Haiping, the distinguished dean of the School of Foreign Studies at the University of Nanjing. During one dinner, Liu argued provocatively that Buck is the only American writer whose work is, in part at least, a product of Chinese culture. As such, she provides an almost unique case study in the complexity of cultural identity.

Beyond that, many young Chinese regard Buck's novels as a valuable historical record – a "treasure trove," in Liu Haiping's phrase – of China's rural life in the early twentieth century.[8] I have recently received a letter from a group of scholars in Chengdu, in Szechuen (Sichuan) province, which confirms Liu's opinion. These men and women, a group called De Heng Fan, are translating Buck's novels into Chinese. "Through [these books]," they write, "we understand the Chinese farmers' hardship, struggle and happiness before the establishment of the People's Republic of China."

In the past couple of years, there have also been a few signs of renewed interest in Pearl Buck in the United States and Europe. In the spring of 1992, Buck's hundredth birthday was marked by a major symposium at Randolph-Macon Woman's College, and the papers from that event have recently been published. In 1993, public television broadcast a widely applauded biography of Buck, called "East Wind, West Wind." More recently, Buck was the subject of a documentary on Belgian national radio. Perhaps, somewhat belatedly, this remarkable woman is being restored to a measure of greater visibility on both sides of the world. This biography is another step in that restoration.

As I have tried to suggest in these prefatory pages, Pearl Buck has several claims on our interest. She lived a richly eventful life on two continents, through years that spanned the remaking of culture and society in both Asia and America. Her career traced a path from late imperial China to the Nobel Prize to America's mid-century struggles for civil rights. Sometimes by choice and sometimes involuntarily, she took part in a number of military and ideological revolutions.

Her life and writing helped to redefine the idea of a woman's place in modern society. She was a major public figure, independent and often pugnacious, who was also the mother of eight children, all but one adopted and including several of mixed race. Beginning in poverty, she earned millions of dollars and spent lavishly on herself, her family, her friends, and her causes. She lobbied successfully to change American attitudes and policies in the areas of immigration, adoption, minority rights, and mental health.

While I happen to agree with many of the cultural and political positions Pearl Buck defended, this book is an essay in historiography, not advocacy. Consequently, I have made a scrupulous effort to tell Buck's story within the thickly detailed context of her own settings and circumstances, not to measure her value by the ideological calipers of a later historical moment. I have tried, in other words, to re-create her own world as she experienced and judged it.

Pearl Buck meets the only three criteria I can think of applying to a biographical subject: her life was uncommonly eventful and interesting; she was a woman of conspicuous significance; and her story provides access to a whole catalogue of social and cultural issues. Any one of these would be reason enough to reconstruct Buck's life and work. Taken together, they make her story compelling.

I have not written a saint's life. Pearl Buck, as I have gotten to know her, was a troubled, conflicted, often limited woman, capable of cruelty as well as kindness. At the same time, this book is not a "pathography," to use Joyce Carol Oates's term for the current fashion of biographical debunking. Whatever my reservations about her commitments or her accomplishments, I have grown to admire Pearl Buck, and I have learned a great deal from her. Her engagement in the major issues of her time is a rare and instructive example of a writer accepting her responsibilities to the larger society and dedicating her energy and influence to serve a vision of the common good.

A note on Chinese proper names

For nearly a century, the most widely used system for romanizing Chinese characters was Wade-Giles. An early form of this system was devised by Sir Thomas Wade in 1859; a modified version served as the basis for H. A. Giles's Chinese–English dictionary of 1912. Wade-Giles and all other systems use Northern (Mandarin) Chinese as the standard language. In 1958, the Chinese government approved the romanization system known as pinyin zimu (phonetic alphabet). Pinyin is now accepted as the official method for romanizing Chinese names. Because Wade-Giles was the standard system throughout Pearl Buck's years in China, I have used it fairly consistently throughout this book. For the reader's information, the first time a Chinese name is used, the pinyin version is given in parentheses following the Wade-Giles version.

A note on proper names in English

Readers will note that Pearl Buck is called "Pearl" throughout this biography. This sometimes creates a tone of dubious familiarity, but no form of address would be fully satisfactory. Pearl Buck did not become "Pearl Buck" until she was in her mid-twenties; she disliked the name "Buck"; and in any case "Buck" would bump up repeatedly against the book's other major "Buck," her first husband, Lossing Buck. My practice has been to call all of Pearl's immediate family and her closest friends – male and female – by their first names, and all others – male and female – by their surnames.

Acknowledgments

My greatest obligation, as always, is to my wife, Terry. Once again, in the midst of a much more demanding schedule than mine, she has found time to listen, to encourage, to improve. She makes it all worthwhile, as she has done for most of my adult life.

Terry and I have shared everything, and what we have shared above everything else is our four children. Jennifer, Alison, David, and Steven are, individually and collectively, remarkable people, and I have always felt privileged to be their father. All of them have read portions of this book at various stages, and have offered shrewd and judicious commentary. And, by demanding my time and attention on a regular basis, they have also reminded me of what is actually important.

IN THE FOUR YEARS I have spent doing the research and writing for this book, I have been blessed by the friendship and support of a great many people, on both sides of the Pacific. Students, colleagues, and administrators at Penn, scholars at other institutions, and a number of editors and journalists have all given generously of their time, advice, and expertise. I am grateful for the opportunity to thank some of them here: Marie Bauers, Nina Baym, Rick Beeman, Andrew Brown, David D. Buck, T. Susan Chang, Pradyumna S. Chauhan, Joel Conarroe, Peter Coveney, Blanch Wiesen Cook, Nancy Cott, Tad Danielewski, Craig Davidson, David DeLaura, Tom Ehrlich, Ruth Engelke, Dave Espey, John King Fairbank, Drew Faust, Al Filreis, Michelle Fine, Paul Fussell, Susan Gallé, Jianmei Gan, W. M. Havighurst, Gao Chun Hua, Robert Geller, Bob Giegengack, Joseph Haentjens, Liu Haiping, Charles Hayford, He Qian, Wyman Hilscine, Paul Howard, Judy Ivy, Randy Ivy, Jin Lei, Tamar Kaplan, Maxine Hong Kingston, Bill Koons, Linda Koons, George Koval, William LaFleur, Nancy Lelli, Ling Dexiang, Elizabeth Lipscomb, Kathleen Lodwick, Donald MacInnis, Harriet Mills, Janet Monge, Kim Morrisson, Elisa New, Donna Lynne Ng, Karl

Otto, Camilla T. K. Palmer, David Palumbo-Liu, Dina Portnoy, Jane Rabb, John Richetti, Donn Rogosin, Carlin Romano, Murray Rubinstein, John W. Service, William Simpson, Helen Foster Snow, Wendy Steiner, Chom Storey, Robert Storey, Grace C. K. Sum, Sun Wei Er, Ross Terrill, James Thomson, Jr., Morris Vogel, Louise White Walker, Edgar S. Walsh, Janice C. Walsh, Wang Ying Guo, Tim Waples, Gerald Weales, Jean Wu, Xu Xin, Grace Sydenstricker Yaukey, Yu Jian Niang, and Michael Zuckerman.

I am also happy to acknowledge the indispensable financial support I received from the National Endowment for the Humanities and the University of Pennsylvania Research Foundation.

Finally, I want to thank the scores of librarians, archivists, research specialists, and government officials who have provided the materials I needed and have patiently answered my questions: D. A. Albrecht, United States Navy; Libby Amann, Swarthmore College; Jody Armstrong, Cornell University; Jean Ashton, Columbia University; John Atterby, Boston College; Kerry Bartel, University of Washington; Emily Batista, University of Pennsylvania; Ronald L. Becker, Rutgers University; Roger Berry, University of California at Irvine; Robert Bertholf, State University of New York at Buffalo; Nancy Birkrem, Mount Holyoke College; Elizabeth Bishop, University of Chicago; Judy Bolton, Louisiana State University; Susan L. Boone, Smith College; Lisa Browar, New York Public Library; Bob Buckeye, Middlebury College; Anne Caiger, University of California at Los Angeles; Andrea Cantrell, University of Arkansas; James W. Carlson, University of Wyoming; David M. Caron, United States Navy; Clark Center, University of Alabama; Althea Church, University of Mississippi; Gould Colman, Cornell University; Lynn Conway, Catholic University of America; Kenneth Craven, University of Texas; Philip Cronenwett, Dartmouth College; Bernard Crystal, Columbia University; Anthony Cucchiara, Brooklyn College; Charles Cutter, Brandeis University; Carolyn A. Davis, Syracuse University; Anne Denlinger, Bryn Mawr College; Leo Dolenski, Bryn Mawr College; Inge Dupont, Pierpont Morgan Library; Susan Ehlert, University of Wisconsin at Madison; Laura A. Endicott, University of Virginia; Elaine Engst, Cornell University; Patricia Etter, Arizona State University; Marie Booth Ferré, Dickinson College; Peter Filardo, New York University; Kirsten Fischer, Duke University; Lizz Frost, Harvard University; La Vonne Gallo, Research Libraries Group; Laura Gaskins, Pack Memorial Public Library; Gene Gieger, Auburn University; Margaret Goostray, Boston University; Howard Gottlieb, Boston University; Joan Grattan, The Johns Hopkins University; Mary Grattan, The National Women's Hall of Fame; Dianne Gutscher, Bowdoin College.

Also: Amy Hague, Smith College; Bonnie Hardwick, University of California at Berkeley; Diana Haskell, Newberry Library; David Hedrick, Gettysburg College; Cathy Henderson, University of Texas; Carmen Hurff, University of Florida; Christopher Husted, University of California at Santa Barbara; Mary Huth, University of Rochester; Karen L. Jania, University of Michigan; Karen Jefferson, Howard University; Tony Jenkins, Duke University; Mary Catherine Johnsen, Carnegie Mellon University; Nancy Johnson, American Academy of Arts and Letters; Edward Joyce, Princeton University Library; Charlene M. Kaufmann, University of Arkansas; Charles J. Kelly, The Library of Congress; Sylvia B. Kennick, Williams College; Carla Kent, University of Florida; Mary Kent, Connecticut College; Kris Kiesling, University of Texas; Tom Kirk, Berea College; Dave Klaassen, University of Minnesota; David Koch, Southern Illinois University; Mitchell Kohl, Clemson University; Diana Lachatenere, New York Public Library; Kay Lauster, Middlebury College; Patience-Anne W. Lenk, Colby College; Erwin Levold, Rockefeller Archive Center; Laura Linard, Harvard University; Dallas R. Lindgren, Minnesota Historical Society; Linda J. Long, Stanford University; Pruda Lood, Stanford University; William H. Loos, Buffalo and Erie County Public Library; Jane Lowenthal, Barnard College; Frank M. Machak, United States Department of State; Jeffrey D. Marshall, University of Vermont; Robert S. Martin, Louisiana State University; William R. Massa, Jr., Yale University; Bettye C. Mayes, United States Department of State; Robert McCowan, University of Iowa; Linda McCurdy, Duke University; Kris McCusker, University of Colorado at Boulder; Sylvia McDowell, Radcliffe College; Lee N. McLaird, Bowling Green State University; Wilbur E. Meneray, Tulane University; Harold L. Miller, State Historical Society of Wisconsin; Martha Mitchell, Brown University; Leslie Morris, Harvard University; Dorothy Mosakowski, Clark University; Margaret Moser, Allegheny College; Carol Moore, Arizona State University; Heather Munro, Indiana University; Gladys Murphy, University of California at Riverside; Clifford L. Muse, Jr., Howard University; Nina Myatt, Antioch College.

Also: Ellen Nemhauser, Emory University; Janet Ness, University of Washington; Jeanne T. Newlin, Harvard University; J. Kevin O'Brien, Federal Bureau of Investigation; Richard Palumbo, Wagner College; Jami Peelle, Kenyon College; Deborah Pelletier, Amherst College; William Peters, Hartford Seminary; Diana Peterson, Haverford College; Linda Pine, University of Arkansas; Michael Plunkett, University of Virginia; Jean Preston, Princeton University; Hilda Pring, University of Pennsylvania; Kevin Proffitt, American Jewish Archives; Lee Pugh, University of Pennsylvania; Roger L. Rainwater, Texas Christian University; Jennie Rathbun, Harvard University; Richard Reilly, The James S. Copley Library; Cynthia Requardt, The Johns Hopkins University; Gene K. Rinkel, University of Illinois; Carley Robison, Knox College; Helen Rutt, Howard University; Sheila Ryan, Southern Illinois University; Joanne M. Sawyer, Hiram College; D. W. Schneider, Louisiana State University; Dina Schoonmaker, Oberlin College; Richard A. Schrader, University of North Carolina at Chapel Hill;

Barbara Sefranek, Allentown Public Library; Margaret M. Sherry, Princeton University; Andy Simons, Amistad Research Center; Daniel Singer, National Archives; Martha Lund Smalley, Yale University; Phillip Smith, University of California at San Diego; Steven Sowards, Swarthmore College; Sandra Stelts, Pennsylvania State University; Susan Sullivan, Presbyterian Historical Society; Dorothy Swanson, New York University; Charles Tamason, University of Michigan; Rebekah Tanner, New York Public Library; Saundra Taylor, Indiana University; Raymond Teichman, Franklin D. Roosevelt Library; Wendy Thomas, Radcliffe College; Robert A. Tibbetts, Ohio State University; Thomas Verich, University of Mississippi; Frank Walker, New York University; William Walker, Metropolitan Museum of Art; Cynthia Wall, Newberry Library; Frances Webb, Randolph-Macon Woman's College; Janet West, Port Washington Public Library; Nancy Weyant, Bucknell University; Thomas M. Whithead, Temple University; Danny Williams, West Virginia University; Patricia Willis, Yale University; Marice Wolfe, Vanderbilt University; Abigail Yasgur, Radcliffe College; Anne Yoder, Swarthmore College; Jim Zink, Southeast Missouri State University.

I

Missionary Childhood

IN APRIL, 1899, six-year-old Pearl Sydenstricker wrote a letter from Chinkiang, China, to the editor of the *Christian Observer*, in Louisville, Kentucky. It was her first published writing, and it appeared under the headline "Our Real Home in Heaven":

I am a little girl, six years old. I live in China. I have a big brother in college who is coming to China to help our father tell the Chinese about Jesus. I have two little brothers in heaven. Maudie went first, then Artie, then Edith, and on the tenth of last month my little brave brother, Clyde left us to go to our real home in heaven. Clyde said he was a Christian Soldier, and that heaven was his bestest home. Clyde was four years old, and we both love the little letters in the Observer. I wrote this all myself, and my hand is tired, so goodbye.

Clyde, barely out of his infancy, was a brave soldier in Christ's army, gathered into his "bestest" home. This sad little allegory came directly out of six-year-old Pearl's fundamentalist upbringing. She may have written her letter all by herself, as she said, but she used the language she had been hearing every day of her brief life.

As an adult, she would completely reject the religion in which she was raised, but it was the source of everything she learned about values as a child. Living in a small Chinese city, she was separated from her own country and its culture almost from birth. She had heard Chinese children make fun of her blond hair and blue eyes, and call her *yang kwei-tse,* a "foreign devil." Four of her brothers and sisters had died, and she had few companions of her own age. Like many lonely children, she depended on her parents for talk and friendship. Her childish Christianity was natural enough, but it had nothing to do with doctrine or belief; her pious enthusiasm brought her closer to her mother and father.

Absalom and Carie Sydenstricker had journeyed to China twenty years earlier as Presbyterian missionaries. Absalom came "to tell the Chinese about Jesus," as Pearl rather sweetly phrases it; for over fifty years, he labored to spread his alien revelation among people he regarded as heathens. He was part of the missionary enterprise, one of the strangest and most compelling episodes in the history of relations between China and the West.

In the nineteenth century, Americans knew almost nothing about China. It was a blank on the map – vast, distant, exotic. Only a handful of merchants, soldiers, and diplomats had set foot in China or in any other Asian country. If Americans thought about China at all, they relied on a cluster of stereotypes. Some were favorable, but most were generally insulting: the Chinese were dishonest, cruel, inscrutable; China was a place of strange costumes and customs. Literally and morally, China was at the opposite end of the earth.[1] Bret Harte's "The Heathen Chinee" (1870) may well have been "the worst poem that anybody ever wrote," as Harte himself said, but it was tremendously popular, and its sly comic hero, Ah Sin, was one of only two Chinese characters – real or fictional – that most Americans had ever heard of. The other was Confucius, who was "known," if that is the right word, only as the author of a number of fairly silly aphorisms.

Devout Christians were no better informed than other Americans, but China had a special importance for them. Because it was the most populous nation on earth, China offered the greatest scope for redemptive effort. Many Protestant Christians in fact believed that the decisive battle with infidelity would be fought in China.

Protestant missionaries began arriving in the 1830s and 1840s. They came, typically, from the small towns of the Middle West, equipped with little more than religious fervor and the degrees they had recently earned at the modest sectarian colleges of Ohio and Michigan and Illinois. They represented all the major Protestant denominations: Congregationalists, Methodists, hardshell and softshell Baptists, several conventions of Lutherans, Northern and Southern Presbyterians, a few Unitarians and Episcopalians, a handful of Christian Scientists.[2]

It is virtually impossible to reconstruct the mixture of attitudes that led thousands of young men and women to China, or even to imagine the unlikely combination of provincialism and daring that defined them. Many of them kept diaries and journals, all of them wrote letters home, some of them published autobiographies. The testimony of their various accounts constitutes an absorbing group portrait, in which piety, fatigue, ambition, illness, disillusion, hope, discovery, homesickness, fundamentalism, and secularism alternate by turns. They uprooted themselves, left behind everything they had known, and lived for years and decades in a society they found inhospitable and utterly incomprehensible.

For most evangelists, the missionary calling satisfied a deep personal need for significant action.[3] Some were attracted by the undeniable glamour of foreign adventuring, and the occasional but real dangers that lay in wait in the Chinese countryside. Many were humanitarians who believed they could improve the lives of the Chinese even as they saved them from damnation. There were undoubtedly opportunists and hypocrites among them, but most were driven by the conviction that they were bringing light to people in darkness. They believed that their exertions would ultimately defeat Chinese heathenism and usher in the Second Coming.

Absalom Sydenstricker embodied the best and worst in the missionary vocation. He was a man of high intelligence and unyielding commitment, indifferent to his own welfare, fearless in the face of danger. He had only one motive. For a half-century, he traveled across central China, from one village and market town to another, relentlessly trying to persuade Chinese men and women to accept Jesus. From his arrival at Hangchow (Hangzhou) in 1880 to his death in Nanking (Nanjing) in 1931, he remained steadfast in his calling. He made few converts among people who found his version of the truth bewildering and often absurd. Nonetheless, despite fifty years of frustration, he clung to the conviction that China was an immense heathen territory ripe for salvation.

When she was a child, Pearl tended to see her father in heroic terms. As she grew older, she decided that he was a simple fanatic, touched with an apocalyptic fever. He had exhausted himself in the service of a futile ambition. He had spent decades in an ancient, complex, and dignified civilization and had seen only a stronghold of Satan. Pearl came to believe that her father was an unfortunately representative figure: "If his life has any meaning . . . it is as a manifestation of a certain spirit in his country and his time. For he was a spirit, and a spirit made by that blind certainty, that pure intolerance, that zeal for mission, that contempt of man and earth, that high confidence in heaven, which our forefathers bequeathed to us."[4] He was insensitive to beauty, to human weakness, to the needs of his family, even to his own suffering. Pearl acknowledged that Absalom's tenacity and sense of purpose had a kind of grandeur. However, his great gifts, his energy and undeniable courage, his sincerity, merely made the waste of his life more poignant.

The person most wounded by Absalom's misdirected idealism was his wife Carie. She had accompanied her husband to China, where she was homesick for the remaining forty years of her life. Pearl regarded Carie as the generous victim of Absalom's commitments, a woman whose life was embittered and shortened by her husband's single-minded and ultimately destructive devotion to his evangelical Work. (When Pearl later wrote about her parents' lives, she often capitalized Absalom's Work, for ironic rather than reverent reasons.)[5] Carie's emotionally impoverished marriage and exile provided Pearl a tragic example of the price that women pay for loyalty to codes and customs that oppress them. It was the most important lesson Pearl would ever learn. Carie Sydenstricker had died in the knowledge that her lifetime of self-denial had brought only suffering; her daughter would not, as Carie had done, collaborate in her own defeat.

Wherever she lived in China, in Hangchow, Chinkiang, or Nanking, Carie always made a flower garden. These were places of beauty and refuge, walled off from the Chinese streets that surrounded them. Carie's gardens, to which she was passionately devoted, and to which Absalom was utterly oblivious, stood for Pearl as a symbol of the distance between her parents. Significantly, throughout the biographies she wrote of both Absalom and Carie, Pearl referred to herself as "Carie's daughter."

In the end, Pearl was inevitably shaped by both her parents. She rejected her father's religious beliefs and his narrow-mindedness, but she inherited his evangelical zeal, his sense of rectitude, his passion for learning. Though she stopped believing in Christian ideas of salvation, she became, in effect, a secular missionary, bringing the gospels of civil rights and cross-cultural understanding to people on two continents. She adored her mother, and took from her a belief in compassion, a stubborn antagonism to abstract creeds, and a commitment to the supreme importance of the family. But she turned away from Carie's conventionally female habits of deference and self-sacrifice. For better and sometimes for worse, the adult Pearl would combine much that was distinctive in both her mother and her father.

LIKE MOST MISSIONARIES, Absalom Sydenstricker was a marginal man. Born in August, 1852, on a farm in western Virginia, he was the second youngest of nine children. The family's ancestors had come from Germany, settling first in Pennsylvania, then moving south at about the time of the Revolution. The homestead was large, though steep hills and thin soil made it difficult to cultivate and unprosperous. There was always enough food, but rarely any money.[6]

Absalom's mother was a quiet woman who became increasingly detached from her large family as she grew older. In her later years, she communed with ghosts. Her husband was a fiercely religious man, always lecturing his family about God and the Devil. He recited aloud from Scripture in all his spare moments, and boasted that he read the entire Bible through every year. He was violent and quarrelsome, with a dangerous temper that drove his children off the farm as soon as they were old enough to move out. After they left, he would curse them for ingratitude.

Absalom was one of seven sons, six of whom became preachers. As a boy, he did his farm work diligently – one of his chores was taking grain to the local mill – but he resented the daily labor and his father's discipline. He loved the Virginia landscape and the changes of season, but he was often lonely and unhappy. His childhood seemed to him mainly a time of fear, anger, and self-doubt.

His earliest memory was a scene of humiliation. When he was six or seven years old, he heard himself called exceptionally ugly by a neighbor woman. The woman consoled his mother by cheerily reminding her that there is usually a runt in every family. This episode loomed over Absalom's life as a symbol of his isolation. He spent his life bitterly insisting that virtue was more important than beauty or talent. Even in old age, he recalled his father as a man who frightened him, and his mother as a woman who seemed to love him less than his brothers and sisters. He retreated into books, partly as a way of escaping from his family, but partly because he had a real talent for learning. His boyhood attachment to reading would eventually lead to a career of modest distinction as a scholar and linguist.

During Absalom's adolescence, the Sydenstricker family was swept up in the turmoil of the Civil War. Four of his brothers, David, Hiram, Isaac, and John, fought for the Confederacy; two were wounded and Isaac suffered for months in a Union prison. Absalom was too young to enlist, but he mourned the Confederacy's defeat, and he maintained sympathy with the South's lost cause throughout his life. Because he missed the great testing of the war, he had further reason to doubt his adequacy. Foreign evangelism allowed him the compensation of lifelong combat against an enemy even more implacable than the Yankees. Fundamentalist Christians have always luxuriated in a rhetoric of constant strife and bloody battle. During his years in China, as he struggled to free pagan souls from Satan's grasp, Absalom would find those images especially appealing.

Absalom's childhood also defined his attitudes toward race. Though his family was poor, they had owned a couple of slaves, and they were untroubled by the moral evil that slavery involved. Absalom was taught to regard racial hierarchy as part of the natural order, which may explain his assured sense of superiority to Asians. He had been made to feel outcast and unattractive among his own people; when he went to China, he knew that he was the agent of a higher civilization.

Aside from fighting with each other and ridiculing abolitionists, the Sydenstrickers apparently had few habits or rituals in common. Religion was their one bond. Each Sunday, they marched dutifully off to the Old Stone Church in Lewisburg to hear the gloomy wisdom of a provincial Presbyterian preacher. Sometimes the service was conducted by a visitor, occasionally a missionary on home leave from China. Following one such service, when he was sixteen years old, Absalom decided that he had heard the call. He kept his vocation secret for several years to avoid conflict with his family. He knew that their conventional Christianity would be affronted at the idea of his going to China. Piety was acceptable and even admirable, but foreign evangelism was considered a form of extremism.

Like his older brothers before him, Absalom was obliged to stay on the farm until his twenty-first birthday. Then he enrolled in Washington and Lee College, in Lexington, Virginia. He was older than the other undergraduates and far more serious in his work than most of them. Tall, red-haired, and extremely thin, he was easily noticed. However, he felt physically and socially awkward, and his habitual reserve was accentuated by his poor eyesight. He was nearsighted, a condition that Pearl eventually decided was symbolic. In any case, in college he kept mostly to himself. He made no friends, but he won "a drawer full of honors," as Pearl later described them. He had no money, and supported himself through the four-year course by working at a series of part-time jobs and living on short rations of bread and cheese. By denying himself any social life at all, he was able to accumulate a small library of books, most of them in history and theology. These were virtually his only possessions. On the day after his graduation, during his last night in the dormitory, a fire destroyed every book he owned.

Absalom returned home penniless. He tried without success to earn a living selling Bibles door-to-door, then announced his missionary intentions. As he had expected, his father found the idea outrageous tomfoolery. His mother, on the other hand, was more conciliatory, in part, apparently, as a way of defying her husband. She promised Absalom her support, but only on the condition that he marry before leaving for Asia. As he later told the story, he had never until that moment thought of marriage, but he agreed to find a wife.[7]

He went about the business of courtship by methodically inspecting the religious convictions of each of the young women he knew. He assumed, sensibly enough, that he needed a wife who shared his beliefs. He was attracted to a woman named Jennie Husted, who had sent him a letter warmly applauding his first sermon, which was published under the title "The Necessity of Proclaiming the Gospel to the Heathen, with Especial Reference to the Doctrine of Predestination." Absalom eventually passed over Husted, in spite of her theological good taste, and proposed to twenty-two-year-old Carie Stulting.

Carie was the descendant of Dutch immigrants. Her grandparents had come to America in the early nineteenth century, refugees from a rare outburst of Dutch religious persecution. Johann Stulting had been a prosperous Utrecht merchant who sold his business and led a band of three hundred pilgrims to the New World in search of religious liberty. The group included Johann's youngest son, Hermanus, and his French wife – Carie's father and mother. After pausing for a season in Pennsylvania, the larger portion of the immigrants eventually settled in Virginia. City people from birth, they learned how to do farm work and eventually prospered.

Carie was born in 1857, and lived with her family in a large white three-story house in what is today Hillsboro, West Virginia, a little town set in the foothills of the Shenandoah Mountains. When she was older, she loved to recall the big maple tree that stood in the front yard and the apple orchard in back, the shelves of round Dutch cheeses and homemade berry wines. The rooms of the house were furnished handsomely, and the walls were decorated with etchings and drawings that her father had made. Bookcases were filled with volumes of poetry, fiction, and biographies. A piano in the front parlor brought the family together for song and laughter in the evenings. Carie learned to play quite skillfully; years later, she lightened the burden of her Chinese exile by coaxing music out of a small organ.

Unlike Absalom, Carie remembered the first few years of her childhood as a time of almost uninterrupted happiness. She was once punished – unjustly in her opinion – for breaking a serving dish when she was three years old. Aside from that single unpleasant episode, however, her early years moved in an agreeable round of play and easy chores. She grew up secure in her parents' affection and confident in her own talents.

In fact, there was a deep flaw in the Stulting family arrangements, but Carie only recognized it after she had grown up. She had especially admired her artistically gifted father because of his attachment to beautiful objects and his scrupulous personal cleanliness. However, because he didn't do his share of the farm's hard work, he doubled the labor of his oldest son, Carie's brother Cornelius. He was, furthermore, the only man in his community who changed his white shirt and collar every day. When she was much older, Carie realized the hardship that Hermanus's fastidious habits had implied. She told Pearl: "It did not occur to me until years later that, after all, there was something cruel about those white collars. Someone – our mother as long as she could and then one of the older girls – always had that collar and shirt to wash and iron every day, no matter how much canning or churning there might be on hand."[8] Carie came to believe that her mother's poor health had been caused in some measure by the charming Hermanus's demands.

The Civil War brought an end to the family's prosperity. Their farm was perilously exposed, lying just a few miles from the border between secessionist Virginia and the new state of West Virginia, which remained loyal to the Union. In a hopeless effort to stay out of harm's way, Hermanus announced that his family would simply remain neutral. Cornelius, who was old enough to fight but refused, spent the war years hiding in a cabin on nearby Droop Mountain. The Stulting farm was ravaged by North and South alike, repeatedly stripped of its food and supplies by hungry soldiers. At one point, the family was reduced to eating a soup made of dandelion greens and a handful of dried beans. Carie acknowledged the violence on both sides, but she was convinced that the Yankee troops were particularly savage. Though she was only eight when the war ended, she never forgave Lincoln or his field commanders. Decades later, in 1900, when the Boxers murdered several hundred foreigners in China, Carie likened them to the armies of General William T. Sherman, who had burned a wide avenue of destruction across the South.

In an important sense, Carie's childhood ended with the war. She had seen bloodshed, starvation, and hate sweep aside the security of her early years. She was old enough to share in the pain and deprivation that settled on her region, but too young to play a part in the task of rebuilding. In particular, she was frustrated by her lack of schooling. All the schools had closed for the duration of the war, and she had received little formal education. She could barely read, and she could not write at all. In the war's grim aftermath, her brother Cornelius began a small school in which she quickly became the best pupil. She read every book she could find, and she also did well in the rudimentary science that Cornelius made available to her.

In the end, the pinched circumstances of the postwar years did not subtract much from Carie's sense of well-being. She had grown into a dark-haired, handsome young woman, an inch or two over five feet tall, ready to laugh, admired by most of the other people in her small community. She enjoyed her studies and felt that poverty was teaching her valuable lessons in self-reliance. Her principal anxiety was for her soul.

Carie spent a good deal of time worrying about God and salvation, and in this she was typical of the young people of her time and place. Some version or other of Christianity was inescapable in nineteenth-century rural America. Children sat through long church services at least once on Sunday, and they recited prayers and heard the Bible read two or three times each day at home. They were subject to continuous interrogation by parents and ministers who probed the state of their souls. The social life in their small communities revolved around the church. In short, young Americans grew up in a culture of piety that reached into every corner of daily life.

Carie would never embrace Christianity with Absalom's immense and solemn finality, but she was an earnest seeker. She wrote in her diary: "During the years between twelve and fifteen I used many times a week to go out into the woods behind the barn and creep into a little hollow in a clump of elderberries and throw myself down and cry to God for a sign – anything to make me believe in Him." Carie thought the sign might have come when her mother died in 1875, at the end of a long illness; she was half-convinced that God had entered the sickroom and eased her mother's last moments. In gratitude, she vowed to devote her life to God's service. She began to think of the foreign missions simply because such a vocation would require the greatest self-denial. Like many ardent young people who experience transports of high religious excitement, Carie instinctively equated personal discomfort with theological perfection.

At this rather precarious emotional moment, she met Absalom Sydenstricker, now an ordained minister of the Southern Presbyterian Church. He had come to Hillsboro with one of his older brothers, who had been installed as the town's new Presbyterian minister. Carie was immediately attracted to the shy, studious younger brother, who kept himself detached from the visiting and gossip that made up Hillsboro's modest social life. She noted that he lacked a sense of humor, but was undisturbed since she regarded her own tendency to laughter as a warning that she might be morally frivolous.

Despite her growing affection for Absalom, Carie did not at first alter her own plans. She wanted more education than her brother's school could provide and, in 1877, she left Hillsboro to spend two years at the Bellewood Female Seminary, near Louisville. Years later, Pearl found two of the essays Carie had written at Bellewood. One was a commentary on Queen Esther that applauded the heroism of self-sacrifice. The other, which won a prize, was a compendium of religious dogma called "The Moral Evidences of Christianity." The light-hearted girl was trying to turn herself into a pious woman.

Like Absalom, Carie had kept her dreams of foreign evangelism secret. Like him, she also met the unequivocal opposition of her father when she made her announcement after returning from Bellewood. Hermanus's resistance only stiffened her own resolve; within a few months, she and Absalom were engaged, mainly on the basis of their shared commitment to a missionary career. If Absalom was capable of passion, Carie never saw the evidence, not even in these early days of their relationship. For her own part, she deliberately suppressed her passion in order to prove her religious sincerity – to herself as much as to God. In place of the more domestic expectations that most nineteenth-century women brought to marriage, Carie was elevated by an apocalyptic vision: she looked forward to "a harvest of dark, white-clad heathen being baptized" as a result of the good work she and Absalom would do together.[9]

CARIE AND ABSALOM were married on July 8, 1880, and almost immediately began the journey west to California where they would board a steamer for China. There was a moment of confusion at the train station because Absalom had forgotten to buy a second ticket. The little episode was comic, but it foreshadowed Absalom's behavior over the next four decades. As Pearl later wrote, he had obeyed his mother and found a wife, but he could never quite remember it.

Absalom had been given no help in preparing for his great undertaking: "Not a word had been said about the importance of being vaccinated; nothing was said about the currency used in China; nothing had been done . . . to secure reduced rates on railways or steamer; no passage had been secured for us."[10] The young couple had to make their way on their own.

1. Carie Stulting and Absalom Sydenstricker at about the time of their marriage in 1880. (Reproduced with permission of the Pearl S. Buck Foundation.)

They traveled across the Pacific on the *City of Tokyo,* which docked in Japan in mid-September. From there they transferred to an old sidewheeler that carried them over the Inland Sea and East China Sea to Shanghai. Carie was seasick through the entire voyage, as she would be each time she crossed the ocean. Absalom spent the trip studying Chinese. The Sydenstrickers, who were the first Presbyterian reinforcements to arrive in China in seven years, received a warm greeting from the small Christian community. They were initially assigned to Hangchow, a hundred miles southwest of Shanghai. They remained here for less than a year, living in a single room. The first of their children, a boy they named Edgar, was born in Hangchow in 1881.

A few months later, they moved to Soochow (Suzhou), where Absalom replaced Rev. H. C. Du Bose, who had gone back to the United States on home leave. When Du Bose returned, the Sydenstrickers were reassigned to Hangchow, where they spent the next year or so. They lived on the upper floor of a small but fairly comfortable bungalow in the missionary compound.

Like most foreigners, the Christian evangelists kept themselves separate from the native populations.[11] They built their houses behind tall brick walls that also shielded their schools and clinics from the local people. Most of them seemed to fear and even despise the native population they had come to save. To his credit, Absalom always felt that the missionaries were too cloistered and prosperous. When he and Carie moved to Chinkiang in 1883, they chose to live outside the foreign settlement (though their house and garden, like those of Chinese gentry, were enclosed by a high wall). Beyond that, Absalom's endless itinerating brought him much closer to the experience of ordinary Chinese farmers and workers. When he wasn't traveling in search of souls, he conducted a boys' school and preached in a street chapel. Carie assisted in the work and tried to re-create as much of America as she could in a foreign land.

Years later, Pearl would write that "the real story of life in a mission station has never yet been told."[12] A small group of white men and women, living huddled together in an isolated compound amid thousands of indifferent or frankly suspicious Chinese, were reminded each day of their alienation.[13] Assigned without regard to their personalities or needs, the missionaries sometimes got along together in their strange, enforced intimacy, but often grew to loathe one another. Alcoholism, opium addiction, disease, incurable depression, and even madness were commonplace consequences of missionary duty, though they were seldom discussed openly. These were the risks that Absalom and Carie faced in China.

Reports about the Sydenstrickers appeared from time to time in the *Chinese Recorder,* a missionary magazine published in Shanghai beginning in the late 1860s. The *Recorder* was the most important of all the missionary publications, and its pages make up an indispensable source of information on the Western effort to evangelize China. It was published under slightly changing names, at first six times a year, then monthly until it expired in 1941.[14] The magazine's growth in the late nineteenth century reflected the expansion of the missionary enterprise; its termination marked the end of the Christian crusade in China.

The *Recorder*'s articles range from ecclesiastical and bureaucratic arguments to studies of Chinese language, history, geography, politics, and culture. Almost every issue incorporates statistics: on conversions, baptisms, school enrollments, hospital beds. Essays on church organization and medical work as an evangelistic activity share space with lessons on etiquette and descriptions of Chinese flowers, even translations of *Poor Richard's Almanac* and Mother Goose rhymes into Chinese. The "Missionary News" provided personal information on the evangelists and their families: arrivals and departures, new assignments and furloughs, marriages, births and deaths. These unadorned, brief announcements summon a vanished world of struggle and faith.

The May–June 1881 issue of the *Recorder* announced the Sydenstrickers' assignment to Soochow. On the same page, the editors printed the following news story, also datelined Soochow: "A proclamation has lately been issued by the

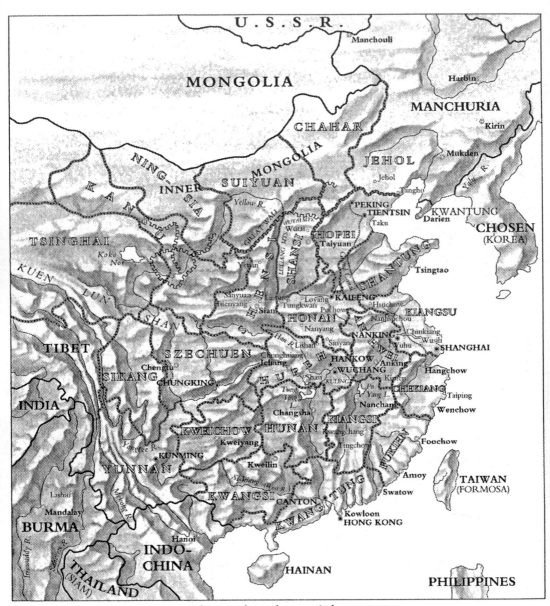

2. China in the early twentieth century.

District Governor warning the public not to molest the missionaries or the natives living at their chapels or school-houses. It has had the effect of stopping some of the abusive language so freely indulged in by the inhabitants of that city toward missionaries or their native assistants."

Aside from suggesting the sorts of hostility the Sydenstrickers would face in their new home, this small item opens a window on an irreconcilable conflict. The curses that Chinese shouted against the missionaries were the consequence and symbol of frustrations that had been growing for generations. Absalom thought of the Chinese people as pagan "fields ripe for the harvest" who should be "gathered in"; in fact, it was revolution and not Christianity that was ripening across the Middle Kingdom.[15]

China in the second half of the nineteenth century was a deeply troubled country. Two centuries of Manchu rule had led to stagnation and a widespread conviction of national failure. The central government was notoriously corrupt. The imperial family lived in the splendid isolation of Peking's Forbidden City, cut off from their own subjects by a gigantic, self-serving bureaucracy. Many in the small but influential group of Chinese intellectuals regarded Western science, technology, and politics with envious admiration, but there was no consensus on what should be done. Some wanted to abolish the monarchy, others to reform it; some continued to believe in the values of a modified Confucian teaching, while others insisted that Confucius must be replaced altogether. Whatever their disagreements, however, nearly all thoughtful Chinese accepted the proposition that broad changes were needed if China was to assume its proper place in the world.

Discontent had been catalyzed by the intrusions of Western economic and military forces. In a matter of decades, beginning in the early nineteenth century, China's relationship with the rest of the world had been dramatically altered. China was one of the oldest continuous civilizations on earth; for most of its history, it dominated nearby nations and ignored the rest of the world. It did not seek foreign contacts either in trade or diplomacy, and it rarely welcomed visitors. The Ch'ien-lung Emperor (Qianlong), a contemporary of George Washington, declared in a famous edict: "Our celestial empire possesses all things in prolific abundance and lacks no product within its own borders. There is therefore no need to import the manufactures of outside barbarians."[16]

Chinese hostility to the West was based on an ancient and durable conviction of superiority. The language itself supported this view. The terms *hua* and *huaxia,* meaning "Chinese," have overtones of culture and civilization; other societies were considered simply less human.[17] The Chinese believed that the Middle Kingdom was "the center of the universe"; consequently, in Warren Cohen's words, they "regarded all cultural differences as signs of inferiority. All who were not Chinese were, obviously, barbarians."

Since the barbarians were ignorant of Chinese values and norms, they were presumed to have "no values or norms at all. Logically, then, they could only be motivated by crude instinctive desires for food and sex, like animals. . . . [T]he Chinese saw them as quarrelsome, stubborn, greedy, and licentious, with little awareness of those finer human qualities, such as flexibility, moderation, kindness and consideration, which were so essential for the smooth functioning of human relationships."[18]

Warren Cohen argues that the Chinese were "probably the most ethnocentric people in the world."[19] Such an estimate is rather hard to dispute but even harder to verify: most societies seem to have adopted a view of themselves as occupying an especially blessed place in the scheme of things. Nonetheless, the general point remains clear. For many centuries, China had stood aloof from the West, complacent in its own self-sufficiency. Starting in the early 1600s, that situation was permanently changed, and by the nineteenth century merchants and traders began to arrive in greater numbers. In their wake appeared the diplomats who represented the power of Western governments, along with the armies and navies that protected commerce from Chinese resistance. China was being simultaneously opened and humbled.

The crisis came with the Opium War (1839–1842), which historian Jonathan Spence has called "the most decisive reversal the Manchus had ever received."[20] British merchants demanded that the Chinese offer themselves as a market for the opium that was being grown and processed under British auspices in India. China's refusal provoked a series of wars which ended in humiliating conquest by Western military forces. That defeat in turn led to the Treaty of Nanking, "the most important treaty settlement in China's modern history."[21]

The twelve main articles of this treaty secured far-reaching privileges and prerogatives for the British throughout Chinese territory. The United States and France quickly followed with their own demands, compelling China to accept similar agreements. Among other things, the unequal treaties, as they were called, forced China to submit to trading terms that ensured lopsided advantages for the West. Five coastal cities, Canton (Guangzhou), Foochow (Fuzhou), Amoy (Xiamen), Ningpo (Ningbo), and Shanghai, were immediately opened to foreign residence and commerce; eventually, more than eighty cities were declared treaty ports. Even more significantly, the Chinese had to accept the concept of extraterritoriality. That is, Westerners were declared exempt from Chinese law; whatever crimes they committed on Chinese territory could only be prosecuted by Western authorities, according to Western laws and procedures.

Finally, the unequal treaties of 1860 guaranteed the right of Christian missionaries to teach their religion. Until this time, it had been illegal to preach the gospel in China; anyone caught doing so, whether Chinese or Western, risked punishment and even execution. China's official attitude was based on its suspicion of foreign ideologies. Beyond that, the Chinese found Christianity especially offensive because of its universal and exclusive claims. Christians did not present their faith as one form of belief among many. Rather, they insisted that their god was the only one who actually existed; they ridiculed other gods, and demanded that other religions be exterminated. They also warned that only those who accepted their god would be saved; everyone else was condemned to eternal suffering. To most Chinese, such notions were bizarre at best, and probably dangerous.[22]

Every Christian sermon was an insult. Regardless of the preacher's motives, regardless of the respect and even affection he might have for the Chinese people, the doctrines he espoused were necessarily abusive to China's culture and traditions. George Santayana, one of Christianity's most strenuous Western critics, understood the demeaning implications of preaching: "A missionary sermon is an unprovoked attack; it seems to entice, to dictate, to browbeat, to disturb, and to terrify; it ends, if it can, by grafting into your heart, and leaving to fructify there, an alien impulse, the grounds of which you do not understand, and the consequences of which you never have desired."[23]

Suspicious Chinese asked missionaries why they had come. Perhaps understandably, they were not satisfied with the answer, "To preach the Gospel," since they had no idea what such a remark meant. Rumors surrounded the foreign evangelists, some of them grotesque: they had come to steal land or find slaves, or they worshiped a pig (a play on the word *chu* in *T'ien Chu,* Lord of Heaven), or they ate Chinese children, or they gouged out children's eyes to make sexual potions.[24]

When the Chinese did listen to Gospel stories, they often found them unpersuasive and even ridiculous. They were skeptical of the Virgin Birth both because it seemed absurd and because it undermined patriarchal authority. Also, since Christ couldn't identify the traitor in his group, was he a person of wise judgment? Since he couldn't protect even himself, could he protect others?[25]

The unequal treaties enabled missionaries to go about their evangelical business legally. Opposition continued, but it became local and often furtive, since Chinese who attacked preachers could now be arrested and punished. Because these new arrangements were enforced by threats of Western military action, missionaries were perceived as simply one part of the growing foreign presence that was reducing China to imperialist subjection.

Many missionaries tried to disentangle themselves from the gunboat diplomacy that was working the Western will on China, but others rationalized the use of force quite enthusiastically. According to historian Stuart Creighton Miller, missionary justification of armed force reflected a nineteenth-century "domino theory" about world religion:

China was the key to world-wide salvation. She was Satan's chief fortress, and the conversion of her huge population would topple pagan defenses elsewhere throughout the world and usher in the millennium. Scriptural warning that the devil's rout would involve turmoil and bloodshed made it that much easier to accept martyrdom as well as to convert the slaughter of countless thousands of "Satan's willing servants" by invading western armies into actions divinely inspired and directed.[26]

To be sure, not all missionaries held such bloodthirsty attitudes. The differences among them were in fact quite striking. Some embraced the idea of Western political supremacy in Asia, others rejected it; some served as agents for government and corporate officials, others refused; some held the whole of Asian culture in contempt, while others believed that – religion to one side – Asia had much to teach the West. Nonetheless, in spite of their particular disagreements, they could be accurately described as "cultural imperialists," since they endeavored to replace an indigenous system of values with their own religious and ethical ideas.

If the Chinese were powerless to resist Western religious incursions, they were able to protest, and they did so, in every available forum. In April, 1899, to give just one example, Wu T'ing-fang, the Chinese minister to the United States, gave a speech to a meeting of the American Academy of Political Science in Philadelphia. He successfully satirized the missionary invasion by reversing the national identities of the preachers and their prospective converts. He asked his audience to imagine that the Chinese had sent bands of Confucian evangelists to major American cities, and that these emissaries of Chinese beliefs had set up temples and schools, filled the afternoon air with their strange music, and converted as many Christians as they could to their Eastern beliefs. Minister Wu described the likely consequences:

If they were to begin their work by making vehement attacks on the doctrines of Christianity, denouncing the cherished institutions of the country, or going out of their way to ridicule the fashions of the day, and perhaps giving a learned discourse on the evil effects of corsets upon the general health of American women, it is most likely that they would be pelted with stones, dirt and rotten eggs for their pains.

Wu asked his audience to consider what would happen if these foreign missionaries demanded police protection and guarantees of safety from Washington. "I verily believe that such action would render the missionaries so obnoxious to the American people as to put an end to their usefulness, and that the American government would cause a law to be enacted against them as public nuisances."[27]

WHEN ABSALOM SYNDENSTRICKER came to China, he saw himself only as an agent of his god. To many Chinese, on the contrary, he was an agent of imperialism, a threat to civil order, a public nuisance. Like many zealots, he was undaunted by the resistance his doctrines encountered. He even seemed to welcome hostility: after all, the struggle with darkness was supposed to be fierce. In any case, the more serious obstacle he and all the Christian missionaries faced was not Chinese hatred but Chinese indifference. The handful of those who accepted Christianity, and the larger handful of active opponents, were dwarfed by the great masses of people who simply ignored the odd-looking missionaries and their curious ideas.

Absalom's arrival in 1880 followed decades of proselytizing that had produced the most meager results. He joined upwards of one thousand missionaries, who had made probably fewer than ten thousand converts altogether. A somewhat more successful future lay ahead, but the numbers of converts would remain paltry.[28] In the first three decades of this century, during the high tide of missionary influence, the number of missionaries passed eight thousand, working under the auspices of several hundred separate missionary societies. The sheer number and variety of Protestant sects, each insisting on its exclusive possession of divine truth, led mainly "to the great confusion of the Chinese," as Pearl Buck herself pointed out.[29] There were never more than a million Chinese Christians in a population that was approaching a half-billion.[30] Furthermore, many of the converts were undoubtedly "rice Christians," less interested in doctrine than in the health care, food, and jobs that baptism often brought in its wake.

Though the direct influence the missionaries had on Chinese beliefs was relatively slight, they played an important cultural role on both sides of the Pacific. In China, the missionaries contributed substantially to the process of modernization – sometimes inadvertently, sometimes by design. As they pursued their evangelical objectives, they frequently addressed questions of literacy, health, women's rights, and agriculture.[31] Jerome Ch'en has claimed that the missionaries, for example, "were the first to draw Chinese attention to the irrational, traditional ways in which men treated women. Polygyny, infanticide, footbinding and the exclusion of women from education all came under attack from the churches."[32] More generally, John King Fairbank argued that missionaries anticipated the Chinese Communist efforts at "the acquisition and Sinification of western knowledge for use in remaking Chinese life."[33] The somewhat ironic case can be made that the missionaries helped to ignite the revolution that would ultimately eradicate them from China.

The political implications of missionary activity were invisible to Absalom Sydenstricker. From the beginning of his long career to the end, he regarded the Chinese only as the object of his religious ministrations. Everything he did, including his rather impressive scholarly work, was propelled by his evangelical ambitions. He mastered the Chinese written language and several spoken dialects, solely as an aid to his preaching.

Even in the context of his fellow missionaries, Absalom represented a conservative point of view. He defended an older orthodoxy that was dogmatic and otherworldly. He was a biblical literalist, and showed almost no interest in the currents of modernism and liberalism that were reshaping Christianity in the late nineteenth century. Many Protestant evangelists tried to adjust their conceptions of Christianity to accommodate the new ideas of social science and Darwinian biology. Absalom remained contemptuous of all such compromises; he called evolution "devilution," and insisted that the Bible contained all the knowledge anyone needed.

He had no interest in the connections between biblical language and historical circumstance, which sometimes led to humorous standoffs. For example, China had few sheep, and Chinese considered sheep cowardly and stupid animals in any case. On the other hand, the dragon had long been regarded in China as an imperial and even divine creature. So, Bible passages that exalted sheep and disparaged dragons were met with disbelief and contempt.[34] Absalom refused to compromise with this sort of heathen ignorance.

He was, in addition, energetically opposed to any involvement in direct social action, an attitude that separated him from many of the missionaries who came to China in the years after he did. To his dying day, he scolded proponents of the Social Gospel for confusing their sacred obligations with such ephemeral activities as education and health care.

Though he was rigid and unyielding in his religious convictions, Absalom's personal manner was usually reserved and even mild. His Chinese audiences, and his children, were often startled by the change that came over him when he stood up to preach. Then he was transformed into a fiery prophet, demanding that the Chinese give up their superstitions and welcome Jesus Christ as their savior.

Most new missionaries spent two years in language study before preaching to the Chinese. Because of his linguistic gifts, Absalom preached his first Chinese sermon just six months after he arrived in the country. Within the English-speaking community, he quickly established himself as something of an authority on the language. Beginning in 1887, he published a series of articles on oral and written Chinese in the *Chinese Recorder*. His subjects included "Variations in the Spoken Language of Northern and Central China," "Southern Mandarin," and "The Dialect of the River and Grand Canal."[35] These are brief, reliable surveys of the major regional differences in Chinese pronunciation, derived from Absalom's own traveling in the countryside. "I have," he wrote, "made it a matter of some care to study the Chinese sounds and their variations from Ningpo to Kalgan, and have certainly convinced myself, if no one else, that the colloquial pronunciation changes more or less every few hundred *li,** and is of almost infinite variety. . . ."[36]

---

*One *li* is about one-third of a mile.

Absalom's preoccupation with colloquial speech determined his opinion in the great debate over biblical translation. He vigorously opposed the use of *wen-yan,* or classical Chinese, on the pragmatic grounds that only a few people in the entire country could read it. In an April, 1888 article in the *Chinese Recorder,* in which he reviewed a new Mandarin version of the Gospel, Absalom wrote: "I am strongly of the opinion . . . that a Mandarin version [of the Gospel] ought to be *thoroughly colloquial* – one that, when read, as in public worship, could be understood as far as possible, even by the illiterate."[37]

Absalom's arguments were learned but completely utilitarian in their purposes. He wanted a Chinese Bible that could be read by more people than just the Confucian literati, and he wanted missionaries who could be understood. The mastery of colloquial and dialectical varieties of Chinese, he wrote, "is highly practical and useful to the missionary as he daily mixes among the people."[38] He would spend many hours over the next thirty years preparing his own translation of the New Testament.

Few American evangelists mixed among the people more energetically than Absalom Sydenstricker. He traveled the countryside, his hair in a long Chinese-style queue, riding a donkey so small that his feet barely cleared the ground. During several of his years in China, Absalom spent more days in the field than at home; he was sometimes gone for a month at a time. To him, these long absences were a signal of his high calling. To his wife, they counted as neglect.

Even when he was home, he was often unavailable to his wife and children. He needed time and privacy to work on his sermons and biblical translations. He also needed money, for books and paper, and grudged his family every dollar spent on clothing or birthday presents. Like other outlanders, on the American frontier and overseas, the Sydenstrickers had copies of the Montgomery Ward mail-order catalogues. For years, Pearl hoped for a baby doll pictured in the catalogue, but she was afraid to ask, and the doll never appeared.[39]

When Absalom went off itinerating, Carie was left alone with her children. The only adults she saw were her Chinese servants and an occasional missionary visitor. She had ample occasion to contemplate the strange outcome of her life. One summer, searching for relief from the heat, she spent several nights in a rented room in a hilltop Buddhist temple. Looking out of the small round window, she pondered the scene before her, the flagstone path and bamboo grove, the enormous incense urn and the chanting, gray-robed priests, and contrasted these alien images wearily with the open meadows and distant hills of her childhood home.[40]

The early years in China severely tested Carie's faith and her physical strength. In September, 1884, her second child, a daughter named Maude, died in infancy. Carie seems to have blamed her death on China and, indirectly at least, on Absalom and his religion. At about the same time, her own health was permanently broken by malaria, dysentery, and a nearly fatal case of tuberculosis. These sorrows drew a line across Carie's spiritual life; from then on, her religious devotion was replaced by skepticism. She decided she had made a tragic mistake in leaving her family and country. She considered returning to America, but elected instead to honor her commitment to her marriage.[41] Her life became a mystery to her, and the world seemed darker. Nearly a century later, when her youngest daughter, Grace, was asked to describe Carie, she replied instantly that she remembered her as especially sad.[42] "I remember her . . . sitting at the piano, or the organ, playing and having to give up because she would begin to weep."[43]

Carie's pain was multiplied by her husband's contempt for her as a woman. Perhaps Absalom was no worse in his attitudes than many other nineteenth-century fundamentalists, but his wife felt the sting of his misogyny throughout her entire married life. He was a man who wished his daughters had been sons; who walked out of church if a woman spoke; who refused to let his wife write a check.

If he had been born in an earlier generation, Pearl later wrote, "he would have burned witches." He harbored "a deep unconscious sex antagonism in him, rooted in no one knows what childhood experiences and fostered, sad to say, by the presence of Carie, that flashing quick mind which he could never comprehend, but against which he struggled to maintain himself. For he could not bear better than another man a woman more clever than himself. Besides, Saint Paul justified him."[44]

Saint Paul ultimately became for Pearl the source and symbol of sexual inequality. Absalom was "imbued," she wrote later, "with the Pauline doctrine of the subjection of the woman to the man and to him it was enough if she kept his house and bore his children and waited on his needs."[45] Pearl's eventual rejection of Christianity had its deepest roots in her irreconcilable anger against traditional Christian views of women. She had watched Carie tormented by the continuous punishment of a theology that belittled her humanity. In one of the most bitter passages she ever wrote, Pearl declared: "Since those days when I saw all her nature dimmed I have hated Saint Paul with all my heart and so must all true women hate him, I think, because of what he has done in the past to women like Carie, proud free-born women, yet damned by their very womanhood."[46]

Carie's grief and doubt never threatened Absalom's serene sense of purpose. Indeed, the most striking and poignant reality of their marriage was the cruel distance that separated Absalom's unshakable tranquility from Carie's abiding regret. He knew that he had made the right choice; she knew with equal certainty that she had chosen badly.

Chinkiang, where the Sydenstrickers lived in the mid-1880s, was a strategically important city. Lying just northeast of Nanking, Chinkiang defends the juncture of the Yangtze River (Chang Jiang) and the Grand Canal. Local records indicated that a few Christian families had lived in the city as early as the fourteenth century.[47] More recently, Chinkiang had been captured by the British during the Opium War, and had become a treaty port, its commerce dominated by the British Concession that sprawled along the river. The crowded lanes bustled with merchants, scholars, messengers, vagrants, lepers, soldiers, and children.

The Sydenstrickers lived in three rooms above a Chinese shop at the edge of the river. Here, Carie nursed her loneliness and her alienation from China. She hated the summer heat, the crowded city alleys and lanes, the omnipresent poverty. Every day, she looked down remorsefully on the Yangtze, which became a symbol for her of everything she feared about Asia: "the flooding, over-powering, insensate life of the Orient."[48] The only sight that gladdened her was the American flag on the masts of some of the trading ships that docked in the harbor.

In 1887, Absalom was transferred to T'sinkiang-p'u, a small city on the Grand Canal, more than a hundred miles north of Chinkiang. "The people are very friendly toward us," he wrote, somewhat wishfully.[49] He found a large, attractive house, in a big courtyard. The rent was low because the house was said to be haunted by the ghost of a former occupant, a woman who had been abused by her husband. Once again, Carie labored hard with paint and furniture to create an American outpost in the Chinese wilderness. The house had a broad front porch, rose bushes on each side, and a view of the valley. The family lived in this house for most of the next decade.

Carie played the organ at Absalom's prayer meetings, but she was more in-terested in bodies than souls. She spent hours talking with Chinese women about their troubles, and did what she could to help them. She showed at least as much facility with spoken colloquial Chinese as her husband; her children, in fact, later recalled that she communicated more easily than he did. While Absalom was urging Christians to resist humanitarian temptations and to show no tenderness for heathenism, Carie was doing her best to ease the suffering of poor women, with affection, Western medicine from a small dispensary she organized, and sometimes food or clothing.[50]

In the summer of 1890, the Sydenstrickers' youngest child, Arthur, died at the age of a year and six months. When Carie and Absalom took Arthur's body to Shanghai for burial alongside Maude in the Christian cemetery, three-year-old Edith contracted cholera and died within a few days. Carie was inconsolable. Three of her first four children were now buried in a single grave; only nine-year-old Edgar had survived. Carie's pain was mirrored by the pathos of the graveyard where her children lay: a small, sad square of land, enclosed by high walls and locked, spiked gates. Such cemeteries could be found in every Chinese city, symbols that the unbridgeable distance between white and Asian endured even in death.

Carie needed to go back to the United States, and the Sydenstrickers, who had now spent ten years in China, were eligible for a year of home leave. They traveled the westward route on the steamer *Bokhara,* which called at Hong Kong, Singapore, and Colombo. From Italy they journeyed through Holland, where Carie traced her family roots, and England. Their furlough ultimately lasted nearly two years; Carie became pregnant and insisted that this baby would be born in America. A daughter, whom she named Pearl Comfort, was born on June 26, 1892, in the Stulting home in Hillsboro. Pearl was Carie's fifth child, the only one born in the United States, and only the second who would survive infancy.

WHEN SHE WAS three months old, Pearl was taken to China – in a market basket, she later claimed.[51] Carie's long visit with her family and the hours she had spent in the West Virginia hills had lifted her spirits. She felt a renewed sense of commitment to the Chinese, and she also felt tied to China by the children she had buried there. Shortly after she returned to T'sinkiang-p'u, she had another baby, a boy she and Absalom named Clyde.

Not long after the family had come back to China, Absalom published an article on "Jesus as a Teacher and Trainer" in the *Chinese Recorder.* Intended as a comment on Scripture, these pages offer a more profound insight into Absalom's character than almost anything else he wrote. In the article, he argued at length that Jesus was best understood as a teacher or trainer rather than a preacher. That is, Jesus's public preaching was less important to his mission than the teaching he did with small groups of disciples. Even the Sermon on the Mount, in Absalom's reading of it, was intended more for the select company of Jesus's friends and followers than for the multitudes. Similarly, Jesus used parables specifically to conceal "from the unbelieving rabble that precious truth which they would only trample under their feet." In all his work, Absalom adds, Jesus "obeyed his own injunction not to 'give that which is holy unto dogs,' nor to 'cast pearls before swine.' "[52]

Though the subject is Jesus and the early church, this essay is autobiographical, an act of self-defense. Only the elite few can appreciate the Christian message; the masses remain on the unenlightened margins. Aside from justifying his religion in the face of almost universal Chinese indifference, Absalom is here reinforcing his image of himself: like the earliest Christians, he is one of the beleaguered, one of the chosen, a true descendant of the Apostles.

In its combination of righteousness, angry isolation, and suppressed anxiety, the essay accurately summarizes Absalom when Pearl began to know him. At a time when Protestant theology was changing, when liberalism or modernism was replacing fundamentalism,[53] Absalom remained true to the more unyielding creed of his youth: "Heaven was actual, a space filled with solid goods. Hell did burn, not only for the evil unbelieving, but far more horrible, for those who died in ignorance."[54]

Absalom was goaded by a terrible urgency to save the Chinese masses from eternal suffering. His dogmatism was absolute, and his cerebral detachment removed him from the circle of intimacy that joined Pearl and Carie. Because of his frequent and lengthy absences in the field, his appearances were momentous and usually unsettling. He figured in Pearl's earliest memories more as a spectral stranger than as a father, a person whose role in the household seemed rather obscure.

Absalom's enthusiasms were exclusively theological. As a Southern Presbyterian, he represented one of the most conservative Christian denominations, and he defended his version of the Gospel with a ferocity that sometimes bordered on the ghoulish or comic. He fought a thirty-year battle with a one-eyed Baptist preacher who continually poached on his territory, warning Absalom's Chinese converts that they couldn't be saved without total immersion. When the Baptist was found one morning, dead in his bed of heart failure, Absalom remarked: "I knew the Lord would not allow that sort of thing to go on forever." Pearl recalled that his tone as he said this was one of "calm and righteous triumph."[55]

The most important people in Pearl's childhood were her mother, her older brother, Edgar, whom she apparently idolized, and her Chinese amah (governess), Wang. Wang had been a pretty woman, with three-inch bound feet, who had been sold by her family as a bride when she was still a girl. After a few years of marriage, Wang's husband had died in the Taiping Rebellion of the 1850s, and she had struggled through the next thirty years, supporting herself mainly as a prostitute. Carie had brought her in off the street and installed her as nurse and governess to the Sydenstricker children. Amah Wang dressed the baby Pearl in a Chinese cap decorated with small images of Buddha – an impropriety for a missionary child that Carie nonetheless overlooked.

In 1896, the Sydenstrickers moved back to Chinkiang, where they remained for the next twenty-five years. Once again, Carie furnished a house and planted a garden, but this time she determined that she would settle down where she was. Though she rarely defied Absalom, she informed him that neither she nor her children would move to another city. She lived in Chinkiang for the rest of her life in China.

Pearl was four years old when her family moved to Chinkiang. Her first several years there lingered in her memory as a kaleidoscope of Western and Eastern images. Throughout her childhood, she lived in two worlds: "the small white clean Presbyterian American world of [her] parents and the big loving merry not-so-clean Chinese world." There was, she later wrote, "no communication between them."[56] She was never quite sure where she belonged, or whether she belonged anywhere.

She was simultaneously an outsider and an insider in two different societies. Her divided situation rather resembled the "two-ness" of American blacks, as W. E. B. Du Bois described it in *The Souls of Black Folks* (1903). In Du Bois's classic formulation: "It is a peculiar sensation, this double-consciousness, this sense of always looking at one's self through the eyes of others, of measuring one's soul by the tape of a world that looks on in amused contempt and pity. One ever feels his two-ness. . . ."[57] Without pressing the analogy too hard, it can be argued that Pearl was one of the few white Americans who grew up experiencing something of the sense of isolation and presumed inferiority that American blacks have known in white America. Her early years as a member of a minority group did much to shape her later commitment to racial equality and cultural pluralism.

To be sure, white people in China in those years usually occupied a protected and even a privileged position. In particular, they enjoyed the immunities conferred by extraterritoriality, which kept them beyond the reach of Chinese justice. Legal entitlement, however, could not conceal the universal evidence of Chinese contempt, nor did it prevent periodic outbursts of murderous violence. All of China's white intruders knew that their presence was resented and their safety was fragile. They knew that, on any given day, they might be attacked because they were foreigners.

While all children experience moments of loneliness, Pearl's situation was exceptional. Growing up in an atmosphere of alienation, she felt continuously disoriented and displaced. She knew that China was not her home, but she had never known any other. The Chinese, even those who were friendly to her, treated her like the yellow-haired foreigner she was. Her parents' house, which might have offered a shelter, was instead a place of restless tensions. Her father was grimly indifferent to her emotional needs and her mother reminded her every day that they were exiles. Carie eased her discontent by instructing Pearl in the heroic tales of men such as Washington, Jefferson, and Madison, Southern men who had built America and bequeathed a legacy of greatness to their political descendants.

Pearl felt in some literal sense abandoned. Her feeling of separation was the central fact of her childhood, and did much to shape her adult relationship to the world. Her lifelong passion for reading and her remarkable self-sufficiency had their roots in her lonely childhood years, as did her inability to make intimate friendships. The large family she later assembled, adopting seven children and

3. An itinerant storyteller in a northern Chinese village. (From J. Lossing Buck, *Chinese Farm Economy*; Courtesy the University of Chicago Press.)

acting as foster mother to many more, was her response to the unsettling and often strangely quiet household Carie and Absalom made for her.

Pearl's odd circumstances also brought advantages. When she was four years old, she could sing "Jesus Loves Me" in both Chinese and English.[58] She grew up fully bilingual, speaking and reading both languages. She learned English in her home, and colloquial Chinese from Amah Wang and the Chinese children she sometimes played with. Though Carie tried to discourage the practice, Wang and the children told Pearl some of the most popular Chinese tales, including "The Kitchen God," "The Jar of Silver," and "Why the Gods Stood Up." Pearl heard stories of devils and fairies, of magic swords and daggers, of the fearsome dragon that was imprisoned in a nearby pagoda.[59]

Pearl also spent many afternoons sitting on the hard benches of the local Chinese theater. Wide-eyed, she watched noisy melodramas in which costumed figures of good and evil battled for mastery. Good invariably triumphed, sometimes at the expense of villains who represented Western invaders. Pearl found herself cheering the massacre of red-haired foreign devils.

Pearl was tutored in *wen-yan,* the classical Chinese language, by Mr. Kung, and in English literature by her mother. She liked to read; when she was still only seven or eight years old she was reading both Chinese and English literature. Her Chinese texts included selections from Confucius, Mencius, and some of the major poets; the English books she remembered best were Fox's *Book of*

Martyrs, Plutarch's *Lives,* the Bible, the poems of Tennyson and Browning, the novels of Scott and Thackeray, and, above all, the works of Dickens.

Unlike almost every other American of her generation, Pearl grew up knowing China as her actual world, while America was the dreamworld, the place of fantasy and imagination. If her life as a missionary child was in many ways provincial, it was also decidedly cosmopolitan. The adults she met included Asians and Europeans, men and women from India, Japan, Korea, Thailand, and Vietnam, as well as France, England, Russia, and Italy.

As a child in the care of a Chinese amah, Pearl learned a great deal about ordinary life in China. She spent hours wandering Chinkiang's streets with her amah, overhearing the talk of ordinary people, and watching the barbers, herbal doctors, food vendors, carpenters, and slaves go about their business. When she had a few copper cash, she bought triangular packages of peanuts or hot sweet potatoes or watermelons from street carts. Goggle-eyed, she stared at the little apes on chains and the dancing bears and the magicians.

Occasionally an aristocratic woman would be carried past in a lavishly decorated sedan chair, borne on the shoulders of four men. Pearl watched New Year's festivals and weddings and funerals, and learned that red was the color of good luck, white the color of death and mourning. She often ate with her family's servants and acquired a taste for the local cuisine.

A girl growing up in a relentlessly patriarchal household, Pearl was especially attentive to the Chinese girls and women she met. She found that they, too, were trapped in a sexual caste system throughout their entire lives, a system even more punishing than the one she had seen at home. She was puzzled at the embarrassment that accompanied the birth of girl children, and she grieved when she learned about the practice of female infanticide. On more than one occasion, she found an unmarked, shallow grave in which the nude body of a baby girl had been buried. At least once, she chased away a dog that had dug the body up and reburied the tiny corpse. She was angry that boys were educated and girls were not. Appalled but fascinated by the bound feet of her amah and other Chinese women, she understood, even as a child, that this barbaric custom symbolized male supremacy.

At the same time, she observed how powerful Chinese women often were. The legends of women warriors, in which heroic, mythical female figures triumphed over men, dragons, and demons, were among the most popular stories in the Chinese common culture. Pearl knew those stories, and she also knew that social fact often echoed folk tale: among farmers and gentry alike, homes were typically ruled by the senior women in a kind of domestic matriarchy. Beyond that, the Chinese nation itself was governed throughout Pearl's childhood by a woman, the Dowager Empress Tz'u-hsi (Cixi), whose remarkable career had taken her from imperial concubine to imperial authority in the 1860s.

Tz'u-hsi served officially as regent, first for her son, Tung Chih (Tongzhi), who died in 1875, then for her nephew Kwang Hsu (Guangxu), whom she personally named Tung Chih's successor. In 1898, Kwang Hsu, influenced by reformers within the Confucian literati, attempted to assert his own authority, by issuing a famous series of liberalizing edicts. Tz'u-hsi responded by deposing him and finally assuming direct control of the country. Her domination of China made her the most powerful woman in the 250-year history of the Ch'ing (Qing) dynasty. Her half-century on (or behind) the Dragon Throne was unprecedented, and undoubtedly required larger portions of leadership and judgment than a male ruler would have needed. She was willing to negotiate when she had to, for instance making concessions to the superior military force of the Western invaders. She was also eager to fight when she thought she could win. Her rivals often disappeared or died, sometimes mysteriously. As a child, young Pearl was dazzled by Tz'u-hsi, and hoped that she might one day grow up to become Empress herself.[60]

In spite of its durability and its outward signs of strength, the Ch'ing dynasty faced formidable problems at the end of the nineteenth century. Tz'u-hsi's attempts to suppress her nephew's liberal reforms were only briefly successful. The modern world, with its technologies and plural ideologies, besieged the old order and could not be permanently held back. Tz'u-hsi herself recognized this, at least from time to time; she shifted back and forth between opposition to reform and alliance with it. She also understood that the rising tide of anti-foreign, anti-imperial sentiment could easily threaten the Manchu Ch'ing, who were still regarded by many of the Chinese people as alien invaders.

Anger against foreign intruders led to an increasing number of violent episodes in the 1890s, culminating in the Boxer Uprising of 1900. The many groups that made up the Harmonious Fists United in Righteousness comprised a miscellaneous collection of intellectuals, farmers, and unemployed workers, as well as a large cadre of women. There was a mystical cast to Boxer ideas, including a belief that they would be immune from harm if they were attacked by guns and swords. They made the missionaries their particular targets, along with Chinese Christian converts; during several months of bloodshed, dozens of missionaries and several hundred converts were killed. Defiant wall posters were emblazoned with slogans and poems denouncing the Christians and their churches:

No rain comes from Heaven,
The earth is parched and dry,
And all because the churches
Have bottled up the sky.[61]

For several months, Tz'u-hsi vacillated. Eventually, she chose to support the uprising, which inspired the Boxers to more furious assaults. The most murderous attack occurred in Shansi (Shanxi) province, where forty-four men, women, and children of several missionary families were killed on the orders of the provincial governor.

These atrocities brought a ruinous outcome to China. In mid-summer, 20,000 foreign troops from Japan, Russia, the United States, Britain, and France battered their way from the coast to Peking. Journalist Thomas Millard, an eyewitness, wrote that "every town, every village, every peasant's hut in the path of the troops was first looted and then burned." The invaders produced a scene of carnage, Millard believed, that "will leave a taint in the moral atmosphere of the world for generations to come."[62] By August, the foreign soldiers had entered Peking and broken the uprising. The treaty that followed imposed crushing financial penalties, together with a long list of humiliating punishments: China was obliged to build a monument to the Western dead, execute the Boxer leaders, and accept a foreign military presence in perpetuity.

Years later, Pearl Buck condemned the punitive Boxer settlement as an act of imperialist piracy. In her view, the episode proved that America was morally indistinguishable from the other great powers that had attempted to dismember China: "We were to be allowed to come and go as we liked over the Chinese earth, our ships of merchandise and our men of war were to be permitted to sail the waters and dock at any port." Not surprisingly, she singled out the religious clauses of the settlement for extended comment. "Our missionaries were given the freedom to live where they wished, to open schools foreign in all they taught, [and] to establish hospitals which practiced foreign medicine and surgery." She called these missionary intrusions a form of "spiritual imperialism." The most pernicious of all the evangelical activities, she argued, was that "these missionaries were free to preach a religion entirely alien to the Chinese, nay, to insist upon this religion as the only true one and to declare that those who refused to believe would and must descend into hell. The effrontery of all this still makes my soul shrink."[63]

In retrospect, it is clear that the Boxer Uprising accelerated the collapse of the Ch'ing dynasty by dramatizing the weakness of the imperial government. Reformers and revolutionaries alike were energized by the failure of China's central authority to protect the country from foreign intrusion. The Empress Dowager embarked on her own campaign of reforms – among other things, the ancient examination system was abolished in 1905 – but she merely undermined her own credibility.

The Sydenstrickers spent several fearful months during the uprising wondering what their fate might be. The violence was centered mainly north and west of Chinkiang, but Westerners along much of the coast and inland as well were molested and killed. Absalom was sometimes stoned and spat on as he went relentlessly on with his preaching. On one frightening occasion, he was tied to a post and forced to watch as an angry mob tortured a Chinese convert woman to death.[64] It was in these days, Pearl wrote later, that the two worlds of her eight-year-old childhood finally split apart. Chinese friends now shunned the family, and Western visitors were fewer; the streets were alive with rumors – many, of course, based on fact – of brutality to missionaries and converts. Carie, Pearl, and the new baby, Grace, were evacuated to the relative safety of Shanghai, where they spent nearly a year as refugees, living in a boarding house near Bubbling Well Road. Edgar was sent to live with relatives in the United States. Carie spent her days sighing for her vanished American home, and telling Pearl stories of the wonderful, Christian country they had lost. Absalom remained at his mission post, apparently quite prepared to add his name to the list of Christian martyrs.

ABSALOM NEVER SPOKE about his experiences in Chinkiang during the dangerous year of 1900–1901, but he seems to have been beaten on several occasions, and he almost surely faced repeated threats to his life. Carie waited anxiously in Shanghai through the long months of separation; she received only a few letters from her husband and fragmentary reports from other refugees. Each night, his daughters, Pearl and baby Grace, would pray, "God, please keep our father from the Boxers." When Absalom finally rejoined his family, he was exhausted, dispirited, and prepared to take another extended home leave.

On July 8, 1901, the Sydenstrickers sailed from Shanghai for San Francisco; they would not return to China until September of the following year. When they landed in California, Pearl was shocked to see white men loading cargo and carrying baggage. "Mother," she asked Carie, "are even the coolies over here white people?" The family spent several days in California, then traveled by train to West Virginia. As always, Carie was delighted to be back in the United States. At the same time, she felt alienated from America in a way that at first surprised and disturbed her. She began to realize that twenty years of exile were slowly but irrevocably separating her from her family and from the land of her birth. The place she had left empty when she went to China had long since been filled by others. She felt that she no longer had a home either in China or in the United States. Carie communicated her mixed feelings to Pearl, who dated her earliest feelings of homelessness to this journey.

The Boxer Uprising that had driven the Sydenstrickers temporarily out of Asia had also created a crisis in relations between China and the United States. For one thing, this was the first time that U.S. armed forces had marched with troops of other Western powers in an assault on Chinese nationals. American newspapers gave the episode fairly extensive coverage, diligently exploiting anti-Chinese hysteria. The "slaughter of the innocents," as some papers called the

4. The Sydenstricker family in about 1901: Pearl, Absalom, Grace, and Carie. Behind them stands Wang, the children's governess. (Reproduced with permission of the Pearl S. Buck Foundation.)

murder of missionaries and their families, merely confirmed the dark suspicions that many Americans had long held about the moral character of the Chinese people.

If, as the Sydenstrickers traveled across the country, they had tried to measure the attitudes of their fellow citizens toward China, they would have found, in the first place, that the great majority of Americans had no opinion at all. Except for moments of international drama such as war and rebellion, neither China nor the Chinese people crossed most American minds from one week to the next. Few Americans, after all, had ever even seen a Chinese person. In 1900, when the population of the United States stood at seventy million, the total number of Chinese in the country was no more than 400,000, and the great majority of those were clustered in a half–dozen cities on the East and West coasts.[65] However, among those Americans who did have an opinion about the Chinese, it seems clear that hostility far outweighed approval. The Boxer Uprising had undoubtedly strengthened that presumption by demonstrating that the Chinese were indeed murderous heathens.

Beginning in the 1870s, immigration had become the principal focus of anti-Chinese sentiment. In the years immediately following the Civil War, when the great transcontinental railroads were being built, Chinese laborers were welcomed. Later, however, when they tried to enter other sectors of the labor marketplace, they began to meet anger, violence, and legislation aimed at their exclusion; this was especially true in hard economic times. As Robert McClellan puts it, "In 1869 the Central Pacific met the Union Pacific in Utah. Nine years later the Nevada mines collapsed. In between these dates the presence of the Chinese had changed from a blessing to a curse."[66]

Resentment against the Chinese, which arose first in California, swept across the country, becoming a national issue in the early 1880s. The first Chinese exclusion act, which suspended immigration for ten years, was passed in 1882; it was extended for another ten years in 1892, through the Geary Act, and for another ten in 1902. (Indeed, it was not until 1943, in the midst of World War II, that the exclusion acts were finally repealed.) Organized labor offered major support for exclusion, since the principal consequence of unlimited immigration was seen then – as it is now – to be increased and unfair competition for jobs.

Economic antagonism was reinforced by cultural and racial polemics. In the songs and jokes of popular culture, the wily and inscrutable Chinaman joined the drunken Irishman and the avaricious Jew as a stock comic figure. Newspaper cartoons, an innovation of the 1890s, quickly began pandering to the national Sinophobia; daily and Sunday strips were filled with the slanted eyes, long queues, and robes of burlesque characters who muttered in pidgin English as they schemed, soliloquized, and eventually came to some bad end or other.[67] Broadway contributed its caricatures, in such musicals as *The King of the Opium Ring, Chop Suey One Lung, Chinatown Charlie,* and *Queen of Chinatown.* The songs introduced in these productions included "Chin-Chin Chinaman," "Toy Monkey," "China Bogeyman," "Chinee Soje Man," "Chinky China Charleston," and Victor Herbert's "Chink! Chink!"[68]

American Chinatowns became tourist attractions, famous for filth and vice and strange odors. Tours were often led by police officers, whose commentary exploited the widespread white fear of Chinese "secret societies" and always included titillating stories of brothels and opium dens. A visitor to San Francisco's Chinatown in the 1890s wrote breathlessly of the "agglomeration of Oriental paganism" she had discovered: "reeking sidewalks, foul with unknown trash; the nauseous odors vomited from black cellars; the wilderness of alleys; . . . and sphinx-eyed, crafty yellow men who glide along the narrow pavements."[69]

Stereotypes could be found in serious journals as well as the sensational press. A writer in *The Galaxy*, for example, proposed that "the Mongol and the Negro are but human saurians who reached long ago . . . their full development, and are now moral fossils."[70] Liberal clergyman Lyman Abbott, editor of *Outlook*, endorsed the 1902 exclusion act with the observation that the Chinese are "a persistently servile and alien population, whose presence is injurious alike to the standards of American labor and American citizenship." Similar comments could be found in such influential magazines as *Scribner's*, *Century*, and the *Atlantic Monthly*.[71]

Unfortunately, the same poisonous attitudes were expressed by the men who managed America's foreign affairs at the turn of the century. Theodore Roosevelt described the Chinese as an "immoral, degraded and worthless race." Roosevelt's first Secretary of State, John Hay, always referred to the Chinese as "chinks."

Missionary testimony did not substantially alter the negative perceptions that most Americans held of the Chinese. While missionaries made contributions to a fuller understanding of Asian culture, most of them seem to have shared the sense of Western superiority that governed American behavior throughout this period. Even those who were relatively sympathetic felt obliged to emphasize China's fundamental immorality and its desperate need for conversion. The Chinese were "sitting in darkness," according to a daily prayer used by the Catholic Foreign Mission Society (the Maryknoll Fathers) as late as the 1960s.[72] Like diplomats, the missionaries believed that China was essentially helpless to save itself. Westerners concurred that the Chinese, whether they realized it or not, needed to import Christianity, democracy, and science, the great gifts of the West that would bring the benighted country into the twentieth century.

In short, missionaries tended to reinforce rather than dispute the basic assumptions on which American policy toward China was based. Politicians could depend on evangelists to affirm that the United States had a civilizing destiny, a responsibility to bring the world's lesser breeds up to an American standard. In the 1890s, the established religions tended to approve of America's entry into the imperialist adventure on which European colonial powers had been embarked for over a century.

After its easy defeat of Spain in 1898, the United States "suddenly became a colonial power."[73] Within two years, the presidential election of 1900 was contested in large measure as a plebiscite on imperialism, and William McKinley's solid victory indicated that after a century and more of resisting foreign entanglements, many Americans were ready to endorse a diplomacy of expansion and intervention. In 1898, Judge H. H. Powers summarized what he took to be a remarkable transformation:

A year ago we wanted no colonies, no alliances, no European neighbors, no army and not much navy. . . . Our role in the world was to be *nil*, and the rest of the new world that of the dog in the manger. The Monroe Doctrine was construed as requiring no constructive action on our part toward the civilized world. The Washington Doctrine was frankly interpreted to mean national isolation. Our position on these points might be questionable, but it was not equivocal. We at least knew our own minds.

To-day every one of these principles is challenged, if not definitely rejected.[74]

The causes of this about-face have been the subject of disagreement among scholars for many years. Manifest Destiny, social Darwinism, capitalist expansionism, the influence of European pro-imperialist propaganda – these are among the explanations historians have offered for America's changed understanding of its proper world role.

A less noted but powerful instrument in the making of American imperial ideology was the influence of what James Reed has called "the missionary mind." As Reed and most other observers have pointed out, American foreign policy in the twentieth century has been marked by a curious combination of arrogance and benevolence, a conviction that other nations can only advance by accepting American help on American terms. That mentality is, in some considerable part, the legacy of the missionary enterprise.[75] The Methodist McKinley, discussing his government's annexation of the Philippines, explained that there "was nothing left for us to do but to take [the islands], and to educate the Filipinos, and uplift and Christianize them, and by God's grace do the very best we could by them, as our fellowmen for whom Christ also died."[76]

The missionaries contributed their share to the patronizing and ultimately self-serving posture of moral obligation that would inform American relations with China – indeed with all of Asia – throughout the twentieth century. The centerpiece of American diplomatic engagement with China in the early 1900s, the Open Door policy, "with its presumption of [American] innocence, friendliness, self-denial, moral leadership," was itself essentially a missionary idea.[77] Furthermore, Christianity was explicitly and frequently invoked by political leaders as one of the "blessings" to be shared with Asian peoples by the West. Finally, in the absence of other mechanisms, the missionary was the chief instrument of educating the policy elite about China and the rest of Asia.

A century ago, American high schools and universities taught almost nothing about Asia. In 1898, when John Fryer was named Agassiz Professor of Oriental

Languages and Literature at the University of California, he was the first faculty member appointed to such a position in the country. Over the following decades, Asian studies slowly emerged as an academic field, but only in a small group of institutions, and even in those places Asian programs were typically underfunded embellishments to more traditional courses of instruction. History textbooks virtually ignored Asia, relying on the usual cluster of derisive commonplaces.[78] In geography books, Asia was scarcely mentioned, aside from a glance at the Great Wall and a reference to China's teeming masses.[79]

Consequently, at the turn of the century, no one in the American foreign policy establishment had ever spent as much as a single day in the formal study of Asia. To be sure, some Americans already suspected that China would play a decisive role in the future. President Theodore Roosevelt sneered at "chinks," but he also shrewdly predicted that "our future history will be more determined by our position on the Pacific facing China than by our position on the Atlantic facing Europe."[80] Yet, because of the systematic neglect of Asia in American schools and universities, practically nothing was actually known about this enormous region of the planet, home to one-quarter of its people. In 1900, eight-year-old Pearl Sydenstricker undoubtedly knew more about the language, literature, and customs of China than Secretary of State John Hay and his principal deputies.

In the absence of organized university programs, missionaries were responsible for most of the Asian scholarship that Americans produced.[81] The missionaries' credentials were in some respects quite impressive. They tended to stay longer in China than diplomats, business persons, or military officers – often, indeed, for a lifetime – and most of them lived nearer to the common people. Above all, the missionaries were almost unique among Westerners in attempting to learn the Chinese language.

Predictably, most missionary writing was theological or autobiographical. However, missionaries also made significant and often innovative additions to the study of China's history and culture. They helped to lay the foundation for twentieth-century scholarship in a dozen different fields.

The publications of American missionaries included J. C. Ferguson's studies of Chinese art, F. H. Chalfant's research on oracle bones, G. B. Cressey's important geographies, and Absalom Sydenstricker's grammar texts. John Lossing Buck (Pearl's first husband) did pioneering work in Chinese agricultural economics, H. H. Dubs produced translations of Chinese chronicles, A. W. Hummel gathered and annotated Ch'ing biographies, and Ida C. Pruitt studied Chinese family life.[82]

Among these missionary publications, by far the most important were those of Arthur H. Smith, in his book on Chinese village life, and especially in his later, legendary volume, *Chinese Characteristics* (1894).[83] Smith was a New Englander who had studied at Beloit and had served briefly in the Wisconsin infantry in the Civil War. He went to China as a Congregational minister in 1872, accompanied by his wife Emma Dickenson; over the next thirty years, his assignments took him to several Chinese cities. Like a good many other evangelists in his generation, including Absalom Sydenstricker, he "insisted as a matter of principle on wearing Chinese clothes and eating with chopsticks."[84]

One student of Smith's work has called him "the sharpest of missionary observers."[85] Another has suggested that he brought an "almost anthropological" way of looking at his subjects, an organizing imagination that reached for general principles to explain social behavior.[86] Smith professed a certain respect for cultural difference, probably to an unusual extent for his generation. He frequently noted the advantages of Chinese customs, and defended China from the charge that it is uncivilized: a "superficial and erroneous judgment," he writes, that "is due to an unphilosophical confounding of civilization and comfort." No one, he continued, would consider "the England of Milton, Shakespeare, and Elizabeth as an uncivilised country, but nothing is more certain than that to the most of us it would now prove to be intolerable."[87]

Nonetheless, Smith, like the other missionary scholars of his generation, inevitably used American and Christian values as his norms. Thus, his comparisons are often invidious, and his analysis frequently bristles with disapproval. His catalogues of what is absent from Chinese society are tantamount to lists of the elements of middle-class Western culture: punctuality, accuracy, public spirit. In Smith's account, the Chinese are indifferent to time, to crowding and noise, to the value of privacy; they know nothing at all of sanitation and they display a stoic disregard for comfort and convenience. They are irrationally sensitive to the loss of face yet at the same time amused by Western notions of guilt. They are notoriously cruel to animals.

Along with most of his contemporaries, Smith believed that in the end Chinese were simply not quite as human as Americans and other Westerners. He drew a line, automatically and almost instinctively, between Chinese behavior and what he would have acknowledged as normal. The most sensational example of his attitude can be found in his chapter on "the absence of nerves" among Chinese, and their insensitivity to pain. As Smith tells it, the Chinese have been equipped by nature with a tolerance for pain that far exceeds Western limits. This in turn helps to explain their allegedly exceptional cruelty in torture and warfare. Such was Smith's portrait of the Chinese, an amalgam of truth, half-truth, and outright fable.[88]

A century ago, Americans read *Chinese Characteristics* to learn about the Chinese; today, his book seems more useful as a guide to the cultural assumptions his judgments reveal. The conclusion is disquieting. Smith's prose is marked by a worldliness and sophistication that many Westerners lacked. It is probably fair to say that *Chinese Characteristics* presents an account of the Chinese people that is somewhat more generous than the turn-of-the-century average. Certainly the nearsighted Absalom Sydenstricker had a far less sympathetic response to China and its people than Arthur Smith. Unfortunately, the comparison suggests that, even at their best, missionary representations of Asia were blinkered and myopic, a species of the "Orientalism" that has consistently bedeviled Western perceptions of Asia.

Historians generally agree that *Chinese Characteristics* was the most widely read and influential work written about China by any American in the nineteenth century. It had a long reach; published in the 1890s, "it was still among the five most read books on China among foreigners living in China as late as the 1920s."[89] Prior to the fiction of Pearl Buck, no extended commentary on the Chinese had so much to do with shaping America's images of Asia in this century. Smith's analysis was superior to the merely vulgar racism that informed much of American popular culture and defined the nation's foreign policy. In the end, however, his views tended to reinforce the widely shared xenophobia that united Americans across class and region.

FEW TRACES SURVIVE of the year Pearl spent in America with her family. Her memories eventually distilled themselves into a handful of pleasant but rather vague images: cousins to play with, an orchard of fruit trees, cows and horses, and unwalled meadow. The Stulting house in West Virginia, so much larger than Chinese houses, was surrounded by acres of open fields, in sharp contrast to the crowded streets of Chinkiang and the minutely cultivated plots of rural Kiangsu (Jiangsu) province. In the summer, red and white grapes hung from the arbor, low enough for a little girl to reach, and the fall brought a radiance to the trees on the hillsides that Pearl had never seen in China. For the first time in her life, she heard English being spoken on the streets and in the shops of the towns she visited.

She enjoyed America, but she was disappointed, as she would be throughout her life, that the people she met seemed to have so little interest in China. She also felt her separation from other children, the roughhousing boys and giggling girls whose behavior she continually found mysterious. Communities are knit together not only by beliefs and assumptions, but by the countless small gestures and tribal customs that everyone takes for granted. Pearl knew that she was an alien in turn-of-the-century America, an outsider indelibly marked by her differences. At eight years old, she was already sequestered in isolation.

One Sunday morning, Pearl announced that she wanted to join the church, mainly to justify putting on a new white dress that she wanted very much to wear. She was received that same afternoon. It was an experience she found frightening in prospect, but rather uninspiring when it actually occurred. In any case, her somewhat ambivalent Christian witness was the most significant episode in an otherwise uneventful year. The family spent several months in Hillsboro, then moved to Lexington, Virginia, to assist Edgar's enrollment as a freshman at Washington and Lee College. There were moments of tension, the unavoidable consequence of the perpetual strain between Absalom and Carie, but for the most part, the American months were tranquil.

Yet even here, thousands of miles from the bloodshed of the Boxer Uprising, Pearl was reminded that the world she was growing up in was a violent place. In September of 1901, shortly after the Sydenstrickers had settled into Hillsboro, President William McKinley was assassinated. There was an historical irony in McKinley's death that Pearl would only detect many years later. The president's murder had nothing to do with Asia – he was shot by a deranged European immigrant, a self-styled anarchist named Leon Czolgosz – but it formed a tragic coda to the most recent chapter in the history of America's relations with China. McKinley had presided over the transformation of the United States into an imperial power; among other things, he had personally ordered American troops to join the allied mission against the Boxers. The murder of the president, on top of the violence she had witnessed in China, confirmed Pearl's growing fears that the adult world on both sides of the Pacific was untrustworthy, often even treacherous.

As the furlough year drew to a close, Carie worried that China's political instability made a return to Chinkiang unwise. Absalom scoffed at his wife's misgivings, and the Sydenstrickers went back to their mission post in the fall of 1902. On the Pacific voyage, they were accompanied by Rev. W. A. P. Martin, one of the most distinguished Presbyterian evangelists of his generation.[90] Martin shared Absalom's view that China was once again safe for Western religious proselytizing.[91]

For a while, Absalom's optimism was apparently vindicated. In the post-Boxer years, foreigners went about their religious and commercial business unmolested, secured from interference by the military power of their several governments. The Chinese, who knew that any opposition would bring swift punishment, grudgingly occupied the status of second-class citizens in their own country. Underneath the surface of their compulsory compliance, however, their bitterness inexorably expanded. As in any situation where cooperation is enforced at gunpoint, the appearance of harmony was an illusion. Those were "strangely hesitant years," Pearl wrote later, a time of misleading, brittle happiness.[92] A day of reckoning was postponed, but it would surely come.

This reality was invisible to Absalom Sydenstricker. Instead, he noted the disappearance of overt dissent and decided that God had worked a miracle in a heathen land. He enjoyed his most successful years in the first decade of the

5. Twelve-year-old Pearl, standing behind Grace, teaches English and hygiene to a class of Chinese girls. (Courtesy Presbyterian Historical Society.)

twentieth century, itinerating endlessly throughout Kiangsu province, preaching every day, accumulating thousands of converts. By 1905, he numbered over two hundred schools and churches in his jurisdiction, a spiritual empire of impressive dimensions. Though he was now in his fifties, Absalom remained strong and was tirelessly energetic in his evangelizing; he never knew a sick day. He still traveled on foot and by mule on his overland journeys. He also outfitted a small junk which he used to navigate the Yangtze canals. In each village he visited, he refused special treatment and always insisted on the most rudimentary accommodations. Where there was no dedicated church facility, he preached in tea shops; he usually slept on a *kang* (a stone or brick sleeping slab) in a peasant home and ate whatever was served.

In a May, 1908 letter to the *Chinese Recorder,* he bemoaned the recent tendency of missionaries to choose indoor work and paperwork over itinerating. "I will not state the reasons which occur to me for this," he concluded, with his customary sense of superiority and his contempt for laziness and physical cowardice. Whatever his faults, he was a brave, hardworking man. In 1910, he was one of the founders of the Evangelistic Association, which was established to promote "the direct evangelistic phase of mission work." To the end of his life, he clung to the belief that a preacher's place was out among the people he hoped to convert.

In a June, 1910 article, "The Importance of the Direct Phase of Mission Work," Absalom insisted that "It is our plain and most important duty to bring the Gospel with all available force directly and unremittingly to bear upon all whom we can reach of the vast multitudes among we are placed who are enveloped in darkness." He estimated that, in spite of their plain duty, fewer than one-third of the missionaries in China were actually engaged directly in the work.

The article concludes with an uncharacteristically personal and rather poignant lament: "Idolatry is not yet dead." Absalom describes himself as an evangelist who "has been itinerating from year to year over a field containing easily one million people, the sole representative of any Protestant missionary society in that field." What he typically found was that towns and even good-sized walled cities contained "not so much as a Chinese evangelist except in two or three places." As a consequence, he has been forced to conclude that "heathenism with all its vices is still living and active. Temples and ancestral halls are constantly being built or repaired . . . the apparent hopelessness of the situation has become well-nigh overwhelming."[93]

Absalom's dedication to direct evangelistic action earned him a portion of grudging respect from his more sedentary colleagues. His reputation as a scholar also flourished in these post-Boxer years. In July, 1908, he was invited to contribute the lead article to a special issue of the *Recorder* dealing with the Chinese language. He was also asked to review the new Mandarin New Testament, a much-coveted assignment. In early 1909, he was unanimously elected a member of the Company of Revisers of the Mandarin Old Testament. The *Recorder's* editorial writer welcomed the appointment: "We think Mr. Sydenstricker admirably adapted to this work."[94]

At home, Absalom remained an aloof and formidable figure. His youngest child, Grace, remembered him as withdrawn and usually solemn. For the first few years of her education, he was her tutor in history, geography, and arithmetic. "When I went to recite to him, I had to stand up. He would be in his study, and I had to stand up, formally, to recite to him." Even his infrequent outbreaks of humor were rather troubling. Grace recalled one of his favorite stories, about a little pig that tried to get through a fence and didn't quite make it: "Someone caught him by the tail and the pig clipped off its tail, and that, to me, was not a bit funny, but he thought it was very funny."[95]

Pearl, seven years older than Grace and now in her adolescence, found herself increasingly alienated from her father. Her deepest loyalties drew her toward her mother, whose life had been blighted by her marriage to a man who kept her always subordinate to his pious work. Because Carie was hobbled by her own traditional commitments, she would never consider divorce or even separation. (A generation later, Pearl would refuse the martyrdom of remaining trapped in a loveless marriage.) Carie's feelings of rejection grew steadily across the long, slow years of her expatriation, and Pearl's sympathetic resentment kept pace.

Furthermore, Carie's health deteriorated in the early years of the century. Unlike Absalom, whose robust constitution was never tested by illness, Carie was often sick during her years in China. Her physical frailty and psychological depression undoubtedly aggravated each other. In particular, she grew to dread the oppressive heat of summer with its heightened discomfort and incidence of disease. She found some relief when Absalom built a small stone cottage at Kuling (Guling), the resort in the Lu Mountains southwest of Nanking that Western diplomats and missionaries reserved for their holiday use. Chinese merchants set up shops outside the white settlement; inside the compound, they were only permitted as servants or, rarely, as guests.[96] Here the air was cool and bracing even in midsummer; the rocky hills were cut by steep gorges, and fast-moving streams tumbled in waterfalls and filled high mountain lakes. Wildflowers covered the hillsides. Carie found the setting more like West Virginia than any place she had ever known in China. For two decades, she spent her happiest hours in Kuling, trying to regain her strength each summer before returning to Chinkiang.

In 1905, Pearl's Chinese tutor, Mr. Kung, died of cholera; Pearl attended his funeral, wearing a white band of mourning. Before his death, he had warned her of the political storm that was gathering across China. He advised her to go back to America for her own safety, and she passed the message along to her parents. But Absalom ignored such threats, believing as usual that they actually vindicated his commitment.

For her part, Pearl felt increasingly displaced. Her anxieties increased dramatically a year or so after Mr. Kung's death, when she saw first-hand the suffering exacted by one of the worst famines in China's history. Absalom remained in the north, where conditions were worst, assisting in the relief efforts there by administering money raised in American Protestant churches.[97] Carie did what she could in Chinkiang, but her small resources were overwhelmed by thousands of refugees who had fled from the devastation in the areas north of Kiangsu province. Each morning, through the whole winter, soldiers came to take away the bodies of those who had died outside the Sydenstricker gates. For the rest of her life, Pearl would remember the groans of starving people, but even more the heart-breaking silence of the dying children.

When conditions improved, Pearl was enrolled in a nearby mission school for girls, where she spent two or three days a week. She continued to read every book she could find, including the novels of Walter Scott, George Eliot, even Mark Twain, though Carie found Twain rather coarse and tried to discourage

Pearl from reading his books. Pearl sometimes irritated her younger sister, Grace, by keeping the light on in the bedroom they shared, as she read far into the night.[98]

Pearl also demonstrated a capacity for minor mischief, as Grace later recalled. "We had one of those old-fashioned beds that had slats across the bottom which held up the springs," Grace said. "It was one of our tricks to try to fix the slats so that they would crash down and the whole bed would sink. And usually she succeeded in tricking me rather than I tricking her."[99]

Practical jokes were one antidote to the restlessness and loneliness that more and more beleaguered Pearl in these years. She wanted to get on with her life, presumably in the United States. Pearl was reluctant to leave her mother but eager to escape from her father's stifling shadow. Between them, her parents had damaged her sense of her identity as a young woman. Her mother had tried to nurture her self-confidence, but Carie's own tear-stained life seemed more of a threat than a promise to a girl on the edge of adulthood. For his part, Absalom's cold detachment and his misogyny had wounded Pearl in ways that would never heal.

At the same time, Pearl took some comfort in her intelligence, her bicultural education, and her physical appearance. She had grown from a pretty child into an attractive adolescent. Standing five feet five inches, she was taller than her mother and almost conspicuously tall among the Chinese girls and women around her. Her blond hair had darkened to a light brown, and her striking blue eyes remained her most arresting feature.

Although Absalom expressed no interest in Pearl's future, Carie had always insisted that both her daughters should attend college. Pearl's first preference was Wellesley, which her parents thought too expensive and too secular. After considerable family negotiation, the choice was Randolph-Macon Woman's College, in Lynchburg, Virginia, a newly founded Christian institution with a strong academic curriculum.[100] The college also appealed to the family because Pearl's older brother, Edgar, was living in Lynchburg with his wife and two children, and working as a newspaper editor. Pearl would have been ready to enter in the fall of 1909, but her parents decided that she would wait until 1910, when Absalom and Carie would be traveling to the United States for another furlough.

To make the best use of the intervening year, Pearl was sent to Miss Jewell's School in Shanghai, once the most highly regarded English school in Asia, now shabby and declining in prestige. From the first day, Pearl heartily despised the place. When she arrived, she was ushered into a gloomy parlor where she sat thinking of *Nicholas Nickleby*. She was greeted by Miss Jewell herself, an elderly woman whose failing health mirrored the decay of her once-proud establishment. The teachers were generally competent but dull, the students narrow-minded and bereft of any intellectual curiosity. Along with that, Pearl's Christianity had already become rather relaxed, and she felt uncomfortable with the high-pitched fundamentalism that characterized teachers and students alike.

The school had little to teach her, but Shanghai, the largest city in Asia, was a revelation. Shanghai, as Pearl herself put it years later, was "the most amazing city in the world's last century."[101] It was a gathering place for people from all over the world, a magnet for commerce, culture, and organized crime.[102] The vast international settlement was a symbol of both worldly diversity and foreign oppression. (While evidence of imperialist arrogance was plentiful, the famous sign that banned dogs and Chinese from public parks was apparently apocryphal.)

Although Pearl had lived as a nine-year-old refugee in a Shanghai mission compound for a few months during the Boxer Uprising, she had seen almost nothing of the city. Her sojourn at Miss Jewell's introduced her to the best and worst of Shanghai, a sequence of experiences that marked her for life. Most memorably, Pearl did volunteer work at the Door of Hope, a shelter for Chinese slave girls and prostitutes.[103]

In the early 1900s, Shanghai had achieved a lurid international notoriety as an immense sexual marketplace. Of course, the problem of prostitution was not new. Chinese women had been bought and sold for centuries before Westerners arrived. Especially among the poor, daughters were regarded as a commodity and a possible source of revenue in hard times. According to Patricia Buckley Ebrey, "To a peasant family, a daughter was worth so much as a bride, so much as a maid, so much as a prostitute. Prostitution in China was treated as a legal contractual obligation in which one owner of a woman sold or pawned her to another."[104]

From the Ming dynasty through 1949, "China had one of the largest and most comprehensive markets for the exchange of human beings in the world."[105] Though the purchase and sale of women went on all over the country, the practice was most active in the cities. Shanghai had by far the largest population of foreigners, and the city's sexual traffic was accelerated by the presence of white men. American journalists routinely noted the corruption that imperialism had brought in its wake. John Gunther called Shanghai "a political ulcer on the face of China," while Edgar Snow frequently referred to the city as an Asian Sodom and Gomorrah.[106]

The Door of Hope, established in Shanghai in 1900, was an ambitious attempt to rescue Chinese women from the degradation and physical abuse that almost always accompanied their sexual servitude.[107] The women who came here had often been tortured, starved, and repeatedly raped. The agency's founder and director, Catherine Bonnel, was a figure of almost mythic proportions in Shanghai's Western community, a Social Gospel Christian who usually favored deeds over prayer. She had spent her entire adult life struggling against the conspiracy

6. Carie, Grace, and Pearl, shortly before Pearl's enrollment at Randolph-Macon Woman's College in 1910. (Reproduced with permission of the Pearl S. Buck Foundation.)

of law, custom, and profit that condemned tens of thousands of Chinese girls and women to varieties of exploitation and slavery.[108]

When Pearl volunteered at the Door of Hope, she was asked to teach the women to sew, knit, and embroider, skills that she had learned from her mother. Because she could speak Chinese, she was also able to talk with the women, who told her stories of incalculable brutality. For Pearl, an adolescent who had grown up in an emotionally reticent household, this must have been a traumatic introduction to sexuality.

Her nascent feminism was undoubtedly nurtured by the squalor and suffering she saw in the Door of Hope, a place that one Western visitor described as "more a sorrowful jail than a bright haven."[109] Here were women and girls whose lives had been crushed solely because of the bad luck of their gender. Pearl also noted how, in Shanghai's commerce in women, racial difference was subordinated to sexual opportunism. Asian and white men, who usually viewed each other with distrust and even hate, managed to reach across the barrier of race to collaborate in the use and destruction of Chinese women.

After Pearl went home for the spring holiday, her mother decided that Miss Jewell's did not, after all, provide a suitable environment; Pearl did not return. A few months later, the Sydenstrickers left Chinkiang for their furlough year in America, during which they would enroll Pearl in college. Carie's fragile health made the prospect of a Pacific voyage even more terrifying than usual. For that reason, and also in part as a kind of pre-college gift to Pearl, the family once again traveled west rather than east: across Russia and Europe, then to the United States by way of the less formidable Atlantic.

2

New Worlds

THE SYDENSTRICKERS SPENT several months making the journey from China to Virginia. After traveling north by canal boat and train from Chinkiang to Peking and then to Manchuria, they endured ten days on the Trans-Siberian railroad to Moscow. The train had no food onboard and no toilet facilities; the whole family shared a single cabin. Pearl was dismayed by the impoverished Russian peasants she saw at every station. The crowds of clamorous beggars represented human deprivation on a scale she had not seen in China except during the worst years of drought and famine. Those scenes remained a vivid memory for the rest of her life. She felt liberated when the family crossed the borders of Western Europe. The Sydenstrickers spent a month in Switzerland, where Pearl was tutored in French, then continued west, sightseeing in Paris and London. In September, 1910, they reached Lynchburg and enrolled Pearl as a freshman in Randolph-Macon Woman's College, one of the few women's colleges in the South.

Creating opportunities for the collegiate education of women was a belated but splendid achievement of the American nineteenth century. The all-male world of higher education was altered in two fundamental ways during the 1800s: through the establishment of women's colleges and through the simultaneous shift toward coeducation in most men's colleges. Between them, coeducational and women's colleges enrolled upwards of 140,000 women by 1910, the year of Pearl's matriculation. Although this figure still represented only a small fraction of the population, women did make up nearly 40 percent of all college students.[1]

Historically, the women's colleges have produced a disproportionate share of female professionals, including scholars, scientists, lawyers, and civic leaders. To give just one example from the early twentieth century, a search of the collegiate background of the 439 female scientists listed in the first three editions of *Men of Science* (1906, 1910, 1921) reveals that a large proportion, 41 percent, graduated from women's colleges.[2] That pattern of accomplishment among graduates of women's colleges has continued up to the present day.

Beginning with the foundation of the Mount Holyoke Female Seminary in Massachusetts in 1837, women's colleges grew to number more than two hundred by the turn of the century. The most distinguished included a group in the Northeast that came to be known as the Seven Sisters – Vassar, Smith, Mount Holyoke, Wellesley, Radcliffe, Bryn Mawr, and Barnard – along with just a few others in the East and Midwest.[3] In a lower tier was Randolph-Macon Woman's College, founded in 1891 on twenty acres of rolling, handsome land in the foothills of the Shenandoah Mountains.

The campus was dominated by a vast central building of vaguely Gothic design, which an early twentieth-century visitor found particularly impressive. "Inside," wrote Mary Caroline Crawford,

the building proves even larger than at first view. The grand corridor itself is, in point of fact, more than a hundred yards long, while upstairs are very many spacious lecture rooms, chemical, physical, biological, and psychological laboratories, music rooms, a beautiful library, a chapel, a large literary hall, a well-equipped gymnasium, and a sky-lighted art studio. Two-thirds of this immense building is devoted to public uses, the remaining third being given over to dormitories.[4]

Aside from the economies of locating so much college activity in a single building, the architecture of Randolph-Macon made a symbolic statement about female community. Religion, learning, physical exercise, art, and sleep all took place under one roof.

Crawford also described a typical day in the life of Randolph-Macon's students, offering a chatty but valuable glimpse of the way Pearl's time was occupied during her undergraduate years. Awakened each morning by a "rising-gong," the students got up at 7:00 A.M., dressed, and presented themselves for breakfast at 7:45. When they finished eating, they walked from the dining room to the chapel for a set of "enjoyable chapel exercises," as Crawford called them. Classes began at 9:00 each morning and continued through the early afternoon; each student attended three or four classes a day. Athletics and reading filled the time between the final class and 6:30 P.M., when dinner was served. After dinner, all the students attended evening worship. Then an evening "study-bell" directed the young women to go to their rooms for homework and reading until the 10:30 "retiring-bell," when everyone was required to go to bed.

Each Sunday morning there was regular Bible study, taught in turn by the members of the college's faculty. Church attendance was, of course, expected. On Sunday afternoons, the Ethical Society had its meetings, where the women discussed such questions as "Meddlesomeness," "College Duties," or "The Proper Keeping of the Sabbath." Sunday evenings featured an hour of religious exercises, usually conducted by an officer of the college or by a visiting minister.

Once a month the Sunday evening service was led by the missionary department of the Young Women's Christian Association, which Crawford called "a body of large membership and broad usefulness at this college."

There were several variations on the daily routine. Mondays were free days; Wednesdays saw a weekly musical performance. After tea on Saturday the students attended a Current Events Club, in which matters of topical interest, including women's suffrage, were addressed. Every other Saturday the college hosted a Social Evening, "when gentlemen who are on the college visiting-list are free to call."

To modern readers, Randolph-Macon's lockstep routines, with its ringing bells, required classes, and obligatory piety, sounds quaint and rather coercive. However, the schedule was intended to promote rigorous scholarship and to encourage the development of women who could assume increasing civic responsibility. The ideal of the liberally educated woman was shared by all of the most demanding women's colleges. L. Clark Seelye, president of Smith in the 1890s, summarized his view of female higher education in a sentence that the faculty and administration of Randolph-Macon would have found altogether congenial: "The college is not intended to fit woman for any particular sphere or profession but to develop by the most carefully devised means all her intellectual capacities, so that she may be a more perfect woman in any position."[5]

The women's college was one of the few institutions in America where women were made to feel welcome, where they were continually reminded that their intellectual gifts were at least equal to those of men. This was especially important for young Pearl Sydenstricker, who was leaving one patriarchal society to spend several years in another. Patriarchy had also been the hallmark of her own family. Her beloved mother was above all an accommodating woman, who had chosen duty over her own desires throughout her entire life. Suddenly, Pearl was introduced to women who had made choices of a quite different sort, who saw themselves as independent agents, who valued their own talents and saw their personal needs as legitimate.

At Randolph-Macon, Pearl also met men who believed in the intellectual capacities of women. Such men were only a minority, to be sure, but they served as an antidote to her father's misogyny. Absalom was almost the only adult white man Pearl had known in all the years of her childhood and adolescence; his systematic contempt for women marked his daughter indelibly. Even as he deposited her at the college, he made it clear that he would have preferred to be spending his money on his religious work.[6]

At Randolph-Macon, for almost the first time in her life, Pearl found herself encouraged rather than diminished because of her gender.[7] "We were soundly taught," she later wrote, "and the curriculum carried no hint that we were young women and not young men." The requirements included mathematics, science, and Latin, and the students "were not corrupted by home economics or dress-making or cookery or any such soft substitute for hard thinking."[8]

The college also kept itself connected to the larger world of national politics. Like other women's colleges in this period, Randolph-Macon was the site of an active suffrage debate. The women might discuss such topics as "meddlesome-ness" at their Ethical Society meetings, but they also addressed the more serious question of their own political rights. There was a suffrage club at the college. And in 1912, suffrage leader Dr. Anna Howard Shaw visited Randolph-Macon. Shaw, successor to Susan B. Anthony as president of the National Suffrage Association, lectured and recruited student supporters.[9] Pearl's later exertions on behalf of the Equal Rights Amendment can perhaps be traced in some part to these college experiences.

In spite of its scholastic sincerity and its lively involvement in current events, Randolph-Macon was in many respects a provincial place. The students were a fairly homogeneous group: Southern, middle-class, Protestant, and almost exclusively white.[10] Pearl was treated as a somewhat exotic outsider by the other women; she was puzzled by their lack of curiosity about China and hurt by their condescension to her unfashionable clothes and hair style. On balance, her first few college months were solitary and generally unhappy.

Emma Edmunds, who would become her closest friend, recalled what Pearl looked like on her first day. Emma herself had come from a small town and felt painfully unsophisticated. Most of the other young women were better dressed than she, poised and apparently comfortable as they greeted each other. "Then," said Emma some years later, "I saw this one girl and she looked even more countrified than me. Her dress was made of Chinese grass linen and nobody else had anything like that. It had a high neck and long sleeves, and her hair was in a braid turned under at the back. Most of the other girls had those little artificial curls stuck on that everybody was wearing, and big puffs. Pearl looked terribly *different.* I felt sorry for her, somehow."[11]

Pearl paused only a few days for self-pity before deciding that she would adapt to her classmates' expectations and become a success. Academic work came easily to her, but she also managed to earn acceptance socially. She changed her hair style, bought a second-hand American dress, and learned the current slang. She wrote short stories that were published in the undergraduate literary magazine, and was eventually chosen for Kappa Delta, the leading sorority at the college. She was elected treasurer of the sophomore class, then president of the junior class. In the spring of 1913 she was named college delegate to the YWCA conference at Bryn Mawr, a coveted honor. (Her friends presented her with a corset when she left for Bryn Mawr, and asked her to wear it in order to maintain

7. Pearl, president of her class at Randolph-Macon Woman's College, stands behind the "even post" in this 1913 picture. (Courtesy Randolph-Macon Woman's College.)

Randolph-Macon's dignity up north. Pearl, who had already detected the oppressive resemblance between corsets and foot-binding, declined.)

Yet, in spite of the academic and social distinctions she earned, Pearl continued to feel like an outsider in the college. Almost all of her formative years had been spent in a distant land, absorbing a culture that her countrymen and -women found alien and strange. Through sheer force of will, she captured a measure of legitimacy, but she never felt entirely comfortable in her new surroundings. She was an object of curiosity, "a freak who could speak Chinese." Three decades later, recalling how "queer" she and her classmates seemed to each other, she confessed that she "withdrew" into herself.[12] Her retreat set a lifelong pattern.

Furthermore, she was perfectly aware that Randolph-Macon was a small, peripheral institution, a school of modest prestige and little visibility on the American educational landscape. Success in such a narrow setting was pleasing but inconclusive. Pearl was nagged by the awareness that she was an outsider in a remote place, practically on the cultural frontier. Her uneasiness followed her for the rest of her life. She would always feel awkward and uncertain about the rank-ordering that American standards and customs imposed. Decades later, when critics treated her fiction with disdain, Pearl could never quite stifle the inward suspicion that they were simply correct.

During her four years at Randolph-Macon, Pearl spent her holidays and some of her weekends at her brother Edgar's Lynchburg home. In the summer of 1911, she had to refuse an invitation to Emma Edmunds's home in Houston because her sister-in-law Alice and her niece Rhoda had both become ill and Pearl was obliged to stay in Lynchburg and "take care of things."[3] She dreaded her immersion in her brother's household, where the strain between Edgar and his wife was quite evident. Neither Absalom nor Carie had approved of Edgar's marriage, and Pearl disliked Alice as well. Eventually, the marriage would end in divorce. The disintegrating union gave Pearl another distressing taste of the anguish that a badly matched couple can cause each other. When Edgar was offered a job in Washington, he accepted, in part to escape his wife, and this in turn caused a crisis in Pearl's senior year. Edgar asked her to move in with his wife and two children. Though she had looked forward to spending her final year rooming with Emma Edmunds, Pearl dutifully agreed.

Moving off campus apparently cost her an expected appointment as editor of the undergraduate literary magazine, but she continued to publish her poems and stories. The most interesting was "The Hour of Worship," in which a missionary woman tries to come to terms with her loss of Christian faith. The autobiographical implications are barely disguised behind the story's slender plot: the woman's disillusion combines Carie's experience as a missionary wife with Pearl's anxieties about religious belief and her emerging disquiet at the missionary intrusion on Chinese society. The tale strongly suggests that Pearl was already moving away from the faith that had caused her mother so much sorrow.

Graduation, in June, 1914, was a somewhat dispiriting exercise for Pearl. Almost all the other women in her class were attended by crowds of relations and other witnesses, but she was alone. Her parents, and her sister Grace, remained in China; even if they could have found the money to travel to the United States to take part in Pearl's commencement, Absalom would not have suspended his work for such an event.

In part because her personal circumstances had periodically subjected her to such moments of isolation, she tended throughout her life to undervalue what she had gained from college. Looking back on her four years at Randolph-Macon, she later concluded: "I am amazed at how little I learned in college. . . . College was an incident in my life and out of its main stream, an experience which remains incidental."[4]

This is a half-truth. Because of its own middling reputation, Randolph-Macon did conspire with Pearl's unusual background to reinforce her doubts about her adequacy and status. At the same time, Pearl derived a good deal of profit out of her college experience. She was well trained by her Randolph-Macon teachers in several subjects, including language and literature. Beyond that, her academic accomplishments, along with her assorted elections and prizes, provided a measure of reassurance that she could compete with her American peers.

More important, by encouraging her to reconsider the relationship of gender to opportunity and achievement and by urging her to aim high, Randolph-Macon contributed significantly to Pearl's embryonic feminism. She had grown up with a powerful father who discounted women because of their sex, and she had first-hand experience of two cultures that had almost nothing in common except their subordination of women. Although she would never completely recover from the self-doubt bred into her by such discrimination, her years at Randolph-Macon provided a glimpse of a more equitable and humane vision of relations between men and women.

Finally, the ideology of most women's colleges, including Randolph-Macon, emphasized the civic responsibility of their graduates. Historian Barbara Solomon has proposed that turn-of-the-century alumnae of such colleges as the Seven Sisters and Randolph-Macon typically sought careers that would prove of benefit to society. They "looked beyond their homes for ways to extend their usefulness."[5] In this, Pearl Sydenstricker would prove to be a triumphantly representative member of her generation of college-educated women. As a writer who tried to promote intercultural understanding through her work, as a vocal spokesperson for equal rights, as an activist for peace, as the founder of an international adoption agency, she would devote much of her life to the search for personal usefulness.

After she graduated, Pearl had to choose not only a career but a country. Though she missed her parents, and especially her mother, she inclined toward America. China offered few opportunities to any woman, and almost none to a foreign woman who had already decided that she would not become a missionary. Pearl's psychology professor had invited her to become a teaching assistant at Randolph-Macon. She accepted the job, in her sister Grace's opinion, simply as "a way of earning her living and being able to stay in America."[16] More than that, the prospect of an academic career suggested itself as a realistic and quite a desirable possibility.

At this moment, Pearl received a letter from her father with the news that Carie was gravely ill. She had contracted sprue, a disease that attacked the digestive system. Though it was not usually fatal, in Carie's case the effect of the illness was multiplied by her long history of medical troubles. Pearl immediately changed her plans; she applied to the Foreign Mission Board for a teaching job in the missionary school at Chinkiang and tried to book passage for China. However, the opening phase of the European war prevented her from sailing until November.

Absalom and Grace met her when her ship docked at Shanghai; Carie, who

8. Pearl's graduation picture, which appeared in the 1914 edition of *Helianthus*.
(Courtesy Randolph-Macon Woman's College.)

was already mortally weakened by her illness, had remained behind in Chinkiang. When she was reunited with Carie, Pearl was shocked by the sight of her mother's emaciated body: "Instead of the strong upright figure I had remembered, wearing her thick white hair like a crown, her dark eyes bright, her lips firm, I saw a small little lady, very dainty in dress as always she was, but shrunken and tiny, so tiny that I lifted her up in my arms when I ran to her."[17] For the next three years, until her own marriage, Pearl spent much of her time and energy caring for her dying mother.

THE CHINA TO WHICH Pearl returned in late 1914 had undergone the most tumultuous political changes in its history. The Revolution of 1911 had ended over two thousand years of imperial government. A political order that had long seemed indestructible simply collapsed. Of course, as Frederic Wakeman properly describes it, the revolution was "not merely a moment or a single discrete event. It must be seen as a continuing process."[18] Political institutions had become moribund; the morale of public officials had declined; Confucianism had lost a large measure of its authority; anti-Manchu nationalism had grown more powerful; intellectuals and military leaders had both become divided in their loyalties.[19] The 1911 Revolution was the product of long-accumulating grievances against Ch'ing incompetence, in particular the failure of the central authorities to defend China from foreign invasion and insult. Tensions rose continuously throughout the first decade of the century, during which the court's responses veered between brutal repression and halfhearted efforts at reform.

Events reached their crisis in the industrial city of Wuhan, on the Yangtze, which was a locus of opposition to the imperial system.[20] A series of skirmishes between radicals and the military escalated following an accidental explosion in the Wuhan city of Hankow (Hankou) in October, 1911. Over the next four months, one province after another rose against the Ch'ing. On February 12, 1912, the five-year-old Emperor, P'u-Yi (Puyi), abdicated in favor of a republic.

Some of the heaviest fighting took place in and around Nanking, not far from the Sydenstrickers' Chinkiang home. On one occasion Carie made a brave effort to rescue a group of refugee Manchu women who undoubtedly faced massacre. (Their unbound feet made them immediately identifiable.) On another occasion, the Sydenstrickers were warned by the American consul to evacuate; they declined to do so. In spite of the violence they saw around them, both Carie and Absalom initially welcomed the downfall of the Ch'ing. With characteristic single-mindedness, Absalom hoped that Christianity might find a more interested audience in a post-imperial China. Carie believed that women would be treated with greater respect in the new order. In fact, in spite of its early promise, the major preliminary result of the upheavals was multiplied confusion.

The conglomeration of groups and individuals who made the Revolution had little in common except their opposition to the Manchus. Once the goal of eradicating the monarchy had been achieved, the coalition began to dissolve into its more radical and conservative elements. Among the radicals, the most widely known leader was an English-speaking physician and Christian, Sun Yat-sen (Sun

Zhongshan), the expatriate head of the Revolutionary Alliance. Sun learned about the Revolution while traveling through the American West on a fund-raising tour. He returned to China to be inaugurated as China's first president, but he resigned almost immediately to make room for Yüan Shih-k'ai (Yuan Shikai), a powerful general who soon began to exhibit imperial tendencies of his own.[21]

Deposing the Emperor proved easier than governing the nation. The history of China for nearly the next forty years, until the Communist victory of 1949, was a turbulent, ceaseless struggle among warring factions for legitimacy and control. One Chinese observer estimated that upwards of twenty million people died in the first two years of the Revolution. Historian Jonathan D. Spence, after acknowledging that this figure might be "vastly exaggerated," adds that "even a figure one-tenth as high is bleak enough, and in the context quite conceivable."[22]

Both at the beginning and end of that chaotic era, the Republican leadership proved itself incapable of governing effectively. Pearl believed that the Republic failed because its politics depended upon faulty, Western assumptions. These notions in turn could be traced to Sun Yat-sen's long exile and his immersion in Western ideas.

"Observing Western countries," Pearl remarked years later, in a shrewd analysis, Sun decided that "a good central government could make all the changes he longed for in China, and that the first and most important step was to change the form of that government." He accomplished this, but it proved to be inadequate. What Sun did not understand "was that central government in China is not important as it is in many other countries, and never has been. The life of the people, their lives and rules of life, have proceeded not from central government but from themselves and out of their family and group life."

Unlike Americans and most Europeans, the Chinese people had never been especially interested in the identity of their central authorities. The country was huge and it had a long tradition of local self-rule, grounded securely in relations of family and clan. The Chinese had frequently been ruled by outsiders and invaders, such as the Ch'ing themselves, who had descended on China from Manchuria in the seventeenth century. The thousands of villages paid their requisite tributes to the court, but otherwise had little to do with their nominal leaders. The Emperor ruled from Peking, and Peking, in a favorite proverb, was far away.[23] A country song captured the attitude of most Chinese:

When the sun rises I work;
When the sun sets I rest.
I dig the well to drink;
I plow the field to eat.
What has the Emperor to do with me?[24]

Neither the warlords nor the Nationalists made any sustained effort to recruit the rural population. As Pearl would argue decades later, it was only the Communists who understood that the countryside and its peasants would have to play a fundamental role in any successful Chinese revolution.

Though China's instability brought occasional threats to the foreign missionary communities, most of the time life went on without interruption. The country's general disorder exposed all Westerners to episodes of hostility; the pages of the *Chinese Recorder* and other missionary periodicals documented violent incidents, including murders, throughout the early Republican period. However, official policies remained tolerant toward Christianity. Few Chinese wanted to risk the sorts of reprisals that had followed the Boxer Uprising. In addition, several of the Revolutionary leaders, above all Sun Yat-sen, were themselves Christian converts. On balance, the first three decades of the twentieth century seemed to offer the most promising opportunities for missionary penetration. Evangelists and their American sponsors alike responded with enthusiasm. Missionaries came in increasing numbers, and chapels, schools, and hospitals were established all over the country.

Among the eager volunteers who arrived shortly after the Revolution was a young man named John Lossing Buck. He would remain in China for nearly thirty years, and would ultimately establish himself as one of the preeminent scholars in the field of agricultural economics.[25] His two books, *Chinese Farm Economy* (1930) and *Land Utilization in China* (1937), were pioneering studies that remained indispensable to researchers for two generations. In those texts and in his teaching, John Lossing Buck applied the methods of statistical analysis to Chinese farming. His conclusions have been the subject of much scholarly dispute, but his work permanently altered the way in which Chinese agricultural questions were addressed.[26]

Lossing, as he was known to his family and friends, was a 1914 Cornell graduate, an earnest, somewhat humorless farmer's son who had taken a degree in the new field of rural economics. Born in 1890 in Duchess County, New York, he had put himself through school by working as a head waiter and managing a boarding house. He had developed an interest in China as an undergraduate, becoming a member of the China Study Club, which met on Sunday mornings. The group gathered under the sponsorship of a graduate student named John Reisner, who would soon become dean of the agricultural college at Nanking University and one of Lossing's principal patrons.

During the first year after his graduation, Lossing worked at a reform school, teaching agriculture to delinquents. It was a frustrating experience that only confirmed his desire to work in China. Though he was not an ordained clergyman, he applied to the Presbyterian Board of Foreign Missions for appointment as an agricultural missionary. His academic credentials made him an attractive candidate, and he was quickly posted to Nanhsuchou,[27] a poor wheat-farming region in Anhwei province, two hundred miles northwest of Nanking. The mission station had been established just two years earlier. The town was chosen in part because a railroad line had recently been completed, which promised future development.

Lossing landed at Shanghai in December, 1915, and settled in Nanking for several months of language study. He rented a large room on the second floor of a new brick and concrete house just a few minutes' walk from the language school. He worked hard at his classes but never mastered the language. He would depend on interpreters throughout his long career in the country.

During his sojourn in Nanking, Lossing discovered the comfort that personal servants provide. The house he lived in had no indoor plumbing, but three servants kept him continuously supplied with both hot and cold water. He bathed every morning, a luxury he hadn't known in the United States. "Everything is done by the servants," he wrote. "I don't even have to black my own shoes." In a letter to his parents, he described the Chinese as a "queer people" who have many things to learn from Western agricultural experts. "I am mighty glad I have come here at least so far. There is plenty of work here. The field is unlimited, almost infinite."[28]

In fact, early twentieth-century American experts were sharply divided in their opinions of Chinese agriculture. Some, including many of the officers in the U.S. Department of Agriculture, agreed with Lossing Buck that the Chinese had much to learn from Western theory and practice. Others, however, were convinced that Asian farmers had proven themselves superior to most others in the world.

Chinese agriculture's most influential defender was F. H. King, whose landmark study, *Farmers of Forty Centuries,* was published posthumously in 1911, on the eve of Lossing Buck's arrival in Asia. King compared Western agriculture unfavorably with that of China, Japan, and Korea. In particular, King admired the Asian habit of conservation, which has traditionally demanded that every resource, including human excrement, be exploited for food production, and that nothing be wasted. This careful husbandry contrasted dramatically with casual and destructive Western practices, which have from the beginning involved unconscionable waste. For upwards of four thousand years, King wrote, Asian farmers "have been conserving and utilizing their natural resources," feeding their densely populated nations on relatively little arable ground.[29] The Western farmer, on the other hand, depends on mechanization and artificial fertilizers, prodigally cultivates vast acreage, and is "the most extravagant accelerator of waste the world has ever endured. His withering blight has fallen upon every living thing within his reach."[30]

Lossing had more respect for Western farmers than King, and more confidence in the benefits of scientific agriculture. Furthermore, he was encouraged in his views by quite a few of the Chinese he encountered. He came to China early in the post–Revolutionary period, when many Chinese intellectuals were convinced that their nation could only survive by modernizing itself, which necessarily meant adopting the politics and technology of the West. The slogan "Science and Democracy" became a watchword among men and women who believed that the future belonged to those who could successfully import Western ideas and adapt them to Chinese circumstances.[31]

In short, Lossing found that his priorities and training made him welcome to many young Chinese who admired his expertise while they rejected his Christianity. He represented a new generation of missionary endeavor. Although he insisted that his intentions were ultimately evangelical, he had no real desire to preach or make converts. He was more interested in China's physical well-being, and less in its collective soul. He believed that churches should provide practical services, such as introducing improved seeds, or information on forming cooperatives. In a typical comment, he suggested that church members "can do a real Christian act by putting enough earth in the middle of the road so that water will run off the road rather than into it."[32] Nothing could have been further from the otherworldly fundamentalism of Absalom Sydenstricker than this sort of humble pragmatism.

Lossing brought an excellent preparation to the task of improving Chinese agriculture. He had begun experimenting with seed varieties when he was still a boy on his father's farm. In college, he had learned the new survey methods of Professor Stanley Warren, who taught his students to visit with farmers to learn their practices first-hand. Lossing also had a genuine talent for administration and fund-raising, which would prove invaluable as he promoted his career over the next three decades.

In February, 1916, shortly after he arrived in Nanhsuchou, he wrote to his family to share his first responses to the area and its people. He had come to one of the most impoverished regions in China.[33] The town itself was rather desolate, a cluster of one-story earth houses huddled inside a ten-foot wall. The surrounding countryside of northern Anhwei was a flat, deforested plain, subject to extreme temperatures, gale-force winds, and periodic flooding. The high water often destroyed the slow-growing Chinese wheat, with famine as the tragic result. Politically, the province was a scene of unrest, caused by local opposition to Yüan Shih-k'ai. Lossing passed along the alarming prospect that civil war might break out in Anhwei at any moment. That threat was lifted by Yüan's death in June of 1916, but the situation remained tense and unpredictable.

Nanhsuchou's farmers were at first puzzled by the questions Lossing asked as he traveled the dirt roads on his bicycle from one village to another. For centuries, the skills of Chinese farming had been passed down by example and instruction from father to son. Agriculture had never been analyzed systematically. The farmers themselves, who were almost universally illiterate, had no interest in written information. They shared advice and ideas among themselves face-to-face, over the communal breakfasts and dinners that began and ended their long work days. Throughout the country, farmers knew little about planting and harvesting schedules, seed varieties, or crop yields from one province to another. Lossing intended to replace these customary arrangements with a comprehensive inquiry that would allow him to determine what actually worked best, and then to publicize his recommendations. In its own way, his conception was revolutionary.

He began his experiments with wheat, which was Nanhsuchou's principal crop. He test-planted sixty-three varieties, from Japan, the United States, and several sections of China. He hoped to discover a more durable, faster–maturing strain of wheat, which would enable farmers to avoid losing their crops to the region's regular flooding. The success of these trials was proven when a number of farmers adopted Lossing's preferred seeds. Later on, he also test-planted twenty–six varieties of barley, eight of American cotton, five of American corn, and twenty of beans.[34]

Like others in the north China missionary community, Lossing spent part of each summer in Kuling. Here he continued his language study and conferred with other agricultural experts. In a July, 1916 letter to his mother, he described the resort as "a cosmopolitan place," with its complements of Britons, Americans, Russians, Germans, French, and "I don't know what other nationalities." A few weeks later, he wrote to tell his mother: "Last Thursday night I had my first opportunity of accepting a dinner invitation by a nice young lady and in her own home since leaving [the] U.S. My but it did seem good. She's pretty nice and a Virginia girl at that altho she has spent all but her four years of college life in China." It was Lossing's first meeting with Pearl.

In mid–September, Lossing returned to Nanhsuchou. Pearl arranged to travel down from the Lu Mountains with him, and they got better acquainted during their long hours together on a Yangtze boat. "She has the most sense of any girl I've seen yet," Lossing commented in a letter home crowded with reports of "the nicest girl in all Kuling." After they had parted at Chinkiang, Lossing had "run down [to] see her for a day," and been treated to dinner and ice cream. "Well, this is enough about girls," he concluded the letter somewhat defensively. "You will begin to think I've fell in love with her which is not the case. She is just one peach of a girl."

Though Pearl and Lossing could only see each other occasionally, and though they each spent some time with other people, their courtship proceeded through the winter. By February, 1917, the couple was engaged. Pearl wrote exultantly to Emma Edmunds: "I am happier every day. Lossing is all any woman could wish him to be, and makes me completely happy. He is so *thoroughly good,* and so fine and true."[35] Shortly after her engagement, Pearl applied to the Presbyterian Board of Foreign Missions for appointment as a missionary wife.

The appointment increased Lossing's salary, and the extra money was welcome. However, Pearl's application was not merely practical and was certainly not cynical. Her formal alliance with the mission board demonstrates that she still regarded herself as a member in good standing of the Presbyterian Church. Her private doubts remained submerged beneath twenty-five years of religious training. She had acquired a habit of belief that would only be broken slowly and reluctantly. Her loyalty to both her parents, in particular to her mother, demanded that she continue trying to honor the faith in which they had lived their lives.

It appears that neither Absalom nor Carie approved of Lossing as a potential husband for their daughter. They considered the young man something of a bumpkin, and believed that his agricultural degree was the worrisome sign of a purely vocational imagination. Absalom was also suspicious about the depth of Lossing's piety. Nonetheless, Pearl and Lossing either surmounted or ignored her parents' misgivings. They were married at Chinkiang on May 30, 1917, in the garden of the Sydenstricker home, and left shortly thereafter to spend the summer at Kuling.

Pearl later claimed that an inner voice had warned her, "This is a mistake. You will be sorry."[36] If the story is true, the voice was prophetic, because the union proved to be a humiliating failure. Pearl's happiness continued for a year or two, then gradually gave way to regret and the leaden conviction that she had made the worst blunder of her life. In her memoirs, written nearly four decades after her wedding, Pearl compressed her final estimate of the marriage into a single, weary paragraph: "The time had come for marriage," she wrote, "as it comes in the life of every man and woman, and we chose each other without knowing how limited the choice was, and particularly for me who had grown up far from my own country and my own people. I have no interest now in the personal aspects of that marriage, which continued for seventeen years in its dogged fashion."[37]

Although the marriage was unsuccessful, Pearl's choice of Lossing Buck was not as inexplicable as this sad backward glance might imply. To begin with, she very much wanted to get married. When she had come back from the United States, she saw that all the Chinese women she had known as a girl were now wives, many with children. Furthermore, she undoubtedly wanted to escape from her parents' house. The care of her mother was becoming an increasing burden, but one that Pearl would never refuse as long as she lived at home.

As she thought about a possible mate, she decided that her basic qualifications were quite simple, and Lossing met them: he was eligible and available, a pleas-

9. Lossing Buck and Pearl Sydenstricker on their wedding day, May 30, 1917. (Reproduced with permission of the Pearl S. Buck Foundation.)

ant-looking American man of about her own age who was not an ordained missionary. Such men were few enough in China in 1917. Beyond that, she was initially attracted by his high moral tone and his energetic dedication to improving the lives of the Chinese masses. She also respected his scientific expertise. Her parents might condescend to his agricultural training, but Pearl placed a great value on technical competence.

She never explained in any detail the reasons her marriage broke down, but her letters, fiction, and memoirs offer a number of convincing hints and suggestions. She was an ardent, ambitious, and independent woman who found that the man she had married stifled her most fundamental needs. Lossing apparently brought to the marriage a set of conventional expectations about a woman's place. Among these was the assumption that Pearl would find her fulfillment as a professor's wife, an unpaid interpreter and research assistant, and, when the time came, a mother.

For her part, Pearl also began with fairly traditional ideas about her role. It was not the institution of marriage, at least not in 1917, that so bitterly disappointed her; it was Lossing Buck. The unfriendly glimpses Pearl has provided in her writing strongly imply that Lossing was a man incapable of intimacy. The distance between husband and wife was, from the beginning, unbridgeable.

As she grew older, Pearl would live her life on quite different terms from those her mother had accepted. Although she deeply admired her mother's strength and tenacity, she refused to imitate Carie's surrender to duty and respectability. At the time of her marriage, however, she was not yet ready to acknowledge her growing distance from her mother, not even to herself. Her sense of her own identity as a young woman was grounded in her devotion to Carie. She still believed that marriage was a woman's natural vocation, and that wives should defer to their husbands. She also remained uncertain about her own talents, and she was not yet ready to think of herself as an independent individual. The autonomy she would eventually discover and cherish would be forged out of her own painful experiences as a wife and mother.

Pearl's identification with her mother may help to explain the odd, alarming, but unmistakable resemblance between Lossing Buck and Absalom Sydenstricker. The similarities are ironic but perhaps not surprising. In effect, Pearl had reenacted Carie's choice. To be sure, Lossing was not, as Absalom was, a religious fanatic, but his temperament and core values were in many respects the same. Like Absalom, he was indifferent to the idea that women might be equal partners in their relationships with men. Like Absalom, too, Lossing disappointed Pearl by proving to be emotionally detached from the daughter they had together. Lossing was fully absorbed in narrow academic pursuits that left little room for companionship with Pearl or their child, or for any sustained attention to family concerns. In this ordering of his life, Lossing bore an uncanny resemblance to Absalom.

Furthermore, just as Pearl grew to have serious doubts about the value of Absalom's preaching, she also eventually questioned the significance of Lossing's research. (She referred derisively to the activities of both men as "The Work.") Both her father and her husband had eye trouble, an ailment she came to view as symbolic. Both men, in her later view, were engaged in various forms of cultural imperialism. "Since the man in the house was an agriculturist," she wrote of Lossing in her memoirs, "it was natural that I accompanied him on his trips into the country."[38] Sounding rather like F. H. King, she added: "I must confess that I had often wondered secretly what a young American could teach the Chinese farmers who had been farming for generations on the same land and by the most skillful use of fertilizers and irrigation were still able to produce extraordinary yields and this without modern machinery."[39]

None of her later misgivings was visible in the first months of the marriage.

Even when she did begin to have second thoughts, Pearl insisted that she tried consciously and continuously to make the marriage work. Some of her examples are undeniably touching. When the couple moved to Nanhsuchou she spent a great deal of time and labor decorating their cottage, trying to turn it into some sort of home. Lossing seems not to have noticed this, nor the other efforts she made to create a setting of domestic comfort.

More seriously, Lossing gave no encouragement to Pearl's writing, and in this, too, he was like Absalom.[40] She often said (whether wishfully or not) that she knew she would be a writer from childhood. However, she chose for a few years to remain in the background of Lossing's career, caring for him and then for their daughter. Her first published essay, "In China, Too," did not appear until 1924, her first story two years later, when she was thirty-four years old. The astonishing pace at which she later produced her work tends to verify her claim that this late start had its source in her commitments to husband and child.

At least part of the "insuperable" distance that separated Pearl and Lossing seems clearly to have been sexual. She was not usually explicit in discussing this topic, but sexual passion is almost always an indispensable part of the successful marriages she depicted in her books. Some of the most vital women she created are ardent lovers whose sexuality is paired with unusual intellectual gifts. The untutored but wise O-lan in *The Good Earth*, the self-taught Jade in *Dragon Seed*, Madame Wu in *Pavilion of Women*, the "vigorous and lusty" Carie Sydenstricker in *The Exile* and *My Several Worlds*, are all women in whom physical passion and high intelligence are evenly matched. They are also women who often suffer at the hands of men who cannot acknowledge and frequently do not even comprehend their emotional needs. Pearl counted herself among these women.

Years later, elaborating on her 1935 divorce from Lossing, Pearl wrote that he was one of those "persons who cannot for temperamental reasons be close to another human being."[41] The technical basis for the divorce was "incompatibility," a bloodless, evasive term that Pearl explicated through an extended comment on *The Forsyte Saga*. Soames Forsyte, she suggested, is Galsworthy's portrait of a successful, irreproachable businessman, decent in many ways, but "simply unlovable for inescapable and yet indescribable reasons." Soames could not understand why his wife, Irene, does not love him: "though we never hear Irene's side of the story from her own lips, yet we feel the loathing she cannot utter, and we imagine the dreadful midnight scene to which she is compelled again and again, and from which she cannot escape."

The sad and often terrifying Forsyte marriage rhymed dismally with Pearl's own experience. She adds that "we pity Soames and we do not blame him, for he is what he is," and yet we clearly see that Irene cannot love him. Generalizing, again with her own history in mind, Pearl writes that "We comprehend that love cannot be compelled, for in a woman sensitive and of quick intelligence, and with a dreaming heart, the flesh is not separate from mind and heart." In Pearl's unforgiving portrait of her marriage, Lossing had failed to respond to her needs as a wife, mother, lover, or writer.

Surely this one-sided account conceals as much as it reveals. Pearl never publicly accepted any responsibility for her failed marriage. Inwardly, on the other hand, she must have acknowledged that her own insecurity played its corrosive role in her unhappiness. She had drifted into marriage because that was what women did, and then became progressively dissatisfied with the narrow reality of her situation. There was nothing in her training, her reading, even in her vocabulary that allowed her to articulate her discontent. Warring against her gathering sense of grievance was a powerful cluster of inhibitions and denials that defined a woman's place. Pearl had to contend with the fear that her demands were self-indulgent, illegitimate, even unnatural. For many years, she would linger in an emotional twilight, caught between conflicting versions of her own integrity.

IN THE SUMMER OF 1917, her marital anguish still lay in the future. Following their honeymoon months in Kuling, Pearl and Lossing moved to Nanhsuchou to begin their life together. A featureless, arid landscape reached to the horizon in every direction, broken only by the clusters of tiny villages and the grave mounds scattered across the countryside. The dust that blew continuously off the dry Anhwei plain settled everywhere and turned the town and its people a uniform, dull brown. The Bucks managed to secure a small but serviceable home that had recently been vacated by a missionary couple. The doors and windows could not keep out the dust, which seeped through every crack and covered all the surfaces in the house.

Pearl's first letters home were the effusive declarations of a contented young wife. When Emma Edmunds married Locke White, in the summer of 1918, Pearl's congratulations were almost violently cheerful: "I was so happy to get your letter and to hear that you are happily married to a good man. After all, it is simply the *only* life for a woman. Of course, one can go on and fill one's life with other things . . . but for fullness of satisfaction with life, there is nothing like marriage and a home." Pearl's description of herself as a wife is nearly a parody of conventional decorum and subservience: "I owe it to Lossing to make his home cheerful and pleasant and be so myself. He has far too heavy a burden, and a man depends so on his wife for his well-being."[42]

Lossing had returned to his surveys, and Pearl helped him by typing reports, reading to him when his eyes were tired, sometimes acting as interpreter. In a typed letter to Lossing's parents in September, 1917, she apologized for her errors, but said she had to practice, because "I want to become proficient enough [as a

10. Farmers threshing wheat in northern China. (From J. Lossing Buck, *Chinese Farm Economy*; Courtesy the University of Chicago Press.)

typist] to help Lossing out with some of the many letters he has to write." Three years after she had graduated with honors from Randolph-Macon, Pearl still thought of herself as her husband's helpmeet, the willingly subordinate creature in an unequal partnership. Indeed, one of the permanent consequences of her quarter-century of self-denial was that her emerging sense of independence would always be cankered by self-doubt.

Nanhsuchou was a much smaller settlement than Chinkiang, subject to a harsher climate, completely lacking in amenities, and vulnerable to bandits and roving soldiers. Carie visited her daughter and was heard to remark with dismay, "Oh, I'm so sorry Pearl has to live in a place like this."[43] The handful of Western inhabitants included Dr. Van Wiltsie, an American physician, and Marian Gardner, a young Smith College graduate who had come to manage a girls' school. In a letter to her mother, Gardner enumerated Pearl's accomplishments. "You can't think how wonderful it is to have Pearl here and to have all the value of her Chinese language and her experience. . . . She has a lot of good sense, too, and is going to be such a comfort to me." Pearl had made a singular impression; Gardner said that she "is pretty and attractive, reads a good deal, and thinks about what she reads. She's thoroughly well bred and generally interesting. . . . [I]t is such fun to go places with Pearl, they understand her very well and she can translate for me. . . . Pearl is a joy in every way."

In spite of Marian Gardner's companionship, Pearl was often lonely in Nan-hsuchou. She made a few Chinese friends but she also found herself, for the first time, alienated from the Chinese life around her. She spent her days in the midst of a grinding, nearly universal poverty. She saw human beings living constantly on the edge of starvation, competing brutally for scraps, and she recoiled with a shudder. Her sympathy was overwhelmed by an undisguised contempt for the primitive hygiene and widespread ignorance around her. The customary beliefs and practices of China's farmers now appeared to her as a bundle of superstitions.

On several occasions, she exemplified her complaints with sad anecdotes. A large number of women – no one knows how many – killed themselves because of the cruelty of husbands or female relatives. Pearl told of one such young woman, driven to attempt suicide by her abusive mother-in-law. The woman hanged herself, but was cut down before she died. She was still breathing slightly when Pearl arrived at the woman's house: "To my horror, I found they had stopped her ears and nose and gagged her so she could not get a breath of air. I told them at once that if she were not already dead she should certainly be smothered." Pearl pleaded with them at least to unwrap the woman's face, but she was refused. "So I had to go away, knowing the girl was being murdered." She explained that the reason for smothering people who hang themselves is that since nearly all breath is out of the body, "they want to keep in what little is left inside." Pearl added the comment: "There is no limit to the ignorance and superstition of these people."[44]

Pearl's debate with China seems to have reached a crisis in her first two Nanhsuchou winters. She wrote a remarkable series of letters to the Buck family, in which she confessed to a weariness that reached nearly to despair. Sounding every bit like a pious Western missionary, she complained about her "constant contact with the terrible degradation and wickedness of a heathen people." The greatest hardships of a missionary life, she continued, were not the material deprivations: "The real difficulty and the greatest hardship is just *all* the time having to deal with and see and know about all kinds of horrible sin."[45] She declared that the Chinese held human life at no value, and that they were steeped in vice. "Knowing these people as I do," she wrote in March, 1919, "it makes me thoroughly angry to have China considered as even a semi-civilized country. There is entirely too much idealism [*sic*] of China in the U.S., and the common idea of her is very far from the sordid truth."[46]

These letters require a comment. To some extent, Pearl was simply exhausted by the daily struggle with hopelessness on a vast scale. More specifically, she was increasingly embittered by traditional Chinese attitudes toward women. Foot-binding, which had been outlawed by the Revolutionary government, was still universal in northern Anhwei. Women here were treated as beasts of burden by their farmer husbands and as servants by their sons. Female infanticide was commonplace; Pearl claimed that nine of every ten Chinese women she talked with had killed at least one girl child, and many had killed several.[47]

The vocabulary in which Pearl complained about the Chinese – her angry talk of degradation and wickedness – demonstrates that her attitudes still conformed to the starkly dogmatic categories of Christian evangelism. This was understandable. After all, throughout her whole lifetime, she had heard her father denouncing the Chinese people in terms like these. She had become accustomed to Absalom's rhetoric of millennial extremism, in which faithful sheep were separated from pagan goats.

Over the next few years, Pearl developed a more balanced and mature estimate of Chinese society. While she would remain critical of rural oppression, especially the treatment of peasant women, her essays and fiction would often celebrate the strength and simple integrity of farming families. Never again, in any case, would she talk about "sin" or "heathens" in her descriptions of Chinese life. She would find her own voice, which would differ at almost every point from her father's theological polemics.

Beneath their explicit statements, Pearl's angry letters were also a veiled but fair measure of her personal frustration. Living on a virtual frontier, she was impatient with the absence of intellectual and cultural stimulation, and with the narrow scope she found for her own activities. In many of the small towns she visited, she was the first white woman the villagers had ever seen. She found herself surrounded by staring crowds, who treated her as if she were a circus attraction. "Look at those eyes," she heard one man say to another; "who has ever seen such a curious color? And the nose like a mountain between."[48] She treated this sort of incident as amusing, but in fact she was depressed by these reminders of the tremendous distance that separated her from the Chinese.

Beyond that, Pearl's outburst against the people and landscape of rural China may also hint at the deterioration in her marriage. She confided to Marian Gardner that she was already becoming dissatisfied with Lossing.[49] In letters home, she continued to talk admiringly about his important work and his "great future," but her private doubts were growing.[50] The prospect of a life buried in the Chinese countryside with Lossing, perhaps for many years, began to loom as a threatening fate. Under such circumstances, the Chinese themselves might well become the targets of her baffled anger.

Pearl's unhappiness deepened in the fall of 1918 when China's political unrest exploded on the Bucks' doorstep. In October, several hundred soldiers under the command of Lung Chi-kwan (Lung Jigan), a small-time Anhwei warlord, occupied the Nanhsuchou railway station. A series of gunfights between Lung's men and the local militia left two dozen killed and wounded on both sides. Pearl, who had now been caught up in Chinese warfare for the second time, was shaken when bullets whistled across her garden. She tried to help one of the civilian casualties, a woman who had been shot in the stomach, but the woman died within a few minutes. "I couldn't forget about it – the way that poor woman looked as she was dying and begging for help, and there was no help."[51]

The episode epitomizes Pearl's feelings of futility. Surrounded by violence, suffering, and death, she was powerless to do anything she considered genuinely useful. She often dreamed of escaping, but she refused to abandon what she took to be her duty. In any case, she was a resilient woman, determined to make the best of her situation. Over time, her circumstances improved and her attitude changed. She and Lossing made plans to move into a newly built larger house, "a pleasant little place" outside the town. Like her mother, she took comfort in cultivating a small flower and vegetable garden. In the summer of 1919, she learned that she was pregnant, which filled her with joy and a renewed sense of purpose. She told her sister Grace that she intended to have a large number of children.[52] She also found satisfaction in keeping busy, combining her housework with teaching and an increased responsibility for mission work among the Chinese women.

She did a certain amount of evangelizing, which the Mission Board expected, but she agreed with Lossing that the emphasis should be practical. "Humanly speaking," she wrote, missionaries had not been successful in China because they had "gone to work at the wrong end." Too often they had preached the Gospel to people "who were starving and cold and homeless, instead of first ministering to their physical needs. A man is not greatly interested in his soul when he is starving."[53]

Gradually, Pearl's response to Nanhsuchou and its people changed, softening from her early repugnance toward tolerance and even affection. Indeed, years later, when she recollected her life in the countryside, she tended to romanticize her experience. She liked to recall the Chinese friends she had made, the peculiar grandeur of the harsh landscape, and the integrity that grew out of the unrelenting hard work of farming. She wrote reverently about Madame Chang and Madame Wu, each of whom presided over a large family compound, but she reserved her warmest comments for the farmers: "the ones who bore the brunt of life, who made the least money and did the most work. They were the most real, the closest to the earth, to birth and death, to laughter and to weeping. To visit the farm families became my own search for reality."[54]

Typically, Pearl and Lossing were having mismatched responses to Nanhsuchou. While she was slowly growing fonder of the town and its inhabitants, he had become discouraged with the halting and insignificant progress of his work. His limited funds disabled him as he wrestled with the entrenched attitudes of the farmers. He tried organizing the effort from the top down, establishing a school for a small group of local landlords, but he discovered that the peasants had little interest in landlord ideas about farming. He also wanted to increase the number of native Chinese workers, and he devised several plans for doing so. Writing in the *Chinese Recorder,* for example, he recommended that missionary schools add agriculture to their curriculums – a utilitarian proposal that tradition-minded educators, both Chinese and American, found shocking.[55] His schemes attracted little attention, and he decided that "the future didn't look bright from the standpoint of really being able to accomplish something outstanding or worthwhile."[56]

At this critical juncture, Lossing received a timely invitation from John Reisner to join the faculty of Nanking University. Lossing was offered a position in the recently founded College of Agriculture and Forestry, where Reisner was serving as dean. Despite some criticism from other missionaries that he would be abandoning his post, Lossing did not hesitate to accept Reisner's offer. He and Pearl moved to Nanking late in 1919. He would remain at the University for twenty-five years, until he was finally driven out in the latter months of World War II.

The Bucks had spent just over two and a half years in Nanhsuchou, a brief period that was decisive for Pearl's career as a writer. She claimed that she had always known she would write, and she had won prizes for her essays and stories at Randolph-Macon. However, it was Nanhsuchou that provided her with her subject, the Chinese characters who would populate *The Good Earth,* and the settings in which they moved.

Nanking represented a dramatic change from northern Anhwei's primitive desolation. Located on the banks of the Yangtze, it was an ancient city with a legendary past, having served as the capital of China in the fourteenth century, the early days of the Ming Dynasty. Along with its political importance, Nanking also had a long and distinguished history as a center of scholarship. More recently, the city was the headquarters of a thriving silkworm industry.

Nanking was lodged at the base of a sheltering range of mountains. The highest peak was the famous Purple Mountain, the site of innumerable temples and shrines, including the tomb of the first Ming Emperor. The city was enclosed within a twenty-four-mile wall, which gave access through nine elaborately decorated gates. Nanking's citizens were proud of their walls, which were forty feet high and broad enough on top for three vehicles to ride abreast. In times of famine, hordes of refugees from the north would sometimes find a rudimentary haven beneath the walls.

When the Bucks moved there, Nanking had a population of about 400,000 people, including a prosperous merchant class. Most of the inhabitants lived in modest one-story houses that lined the narrow, crooked streets of Nanking's poorer sections.[57] Pearl would grow to love the city's streets, especially at night: "the old winding cobbled streets of Nanking, lined with little shops all open and

11. One of the gates in the Nanking city walls at about the time Pearl and Lossing moved to the university (1919). (From J. Lossing Buck, *Chinese Farm Economy*; Courtesy the University of Chicago Press.)

revealing by glimmering candlelight or flickering oil lamps the solid family life of the people within."[58]

Nanking's public buildings and the houses in the more affluent districts included superb examples of traditional architecture. Though many sections were crowded, the city's great size provided room for a number of small farms within the walls. This gave Nanking a limited agricultural self-sufficiency, and thus afforded a fragile defense against siege. Over the centuries, the city had often been attacked. Because of its strategic location and storied past, Nanking was a rich prize in any struggle for control of China's northern provinces. The streets were littered with the evidence of past battles. Entire blocks of burned houses, destroyed decades earlier during the Taiping rebellion of the 1850s and 1860s, could still be seen when the Bucks moved to the city.[59] The Chinese regarded the ruins as bad luck, relics and reminders of the danger that might return at any time.

When John Reisner invited recruits such as Lossing Buck to the university faculty, he promoted the comforts that Western academics might expect to enjoy: "Living conditions in Nanking are very good indeed. We live in foreign, or semi-foreign houses in the very highest and nicest part of the city." There were no significant health problems, though "there are certain precautions to be taken." Reisner admitted that Nanking winters were damp and cold, but hastened to add that the lovely spring season was a full compensation. (He neglected to mention the appalling heat and humidity that have always made Nanking's summers notorious.) Of special interest to parents, or parents-to-be, such as the Bucks, Reisner pointed out that the city contained a school for American children. Finally, through the university and other Western institutions, new settlers had the companionship of a foreign community of about four or five hundred people.[60]

Pearl and Lossing settled into a faculty house in the university compound. The university's residences boasted the luxuries of electricity and running water, though both services were thoroughly unreliable. Lossing taught courses in scientific agriculture and farm management, while Pearl made arrangements to teach English at both Nanking University and the Chinese-governed National University. The couple lived on their missionary stipend. Though their income was much smaller than what consular staff or Standard Oil executives earned, they could afford to employ two or three servants. Almost every white family in the city enjoyed such help.[61]

Since Nanking was only two hours by train from Chinkiang, Pearl could now visit her parents more regularly. This was a matter of some importance, because Carie's illness was obviously entering its final stages. Pearl's health at this time, on the other hand, was excellent. Her pregnancy advanced without apparent complication, and she looked forward to the birth of her child, which was anticipated around Christmas of 1919.

It was not until March 4, 1920, that the baby was born: a girl, whom Pearl named Carol Grace. Smooth-skinned, chubby, and – in Pearl's maternal opinion – seraphically beautiful, Carol's appearance gave no indication of the tragedy that lay ahead. She was a victim of phenylketonuria (PKU), an inherited metabolic disease which, if untreated, leads to profound mental retardation. In 1920, neither the illness nor its cure had been identified.

Pearl spent three weeks in the hospital recuperating from Carol's birth. When she came home, Lossing wrote to his parents that both she and Carol were "getting along fine, [though] it is taking Pearl quite a while to get her strength back."[62] Pearl was not getting along fine. Dr. Horton Daniels, who had attended the birth, discovered a few weeks after the delivery that she had a tumor in her uterus; he insisted that she return to the United States for surgery. Pearl, Lossing, and Carol reached the Buck farm in Pleasant Valley, New York, in late June. In mid-July, doctors at New York's Presbyterian Hospital removed Pearl's appendix and a benign tumor. Although the operation was successful, Pearl learned that she would no longer be able to bear children. As one consequence of the crushing news, she determined to lavish her affection abundantly on Carol.

During Pearl's convalescence, Lossing made a trip to Ithaca, to renew acquaintances and confer with Cornell's agricultural faculty. He also visited Washington and consulted with officials in the Department of Agriculture. In both places, he discovered that his innovative work had already made him a minor celebrity in the community of Asian specialists. He and Pearl went back to China with Carol in October. The coming year promised to be especially exciting, because Lossing had been named acting dean of the agricultural college, during John Reisner's leave. The appointment was a conspicuous vote of confidence in the young man's abilities. Just before the Bucks sailed from San Francisco, Lossing wrote to Reisner, who had already begun a research trip through the south of China. Most of the letter was taken up with academic chat and miscellaneous comments on farming, but Lossing closed with an encouraging if perfunctory reference to his wife: "I am certainly a happy man going back with Pearl so well."[63]

When Pearl wrote to the Buck family from Nanking in November, she reported that her house, behind a wall on Big Horse Road, was handsomely located in a large yard, "all trees and grass and a bamboo grove at one end." Since she and Lossing had sold their dining room furniture to pay for medical expenses, they were waiting for a new wicker table to be delivered. An outbreak of cholera put Pearl under temporary strain, but for the most part her life settled into a daily routine of housework and teaching. The Bucks' small staff of Chinese servants relieved Pearl of most of the burdens of cooking and housecleaning. Her main anxiety was caused by Carol's persistent eczema, which she was trying to cure with vegetable and fruit juices.[64] Though Pearl could not know it, the eczema was a symptom of Carol's phenylketonuria.

By the fall of 1921, Pearl had begun to suspect that Carol was not developing normally. She tried to reassure herself by collecting stories from friends and neighbors of healthy babies who had been slow to walk and talk in their first years. She hid her growing fears from her father and mother, partly out of shame and partly because her mother was now near death herself, and Pearl wanted to spare her further distress. Carie had never recovered from the sprue she contracted in 1915; she struggled against her disease through six years of alternating remission and relapse. Anemic and unable to eat, she was now also suffering from pellagra and losing strength more rapidly.

She spent her final summer at Kuling, then came back to Chinkiang to die. Her bed was moved over to the window so that she could look out over the city in which she had lived during the last three decades of her exile. To break the silence of the sickroom, she asked for music. However, when someone put a familiar hymn tune on the phonograph, "O rest in the Lord, wait patiently for Him," Carie reacted angrily: "Take that away. I have waited, and patiently — for nothing."[65]

Images of Carie's terminal despair clung to Pearl for decades. In "The Angel," a story that she wrote almost twenty years later, Pearl's main character is a missionary woman (significantly, unmarried) who is driven to suicide by the burden of her loneliness and doubt. The woman leaves a note that reads, in part:

Here in my tiny poor garden my life is a struggle against weeds, against dirty footsteps, even against incessant spittle upon my walks, for this is the distressing habit of casual persons here. Indeed, my life, which once I planned so nobly, has, now that I look back upon it, resolved itself into nothing but a battle against filth and laziness — and I have lost. I might as well have tried to stop the dirty muddy Yangtze River as it flows past this heathen city.[66]

Carie's garden, overmatched by weeds and spittle and indifference, eventually became a metaphor for her defeat.

At the very end of her life, Carie would not allow Absalom to visit her. "You go along and save your heathen," she told him. She refused the consolation of prayer and removed herself from the ranks of Christian believers. Her act of renunciation lingered in Pearl's memory as a poignant confession of failure. At the same time, there was also something heroic about the spectacle of this feeble, emaciated woman putting aside the commitments of a lifetime, in effect defiantly remaking herself in her last days. In a brief ceremony on a rainy day, Carie was buried in Chinkiang's walled Christian cemetery.

Carie's death was devastating for Pearl. As she watched her mother die, she felt her "very flesh being torn from" Carie's.[67] At a time when Pearl's life was clouded by growing uncertainties, she believed she was losing her main support. As a way of mastering her sense of loss, she began to write her mother's biography. This became her first book, a loving memorial originally intended as a private, family document, a record to be shared with Carie's grandchildren. Fifteen years would pass before the book was published as *The Exile*.

WHEN PEARL FINISHED this first book, she was thirty years old; she had not published anything since college, and had not even written anything except letters and reports for nearly ten years. Nonetheless, she decided that she would begin writing in earnest. Paradoxically, Carie's death brought Pearl a measure of freedom. It gave her the opportunity to create a more visible identity for herself than her mother had chosen, without risking Carie's disapproval. Writing offered Pearl an untraditional role and at least a chance of gaining the independence that an extra income might bring. At the same time, it was a career that could be adjusted to make room for her other obligations. With the help of her servants, she could write and also carry on her assorted duties as wife, mother, occasional hostess, and part-time teacher.

Pearl Buck began her career as a writer at a time of unusual cultural turbulence all over the world. The early decades of the twentieth century witnessed an astonishing sequence of literary and artistic transformations, both in China and across the Western world. In Europe and America, a concentration of energy unmatched since the Renaissance brought fundamental change to painting, poetry, fiction, architecture, and music. Picasso, Matisse, Yeats, Pound, Joyce, Frank Lloyd Wright, Stravinsky, and dozens of others collaborated to invent the varieties of modernism that would dominate twentieth-century culture on both sides of the Atlantic.

China also experienced a literary revolution in these years. It was a nationwide uprising, but it was headquartered at Peking University, and led by prominent scholars such as Ch'en Tu-hsiu (Chen Duxiu), Hu Shih (Hu Shi), and Ts'ai Yüan-p'ei (Cai Yuanpei). The dissidents called for a radical reconstruction of China's literary culture, and of its philosophical and political traditions as well. To promote the cause of change, Ch'en Tu-hsiu founded *New Youth* magazine in 1915; it quickly became the most influential intellectual journal in China.[68] The pages of *New Youth* were filled with articles attacking Confucianism, endorsing the value of science and democracy, and demanding the use of *pai-hua,* the Chinese spoken language, in place of *wen-yan,* the classical written language, in all professional and educational publications.

The political implications of this linguistic debate were clear enough. The classical language was the property of the educated elite, a minuscule fraction of the population. In the view of Ch'en Tu-hsiu, and of Hu Shih, who had done graduate work at Columbia with John Dewey, the masses would never share in China's progress unless they had access to literacy. The failures of the 1911 Revolution seemed to confirm that more basic changes were necessary if China was to reform itself and join the modern world.

On February 1, 1917, Ch'en Tu-hsiu published a literary manifesto in *New Youth;* the essay became a rallying cry for the proponents of cultural change. The campaign that followed was surprisingly successful, forcing changes in official policies and customary practice. Among the educated classes, simple clarity replaced elegance as a literary criterion. The vernacular language came into use around the country; by 1920, the Ministry of Education had decreed that *pai-hua* be taught in the elementary schools.[69] Literary journals began to appear in luxuriant abundance, "and the so-called New Literature was brought into being."[70]

Pearl Buck saw much of this cultural insurgency first-hand, and recognized it as "a fresh force in modern China," capable of freeing energies that had been "suppressed for centuries." She numbered among her friends and students some of the men and women who were trying, as she said, "to create the new China."[71] She was among the few Westerners who read the arguments of Ch'en Tu-hsiu and Hu Shih as they appeared in *New Youth*. Hu Shih's essay defending the Chinese novel was of special importance to her. Scholars had traditionally accused fiction of vulgarity because of its association with the common people and common speech. Pearl, who was an avid reader of Chinese novels, welcomed Hu's lively polemic, in which he praised the vitality of the old stories as a sign of their cultural authenticity.

Pearl called that period, without exaggeration, "a fantastic era." It was an urgent, tumultuous moment in China's political and cultural history. While young people vigorously debated every subject from poetry to equal rights to Confucius, a stumbling republican government competed with dozens of regional warlords for sovereignty. The stakes were high. The Chinese people lived in constant fear of civil war and of outside invasion. The territorial integrity of the nation itself remained under threat from Western predators and the newly assertive empire of Japan. Everyone understood that political and cultural forces were closely linked as China groped toward its post-imperial identity.

At the end of World War I, the agitation for a new literature was absorbed into the so-called May Fourth movement. On May 4, 1919, Peking exploded in a student protest directed against the shameful terms of the Versailles Treaty. Among other things, the Allies had agreed to turn over German concessions in Shantung (Shandong) to the Japanese. Because of Western treachery and ignorance, one imperialist intruder was to be replaced by another. Thousands of students, from a dozen Peking universities, responded with strikes, demonstrations, and occasional violence. The police imposed an uneasy peace, but the spirit of protest spread across the country, attracting merchants, scholars, the new labor unions, and some sections of the military.[72] Simultaneously iconoclastic and nationalistic, the events of May Fourth unleashed a torrent of criticism and searching. "May Fourth" became a summary term for Chinese efforts to redefine the nation's culture and to assert China's proper role in the modern world.[73] The outcome was incoherent and indecisive; one scholar has described the movement as "an eclectic jumble of Marx, Ibsen, Freud, Dewey, Russell – even Confucius," but an important turning point had undeniably been reached.[74]

For Pearl Buck, this was a heady moment in which to begin writing about China. She had a privileged vantage point from which to judge the turmoil around her: she knew the Chinese language and a good deal of China's classic literature, she had lived in the country most of her life, and she had access to some of the people who were making the new culture. Indeed, her situation was unique in American literary history. No other American writer of equivalent significance has come to literary maturity so completely absorbed in the intellectual life of a foreign country.

Not surprisingly, cultural upheaval was the subject of Pearl's first professionally published work. This was an essay called "In China, Too," which was written in 1923 and appeared in the *Atlantic* in January, 1924. Couched in the florid style of much contemporary travel writing, the article compares social changes in China with those sweeping across the United States and Europe in the 1920s. Pearl's major point is that the forces of modernity are also reshaping Chinese public and private life, despite the fact that China is a far more ancient and more conservative society than any in the West.

Significantly, the essay's principal focus and its most extended illustrations concern the position of women. In less than a generation, according to Pearl, young women have redefined their roles, casting aside the custom of bound feet and everything symbolized by that brutal practice. Women now insist on education, a chance for employment, a measure of equality in marriage, even cigarettes and Western fashions.

Throughout "In China, Too," Pearl identifies herself as a middle-aged, stiff-necked supporter of the status quo, uncomfortable with the new Chinese woman and her demands. In part, this is a narrative pose, a mechanism for throwing her liberated women into sharper relief. In some further part, however, this stance reflects the rather conservative views she still held. Yet her own attitudes were under revision even as she addressed the shifting scenes around her. The essay's final paragraph predicts the future course of her opinions. Here, she abruptly allies herself with China's rebellious women, conceding that their revolt is part of a "new era of general enlightenment and clear thinking . . . a struggle for better things." Over the next decade, Pearl would come to speak unequivocally for these women as well as their counterparts in America.

Pearl's first steps to establish herself as a writer coincided with further disruptions in her domestic life. Following her mother's death, she had taken on a much larger responsibility for her father's care. Absalom had never treated Carie with visible affection, but he had become bound to her by a lifetime of dependence. Among other things, she had loyally defied his critics and had shielded him from most routine obligations. Like many old men suddenly deprived of their wives, Absalom declined overnight into a ghostly passivity.

He had never been popular with other missionaries, in particular the younger men who resented his irascible condescension and found his fundamentalism an archaic embarrassment. On his seventieth birthday, just a few months after Carie's death, he was informed of a recent regulation that required missionaries to retire from active service at seventy. (The new rule may have been drafted with Absalom in mind.) When he appealed for an exception, he was presented with evidence of his bad management. He had never been careful in accounting for either money or souls. Accused of making converts who were not sincere, he replied imperiously: "It was not our part of the work to attempt to gather the tares out of the wheat. . . . The Lord of the harvest will see about the separation of the wheat and the tares."[75]

His critics were unconvinced by such rationalizations, and he was relieved of his authority. He tried to carry on without the support of the Mission Board. He visited his native churches, only to discover that they had been rapidly reorganized, his assistants summarily fired and replaced by new men. On his final itineration, he suffered a slight stroke, which left him physically weakened for almost the first time in his life.

Pearl rescued her father from his defeat by finding work for him on the faculty of Nanking Theological Seminary. Without telling him of her plans, she proposed to the seminary's officers that Absalom be put in charge of a correspondence course in preaching. The idea was repeatedly turned down, but Pearl persisted. Day after day, she invaded the offices of the dean and president, patiently rehearsing Absalom's credentials and his long years of evangelizing. As she would prove throughout her life, she was a woman of exceptional tenacity. Within a few weeks, Absalom was appointed dean of the seminary's new correspondence division.

Pearl invited her father to live in her Nanking University house. The Chinkiang cottage was vacated, its few furnishings sold or removed to Absalom's new home. Shortly after he moved in, under Pearl's prodding, he reluctantly wrote a short autobiography, which he called *Our Life and Work in China*. The manuscript inadvertently confirmed much of his daughter's view of his values and priorities. The sixty-page, handwritten text is an airless, unadorned history of

Absalom's religious vocation, a recitation of his language study and itinerations and conversions, with almost no reference to friendships or family relations. His pride was all in the work: "It has been my duty to do more pioneer, itinerating and opening work than any other missionary in connection with our whole China mission, [including] the Japanese and Korean missions; and more than any other man in any mission laboring in the lower Yangtze Valley. I have had my home in no less than 20 dwellings."[76] Through the whole of this strange document, Absalom's children are barely mentioned, and neither they nor Carie are ever named.[77]

At about the time that Absalom joined the Bucks' household, Pearl's college friend, Emma Edmunds, arrived in Nanking with her husband Locke White. The Whites had also come to China as missionaries, and had been assigned to Nanking for language study. They were frequent guests at the Buck home, and Emma later recalled the steady stream of visitors who succeeded each other in the large Buck living room.[78] Pearl did quite a lot of entertaining; according to her sister, she usually invited people who might be useful to Lossing's career.[79] From the evidence of Lossing's correspondence in these early Nanking years, he was apparently busy and happy in his work. As professor of agriculture and as acting dean for a year, he was at the center of a rapidly expanding academic enterprise. He was teaching, pursuing his research, and cultivating new sources of support, including the Rockefeller family and Cornell University.[80]

Lossing's relationship with Pearl had apparently reached an unsatisfactory but resigned stasis. Both of them came from a religious background that made separation difficult and divorce unthinkable. Their temperamental differences, however, had become more pronounced over time. Lossing was increasingly absorbed in his work, while Pearl was becoming frustrated within the confines of her domestic role. The marriage was weakened further by Carol's failure to develop normally. At three years old, she was still not speaking, and her movements were uncoordinated. Friends later recalled the growing anxiety and fear that pervaded the Buck home.

Pearl erected a wooden screen in a corner of the living room, creating a tiny, improvised study. The screen was a paltry symbol of her emerging sense of separation from her family troubles: whenever she could, she retreated into her minute private space to write. She started working on "a big novel,"[81] which was never completed. In the summer of 1924, she received a flattering commission from the editors of *Forum* magazine. Impressed by her *Atlantic* article, they wrote asking her to send something to them. She immediately responded with a long essay, "Beauty in China," which appeared in *Forum* in March, 1924.

The opinions and techniques in the opening part of the article are, by and large, fairly conventional. Pearl contrasted American and Chinese beauty, locating the beauty of America in its natural landscapes, while China's was to be found in the arts and crafts of an ancient civilization. In the most interesting section of the essay, Pearl moves beyond connoisseurship to social commentary. Briefly, she qualifies her admiration for China's artistic achievement by noting that Chinese beauty has always been the exclusive possession of the rich. The masses have lived in squalor, forced to subordinate whatever instinct for beauty they might have to a daily struggle for survival. Though "Beauty in China" is not overtly political, it implicitly endorses radical social change. For centuries, unjust circumstances have deprived the poor of one of their basic rights. Only a new ordering of society will ensure the equitable distribution of spiritual, as well as material, goods.

By the spring of 1924, Pearl was no longer able to pretend that her daughter was simply developing slowly. Carol could only carry out the most elementary tasks, and she still didn't speak. Her eyes were often set in a vacant stare. The coming year was Lossing's sabbatical, which he planned to spend at Cornell, working toward his master's degree. It became clear to both parents that the second purpose of the home leave would be to have Carol properly diagnosed. At about this time, Pearl attended a lecture by an American pediatrician, and later questioned the doctor closely. She was continuously alarmed, even panic-stricken. A Nanking neighbor later recalled Pearl coming to her in tears, asking repeatedly, helplessly, "What am I going to do? Oh, God, *God! What am I going to do?*"[82]

PEARL AND LOSSING settled into two rooms in a small, rented house in Ithaca in the late summer of 1924. Both of them enrolled in Cornell's graduate school. Lossing intended to use his survey results as the basis for a master's degree in agricultural economics. Pearl decided to pursue a master's in English; she divided her time between housework, classes, and caring for Carol. She also managed to finish some writing for publication, including an essay, "The Chinese Student Mind," which appeared in the *Nation* in early October, 1924.

Like "In China, Too," the principal theme of "The Chinese Student Mind" is cultural and social revolution. Speaking with the authority of a person who has lived all her life in China and as a woman who has taught several hundred Chinese students, Pearl describes the confusion of young people "caught as help-less victims between the impact of two totally different civilizations," those of ancient China and the modern West. Their parents have trained them in "the conservatism, obedience, and dependence of the old patriarchal system of family life." As always, Pearl was especially sensitive to the gender hierarchy of the old order. "From birth it has been impressed upon [the university students] that they are Chinese and males and therefore invincibly superior. They have always been given special privileges as males, and have therefore received the best possible education, the best possible clothes and perquisites which the family finances could procure, and, in addition, anything else they could reasonably demand or unreasonably desire."[83]

When these young men go to school to learn English and other Western subjects, they are shocked to find "a modern civilization which does not at all admire the old, and which is nervous, tense, energetic, and iconoclastic." Faced with the failures of their own society, many young Chinese have turned to the West for guidance, only to discover the bitter distance between Western ideals and the behavior of Western individuals and nations.

Propagandizing Western teachers, including many missionaries, promote the idea that America and the nations of Europe "are Edens of pure delight." Then, the students see for themselves "those white people who live so besottedly that one hates to call them human beings for the sake of the rest of us." Following World War I, the students were also instructed in the facts of "international jealousies and land-grabbing," and they learned "what spheres of influence really are, and indemnities and retributive measures and all the rest of it." Finally, these students eventually learn "that America, *even America,* is pouring morphine into China through Japan; and England, not to be left behind, is hastening with extra supplies of opium; and, after all, cigarettes are more successful than the Gospel."

The *Nation* was a prestigious liberal magazine, and Pearl was pleased to have her opinions published there. It was something of a triumph for a woman who still described herself as a housewife to find her comments on foreign affairs appearing alongside articles by H. L. Mencken and Walter Lippmann.[84] Her year in Ithaca offered a few other moments of satisfaction. One of the most memorable occurred when Eleanor Roosevelt came to lecture at the university, and Pearl was named to the welcoming committee. Pearl later recalled Roosevelt's energy, which made her shyness, her high-pitched voice, and her nondescript clothes irrelevant. After the speech, Roosevelt and her hosts ate a lunch that Pearl said was "invented" by the Home Economics Department: "It seemed to be mostly raw cabbage. . . . It was an uneatable meal so far as I was concerned," Pearl said. Eleanor Roosevelt, however, demonstrating the political instincts that made her indispensable to her husband's career, "ate it with great gusto . . . and congratulated the head of the department on having achieved this meal."[85]

Such excitement was rare during Pearl's Cornell year. She was virtually trapped in two badly furnished rooms through an unusually cold winter, thousands of miles from her own home, troubled in her marriage, and deeply worried about her daughter. She took Carol to a succession of doctors and psychologists, traveling as far as Rochester, Minnesota, to consult specialists at the Mayo Clinic. Reluctantly, she accepted the diagnosis of permanent impairment. Nothing could be done for her daughter.

Carol's tragic illness had profound consequences for Pearl and for her marriage. Like so many parents of retarded children in her generation, she staggered under the weight of guilt and shame. The consciousness of Carol's condition tormented her night and day, gnawing at her fragile self-confidence. She was lacerated by the fear that Carol's very existence was a proof of her failure as a woman.

At the same time, searching for whatever consolation she could find, Pearl chose to blame Lossing for Carol's deficiencies. Although she had no medical basis for this cruel hypothesis, she added it as another indictment to the growing list of charges she had drawn up against her husband.[86] In an effort to ameliorate their grief over Carol, Pearl and Lossing also decided to adopt another child. At Christmas, they paid a courtesy visit to the congregation of the First Presbyterian Church of Troy, New York, which had provided some of the money for Lossing's work. In a small Christian orphanage in Troy, they found a pale, thin, three-month-old girl. Janice became the Bucks' second child, and the first of seven that Pearl would adopt over the next two decades.

Working under extreme personal pressure, Pearl made a distinguished academic record in her Cornell year. Because the Bucks were desperately short of money, Pearl decided to compete for the best-paying graduate award, the Laura L. Messenger Memorial Prize, which included a stipend of $250.00. This honor was given annually for the essay "giving evidence of the best research and the most fruitful thought to the field of human progress or the evolution of a civilization." Warned by an English professor that the prize almost always went to a student in history, Pearl nonetheless submitted a 140-page thesis, "China and the West." The rules of the competition stipulated that entrants use pen names to ensure impartiality. Pearl chose the name "David F. Barnes," calculating that a masculine identity would protect her from discrimination at the hands of the all-male professorial jury. She won the prize and spent the money immediately on new clothes for the family.

"China and the West" is an impressive combination of scholarship and analysis that traces the complex patterns of Western influence on Chinese society.[87] Beginning with a sketch of Chinese culture in the sixteenth century, on the eve of extensive international contact, the essay moves on to a detailed assessment of the changes that three centuries of Western presence has brought – in politics, religion, literature, and aesthetics. With one exception, Pearl eloquently defends the integrity of traditional Chinese social values and the high achievements of Chinese art and philosophy.

Her sole criticism of the old order reflects her anger at China's treatment of women and girls. Noting the pernicious consequences of Confucianism for women, Pearl concludes that "any student of society" would be compelled to admit that "the inferior education given women and the inferior position of woman had an evil effect on ancient China."[88] According to Pearl, the qualities that have been most esteemed in Chinese wives are more suitable for servant girls than for adult women. Trained from birth in routines of deference and submissive silence, Chinese women are expected to endorse their own lesser humanity.

Pearl gives Christian missionaries some credit for persuading the Chinese to improve the status of women. More generally, anticipating later historians, among them John King Fairbank, she puts the missionaries near the center of her commentary on all of the revolutionary changes that have convulsed China in its recent history. In her view, the missionary record was mixed. She denounces the "unwise and dogmatic teachings of many missionaries," who had reviled Chinese culture as "heathen and irreligious because it was incompatible with a narrow view of religion." At the same time, she acknowledges the role that missionaries played – indirect and unintended though it was – in undermining traditional systems of value and thus helping to accelerate radical change. It was they who had attacked Confucianism, who had promoted the emancipation of women, who had set up schools and medical clinics for the masses. At one point, Pearl cited a well-known, non-Christian Chinese leader, who was asked, in 1918, when the Revolution began. He replied, "When Morrison first came to China."★

Beyond its shrewd anatomy of the missionary enterprise, Pearl's essay resonates with intriguing biographical overtones. "China and the West" can be read as part of her long debate with her father. On the one hand, Absalom quite precisely exemplified the dogmatic, narrow-minded evangelist whose contempt for China's heritage Pearl scorns. On the other hand, he was also indifferent and even hostile to the Social Gospel and the progressive upheavals that Christianity provoked, sometimes in spite of itself. In short, Absalom stands accused by both halves of Pearl's argument about the significance of the missionary effort in China.

It may be that Pearl's use of a pseudonym liberated her to declare publicly things she would not yet have said under her own name. Despite her deep disagreements with her father, she still hesitated to argue with him, not out of fear, but because of her enduring filial piety. "David Barnes" was a shield; it was not likely that Absalom would hear anything about this fictitious scholar or his obscure essay unless Pearl told him. Needless to say, she never did.[89]

The essay's concluding pages contain a hardheaded estimate of China's growing anti-foreign sentiment. The Revolution had brought an initial period of enthusiasm for all things Western. Subsequent events in Europe and America, above all the carnage of the world war and the several treacheries of the Versailles conference, had undercut Western credibility as a relevant political model for

★Robert Morrison, the first Protestant missionary to come to China, arrived in 1807.

most Chinese intellectuals. Even the United States, which had probably enjoyed the largest measure of Chinese respect, had come under increased suspicion.

In an astute and prescient paragraph, Pearl described China's increasing resentment against American imperialism and American behavior toward people of color: "In the policy of not granting independence to the Philippines, China sees nothing but the sheerest self-interest on the part of the Americans. One may hear the Chinese say repeatedly, what they firmly believe, that the United States has gained far more by her Philippines possessions than she has ever spent upon them." Turning from America's foreign policies to its domestic legislation, Pearl described the exclusion of Asian immigrants as an insult: "In the Exclusion Act [China] sees the significance of a rising race feeling on the part of the white race and a determination to maintain supremacy on the grounds of color. She is being told anew by Japan and the Indians that the East must stand together in the final struggle which will eventually come against the white race." As early as 1925, Pearl was predicting the eventual realignment of the world's politics according to color and race. She was also, somewhat courageously, joining the tiny cohort of Americans willing to oppose the colonial and racial policies of the United States.

Pearl and Lossing both received their master's degrees in Cornell's June commencement, and then stayed in Ithaca through the summer before returning to China. Pearl's older brother, Edgar, spent some time with them. Edgar was establishing himself as an authority in the new field of public health. He and Lossing had several long talks debating whether the survey methods Lossing was using to study Chinese agriculture would also be applicable to research on rural health questions. Pearl joined in these discussions, and also kept busy with her writing. Shortly after commencement, she learned that *Asia* magazine had accepted her first short story, and had scheduled publication for the following spring.

"A Chinese Woman Speaks" is a fairly long story that eventually appeared in two installments. Told as a monologue by a young Chinese woman, the story addresses the tensions that modernization was bringing to private lives in contemporary China. Kwei-lan, betrothed at birth to a man of good family, embodies the traditional female role. She accepts her position and fate, including the bound feet that will make her more attractive to her husband. She has been thoroughly schooled in domestic skills, and she intends to disappear into her husband's identity after she is married. Her mother proudly reviews the education she has given Kwei-lan to prepare her for her life as a wife: "The behavior of a hostess, the subtlety of smiles, the art of hair decoration with jewels and flowers, the painting of your lips and finger-nails, the use of scent upon your person, the cunning of shoes upon your little feet – ah, me, those feet of yours and all the tears they have cost."[90]

For centuries, Chinese men admired the mutilated "lily-feet" of Chinese women: " 'Surely no one could prefer huge, coarse ones like those of a farmer's daughter,' " Kwei-lan herself remarks. Few of the practices that have been devised to subordinate women have been as grotesque as foot-binding. Beginning as early as her fifth birthday, a girl's feet were wrapped in strips of long cloth, tied tightly enough to cut off circulation, break the bones, force the big toe under the sole, and eventually shrink the foot to a few inches. In many cases, infection and gangrene set in, toes dropped off, and feet were reduced to rotted stumps. This is the pain Kwei-lan has endured.[91]

To her surprise, she finds that her husband, a Western-educated physician, is a man of progressive views who wants her to abandon her customary subordination and join him as a partner. She is wounded when she realizes that he is dissatisfied with her obedience, silence, and lack of intellectual curiosity. He even insists that she unbind her feet.

On their wedding night, instead of making love to her, Kwei-lan's husband makes a speech: " 'I wish to regard you in all things as my equal. I shall never force you to do anything you dislike. You are not my possession – my chattel. You may be my friend, if you will.' " Kwei-lan is understandably amazed: "I equal to him? But why? Was I not his wife? If he did not tell me what to do, then who would?"

Kwei-lan's dilemma takes the form of an exquisite, suffocating irony. She accedes to her husband's demand that she be his equal, but only because he wants her to and she is thus obeying him in doing so. Symbolizing her paradoxical emancipation, her husband unbinds her feet himself, commenting on the needless ruin and pain she has suffered. "The tears came into my eyes at his words. I saw the white-faced little girl sitting wide-eyed through the long night, feeling life insupportable with pain and yet remembering her one great purpose of pleasing her husband. And now this husband was making useless all the sacrifice and demanding even a new sacrifice."

"A Chinese Woman Speaks" is a neglected but illuminating document in the history of Western efforts to represent Asia. The title itself is an act of defiant feminist affirmation, encapsulating Pearl Buck's pioneering desire to give voice to the voiceless women of China.[92] In the vast library of Western books about China that had been produced since the sixteenth century, women were rarely discussed except in their familial roles, and they had almost never spoken for themselves. Pearl Buck set out to correct that imbalance, and she did so. Nearly seventy years later, Maxine Hong Kingston publicly acknowledged Pearl's work as a precedent and model. Kingston began her own career by searching for literature in which she could see her own image and hear her own voice. She said that she first found what she was looking for in the writing of Pearl Buck.[93]

When Pearl wrote "A Chinese Woman Speaks," the clash between tradition and innovation was engulfing men and women all over China. The characters and plot are securely anchored in historical reality and in Pearl's intimate knowledge of Chinese family life in the early decades of the century. Equally important, there is no trace of condescension or parody in Pearl's portrait of Kwei-lan. As the young Chinese woman struggles toward modernity, she proves herself to be a person of dignity, high principles, and good judgment.

The story is filled with finely observed details of clothing, furniture, and family ritual. It is uncontaminated by the "orientalizing" that has marked so much Western writing about Asia, the pandering appeal to notions of an exotic, mysterious East.[94] The main reason, quite simply, is that China had been for decades a daily round of commonplace facts for Pearl, not a cluster of demeaning stereotypes. She had known a hundred women like Kwei-lan, strong but ill adapted for a revolutionary world, trying to make their way through a maze of swiftly changing circumstances. In addition, Pearl's representations of Asia were undoubtedly affected by her gender. Orientalist images have typically been feminized: the languorous, decadent East is quite often figured in female terms. Pearl aggressively defied that insulting equation. For her, neither Asia nor women signified "the Other."

Indeed, it is the West that appears somewhat exotic in the story. Adhering scrupulously to Kwei-lan's point of view, the narrative registers the shock that a first contact with Westerners has on a sensitive but cloistered imagination. Kwei-lan's husband takes her to visit a Western house, where she sees an adult foreigner for the first time:

I knew he was a man because he wore clothes like my husband's. But he was much taller than my husband, and, to my horror, his head, instead of being covered with human hair, black and straight like that of other people, had on it a fuzzy red wool! His eyes were blue, and his nose rose up like a mountain from the middle of his face.[95] Oh, a frightful creature to behold, more hideous than the God of the North in the temple.[96]

On one level, of course, this is merely broad humor, but it offers the unusual example of a Western writer trying to capture the oddity of Western appearance to a Chinese. It might be called a kind of "occidentalism," in which Asian images have become the norm and the West is the source of comic deviance. Kwei-lan decides that the white woman in the house is less hideous, but her hair is unfortunately yellow, and her feet are "rice-flails for size." Along with their physical defects, Kwei-lan also notes the white couple's failures of breeding. They serve her before her husband, for example, and address comments directly to her. They risk bad luck by dressing their babies in white, the color of mourning. Generously, she forgives the foreigners their limits, since they have been brought up outside China.[97]

Slowly, Kwei-lan learns that the West also contains an old and valuable civilization, that "foreigners have a history and a culture." She also learns to take what she needs from the West and adapt it to her Chinese context. The story offers a homely emblem of this transaction when Kwei-lan, now pregnant, visits a friend, the Western-educated Mrs. Liu. This woman has mastered the art of accommodation: her baby's underclothes are all hygienically white, but they are covered with colorful red and flowered fabrics. Mrs. Liu advises Kwei-lan: "Learn the good that you can of the Western people, and reject the unsuitable." This was more or less the view of the majority of May Fourth intellectuals. In the end, "A Chinese Woman Speaks" celebrates tolerance and a version of cultural pluralism: it was a point of view that Pearl Buck would continue to promote for the rest of her life.

The Bucks were back in Nanking by the time this story appeared in *Asia*. Accompanied by Pearl's brother, Edgar, they had come back to find a country sliding deeper into civil war. The dangers that Pearl had lived through in 1900 and 1918 were about to be repeated, as the armies of the Kuomintang, the Communists, and assorted warlords moved erratically but relentlessly closer to the Bucks' university home. Within two years, Pearl and Lossing would find themselves swept up in a bloody conflict that would threaten their lives.

3

Winds of Change

THROUGHOUT THE LATE SPRING of 1925, as the Bucks prepared to return to Nanking, anti-foreign sentiment was increasing dramatically throughout China. Events reached a crisis when Chinese laborers organized a series of strikes against Japanese-owned textile mills in Shanghai and other cities. On May 30, 1925, several thousand Chinese strikers and students staged a rally in Shanghai to protest the death of a worker in an earlier demonstration. As the crowds marched through the International Settlement, they were attacked by a police detachment under the command of a British inspector. At least twelve Chinese died in the shooting, and another two dozen were wounded.

The tragedy, which became known as the Shanghai Incident, marked a fundamental turning point in China's relations with Japan and the West.[1] The May 30th Martyrs, as the victims were called, were immediately transformed into symbols of foreign oppression. "The patience of the Chinese . . . was at an end," in historian Dorothy Borg's laconic phrase; "underneath was revealed an amount of hostility that astonished even the most experienced observers."[2] Anti-foreign hatred, which had been rising for a century, now crystallized into an explicit and central feature of Chinese political life.

Many Chinese would have preferred to see Westerners simply thrown out. Short of that, protest leaders concentrated on two issues: they called for substantial revision of the unequal treaties and an end to extraterritoriality. Surprisingly, there was a great deal of Western support for reform. True, Western merchants and some diplomats argued for maintaining the inequitable status quo.[3] At the same time, a considerable portion of American and European opinion, including a majority of the Protestant missionaries and their home boards, supported Chinese demands for fairness. Speaking for the pro-Chinese evangelists, for example, the influential editors of the *Christian Century* denounced extraterritoriality as "the perfect fruit of western imperialism in China." The missionary enterprise, the magazine continued, "must be ready to trust itself to the same conditions of life and work which obtain for the Chinese. Either that, or it might as well quit."[4] To most Chinese, the relatively progressive attitude of the Christian establishment was welcome but trivial and belated. Sympathetic rhetoric did not erase the missionary role in a century of exploitation.

Agitation against foreigners and their privileges added to China's growing instability. The vacuum created by the collapse of the Ch'ing in 1911 had never been effectively filled; for years, private armies and roving bandits brought continual chaos to many villages and provinces. Local anarchy was repeated on the national level as well. Sun Yat-sen's untimely death in March, 1925, removed the country's most prominent political leader. National authority remained divided among warring regional and political factions, including the small but growing Communist Party. As leader of the Nationalist Party, the Kuomintang (KMT), Sun was succeeded by his chief military aide, Chiang Kai-shek (Jiang Jieshi), who reluctantly forged a temporary and uneasy alliance with the Communists in the summer of 1925. Most observers predicted a future of continuing turmoil as the factions struggled for predominance.

Lossing and Pearl watched events in China as closely as they could from upstate New York. The few reports that appeared in the American press were brief and uninformative. For first-hand accounts, the Bucks depended on correspondence from colleagues at Nanking University. One of the letters they received in the summer assured them vaguely that "matters are settling down," and that everyone associated with the university, including the Bucks, "should go ahead with plans as usual for the fall."[5] After delaying their return until September, Lossing and Pearl sailed from San Francisco, accompanied by Carol, baby Janice, and Pearl's brother Edgar.

Coming back to Nanking in the fall, the Bucks had managed to escape the worst of the summer's heat and humidity. On the surface, the beautiful old city they found was unchanged: massive walls and watchtowers stood intact, shops and restaurants were busy with customers, crowded streets echoed with the shouts of peddlers and ricksha men. Politically, however, Nanking had been transformed in the year the Bucks had been absent. Daily rumors besieged the foreign community, each more threatening than the last. English-language newspapers carried stories of anti-foreign harassment and violence. Westerners, who had been sheltered by privilege for nearly a century, now felt themselves particularly vulnerable. At Nanking University, Pearl and Lossing and their friends went about their business in an atmosphere of mounting desperation, trying to sustain an elaborate pretense of normality as they waited for the disaster that most of them felt was inevitable.

Pearl and Lossing moved back into their university house. They hired new servants and added a few pieces of furniture. Pearl discovered that the summer's heat had killed all her flowers, but she determined to replant everything she had lost. Like her mother, she needed a garden as a place of escape from a house she found unhappy and claustrophobic. She was thirty-two years old, estranged from her husband and struggling with the burden of a retarded daughter.[6] She was gaining weight – becoming a balloon, as she put it – which depressed her. She had a lifelong tendency to lose or add as much as twenty or thirty pounds in times of exceptional stress.

A story she wrote at about this time, called "The Rainy Day," contains a coded statement of her desperation. The story's main character, Li Teh-tsen, is an eldest son who has gone off for eight years to America, earned a college degree, and returned to his village. He is filled with a zeal to put his new learning at the service of the nation. His family, on the contrary, expects him to pick up his customary duties where he left them. He wants to be a teacher, and to marry as he chooses; they insist that he take a job with a bigger salary, and marry the young woman they have selected. Trapped by the invincible force of tradition, his anger gives way to embittered resignation. He wrestles with his frustration through a long rainy day, tormented by visions of his own future children, who beg not to be born into such circumstances. In the end, Teh-tsen decides that only death can release him. He commits suicide by taking an overdose of opium.[7]

The story is a modest but passable drama of the conflict between old and new China in the early days of the Republic. Western ideas were challenging received beliefs and practices, often with tragic consequences. At a deeper level, however, Teh-tsen is a Chinese and masculine embodiment of Pearl Buck's own feeling of intellectual and sexual imprisonment as she returned to Nanking with Lossing. Significantly, Teh-tsen had been an honors graduate of his American college, and had even won a prize for his thesis, a comparative study of Eastern and Western philosophy. Pearl herself had just won a similar prize for a similar thesis, which she had published under a male name. Her moment of intellectual triumph had been submerged in her duties to a marriage without passion and a daughter who brought only sorrow.

Pearl found a measure of consolation in Janice, who was developing into a beautiful and talented child. She also put more of her energy into her work, writing essays and stories, and teaching education, English, and religion at several Nanking institutions. In the 1925–1926 school year, Pearl taught three classes in the university, another at Ginling College for women, and a fifth at Hill Crest school. The work was exhausting, but it enabled her to disappear for long stretches of time into paper grading and class preparation, private conferences and office hours.

Her favorite class was education, which she taught both at Nanking University and Ginling College. Her religion classes, as she reported to the mission board in New York, were less successful. She wrote that she had begun to feel a "profound dissatisfaction . . . with the whole method of trying to teach religion through the classroom." Her students were also discontented; she felt that her education classes actually provided better Christian teaching than the formal curriculum in religion.[8] Though Pearl's statement is sincerely pious, it also represented another step away from her father, who insisted that only formal teaching in religion was worth the Christian teacher's effort.

Pearl's new writing included a short story, "Lao Wang, the Farmer," which was published in the *Chinese Recorder* in April, 1926.[9] The story recounts an uneventful day in the life of its title character, an aging peasant. Lao Wang is widowed and semi-retired from long years of labor. He spends his mornings listening to gossip in the local teahouse, then a few hours each day working on the tiny farm he shares with his son. His pleasures consist in his morning tea, the sun that warms him in the afternoon, and the company of his ten-year-old grandson in the evening. He dreams of wealth but knows that he will die poor; he is dazzled by tales of big-city excitement, but prefers the dull security of the countryside. Above all, he is terrified by occasional rumors of war, and prays that China's spreading violence will not reach his obscure village.

Though it is little more than an anecdote, the story is an impressive narrative performance. Lao Wang is presented as a credible human being, limited but sensible and rather dignified, a man who has known only hardship and longs for a few final years of peace. Pearl Buck assumes his point of view without a hint either of condescension or mystification, convincingly situating him and his family in the strong but troubled world of rural China.

The warfare that frightens the fictional Lao Wang was spreading throughout the country in the late 1920s. The Kuomintang had successfully established itself in Canton and the southern provinces. The north lay under the uncertain and shifting rule of three principal warlords: Chang Tso-lin (Zhang Zuolin), who controlled Mongolia and the seacoast south to Shantung (Shandong); Feng Yu-hsiang (Feng Yuxiang), whose strength was concentrated in the northwest, including Kansu (Gansu) province; and Wu Pei-fu (Wu Peifu), the chief military figure in the Yangtze valley. Relations among these three leaders and their many lesser adversaries and subordinates lurched through an unpredictable, bewildering sequence of open warfare, uneasy truce, and opportunistic alliance.

Anna Louise Strong, the radical American journalist, visited China's several competing armies in the summer of 1926, and filed a useful report in *Asia* magazine. Aside from sorting out the various generals and their spheres of influence, Strong observed that the peasants she spoke with in each region seldom knew or cared about the military winners and losers. Their concern was survival. To the small farmers and their families, scratching a meager subsistence out of the stubborn earth, soldiers were no better than bandits. In fact, Strong suggested, the peasants often preferred the bandits, since they were less rapacious. "If hospitably treated, with food and opium," Strong wrote, bandits "frequently retire with no further plundering. But soldiers, being better organized, take all the spoil they can carry and then steal horses on which to load the surplus."[10] Pearl Buck's Lao Wang stood accurately for millions of his countrymen; he spoke for Pearl as well, who was about to join the countless victims of China's civil wars.

In 1926 and 1927, Kuomintang forces under the leadership of Chiang Kai-shek mounted a successful Northern Expedition, eventually establishing Nationalist control over much of the country. The KMT's victories rested precariously on a strained partnership between Chiang and the Communist cadres within his party. Six main armies marched northward from Canton to Hangzhou, Wuhan, and Nanking, bribing, conquering, or absorbing the small warlord forces they encountered.[11] In March, 1927, the battle reached the gates of Nanking. March 23 and 24, two days of violence and bloodshed that became known as the Nanking Incident, left hundreds of Chinese and at least six foreigners dead. Nanking University and the homes of missionaries were among the targets.

The assault on Nanking had been preceded by weeks of rising tension throughout much of the country. For Western missionaries, the first months of 1927 were a dangerous time, as the opposing armies disrupted one mission station after another. The result, in James Thomson's phrase, was a "collective trauma: lives endangered, possessions looted, property destroyed, and a mass exodus."[12] Pearl's sister, Grace, her husband, Jesse Yaukey, and their young son, Raymond, left their missionary outpost in rural Hunan and moved in with Pearl and Lossing.

By early March, as Pearl explained to Emma White, thousands of soldiers – "cordially hated by the people" – had overrun the city and the surrounding plain. These were Northern troops, moving south to oppose the KMT. Cannons on Purple Mountain could be heard booming "for practice. It was rather nasty to hear."[13]

In her letters, Pearl assured her friends that there was no reason for alarm. She adopted a downright breezy tone in a note to New York editor Lewis Gannett, whom she had met a few months earlier when he had stopped in Nanking on a tour through China. "I fancy you would enjoy being with us these exciting days," she told Gannett; "we expect a battle here any day." She added that she and Lossing "have decided not to evacuate with the crowd. The decision was arrived at with some trepidation on account of the two infants, but we could not bear *not* to see what is going to happen."[14] In another letter, Pearl remarked that the "big battle" would probably take place somewhere else. She enjoyed passing on what she called "rank gossip" about other Nanking foreigners, and reported on their panic with amused contempt. Mrs. Holroyd and Mrs. Plumer looked "half-insane"; the Hutchinsons and Richardsons "expect the most absurd things to happen . . . they swallow every rumor whole"; several families fled to Shanghai.[15] Just two weeks later, Pearl would join the refugees fleeing Nanking.

On the evening of March 23, the troops defending Nanking were routed and Kuomintang forces poured into the city. Discipline collapsed on both sides, with devastating results. In Nanking's crowded streets, the main military engagement dissolved into a hundred skirmishes, blanketing the city with smoke and noise. Thousands of soldiers ran through the streets, attacking and retreating, firing their rifles and pistols at random, pausing only to steal whatever they could carry from houses and shops. Mobs of terrified civilians, desperate to escape the danger that assailed them from all sides, thronged the narrow lanes and back alleys, carrying their elderly relatives and children on their backs, and pushing rickety carts piled high with their belongings. For two days, fear and confusion gripped the city.

Chinese were no better able to estimate the situation than foreigners. In the midst of the chaos, the veteran activist Liang Chi-ch'ao (Liang Qichao) wrote a letter to his two sons, who were studying in the United States: "The Nanking situation is in complete flux, and I am not completely sure what is going on. Outsiders are exaggerating everything, but though what has happened was unavoidable, there is certainly a group within the army that is intent on stirring up trouble; . . . it's an incredibly desperate situation."[16]

At first, the members of the foreign community felt reasonably secure. They had not been molested by the Northern troops, and Chiang had guaranteed the safety of Nanking's foreign inhabitants when his Kuomintang armies marched into the city. Furthermore, many Westerners, including Pearl and Lossing, were sympathetic with Nationalist objectives. Lossing had written to the foreign missionary board that the hundred or so Nanking missionaries "support the Nationalists' principle of China for the Chinese. It is the best for mission work."[17] Somewhat naively, the Westerners believed that such sentiments would protect them from anti-foreign harassment.

There were eight members of the family gathered in the Bucks' university home when the attacks began: Pearl and Lossing, her father Absalom, Grace and Jesse Yaukey, and the three children, Carol and Janice Buck and Raymond Yaukey. All of the adults had seen Chinese warfare before, and they felt at first only slightly threatened. However, when they received word that Dr. John Williams, vice president of Nanking University, had been shot and killed in his office, they realized they were in mortal danger. Frightened servants rushed in, warning them that foreigners were being killed in all parts of the city. For several hours, the family huddled in the Bucks' living room, waiting for disaster to find them. Eventually, they took refuge in the poor house of one of their Chinese servants, a woman named Mrs. Lu.

Throughout a day of looting and bloodshed that seemed interminable, the Bucks hid silently in a tiny, windowless room not far from their own home. Amid the gunshots and screaming, they could hear their house being looted. Troops raced back and forth all day near their hiding place, sometimes at a distance, sometimes apparently stopping outside the door. When the shouting grew louder and nearer and capture seemed inevitable, Pearl and Grace vowed to each other that they would kill their children rather than permit them to be murdered by the soldiers.[18] Pearl was convinced that she and her family would die, not for any crimes of their own, but solely because they were white.[19]

The danger came to an end, abruptly and unexpectedly. American and British gunboats, stationed in the Yangtze River several miles away, began shelling the city.[20] The soldiers, who had been about to break into the room where Pearl and the others were hiding, were thrown into panic by the tremendous explosions and ran from the neighborhood. For several hours afterward, Pearl and her family sat in darkness, surrounded by an unnerving quiet. Finally, a Chinese friend came to the hut and suggested that it would be safe enough to walk to the university, under the protection of a guard of Kuomintang troops.[21] They had spent thirteen anxious hours in hiding. When they got to the university, the Buck family joined a large number of the city's white residents, all being held under guard in a large room on the third floor of Bailie Hall.

The stories they shared indicated that only a small number of Westerners had actually been wounded or killed in the violence. Nonetheless, the white residents of Nanking had been through a harrowing time. Men and women alike had been beaten and robbed, sometimes stripped and searched for hidden valuables. A number of women had been sexually assaulted. Professor R. H. Porter of Nanking University's plant pathology department had been captured in his office with his co-workers. He gave a chilling account of the moments that followed the arrival of troops at his office door:

They called for us to come out, we heard them draw the bolts of their guns and we knew they would shoot into the doors so we decided the best thing to do was to come out. Accordingly everyone came out and there before us were about eight men, or rather boys about seventeen to eighteen years of age, armed with rifles, bayonets, and knives. They began a systematic search of every one, taking anything of value, jewelry, money or clothing. Unfortunately, most of the people had been robbed in their homes so that the soldiers were not pleased with their booty. Accordingly they became desperate and two or three stepped back, drew the bolts in their guns and threatened to shoot us if we did not give them money. I remember distinctly that the worst one of the lot stood directly in front of me with his bayonet within a few inches of my heart region and I expected any minute either to be run through or shot.[22]

Porter's story was duplicated by many of the other men and women in the group.

After two days of imprisonment, the hundred or so foreigners were taken to the docks and transferred to an American destroyer. Their release had been negotiated by the American consul, John Davis, who had threatened to bombard the city unless all the foreigners were turned over to his custody.[23] The destroyer took its sad cargo of Western refugees downriver to Shanghai. The trip was a brief nightmare of overcrowding, bad food, illness, and weeping. Pearl spent several hours nursing the sick, then sat hunched over a copy of *Moby-Dick,* which she had never read before. The book, she later said, "restored my soul."[24]

Since the fate of Shanghai itself was uncertain, Lossing and Pearl remained there only a few days before sailing to the Japanese town of Unzen, a small coastal city near Nagasaki. As she reflected on the tumultuous events of the past weeks, Pearl remained loyal to the Chinese and their national aspirations. She wrote bitterly about the Communists, as she believed them to be, who were responsible for the destruction of her house and the murder of her friend, John Williams. But she continually emphasized the humanity of most Chinese, and she spoke sympathetically about Chinese anger against foreign exploitation.

Commenting on the Western ships that saved her, she later wrote, "I was glad not to die, but I wished that I had not needed to justify, against my will, what still I knew to be wrong."[25] The presence of gunboats in China's waters was "an act of imperialism which cannot be tolerated" by any government that wanted to preserve its integrity and self-respect.[26]

Pearl had fled from Nanking with her children and the clothes she was wearing. She had lost everything else she owned, including the manuscript of her first novel. She claimed that she felt strangely exhilarated, filled with a "curious sense of pleasant recklessness," because she was free of obligations and possessions.[27] She had been uprooted from the city she knew better than any other, and she suspected that she would not return. She had become a displaced person, one of the tens of millions of homeless refugees created by the wars of the twentieth century.

THE LANDSCAPE OF UNZEN is a picturesque combination of pine woods and mountains that rise out of what Pearl called "the most beautiful coastline in the world."[28] Lossing, Pearl, and their two children moved into a small wooden house on a hilltop and spent several months of recuperation. The other members of the family dispersed. Absalom, who was nearing eighty, refused to rest, and instead sailed off to Korea to examine Christian mission work in the Hermit Kingdom. The Yaukeys moved to the larger city of Kobe; Grace was expecting another child and needed access to decent hospital facilities. Margaret and Claude Thomson and their two sons, who had been the Bucks' closest friends at the university, moved in as Unzen neighbors.

Since there were no Western reporters in Nanking at the time of the riots, initial descriptions of the Nanking Incident in the American press were scanty and confused.[29] Shortly after settling into her temporary Japanese home, Pearl wrote a rather detailed but somewhat sanitized four-thousand-word report which she mimeographed and sent to the Presbyterian mission board and to several

friends in the States. Intended for more-or-less public consumption, this document laid out the events in a fairly detached tone, and ended with hopeful
predictions about the return of the white community to Nanking.

Less guardedly, Pearl wrote to Lulu Hamilton that she was having nightmares
filled with the lurid scenes she had witnessed or heard. Her prose collapsed into
breathless fragments as she recalled "the awful yelling and shouting . . . and the
sound of burning houses falling – Polly Small nearly raped – soldiers with their
trousers unbuttoned – everything ready – saved at the last instant . . . Mrs. Cooke
just escaping by a mere chance from having her finger cut off for her rings –
Dr. Price stood up to be shot half a dozen times and beaten. . . ." Contradicting
the artificial optimism of her formal report, she confided to Lulu: "Personally I
don't believe there is the least chance of going back." Aside from Nanking's
potentially lethal politics, the university had been taken over by Chinese administrators and faculty; there would probably be no room for foreigners.[30]

Unzen's scenery and weather reminded Pearl of Kuling. For the first time in
her adult life in Asia, Pearl had no servants to help with child care and cooking.
In May, Pearl wrote to Emma White that she and Lossing were doing all "our
own work." She immediately added this impatient amendment: "That is, I do
the house work and look after the children and Lossing is busy writing up some
of his University research stuff."[31]

Lossing had saved his survey manuscript when he left Nanking. He was absorbed in his maps and calculations, insisting that no one interrupt his work
between eight and twelve in the morning and one and five in the afternoon.[32]
He tried to maintain contact with the Chinese staff at Nanking University, urging
them in letter after letter to protect his extensive files of data. Unlike Pearl, he
fully expected to return to Nanking after order was restored by the Nationalist
government. In the annual report he prepared in the summer of 1927, he strongly
endorsed the principle that Chinese institutions, including the universities, should
be managed by the Chinese. He declared that he and other Western scholars
should return only "if the Chinese want us, as their colleagues at their invitation
and under their direction."[33]

The summer passed uneventfully. Absalom returned from Korea, filled with
opinions about the work that could be done there.[34] Pearl sometimes took Carol
and Janice for walks on the mountainside and modest picnics in the surrounding
woods. They ate sandwiches that Pearl made with bread she baked herself.[35] Lulu
Hamilton sent a large parcel of clothes, including hats for Pearl and Margaret
Thomson and shirts and sweaters for the children.[36] Pearl found Unzen restful,
in spite of the unequal division of household chores. In any case, in mid-summer,
her Nanking housemaid, Li Sau-tse, suddenly appeared on her Unzen doorstep,
demanding support and a job.[37] For the remainder of her Japanese sojourn, Pearl
was able to delegate many of her domestic tasks.

As the shock of March 24 receded, she became increasingly concerned that the American press was doing China a disservice with its bellicose anti-Chinese reporting. "I do rebel," she wrote to a friend, "against the vengefulness that calls the [incident] Chinese and Oriental – no nation can be branded, especially in times of stress." Blaming all Chinese for any single episode, Pearl said, would be as logical as blaming all Americans for a bombing outrage in the New York City subways. Beyond that, she believed that "none of us is guiltless, if history be read rightly."[38]

Similarly, in a letter to Lewis Gannett, she vigorously distanced herself from the crude stereotypes that defined Western accounts of Chinese behavior. Lying just under the surface of such reporting, Pearl heard the echoes of old clichés about Asiatic cruelty and treachery:

Of course I have no sympathy with the "Saturnalia of Oriental crime" stuff. It was not Oriental crime. There is no such thing, any more than there is American crime or English crime or any other kind of wholesale crime. I suppose one must call the individuals who planned and executed so cruel a plot . . . criminals. But it is nonsense and injustice to blame the affair on the Chinese people.

Pearl insisted that the Chinese themselves were the chief victims of China's turmoil, oppressed simultaneously by their own leaders and by interfering outsiders. More than ever, the common people of China deserved her loyalty and support. She said that she considered herself "bound to China and the Chinese now as never before."[39]

By late June, Pearl had become more hopeful about returning to China. She wrote to Lulu that "it seems more and more evident that a good many of us are going to be wanted back." She had even decided that the violence had been useful, in permanently purging the most reactionary missionary elements from the Chinese scene. She called them "dead wood," and she was convinced that "this cleaning out of a lot of the ultra fundamentalist-minded-missionaries – and they have gone home by the hundreds – has done no small amount of good."[40]

Pearl didn't mention that her father, who had every intention of going back to Nanking, was among the most unreconstructed fundamentalists in the entire Christian community. Perhaps she simply assumed that Absalom was too old for much more evangelical exertion. Her hostility toward the missionary enterprise, which had long been gathering force, now became one of her leading convictions. Pearl remained loyal to her Christian faith, at least in public statements. However, as she brooded on the Nanking Incident and its deeper causes, she decided that the missionaries bore much of the responsibility for Chinese hatred of the West. She came to believe that, for too long, the missionaries had served as both agents and symbols of imperialism.

Pearl admired Japan as an efficient, modern society, in many ways more comfortable than Chinkiang or even Nanking, but she was drawn back to China by a tangle of obligations and affections. By the end of July, though Pearl remained deeply ambivalent, the Bucks had begun planning a return to Nanking. Pearl passed this information along to Lulu, after thanking her for sending a pair of silk bloomers as a gift – the first pair of store-bought bloomers Pearl had ever owned.

China's political situation remained volatile. The final split between the Kuomintang's Communist and conservative factions had occurred just a few weeks after the Nanking Incident. Chiang had made a raggedly triumphant entry into Shanghai in April, and immediately attacked his erstwhile allies, the left-wing labor unions and youth groups who had held the city on his behalf.[41] Chiang waged a particularly lethal campaign against Shanghai's workers and students, imprisoning and executing thousands without trial or appeal. After taking control of the city, he marched back to Nanking, where he set up his government. The symbolism of his strategy was clear; he had chosen the ancient capital of the Ming emperors to dramatize his ambitions for Chinese unity and to signify his own authority. He was also trying to legitimize his descent from Sun Yat-sen, who in 1912 had hoped to locate the capital of the new Republic in Nanking.

This was a turning point in twentieth-century Chinese politics. At this moment, in John King Fairbank's summary of the situation, "the latent split between the right and left wings of the revolution became complete."[42] In the long run, Chiang's methods and ideology would lead to disaster for the KMT. Twenty-two years later, comrades of the Communists whom Chiang expelled, hunted down, and murdered would take control of China. In the summer of 1927, however, his tactics seemed brutally effective. He decimated the Communist leadership, which retreated into the mountains of Kiangsi (Jiangxi) province. Chiang had become the country's dominant military and political figure. He controlled the cities of the south and the Yangtze river, and began to create the administrative apparatus of a national government. In the spring of 1928, Chiang led another Northern Expedition, which occupied Peking in June. (He wishfully renamed the city Peiping, or "Northern Peace.")[43]

As he consolidated his control over the country, Chiang also managed to pacify the foreign powers. Although a few jingoist politicians in the United States, Britain, and Japan demanded reprisals and even invasion, all three countries adopted a milder official policy. Calvin Coolidge and his Secretary of State, Frank Kellogg, determined that the United States would not interfere in China's internal affairs. British Foreign Secretary Austen Chamberlain denounced what he called "the Nanking Outrages," but coupled his belligerent rhetoric with a half-hearted declaration of support for the Nationalist government.[44]

From her closer vantage point, Pearl also endorsed Chiang as the only feasible

alternative to warlord anarchy or Communism. By late summer, she had begun
to reinterpret the Nanking Incident, defining it both as a pogrom and a great
patriotic gesture. In a letter to Lewis Gannett, she insisted that it was a major
event in the Chinese revolution, "really a sort of Boston tea-party for them – a
declaration of independence of a very gruesome sort to tell the world that they
[are] no longer afraid of foreigners." She defended Chinese demands for justice,
but she worried that Chiang's fragile authority might evaporate at any moment.[45]

Understandably, revolution was much on Pearl's mind in these days. She told
a friend that she was reading widely in the history of revolutions, trying to situate
China's upheavals in the context of the past. She eventually reached a pessimistic
conclusion, which she summarized for Lewis Gannett. The Chinese revolution,
she wrote, "seems to be following pretty faithfully the past history of other
revolutions, which have gone through a period of just such disintegration and
demoralization."[46]

Pearl's skepticism about revolution took shape in a long story that she began
writing while she was still in Japan, and published the following year in *Asia*
magazine. "The Revolutionist" is the story of Wang Lung, a poor farmer who
lives with his wife and three daughters in a village near Nanking. He works hard,
regularly abuses his wife for producing only girl children, and has little hope for
the future. The time is unspecified; the events in this story could have occurred
anytime in the chaotic years leading up to the collapse of the Ch'ing dynasty.

On a visit to the city to sell his vegetables, Wang stops in a teahouse where
he listens to a young man attacking foreigners and rich Chinese, and preaching
the need for violent revolution. Initially, Wang, who has never heard such terms
as democracy, imperialism, or capitalism, is more interested in the young man's
expensive clothes than in his radical message. When he is asked whose name he
would write on a ballot for president, he explains that he cannot read or write,
doesn't know what the term "president" means, and has no idea why anyone
would ask his opinion about such matters.

Wang Lung's indifference reflects his distance from the military and ideological struggles that are convulsing China. He regards the identity of his rulers as
a matter of small consequence, compared to the more fundamental realities that
define his life, such as soil and rainfall, seed and manure, work, good or bad
luck, above all his yearning for sons. Nonetheless, he is electrified by one statement the young orator makes: after the revolution, the poor will become rich.

As he walks down Nanking's streets, Wang Lung indulges himself in fantasies
of wealth. He decides that his long, unwashed queue would be unfashionable;
on a whim, he pays a traveling barber a few pennies to shave it off. Without
knowing it, Wang has become a revolutionist. The long braided queue had been
imposed as a mark of subordination on Chinese men by the Manchus centuries
earlier. A man who cut off his queue was publicly declaring his defiance.

When he returns to his village, Wang becomes the target of his neighbors' amusement. They call him "Wang the Revolutionist," a teasing title that embarrasses him because he doesn't know what it means. On his next visit to Nanking, he sees a young man arrested as a revolutionist, and he hears that revolutionists are being rounded up and executed. Guided by whispered rumors that sweep through the crowds, Wang runs to the Bridge of the Three Sisters, where he is confronted by a horrific scene:

There at the bridge, upon seven bamboo poles, were seven bleeding heads, bent on ragged, severed necks; heads with fringes of black hair hanging over their dull, half-closed eyes. One head had its mouth open and its tongue thrust out, half bitten off between set white teeth.[47]

A mob of old and young men curse at the heads, jeering that this is what happens to revolutionists. Wang is sickened with fear. If someone he knows were to call out to him: "Ha! Wang the Revolutionist!," the joke could be fatal. He returns to his village, haunted by the vision of his own head on a pole. Over the next months, he retreats into a frightened, embittered silence, waiting to be dragged off and beheaded for ideas he has never held. Immobilized by dread, he even stops beating and berating his wife.

The story's conclusion turns on a final irony. An army of vaguely defined "revolutionary" soldiers marches through Wang Lung's village on its way to Nanking, carelessly destroying all of his crops except a few turnips. The soldiers encourage the people to attack the homes of privileged foreigners. Wang Lung, still more bewildered than eager, joins in the looting but comes away only with a single dollar, a couple of books he cannot read, and a few torn pieces of clothing.[48] Clutching his trifling plunder, Wang walks home, exhausted and ashamed, past the bodies of the dead that litter the roads. His long-suffering wife gets the story's last words: " 'These books are fit for nothing but to make shoe soles, but at least this dollar will feed us until the turnips can be eaten.' "

Aside from presaging the main character and some of the events that would appear several years later in *The Good Earth*, "The Revolutionist" offers a mordant comment on contemporary Chinese politics. The story argues that abstract demands for justice more often than not give rise to bloodshed and chaos. In China, as in other countries before and since, utopian dreams typically collapse into brutality, leaving peasants such as Wang Lung no better off than they had been. Attacks on foreigners might be therapeutic, but in the end they would do little to solve the problems of the Chinese masses. Poverty and exploitation were ancient, indigenous realities, embedded in the hierarchical structure of Chinese society for thousands of years.

Pearl's satire had its obvious sources in her own predicament. She was still recovering from the trauma of her recent danger, and uncertain about her future. Her thinking revolved around a set of opposed attitudes. She was sympathetic to China's nationalist aspirations, but she was appalled by the violence that attended nationalism. She was angry at the Communists, but she was chastened by the insight that hostility against foreigners was no Communist invention. (She said that if she went back to China she wanted to live in a "less pretentious-looking home.") She was increasingly convinced that missionaries had no real function in China, but she clung to her shrinking faith as a buttress against despair. She still saw her vocation as wife and mother, but she was finding more satisfaction as a teacher and especially as a writer.

Under the combined pressure of personal and political disappointments, Pearl was divided against herself. She was still groping with the pain of her failing marriage and the guilt she felt in Carol's illness and her own sterility. Her life seemed to teach the lesson that passion and commitment inevitably led to disappointment. She was approaching her late thirties, assailed by self-doubt, worried that she had accomplished nothing.

From this period forward, she would continue to carry the burden of her insecurity, but she also took steps to protect herself emotionally. She became more cautious in bestowing her affections, more private, more selective in sharing confidences, even with women friends. She also placed a higher value on her own needs, exchanging the familiar conventions of female service and sacrifice for a new conception of her opportunities and entitlements.

Put less generously, as her husband would have done, she became more selfish. She had begun to realize that, because she was a woman, she was less likely to be taken seriously as a writer and professional than male colleagues. She sometimes joked that she needed a wife to provide the space and time her work required. Since that was impossible, she could at least refuse to submerge herself in tending on those around her. If she was often disappointed with herself, she had also been disappointed by others. Her parents had squandered their chance of happiness by chasing an evangelical mirage. Her husband was more interested in his statistical charts than in her. Her birth child was the cause of daily pain. Whether she would ever find satisfaction in herself or not, she had learned that she could not rely on others to create contentment for her.

Pearl was not yet articulate, even with herself, about the changes she would make. Like most women in her generation who became discontented with the gendered status quo, she did not yet have a vocabulary in which to describe an alternative. Nonetheless, she had decided that she would only survive by re-creating herself as an independent person. She mistrusted her own talents, a habit of anxiety bred into her by almost four decades of experience. At the same time, she realized that she had to take charge of her life and renegotiate her relations with those around her, including the members of her family. Ultimately, she would not recognize any claim except Carol's as automatically legitimate, and she would even devise a strategy to separate herself from Carol's constant care.

THE BUCKS RETURNED to China in October, 1927. Since conditions in Nanking were still dangerously unsettled, they moved into a large but shabby house in Shanghai, on the avenue Joffre in the foreign concession. Living on a small allowance from the Foreign Mission Board, they had to share their accommodations and expenses with the Yaukeys and another American family, the Bateses. Absalom continued to add his crotchety demands to Pearl's burdens. On the other hand, Grace Yaukey was quietly helpful, and the Reisners and Thomsons lived nearby, providing Pearl some companionship outside her family.

In fact, the situation in Shanghai was only marginally more secure than in the rest of China. Always overcrowded, the city's population was now swollen with Western and Chinese refugees, including thousands of White Russians. Carrying their obsolete Czarist passports or their refugee identity papers, the Russians faced certain death if they went home and an uncertain future in China. Pearl made friends with one of these Russian émigrés, a former professor of literature, now working as a watchman at a Chinese house, barely surviving on the few pennies he earned each day.

Even for the city's legal residents, existence was brutal and often short. Boys and girls as young as ten years old, bought from their parents, were imprisoned in brothels. Others worked twelve or fourteen hours a day in factories, hunched over dangerous machinery, breathing toxic fumes, burned by chemicals and exposed electrical wiring. Thousands of children working in cotton mills developed tuberculosis.

Little girls worked in silk-winding mills "so full of steam that the fingers of the mill-girls are white with fungus growths." In one mill, if the exhausted children ever slacken their pace, "the overseers often plunge their elbows into the boiling water as a punishment."[49] The windows of the stifling silk factories were always kept tightly sealed, even in summer, to prevent any breeze that might break the fragile silk threads unwinding from cocoons.[50] Temperatures rose to over 110 degrees Fahrenheit; children regularly passed out and fell into the machinery, maiming or killing themselves by the hundreds.

Shanghai was a city of pain and fear. Along with victims of war, the transients included outlaws and criminals who brought their violence inside the city's borders. Law enforcement gave way to the rule of private gangs and enterprising thugs. The hordes of homeless put a major strain on Shanghai's primitive sanitary and health facilities. Food was often in short supply, reducing everyone but the rich to a struggle for mere survival. Disorder and epidemic hovered over both the Chinese and Western sections of the city.[51]

The winter of 1927–1928 was an unhappy time for Pearl. She was living in rented, shared quarters, surrounded by squalor and rising tension. Lossing, showing as much domestic indifference as bravery, went back to Nanking with Claude Thomson and John Reisner to work on his survey. Pearl was left to care for the children. Once again, she found herself displaced and lonely. She told Lulu Hamilton she was convinced that foreigners would never again be welcome on the Nanking University staff, adding bitterly: "That is my private opinion to you and not to be quoted, since I am a mere female."[52]

The day after Christmas, Pearl wrote to two American friends, coupling a pathetically optimistic report on Carol's progress with a glum appraisal of Chinese politics.[53] She reiterated her contempt for "Bolshevism" but condemned Chiang Kai-shek's savage suppression of the Communists. The Nationalists, she declared, had already failed: they were employing "the old militarist methods – heavy, illegal taxes, corruptly used." She accused Chiang of serving his own interests, becoming a millionaire at the expense of China's poor.

At the same time, still sounding a little like her missionary father, Pearl blamed the nation's troubles primarily on "the moral weakness of her people."[54] In particular, she was appalled by the "wanton extravagance and carelessness of the Chinese rich." Shanghai, in her view, resembled Bourbon Paris on the eve of the French Revolution: "The streets are crowded with hungry, sullen, half-starved people and among them roll the sedans and limousines of the wealthy Chinese, spending fabulous sums on pleasure, food, and clothes, wholly senseless [*sic*] to others." Pearl prophesied that if Chiang was unable to reform Chinese society, others would, and far more dramatically: "This cannot go on forever. Personally I feel that unless something happens to change it, we are in for a *real* revolution here, in comparison to which all this so far will be a mere game of ball on a summer's afternoon." She concluded by asking her friends, as "an act of Christian charity," to send her any funny book or magazine they happened to find – a lighthearted confession that her daily life was indeed grim.

At about this time, Pearl hired a literary agent, choosing David Lloyd from an advertisement in a dog-eared trade magazine that she found in a Shanghai book shop.[55] Although she had now published a handful of stories, essays, and translations in the *Chinese Recorder, Asia,* the *Nation,* and other journals, she still felt disadvantaged by her ignorance of the American literary marketplace and her distance from New York. Lloyd was one of two agents she wrote to; the other one, Carl Brandt, declined to represent her because, as he explained, "no one was interested in Chinese subjects."[56] Lloyd, on the other hand, eagerly agreed to work with her, commencing a relationship that lasted for three profitable decades.

Pearl set out to become a professional writer for the best of motives: she needed the money. She had always lived in pinched circumstances; at thirty-five, she yearned for something better. She and Lossing both earned small salaries, and his surveys routinely consumed funds that might have been spent on household furnishings or clothes and toys for the children. Worse, Pearl had no control over her finances. One of her Shanghai housemates later recalled her shock when she learned that Pearl was expected to sign her income over to Lossing and then ask for an allowance.[57]

Pearl wanted her independence. Above all, she intended to provide adequately for Carol for as long as the child might live, and to do so without any help from Lossing. She had only a vague plan in mind, to find Carol a school of some sort where she could live happily, but she knew that any such scheme would be expensive. She was haunted by the fear of dying and leaving Carol unprotected in a strange land. Whatever other motives compelled Pearl to sit down at her typewriter every time she could reserve ten minutes or a quarter-hour from household chores, her fears about Carol were the most urgent. It goes only a little too far to say that Pearl Buck's entire career as a writer was anchored in her anxiety for her child.

Early in January, 1928, Pearl told Emma White that she had lost forty-five pounds, though she had not been dieting. While she welcomed the change, which made her look more "like her old self," she also interpreted her weight loss as another sign of the unrelieved stress she was enduring. Nightmares still disturbed her sleep with images of her brush with death the previous March: "I did not dream that human faces could become so frightful – worse than the faces of the insane, because they were so malignant."

She warned Emma to remain in the States with her children, telling her that China had become a lawless frontier place, like the American old West, and "people with families can't go in for pioneer work."[58] Pearl, too, longed to escape from China, at least for a little while, but Lossing's work had to go on, so she had no alternative but to stay. She faced each day with a sense of foreboding, sharing in the nation's universal uncertainty: "It is like living in a dense fog all the time," she wrote on the anniversary of the Nanking Incident.[59]

The emotional distance between Pearl and Lossing reached a further crisis at about this time. Pearl accused Lossing of behaving suggestively with young Chinese women at the University. She later told Marian Craighill that she sometimes discovered "foolish letters" that Lossing had written "to his old girls." Whether Lossing's indiscretions reached as far as sexual relations is not clear. But it was about this time that Pearl moved her bed into a separate room and began to sleep alone. When Pearl's sister, Grace, visited the Bucks, she was herself occasionally surprised to wake and find Lossing standing over her bed. Sixty years later, Grace still found Lossing's intrusions rather shocking.[60] According to Grace,

Lossing was unfaithful to Pearl; she said that he "had his women," both before and during his marriage to Pearl.[61] Pearl believed that his assorted "silly secret episodes" repudiated "all the mutual fine loyalty of feeling and understanding that makes a marriage real."[62]

Perhaps in retaliation, Pearl took a lover, an extraordinary Chinese poet named Hsu Chih-mo (Xu Zhimo). The affair probably began in Shanghai and continued intermittently until Hsu's death in a plane crash in November, 1931. The evidence suggests that Pearl had been faithful to Lossing throughout the decade of their marriage. She met Hsu at a time of intense personal need, and apparently found a brief joy that was canceled by the tragedy of his death.[63]

Born in 1896, Hsu was a figure of conspicuous literary and political influence throughout his short career. He went to England to attend Cambridge University in the mid-1920s, and affiliated himself with the literary radicals of the May Fourth movement when he returned. In her memoirs, Pearl described him along with others who had adopted the fashion of imitating the dress and manners of Western poets. She never hinted at any personal connection:

[O]ne handsome and rather distinguished and certainly much beloved young poet was proud to be called "The Chinese Shelley."[64] He used to sit in my living room and talk by the hour and wave his beautiful hands in exquisite and descriptive gestures until now when I think of him, I see first his hands. He was a northern Chinese, tall and classically beautiful in looks, and his hands were big and perfectly shaped and smooth as a woman's hands.[65]

A quarter-century after Hsu's death, Pearl memorialized her relationship with him in a novel, *Letter from Peking*. The novel is told in the first person by Elizabeth Kirke, an American woman who has been separated from her Chinese husband by World War II. *Letter from Peking* disguises the affair between Hsu and Pearl in a cluster of heavily altered details. The husband, Gerald MacLeod, is only half-Chinese, the son of a Scottish father and a Chinese mother; Gerald's and Elizabeth's relationship leads to marriage and two children; the dates of the connection are moved forward from the 1920s and 1930s to the 1940s. (Written in the mid-1950s, the book savages the Communist regime.) What emerges vividly from the narrative, however, is the sexual and intellectual excitement of a union that defied disapproval and reached across the barrier of race.

There was never any question of marriage between Pearl and Hsu. Both were married, and, despite the fantasies of *Letter from Peking*, neither of them would actually have married across racial lines. For Pearl, a missionary's daughter still living mainly inside a circle of Christian piety, the need for discretion was obvious.

So, in spite of her misgivings, Pearl returned to Nanking with her children to rejoin Lossing in late July, 1928. She almost choked with anger at what she found. Her house and garden had been ruined by the Nationalist soldiers who had been billeted there for the past year. Most of her furniture had disappeared, and the rooms were covered in accumulated filth. Horses had been stabled in the ground-floor rooms. The garden was gone, replaced by shoulder-high weeds. Every shrub and hedge had been destroyed; only the large trees remained. Where Pearl had cultivated roses, the soldiers had jury-rigged a communal toilet. Amid much complaining on all sides, Pearl hired local Chinese workmen and began the task of reconstruction.[66]

The city of Nanking was also being rebuilt. In China's ancient capital, Chiang Kai-shek had established the most promising Chinese government since the Revolution of 1911. The new Republic was based on a constitution that divided power into five *yuan,* or bureaus, including (on paper, at least) a system of checks and balances. Chiang embarked on a large-scale construction and renovation program in Nanking, clearing slums and adding handsome new buildings for his various ministries.

The next ten years, sometimes called "the Nanking Decade," witnessed Chiang's unending struggles to establish and maintain control over all of China. He faced three principal challenges. To begin with, his Kuomintang government was hobbled by its own internal weaknesses. Too many of the leading figures were corrupt, and too much power resided exclusively in Chiang's hands. The five *yuan* had little authority; they served mainly as bureaucratic devices that Chiang manipulated to carry out his own decisions. The KMT's dictatorial tactics, including its casual resort to censorship and political arrests, stained its credibility. So too did the regime's alliance with organized criminals, in particular Shanghai's notorious Green Gang (which enrolled twenty thousand or more members).

Even if Chiang had been a more enlightened leader, surrounded by less self-serving lieutenants, his reform program was almost surely doomed by the sheer scale of the problems he faced. The overwhelming majority of China's four hundred million people were units in a decentralized agricultural economy that long predated the industrial revolution. Chiang's vision of limited change and gradual modernization was helpless against such obstacles. In the 1920s, China's entire industrial production was smaller than Belgium's, a country with about 1 percent of China's population. Chinese standards of living and life expectancy rates were among the lowest in the world.[67] Only a program more radical than Chiang's, undertaken even more ruthlessly, would move China forward.

Kuomintang corruption and China's gigantic backwardness constituted two of Chiang's problems; the third was Japanese militarism. Taking advantage of China's continuing disarray and the West's distaste for involvement, Japan became increasingly aggressive throughout the Nanking Decade. In 1931, Japanese troops attacked Manchuria, annexed the huge region and renamed it Manchukuo

(Manzhouguo), and installed the last Manchu emperor, P'u-Yi, as puppet ruler. In 1932, after a long campaign of bullying the municipal government of Shanghai, the Japanese bombed the city in a raid that inflicted hundreds of civilian casualties. Finally, in 1937, the Japanese army marched into China proper, opening World War II in Asia. In short, almost from the day of its founding, the Nationalist government faced the power of an expanding, militarized Japan.[68]

Not all of these troubles were visible to Pearl or to anyone else in the summer of 1928. However, because of her privileged vantage point on the scene and her experience of Chinese politics, she was less enthusiastic about Chiang than many other Westerners. A large number of outsiders, including the makers of foreign policy in Europe and America, were attracted to Chiang by his apparent personal integrity, his anti-communism, and his glamorous Christian wife, Soong Mei-ling (Soong Meiling). A Wellesley graduate and a younger sister of Sun Yat-sen's widow, Soong spoke impeccable English and served for many years as the Kuomintang's most effective spokesperson in the West. Chiang never learned to speak English, but he converted to Christianity and divorced his three wives at the time of his marriage to Soong.[69] Both decisions helped to shore up his support among the Western powers.

Pearl had a more skeptical reaction to Chiang. She was indifferent to his sudden embrace of Christianity and amused at his opportunistic marriage. In spite of his limits, she sometimes counseled patience with Chiang's policies, for example reminding a friend that it might be "too early to judge of this government when one remembers amid what storms our own small republic was begun." Furthermore, she was buoyed by signs of an emerging national consciousness among the common people and a new habit of loyalty to ideas and principles rather than individual leaders.[70]

In the end, however, as Pearl tried to judge the currents of change rippling across the country, her moments of optimism alternated with more fixed moods of despair. She noted Chiang's virtues, especially his anti-Communism, but she never believed that he could reform or lead China. In her view, he was condemned to fail because of his alienation from the masses. Furthermore, the Western powers only supported him because he threatened less disruption of the inequitable status quo than more radical leaders. For that reason, she predicted, he would come to be seen as an agent of the West, wearing a badge of dependency that would eventually make him a target of anti-foreign hatreds.

Pearl had not yet heard the name Mao Tse-tung (Mao Zedong), who in the late 1920s was reconnoitering in the countryside, evaluating the revolutionary stamina of the peasantry.[71] Indeed, the Communists were uniformly nameless and faceless to her. Nevertheless, her experience compelled her to take them seriously. Kuomintang incompetence and misbehavior handsomely served Communist purposes: "the Communists flourish on this [the corruption in Chiang's government] as propaganda, of course, and are beginning to lift up their heads in various parts of the country. Personally I look for worse times yet to come from them."[72]

THROUGHOUT THE FALL, Pearl supervised the restoration of her home. When she didn't like the work that was being done, she would sometimes shout at the workmen, climb a scaffold or get down on her knees to show them how a floor should be sanded. Rummaging in a small closet, she had a pleasant surprise when she found a wooden box, overlooked by the looters and soldiers who had walked off with most of her possessions. In the box, undisturbed, lay the Dickens novels she had read as a child, along with the manuscript of *The Exile,* her biography of Carie. The discovery seemed a good omen, encouraging Pearl to keep writing. She sent David Lloyd her story "A Chinese Woman Speaks," along with an unpublished supplement, suggesting that the two parts might make a novel under the title *Winds of Heaven.* She also continued working on a new novel, which she had begun in Shanghai, called "Wang Lung."

In some respects, Pearl's return to Nanking merely intensified her discontent. For one thing, the city seethed with anti-foreign sentiments that threatened to erupt in violence at any time. On one occasion, when Pearl joined a Chinese crowd to listen to a street-corner revolutionary, the angry speaker suddenly cursed and spat on her.[73] Though several people came to her assistance, the incident was a painful reminder that her years in China did not immunize her against nationalist hatred.

She also chafed against her personal circumstances. She was a strong, impatient woman, schooled to grudging conformity only by circumstances she couldn't alter and by a deep-rooted sense of obligation. There was no real job for her in the university, and her memories of the Nanking Incident remained vivid as a warning of the dangers that could erupt again at any time. The empty Christian chapel on the university campus was haunted by ghosts. The sound of unexpected voices at the gate made her shiver with fear. She planted cabbages, spinach, larkspur, and violets in her reclaimed garden, not knowing if she would ever harvest them.

She wanted to go back to America – "not permanently, but for a few years," as she wrote to Emma White in early 1929. She wanted time to find a school for Carol: "I realize I must leave her in some place . . . and my heart is wrenched in two at the thought." She confessed to friends that Carol's daily presence had become unendurable. "The years do not make me resigned," she wrote. "Sometimes I can scarcely bear to look at other children and see what she might have become."[74]

Pearl admitted, with shame, that she was often embarrassed by Carol, who would sometimes cry and scream continuously for attention. The hours Pearl spent trying to teach her daughter only led to tears and frustration on both sides; any little progress Carol made in speaking or reading seemed to evaporate after a day or two. Pearl felt a stab of guilt whenever she contemplated putting her daughter in an institution, but she had concluded that it was the only way to save herself from suffocating.

She accused Lossing of withdrawing emotionally from both her and Carol: he "felt the child was not worth bothering about," she said bitterly.[75] She did acknowledge that she was "rather proud" of Lossing's forthcoming book – the tribute of one writer to another. However, in her letters to American friends, she took less trouble than she had in the past to disguise the rift with her husband. The Bucks remained in China, Pearl said, solely because "Lossing never really wavered in his decision to stick by China for better or worse. And so stick we will."[76]

Throughout the winter, Pearl closely watched the city's largest building project, the construction of Sun Yat-sen's tomb on the side of the Purple Mountain. The elaborate mausoleum was only coincidentally a tribute to China's fallen republican hero, whose body had been lying above ground, rather scandalously, for almost four years, waiting for burial. The real point of Sun's tomb was not reverential but political. Chiang was still campaigning to establish himself as Sun's legitimate ideological heir. Sun's three Principles of the People – nationalism, people's rights, and people's livelihood – had been embedded in the Kuomintang platform. His tomb was intended as a proof of continuity, a visible reminder to the citizens of Nanking that the responsibilities of leadership were in good hands.

Sun's funeral, in June, 1929, was a grand state occasion. Though Pearl and other foreigners had feared that the Communists would take the opportunity to provoke some sort of violence, the ceremonies took place peacefully. Since the city was crowded with visitors, Pearl and Lossing found room for two house-guests, Dr. Alfred Sze (Shi Zhaoji), the Chinese minister to the United States, and a Dr. Taylor, an American physician who had embalmed Sun's body several years earlier and had then periodically touched up the corpse. Taylor worried that Sun's body might disintegrate in the June heat, especially when the cata-falque was jostled during the long procession through the city.[77] (In the event, only Sun's hands decomposed, and they were hidden from view.)

A wide new road had been carved through Nanking to accommodate the funeral marchers. Thousands of men, women, and children took part in the procession, carrying banners that represented schools, youth groups, political organizations, and military units from all over the country. Delegates from Britain, Japan, the United States, and several other countries also joined the march. The route was six miles long, across the fields that separated the Purple Mountain from Nanking's walls.

Pearl, who stood for several hours in the crowd as the long cortege went by, had her first glimpse of Chiang as he passed her at the head of the mourners. In a report that she filed a few days later to the Mission Board, she described him in flattering terms: "His eyes were the most remarkable feature. They were very wide, fearless, direct in gaze, and commanding in expression."[78] Pearl transformed Chiang into a symbolic figure, representing China's transition from past to future: "Young China stands looking out across the great land it has made its own, its eyes fixed fearlessly on the future."[79]

Pearl assumed that her report would be treated as a relatively public statement, which explains its infatuated tone. As her letters from the same period make clear, the heroic sketch she drew of Chiang in these pages varied quite sharply from her private estimate. She did admire Chiang's personal courage, but she did not think that he actually embodied China's future. She tempered her opinions to suit the preferences of her readers back in the United States, the dignitaries of the mission establishment who had already adopted Chiang's cause as their own.

Yet even in this calculated document, Pearl balanced her approval with a characteristically tough-minded analysis of how much Chiang did *not* represent. It would "not be fair," she continued, "to close this letter without some reference to the millions who did not come to the funeral and who perhaps scarcely knew it was going on." As she would do throughout the following decades, Pearl was speaking for China's peasants, the nameless masses on whose alleged but unwitting behalf revolutions have been made. "The common people, the workers, had no great share in the day and the hour," she wrote. Vast numbers of Chinese proletarians and peasants were excluded from Young China's day of self-congratulation.

One gauge of Pearl's more troubled analysis of Sun's funeral and Chiang's behavior can be found in her response to the new road that was built as a stage for the procession. As work on the road progressed in the months prior to the funeral, she remarked several times on the "barren strip" that Chiang's bulldozers were driving through the colorful old city.[80] Hundreds of houses and shops were leveled to create the grandiose boulevard that Chiang decreed, in spite of the protests of their owners. The work produced a broad avenue of demolition, victimizing countless ordinary citizens who instantly became enemies of the Republic. Pearl personally watched some of the destruction, in which she saw a fearful emblem of Chiang's megalomania and his alienation from his own people.[81] She later said that the Communists gained their first major victory without firing a shot on the day that Chiang ordered his splendid road.

The scenes of devastation she witnessed became the basis for a story that she wrote a few months later. "The New Road" describes the project from the point of view of Lu Chen, a fifty-year-old grandfather who is displaced by the demolition. All his life, Lu has made a meager income by selling hot water in a tiny shop in one of Nanking's cluttered alleys. Every day, starting before dawn and ending after dusk, Lu heats water in two huge caldrons, ladling it out to his customers. Workers buy a cupful for their tea; slaves fetch it in buckets for the baths of wealthy ladies in the nearby great houses. Lu inherited his shop from his father and grandfather; in turn, he plans to leave it to his son and grandson.

When the new government moves to Nanking, Lu is initially untouched by it. Revolution is a word he sometimes hears, but the idea of essential change seems to him wrongheaded. At the level of the body's needs, life makes its demands without regard to politics: " 'There is never great change,' " Lu declares. " 'Emperors and kings and presidents or whatnot, people must drink tea and must bathe – these go on forever.' "[82] The only changes he has seen have been disruptive. His son has become lazy and disrespectful, and his high-spirited grandson is not properly obedient. If these are the consequences of revolution, then Lu wants none of it.

Lu's world is abruptly turned upside down when a young officer comes to his door and tells him that his shop stands in the way of the new road. He is given fifteen days to vacate. When he demands compensation, the brutal Republican officer threatens to punish him for his complaint, and declares that his shop is his contribution to the new regime. Fifteen days later, precisely on schedule, workmen arrive and dismantle Lu's house and shop around him. He refuses to leave, stubbornly sitting on his bench through a long day of destruction:

There were the great copper caldrons, firmly embedded in the clay of the ovens. Two workmen hacked at them with pickaxes. "My grandfather put those in," he said suddenly. "There are no such workmen nowadays."
But he said nothing more while they took the tiles from the roof and the light began to seep down between the rafters. At last they took the rafters, and he sat there within four walls with the noonday sunshine beating on him. He was sick and faint, but he sat on through the long afternoon, and, when evening came, he still sat there, his shop a heap of bricks and tiles and broken rafters about him. The two caldrons stood up naked out of the ruins. People stared at him curiously but said nothing, and he sat on.

This is a moving scene, an image of the pain and loss that ordinary men and women often suffer in the midst of social turmoil. Lu is finally led away to his son's small cottage on the city's outskirts. There he spends the next several months in stupefied despair, disconnected from his family, silent, virtually motionless.

Yet Lu's paralyzed grief is not the story's final comment on revolution. Though Pearl mistrusted Chiang and hated the Communists, she also knew that fundamental change was inevitable. In spite of her misgivings, she wanted to believe that the indeterminate future might bring progress to China's masses. So, Lu Chen's story ends with a hint of hope. His son joins the revolution, and proves himself a talented builder. Hardworking and useful, he also becomes more courteous toward Lu. The plot suggests that, paradoxically, change can strengthen rather than diminish the bonds of filial piety.

In the story's last scene, Lu Chen summons up the courage to go look at the road that has caused him so much misery. To his own surprise, he is thunderstruck with admiration. The road is longer and wider than anything he has seen before. "Well," he thinks to himself, "here was a thing. Not even emperors had made a road like this!" For the first time, Lu does not use the word "robbery" when he thinks about his vanished shop. Instead, he asks himself, "Had it taken this road to make his son a man?" The story ends with a question: "This Revolution – this new road! Where did it lead?"

That concluding interrogative tone lifts the story above mere polemic. Though Pearl was engrossed in the political events taking place around her, she was drawn above all to the large theme of change itself. In 1911, a status quo that had lasted for over two thousand years had been knocked to rubble, like Lu Chen's hot-water shop. In the decades that followed, the country was engaged in an enormous experiment. Any number of new societies might eventually rise in place of the ancient empire, but, for better or worse, all of them would inflict tremendous penalties on traditional values and structures.

Given the country's size, China's internal struggle for self-definition was perhaps the most important political and cultural conflict of the twentieth century. As she watched the debate unfold before her, Pearl was irremediably ambivalent. On the one hand, she had seen poverty and its fierce consequences. She was also a woman growing more rigorous in her demands for justice for herself. For these reasons, her sympathies were engaged on the side of China's masses, both the nation's men, such as her fictional Lao Wang and Lu Chen, and especially its subordinated women and female children. Change was obligatory if people like these were ever to have decent lives.

On the other hand, as a student of China's classic culture, Pearl mourned the passing of the old order. She acknowledged the entrenched inequities and narrow-mindedness of Chinese customs and beliefs, but she also believed that traditional China had discovered and invented much of what deserved to be called civilization. In any case, she had seen too much of both natural disaster and human cruelty to be seduced by the utopian schemes of any party, whether on the left or the right.

IN THE SPRING of 1929, the Rockefeller Foundation offered Lossing a major grant to expand his survey work. Negotiations over the details required a return to the States, and the family left Nanking in July. Pearl's main task during the five-month trip was to find a suitable institution for Carol. She visited several schools, collecting a set of discouraging impressions. At one high-priced institution, for example, retarded children were taught to hold cards as if they were playing bridge, though they did not understand the game.[83] Many schools were managed as warehouses, in which children were simply stored until they died.

Eventually, Pearl settled on the Vineland Training School in New Jersey. It was a modest facility, but she was impressed by the director, Dr. Edward Johnstone, who treated the children as human beings and not merely medical problems. Vineland was committed to an educational program, training each child to the limits of his or her abilities. This is where Pearl brought Carol, in September, and where Carol would live for more than sixty years.

Vineland's annual fee was $1,000, more money than Pearl could afford, even if Lossing agreed to the expenditure. She borrowed $2,000 from the Presbyterian Mission Board to pay for two years in advance. In exchange, the Board asked her to write a story about missionaries for children. Pearl agreed thankfully, but when she delivered the money to Dr. Johnstone, she had no idea where the fees would come from in the future.

Though Pearl was convinced she had made the right choice, for Carol as well as herself, parting from her daughter was one of the most anguished moments of her life. They had almost never been separated, and this separation, she later wrote, was "almost as final as death."[84] She was convinced that nothing could ever repay her for the agony of leaving Carol behind. She was tormented by the image of her last moments with her daughter: "She clung to me so desperately at the end – I had to pull her little arms away from my neck . . . it was rending flesh from flesh."[85] It was a scene she would never forget.

When she left Carol at Vineland, Pearl was torn by conflicting emotions of relief, guilt, and anger. For the first time in her life, she was "on the constant edge of weeping – and I feel if I once began to weep I should go to pieces and never stop again." She wanted to cry, she said, not just because she had to give Carol up. Rather, "it is weeping for all that I have never had of my only child and never can have."[86] She was mourning the loss of Carol's "precious life" and of "other lives that might have come from hers – oh Lulu, nobody knows who hasn't had it, and I am glad for everyone who doesn't know."[87]

She concealed Carol's existence for the next two decades. She systematically avoided any mention of her daughter in the autobiographical sketches she provided to publishers and journalists when her popularity aroused public interest just a year or two later. The text of one such pamphlet, from 1932, is illustrated with a photograph of Pearl and Janice, and concludes with the accurate but misleading statement: "I have two little daughters. One is away at school and one . . . is at home with us." Pearl claimed that her motive in such evasions was not shame, but a desire to protect Carol's privacy. Perhaps. However, at a time when mental illness was still powerfully stigmatized, it seems likely that she was protecting herself as well.

On this visit to America, Pearl also received much better news, a cable from David Lloyd telling her that the John Day Company had offered to publish her first novel, *East Wind, West Wind*. Lloyd had sent the manuscript to more than two dozen publishers – "every publisher in New York," as Pearl later told it. John Day was the last company on Lloyd's list; if they refused the book, he intended to withdraw it. Pearl went to the John Day offices to sign a standard contract: a royalty rate of 10 percent, rising to 15 percent after five thousand copies. The book's list price would be $2.50, and its title would be *East Wind, West Wind*, not Pearl's proposed *Winds of Heaven*.

The price and change of title were personally negotiated by John Day's president and publisher, Richard Walsh. From that day until his death thirty years later, Richard would publish everything Pearl wrote. The two became friends on the spot; within a couple of years they would be lovers. In 1935, after they were divorced from their first spouses, they married. The marriage, which lasted until Richard's death in 1960, encompassed what Helen Foster Snow has called the most successful writing and publishing partnership in the history of American letters.[88]

When Pearl met him, Richard Walsh was forty-two years old, a writer-businessman presiding over a young and unprofitable publishing house. He had graduated from Harvard in 1907, where he had written humor for the *Lampoon*, trading jokes with classmate Robert Benchley. He had taken a job at Curtis publications and moved up to promotion manager, leaving the company after the world war to work for Herbert Hoover as a relief administrator. In 1927, he had taken over the fledgling John Day Company, following a safer but less exciting sequence of jobs in the mid-1920s in which he had written copy for an advertising agency, worked on the staffs of *Judge* and *Woman's Home Companion*, and edited *Collier's*. He lived in a handsome house in suburban Pelham, just north of New York, with his wife, Ruby Abbott, and their three children.

Richard had published his first book, *The Making of Buffalo Bill: A Study in Heroics*, in 1928. As the title suggests, this volume is not so much a biography as an analysis of the public relations campaign that turned William Cody, an energetic but only moderately interesting Indian fighter, into a legendary figure. "Buffalo Bill," Richard concluded in his "Foreword," was the beneficiary of "the deliberate and infinitely skilful use of publicity."[89] Throughout the book, Richard is simultaneously skeptical of manufactured celebrity and dazzled by the power of press agentry to manipulate public taste. Instructive on its own terms, the book also provocatively anticipated Richard's relationship with Pearl over the next three decades. She produced the fictional commodity; he delivered the market.

In their first meeting, Richard told Pearl that his staff had been evenly divided on her book. He had cast the deciding vote in favor, not because he thought *East Wind, West Wind* was very good, but because he believed her next novel would be better. In choosing to publish Pearl's work, Richard was challenging what he called "the well-known wall of prejudice against Chinese books."[90]

Richard didn't tell Pearl or her agent that he also badly needed a successful book. The early days of the Depression had sharply reduced revenues across the book publishing industry. The John Day Company, which had opened just two years before the crash of 1929, was especially vulnerable. As a new company, John Day had no established authors or reliable backlist. Richard kept the company going by reducing staff, cutting his own salary, and using his children's Liberty Bonds as collateral for loans.

Having taken personal responsibility for *East Wind, West Wind*, Richard suggested a hundred changes, nearly all of which Pearl accepted with docility. She defended only one phrase, on the basis of Chinese usage. Richard objected to the exclamation "Oh my mother," which was used several times in a funeral sequence. Pearl retorted that it accurately rendered a repetitive Chinese mourning cry, and was therefore a necessary rhetorical device.[91]

Here, for the first time, she was defending her stylistic choices on the basis of her knowledge of Chinese language and customs. She often said that she first composed her novels mentally in Chinese, and then translated them into English. Her stylized and often stilted prose originated in her effort to reproduce in English the altogether different cadences of Chinese speech.

East Wind, West Wind received a fair amount of comment for a first novel, much of it favorable. Pearl said that reading the fulsome notices was like reading her obituary.[92] Several reviewers praised the book's authenticity, though the compliment was gratuitous, since few American readers knew enough about China to have any basis for judgment. The book is divided into two parts. The first reprints, more or less verbatim, Pearl's story "A Chinese Woman Speaks," in which the sheltered young woman, Kwei-lan, describes her confusing encounter with the modern world in the figure of her progressive husband.

In the novel's second part, Kwei-lan tells of her older brother's return from study in the United States, accompanied by his American wife. For Kwei-lan's mother, the marriage is a calamity, and the white woman's pregnancy even worse, since she refuses to acknowledge any son of a racially mixed couple as a legitimate member of her family. (If the child is a girl, of course, then it will be of no consequence.) The plot may have its basis in Pearl's relationship with Hsu Chih-mo, but the issues at stake in the tale are those that she would always be drawn to: the contest between tradition and modernity and the risks and possibilities of human connection across racial and cultural lines.

In particular, the novel questions the traditional status of women in Chinese society. In her own way, Pearl was anticipating a central issue that philosophers have only formally addressed quite recently: the relation of gender and family structure to the definition of justice. Kwei-lan's husband notes that " 'our old customs have held women lightly,' " and Kwei-lan herself recalls what she learned "in the Sacred Edicts" of Confucius when she was just a child: "a man must not love his wife more than his parents. It is a sin before the ancestral tablets and the gods."[93] By giving Kwei-lan a voice, Pearl Buck was attempting to destabilize the received notion of woman's place in the Chinese family. Since the family, in turn, has been at the very center of China's ethical world for centuries, the issues Pearl raised also spoke to the organization of society itself.

Lossing and Pearl returned to Nanking with Janice in January, 1930. Pearl's voyage across the Pacific was shadowed by sorrow and doubt. Writing to Lulu Hamilton from the *Empress of Asia,* she was inconsolable: "If I had known how hard this leaving [Carol] was going to be, I simply couldn't have done it. Left to my choice, I simply should have given up China absolutely and without question." She blamed her husband for her pain. "It has been a dreadful time — having to go back, because Lossing has felt equally without question that he must go, and wanting myself to stay, and yet his absolute unwillingness to let me stay behind, even for a year or two."[94]

Pearl's separation from Carol ended a decade of testing that had profoundly altered her view of herself and her obligations. She regarded her marriage as a slow martyrdom. She believed, probably accurately, that she had come close to death in the Nanking Incident. She had lost confidence in the missionary enterprise. Above all, she had gone through Gethsemane with Carol.[95] These were the sad thoughts that preyed upon her as she looked out across the Pacific. To make matters worse, she was almost constantly seasick. Like her mother, she hated ocean travel.

In contrast to Pearl, Lossing was exhilarated by his return to Nanking. His own views on his marriage are not known, though he was presumably aware that a crisis lay in wait. His scholarly career, on the other hand, had taken a leap forward. At forty years old, he had established himself as one of the preeminent authorities on Chinese agricultural economics. His book, *Chinese Farm Economy,* was to be published by the University of Chicago Press in the fall; it would receive admiring reviews in the relevant learned journals. His Rockefeller Foundation grant would support the major research project that would occupy him through much of the 1930s.

The struggle that dominated the Bucks' intimate life had ironically and quite accidentally spilled over into a public contest for recognition. Lossing and Pearl published their first books within months of each other, and both volumes were warmly welcomed by the press. Just a year later, when she published *The Good Earth*, Pearl would become a household name all over the world. However, in 1930, Lossing probably had more visibility than his wife. His book and the decade of articles that preceded it had given him high standing among students of Asia.

Chinese Farm Economy summarized the profound changes that had overtaken Lossing's agricultural evangelism. He had set out for China fifteen years earlier with Christian intentions, inspired by the pious hope that he could improve Chinese farming and save Chinese souls. Though his evangelical impulses were never urgent, he had become a leading figure in the agricultural mission field, much in demand as a speaker and consultant. He helped to organize the two Nanking University conferences, in 1924 and 1926, that "represented the apogee of talk about the subject."[96]

By the time his book appeared, the Christian perspective that had motivated Lossing in the beginning of his career had given way to a thoroughly technical and scientific point of view. The five hundred densely printed pages of *Chinese Farm Economy* make no reference to religion at all. Instead, the book mounts a massive display of graphs, charts, and maps, which assemble and present data on 2,866 farms in seven provinces. It was the first study of its kind, and it has remained permanently influential. Though later experts have often argued with its methods and conclusions, they rarely ignore Lossing's work.[97] John King Fairbank has called Lossing a "pioneer" who sent his students "out into the villages to find out how the farmers did things, and whether they could be helped with modern agronomic science."[98]

Gradually, Pearl's morale improved. Though her relations with Lossing would continue to deteriorate, she had begun to think about the new start that a divorce might bring. On the biographical fact sheet of her annual report to the Mission Board for 1929, Pearl still identified her occupation as "housewife," but she was now using that comfortable term almost ironically. Her first novel had been accepted, albeit by a marginal press. She had established an immediate friendship with her publisher, who had encouraged her to think of herself as a professional writer. She was busy at work on her second novel, telling a few friends that she hoped the royalties would guarantee her daughter's care.

Pearl never escaped the guilt she felt for putting Carol in an institution, but she decided that she had made the best arrangements she could manage. Friends in the States, including Lulu Hamilton and Emma White, wrote to assure her that her daughter was happy at Vineland; in fact, Carol gave no sign that she missed her mother at all.

By mid-February, 1930, the Bucks had settled back into their university house. The winter had been unusually cold; along with rapidly rising inflation and lingering Chinese hostility, the bad weather added to the discomfort of the for-

12. Pearl and Janice in Nanking, about 1930. (Courtesy Bettman Archives.)

eign community. Though Pearl was tormented by Carol's absence, listening for her step on the stair or her nighttime calls for help, she was soon busy again with her teaching and absorbed in Nanking's politics and social gossip. Janice was happily attending kindergarten at Hill Crest school, where her classmates included the children of H. H. Kung, Chiang Kai-shek's finance minister and brother-in-law.[99] Each morning, Mme. Chiang herself brought the three Kung children to class, conferring a daily portion of prestige and excitement on the little school.[100]

In February, Pearl published an article on the Chinese novel, "China in the Mirror of Her Fiction."[101] The essay is frankly populist in its point of view, a defense of the novel, which had always been despised by Chinese scholars as non-literary *hsiaoshou,* small talk. As Lu Hsün (Lu Xun) said in a 1934 essay, "Fiction was never thought of as literature in China."[102] For Pearl, as for Lu Hsün, the stories that make up Chinese fiction are valuable precisely because they have been the property of the common people for centuries. Before being transcribed, they began as tales handed down orally from one generation to another. Consequently, the novels provide a more revealing portrait of China's ordinary men and women than the abstract writings of philosophers can offer.

Anticipating what later historians would call "history from the bottom up," Pearl attacks the tendency of Western academics to generalize about China from the writings of a few exceptional men. She traces "the root of our confusion about China" to the mistaken belief that the country's reality could be found "in the ice-pure pages of her wisdom literature [where] the lonely figures of Confucius, Mencius and Lao-tse have passed in stately isolation."

The teachings of sages and philosophers are known and "reverenced devoutly by a few hermit scholars." Those texts have produced "the high civilization of the few" – in Pearl's words, China as "she likes to be quoted and above all as she likes to quote herself." The lives of the people are to be found elsewhere. Pearl doesn't deny the extraordinary significance that Confucius and other thinkers have had on Chinese culture. She does argue that their writings do not reveal "the rich wild life" of the nation.

Against the discipline, regulation, and decorum of Confucius or Lao-tse, such novels and stories as *Shui Hu Chuan (Shuihuzhuan)* and *San Kuo (Sanguozhi)* disclose a world of magic, passion, and primitive violence. The mirror of fiction suggests that the Chinese are not the sober, peace-loving people idealized in their ancient ethical texts. The country's novels, like its history, are filled with warfare and bloodshed, often recounted with relish. Some stories

tell of the devouring of human hearts, a practice not unheard of still among the wilder mountain bands.[103] The victim's breast is slashed and the sides pressed until the quick heart leaps into a bowl prepared to receive it. It is thus eaten and is supposed to endow the eater with phenomenal qualities of courage. All this is told in the matter-of-fact way in which a cook book gives a recipe!

As for love, "the Chinese have frankly put the relation of the sexes upon sex and sex alone. Lust is a glory, not abnormal or out of a diseased imagination, but robust and with open delight in the body and its acts." For instance, a lover who praises "the moth eyes of his mistress proceeds as the next and natural step to the possession of her person." Significantly, descriptions of such sexual scenes "are given with an item-to-item clarity, shocking perhaps to the spinster mind," but "fascinating" to Pearl. In short, "love and lust are one and unashamed."

The note of defiance in this essay undoubtedly had several sources. Pearl's embrace of the earthy and ungovernable lives of China's common people was directed in the first place at the stuffy conventions of pre-revolutionary cultural criticism. Like many of the dissidents of the May Fourth movement, she wanted to make room for a literary form that had too long been held in contempt. In addition, Pearl was making a political statement, expressing her solidarity with the Chinese masses, who were abused, as their stories were, by the privileged classes.

Finally, by identifying herself with the anarchy and excess represented in Chinese novels, she was also rejecting the frowning puritanism that had deformed her own religious and cultural background. Even the rapacity and grotesque cruelty that these books sometimes endorsed seemed superior to the narrow moral and aesthetic boundaries that had been her pious legacy. To be sure, some of this was mere swagger. However, her celebration of sexual candor was utterly serious. Over the years, she insisted that relations between women and men were always damaged by euphemism and evasion.

In the spring, Pearl's brother Edgar came to lecture at Nanking University and stayed with the Bucks for several weeks. Edgar was making steady progress in his career, though his personal life was troubled by alcohol and an impending divorce. He had become director of the Research Division of the Milbank Memorial Fund in New York, an important public health foundation. He had come to China principally to arrange a grant for James Yen (Yan Yangchu), who had founded the Mass Education Movement to bring literacy to the vast rural populations.

Edgar's visit to China gave him the chance to consult with members of Lossing's department about a proposed population study. During his stay, he also gave a series of lectures on statistical methods.[104] Pearl's affection for Edgar had become strained by his drinking; she felt she could no longer rely on him to help look after Carol. She complained about him in an April letter to Lulu Hamilton. In the same letter, she announced that she was working hard on her second book: "I hope a bigger, better affair than my first."[105] By late May, 1930, she had finished the book, still called *Wang Lung,* and sent it off to David Lloyd.

At the same time, fighting had begun again: soldiers were "marching – marching – marching – through the streets." There was heavy fighting north of the city, and Communist uprisings were reported in several provinces, including Kiangsi.[106] B. A. Garside, head of the New York board that supported Lossing's work, wrote to commiserate, resorting to a lumpish humor to conceal his concern: "You and Mrs. Buck arrived in Nanking just in time to have ringside seats for the usual spring war."[107] Once again, Nanking's foreign residents faced the threat of attack and evacuation. Furthermore, the Communists controlled the area around Kuling. Even if the foreigners were not forced out of Nanking, there would be no mountain vacations to escape the city's summer heat. One frightening rumor involved a Communist plot to burn most of the public buildings in Nanking, including the mission schools, the residences of foreigners, and the university.

Throughout this first year of separation from Carol, Pearl's letters were filled with worried questions and directions about her. She was told by the school that Carol had developed some sort of spasm, and waited anxiously until she was reassured that the disorder had cleared itself up. She repeatedly listed the clothes and toys that she wanted her friends to buy, always promising that whatever money they needed she would somehow provide. In the fall, she asked Lulu Hamilton to organize a "nice big box" for Carol's Christmas: "buy her a pair of silk stockings, a pretty sweater, toys, candy, peanuts – she loves peanuts!"[108]

Several paragraphs after this poignant inventory, Pearl also mentioned that her new book had been accepted, "with much enthusiasm," by her publisher. She had not yet seen any royalties from *East Wind, West Wind*, but she hoped that two books on the market would bring her "a nest egg toward the sum I have to make for Carol." As an aside, she complained that Lossing's book, which "looks very well," would earn them no money at all: "All of his royalties go to the University – worse luck!"

Richard Walsh did accept Pearl's new novel with great optimism, raising only three questions. First, he wanted the title changed. *Wang Lung,* he said, was "quite impossible"; it was unpronounceable and would be an irresistible target for ribald humor. Richard argued that the title should have "a good deal of sweep and romance," and proposed "something like *The Good Earth*."[109] In addition, he wanted several cuts made in the second half of the novel, where he thought the pace of the narrative became too slow. Finally, Richard suggested that publication be deferred until the summer or fall of 1931. He wanted to see "how fast the fiction market recovers from the present depression."[110] He also hoped that the new book might profit from Pearl's growing reputation as a writer and interpreter of Asia. *East Wind, West Wind* was proving to be "more than a one-season book." Sales, boosted by continuing good notices, were slowly climbing all over the country.

The London publishing house, Methuen, had bought the British rights and was planning to bring out its edition in the spring. The John Day Company had received inquiries from publishers in several countries concerning translations. In Richard's opinion, the "general prejudice against books about China" still presented a problem, but Pearl was single-handedly doing much to overcome it. She had begun to cultivate a large audience which looked forward eagerly to her second book.

Although she enjoyed the praise that was beginning to come to her from critics and readers around the world, Pearl felt less welcome at home. Lossing congratulated her on her good fortune, but made it clear that he regarded his own work as far more significant. At some level, Pearl probably agreed. She would never outgrow a puritanical suspicion that novel writing was merely a distraction from life's duties. Nonetheless, Lossing's condescension punished Pearl's fledgling and fragile self-confidence.

Absalom hardly acknowledged his daughter's success.[111] In part, his neglect was habitual. He had never taken women seriously, including those in his own family, and he had no patience with the triviality of any aesthetic pursuit. Furthermore, Absalom's mind was beginning to fail. Though his body was still strong, he now suffered periods when he didn't know where he was or who was with him. He was nearer death than either he or Pearl knew, but his baffled resistance to Pearl's ambitions would continue to the end of his life.

4

The Good Earth

IN JANUARY, 1931, Lossing and Pearl spent several weeks sailing south along the Chinese coast toward Hong Kong and Canton (Guangzhou). Lossing was trying to make arrangements for an expanded survey of agriculture, while Pearl was exploring parts of China she had not seen before.[1] Several times, the Bucks nearly stepped into the fighting that swept back and forth across the countryside, devastating thousands of farms and keeping the peasants in a constant state of terror. Armed struggle had spread everywhere. Bandits were fighting Chiang Kai-shek's Kuomintang troops and each other, the KMT was battling Communists as well as local warlords, Communists were harassing KMT soldiers at every opportunity and also attacking bandits and landlords. On more than one occasion, the armed men who fought and killed each other literally did not know who their enemies had been. The slide into *luan*, chaos, which the Chinese feared above all else, seemed to have become irreversible.[2]

When the Bucks got back to Nanking, Lossing went immediately to the local dentist to have several bad teeth removed. His eyes were also giving him trouble, and his physical problems interfered with his work. Pearl was dismayed to find that Janice, who had stayed in Nanking with friends, had come down with a case of whooping cough.

Janice quickly recovered, but Pearl remained distraught about Carol. Though she confessed it to no one, she wished Carol would die, she even prayed for it.[3] For one of the few times in her life, Pearl was immobilized by sorrow. Ordinarily, she resisted depression with work: writing, teaching, cooking, cleaning house, gardening – anything to keep busy. However, in these early weeks of the new year, she couldn't anesthetize her unhappiness with activity. Day after day, she sat motionless, sometimes for hours, staring at a photograph of Carol, and thinking about her retarded daughter now living half a world away in America. She tried to visualize what Carol's Christmas had been like at Vineland – the first Christmas that mother and daughter had been separated since Carol's birth nine years earlier.

Pearl was jolted out of her stupor at the end of January, when she received an excited telegram from Earl Newsom, a colleague of Richard Walsh at John Day. Newsom told her that *The Good Earth* had been chosen for the Book-of-the-Month Club. Pearl wrote to Lulu Hamilton: "I don't know just what that means, but from the enthusiasm of my publishers in cabling me the news I gather it is very desirable."[4] To Richard Walsh, she wrote: "It was very nice if the Book of the Month Club chose me if it pleases you so much, but do they know that I am not a member of their club?"[5] Living in China, Pearl had never heard of the Book-of-the-Month Club, a relatively new and oddly American institution that would exert a considerable influence on the nation's reading habits for the rest of the century.

Founded in 1926 by an enterprising promoter named Harry Scherman, the Book-of-the-Month Club was a triumph of mass marketing. A panel of literary advisors selected one book from the hundreds of new titles published each month. The panel's choice was then offered to Club members, along with a brochure that spelled out the volume's merits at effusive length. The five original advisors, Henry Seidel Canby, William Allen White, Dorothy Canfield Fisher, Christopher Morley, and Heywood Broun, were well known as popular writers and literary journalists. Their participation in the project was intended to assure prospective Club members that the books chosen would be significant and – at least as important – dependably readable.

From the beginning, cynics dismissed the Book-of-the-Month Club as one more demonstration of middle-class America's cultural anxieties. Unable to decide for themselves what novels or nonfiction books were worth reading, educated but insecure men and women were grateful to be told which volumes they should add to their collections. The Club's defenders, on the other hand, portrayed it as an honorable experiment in public education, which encouraged adults in the habit of serious reading and broadened America's literary horizons.[6]

Whatever the merits of the arguments on either side, the Club had an extraordinary success. The initial membership of 4,750, shrewdly solicited from the New York Social Register, grew to 50,000 within a year, then to 110,000 by 1929. The Depression pushed the numbers down temporarily, but enrollment climbed again in the second half of the 1930s, reaching 350,000 by the end of the decade.[7] A novel, biography, or volume of history that appeared on the Club's list was guaranteed high visibility and excellent sales.[8]

The Good Earth was the first of fifteen of Pearl Buck's works chosen over nearly four decades as a Book-of-the-Month Club selection. It was Dorothy Canfield Fisher who strenuously promoted the novel with her fellow panelists. Her initial reaction, after a glance through the page proofs, had been casually dismissive: the book "seemed to be about agriculture in China," not a subject likely to interest America's general readers. Nonetheless, she took the pages with her on a five-hour train ride from Virginia to New York, to give the book a more careful reading. She told the rest of the story some years later:

> As the train pulled out of Arlington, I opened it [*The Good Earth*], and by the end of the first twelve pages I was sitting up just electrified by the quality of it, and read it, nearly putting my eyes out, all the way to New York. I hadn't begun to finish then — sat up in the hotel bedroom until I had finished it.[9]

At dawn, Fisher walked to the Club's empty midtown offices and left a note for Scherman and her fellow panelists announcing that she had found a book "of first importance." At the next panel meeting, *The Good Earth* was a unanimous selection.

A few months earlier, Richard Walsh had considered holding back publication until the fall, to capitalize on the slowly rising sales of *East Wind, West Wind*. However, his own enthusiasm, confirmed by the Book-of-the-Month Club decision, led him to revise his timetable. At the Club's strong urging, the book was rushed into print. With Pearl watching rather quizzically from 10,000 miles away, her novel was published on March 2, 1931.

In a flurry of letters in February and March, Richard gave Pearl an almost daily account of the reception *The Good Earth* was enjoying from readers and reviewers. Every leading newspaper and magazine gave the book a major notice, and almost all the reviews were ecstatic. Sales were so strong that Richard had to borrow copies from the Book-of-the-Month Club inventory to meet bookstore demand. *The Good Earth* would eventually prove to be the best-selling book of both 1931 and 1932.[10]

Since Pearl was unknown and virtually out of reach in Nanking, John Day's publicity department had little material to work with. "It is a curious feeling," Richard said in one of his many letters, "writing to you at so great a distance about these matters. We sit here in a genuine whirl of excitement about the book which you have written and you the author are completely detached from it."[11] Pearl turned back Richard's pleas for detailed biographical information, taking the lofty (and allegedly "Chinese") position that the work was more important than the author. Though she lived in China, Pearl had a good deal of insight into the metamorphosis that was taking place in America, the shift toward the cult of celebrity that would become the hallmark of artistic value.

More pertinently, she wanted to protect her own privacy and conceal Carol's condition from the public's remorseless curiosity. Carol's tragedy also subtracted from any happiness Pearl might have felt in her accomplishment. As she explained to Emma White, "If the success had come earlier, or if my life had been different as regards Carol, I think I would have been wildly thrilled. As it is, nothing means overwhelmingly much to me, since the fundamental inevitable for me must remain inevitable."[12] She repeated to Emma what she told other close friends in those first days of her sudden fame: the money would be welcome because it would enable her to provide for Carol's permanent care.

The book that changed Pearl Buck's life forever was at once innovative and familiar, groundbreaking in its subject matter but thoroughly conventional in its techniques. *The Good Earth* is set in Anhwei province, in a rural landscape identical to that of Nanhsuchou, where Pearl and Lossing had spent the early years of their marriage. The novel's simple but eventful plot follows the life of its principal character, the Chinese farmer Wang Lung, from his marriage day to his old age. Wang Lung's triumphs and defeats map the encounter between traditional China and the revolutionary future.

Wang Lung's identity and motives are shaped above all by his relationship to the land. He has grown up in an isolated, illiterate community, where patriarchal piety is the core value, and survival depends on an endless round of crushing physical labor. The property he farms has been in his family for generations; the soil is thin and unforgiving, but it represents the sole security he can imagine in an utterly untrustworthy universe. Victimized in turn by famine, flood, locusts, and bandits, he knows that only the land endures.[13]

Because he is the son of a poor farmer, Wang Lung has few options in choosing a wife. To save money, his father has directed him to buy a slave from the House of Hwang, the leading family in the region. O-lan, the woman he buys for his wife, is the novel's most memorable character. She accepts her status and fate without complaint, submerging whatever personal desires she might have in her tasks of wife, daughter-in-law, and mother. At the same time, she is portrayed as the story's moral center, a figure of courage, perseverance, and instinctive common sense. And, as Adrienne Rich, among others, has pointed out, the scenes in which O-lan gives birth to her several children were among the few such episodes in American fiction.[14] Both in herself and in her functions, she represents Pearl's feminist affirmations.

Through the first section of the novel, Wang Lung prospers. His first two children are male, a particular sign of good fortune in a culture where boy babies are called "big happiness" and girls are only a "small happiness." Working every day from dawn to dusk, with O-lan beside him, Wang Lung accumulates more land through self-discipline and thrift. He buys some of his new acres from the decadent House of Hwang, which is squandering its wealth in pursuit of pleasures, including the purchase of expensive slave girls for the family's patriarch and opium for his first wife. In the early pages of the novel, the only event that darkens Wang Lung's life is the birth of a daughter who proves to be retarded. This nameless child, who serves throughout the novel as a symbol of humanity's essential helplessness, is Pearl's anguished, barely disguised memorial to Carol.

Wang Lung's prosperity is short-lived. In the naturalist environment of *The Good Earth,* as in the subsistence economy of rural China itself, effort and intentions are only vaguely linked to consequences. The novel's most powerful episode tells of a killing famine that slowly annihilates the entire countryside, reducing Wang Lung and his neighbors to poverty and near-starvation. When their food is exhausted, the people begin to eat the roots of plants, then their precious supply of seeds, then a kind of clay called "goddess of mercy earth," which provides the flavor of food but no nourishment.

Scourged by hunger, desperate men and women sink into brute appetites. There is talk of cannibalism in the village, which Wang Lung's father says he has seen before, in another famine when he was a boy. Women resort to the terrible practice of female infanticide. O-lan gives birth to a daughter whom she immediately smothers. Wang Lung wraps the body in a piece of broken mat and lays it next to an old grave: "He had scarcely put the burden down before a famished, wolfish dog hovered almost at once behind him."[5] Wang Lung is too exhausted to drive the dog away; after he turns back to the house, the hungry animal will feed on the infant corpse. Pearl had been witness to such a scene when she was a child.

Defeated by the drought, Wang Lung and his family join the hordes of peasants fleeing south. They become part of an army of displaced refugees who seek shelter in Nanking, living in makeshift huts under the city's walls. O-lan teaches her children to beg, telling them where to stand and how to cry out to attract pity from the men and women who pass by. Wang Lung finds work pulling a ricksha, becoming a human beast of burden and destroying his body for a few pennies a day.

All around him, Wang Lung hears talk of revolution, but it is a word he has never heard and does not understand. As far as he can tell, the enemy is not the Emperor or the economic system or Confucianism or any abstract ideology. The enemy is drought, an unfriendly fate, and bad luck. Wang Lung does not want to overthrow the established order; he wants to find the money that will enable him to return to his farm and rebuild his life.

Ironically, it is a revolutionary uprising that restores Wang Lung's fortune, though only in an accidental way. When an army smashes open the gates of a rich Nanking house, Wang Lung and O-lan join the looters, not for any political reason, but out of curiosity and desperation. Recalling what she had learned in her years as a slave in a similar house, O-lan discovers a cache of jewels hidden behind a loose brick in a wall. With the money he gets from the sale of this treasure, Wang Lung can go back to his farm. The same blind chance that brought him to the edge of starvation has restored his fortunes.

The middle third of the novel documents Wang Lung's increasing prosperity, a rising affluence that reaches a symbolic climax when he buys the great house of the Hwang family and moves into it with his own sons and grandchildren. He sends his two oldest sons to school, so that they will be more efficient stewards of his property. Tired of O-lan, he purchases a young sing-song girl named Lotus, and installs her in a separate apartment in his house.[16] The new arrangements lead to trouble almost immediately. When Wang Lung discovers that his eldest son has visited Lotus secretly, he banishes the young man, an act that affirms his authority but threatens the stability of his family. As the family becomes increasingly disoriented, O-lan falls sick, weakens, and dies.

In the novel's final section, a chronicle of natural calamity and political turmoil, Wang Lung's familiar world is turned upside down. His farms are ruined by a flood of unparalleled proportions; shortly afterward his house is occupied by a unit of the revolutionary army. He survives these upheavals, but the book's last scene is a prophecy that disaster lies ahead because his sons do not share his commitment to the land. These are modern men, contemptuous of their peasant father and his antique values.

The critical response to *The Good Earth* was virtually unanimous. In particular, reviewers saluted the novel for rigorously avoiding stereotypes and for rendering Chinese life as recognizably human and even ordinary. The notice in the *New York Times* argued that Pearl Buck had presented "a China in which, happily, there is no hint of mystery or exoticism. There is very little in her book of the quality which we are accustomed to label, 'Oriental.' " Similarly, Florence Ayscough, in the *Saturday Review of Literature,* said that "the China of fantasy so often exploited is absent from its pages."[17] The anonymous reviewer for Britain's *New Statesman and Nation* made the same point more elaborately: *The Good Earth* represents the Chinese peasant absolutely free of "those screens and veils and mirrors of artistic and poetic convention which nearly always make him . . . a flat and unsubstantial figure of a pale-colored ballet."[18]

There were a few dissenters. Younghill Kang, an expatriate Korean writer and editor, complained that Pearl had falsified the reality of Chinese gender relations, first by involving her main characters in a "western-style" romantic plot, and then by depicting a landlord's sexual use of his slaves, which Kang claimed – erroneously – could not happen.[19] Kiang Kang-hu (Jiang Kanghu), in the *Chinese Christian Student,* insisted that Wang Lung and O-lan were merely "peculiar characters from a special section of the interior," not typical Chinese.[20] Pearl's mistaken impressions about the Chinese, Kiang added, with more confidence than accuracy, were based on her inability to read Chinese literature in the original. If she had been able to read the classic Chinese texts, she would have presented a different China, instead of relying on the testimony of "coolies" and "amahs" for her information.

Pearl published a lively rebuttal to Kiang Kang-hu in the *New York Times Book Review.* Charitably, she didn't mention her competence in the Chinese language. She did argue that Kiang was one of those who "want the Chinese people represented by the little handful of her intellectuals, and they want the vast, rich, somber, joyous Chinese life represented solely by literature that is ancient and classic." But this, she argued, would leave out the mass of common people, men and women she sympathetically called "the proletariat."

In effect, Pearl regarded herself as the victim of a class-based attack. She said in this essay, and often elsewhere, that China was doomed until its sheltered academics and intellectuals learned to honor the country's peasants and its urban poor, rather than despising them. Among China's warring factions, only the Communists seemed to understand this.

The Good Earth received a number of admiring reviews in Chinese journals.[21] Nonetheless, Pearl's conflict with the literati became a staple of gossip in both the native and foreign communities in China in the early 1930s. The young journalist Helen Foster, arriving in China for the first time in 1931, was greeted by the debate over Pearl Buck. In Foster's opinion, Pearl was unpopular with the scholars and rich gentry because she told truths about poverty and inequality they found embarrassing. Foster later recalled her conversations with Chinese scholars and students about Pearl's book:

I was surprised to find how the young intellectuals hated it. . . . They would say, "She ought not to write about all those horrible people; why doesn't she write about . . . civilized people?" These Western-educated Chinese hated it because they didn't want foreigners to learn anything unpleasant about China; they were trying to hide the truth. I couldn't understand this point of view at first. . . . When she wrote *The Good Earth* she was actually trying to break through this tissue of lies and expose the real conditions, which they were covering up for political reasons.[22]

Over the next six decades, Pearl Buck has remained a controversial figure in China, alternately attacked and rehabilitated as the political winds have shifted.

THE MISSIONARY COMMUNITY, which read *The Good Earth* with particular interest, had a deeply divided response. To begin with, those who knew of Pearl's lifelong association with the missionary enterprise were startled by the complete absence of Christianity from the novel. The Chinese characters routinely invoke their traditional gods, praying for rain or good harvest or sons, but their lives are fundamentally secular, and Western religion has no effect whatever on them.

The single, brief scene in which a missionary appears only underscores the irrelevance of Christianity to Wang Lung and his family. During their sojourn in Nanking, Wang Lung is confronted by a tall, thin foreign man who hands him a piece of paper. The man has blue eyes, a hairy face and hands, and "a great nose projecting beyond his cheeks like a prow beyond the sides of a ship." The paper he hands Wang Lung includes characters that he cannot read and the picture of a nearly naked dead man hanging on a cross.

Wang Lung is baffled and understandably horrified. Later that night, he discusses the bizarre picture with his father, who offers the only plausible explanation: " 'Surely this was a very evil man to be thus hung' " – a logical inference for someone who had never before seen a representation of the Crucifixion and could only interpret the image by his own experience. The episode demonstrates Pearl's effort to remain consistently inside the novel's Chinese point of view: here is the strange, inscrutable Occident, as it might appear to a skeptical, worldly Asian. A sacred Western icon is merely a gruesome scene of execution.

O-lan, for her part, has a typically utilitarian response to the matter. Unlike Wang Lung and his father, she has no interest in the meaning of the characters or symbols. She is a poor woman, who knows that the heavy paper itself is rare and valuable; she uses it to line the soles of a pair of shoes. The Christian message is put to a good purpose.[23]

Despite Pearl's realistic and therefore unfriendly handling of Christianity in *The Good Earth,* quite a few religious readers counted themselves among the novel's admirers. The evangelical *Living Church* called it a "strong, absorbing book." The *Catholic World,* though squeamish about the "many over realistic pages," nonetheless called the novel "an intimate and accurate picture of Chinese peasant life and customs." And the *Chinese Recorder,* which had published several of Pearl's stories and essays, congratulated its sometime contributor as the author of a masterpiece.

On the other hand, *The Good Earth* also provoked a good deal of resistance from more pious Christians. Pearl's old friend Emma White wrote that she had been trying to defend the book against charges that it was "not nice." Pearl replied with amusement: "I felt like giving you a good hard hug and laughing a little too at the vision I have of you trying to make *The Good Earth* into a 'nice' book. . . . [Because] it *isn't* a nice book! Your friends or whoever they were who said it was a coarse book are perfectly right."[24] Or rather, Pearl added, it was coarse by the genteel standards of American readers. In China, she said, the body's functions, including sex, were approached with healthy candor. Americans, on the other hand, respond to sex with a collective immaturity that reveals their "secret, pernicious" obsession with sexual matters.

In late March, Pearl received a more serious reprimand, a disapproving letter from Courtenay Fenn, Executive Secretary for China of the Overseas Mission Board in New York. Adopting a somewhat glutinous, paternal tone, he confided his "disappointment and distress" at Pearl's book. Fenn acknowledged the literary excellence of her work, but scolded her for not adopting "the missionary point of view." For a faithful missionary, he said, "the fact that a thing is 'true to life' is not a sufficient reason for its publication." With an admirable if unintended candor, in other words, Fenn confessed that he disliked *The Good Earth* precisely because Pearl had told the truth about China.

Fenn regretted that "the artist in you has apparently deposed the missionary." Somewhat more ominously, he assured Pearl that "there is no thought of public denunciation of your book" – a clear indication that such a response had at least been discussed at Board headquarters.[25] By now, as her novel itself made perfectly clear, Pearl had become disillusioned with the missionary enterprise. And she was no longer willing to take dictation from anyone about either her beliefs or her writing. Fenn's patronizing and vaguely threatening remarks only stiffened her resolve to hold fast to her own ideas. This was the opening round in a contest that would lead, within eighteen months, to a notorious public dispute between Pearl and the Presbyterian leadership.

Fenn warned Pearl against the temptation to be a best-selling writer, since that would mean she had come "down to the world's point of view." It was not a temptation Pearl intended to resist. She had certainly identified the world's point of view: from the day of its publication to the present, *The Good Earth* has been one of the best-selling books of the twentieth century.[26]

Beyond that, the novel was significant for its attempt to negotiate the profound differences of language and culture that separate East and West. To most Americans in the early 1930s, difference was still the sign of deviance. Western customs and practices, no matter how arbitrary, were taken to be the human norm. A classic statement of the case appeared in a famous "Believe It or Not!" cartoon by Robert Ripley. The drawing, which first appeared in newspapers in May, 1932, titillated its readers with the revelations that Chinese coins have holes in them and that the Chinese character for "peace" is a pig under a roof. The question "Can a Chinaman Whistle?" filled one box; another box, under the label "The Heathen Chinee is Peculiar," offered the apparently shocking news that Chinese use the color white to signify mourning, that the Chinese calculate age and write fractions differently, and that Chinese men remove their shoes instead of their hats when entering a house.

This sort of nonsense – Orientalism with a vengeance – still determined American assumptions about China when *The Good Earth* appeared. Pearl's novel battled against these derisive attitudes, exchanging the stereotypes of earlier American representations of Asia for a more firmly grounded portrait. She countered Robert Ripley's amused condescension with compassion, replacing the "inscrutable Oriental" and the "heathen Chinee" with a hardworking, ordinary farming family. Pearl did much to alter American attitudes toward China, encouraging a sense of solidarity between the two nations that would have important strategic implications over the next decade.[27]

Chinese readers themselves were among those who insisted on the difference between Pearl's images and the usual Western practice. In a 1933 article called "Mrs. Buck and Her Works," Chuang Hsin-tsai (Zhuang Xinzai) sketched the rudiments of most Western novels and travel books that treated China. To begin

13. The Chinese people according to Robert Ripley's "Believe It or Not." This syndicated newspaper cartoon was first published in May, 1932.

with, Chuang observed, the characters in such literature are depicted "as an archetype: men with long pigtails and women with bound feet, all skinny with running noses and dirty, ugly faces. Their deeds are always connected with theft, burglary, raping, plotting and assassinations. For centuries, this has been the image the Western mind has [had] of the Chinese."[28]

As Chuang and other Chinese readers pointed out, Pearl's novel diverged from these debased clichés in almost every line and scene. *The Good Earth* was a pioneering exercise in what might be called authentic multiculturalism. Critic Robert Hughes has recently defended such multicultural efforts, which honorably assert that people "can learn to read the image-banks of others, that they can and should look across the frontiers of race, language, gender and age without prejudice or illusion. . . ."[29] Pearl had spent forty years immersed in the "image-banks" of China. Her accounts of the Chinese people were rooted in a more extensive personal acquaintance than almost any Western writer before or since has brought to the task.

At the same time, given the American public's longstanding indifference to books about China, the spectacular sales of *The Good Earth* and its profitable six decades in the book market actually require some explanation. There was no precedent in American fiction for the success of Pearl's tale of two Chinese peasants and their family living out their lives in the distant landscape of north central China. Why was *The Good Earth* so popular? To begin with, Pearl was a fine storyteller. The tale of Wang Lung is consistently engaging and often exciting. The novel's descriptive passages also communicate a fully rounded feeling of rural existence. Drawing on decades of experience and observation, Pearl filled *The Good Earth* with the sights and sounds of China's daily life: the landscape and houses of a small village, the tools of the working men and women, the clothes the people wear and the food they eat, the rituals of marriage and death. At the same time, the novel is narrated in a formal, quasi-biblical rhetoric that lends a degree of dignity to the events. Many readers warmly admired the style, arguing that it helped to lift the plot toward a sense of universality.

Furthermore, Pearl's timing was lucky. Underneath its alien details, the novel is a story of the land, a rather familiar American genre. And the formula that depicts the struggles of farmers on their soil had a particular appeal to Americans in the Depression decade. Throughout the 1930s, millions of farm families were pushed off their homesteads, victims of economic collapse and the natural disasters of drought and dust bowl. In those circumstances, it is not surprising that the suffering and endurance of farmers would become a special subject of fiction. Several of the major novels of the decade, *Gone With the Wind*, *Tobacco Road*, and *The Grapes of Wrath*, to name only three in addition to *The Good Earth*, share this theme.

Beyond that, all of these books and others, such as the Depression photodocumentaries *An American Exodus* (1939, by Dorothea Lange and Paul Taylor) and *Let Us Now Praise Famous Men* (1941, by James Agee and Walker Evans), celebrated the traditional American virtue of simplicity. From the Puritans through Jefferson and Thoreau to the twentieth century, American culture has continuously placed high value on the simple life, treating it as an emblem of democracy, in contrast to the ostentatious rigmarole of European aristocratic societies.[30]

Again, *The Good Earth* perfectly exemplifies this attitude. Wang Lung is not an idealized character, but the strength he possesses is tied to his undecorated personal exertions. When he becomes too wealthy, he loses his moral bearings.[31]

In short, *The Good Earth* consisted of a rather brilliant if uncalculated hybrid, which treated its unfamiliar subject matter in the thematic terms of much popular fiction. If this did not represent the highest literary achievement, it did assure Pearl Buck's commercial future. Richard Walsh sensed her financial potential and moved with almost unseemly haste to secure her long-term commitment. He sent her a contract that promised her next three novels to John Day and to him personally. Pearl signed without hesitation; she was grateful to Richard for his confidence, and gave him much of the credit for her success.

The spring was unusually wet and cold. In spite of *The Good Earth*'s friendly reviews and brisk sales, Pearl remained depressed about Carol. She yearned to go back to the United States to be nearer to her daughter, but she recoiled from the prospect of answering questions about Carol's condition. She wrote to Polly Small that she was unable to resign herself to Carol's fate, and was always on the edge of weeping. She admitted that she found satisfaction in the success she was having with her writing, but she added the poignant comment that "I would gladly have written nothing if I could have just an average child in Carol. Average children seem such a wonderful joy to me – I wouldn't ask for a clever, bright child if I could have had her just average."

Pearl confessed that the mere sight of other boys and girls who had been babies with Carol caused her to grieve. Even worse, the tactless comments of her women friends about their children created a daily purgatory for her: "My friends do nothing but talk about their children – their children. Of course, they do not think what pain it is to me to sit and hear this." Ordinary conversations had become a harrowing trial.

"I am afraid," she added revealingly, that "it makes me draw away from my friends."[32] People who knew Pearl only in the 1930s or later often found her distant, emotionally cautious, barricaded behind an impenetrable reserve. In a quite conscious way, she was protecting herself. Her suffering as Carol's mother had compressed a lifetime of disappointment into a decade. Above all, her decision to institutionalize Carol, whether it was the best choice or not, amounted to a self-inflicted wound. Her frequent declarations that she didn't feel either guilt or shame only proved how much those feelings troubled her. In letter after letter, she pleaded with friends not to mention Carol's existence to the press. After the trauma of these years, she would never again share herself fully with anyone.

In the spring, Pearl learned that she had been inducted into Phi Beta Kappa by Randolph-Macon. She proposed the moral of this belated honor to Lulu Hamilton: "you needn't study in college," provided you did something more or less distinguished after graduation. At about the same time, she took Janice on a brief visit to Peking. After five years of work, Pearl had completed her translation of the classic novel *Shui Hu Chuan*. She wanted to spend some time in Peking's National Library in the hope of finding illustrations for the book in old Chinese editions.

While Pearl was in the northern capital, she met the great Chinese actor and female impersonator, Mei Lan-fang. She also had dinner with Owen Lattimore and his wife. Owen Lattimore had already established himself as the leading Western expert on the people of Mongolia.[33] The dinner in Peking was the first meeting between Pearl and the Lattimores; over the next twenty years, their paths would cross again as Owen rose to academic prominence and was then smeared and harassed in the witch-hunts that followed World War II.[34]

By the late spring of 1931, Pearl resolved that she would eventually have to leave China and settle in the United States. The decision was probably inevitable, but it was hastened by the warfare that was "thickening again about us," and the anti-foreign violence that erupted periodically in the cities and the country-side. In addition, Pearl was deeply shaken by the calamitous Yangtze floods of July.

Throughout the spring, unusually heavy rains had swollen the rivers that con-verged at Wuhan, southwest of Nanking. Eventually, the water rushed over banks and dikes and covered the entire surrounding countryside – an area the size of New York State. The waters did not recede for two months. As many as two million people may have died, some from drowning, most from dysentery, cholera, and famine. Another fourteen million were made homeless.[35] The Yang-tze floods of 1931 undoubtedly rank among the most destructive natural catas-trophes of the twentieth century.[36] The American aviator Charles Lindbergh came to China to help with relief flights; Pearl attended a dinner at the American consulate for Lindbergh and his wife, Anne Morrow. She found Morrow at-tractive, but judged Lindbergh to be self-absorbed and quite unsophisticated in his political opinions. He was only really animated when he could direct the conversation to airplanes and flying: "He either talks aviation or is silent," Pearl wrote to Emma White, "but mostly talks aviation!"[37]

Nanking was not the scene of the worst devastation, but the situation was grim enough. Pearl wrote that the nearby countryside was like "one vast lake," with Purple Mountain rising up like an island in the northeast.[38] Houses in the low-lying fields around the city were under two and three feet of water; people were living on scaffolds and in the streets; bodies lay unburied on the high ground or decomposed in the rivers and canals.[39] Pearl was an eyewitness to the flood and some of its victims. Out of her observations, she wrote a series of memorable stories that translate statistical abstractions into the more accessible tragedies of individual men and women.

The point of these stories is simple: though China's peasants always face a hard, precarious existence, the floods have reduced them to abject misery. "Barren Spring" is no more than a vignette, a four-page sketch of a farmer named Liu who has lost everything he owns and sits in the door of his one-room house, waiting to die. In "The Refugees," a starving column of displaced peasants shuffles through the streets of Nanking, hoping without hope that someone will feed them. "Fathers and Mothers," the most bitter of these stories, tells of a young father who murders his two girl children so that he and his wife and their three sons might survive the famine that has driven them all to the point of death.

In late August, while the flood waters were still high throughout the Yangtze valley, Pearl's father died. Nearly eighty years old, Absalom had continued working at his missionary calling until the end of his life. In the decade following Carie's death in 1921, while he managed the correspondence department of the Nanking Theological Seminary, he had lived in a single room in Pearl's Nanking University house. He regarded his translation of the Bible as his main contribution to the evangelical enterprise, and he kept tinkering with it until the day he died. He also published a number of articles in the *Chinese Recorder* on language and theology.

Absalom in old age held fast to the fundamentalist beliefs that he had brought to China nearly half a century earlier. In June, 1929, he sent a long letter to the *Recorder,* in which he vigorously defended the old orthodoxy against any need for modernizing. He directed his polemic principally against those who confused preaching with social reform: "The Message that we are sent to deliver," Absalom insisted, "has no immediate reference to civilization, to education, to politics, to family, to science"; it is directed exclusively at the soul.

Absalom also rejected the latitudinarian drift of many younger missionaries, who tried to find agreeable likenesses between Christianity and native religions as a way of building bridges between Eastern and Western faiths. Absalom, on the contrary, demanded that evangelists acknowledge the unique truth of Christianity, whatever the price to be paid in cross-cultural tension. He admitted that other creeds possessed some murky vision of divinity. However, "all the good that there is in all of these religions is also embraced in the Gospel of Christ, and this in a perfect manner. There is no need for bringing anything from the outside in an attempt to make the teaching of the Gospel more perfect." For Absalom, changing the message was unnecessary and even dangerous.[40]

Absalom's last two publications in the *Recorder,* in April and June, 1931, defended the doctrine of the Virgin Birth. It was a splendid valedictory gesture, with the old fundamentalist stoutly affirming an article of faith that liberal theologians found quaint or embarrassing and usually passed by in silence. Shortly afterward, on August 31, 1931, Absalom died at his summer home in Kuling. His younger daughter, Grace, was with him. He had spent just over fifty-one years preaching the Gospel in China. Because of the floods, Pearl could not reach her father before he died. Grace arranged for a brief ceremony, after which Absalom was buried in Kuling's Christian cemetery.[41]

Several years later, when Pearl wrote her biography of Absalom, she used the *Century Dictionary*'s definition of "angel" as one of the book's epigraphs: "an order of spiritual beings, attendants and messengers of God, usually spoken of as employed by him in ordering the affairs of the universe, and particularly of mankind. They are commonly regarded as bodiless intelligences." Pearl claimed that this quotation demonstrated her "warmth and reverence" for her father.[42] Of course, it did no such thing. Instead, it summarized her alienation from a man whose spiritual, cultural, and sexual values had become precisely antithetical to her own.

In Pearl's view, Absalom's half-century of exertions had made him the only completely happy person she had ever met. It was a happiness, however, that he had paid for by divorcing himself from most of ordinary reality. She wrote that missionaries like her father were happy because "their hearts were empty and swept, the light in their minds extinguished."[43] To his dying day, Absalom had treated her with contempt. In one of their last conversations, Absalom thanked Pearl for the copy of *The Good Earth* she had given him, but told her that he would not have time to read it.[44]

Absalom's death, coinciding with the international publicity that had grown up around *The Good Earth*, marked one of the turning points in Pearl's life. She felt a sincere if measured grief at her father's loss. At the same time, she was also profoundly relieved, liberated from forty years as a missionary daughter. Rather suddenly, she had created a new identity, a prelude to other changes that were soon to follow. Independence had become a plausible alternative, not merely a wishful secret. Within a few months, she would be rich; within a couple of years, she would noisily separate herself both from the Presbyterians and from Lossing Buck.

THERE SEEMED TO BE NO LIMIT to China's troubles in 1931. Along with the interminable civil war and the starvation that came in the wake of the Yangtze floods, Japan invaded Manchuria in September. It was, in effect, the opening action of World War II. The Japanese had been preparing for years to extend their military hegemony throughout Asia. They opened their campaign in Manchuria, an undeveloped area rich in natural resources, because they knew that the Chinese government would be powerless to defend its northern territory. After a quick and almost bloodless victory, Japan renamed the region "Manchukuo," installed the last Ch'ing emperor, P'u-Yi, as ruler, and immediately began building highways, railroads, and communication lines across the vast northern wilderness. During the fourteen years of Japanese occupation, Manchuria would become the most productive industrial section of China.[45]

Pearl reported nervously to her American friends on Japan's aggression, which had raised tensions throughout China. On one occasion, angry Chinese students surrounded the Japanese consulate in Nanking shouting insults and threats. Pearl decided that the "fearful turmoil" was becoming intolerable.[46] She and Lossing made definite plans to return to the United States in 1932. Lossing intended to complete his Ph.D. at Cornell; Pearl wanted to spend more time with Carol. Lossing was committed to returning to China after he finished his studies. Although he simply assumed that Pearl would once again accompany him, she had begun to imagine a life apart.

Pearl was now in demand as a speaker and celebrity. In October, she was invited to address a joint meeting of the American Women's Club and the American Association of University Women in Shanghai. It was a difficult but important event. Pearl was nervous about her looks, her clothing, her lack of experience as a public speaker. She was frightened by the crowd, which she called "the greatest mob of women I have ever seen."[47] At the same time, she enjoyed her new authority. Her opinions were suddenly important. As she would frequently do over the next forty years, she tried to shape the occasion into a dialogue between Asian and Western cultures.

She gave a talk called "East and West and the Novel," a historical survey that compared the development and structure of Asian and Western fiction. Pearl explained that the Chinese novel differs at almost every point from the fiction of Europe and America. Typically, Chinese novels are collections of old folk tales, gathered together over time rather than written in the Western sense. As one consequence, the Chinese are indifferent to Western notions of originality. Authors are usually unknown, and storytellers have borrowed freely from each other for generations. What Westerners would call plagiarism the Chinese regard simply as a technique. Finally, since Chinese novels are cobbled out of miscellaneous stories, they often lack either a main character or a coherent plot.

Not surprisingly, according to Pearl, Western critics tend to find these Chinese novels "badly coordinated and sometimes very confused." She acknowledges the defects, but insists on some evident virtues as well:

In the first place in this formlessness there is a remarkable likeness to life. Life has no plot, no subplot. . . . We meet people, their time coincides with ours for a short space, they walk away out of the story and we never see them again nor do we know their end any more than we know our own. This fragmentariness is the impression which the Chinese novel gives us, primarily. Events come and pass, people walk on and off the stage, perhaps to return, perhaps never to be seen again.

Pearl's argument on behalf of the Chinese novel shades into an appeal to reality. It may be, she admits, that a lack of formal unity denies the Chinese novel the status of art. "I have no definition of art, and I cannot say whether it is art or not, but this I do know, it is life, and I believe in the novel it is better to have life than art, if there cannot be both."[48] Some years later, she would be repeating ideas like this in defense of her own fiction.

The Chinese novel that Pearl knew best was *Shui Hu Chuan,* a huge, sprawling book that she had just finished translating into English.[49] The novel goes back at least to the Ming era, and was first published in its modern form in the seventeenth century, early in the Ch'ing period.[50] *Shui Hu* records the legendary tales of 108 twelfth-century bandits who have made their hideout and headquarters on a mountain, Liang-shan, in Shantung province.

The novel is a vast social panorama, whose characters include nearly all the types and occupations of China. Priests and courtesans march across the pages, along with merchants, scholars, tavern keepers, politicians and minor officials, farmers, fishermen, slaves, aristocrats, and children. There is even a succession of mythical animals. At the center of the action is the robber band, enforcing rough justice in a bad world.

In the course of their numberless adventures, the Liang-shan outlaws face warfare, execution, mutilation, treachery, hand-to-hand combat, battles with tigers and leopards, attacks from outraged landlords – one perilous brush with death after another. The book has properly been called the most lurid and savage text in all Chinese literature; for several hundred years, it has also been one of the most popular.[51] Though the robbers are violent, often bloodthirsty men, they are entertaining swashbucklers whose hair-raising exploits are still familiar to Chinese schoolchildren. Furthermore, these cunning and courageous outlaws have been driven into crime in the first place by the injustice of a tyrannical government. Consequently, they have traditionally been revered as heroes by the Chinese people.[52] Mao Tse-tung's reading of *Shui Hu Chuan* helped forge his revolutionary consciousness.[53]

Pearl's *All Men Are Brothers* was the first complete translation of *Shui Hu Chuan* into English. It is an extraordinary accomplishment, reaching over one thousand printed pages.[54] The novel's Chinese title is usually rendered literally, as "Water Margin," which describes the locale of many of the book's events. Pearl decided that this would be meaningless to Western readers, so she called her translation *All Men Are Brothers,* using a famous phrase from the Confucian *Analects:* "Around the four seas, all men are brothers." (In 1925, Pearl had used the same quotation as the epigraph to her Cornell master's thesis, "China and the West.")[55] Pearl's decision to translate the novel was probably intended, in some part, as another rejoinder to her father and his beliefs. He had translated the English

14. A woodcut from a Chinese edition of *Shui Hu Chuan*. This is one of a series of photographs Pearl had made on her visit to Peking in 1932. (Reproduced with permission of the Pearl S. Buck Foundation.)

Bible into Chinese for the edification of the heathen; she made an earthy Chinese text accessible to Westerners.

Pearl admired the novel's colloquial language, which has had a profound influence on the history of Chinese fiction.[56] More important, she was attracted to the political substance of the book. Like Mao and the Communists, she applauded the novel's sympathy with the common people.[57] She regarded the basic conflict in the book as "the struggle of everyday people against a corrupt officialdom."[58] For many Chinese, the robbers of *Shui Hu* resembled the outlaws who followed Robin Hood in medieval England, renegades not by choice but by circumstance, resourceful citizens who challenged a morally bankrupt establishment.

The novel seemed to have a particular relevance in China in the 1920s and 1930s. The anarchy and fumbling government of the northern Sung period in the twelfth century were being tragically re-enacted eight hundred years later. *Shui Hu* was not just a famous literary document from a safely distant epoch; it was an angry and quite timely commentary on the turmoil of the Chinese Republic.

Pearl's five years of work on *Shui Hu Chuan* concluded a lifetime of reading in classic Chinese fiction. That experience had a considerable effect on her own prose style. Her tendency to rely on formulas and stock phrases, her preference for narrative surface over psychological depth, her use of episodic plots, her desire to entertain, her naturalism – all these writing habits were influenced by her long immersion in texts such as *San Kuo (Three Kingdoms)*, *Shui Hu Chuan,* and *Hsi Yu Chi (Travels to the Western Regions)*.

Shui Hu Chuan provided the proximate background to Pearl's next novel, *Sons,* which she wrote while she was revising and completing her translation. At five hundred pages, *Sons* is one of the longest books Pearl wrote. The novel is ostensibly a sequel to *The Good Earth,* but it is also a twentieth-century tribute to early Chinese fiction. The title refers to the three sons of Wang Lung, all of whom reject their father's commitment to the land to follow some other vocation. The eldest settles into the parasitic life of a landlord, the second prospers as a merchant and mean-spirited moneylender, while the youngest becomes a soldier. This third son, known as Wang the Tiger, is the book's principal character. He is a ferocious warrior, idealistic and self-serving by turns, who might have stepped out of the pages of *Shui Hu Chuan.*[59] As a boy, he had read the stories "of the robbers that bordered a great lake," and had dreamed of "the old days, even five hundred years ago, when good brave fellows banded together to punish the rich and to protect the poor." The original army he raises has exactly 108 men, the same number as the Liang-shan bandits.[60]

Along with its literary echoes, *Sons* also reflected Pearl's own experience. The book is set in the geography of Kiangsu and Anhwei provinces, and the battle scenes recall the fighting Pearl had seen in Nanhsuchou and Nanking. The main characters, although they are flattened into generalized types such as the predatory landlord and the scheming moneylender, were loosely based on men that Pearl had in fact known during her years in China.

Sons is an allegory of contemporary China, a morality play in which ambition and greed become instruments of self-destruction. The novel's events trace an ironic arc, as each of the overreaching brothers is humbled, and their father's primitive devotion to the soil is ultimately vindicated. The two elder sons exemplify the opportunists who corrupted the revolution. They are masterless men who have no conception of personal honor or national identity. Wang the Tiger is a just man who inevitably declines into mere egotism and cruelty in his old age. In the end, he is repudiated by his own son, who prefers obscurity to the indecencies of power and retires to Wang Lung's original homestead.

The events Pearl had lived through in her nearly four decades in China had made her deeply skeptical of revolution. While she despised the inequities of the old order, she suspected that political instability would only multiply the suffering of China's ordinary people. The rulers would change, but justice would remain the hostage of force. When *Sons* was published, two decades after the last emperor had abdicated, peasants were dying by the hundreds of thousands in famine and flood, bandits and warlords controlled much of the countryside, the Japanese had annexed the northern quarter of the nation, and China's major political-military force, the Kuomintang, was notoriously corrupt.

Pearl's political fatigue had much to do with the point of view she adopted in *The Young Revolutionist,* the only novel she ever wrote on salary. This was the children's book she promised the Presbyterian Mission Board when they had loaned her the money she needed to place Carol in Vineland.[61] In exchange for the story, the Board subtracted $500 from her $2,000 debt.

Under ordinary circumstances, such a book might have gone unnoticed. However, since *The Young Revolutionist* appeared directly in the wake of *The Good Earth,* it received considerable attention, including a number of friendly reviews. Pearl, who regarded the little story as a piece of evangelical ephemera, immediately tried to distance herself from it.[62] She didn't want to be associated with a book that the *New York Herald Tribune* approvingly called a "modern Christian parable."[63]

In fact, in spite of a burst of piety at the end, the novel is more interesting and considerably less orthodox than most readers seem to have noticed. The title character is a teen-aged peasant named Ko-sen who joins the Republican army and embraces a fervent nationalism that serves as his religion. Then, after a bloody and pointless battle in which all his comrades are killed, Ko-sen's patriotism is overwhelmed by despair. He transfers his allegiance to a Western Christian doctor who had ministered to the dead and dying on the battlefield. Ko-sen believes the man's name is "Jesus," and on the book's final page he decides to serve in the hospital where he met this saintly figure.

Of course, this Jesus is a man, not a god; Pearl calculated the mistake so that she could honor her own scruples silently even as she appeared to suit her missionary benefactors. She had long since stopped believing that dogmatic Christianity could be any part of the solution to China's problems, but she did feel there was a role for Western medicine and education. It is human compassion, not the Christian faith, that Ko-sen actually embraces. The kindly Christian doctor is utterly different from the Jesus that missionaries such as Absalom Sydenstricker had tried to import into China.

Pearl completed *The Young Revolutionist* and *Sons* more or less simultaneously, in the fall of 1931. In October, she sent the typescript of *Sons* to David Lloyd, with a note apologizing for its length. Lloyd was perfectly content: he turned down an offer from the Book-of-the-Month Club, which would guarantee only $5,000 or so, in order to accept a $30,000 fee from *Cosmopolitan* for serial rights.

Pearl wrote hopefully about the new book to Emma White; she also mentioned that *The Good Earth* had already appeared in several translations, including German, French, Dutch, Swedish, Danish, and Norwegian. In addition, she had received several offers from Chinese scholars who wanted to translate the book into Chinese.[64] To cap off her success, Metro-Goldwyn-Mayer had offered $10,000 for the film rights to the novel. David Lloyd shrewdly advised Pearl to refuse; as he predicted, MGM quickly came back with offers of $30,000 and finally $50,000, the largest fee Hollywood had yet paid for movie rights to a book. Pearl accepted.

Ironically, Pearl was becoming wealthy in the worst years of the global Depression. Lulu Hamilton had sent a letter itemizing the hard times Americans were facing in the early 1930s, the unemployment, bread lines, and Hoovervilles. "Times in America sound dreadful," Pearl acknowledged. "But as usual China, I suppose, is worse. The famine is really colossal here, this year. What suffering there is everywhere!" Pearl added that she was in bed trying to recover from influenza, and was "still very miserable."[65]

Early in the new year, Pearl wrote Polly Small describing the famine that continued to ravage much of eastern China. In an area as large as one-third of the United States, trees, crops, and seeds were all gone. Tens of thousands would die, Pearl predicted, and the world would not even notice: "people are used to tens of thousands of Chinese dying."[66] Lossing was active in famine relief. He put his squadrons of survey research workers at the service of government and private agencies that were taking convoys of food to the starving countryside.

In February, 1932, Japanese gunboats appeared in the Yangtze River, just a mile or two from Chiang Kai-shek's Nanking capital. The city went into a panic;

foreign residents expected a bloody reprise of the Nanking Incident of 1927. Like many others, Pearl blamed Chiang's appeasement for the Japanese effrontery. In the months since Japan had invaded Manchuria, Chiang had dithered and vacillated. Instead of resisting aggression, he preferred to hunt down Communists, a policy that merely encouraged Japan's imperialist ambitions.

Although the Japanese menaced Nanking for several weeks, they shelled the city only once: "one night's bombardment," Pearl wrote, when "we learned what it was to tumble out of bed in the dark and dress without lights while the house shook with cannon reports."[67] Occasionally, small-arms fire was exchanged between Japanese and Chinese soldiers, but both sides generally observed an unspoken, uncertain truce. Japan was apparently more interested in humiliating Chiang than attacking him in force. Nonetheless, the tension was excruciating, and foreigners were advised to evacuate. Pearl, who still had nightmares about the 1927 incident, readily agreed to leave the city. With the help of the American consul, the Bucks found seats on a train for the north. They spent the next several months in Peking, returning to Nanking in the late spring.

During her sojourn in the north, Pearl was delighted to receive a copy of the March issue of the *Yale Review,* which printed her article "China and the Foreign Chinese." Pearl was in distinguished company; this issue of the *Review* also included articles by John Maynard Keynes (on currency markets), Harold Laski (on India), Julian Huxley (on Russia), as well as reviews by F. S. C. Northrop, Mary Ellen Chase, B. H. Liddell Hart, and William Ernest Hocking.

Pearl's article, though it is typically anecdotal and self-effacing, makes an important cultural argument.[68] She insisted again, as she had done in her earlier stories and essays, that the reality of Chinese society should be sought in its masses rather than its small group of educated elite. Confucian texts supply subjects for scholarly meditation, but have no relevance to the vast majority of China's people. The "chief usefulness" of Confucian proverbs and pronouncements, she wrote, "seems to be as decorations, just as the sayings of Jesus in Western countries seem to be mainly decorative."[69]

Specifically, Pearl contrasted the tremendous emphasis Confucius put on self-restraint with the actual behavior of the Chinese people. For example, propagandists for China often liked to create the impression "that the Chinese are a peaceful and peace-loving people. Nothing could be farther from the truth." Confucian maxims about the reign of harmony were to be found only in books, not in the lives of the people. Juxtaposing her observations – and common sense – against sentimental images of a land ruled by tranquil men of learning, Pearl points out that "power in China has always been in the hands of the physically strong, and the military rather than the civil official has had the true government." In every village, the chief man "is the bully, not the scholar."[70]

By mid-May, the Bucks were back in Nanking. The Japanese warships had disappeared, at least temporarily, but tensions in the city remained high. Chiang's inaction was breeding discontent, and the Communists gained new recruits every day with promises that they would resist Japan's aggression. Lossing and Pearl only planned to stay a couple of months in the city before leaving for America.

As soon as she reached Nanking, Pearl received a cablegram informing her that *The Good Earth* had won the Pulitzer Prize.[71] She wrote to her sister Grace that she was astonished: she had thought that a novel had to be set in the United States to be eligible. To Lulu Hamilton, Pearl wrote that the Pulitzer made her feel like a "common brown hen . . . who has seen a phoenix emerge from what she thought was an ordinary egg!"[72] The book's sales, which had been exceptional for a full year, accelerated again in the wake of the Pulitzer.

As she packed for the journey to the United States, Pearl worried that her return threatened to become triumphal. She became preoccupied with protecting her privacy. She repeatedly instructed Richard Walsh and others that she wanted to conceal her itinerary, keep her addresses and phone numbers secret, and avoid interviews and formal social occasions. She even considered traveling in some sort of disguise. She said, rather primly, that she found the prospect of public exposure vulgar. That was part of the truth: crowds would always make her uncomfortable. More important, although she didn't mention it in her letters, she was terrified that reporters would pry out information about Carol and torment her with questions.[73]

Whatever Pearl's motives, Richard was prepared to cooperate. The author of *The Good Earth* had single-handedly rescued his company and turned it into a solvent if not flourishing concern. He wanted to take advantage of her American visit, but he was willing to manage her relations with public and press on whatever terms she stipulated. Working with David Lloyd, Richard arranged for the Bucks' almost clandestine arrival in July. He met their train in Montreal, took them to the Buck home near Poughkeepsie for a reunion with Lossing's family, and arranged for Pearl's New York hotel. Richard helped her sort through her mail, suggesting whose invitations she should accept. She turned down most, but agreed to lunches with Lewis Gannett and Christopher Morley. She shared a table at a PEN dinner with Thornton Wilder, and entertained Will Rogers in her hotel apartment.

One of Richard's most important tasks was to screen the reporters who wanted access to the woman who had become the country's most popular writer. It turned out that Pearl's reluctance to meet the press was also good business. As Richard was clever enough to guess, there was a certain glamour in Pearl's remoteness, which whetted the journalistic appetite. She became a figure of mystery, which led even to a moment of speculation that "Pearl Buck" did not exist! After all, as one exasperated journalist explained, "Would anyone . . . venture upon a literary career with such a name? [Perhaps] the whole thing was a hoax behind which lurked someone of the stature of George Bernard Shaw or of Theodore Dreiser."[74]

From this time forward, Richard became indispensable to Pearl. He had already served her as editor and publisher; now he quickly became her manager, advisor, spokesman, and public relations director. He admired her talent and she trusted his judgment. Their shared interests and their sheer delight in the magnitude of Pearl's success brought them intensely together. Pearl was forcefully struck by the contrast between Richard and Lossing, between the sophisticated, expansive New York literary man and the humorless technocrat. Richard released Pearl from fifteen years of marital claustrophobia. Over the following months, spending almost every day in each other's company, their mutual regard ripened into friendship and then love.

PEARL RETURNED TO AMERICA in the third year of the Depression. The crash of 1929 had precipitated the most wrenching domestic crisis since the Civil War. An economic structure that had seemed unshakable simply disintegrated, and no one could explain why. By the middle of 1932, American industrial production had been cut in half, and wages for workers who still had jobs had dropped almost as steeply. Unemployment was nearing one-quarter of the workforce, the largest figure in the nation's history. The prices of stocks fell by as much as 90 percent. Under the statistics lay millions of individual tragedies, which bred an unprecedented mood of national anxiety and doubt.

A great many writers joined the political struggle, most of them on the left. In a pamphlet called *Culture and Crisis,* fifty novelists, poets, and critics clamorously endorsed the Communist Party's presidential candidate, William Z. Foster. The signers included some of the most prominent names in American letters, among them Edmund Wilson, Sherwood Anderson, Langston Hughes, John Dos Passos, Lincoln Steffens, and Malcolm Cowley. Proletarian literature, which subordinated aesthetic standards to the purposes of the revolution, enjoyed a vogue that would continue through the 1930s.

Though Pearl occasionally called her own characters "proletarians," she played no part in the political debate. The presidential campaign in which Franklin D. Roosevelt challenged Herbert Hoover was the first she had been able to watch from within the States for twenty years, and she followed it with attention. She had a slight personal interest in Roosevelt's fortunes, since she had been favorably impressed when she met Eleanor Roosevelt at Cornell several years earlier. However, she made no public declaration in support of either man.

On August 3, Pearl briefly interrupted her self-imposed seclusion. She agreed to be the guest of honor at an immense dinner in the new Waldorf-Astoria.

Two hundred people gathered in the ornate Jade Room, among them some of New York's most familiar literary people. The guests included writers Fannie Hurst, Carl Van Doren, Christopher Morley, Gertrude Emerson, and William Rose Benet; editors J. Donald Adams of the *New York Times Book Review*, Bruce Bliven of the *New Republic*, Edward Weeks of the *Atlantic Monthly*, and Harold Ross of the *New Yorker*; and publishers Donald Brace, Guy Holt, Richard Simon, and Max Schuster. Harry Scherman and Henry Seidel Canby represented the Book-of-the-Month Club. The sprinkling of academics included historians Harry Elmer Barnes and Foster Rhea Dulles and economists Richard Ely and Rexford Tugwell. Henry Luce, the young publisher of *Time* and another child of Presbyterian missionaries in China, attended, along with lawyer and literary patron John Quinn. Even cartoonist Rube Goldberg was there.

On a fiercely hot and humid evening, the assembled worthies sat down to an international menu that opened with a "coupole of melon tricolor," and proceeded through courses of Russian borscht in jelly, filet of English sole, breast of chicken on Virginia ham, and "Starlight Salade." Speeches saluting Pearl accompanied the dessert and "café," notably a brief and graceful tribute by the Chinese consul-general, H. K. Chang.

Pearl was nearly paralyzed with nervousness. One eyewitness recalled that "she was a shy creature, and mousy, and looked about to run away." She was wearing a plain blue dress that seemed obviously homemade: "It actually had sleeves — unheard of at that time for evening wear — and a high V-neck." Her hair was parted in the middle and pulled back into a bun."[75]

Alexander Woollcott, who had been relegated to the thirty-fourth and last table in the hall, wrote a cranky account of the event for his "Shouts and Murmurs" column in the *New Yorker*. He complained about the heat, the food, most of the speeches, and in general the Barnumism and ballyhoo of New York's literary life. In spite of himself, on the other hand, he found the guest of honor irresistible. Woollcott assumed — correctly — that Pearl dreaded these "grisly occasions" as much as he did. Nonetheless, when she finally rose to speak, though she was inexpert and somewhat fuddled by the ranks of "curious gentry," she mastered the occasion. In Woollcott's words, she read a "lovely old fabric of miraculously apposite Chinese prose transmuted with a cadence which is half the secret of her alchemy and thereby turned the evening at last into a quiet triumph."[76]

In the eighteen months since the publication of *The Good Earth*, Pearl had earned well over $100,000.[77] This caused some envious grumbling among her missionary colleagues, who thought her salary as a missionary wife should be subtracted from her royalties.[78] For her part, Pearl had already suggested that the Mission Board reduce her salary. She also reminded Board officer George Scott that she still faced the heavy expenses of supporting her retarded daughter and that the Board had never increased her stipend when she adopted Janice because of a barbaric but longstanding policy discriminating against adopted children.[79]

Pearl's income did enable her to make permanent arrangements for Carol. With a check for $40,000, she established an endowment at the Vineland Training School that ensured Carol's care for life. At Pearl's direction, a separate, two-story residence was built on the grounds of the school, with a kitchen, bathroom, and several bedrooms. There was a pleasant front porch and a wading pool in the back. Known as "Carol's cottage," it housed Pearl's daughter and several other girls her own age.[80] Because Carol loved music, the cottage was equipped with a phonograph and a collection of records.

Now that Pearl was back in the States, she spent as much time as possible at Vineland, driving down from New York and staying at a nearby guest house for a day or two every week. Building Carol's cottage, she wrote with some exaggeration to Lulu Hamilton, "has about cleaned me out financially."[81] She presumed that her investment entitled her to opinions about the school's management. When she concluded that the director was too old to manage efficiently and that his deputy was "utterly unfit," she lobbied the trustees to appoint an assistant who could be groomed for succession.[82]

Vineland was conveniently close to Philadelphia, where the stage version of *The Good Earth* was in summer rehearsals. The play was scheduled to open the Theatre Guild's fifteenth New York season. The adaptation was written by Owen Davis, a Broadway veteran with upwards of two hundred plays to his credit, with assistance from his son, Donald. Philip Moeller directed.

Pearl had a remarkable clause written into her contract with the Davises, making her the final arbiter of "all points of racial and national accuracy . . . a court of last resort in respect to any questions as to . . . Chinese civilization, life and custom."[83] She busied herself in every aspect of the production, in particular offering her opinions on costumes and settings. She urged that Moeller scrupulously avoid the use of embroidered gowns and mandarin robes, "quasi-Oriental costume" which "no one has worn in China since ancient times and which are never seen except in stage farces and on the backs of tourists."[84]

The play had its preview at Philadelphia's Chestnut Theater in late September, and opened to generally mediocre reviews at the Guild's Nixon Theatre in New York on October 17. It was a big production: three acts, twelve scenes, and a cast of forty. Claude Rains played Wang Lung, Henry Travers took the part of the father, and Alla Nazimova was cast as O-lan. Sydney Greenstreet took the small part of Wang Lung's rascally uncle. Publicly, Pearl assured interviewers that she liked the play. In private, she complained that it was impossible for Europeans and Americans to impersonate her Chinese characters credibly.[85]

Most critics agreed. Alla Nazimova received a few warm comments, but most of the reviewers concluded that the play had failed to reproduce the novel, in large part because the actors were too remote from their Asian characters. In his *New York Evening Post* notice, the influential John Mason Brown summed up the problem: "Dragged indoors; played by white actors with English accents and Occidental hearts, who wear pigtails and Chinese costumes; set before a wrinkled cyclorama that is supposed to represent the sky . . . 'The Good Earth' does little more than demonstrate the limitations of the theater as a medium."[86] Almost unanimously, the critics who skewered the play lavished praise on the novel; it was precisely the play's failure to capture the spirit of the book that caused much of the complaining.

The audiences were not much kinder than the critics. After the first couple of weeks, *The Good Earth* played to a half-empty house; it closed after fifty-six performances. Pearl herself, on the other hand, was given a warm welcome when she was recognized sitting in the manager's box. Too nervous to attend opening night, she went to the second performance and received a standing ovation. It was a heady experience. Just two years earlier, Pearl had been a missionary wife, toiling in obscurity, looking forward to the publication of her first book. She was now one of the best-known writers in the world.

Pearl had decidedly mixed feelings about her new-found fame. She had spent too many years in the shadows to feel comfortable in the light. More to the point, she mistrusted her own talent. Although she pretended to be indifferent to hostile opinion, she was sensitive to the condescension that she suffered at the hands of the serious quarterlies and advanced tastemakers. Brought up in a tradition of rigorous morality, she was always haunted by the fear that her celebrity was undeserved and would lead to humiliation.

At the same time, she was growing accustomed to the money and influence that her success was bringing in such abundance. She had just passed her fortieth birthday; few persons at that age have seen their lives change as dramatically and as suddenly. Pearl had spent most of her life inside a small, closed circle of rigid fundamentalism. For four decades, two different cultures had tutored her in the inferiority of women. She had spent much of adulthood pent up in a loveless marriage and caring for a disabled child. She would never escape her history, but she would try to arrange her life on altogether different terms.

For a while longer, she remained the outwardly dutiful wife. When Lossing moved back to Ithaca in September, Pearl went with him. She considered staying behind in New York, which was closer to Carol and Richard, now the two most important people in her life. However, she wasn't yet ready for a public break with respectability. Beyond that, the remoteness of upstate New York brought certain advantages, making it easier for her to protect her privacy and giving her more time to write.

Sons was published shortly after Pearl was settled in Ithaca. Within a few days,

Richard was able to report on the "phenomenal" sales and uniformly good reviews.[87] When a few critics complained about the novel's melodrama, Pearl responded defensively that life in present-day China "*is* a melodramatic life, and warlords are strange, melodramatic, Napoleonic figures – cruel, ignorant, impulsive, emotional, lonely figures."[88] Yale's William Lyon Phelps called *Sons* "one of the outstanding works of our time."

Comparisons with *The Good Earth* were inevitable. Interestingly, a good-sized proportion of critical opinion actually felt that the new book was the better of the two. Writing in the *New York Times*, J. Donald Adams announced that "Mrs. Buck has enriched her wide canvas" with *Sons;* Juliet Stern, in her *Philadelphia Record* notice, wrote that "there is more power in the new book, and a wider scope."[89] Some of the praise came from unexpected quarters. General John J. Pershing, the revered leader of American forces in World War I, sat next to Pearl at a dinner party and told her that *Sons* was a much better book than *The Good Earth*.[90]

Throughout the fall, Pearl continued to turn down almost all speaking engagements. She made an exception when she accepted an invitation from a group of Presbyterian women to address a luncheon on November 2. Her decision would prove fateful. On a warm and sunny afternoon, Pearl faced some two thousand men and women in the main ballroom of the Astor Hotel.[91] The guests included some of the city's most prominent clerics, among them Dr. Cleland Boyd McAfee and Dr. Henry Sloane Coffin.

In place of the ceremonial or pious remarks that such an occasion might have evoked, Pearl delivered a long speech that instantly became the subject of international controversy. She announced as her title the question, "Is There a Case for Foreign Missions?" Her answer was a qualified but unmistakable "No." She continued to identify herself as a missionary, and she insisted that her criticisms had nothing to do with the essential message of Christianity. She even weakly endorsed the continuation of missionary work. By far the most memorable passages in the speech, however, portrayed the typical missionary as "narrow, uncharitable, unappreciative, ignorant." Pearl devoted most of her text to a root-and-branch exposé of evangelism's defects, its superstition, cultural arrogance, and cruelty:

I have seen missionaries, orthodox missionaries in good standing in the church – abominable phrase! – so lacking in sympathy for the people they were supposed to be saving, so scornful of any civilization except their own, so harsh in their judgments upon one another, so coarse and insensitive among a sensitive and cultivated people that my heart has fairly bled with shame.[92]

Pearl went out of her way to implicate the audience before which she stood in her indictment. Over and over again, she blamed American Christians for their indifference, narrow-mindedness, and racism.

Pearl's remarks caused a genuine sensation, and were printed both in the December issue of *Harper's Magazine* and as a John Day pamphlet which sold thousands of copies.[93] The reaction, both among those who heard the speech and those who read it a few weeks later, was predictably fierce. The Mission Board was deluged with letters from American and overseas church members. A few supported Pearl's position or at least defended her right to speak; most, however, demanded that she be punished for her views. The controversy continued for a full year, attracting attention around the world. Pearl's prominence made her comments newsworthy in papers from Shanghai to Montreal, from Rio de Janeiro to Paris.[94]

With her speech, Pearl had stepped into the middle of a debate that had been gathering force for nearly a decade. In the years after World War I, missionaries had been subject to a rising tide of criticism. Much of the opposition was grounded in recent anthropological ideas, which equated missionary activity with the destruction of foreign cultures.[95] The mainstream churches themselves often joined in the attacks. From the mid-1920s on, the progressive *Christian Century* ran a series of articles with such titles as "Can a Missionary Be a Christian?" (1930), "End Mission Imperialism Now!" (1934), and "I Don't Want to Christianize the World!" (1935).[96]

Popular culture also reflected the growing disenchantment of Americans with their overseas missionaries. One of the movie hits of 1932 was *Rain*, with Joan Crawford and Walter Huston.[97] Crawford plays Sadie Thompson, a good-natured whore who has been stranded by a monsoon on a Pacific island for several days. Her companions include a ranting, Bible-quoting Protestant missionary, Reverend Davidson, played by Huston. Davidson spends several days denouncing Thompson, then spends a night in her bed. The film implies that the evangelist, as a type, is a fanatic, a sanctimonious prig, and ultimately a hypocrite. The missionary, who had been a heroic figure in the nineteenth century, had become shrunken and even ridiculous, a symbol of America's misplaced desire to reform the world on Western terms.[98]

The missionary enterprise was decisively repudiated in a widely read book called *Re-Thinking Missions*, published in October, 1932, within a few days of Pearl's Astor Hotel speech. The book contained the three-hundred-page report of the "Laymen's Inquiry Commission," which had been appointed by a confederation of seven Protestant denominations. Sixty-year-old Ernest Hocking of Harvard, one of the country's most distinguished philosophers, served as commission chairman.

Ironically, a study that was initiated to reform and save missionary work had the effect of writing its epitaph. Although the report is punctuated with statements of admiration and respect for the work of American missionaries, in the end Hocking and his colleagues demolished the foundations on which a century of Christian evangelizing had been built. *Re-Thinking Missions* enumerated a whole list of liberal recommendations, which had the collective effect of condemning most practicing evangelists as irrelevant and obsolete.[99]

Henceforward, according to the report, preachers ought to back away from such doctrines as eternal damnation and appeal instead to notions of divine love and universal brotherhood. Indeed, Hocking's group advised missionaries to stop insisting that Christianity is the only true religion and acknowledge the value of other systems of belief. There is "at the core of all the creeds a nucleus of religious truth," and the missionary's job is to celebrate the likenesses between native faiths and Christianity.[100]

Trying to accommodate traditional piety to revolutionary new circumstances, *Re-Thinking Missions* virtually acknowledged the defeat of the missionary dream. The report infuriated the fundamentalist community.[101] In the view of veteran evangelists, *Re-Thinking Missions* was an exercise in soft-headed sentimentalism. The point of mission work was to save souls, not to pamper the sensitivities of unbelievers. Above all, the idea that Christianity was to be presented as merely one religion among many mocked the assumption that had principally governed generations of missionary work.[102]

Pearl Buck warmly welcomed the commission's findings and recommendations. She had met Ernest Hocking in China, entertaining him in her home during his tour of investigation, and she had been stirred to deep admiration.[103] When *Re-Thinking Missions* appeared, she published a long review article in the *Christian Century* in November, 1932, which was immediately reprinted as an eleven-page pamphlet. Though she referred to herself as a missionary – "We missionaries find ourselves now [among] the most criticized bodies in the world" – she distanced herself from the typical missionaries she had known, men who were "limited in outlook . . . lacking in appreciation and understanding" of other cultures and religions, in a word, "mediocre." The missionary, she concluded, is simply "not big enough for his job."

Pearl placed much of the blame for what she called a "hideous situation" on the dogmatic, money-minded, convert-counting atmosphere in which missionaries were forced to operate. She singled out preaching for special contempt. "I am weary unto death with this incessant preaching," she wrote, perhaps with the sound of her father's sermons still echoing in her ears. Preaching, she continued, "deadens all thought, it confuses all issues, it is producing in our Chinese churches a horde of hypocrites." Rather than words, Christians should offer tangible service to the Chinese, in medicine, education, sanitation. She concluded by endorsing the continuation of mission activity, but her attack had been so relentless that this gesture of conciliation seemed perfunctory.

Pearl's critique originated in her long years of silent alienation from her father. Just a little more than a year after Absalom's death, Pearl was publicly signaling her repudiation of her father's creeds and values. Unconvincingly, she told family friends that she considered her father exempt from her charges. In fact, Absalom's entire career had exemplified precisely the excesses and misunderstandings that had, in his daughter's view, doomed evangelism to failure.

Between them, Pearl's Astor Hotel speech and her review of the Hocking report instantly made her the country's most visible critic of the missionary enterprise. The public waited eagerly for each accusation and response in the argument. It was a time when religious debates were commonly front page news. Just a few years earlier, the Scopes "monkey trial" in Tennessee had divided the entire nation on the issue of the Bible's literal truth. The missionary question generated almost as much controversy, and Pearl found herself at the center of the storm.[104]

Pearl's commitment to equality, which anchored her analysis of evangelism, also had significant implications for her view of American race relations. Her long association with the civil rights movement dates from these months in the fall of 1932, when she first made contact with a number of leading African-American organizers and journalists. Elmer Carter, editor of the Urban League's magazine, *Opportunity,* concluded from his reading of *The Good Earth* that Pearl understood "the whole question of race. This was no sugar-coated philanthropy; [rather] it was basic understanding."[105]

Pearl accepted an invitation from Carter to attend a discussion of black problems that took place in Harlem in late December. Roy Wilkins, then a young columnist, covered the event for the African-American *Kansas City Call.* He described Pearl as "a charming, gracious lady," who had nonetheless "given some hard blows to white people and their prejudices against colors and races." He quoted with particular relish Pearl's statement that the behavior of white Americans often made her wish that she didn't have "a drop of white blood in my veins." She told her listeners: "I have seen white men and women so stupid in their ignorance and arrogance, so much a disgrace to the very race in which they took pride that I have despised them and been ashamed that my skin was like theirs." Pearl counseled blacks to be proud of their identity and achievements as Americans, as she was proud to be their "fellow-countryman."[106] She concluded by reminding them that, among the populations of the world, white people were a small minority.

In a conversation after her formal remarks, Pearl traced her opinions about race to her own experiences in China. As a person who had once faced death because of her color, she said she was particularly sensitive to injustice based on racial prejudice. From that afternoon forward, Pearl remained active in civil rights work. A dozen years after this Harlem meeting, in the midst of World War II, Elmer Carter said that "All Negroes have implicit faith in Miss Buck. They have greater confidence in her than in any other white person in public life."[107]

ON SEVERAL OCCASIONS in that busy New York winter, Pearl had lunch or dinner with her older brother, Edgar. He was still working at the Milbank Foundation, with responsibility for funding development projects in China. Edgar had once been Pearl's idol. Now he seemed to be an old man at fifty, drinking too much and about to embark on a second marriage that Pearl predicted would also turn out badly. The visits depressed Pearl, but they cheered Edgar up; he wrote to Grace that Pearl seemed "to have the world wrapped around her finger, and yet she is exactly the same."[108]

In the early months of 1933, Pearl spent less time in Ithaca. She moved into a suite of rooms at the Murray Hill Hotel on Park Avenue, and commuted weekly between New York and Vineland.[109] Wherever she was, she reserved her mornings for writing. This was a habit she had developed in China and would continue to the end of her life. When she was in New York, she spent most afternoons working with Richard at the John Day offices. Evenings were divided between family engagements and a few literary and political dinners. In late January, she was guest of honor at a Town Hall testimonial sponsored by the League for Political Education.

A couple of weeks later, Pearl went to Washington to speak at a meeting on the subject "Birth Control Comes of Age." She identified herself as a fervent supporter of birth control; her years in China, she said, had shown her the terrible cost that overpopulation brings to a nation and to its women. She saluted Margaret Sanger, who had brought "into the light of science and of common knowledge a matter which involves every human being vitally and which for generations has not been discussed except in secret and obscene ways."[110] She concluded by attacking America's sexual prudery, which made the rational discussion of contraception impossible. "No cause," she said, "has been fought against more stupid, blind social injustice."

This was the first of dozens of speeches Pearl would make over the next two decades in support of family planning. It was also the beginning of a long friendship with Margaret Sanger. Along with civil rights for African-Americans and women, Pearl would make birth control one of her principal political commitments in the 1930s and 1940s.

Because of her travel schedule, Pearl was unable to attend a tribute dinner for Eleanor Roosevelt in New York in January. However, in mid-February the two women shared the stage as principal speakers at a symposium organized by Cornell's College of Home Economics. Roosevelt gave a talk called "The Widening Interests of the Family," after which Pearl spoke on "Women in China Today." Her principal point was that Chinese women, in spite of their legal and traditional inferiority, were actually a good deal stronger than Chinese men, who had been weakened by a system that indulged them from birth.[111]

Eight years earlier, Pearl had been a graduate student member of the committee that welcomed Roosevelt, then the wife of New York's governor, to Cornell. Now, she was a prize-winning novelist getting as much attention as the wife of the president-elect. The university's press release made the point in its evenhanded headline: "College Features Two Noted Women, Eleanor Roosevelt and Pearl S. Buck."

Back in New York City, Pearl's calendar became more crowded every day. The guests who came to her Murray Hill apartment included Vita Sackville-West, poet Witter Bynner, and Gertrude Lane, publisher of the *Woman's Home Companion,* who wanted Pearl to write something for the magazine's sixtieth anniversary issue.[12] Christopher Morley paid a call, leaving a copy of his *Poems and Translations from the Chinese* as a gift.

In March, Pearl was part of a large Waldorf-Astoria audience that heard Albert Einstein call for "moral intervention" against Hitler. A few days later, she called Will Rogers to thank him personally for an extraordinary remark he had made about *The Good Earth,* which the *New York Times* had printed in a page-one box. Among other things, Rogers said, "It's not only the greatest book about a people ever written but the best book of our generation." Since Rogers was one of the most popular entertainers of his time, his comment caused a predictable surge in the novel's sales.

Lossing remained sequestered in Ithaca, studying for his final exams. Pearl reported, with exasperated amusement, that she was often asked, "*Is* there a Mr. Buck?"[13] Richard was her constant companion. When Pearl wanted a weekend away from New York, she and Janice often stayed in Richard's suburban home. When they were not together, Pearl wrote frequently, asking for advice, commenting on the day's news, or thanking him for some kindness or other. In one of these notes, she rather impulsively made Richard the owner of all her manuscripts: "I want all those manuscripts you now have, and all those I shall send you in the future, to belong to you personally, to be kept by you and disposed of as you see fit, as your private and personal property."[14] Like all her letters to Richard, this one was decorously addressed to "Dear Mr. Walsh," and signed "Sincerely, Pearl S. Buck." However, the extravagant gesture indicates the progress of Pearl's trust and affection.

She depended on Richard for support as her conflict with the Presbyterians escalated in the late spring. She was shaken by rumors that a church court planned to put her on trial for heresy. The report proved untrue, but a crisis of some sort had clearly become inevitable. In the months following her Astor Hotel speech, she had become the target of a bitter campaign, directed by conservatives on both sides of the Pacific. The attacks were typically intemperate and personal. Rev. James Graham, who had succeeded Absalom in the Chinkiang mission, accused Pearl of betraying her mother and father. She had "lost her bearings," said Graham, "run amok . . . prostituted her genius . . . debased her woman-hood."[115]

Pearl assured Cleland McAfee and other Presbyterian leaders that she wanted some sort of reconciliation. At the same time, she refused to back down from her criticisms of Christian extremism and missionary misbehavior. Indeed, while the church was still debating how to deal with her, she sharpened her dissent in an article called "Easter, 1933," which she published in the May issue of *Cosmopolitan*. She likened Christ to the Buddha, declared that Christ's historical reality was irrelevant, denied the necessity for any specific dogma, and located the truth of Christianity in "the essence of men's highest dreams."[116] As the *New York Times* accurately suggested in its report on the article, Pearl had apparently adopted "a creedless faith."[117]

"Easter, 1933" demonstrated that Pearl could no longer serve as a Presbyterian missionary. All that remained was to negotiate the manner of her separation. Fundamentalists, led by Dr. J. Gresham Machen, a professor at the Westminster Theological Seminary of Philadelphia, vehemently demanded that she be publicly rebuked and dismissed.[118] However, the majority of the members of the Board of Foreign Missions were reluctant to act so decisively. Some members feared the consequences of a public dispute with a world-famous novelist, while others admired her sincerity and courage, and a few even expressed a degree of sympathy for her views.

On May 1, Pearl ended the discussion by resigning from her missionary position; the Board officially accepted her resignation "with regret." Machen tried to keep the controversy alive. The May 2 *Philadelphia Ledger* quoted his denunciation of the Mission Board as unworthy of confidence because it had let Pearl resign "without expressing any condemnation of her radically anti-Christian views." Machen was almost alone in his zeal to continue pursuing the matter. His shrill demands went unanswered, he and his few allies were defeated at the General Assembly later in May, and the Pearl Buck affair disappeared from the Presbyterian agenda.

A few of Pearl's critics suspected that she had deliberately stirred up the controversy as a publicity stunt. While there is no evidence that this is true, it is undeniable that the charges and countercharges kept her name constantly in the news. She also took more pleasure than she admitted in the agitation she was causing. She was settling some old scores, speaking out for tolerance against bigotry, for Asia against the colonizing West, for women against patriarchal institutions, for herself against her father. When she resigned, she was treated as a hero by much of the press. The African-American *Chicago Defender* insinuated that she had been "lynched," and stated flatly that she had been forced out "under a barrage of criticisms because of her attitude of fairness and justice toward darker races."[19]

Pearl's confrontation with the Presbyterians nourished her confidence in her public role. With Richard's encouragement, she began to make herself more available to academic and professional groups. In April, she gave a speech on American policy in China at the annual meeting of the American Academy of Political and Social Science in Philadelphia. A few days later, she talked again on race relations at a seminar hosted by a group of Philadelphia Quakers. She gave a lecture on Chinese humor at Bryn Mawr, and spent an evening with Chinese students at Columbia discussing fiction. At the request of Edward Carter, she agreed to serve on the American Council of the influential Institute of Pacific Relations. She presided over a China Society dinner in honor of Dr. T. V. Soong, Chiang Kai-shek's finance minister and brother-in-law.

In early June, Pearl traveled to Lynchburg to give the Alumnae Address at Randolph-Macon's commencement. Her old classmates were impressed by her appearance. Her costly new dress contrasted with the peculiar clothes she had worn when she had arrived at the college as a freshman more than twenty years earlier. From now on she would dress expensively, sometimes even ostentatiously. She bought clothes, and later spacious houses and oversized cars, to repay herself for years of poverty and obscurity. She needed to prove the scale of her success – to herself as much as to anyone else. Though she remained intractably modest, to the point of insecurity, her self-doubt now coexisted with a hard, competitive instinct. Her exceptional accomplishments engendered a slow-growing but understandable pride. Returning to Randolph-Macon, she savored the admiration of her old teachers and friends. Her visit was a kind of fairy tale homecoming, in which the awkward outsider was transformed into a star.

Pearl began with a paragraph of self-deprecating irony. She told her audience that she had personally devised the title of her talk: "Women and International Relations." This, she said, had sounded like an interesting subject when she proposed it; and it still did. However, she had discovered in trying to write her lecture that she had nothing original or useful to say about women and international relations, so she would speak instead "On the Writing of Novels."

Half-jokingly, she advised her listeners to avoid novel writing at all costs: it led to isolation, hypersensitivity, and anti-social behavior. She went on, more seriously, to argue that the technical experiments of modern writers do not automatically lead to a superior fiction. "There is," she told the assembled graduates, "no evolution toward the perfect novel. There is no road marked and to be discovered by even the most eager soul, at whose end there is to be found waiting the Absolute Novel." On the contrary, she said, there are only good and bad novels, some brand new and some that are centuries old.[20] The obser-

15. Pearl at the "even post" during her visit to Randolph-Macon in 1933. (Courtesy Randolph-Macon Woman's College.)

vation is true enough, though there was a palpable measure of self-interest in her endorsement of old-fashioned narratives.

Lossing had completed his doctoral work and wanted to get back to China as quickly as possible. Pearl agreed to go with him, though she added the surprising announcement that Richard and Ruby Walsh would join them for the European portion of the journey. Just before the Bucks sailed from New York, Pearl drove up to New Haven, where she gave a talk at the annual meeting of Yale-in-China. The next day, she received an honorary degree at Yale's commencement. William Lyon Phelps, who had proposed her name, also served as the university's official orator. At the ceremony, he opened his citation with a bit of humor − "she had the original idea of not writing a book until she had something to say" − but went on more solemnly to call her "the ablest living interpreter of the Chinese character." Phelps proposed that Yale's long association with China made Pearl's degree especially appropriate.

By a friendly coincidence, Pearl received her honorary Yale degree in the same week that her newest book was published. *The First Wife and Other Stories* gathered together fourteen of her shorter works, including her sketches of the Yangtze floods and the Chinese revolution. The collection was Richard's idea. Except for Pearl's book and Franklin Roosevelt's *Looking Forward,* a volume of political platitudes that had brought a certain luster but few receipts, the John Day Company was facing financial trouble. Knowing that sales of Pearl's three novels would eventually slow down, Richard wanted a new title that would keep her name as visible as possible in the book markets. He also wanted to take advantage of her notoriety. He was preparing *All Men Are Brothers* for publication, but he sensibly assumed that a two–volume translation of a classic Chinese novel had few commercial prospects, however much it might add to Pearl's prestige.

First Wife performed exactly as Richard had hoped. Unlike most anthologies of reprinted stories, Pearl's book received important and prominent reviews on both sides of the Atlantic, almost all of them enthusiastic. Margaret Cheney Dawson, in the *New York Herald Tribune,* said that "at least four" of the stories "are good enough to be called great," while the anonymous reviewer for the *Times Literary Supplement* concluded that all the stories "are alike in the high level of their writing, their power of observation and . . . understanding." Graham Greene, writing in the *Spectator,* applauded Pearl's dispassionate realism and her single-minded effort "to present life with truth."[121]

The title story, the longest and most substantial in the book, dramatizes the collision between new and traditional values in revolutionary China. A young husband, Li Yuan, returns to his wife and parents in their backwater village after seven years of study in the United States. He brings with him a cluster of liberal ideas, including progressive opinions about the emancipation of women. As an ironic result, he finds his wife unsatisfactory; she is dutiful, uneducated, and hobbles on bound feet. After months of mutual frustration, Li Yuan deserts his family, moves to a coastal city, and sends word that he plans to marry a more suitable woman. Faced with disgrace for reasons she cannot understand, the first wife hangs herself.

Staying close to the woman's point of view, the story exhibits an excruciating balance of sympathies. Using foot-binding as a cruel symbol, Pearl delivers an unblinking critique of China's systematic diminishment of women. At the same time, she is sensitive to the destructive consequences that "progress" can have for traditional women themselves. The wife suddenly finds herself expelled from her home and robbed of the only identity she has ever known.

Lossing, Pearl, and Janice sailed for England in July aboard the *Duchess of Bedford.* Pearl was carrying a letter of introduction to Edith Wharton, which she had been given by the anthropologist Bronislaw Malinowski. Pearl never did search out the expatriate American writer, though she did meet a long list of prominent people. She spent a day visiting Beatrice and Sidney Webb, the venerable English socialists. Sidney talked continuously through lunch; at the end

of the meal, Beatrice aimed an accusatory index finger at Pearl and demanded
to know why she had ignored Chinese homosexuality in her fiction.[122] The
question left Pearl more or less speechless.

The Bucks and Walshes did some sightseeing together in England, Sweden,
Italy, and France. They saw *A Midsummer-Night's Dream* at the open-air theater
in London's Regent's Park, and John Gielgud's *Richard of Bordeaux* at the New
Theater. They went on a Thomas Cook tour of the East End, then spent a
couple of days in Stratford, where they attended a production of *Much Ado About
Nothing*. In Paris, they joined the other tourists at the Folies Bergère. In Stockholm, Pearl had her picture taken with fellow Pulitzer winners Louis Bromfield
and Marc Connelly, who were also vacationing there.

On their own, Pearl and Richard visited the military cemetery at Verdun,
where Pearl wept over the thousands of white crosses that marked the graves.
She brooded about the likelihood that America would soon be fighting another
war, this time in Asia. It was a forecast that brought particular pain because she
was now "haunted by the similarity of the condition of the Negroes in my own
country and that of peoples in colonial Asia." If white Americans couldn't treat
black Americans with decency in their own country, what moral principle would
justify a white war against people of color on the other side of the world?

After Richard and Ruby had returned to the States, Pearl and Lossing set out
for China, first traveling to southern France. When they got to Nice, Pearl told
her husband that the marriage had come to an end. She asked for a separation.
The announcement was abrupt but not unexpected. Lossing claimed that he had
known about Pearl's growing intimacy with Richard: "I was prepared, I'd seen
it going on, they were pretty brazen about it. I *cared*, of course. But it's foolish
to protest."[123]

It is not clear whether Lossing ever understood why Pearl left him. She herself
usually only spoke of her motives in vague terms: "There were no differences –
only a difference so vast that communication was impossible, in spite of honest
effort over many years."[124] The distance between them was sexual as well as
temperamental; Lossing had been unable to gratify either her passion or her mind.

Because Pearl was still part of a society in which divorce was regarded both
as a scandal and as an admission of defeat, it would take her nearly two years to
go through the process and secure her final decree. However, she was now firmly
committed to ending her marriage. Having made her decision, she and Lossing
traveled back to China separately. She suffered through a sad and solitary voyage,
a month-long journey on the S.S. *Conte Rosso* that took her from Italy to China
by way of Bombay, Colombo, Singapore, and Hong Kong.

Midway through the trip, she exposed her marital torment in a long, candid
letter to Emma White. She pleaded with Emma to agree with her that the present
impasse was intolerable: "You can see how impossible everything is, Emma, do

you think it is possible to go on like this year after year?" Before she had met Richard, Pearl said, she could simply ignore her failed marriage and go through the motions of domestic life. But her love for Richard made her sham marriage unacceptable. In particular, she could never again have sexual relations with Lossing: "My whole soul and body turns sick at the thought. Surely it is not right to violate one's self like that."

In an apparent reference to Hsu Chih-mo, Pearl reminded Emma: "I once loved someone – I told you, you remember – but I beat that down, year after year. But it was no such love as this and no such man as Richard." Defending herself from charges of selfishness, Pearl mentioned that she had provided financially for Lossing and his parents. More importantly, she insisted that she had done everything she could think of to be a good wife, "for no return in joy, companionship – nothing." She said she had become quite desperate, and she begged her old friend to "think of it humanly, Emma, and not as a preacher's wife."[125]

Pearl landed in Shanghai on October 2, 1933. She paused only for a few days, during which she met the young critic Lin Yutang at a dinner party; then she moved on to Nanking. She stayed in touch with Richard by mail and cable, though their correspondence was cautiously restricted to business matters, including questions and answers about sales and royalties. Pearl reported on the tribulations of the MGM film crew that had come to China to begin work on *The Good Earth*. Progress was slow because of the opposition of a couple of interfering officials, who thought that a movie about peasants would be bad for the government's image. One irritated agent was heard to complain that "in spite of the utmost vigilance of the government there will be a few servants with dirty aprons and some women with bound feet in this picture."[126]

Janet Fitch, a missionary living in Peking at the time, wrote in her diary about the tug-of-war between Pearl and the bureaucrats. "Pearl wants the shots to be absolutely authentic, as she knows them. The Chinese officials, who give out the permits, will lose much face here and abroad unless everyone, down to the last extra, is in new clothes and the buildings are freshly painted." Pearl won, but her victory was hollow. The camera crew was finally permitted to take shots of peasants and their farms, along with teahouses, mud huts, and work animals. However, when the crew brought the footage out of China, the Kuomintang arranged to have all the containers X-rayed. A few weeks later, several thousand feet of blank film arrived in Hollywood.[127]

Richard's news was better. He informed Pearl that sales of *All Men Are Brothers,* aided by Owen Lattimore's admiring notice in the *New York Times,* were surprisingly good. He also mentioned that he had concluded arrangements to take over as editor of *Asia* magazine, an illustrated, upmarket monthly that served mainly to advertise luxury cars and glamorous Asian tours. The magazine's publisher, a Briton named Leonard Elmhirst, was receptive to Richard's proposal that *Asia* should become a more serious journal. Richard argued that Americans were becoming more interested in Asia, and would pay for solid, well-written articles on the region's politics and culture.

Pearl's career and her personal needs were both drawing her inevitably back to America. In a letter to her new friend, William Lyon Phelps, she confessed that she was beginning to feel alienated from China. At times, she still thought it was "the most beautiful country I have ever seen." At other times, however, the Chinese landscape can be "ugly and sordid and evil looking." Centuries of continuous human occupation have permanently marked every foot of soil: "the land seems man-possessed, utilized by both living and dead until the very contours of the landscape have a strangely human look." She was increasingly attracted to America's open spaces.[128]

At the end of 1933, Pearl and Richard were reunited when Richard came to Nanking for an extended visit. Ostensibly, he had come as a tourist and businessman, though his arrival prompted Lossing to decamp for a research trip of several months to Tibet. Leaving Janice in the care of Adeline Bucher, Pearl took Richard to rural Yoyang (Yueyang) to meet her sister, Grace. From there, the couple traveled ambitiously through Southeast Asia: they stopped in Indochina, India, Thailand, and Burma.

In rural India, Pearl encountered poverty on a vaster scale than anything she had seen in China. She placed much of the blame on Britain's colonial rule, which had relentlessly stripped the Indian people of their dignity and initiative. The average life expectancy of the Indians was just twenty-seven years, a statistic that Pearl interpreted as a shocking summary of the consequences of British rule.[129]

Eventually, the couple circled north to Peking, where Pearl showed Richard around her favorite city. Richard did do a little work in Peking, recruiting H. J. Timperley, an Australian who represented the Associated Press and the *Manchester Guardian* in China, as a talent scout for *Asia* magazine.[130] Pearl and Richard also spent a day with Helen and Edgar Snow, who were then studying Chinese and teaching English to supplement their small journalists' income. The four Americans immediately began a friendship that would last for many years.

In February and March, 1934, Pearl and Richard went on another long trip together, this time traveling through Hong Kong, the Malay States, and the Philippines.[131] They returned to Nanking and made preparations for a long visit to the United States. On May 30, Pearl sailed for Canada on board the *Empress of Russia* with Richard, Janice, and Adeline Bucher. She was not sure when she would return to China, but she took it for granted she would be back someday. She had never been away for longer than a few years, usually not longer than a few months.

16. Richard Walsh on his visit to China in 1933. (Reproduced with permission of the Pearl S. Buck Foundation.)

History had other plans; in the event, she never set foot in China again. A combination of political circumstance and personal choice would separate her permanently from the country in which she had lived most of the first forty years of her life.

5

An Exile's Return

IN 1934, THE YEAR that Pearl Buck moved back to the United States, Malcolm Cowley published *Exile's Return*, his anecdotal history of the "lost generation." Cowley chronicled the private lives and transatlantic travels of a group of writers who had come of literary age in the years after World War I: F. Scott Fitzgerald, E. E. Cummings, John Dos Passos, Ernest Hemingway, and Edmund Wilson, among others. Born in the 1890s, they were white, male, mainly middle-class, and mainly college-educated. Although they differed from each other in all sorts of ways, they were linked by what Cowley called their "common adventures" – in particular the war and the disillusionment that had followed.[1]

They also shared a belief in "salvation by exile," the idea that Europe was a place more hospitable to their talents and aesthetic commitments than America. Throughout the 1920s, they all spent months and in some cases years overseas, often in Paris or the south of France, taking advantage of a favorable exchange rate and searching for kindred artistic spirits. Though all of them returned to the United States sooner or later, their decision to leave America was a highly premeditated gesture.[2]

By contrast, Pearl Buck had been an involuntary expatriate. She had not chosen China; she had simply found herself growing up there, absorbed in a society radically different from America at almost every point. As a consequence, she had gained a uniquely cosmopolitan perspective, which equipped her to make valuable comparisons between Eastern and Western cultures. At the same time, she was uncertain where she actually belonged. In different ways, both China and the United States were foreign countries to her. She had no home in either Asia or America. If exile and displacement are the characteristic marks of modern experience, then a credible case can be made that Pearl Buck's life uniquely summarized the leading themes of her time.[3]

Needless to say, neither Pearl's years in Asia nor her return to the United States was memorialized by Malcolm Cowley in his survey. Her reputation already lay outside the borders of high culture. There were several reasons for her

neglect by the makers of taste. To begin with, she was an accessible and tremendously popular novelist working in familiar forms. Those facts alone made
her books almost automatically ineligible for the new list of masterworks that
was being constructed, by literary journalists and academic critics, largely on the
basis of stylistic experiment.

In addition, Pearl was a woman who wrote mainly about the unglamorous
daily lives of women – a subject to which the men of the lost generation and
their champions were collectively indifferent. She also took religious questions
seriously, which linked her closely to most Americans but separated her from
the intellectual establishment.[4] Finally, her books were set in Asia, which made
them seem alien and merely exotic. For most American critics and academics,
Europe remained the place where significant cultural questions were asked and
answered.[5]

In the early months of her return, Pearl had a hard time adjusting to her new
country, which she found continually bewildering. Her daughter, Janice, one
day cannily remarked to her: "Mother, I guess you know a lot in China, but
when you are in America, you don't know *anything* hardly!" Pearl didn't argue
with Janice's eight-year-old wisdom. On the contrary, she saluted what she called
the "fatal penetration of the very young!"[6] At first, Pearl responded to the United
States more like an anthropologist than a settler, noting the distinctive and sometimes odd customs of the natives. Like an anthropologist, too, she usually tended
to keep a wary distance from her countrymen.

She was fascinated by the diversity of American life, the unmatched variety
of its landscapes, traditions, races, and religions. Beyond that, she noted the
enormous social contrasts: "Surely no country in the world can boast at the same
time so high a rate of college education and illiteracy, of high artistic culture,
and such complete primitive life . . . of wealth and terrifying poverty."[7]

On another occasion, she observed that white Americans had a peculiar smell.
She had lived so long among the Chinese and had eaten their food so consistently
that she ate very little meat and avoided milk and butter altogether. "Therefore
among my own people," she wrote, "I smelled a rank wild odor, not quite a
stink, but certainly distressing and even alien to me at the time, compound as it
was of milk and butter and beef. I remembered how my Chinese friends had
used to complain of the way white folk smelled, and so they did."[8] Pearl had
upended a favorite Anglo-Saxon stereotype: body odor as a bizarre sign of racial
superiority.[9]

As she groped her way into American attitudes and beliefs, Pearl was undoing
the misleading, patriotic lessons her mother had taught her as a child. For years
and years, as Carie dreamed of the American home she had lost, she had drilled
into her children the idea that the nation's reality was actually contained in its
celebratory myths and outsized heroes. America, she assured Edgar and Pearl and

Grace, was in literal fact a land of milk and honey, rooted in equality, ruled by just men. Pearl had spent enough time in the States to know that Carie's sentimental view was no more than a species of pleasant folklore. Still, like many immigrants, she believed resolutely in America's democratic aspirations, and each revelation of the gap between the nation's ideals and its day-to-day reality came as something of a shock.

This is to say that Pearl's progressive politics had been shaped, inadvertently, by Carie's tales of America. Pearl would spend the rest of her adult life trying to force America to live up to its own promises, to become the country Carie had told her about when she was a girl. Her exertions would do belated honor to her mother's memory. In that sense, reform would also be an act of restoration, in effect bringing the country back to the sanctity it had enjoyed in Carie's imaginings.

Pearl was fascinated by the American religion of consumption and by the advertising business that spread the gospel of materialism. She observed that in America everyone worshiped wealth, including intellectuals and would-be intellectuals, despite their pretenses to the contrary. She was repeatedly struck by the nervous, twitchy rhythm of American life, especially in the cities, and the frantic rate at which fashions came and went in everything from clothes to literature to architecture.

She found out more about the country's tragic racial divide. She read about the Scottsboro case, in which nine young Alabama blacks had been convicted of rapes they did not commit. The first trial had taken place in 1932; by the time Pearl left China for the United States, in 1934, the case had become a slowly unfolding tragedy, the subject of daily coverage in the Northern press.[10] She also attended an art show in Harlem that featured pictures of lynchings. She was appalled to discover that this brutal form of murder continued to be a common feature of American life.[11] Most Americans had become oblivious to the outrages, despite the fact that lynchings still occurred at the average rate of twenty-five every year during the 1920s and early 1930s.[12]

National politics remained meekly subservient to white Southern pressure.[13] Franklin D. Roosevelt, for example, calculated that he needed the support of senators and congressmen from the deep South to keep the New Deal moving forward. In partial payment, in his dozen years as president, he refused to lend any support to even the most feeble federal anti-lynching bills. To Pearl, such behavior was inexplicable.

She was, of course, especially interested in the condition of American women. They were usually better educated than women in China, and more likely to work outside the home. Nevertheless, they seemed to lack a clear perception of their identity and role. China's traditional society offered women the security of a time-honored if inferior status. In contrast, American women were being disoriented by profound but inconclusive changes. Pearl applauded the progress American women had made, from the right to vote, which they had only recently acquired, to the home appliances that saved middle-class women from domestic drudgery.

At the same time, while women could be replaced by machines in their homes, they were not welcome in the male domains of industry, politics, and commerce. So, without having gained a real foothold in the outside world, they were at the same time becoming marginal in their own families. The demands that many American women were making for equality collided with long-cherished cultural attitudes about the physical and intellectual superiority of men. Women were becoming restless, dissatisfied, and potentially explosive as well. Pearl would later coin the phrase "gunpowder women" to describe them.

Eventually, after she had educated herself in the culture of her new home, Pearl would turn to the stories of American women for her novels. Until then, she continued to draw on her experiences in China for fictional material. Her next book, *The Mother,* was the most ambitious attempt she had yet made to portray the life of a Chinese woman.

Pearl had written a first draft of the novel several years earlier, soon after completing *The Good Earth.* She had initially considered throwing the pages in the wastebasket. She claimed this was because she had doubts about the quality of what she had written.[14] That may be true, though she rarely discarded anything she wrote. More plausibly, she thought of suppressing the book because it veered perilously close to a personal confession, an unguarded glimpse into the secrets of her sexual and maternal frustrations. She said later that the model for the novel's protagonist was Li Sau-tse, her longtime Nanking housemaid. Another, unacknowledged, source was Pearl herself.

She might never have allowed the book to be published if Richard Walsh had not put her under exceptional pressure. In spite of the success of her earlier books, the John Day Company was losing money.[15] Pearl's own royalties, which were payable quarterly, were delayed several times, and the company's other creditors often went unpaid as well. Richard borrowed against his life insurance, laid off most of the staff, and began doing almost every job in the office himself. Pearl did what she could to help. She accepted her royalties on an erratic schedule, and she bought several hundred copies of *All Men Are Brothers* as expensive gifts for her relatives and friends.

These stratagems bought Richard a little breathing space. What he needed, however, was a new book from his leading writer. He pleaded with Pearl to give him something – anything – that he could use to increase revenues. She was working on a novel that would complete the trilogy begun in *The Good Earth* and *Sons,* but that book was progressing slowly. Against her own instincts to protect her privacy, she reluctantly sent the typescript of *The Mother* to Richard in late 1933.

Commercially, at least, it was a shrewd decision. Advance sales, which Richard described as "perfectly extraordinary," reached nearly 50,000 copies.[16] *Cosmopolitan* magazine paid $35,000 for serial rights. When the book appeared in late January, a date Richard chose to avoid a conflict with the new Sinclair Lewis novel, *Work of Art*, the reviews were generally good.[17] In a front-page notice in the *New York Times Book Review*, J. Donald Adams suggested that *The Mother* might be Pearl's best novel. He praised the book's "architectural unity" and its "driving simplicity and strength."[18] Most of the other reviews greeted *The Mother* with similar admiration. Brisk sales meant that, for the time being, the John Day Company could meet its obligations.

The Mother tells the story of its central character from the early years of her marriage to her old age. Like everyone in the novel, she is unnamed, perhaps an effort on Pearl's part to universalize her story.[19] She is a woman who is "all mother," as Dorothy Canfield put it, a mother because "her nature allows her to be nothing else," a study in maternity itself.[20]

In the novel's opening pages, the mother presides over a poor but productive farming family. She lives in a one-room, mud-walled home with her husband, her ancient mother-in-law, and her three children – two healthy sons and a daughter who is losing her sight. Her husband is a handsome but discontented man, unhappy with his bondage to the land. Early in the book, he deserts his family and never returns. To save face and protect herself from the cruel gossip of her neighbors, the wife has letters written to herself as if they were from her husband, and pays to have them delivered once each year.

The rest of the novel is a sustained portrait of loneliness, sexual frustration, and despair. Pearl drew on her own feelings of marital abandonment, and what she thought of as her maternal failure, as she delineated the corrosive sorrow that accompanies a lifetime of disappointment. The female character she created was always eager in sex, and longed for more pregnancies to enlarge her family with sons. Suddenly, she is condemned by circumstance and the customs of her culture to a permanent, unwanted celibacy. Her nostalgic recollections of intercourse and childbirth are overwritten and sometimes unconvincing, filled with Lawrentian talk of heat and hunger and thundering blood. Nevertheless, the remarkable candor and intensity of the prose suggest how much of Pearl's own intimate history is entangled with her character's story. Intrusively so, perhaps: in shaping the mother's psychology to serve her own therapeutic needs, Pearl superimposes a Westernized sexuality on a Chinese subject, and thus could be charged with the sort of cultural appropriation she usually avoided.

This mother is a woman of abundant fertility. Just once in the long years after her husband leaves, she yields to sexual temptation, with a landlord's agent, an oily figure out of melodrama, and she becomes pregnant:

Well she might have known that with her own body all hot and open and waiting as it had been, her mind all eaten up with one hunger, well she might have known it was such a moment as must bear fruit. And the man's body, too, so strong and good and full of its own power – how had she ever dreamed it could be otherwise?[21]

Ironically, this is a baby she cannot have. In one of the novel's most scarifying scenes, she drinks a powerful mixture of herbs to induce an abortion that nearly kills her. The cousin who helps her through the ordeal tells her that the child would have been male; she tells her as well that she will never conceive again.

The woman's plight has clear sources in Pearl's personal afflictions. Pearl, like the mother she invented, was a passionate woman whose sexual needs had been stifled and whose childbearing had ended in tragedy. Another connection between character and author is the fictional mother's only daughter, the source of some of her deepest anguish. Like Carol Buck, this child is damaged: she is the victim of an eye disease that gradually leaves her blind. The passages in which this girl is described, rubbing her sightless eyes in pain, or stumbling as she tries to be useful around the farm, or learning to use her walking stick and bells, are among the most moving Pearl ever wrote.

As she grows older, the girl becomes a burden to her older brother, the mother's elder son, who has married and is now head of the family. Unable to find an alternative, the mother agrees that her daughter will be married off to an impoverished family many miles away. The mother is fearful for her child, but finds little sympathy among her friends and kinfolk. As the village match-maker repeatedly reminds her, she should consider herself lucky to have found any husband at all for a blind daughter.

Not long afterward, the worried mother undertakes the long journey to visit her child. She is directed to a hillside hut, little more than a pigsty, where she finds that her daughter has died just hours earlier, after months of abuse and neglect. The wasted body lies on a rude table, surrounded by a family of filthy, threatening halfwits. The lurid scene comes directly out of Pearl's long immersion in Dickens, whose grotesque villains and tear-stained deathbeds always made up her favorite reading.[22]

The scene is the thematic center of the novel. The pathos of the dead, blind daughter not only recalls Dickens's techniques but also embodies what might be called Pearl's Dickensian morality. While she was radical in her ideas about race and gender, she was also in many obvious ways a belated Victorian, whose analysis of society was couched in familiar ethical categories. Or, to put it more precisely, she tended to evaluate political questions in personal, moral terms. George Orwell once wrote, in a famous passage, that "Dickens's whole message is one that at first glance looks like an enormous platitude: If men would behave decently the world would be decent."[23] Platitude or not, the remark was intended as praise, and it can apply to Pearl Buck as well. She lacked much of Dickens's versatility and nearly all his humor, but she shared his devotion to social justice and simple personal integrity.

The death of the blind daughter is not the final tragedy that the mother endures. Soon afterward, her younger son is arrested as a revolutionary and beheaded in a public courtyard. Two of her three children are dead, leaving her numb with grief. In the novel's last few pages, Pearl contrived a happy ending of sorts, compensation to the woman whose misfortunes echoed her own. As the mother sits on a grave mound near her village, mourning for her children and her own abandonment, she learns that her daughter-in-law has borne a son. The mother's suffering is redeemed in this new life, which ensures her claims on posterity.

ONCE PEARL DECIDED that her return to the United States was permanent, she set about finding a suitable place to live. She had installed herself in a rented apartment on East 52nd Street, overlooking the East River, but she wanted a home of her own. She knew that until she settled somewhere, she would continue to feel uprooted, a refugee from her past and a stranger in her own country. Furthermore, although she was still married to Lossing, she had already begun to sketch out her future life with Richard. She intended to adopt more children – lots of children, she often told her friends – and she wanted them to grow up outside the city, in a large house with open spaces around it.

Pearl had the money to live anywhere she chose. She was briefly attracted to the idea of moving back to the South, where she had been born, where her parents had grown up, and where she felt a slender claim of kinship. However, the South's perverse loyalty to segregation made it impossible for her to imagine family life there. "I could not live," she wrote, "where the colonial atmosphere prevailed, and where I would have always to look at signs to see where I belonged in railroad stations and restaurants."[24]

In a short time, she found what she was looking for: Green Hills Farm, an ill-preserved stone house in Bucks County, thirty miles north of Philadelphia. In her memoirs, written twenty years after she bought her home, Pearl carefully recorded that the farmhouse and its forty-eight surrounding acres cost $4,100 – a Depression-deflated bargain.[25] Since she was ordinarily secretive and vague about her financial transactions, the precision of this detail is surely significant. Pearl felt pride in her hard-earned independence. She no longer relied on any person or institution for support – neither parents, nor husband, nor missionary board.

Beyond that, she wanted it known that she was a good businesswoman, with a knack for getting her's money's worth. Green Hills Farm proved to be a superlative investment, multiplying more than twenty times in value over the thirty-five years she lived there. She turned the farm into the headquarters for half a dozen schemes, from publishing to filmmaking to children's welfare programs. In everything she took on, Pearl displayed an uncommon entrepreneurial aptitude and a prodigious appetite for work. She intended to prove, over and over again, that she could compete successfully in a man's world.

Her first major financial project was Richard. Because his business instincts were less certain than her own, she set out to help him in any way she could. She volunteered to become the John Day Company's principal literary advisor, in the hope that her editorial association with the press would attract new authors. She would have done the job for nothing, but Richard insisted that she accept a token annual stipend of $1,000.

More important, she sought out the most lucrative offers she could find for her own work, so that she could invest directly in John Day. In spite of the Depression, Pearl was one of several writers who could routinely command fees of $2,500 or $5,000 for a single story in such magazines as *Saturday Evening Post*, *Cosmopolitan*, and *Woman's Home Companion*. After her long years of threadbare living and facing heavy financial obligations, she found the money irresistible. Somewhat defensively, she claimed that the stories she produced under these circumstances were only potboilers. Many of them were. Whatever their literary merit, however, almost all of them comment usefully on Pearl's frame of mind at this moment in her life.

In particular, "Fool's Sacrifice," which Pearl sold to *Cosmopolitan* in the spring of 1934, is a revealing autobiographical document. The fool of the title is Freddy Hill, a British businessman stationed in Shanghai. He has been married for fifteen years to an Englishwoman named Marian. Freddy, who is conventional and utterly dull, believes that his marriage is blissfully happy.

The story opens with Marian's bitter revelation that she has in fact felt lonely and trapped since a week after her wedding, and that Freddy has simply been too stupid to detect her unhappiness. She also announces that she has found someone else, a more literary and interesting man whom she met on a recent visit to England. Because she takes her marriage vows seriously, she has returned to China to continue living as Freddy's wife. However, she warns him that she will never again have sexual relations with him. When he presses her about his "rights," she threatens to commit suicide if he touches her.

In the story's latter pages, Freddy rather generously acknowledges that he has indeed been insensitive and inadequate as a husband. He pretends that he has taken a lover, which frees Marian to return to England and start a new life. This is his sacrifice. When she gets on the boat in Shanghai harbor, "she seemed not wildly happy so much as dazed, as one is dazed when a long enduring pain is suddenly gone, or a load unexpectedly removed."[26]

Despite the loose-fitting English disguises, the parallels between Marian's situation and Pearl's are insistent. After fifteen years of stultifying marriage with a narrow-minded technician, Pearl, too, had fallen in love with a more cultivated man, and had refused to have any further sexual contact with her husband. Like Marian, she was compelled to redefine the limits of her marriage to meet her emotional needs.

In its plot, "Fool's Sacrifice" is little more than an unpleasant fragment of fictionalized recollection, as if Pearl had strip-mined her own experience to get something written as quickly as possible. However, the story's narrative technique makes the whole exercise a good deal more provocative. Everything is told from Freddy's point of view. When Marian rejects him, he sulks briefly, but then almost instantly concedes that he was not good enough for her, not clever enough, not capable of appreciating her gifts.

To put it bluntly, Pearl forces Freddy to confess, as Lossing never did, that the blame for his failed marriage lies solely with him. This is a wishful, even cold-blooded manipulation, which permits Marian, as Pearl's surrogate, to have it both ways. She can enjoy a fairy-tale happy ending with her new lover while also occupying the moral high ground: even her husband agrees that she is doing the right thing to leave him. Although Freddy's magnanimous reactions defy probability, Pearl presumably found her fable gratifying, since it permitted her to exact a kind of revenge against the man she blamed for ruining her middle years.

Lossing had stayed behind in China when Pearl and Janice returned to the United States. In his absence, Pearl and Richard spent even more time together, now talking quite frankly about the life they would share after both of them were divorced. They became partners in virtually everything they did. By September, Pearl had been named a shareholder in the John Day Company. She also assumed increasing responsibilities at *Asia* magazine.

Richard had taken over as editor of *Asia* with the January, 1934 issue, and moved the magazine's editorial headquarters to the John Day office at 40 East 49th Street.[27] In his inaugural issue, he published a high-minded statement of purpose, declaring that *Asia* was no longer going to be a tourist handbook. Aimed at readers who wanted serious reporting and analysis, the magazine would rely on experts to comment on Asian history, society, and culture. Richard promised that no subject, from ancient philosophy to contemporary politics, would be off limits, and that every question would be addressed with scholarly impartiality. *Asia* would "look upon Communism as objectively as upon art, and bring to a religious concept as open a mind as we bring to an economic problem."[28]

Richard's lofty point of view quickly led to both commercial and political trouble. Serious readers, for example Helen Foster Snow, congratulated him on "getting away from the pretty-pretty stuff."[29] His advertisers, on the other hand, especially the steamship lines and travel agencies promoting glamorous cruises to the mysterious, exotic East, were unhappy with Richard's turn toward sober realism. Similarly, his commitment to what he called an "international" rather than an "American" editorial policy, and his promise to use a larger number of Asian writers, caused predictable alarm in conservative quarters. And the magazine's evenhanded approach to Chinese and Russian Communism brought numerous complaints and threats.

Richard spent a good deal of time over the next few months defending himself. Despite the grumbling from Madison Avenue, *Asia* survived. Indeed, with an assist from events overseas, the magazine did quite well through the second half of the 1930s. In those years, while Americans still faced the problems of a lingering Depression, they reluctantly shifted some of their attention to Asia and Europe. Each day's headlines warned that another world war was becoming more likely. Within the space of a few years, Japan invaded Manchuria, Mussolini sent Italian armies into Ethiopia, Hitler unilaterally revoked the Versailles treaty by re-arming Germany and marching into the Rhineland and the Sudetenland, and Spain erupted in civil war.

Although most Americans were more interested in Europe than Asia, Japanese aggression provoked a growing demand for reliable reporting on Asian events and conditions. No other journal was as well positioned to take advantage of the situation as *Asia*. The magazine's subscription list expanded every time Japan made a saber-rattling statement or redeployed its troops.

As he promised, and with Pearl's help, Richard recruited a formidable list of well-known writers as contributors. Articles by Lin Yutang, Bertrand Russell, Lowell Thomas, and Charles Beard appeared in the first few months of Richard's tenure as editor, along with pieces by Owen Lattimore, whom Pearl had known in China, and Walter Duranty, the legendary fellow-traveler and Moscow bureau chief for the *New York Times* in the 1920s and 1930s. Notable women who wrote for the magazine included Agnes Smedley, Nym Wales (Helen Foster Snow), Margaret Mead, and Anna Louise Strong, who looked forward to the "rotting of capitalisms" in an article called "The Last Word in the Far East."[30] The magazine also carried fiction, including stories by Pearl herself and Rabindranath Tagore, the Indian writer who in 1913 had become the first Asian to win the Nobel Prize in literature.

Richard and Pearl stamped *Asia* with their cosmopolitan and generally liberal politics. The magazine was consistently anti-imperialist, arguing in a number of essays that both Eastern and Western interests would be well served by an end to the colonial system. An historic statement of this position was laid out in

Jawaharlal Nehru's "Prison Letters to Indira," which appeared in four installments in late 1934. Publishing this nationalist manifesto was a timely and rather brave gesture of support for Indian independence and the Congress Party, in a period when the mainstream American press lopsidedly endorsed Britain's continued colonial rule.

Pearl reaffirmed her commitment to Nehru when she reviewed his autobiography in *Asia* in 1936. After denouncing British imperialism as "unjust . . . relentless . . . cruel," Pearl saluted Nehru as a genuinely great leader, a visionary and revolutionist who opposed British madness with courage, integrity, and sanity.[31] Nehru and his influential sister, Mrs. Vijaya Lakshmi Pandit, repaid Pearl and Richard for their help by embracing them as lifelong friends.[32]

For the next decade, Pearl would continue her agitation for Indian independence. Shortly after publishing Nehru's prison letters, she used the occasion of a book review to make one of her most vigorous attacks on the British position in India. Commenting on *The White Sahibs in India*, by Reginald Reynolds, Pearl declared without flinching that the British treatment of India was comparable to Hitler's treatment of the Jews. She wrote that Great Britain was responsible for "one of the longest and cruelest tyrannies in human history."[33]

Along with colonialism, another of *Asia*'s principal topics was the condition of women in Asia. There were articles on women in Tibet and India, on the persistence of foot-binding in republican China, on the system of purdah among Muslims, on the family structure of New Guinea's tribes. An essay on "Birth Control in India" consisted of unabashed propaganda for contraception.[34] Another, on "The Traffic in Women," reported on a League of Nations conference devoted to the eradication of prostitution and child slavery.[35]

Aside from occasional stories, Pearl also contributed essays and book reviews. Her disappointment with Chiang Kai-shek's policies formed a major theme of much of this writing. For example, "Shanghai Scene," the fictional study of a university-educated man forced to take a job as a railroad guard, offers a sad glimpse of the growing gap between rhetoric and economic reality in contemporary China. Similarly, in a review of Tan Shih-hua's *Chinese Testament*, Pearl ridiculed the intellectual weaklings around Chiang who had helped deform the revolution into a self-serving and corrupt "bourgeois government."

Pearl believed that Chiang's regime had lost its way. She elaborated her case in a two-part essay, "The Creative Spirit in Modern China," which she published in *Asia* in the fall of 1934. The essay combines an effusive tribute to China's history and culture with a relentless attack on the failures and decadence of the revolution.

She had rarely written with such passion about the beauty of the Chinese people and their landscape. She called the people the most handsome in the world, the countryside the most beautiful. The "real beauty of China," she argued, was not to be found in the legendary mountains and picturesque lakes, made famous by generations of poets and painters, but in the commonplace scenery of farms and villages:

the somber crumbling tombs of the Mings turning slowly to brilliant dust under a glittering, heartless, blue sky; the sandy northern hills, the treeless walled cities set sharply square in the desert, the windswept plains . . . all sand-colored against the relentless sky; the gradually approaching green of Central China, the deepening pools and rivers, the treeless hills, jade-colored in spring against a soft sky, ruddy brown in autumn; the cobbled village streets, filthy to the sensitive western eye and nostril, but how rich in life and color to the appreciative human mind.

Perhaps Pearl had begun to acknowledge that she would not soon be returning to China, a country she had grown to love as her own: her catalogue of the Chinese sky and scenery has the affectionate tone of a backward glance. Beyond that, her tribute serves as an ironic preface to an indictment of China's current troubles. She felt that the nation under Chiang Kai-shek was paralyzed by corruption and chaos, that it had squandered its creativity and betrayed its own proud history.

Pearl's opinions were shared by many observers inside and outside China. Chiang himself had become disillusioned by the Kuomintang he headed, and was drifting toward fascism as a vehicle for strengthening his control. He created the Blue Shirts, an elite corps of men loyal to him personally, which was modeled on the Black Shirts and Brown Shirts of fascist Europe. In 1934, he inaugurated the New Life Movement, which tried to secure his rule in revived Confucian notions of piety and obedience. He invited officers of Nazi Germany to train his troops.[36] Chiang's embrace of totalitarianism and his stubborn preference for fighting Chinese Communists rather than Japanese invaders would ultimately prove fatal to his Nationalist government.

Since Pearl was recognized as one of America's leading China watchers, her reservations about Chiang attracted wide notice. Though she remained anti-Communist, she had reluctantly concluded that the Communists were more likely to win the allegiance of China's peasants. Chiang's inability to stop the corruption around him induced national cynicism, and his opportunistic conversion to Christianity, which helped to shore up his Western support, further alienated him from the Chinese people.

Pearl's criticisms of Chiang, together with her populist rhetoric and her sympathetic references to the world's struggling masses, earned her a reputation as a writer on the left. Mark Van Doren, for example, said that *The Mother* was the kind of novel "that many may write during decades to come when, happily or unhappily, classes are likely to be considered more interesting than individuals as material for fiction."[37] In fact, Pearl did not think of her work as definably left-wing, in particular because her experiences in China had made her a devout opponent of Communism. Nonetheless, she was sometimes labeled a "proletarian" writer.[38]

The cultural leadership of the Soviet Union apparently found Pearl's books and ideas congenial. In the early 1930s, she was one of the relatively few American writers whose work was admitted into Soviet Russia. At a time when Communist publishers were searching for writers who were entertaining as well as ideologically acceptable, Pearl joined an ill-assorted collection of novelists and journalists whose works were deemed worthy to be officially circulated. Along with Pearl, the list included John Dos Passos, Ernest Hemingway, Sherwood Anderson, Theodore Dreiser, Langston Hughes, and Agnes Smedley.[39]

BY MID-SUMMER OF 1934, it was evident that the financial problems facing the John Day Company had not been solved. After an encouraging two or three months, sales of *The Mother* slowed to a disappointing trickle. The company's big spring book, Franklin Roosevelt's *On Our Way*, also sold far fewer copies than Richard and Pearl had expected. Pearl's own income kept growing, but much of the money came from magazine sales and foreign royalties. She had already found the world audience that she would command for several decades. Her books were being translated into a dozen languages almost as soon as they appeared.

In the fall, Richard decided on a dramatic reorganization of the publishing operation, contracting with Reynal & Hitchcock to manufacture John Day's books. The arrangement subtracted from potential profits, but it saved the company from bankruptcy, and freed Richard from the job of production. Henceforth, he worked almost exclusively as an editor and publicist, selecting manuscripts and developing promotional campaigns.

Pearl had begun reading manuscripts as Richard's principal advisor. One of the first writers she signed up for John Day was the Chinese expatriate scholar and critic, Lin Yutang, whose work had already appeared in *Asia*. His first book, *My Country and My People*, an urbane and stylish survey of Chinese culture, was a surprising best-seller.[40] The Walshes became close friends with Lin and his wife, who stayed at Green Hills Farm while they looked for a place to live. When the Lins were denied housing in Princeton because a professor's wife would not rent to a Chinese, Pearl reported to Emma White that she "got perfectly furious and wrote a terrific letter to the woman," attacking her for her "appalling ignorance," her "superstitions and prejudices."[41] To her sister Grace she wrote even more angrily: "I *loathe* the American woman!"[42]

Between her writing, reading, and correspondence, Pearl sometimes worked fourteen or sixteen hours a day. She put in long hours because she enjoyed being busy and because she was well paid for her literary labors. In addition, her crowded schedule shielded her from some of the continuing tumult in her private life. She was still "sore to the touch," as she frequently described it, about Carol, and bitter about Lossing. Furthermore, she was now helping her sister Grace cope with a tragedy in her own life. Grace's new baby, a daughter named Anne, had been seriously injured during delivery. Several specialists had examined the child and concluded that she would be permanently crippled. Grace was inconsolable and Pearl was lavishing support and advice on her younger sister.

The episode is worth pausing over, because it discloses something of Pearl's strengths and weaknesses. Her formidable competence often disabled those around her, and her impatience could add to the burdens of those she set out to help. When Anne had been born, Grace and her husband Jesse were stationed in a small village mission in inland China. Obstetric care was largely in the hands of the village's Chinese doctor, half-trained in Western medicine. Grace had often encouraged her Chinese women friends to use this doctor, as an alternative to the practitioner of traditional herbal medicine. As the time for her baby's birth neared, Grace faced what she regarded as a moral dilemma: whether to rely on the local man or travel to Peking to take advantage of the excellent facilities at Peking Union Medical College (PUMC), the finest Western medical center in China.

Pearl strongly urged Grace to go to Peking and get the best care she could. What Grace interpreted as an ethical choice, Pearl dismissed as irrelevant scruple. In the end, Grace used the local doctor, largely as a sign of solidarity with the Chinese women in her village. The result was calamitous. The baby took a transverse position just before birth and was mutilated in the delivery. The doctors at PUMC would undoubtedly have handled the emergency more competently.

Talking about the events nearly sixty years later, Grace insisted that when she informed her sister of the tragic outcome, "Pearl was lovely about it; she never said anything that intimated, you know, 'I told you so.' " But Grace felt that Pearl's silence was saturated with disapproval. When Grace returned to the States with Anne a few months later, Pearl briskly took charge. She provided housing for mother and daughter and arranged for a battery of tests. She was efficient, useful, indispensable. Grace was pathetically grateful, but she had been lacerated by Pearl's unspoken judgment. In this case and in many others, it proved hard to be Pearl's younger sister. "All the time," Grace said, "it was always superior – inferior. And this finally had quite a psychological effect on me, years later."[43]

Pearl treated her brother Edgar with the same combination of detachment and efficiency. In spite of a bad heart, alcoholism, and a failed private life, Edgar had done important work at the Milbank Memorial Fund and in the United States Public Health Service. He was a pioneer in the science of epidemiology, experimenting in the application of statistics to disease control. Among other accomplishments, Edgar had published a major study of pellagra among South Carolina mill workers that had identified the link between the disease and nutritional problems. In 1934, he was hired by the Committee on Economic Security of the U.S. Congress and helped draft the legislation that would eventually become the Social Security Act.

At Pearl's invitation, he moved into a separate house on the Green Hills property, but the arrangement led to tension and hard feelings on both sides. Pearl kept urging Edgar to get a grip on himself and put his life in order. Pearl didn't conceal her disappointment with her brother's weakness; Edgar resented what he understood to be his sister's insensitive interference.

It seems clear that Pearl's capacity for spontaneous affection had been truncated by the loneliness she had suffered for so many years as daughter and wife. Like many philanthropists, she was tenaciously committed to the welfare of humanity in general, but she had trouble in returning the love of the people around her, including her own children. Her oldest adopted child, Janice, sadly acknowledged that Pearl's multitudinous responsibilities often prevented her from nurturing her own family. "Although she provided for our material needs," Janice later recalled, "she often did not have the time to take care of our emotional needs. . . . And even when she had time to spend with us, I often felt that she lived in another world from ours, and really did not understand simple, everyday family life."[44]

Pearl's habit of self-reliance had cut her off from the circle of ordinary affection. Her fierce struggle to establish and sustain her independent identity brought an immense success, but at the cost of permanent isolation. Here, then, was another reason for Pearl's ever-lengthening schedule: her myriad tasks stood between her and emotional demands she did not feel prepared to satisfy.

Only Richard proved a partial exception to this generalization: from the beginning of his relationship with Pearl, he was admitted to an intimacy that others were denied. His privileged access had its deepest source in the affection and mutual admiration these two remarkable people felt for each other. Friends like Helen Foster Snow remarked that when Pearl and Richard were together, they were always completely absorbed in each other, joined in a bond of friendship that was nourished by shared interests and energized by an unmistakable erotic charge.[45] Beyond that, Pearl was grateful for Richard's tireless devotion to her career. Most men are unable to accept women whose fame overshadows their own. Richard, on the contrary, submerged himself for nearly three decades in the job of promoting Pearl's success.

The closing days of 1934 were typically hectic. Domestic troubles occupied much of Pearl's time. Janice had broken out in mysterious spots, and Pearl had spent $300 on doctors, only to be told that the ten-year-old girl was approaching adolescence and needed "plenty of nourishing food!" Even more irritating, Lossing suddenly returned to the States in December for a conference at the U.S. Treasury. He demanded several meetings with Pearl, including one at Vineland. Pearl's response: "I'll get through somehow."[46] In a happier episode, Pearl met Helen Keller, "to my great excitement," as she said. She found Keller to be a "marvelous, eager, sensitive personality bursting through" the barriers of her handicaps.

Just after Christmas, Pearl delivered two prestigious lectures, one at the University of Chicago, where she had been personally invited to speak by President Robert M. Hutchins, the other at Yale. In the Yale lecture, called "Advice to Unborn Novelists," Pearl offered the warning that novelists should arrange to grow up in their own country. In her own case, she said, her years in China had made her an expert in materials that most Americans weren't interested in. She also acknowledged that her childhood immersion in the Chinese language had made her permanently uncomfortable with idiomatic English.

The lecture was generally lighthearted, except in its references to the missionary community. She told her audience that even as a girl she had chosen Kwan yin, the Buddhist goddess of mercy, over the jealous, angry God of the Bible. This, Pearl said, was her main advice to a novelist: "do not be born under the shadow of a great creed, not under the burden of original sin, not under the doom of salvation. Go out and be born among gypsies or thieves or among happy workaday people who live in the sun and do not think about their souls."[47]

In January, 1935, Reynal & Hitchcock published Pearl's latest novel, *A House Divided,* the final volume of the trilogy that had begun with *The Good Earth* and continued with *Sons.* A chronicle of the third generation of the Wang family, *A House Divided* extended Pearl's inquiry into China's civil wars and the consequences of national turmoil for individual men and women. The novel's main character, Wang Yuan, son of Wang the Tiger and grandson of *The Good Earth's* Wang Lung, sets out to be a scholar and poet, rejecting his father's rough and dangerous military vocation for a life of learning and refinement.

Wang Yuan represents Young China, the rising generation trapped between the future and the past, disillusioned equally by Confucius, Chiang Kai-shek, and Communism – youthful men and women unable to make any lasting commitments at all. Though Wang Yuan is intelligent and introspective, he is ultimately paralyzed by ambivalence and indecision. He dabbles in revolution, but cannot embrace revolutionary certitude or violence. He is appalled by the sufferings of the peasants, but cannot quite believe that the peasants are fully human. He spends six years in the United States, graduating at the top of an American university class, but in the end he knows that most of his book learning is useless in China's chaotic circumstances.

In short, in the midst of China's great crisis, Wang Yuan is unable to act usefully, or even to imagine what a useful course of action might be. He is a casualty of history. As such, he embodies Pearl's growing skepticism about China's future. The abolition of the ancient monarchy had brought only warfare and disorder. Neither Wang Yuan nor his contemporaries were equipped to build a meaningful future.

In particular, the debates and manifestos that Young China indulged in were irrelevant to the millions of China's poor people, the masses whose misery had not been relieved by twenty years of warfare and political maneuvering. Some of the most vivid passages in *A House Divided* represent the plight of the urban and rural poor. This scene, describing the hordes of poverty-stricken peasants living in houseboats on the Yangtze River near Nanking, crushed by the August heat, evokes the squalor in which the Chinese masses were trapped:

This was the eighth month of the year, and though it was scarcely more than dawn the day was thick with heat. There was no great light from the sun, the sky was dark and low with clouds, pressing down so that it seemed to cover the water and the land, and there was no least wind anywhere. In the dull sluggish light the people pushed their boats aside to make way for the ferry, and men scrambled out of little hatches, nearly naked, their faces sunk and sodden with the sleepless night of heat, and women screamed at crying children and scratched their tangled hair, and naked children wailed, hungry and unwashed. These crowded tiny boats held each its fill of men and women and many children, and from the very water where they lived and which they drank the stench arose of filth they had poured into it.[48]

China's long-suffering common people remained Pearl's principal concern.

As usual, the critics were generally kind to Pearl's new book. Admiring, page-long notices in the *New York Times* and *New York Herald Tribune* were typical of the friendly response the novel evoked around the country. Even readers not disposed in Pearl's favor found reasons to praise the authenticity of her Chinese portraits. Malcolm Cowley, for example, compared *A House Divided* with *Man's Fate*, André Malraux's powerful story of Chinese revolutionaries who die for their beliefs. Cowley preferred Malraux's politics and his more sophisticated prose style. At the same time, he confessed that Pearl's lifelong acquaintance with China made Malraux and other Western writers seem "like tourists dropping ashore from a round-the-world cruise."[49]

In an era of criticism that placed special value on authenticity, this was high praise, and Pearl had earned it. For her part, she was more like a tourist in America. Wang Yuan's sojourn in the United States memorializes Pearl's own eager but bewildered encounter with her new country. His experiences make up a catalogue of the virtues, vices, and peculiarities that Pearl discovered when she returned to her native land. Like Pearl, Wang Yuan is shocked by the racism of white Americans and offended by their slightly goatish smell. On the other hand, and again like Pearl, he is enchanted by the American landscape, fascinated by the changing roles of American women, and attracted by the energy and optimism of ordinary citizens.

The autobiographical implications of the novel were transparent. Reviewing *A House Divided* in the *New York Herald Tribune,* Pearl's old friend Lewis Gannett said that "between the lines, one descries . . . the story of a repatriated American." For Gannett, this made the book more valuable and more timely, he said, because "We are all coming home, rediscovering America."[50]

Gannett was reporting accurately on one of the most significant cultural developments of the 1930s. American myths of equality and limitless opportunity had been unsettled by the shock of the Depression. The nation's collective anxiety provoked an energetic search for America, in which dozens of writers traveled the country, sought out ordinary citizens, and filled a library shelf with their findings. Sherwood Anderson's *Puzzled America* (1935), Edmund Wilson's *American Jitters* (1932), Theodore Dreiser's *Tragic America* (1931), and Dorothea Lange and Paul Taylor's *An American Exodus* (1939): these were just a few of the books that resulted from the national introspection. Like Pearl, all of these writers were "rediscovering America."[51]

Pearl's repatriation brought her closer to Richard and Carol, but it also precipitated an unexpected crisis in her writing. While she had enjoyed tremendous success for her novels about China, she also knew that China was now part of her past. She believed that novelists should make use of the materials they know best, what she called their "everyday environment."[52] For her, that now meant America. These aesthetic opinions were reinforced by commercial calculations. She suspected that the American public would quickly lose its appetite for stories set in Asia. After all, her own first success had been anomalous – she had been the first and only American novelist to publish a best-seller about China – and her sales had recently declined. In mid-1935, trying to make whatever additional profits she could from her China fictions, she republished *A House Divided,* together with *The Good Earth* and *Sons,* in a one-volume trilogy under the collective title *The House of Earth.* Sales were not encouraging.

Pearl decided that her next book should be set in America, but she felt unready for the task.[53] In rapid succession, she produced a sequence of American stories, including "Now and Forever," a thin harlequin romance serialized in *Woman's Home Companion.* She also wrote a fictional confession of her own marital troubles that included a heartbreaking portrait of Carol. Richard and Dorothy Canfield Fisher worried that the book would cause unwanted controversy, especially for its unflattering accounts of Lossing's parents. Pearl agreed to put the book aside, though she refused to destroy it. Thirty years later, she published the novel under the title *The Time Is Noon.*

She kept writing steadily during her first American years, but her published work was restricted mainly to nonfiction and occasional stories. Many of her essays and book reviews appeared in *Asia,* where she was increasingly active as an editor and contributor. In February, 1935, she published a political survey called "The Rulers of China," in which she repeated the warning she had been making for a decade: unless the revolution reached the common people, it could never succeed.

In April, Pearl took charge of the "Asia Book-Shelf" column for the magazine, assigning books for review and writing many of the notices herself. Over the following months, she commented on dozens of works of fiction and non-fiction. She did a prodigious amount of reading for each monthly issue. In the April column alone, she reviewed seven books, including Nathaniel Peffer's *Must We Fight in Asia?* Drew Pearson's *The American Diplomatic Game,* Reginald Johnston's *Confucianism and Modern China,* and Vincent Sheean's *Personal History.*

Pearl was also much in demand as a lecturer. Under Richard's watchful eye, she accepted only a few invitations, choosing settings and subjects that interested her. One such request led to an important speech at a fund-raising dinner in Washington, D.C., sponsored by the National Committee on Federal Legislation for Birth Control. The dinner was a tribute to Margaret Sanger, whom Pearl described as "one of the most courageous women of our times," who had led "the most important movement" of the twentieth century.[54] Pearl assured her audience that the battle for birth control would soon be won, freeing women from one more sign of their servitude and second-class status. In particular, poor women would welcome the protection that dependable and affordable contraception would bring.

As a child and woman in China, Pearl had personally witnessed the poverty and maternal suffering associated with uncontrolled pregnancies and births. She constantly sought medical advice on contraceptives that would be safe, relatively reliable, and above all cheap and easy to use. The Chinese, she explained, needed a contraceptive that would "cost almost nothing" and be simple. She described a new contraceptive device that she thought would be especially useful for poor Chinese women: "simply a chemical mixed with water and a small sponge soaked in it. It costs almost nothing and would be extremely practicable . . . even for very poor people." This last point was especially important to Pearl, because she was not interested in "providing contraceptives for well-to-do people" or "birth control for the upper classes."[55]

SOMETIME IN THE SPRING of 1935, Pearl concluded that her long marital stalemate had to be resolved. She traveled to Washington for several unpleasant meetings with Lossing, who was working as a consultant to Treasury Secretary Henry Morgenthau.[56] In April, Pearl wrote to Emma that she would soon be leaving for Reno to get her divorce. She described the arrangements she intended

17. Pearl, Margaret Sanger, and Katharine Houghton Hepburn at a dinner in Sanger's honor in 1935. (Courtesy Bettman Archives.)

to make: "I am giving Lossing the furniture in both the Chinese house and Duchess County farmhouse and will help him some financially if necessary. He will have good homes at both ends of the world." Pearl's bitterness was unrelieved by the prospect of freedom: "I ask nothing of him for myself and the children, only ask, that is, not to have to live with him. He has never seen or understood anything."[57]

Somewhat remarkably, Pearl traveled to Reno with Ruby Walsh, who had agreed to Richard's request for a divorce. The two women shared lodgings throughout the six weeks required by Nevada law to establish their local residence. Pearl passed some of the time in the hands of a masseuse named Madame Kolak — whom she later recalled as "the largest woman I had ever seen" — trying to lose a few of the extra pounds she had put on since returning to America.[58]

On June 12, 1935, the *New York Times* carried the news of Pearl's divorce from Lossing Buck and her marriage two hours later to Richard Walsh. Pearl, who attended the divorce proceedings wearing a white summer dress, a cape and a blue straw hat, borrowed a cigarette and smoked "nervously" throughout the hearing.[59] The Bucks' marriage was dissolved in twenty minutes, the Walshes' in five. For the record, Pearl filed a charge of incompatibility against Lossing, and Ruby charged Richard with cruelty.

Some of the tabloids titillated their readers by speculating on the love affair that presumably preceded Pearl's speedy new marriage. Pearl grandly insisted that she was indifferent to such gossip. She knew that the hasty scene in the Reno courtroom was merely the final chapter in a story of marital suffering that went back nearly two decades. In a letter that she wrote to Emma White the day before her divorce and remarriage, Pearl referred to the strain she had been under for so long. "Some day," she added, "I shall put into a book the wickedness of a marriage without love, the evil that comes from it."[60]

To Margaret Thomson, her old friend and neighbor from Nanking, Pearl wrote that she was really happy "for the first time in my life . . . I have everything right – at the center – now."[61] She and Richard spent a few days in Lake Tahoe and then returned to the East Coast. Ten-year-old Janice, who had previously referred to Richard as "Uncle Dick," was instructed to call him "Daddy" from now on. Always eager to oblige, Janice suppressed her misgivings and complied.[62]

As usual, Pearl refused to talk in public about her personal life. However, in her "Asia Book-Shelf" column for June, which was published in the same month as her divorce, she made a coded statement about her feelings. One of the books she reviewed was *I Change Worlds,* Anna Louise Strong's memoir of her life as a radical. Pearl commended Strong for persuasively explaining the appeal that Communism had for young idealists around the world. However, she distanced herself from the book's romantic conclusion, in which Strong describes how her political commitment was energized by love and marriage. Pearl reacted argumentatively: "We are not quite satisfied to realize that Miss Strong does not really change her world until she marries. Is this an answer for modern women?" Answering that rhetorical question from the vantage point of her own experience, Pearl concluded, "There are many for whom it cannot be."

Pearl had long since come to believe that a woman must locate her identity in herself, outside the assorted relationships and roles that are implied and usually dictated by her gender. It was an insight Pearl had achieved by way of her own experience. She welcomed the companionship and intimacy that a good marriage could bring, but she refused to define herself in terms of her husband. American women, she said in a short article she wrote at this time, were "only just beginning to be liberated from that most insidious of prisons, the prison of chivalry."[63] Pearl wanted equality, not the systematic discrimination that masquerades as the "spurious nobility" of special treatment. Chivalry, Pearl suggested, allows men to feel virtuous because they pick up a woman's handkerchief while denying her a job for which she is qualified.

As she had expected, Pearl's divorce and remarriage was treated as a scandal in conservative circles. Presbyterians pelted their leaders with demands that Pearl be somehow punished. Courtenay Fenn, secretary of the Foreign Mission Board, sent a letter of condolence to Lossing, in which he declared that Pearl's "literary talent, misused as I have always felt, has been her undoing." Fenn concluded his note, somewhat sanctimoniously, by assuring Lossing that "We are all ready to pray that she may be forgiven if, some day, she comes to herself and asks forgiveness of God and man."[64] Had she had known of it, Pearl would have found Fenn's presumption intolerable.

Even secular institutions were caught up in the reaction. A few months before the divorce, President Clarence Barbour of Brown University had offered to confer an honorary Doctor of Letters degree on Pearl at the June, 1935 commencement. (Barbour had been a member of the Hocking Commission, which had produced *Re-Thinking Missions,* and had met Pearl in Nanking.) When the divorce became a widely publicized event, Barbour confessed his relief that Pearl considerately withdrew from the occasion. We "would be greatly embarrassed," Barbour wrote to Dean Margaret Morriss of Pembroke College, if Pearl were to come to Brown while her personal life was front-page news.[65]

The University of Virginia was less squeamish. When Pearl offered to cancel a long-scheduled pair of lectures at the university's Institute of Public Affairs, she was told to come as planned: "This is an Institute of Public Affairs, not private affairs."[66]

Her first talk, "Conflict and Cooperation," argued that ideology had overtaken nationalism as a cause of world tension. This was a widely shared view in the supercharged atmosphere of the 1930s. The conflicts of the present day, Pearl said, which appeared to be struggles between nations, actually involved competing systems of economic and political organization. Japan's pottery, China's silk, and Ceylon's rubber all symbolized the international competition for access to resources, labor, and markets. Pearl predicted that the battles of the future among Communism, fascism, and democracy would be latter-day religious wars, and therefore "the most bitter and cruel wars of all."[67]

Later on the same day, Pearl gave another talk, this one on differences between East and West. Imagine, she said, a hypothetical situation, in which a young man tries to save a drowning stranger and loses his own life in the attempt. If the man is American, he will be considered a hero, who has brought honor to his grieving family. If the man is Chinese, on the contrary, he will have behaved shamefully, since he owes his life to his parents, and other loyalties are subordinate or non-existent.

Pearl uses this example to illustrate two important ideas. First, neither the Chinese nor the American system is superior; each quite adequately expresses ideals and values that are anchored in historical experience. Second, the contrasts between East and West are not based on race, a concept that is "extraordinarily meaningless in explaining fundamental differences."[68]

Pearl's analysis reflected and reinforced the more enlightened cultural theories of the mid-1930s. Under the influence of progressive social scientists like anthropologist Franz Boas, Americans were gradually coming to embrace relativizing, non-racial explanations of cultural difference. This was an important development. For nearly a century, European and American science had collaborated in affirming theories of racial superiority and inferiority.[69]

The decisive change in that barbarous point of view occurred in the 1930s.[70] Henceforward, racism would continue to flourish in the back alleys of the American imagination, but it would no longer have the support of science, as it had throughout the nineteenth century and the first decades of the twentieth. In her essays and lectures, Pearl made a significant – and generally unacknowledged – contribution to that epochal transformation.

In 1937, for example, she wrote an admiring review of Jacques Barzun's *Race: A Study in Modern Superstition,* in which she rebuked "our absurd modern belief in the inherent superiority of one race over another." From an anthropological point of view, she insisted, "there is no basis for the superstition."[71] She went further, pointing out that race could not even be defined in any scientific, consistent, or rational way.[72] In another review, Pearl argued that, even if the term "race" could be adequately defined, there are no pure examples, because "miscegenation is going on constantly between all peoples." Similarly, "there is no such thing . . . as a pure culture"; all cultures are hybrids and amalgams.[73] This opposition to racist hierarchies would become a major theme of Pearl's writing through the rest of her American career.

A week after her two talks at Virginia, Pearl was the principal speaker at a summer seminar on Chinese and Japanese Studies at Columbia University. Typically, in these appearances, as in her lectures at Yale and the University of Chicago, she was asked to comment on quite broad issues affecting China and its relations with the West. Pearl had earned an enviable status, not merely as a popular writer, but as an acknowledged expert on Asia. Over the next two decades, she would exert more influence over Western opinions about Asia than any other American; her only competitor was Henry R. Luce, founder and publisher of *Time* magazine, whose parents had also been Presbyterian missionaries in China.[74]

In the summer of 1935, "while governments prepare for approaching war," as she put it in one of her "Asia Book-Shelf" columns, Pearl associated herself with the peacemakers.[75] An exchange of letters with Mabel Vernon over the summer initiated Pearl's long association with the Women's International League for Peace and Freedom. She signed the "Peoples' Mandate," a petition circulated by WILPF that demanded an end to the arms race and a world treaty on disarmament. And she spoke on behalf of the Mandate on NBC's International Broadcast in September.[76]

Pearl never embraced pacifism. She supported the Chinese in their war against Japanese aggression, and, after Pearl Harbor, she endorsed American entry into World War II. However, even in wartime she remained deeply suspicious of militarism, considering it a form of "degeneration." She wrote, only half-facetiously, that "some recessive strain appears" in the military mind, which makes it blind to all reason and humanity.[77]

Along with her speeches on behalf of world peace and birth control, Pearl continued to work with human rights organizations. In August, she participated in an Institute of Human Relations at Williams College, sponsored by the National Conference of Christians and Jews. The particular focus of the institute was the role of women in the effort to build harmony among religious groups. Eleanor Roosevelt also attended, at Pearl's personal invitation.

In October, she asked Elmer Carter, editor of the Urban League's magazine, *Opportunity,* to send her a package of materials on racial discrimination in labor unions.[78] Her efforts to open unions to black membership would continue over the next decade, in particular during World War II, when she repeatedly attacked organized labor for excluding African-Americans at a time when black soldiers were dying in Europe and Asia.

Increasingly, Pearl also turned to the conflicted experience of Asian-Americans as one of her subjects. Reviewing a history of San Francisco's Chinatown, she remarked on "the shocking persecutions" which Chinese have suffered on American soil. The history of Asians in America, she wrote, has been a sad chronicle of "robbery, injustice, pillage, murder and massacre." Enjoying the irony, she turned missionary rhetoric upside-down, calling the nation's treatment of its Asian population "as heathen a tale as any to be found."[79]

Pearl's political activism enhanced the notoriety that had come with her sexually candid novels, her dispute with the missionary establishment, and her divorce. Her books still generated controversy. In the fall of 1935, the Kansas City Superintendent of Schools removed *The Good Earth* from a list of suggested readings. He acted on the complaint of a Mrs. E. B. McCann, who said that Pearl's novel was "filth": the kind of book that used to be read "behind the barn."[80]

Publicity of this sort did Pearl no harm, of course. While she was banned in Kansas City, she was frequently the guest of honor at literary luncheons and teas in New York, Philadelphia, Washington, and New Haven. In mid-October, she was toasted at a reception at New York's Pen and Brush Club, a women's literary society. After Pearl spoke to the members on the subject of "The Proletarian

Novel," club president Ida M. Tarbell declared breathlessly that the presentation was "the finest talk on writing she had listened to in a generation."[81]

A few weeks later, under the auspices of the League for Political Education, Pearl gave a lecture comparing Chinese and American society at Town Hall. She was one of several prominent speakers on the League's fall program. Other lecturers and their topics included Dorothy Thompson, discussing contemporary European politics, John Mason Brown, who surveyed the Broadway scene, and Amelia Earhart, whose title was "My Flight from Hawaii to California."

Just before Thanksgiving, Pearl received the cheering news that the American Academy of Arts and Letters had awarded her the prestigious Howells Medal for *The Good Earth*. Named for William Dean Howells, the Academy's first president, the medal was given each fifth year "in recognition of the most distinguished work of American fiction published during that period." (Pearl received the third Howells Medal; the two previous recipients had been Mary Wilkins Freeman and Willa Cather.)[82]

Novelist Robert Grant, in presenting the award, commended Pearl for having given "the intelligent world a far better understanding of the common man in China than it ever had before." Glancing at the debates currently thrashing America's literary waters, Grant added: "Except that I abhor the term as used by some in these United States to distort art, [*The Good Earth*] is a proletarian novel in the best sense. The author . . . takes life as it is."[83] Pearl made a brief, graceful response, thanking the Academy for another demonstration of America's "generous, often too generous, recognition" of her work. Tactfully, she didn't enumerate the writers she had competed with in taking the award: in the five years between 1930 and 1935, Ernest Hemingway, F. Scott Fitzgerald, John Dos Passos, William Faulkner, and Thomas Wolfe had all published major novels.

A few weeks after she won the Howells Medal, Pearl was honored again by the American Academy, which elected her to membership in the National Institute of Arts and Letters. This was the sort of upscale recognition she particularly longed for, since it suggested that she was earning at least some respect from literary tastemakers. She accepted the distinction with thanks, and made another visit to the Academy headquarters for her induction.

The early months of 1936 were also brightened by the reviews and revenues earned by Pearl's latest book, *The Exile*. This was her biography of Carie, which she had written fifteen years earlier, as a way of coping with her mother's death. Out of respect for Absalom, who is treated harshly in the story, she waited to publish it until a few years after he died. Critics and public alike met the book with unanimous enthusiasm, restoring Pearl's confidence in her work and temporarily repairing the beleaguered finances of the John Day Company.

The Exile earned such a stunning success that Pearl immediately wrote a sequel, a biography of her father called *Fighting Angel*. Richard made a shrewd deal with the Book-of-the-Month Club, which published a special boxed edition of both biographies and offered the package to members for $2.75 (just over half the list price of $5.00). The collective title of the two volumes, invented by Richard, was *The Flesh and the Spirit*. Through these books, Pearl paid public tribute to her mother and settled old accounts with her father. In spite of her unconcealed partisanship, however, Pearl created one of the most richly detailed and evocative narrative accounts ever written of the missionary world. *The Exile* and *Fighting Angel* are monuments to the story of Protestant evangelism in China, a vital but neglected chapter in American cultural history.

Pearl's biographies of her parents appeared within a year of her divorce and remarriage. These events, together with her brother Edgar's death in March, 1936, effectively brought her old life to a close. She began to order her new life almost immediately, when she and Richard adopted two children in the spring of 1936. She was forty-three, Richard was fifty, and, as she said in a letter to Margaret Thomson, "Lots of my friends think this is insane."[84] Nonetheless, after consulting with Janice, and then subjecting themselves to the customary intrusions of social workers, the Walshes traveled to The Cradle in Evanston, Illinois, where they picked up two infant boys. The babies were both one month old; Pearl and Richard named their new sons Richard Stulting Walsh and John Stulting Walsh. A year later, two more adopted children were added to the family, a boy named Edgar and a girl named Jean.

Rather suddenly, the Walsh family had grown from four (counting Carol) to eight. The costs of food, clothing, and child care rapidly mounted. In addition, Pearl also continued to maintain two residences, an apartment at 480 Park Avenue and Green Hills Farm, where she had begun extensive renovations, adding bedrooms for the children and libraries and work rooms for Richard and herself. More than ever, she needed the sort of money that popular magazines, foreign sales, and the Book-of-the-Month Club represented. In the years from 1935 through 1937, Pearl's income ranged between $50,000 and $70,000 annually.

At the same time, she was always willing to accept speaking engagements without fee when she found the setting interesting or the cause deserving. In April, 1936, Pearl gave a lecture in front of 2,500 people at Constitution Hall in Washington, with the proceeds benefiting the research department of the Vineland Training School. Talking from a handful of notes held together by a safety pin, Pearl held the stage for over an hour, entertaining her audience with anecdotes and personal recollections.

She set out, as she said, to demystify China and to suggest likenesses between Chinese and Americans. Both peoples, she said, were materialistic, pragmatic, undisciplined, instinctively democratic. In contrast, the Japanese resembled the British: authoritarian, insular, devoted to monarchy and aristocracy, ambitious

18. Richard and Pearl with their new sons, Richard and John. (Reproduced with permission of the Pearl S. Buck Foundation.)

for empire.[85] In short, it was not some racial essence that defined a people's identity – some essential Oriental or Caucasian characteristics – it was geography, culture, and collective experience.

Pearl was introduced at Constitution Hall by Eleanor Roosevelt, who had also presided over a White House dinner in the Walshes' honor before the lecture. Pearl reported that the menu was quite simple: corn soup, pork chops, apple sauce, cauliflower, string beans, lettuce and tomato salad, and floating island for dessert. A couple of months later, Pearl invited Roosevelt to speak at Vineland, but the pressures of the 1936 presidential campaign made the visit impossible.

While she was eager to take on fund-raising responsibilities for Vineland, Pearl was still unwilling to see Carol mentioned in news stories or press releases. An-

19. Pearl at Green Hills Farm in the mid-1930s. (Reproduced with permission of the Pearl S. Buck Foundation.)

other fifteen years would pass before Pearl would publicly acknowledge her retarded daughter. In September, 1936, the *Akron Times* carried an interview with Mrs. W. C. Lowdermilk, who had been one of Pearl's neighbors at Nanking University in the 1920s. Lowdermilk talked about Carol's condition in considerable and painful detail. Pearl, who was still trying to maintain a wall of silence around Carol, did what she could to discredit and suppress the story.

Pearl's volunteer work for the Vineland Training Center helped her to cope with her lingering grief over Carol's condition. Along with raising money for research on retardation, Pearl also spent a good deal of time analyzing Vineland's instructional programs. She had been a teacher herself. Now, with six children, she had become an advocate for schools and learning. She believed that personal growth and meaningful work both depended on a good education.

In particular, she argued that quality education was crucial to the aspirations of those who were disadvantaged by handicap or race or sex. In early 1937, Pearl published an essay called "On the Cultivation of a Young Genius" in *Opportunity,* the journal of the Urban League. Sounding like W. E. B. Du Bois, who had called upon the "talented tenth" to take responsibility for the African-American struggle, Pearl connected the fate of all societies to the leadership of their most gifted members.[86] Pearl described a Chinese custom that both African-Americans and American Caucasians might fruitfully imitate. When a gifted child is born into a Chinese village, the townspeople erect a stone arch in celebration:

20. Eleanor Roosevelt and Pearl on the evening of Pearl's Constitution Hall speech in April, 1936. (Courtesy Bettman Archives.)

"not for the child's sake," but in the hope "that he might use his matured ability for all the people of the village and of the nation." Pearl believed fiercely that "the genius child may be born of any race and class."[87] This was the fundamental promise of democracy.

METRO-GOLDWYN-MAYER's adaptation of *The Good Earth* opened in theaters across the country at the end of January, 1937. The years of preparation included half a dozen scripts and filming on both sides of the Pacific.[88] Three directors worked on the project: George Hill, who had supervised the ill-fated 1934 location shooting in China; Victor Fleming, who was hired after Hill committed suicide; and Sidney Franklin, who finished the work and received on-screen credit.[89]

The reviews were rapturous. As Pearl said, "even the cynical *New Yorker*" was enthusiastic.[90] Frank Nugent began his *New York Times* notice by gushing that MGM had "once again . . . enriched the screen with a superb translation of a literary classic." Nugent praised everything about the film: "The performances, direction and photography are of uniform excellence, and have been fused perfectly into a dignified, beautiful and soberly dramatic production." The movie did exceptionally well at the box office both in America and in Europe: film historians estimate that ticket sales eventually exceeded twenty-five million. *The Good Earth* earned several Academy Award nominations, and Luise Rainer won an Oscar for her portrayal of O-lan.

The Good Earth was Irving Thalberg's last project, and the only MGM film on which his name appeared. When the legendary producer died before the movie was completed, studio executives inserted a title into the opening credits dedicating the entire project to him. Despite his death, Thalberg left his unmistakable stamp on the film. The panoramic cinematography, the script's insistence on romance, and the manufacture of an uplifting conclusion reflected Thalberg's characteristic emphases.

The filmscript took all sorts of liberties with the novel, especially in its portrait of O-lan. The general effect of the changes is to suffuse Pearl's unblinking naturalism and sexual candor in a haze of Hollywood sentimentality. In the novel, O-lan, an unattractive slave who serves her purposes of work and childbearing, is supplanted by the sing-song girl, Lotus, and dies a worn-out woman just over halfway through the story. In the movie, O-lan is transformed into a glamorous creature who quickly claims Wang Lung's erotic interest. Her death is postponed until near the end of the film, and Wang Lung is grieving for her in the final frames.

To underscore O-lan's enlarged role, the film introduces an elaborate symbolic pattern that links O-lan and the earth. Early in the script, O-lan plants a peach pit in the front yard of Wang Lung's farmhouse. Images of the growing tree punctuate the film, signifying O-lan's beauty and strength, her fertility, and her indispensable place in Wang Lung's life. The entire motif was invented by Frances Marion, one of the first writers to work on the film.[91]

The movie reshapes the relation between Wang Lung and O-lan into a Westernized boy-meets-girl drama, in which marital loyalty ultimately triumphs. Lotus is reduced to the conventional "other woman," who serves mainly as a foil to O-lan's virtues. Needless to say, there is no mention at all of Pear Blossom, the twelve-year-old girl whom the aging Wang Lung takes as his concubine in the later chapters of the novel.[92]

In the film, Wang Lung treats O-lan with an egalitarian respect almost completely at odds with the traditional patriarchal assumptions that guided Pearl in writing her novel. On their wedding night in the movie, along with some unlikely sexual teasing, Wang Lung tells O-lan that his land now "belongs to us both." This is a declaration that the novel's Wang Lung would not conceivably make. O-lan is made less competent as well as more ornamental. In the novel, for example, she discovers the jewels during the revolutionary attack on the great house in Nanking because she knows where to look and keeps her wits about

21. A scene from the MGM production of *The Good Earth* (1937). (Courtesy Movie Star News.)

her. In the film, she is knocked unconscious in the attack, and simply finds the jewels lying next to her when she wakes up.

Pearl's story and characters were softened in other ways as well. Wang Lung's uncle, who is a genuinely sinister figure in the novel, an ally of bandits and murderers, is in the film reduced to a clown, in a nice comic turn by Walter Connolly. Similarly, the formidable gatekeeper at the House of Hwang is played exclusively for laughs by William Law.

Most significantly, by ending the film with O-lan's death and Wang Lung's grief, the script suppressed the hard-edged irony of the novel's final scene. At the novel's conclusion, an elderly Wang Lung pleads with his sons to remain true to the land as the narrator makes clear that they will not. Where the book declined into a whisper of resignation over human frailty, the movie closes with a shout of love and loyalty.

In spite of its failure to capture the tone of Pearl's book, the film accomplished a great deal. To begin with, the movie creates powerful, authentic images of Chinese rural life. Almost $3 million was spent on the project, and much of it went into the carefully researched sets that reproduced farmhouses, tools, clothing, and furniture. Some of the best scenes in the film are extended sequences that depict the relentless pace and human cost of subsistence farming: oxen straining as they pull heavy plows through thick soil; men sweating through a long day harvesting grain; women wearily turning heavy stone querns to grind their wheat.

The cinematography, which is consistently first-rate, yielded a dozen or more memorable vignettes. Wang Lung's timid first entrance into the magnificent House of Hwang anticipates Dorothy's entry into Oz in the classic scene that Victor Fleming would direct just two years later. (Even the musical background is similar.)[93] Revolutionary warfare and mob violence are impressively portrayed, along with the famine that ravages the province in the middle of the film.

The most elaborate sequence, a triumph of camera work, cutting, and special effects, re-creates a swarm of locusts that threatens Wang Lung's farm. The scene is based on a brief, understated episode halfway through the novel, which Sidney Franklin transformed into a plague of biblical proportions, using hundreds of extras and occupying over fifteen minutes of screen time. Franklin intercut long shots of the descending swarm with closeups of the struggling farmers and even tighter, near-hallucinatory shots of individual locusts. The camera moves with tremendous speed, lurching between the marauding insects and the frantic efforts of the men to beat them back with fire and flood. Franklin crafted an apocalyptic sequence, an emblem of humanity's elemental struggle with nature's overwhelming force.

For viewers who come to the film of *The Good Earth* in the late twentieth century, sixty years after it was produced, the most noticeable defect is that a white actor has been cast in every major Chinese part. Along with Luise Rainer as O-lan, the actors included Paul Muni as Wang Lung, Charley Grapewin as Wang Lung's father, and Tilly Loach as Lotus. A half-dozen Asian and Asian-American actors had speaking parts in the film, including Soo Yong, who played the aunt, Keye Luke, cast as Wang Lung's first son, and Chingwah Lee, who played Ching. However, these were all secondary roles.

Pearl herself had proposed that Chinese actors be used in the film. MGM ignored the advice.[94] The studio's discriminatory casting decisions capitulated to the assumed prejudices of American audiences. There were only a few celebrated Asian characters in 1930s films, and they were always played by Caucasians. Akim Tamiroff played the villainous General Yang in Paramount's *The General Died at Dawn* (1936). In the later 1930s, Peter Lorre portrayed the Chinese detective Mr. Moto in a few films. The Moto character was preceded by the far more famous Charlie Chan, based on a fictional detective invented by Earl Derr Biggers. Beginning in the late 1920s, Warner Oland and Sidney Toler starred in a series of Charlie Chan mysteries that had considerable commercial success. Except for

22. Luise Rainer as O-lan and Paul Muni as Wang Lung in the MGM production of *The Good Earth*. (Courtesy Movie Star News.)

the characters in *The Good Earth,* Chan was unquestionably the most widely known Asian in the movies of the 1930s.

A distinction needs to be made. In spite of the conventional wisdom, the Charlie Chan movies did not simply propagate derisive stereotypes about Chinese. To be sure, Chan's sons (one of them often played by Keye Luke) are typically presented as eager fools, and Chan's own excursions into fake Confucian proverbs are a species of low comedy. On balance, however, the Chan character is an estimable combination of intelligence, courtesy, and good sense. As in most formula detective stories, the truly bungling characters are the officers of the regular police force. White men like the detective sergeant played by William Demarest in *Charlie Chan at the Opera* (1936), perhaps the best of the Chan movies, are simultaneously arrogant, tactless, and stupid.

A fair appraisal of the Charlie Chan films suggests that the images of Asia current in the 1930s were not universally one-dimensional and demeaning.[95] Nonetheless, MGM's *The Good Earth,* like Pearl's novel six years earlier, constituted a long step forward in the way American popular culture represented the Asian experience. Here the Chinese characters are constructed as ordinary people, unremarkable men and women making the best they can of their difficult circumstances. Instead of pandering appeals to the inscrutable or exotic East, the movie offered access to a recognizable world of human conflict and ambition.

Whatever its merits, Pearl did not much like the film. She thought it was too long and too noisy, in general "too *much* – too much storm, too much locusts, too much looting." Pearl noted the effect of the changes MGM had introduced: "O-lan gets the pearls, the second wife is dismissed, Wang returns to the land – the American romance in other words."

Pearl continued to believe that the characters should have been played by Chinese actors. Paul Muni, she confided to Emma White, was "simply wrong" in the part of Wang Lung, and Tilly Loach was "horrible" as Lotus. "None of the white actors are really good except Rainer and the old rascally uncle." Luise Rainer was more than good: hers is "such a perfect performance that it's incredible she isn't Chinese."[96]

A businesswoman as well as a critic, Pearl kept her dissenting opinions to herself. She provided a few guarded sentences for the MGM publicity packet, praising the movie's ambitious scope. Similarly, when the movie opened, she concealed her reservations behind a screen of friendly irrelevance, telling an interviewer for the *New York Evening Post:* "The book I wrote has taken on a new life of its own . . . a life beyond my conception . . . in an art foreign to me but which I appreciate."[97] She even wrote a tepidly approving review of the film for *Asia,* in which she spent most of her column distinguishing at unnecessary length between moving pictures and novels.

The tremendous success of the film multiplied the invitations Pearl received for lectures and articles from college presidents, magazine editors, and leaders of human rights groups. Everyone wanted her opinions: on Asia, on women's rights, on segregation, on the prospects for war. She turned down most requests, but accepted an invitation from Victor Weybright, editor of the left-leaning *Survey Graphic,* who asked her to write an article on immigration.

This was a subject of increasing controversy in the 1930s. The numbers of immigrants, which had reached as many as a million and a quarter a year before World War I, had shrunk to a trickle after passage of the restrictive Immigration Act of 1924. In the early years of the Depression, the numbers were pushed even further down. Reacting to the combined pressure of nativists and organized labor, the Secretary of State ordered strict enforcement of the provisions of the law that excluded "persons likely to become a public charge." One notorious outcome of the hard-line attitude was that Jews and other refugees fleeing Hitler's Germany were turned back, sometimes with tragic consequences.[98]

Pearl hated the exclusion and quota laws, and used her *Survey Graphic* article to argue the case for opening America's doors. Editor Weybright apparently had a somewhat scholarly piece in mind. After Pearl accepted the assignment, he shipped off cartons of factual material to her, including reports of the Immigration

Restriction League, a Boston organization that had been leading the fight against immigration since 1894. However, statistical and abstract debate was not Pearl's style. She made her case instinctively, rhetorically, anecdotally. Like her father, she was a preacher, not an explainer.

Pearl called the article "On Discovering America," and in it she adopts the pose – a more or less accurate pose – of an immigrant herself. Having come from a country that was actually homogeneous, her answer to American nativists is simple: there is no essential or even typical "American." Not one of us, she writes, "is really native in any profound sense. Everybody in the United States, except the Indians, is now or was once, foreign-born." To be sure, our differences have led to tension and even hate: "hatred that burns like wildfire in a hundred different directions," between blacks and whites, Jews and Christians, Protestants and Catholics. Nonetheless, Pearl concluded, our diversity remains "our strength, our nature [and] our safety."[99]

Several members of the *Survey Graphic* staff were disappointed by Pearl's article. One of the anonymous notes in the magazine's files complains that, while the piece is "personal and charming and will delight many people," it is "neither factual nor thought out." Another staffer passed the essay along with the comment: "Well, there it is. And I find it very moving. I'm not sure if it makes sense, but it's swell uplift."[100]

Whatever editorial misgivings Pearl's essay aroused, the public response was extraordinary. Orders for reprints came in from all over the country, from high schools and colleges, from ministers and priests, from cultural and civic associations. Eleanor Roosevelt discussed the article favorably in her "My Day" column. *Reader's Digest* printed an abridged version. Louis Bamberger, of the Institute for Advanced Study at Princeton, asked for 10,000 copies, then wrote again to order 30,000 more.[101]

As she usually did, Pearl coupled her public statements with action. One example is instructive. Along with other prominent citizens, Pearl took advantage of an exception in the immigration law that enabled several thousand European refugees to reach America. Prospective immigrants could meet the test that they were not "likely to become a public charge" if they could present an affidavit of support, signed by an American citizen, who agreed to take personal responsibility for the refugee.

In 1938, after Pearl had signed as many of these affidavits as the law permitted, she received a letter from Anne Polzer, a Viennese Jew who was desperate to get out of Austria with her husband, Viktor. Polzer, who was working as executive secretary to a leading publisher, Paul Zsolnay Verlag, had translated Pearl's *First Wife and Other Stories* into German. Though the translation had been a success, she and Pearl had never been in direct contact. Polzer herself has recently told the rest of this remarkable story:

When Hitler marched into a delighted Austria (don't try to tell me otherwise because I witnessed it), we had to get out as fast as possible. At that time, two things were required for obtaining an immigration visa: a quota number, and an affidavit of support from an affluent American citizen. . . . Now we did have the quota number, because my husband applied for it at the Vienna Consulate one day after Hitler marched in. But we didn't know a soul in America – except by a stretch of imagination due to despair: Pearl Buck. So I sat down and wrote her asking whether she could help us. It was like asking for a miracle, and lo and behold the miracle happened.

Because she could not legally sign any more affidavits herself, Pearl recruited friends to assist the additional refugees who appealed to her. In the Polzers' case, she persuaded publisher Bennett Cerf to sign.

When she recalled these events more than fifty years later, Anne Polzer concluded that, quite simply, Pearl Buck "saved my and my late husband's life." The Polzers arrived in New York, penniless but free, in early 1939. Though Bennett Cerf made it clear he never wanted to hear from either Polzer or her husband, Pearl and Richard kept in touch, doing what they could to help the two refugees find work. Among other things, Pearl provided a letter of reference that Anne Polzer presented to Henry Luce at *Time* magazine.[102]

Commuting weekly between New York City and Green Hills Farm, Pearl continued to juggle the demands of her daunting schedule. She was managing two households and their employees, writing articles and reviews, lecturing, and attending meetings on civil rights and world peace. She wrote several plays, including *The Empress,* based on the life of the Dowager Empress Tz'u-hsi, and met several times with Katherine Cornell and Guthrie McClintic to discuss the possibility that Cornell might play the leading role. Like many American novelists, Pearl very much wanted to succeed as a playwright. The prospect that Cornell, whom Pearl considered the leading actress of her generation, might appear in *The Empress* filled Pearl with an almost childlike enthusiasm. After months of negotiation, however, Cornell declined. Pearl's disappointment, and her irritation, were both sharp.[103]

Although she didn't always find enough time for her growing family, she reported proudly on their development to Emma White. "The babies are all thriving. The two tinies [*sic*] are exceptionally splendid. Little Edgar at six months weighs twenty pounds, is already up on his hands and knees to creep, and is a wonder for intelligence. Jeannie is very close to him, and is *very* pretty, with bright blue eyes and black hair. John and Richard are no longer babies at all." Pearl reported that Janice was doing straight A work in school, and had grown quite tall.[104]

With customary efficiency, Pearl used the long car rides back and forth between New York and Bucks County to read and write. The evidence of her essays and reviews in *Asia* suggests that her curiosity remained omnivorous. She reviewed all sorts of books, from journalism and memoirs to political and social history to studies of Asian art, religion, law, and music. She argued in favor of free trade, cultural exchange, and human rights; she attacked colonialism, racial discrimination, and militarism.

She tried to make space for books translated from Asian languages. As she said in one of her essays, she wanted to give Asians the chance to speak in their own voices. (She acknowledged the limits of translations, but pointed out that almost no one in the West could read any Asian language in the original.) "The whole literature of the East is closed to the West," she wrote, despite the fact that Asia has produced "a literature far vaster in extent and in age than that of Europe. Yet oriental languages are never compulsory and seldom even available in western universities." She judged the West's cultural loss "incomparable," and difficult to fathom "except on the grounds of extreme provincialism."[105]

In March, 1937, reviewing *Living China,* Edgar Snow's pioneering anthology of contemporary Chinese short fiction, Pearl decided that, even in translation, the best of these stories "are still better, more vivid, more simple, more profound than the best of modern American stories." She singled out the work of such writers as Lu Hsün, Jou Shih (Zhou Shi), and Mao Tun (Mao Dun) – major figures who were unknown in America – and rather proudly reminded her readers that some of these stories had originally appeared in *Asia*. Pearl was probably the first American critic to declare that Lu Hsün should be recognized as one of the twentieth century's leading prose writers.

FOR SIX YEARS following the Japanese invasion of Manchuria, an uneasy stalemate had marked the situation in China. Japan's soldiers and warplanes occasionally raided into China proper, and the ambitions of Japanese generals were encouraged by Chiang Kai-shek's reluctance to oppose their incursions. In July, 1937, Japanese and Chinese soldiers engaged each other at the Marco Polo Bridge, ten miles east of Peking. While the skirmish was almost accidental and initial casualties were light, the encounter proved fateful. In Jonathan Spence's words, the fight at the Marco Polo Bridge "can be considered the first battle of World War II."[106] For the next eight years, China and Japan would wage one of the bloodiest and most bitter wars in history.

Pearl's response was predictably desperate. Citing the testimony of the Japanese themselves, she assailed Japan's militarist culture and its expansionist foreign policies. In January, 1938, she and Richard decided to publish in *Asia* a translation of an article written by Michitaka Hiramoto, a lieutenant commander in the Imperial Japanese Navy. The article had the smirking title, "Our Little Visits to Nanking." It described the Japanese bombing raids that had supported the "rape of Nanking," the notorious attack on the Chinese capital in December, 1937, that had left tens of thousands of civilians dead, including thousands of women who were raped before and even after they were killed.

Hiramoto's article is permeated with a macabre exhilaration: the order to bomb Nanking brings Hiramoto "the thrill of a lifetime"; as the bombs fall, "death reigned supreme over the ancient city." Shells explode in "riotous bursts of color that bloom in the night sky"; in comparison, "the gorgeous annual fireworks display at Tyogoku Bridge in Tokyo . . . is but a mere sickening flicker of dying match." On the flight back to Japan, "all was well with the Rough Eagles of Nippon," their dreamless sleep is the "gift of Heaven to men who have done their work well."[107]

Pearl's anger was intensified because Nanking, the beautiful old city that was pulverized in this attack, had been her home for so many years. She attached a brief comment, under the title "The Mind of the Militarist," to Hiramoto's article. She disputed his facts and denounced his misplaced enthusiasm. Extensively quoting his own words, she assailed his "hideous gaiety," his "incredible, maniac light-heartedness," his "horrible false conception of duty." Furthermore, she sadly concluded that Hiramoto accurately represents "the mind of Japan"; its traditions of order and obedience have led to a savage outcome.

At the same time, Pearl also blamed China for its failure to reform and to prepare for its own defense. "For twenty five years," she wrote to Emma White, "the Chinese have known this day would come and they have gone right on grafting and pocketing money that should have been used for national defense. Dick's son-in-law, who works in the Chase bank here, says the greatest fortunes in the bank belong to Chinese war lords."[108]

Outraged by the atrocities committed on both sides in the early months of the war, Pearl wrote an intemperate essay, "Western Weapons in the Hands of the Reckless East," in which she portioned out blame to China and Japan equally for the deaths of thousands of innocent people. Prompted by anger and sorrow, she indulged in the stereotypes she usually avoided, accusing both Asian nations of unusual cruelty, and warning that "the Oriental is not hampered by pity or sentiment about right or wrong."[109]

Never again would Pearl descend to this sort of name calling. A few weeks later, in her November book review in *Asia,* she published a less direct but a much more interesting response to the war, when she commented on Rudolf Hommel's landmark study, *China at Work.* Hommel's book, Pearl said, reminds us that "the real life of peoples is not war. . . . War is a period as abnormal as disease." Rather the real life of a people is in their daily work.[110]

China at Work is one of the most undervalued cultural documents of the 1930s. Based on the eight years that Rudolf Hommel spent traveling throughout China, the book's 350 double-columned pages offer an encyclopedic survey of rural China's material culture. Each of the five long chapters catalogues and describes

Chinese tools: tools for making other tools and for producing clothing, tools to procure food, to provide shelter, to enable transportation. Here are plows, hand mills, axes, fish nets, stoves, eating utensils, the blacksmith's hammer and anvil, wheelbarrows, saws, the potter's wheel, roofing tiles, brooms, bricks, scissors, and shoes, to list just a few of the items included – over a thousand entries in all. The scrupulously detailed texts are accompanied by over five hundred photographs and diagrams.

The significance of *China at Work* is twofold. First, Hommel's text addresses its Asian subject matter in a thoroughly dispassionate, evenhanded way. The descriptions of Chinese tools are never touched by a hint of condescension. Indeed, rather like F. H. King's studies of Chinese farming thirty years earlier, Hommel's rare comparisons of Asian and Western tools and techniques usually favor Asian alternatives.[111] He praises the skill of Chinese craftsmen, their unerring sense of proportion, and their economic use of scarce resources.[112]

The second reason for the importance of Hommel's book is suggested in its subtitle: "An Illustrated Record of the Primitive Industries of China's Masses, Whose Life is Toil, and Thus an Account of Chinese Civilization." That is to say, Hommel redefined the idea of "civilization" away from the artifacts of high culture usually found in museums of Asian art – scroll paintings, vases, silk robes, rosewood furniture, jade carvings – to encompass the ordinary objects used by the rural masses in their daily struggle for survival.

In short, Hommel was committed to writing Chinese history "from the bottom up," to use the phrase of a later day. This was a populist attitude shared by a number of other American historians and social scientists, including Henry Mercer, the colorful Doylestown, Pennsylvania, millionaire and collector who had sponsored Hommel's expedition. Earlier in the century, Mercer had gathered tens of thousands of the objects that Americans used in their daily lives – from baking pans to barber poles to fishing rods – and put them on permanent display in his five-story, reinforced concrete Gothic castle in Doylestown. (Pearl called the building "an inspired monstrosity.") Mercer hoped to create a new kind of history, which would put the daily lives of ordinary men and women at the center of attention.[113] Rudolf Hommel's long sojourn in China gave international scope to Mercer's historical theories.[114]

All of this dovetailed perfectly with attitudes Pearl had long held. In several of her essays, she had argued that the reality of China was better found in the country's villages and colloquial tales than in imperial palaces, Confucian texts, and classic novels. And she had defended *The Good Earth* against intellectuals who had reproved her for putting peasants at the center of her novel. Hommel's vast survey vindicated Pearl's own ideas of Chinese reality: "I do not know of any book on China which is more fundamental than this one. At least eighty per cent of China's millions daily handle these tools, earn their living by them, make shelter and clothing and food by them. When we read this book we are reading of actual Chinese life."

For Pearl, *China at Work* was a testament to the endurance of the Chinese people. In the early days of a brutal war, she found it consoling to recall that China's rural culture had survived for four thousand years. She believed that the Japanese invasion would inevitably fail. In a July, 1938 article in *Redbook*, optimistically titled "Japan Loses the War," Pearl saluted China's stamina and courage, and she described the guerrilla tactics that were "nagging and harassing the Japanese by trickery and surprise attacks." In another article, this one in *Asia*, she argued that Japanese aggression had produced the welcome result of uniting China's factious politicians."[15]

In the spring of 1938, Pearl and Richard began working for a variety of agencies that were raising money for Chinese war victims. In her first fundraising efforts, Pearl sent out hundreds of letters on behalf of the New York-based China Famine Relief. Taking advantage of her identification with the Chinese people, Pearl reminded her potential donors that Americans had given $11 million to Japan after the Tokyo earthquake of 1923. Yet, during the present war, "the major disaster of China's history, we have not sent even one million dollars to relieve the millions of people who are wounded, homeless, and starving."

Although Pearl's solicitation proved impressively successful, she soon broke with the organization. She gave her reasons in a letter to administrator Florence Lurty: "I have been somewhat disturbed by various reports which have been brought to my attention in one way or another that the China Famine Relief is being more closely brought under the supervision of religious organizations. If this is true, I must ask that my letter be withdrawn, because I make it a policy never to associate myself with religious organizations."[16] Eventually, Pearl and Richard would undertake their own fund-raising efforts.

After the outbreak of the Asian war, Pearl devoted even more of her reading and writing to political subjects. In rapid succession, she published a series of six articles in *Asia*, commenting on such subjects as military tactics, American neutrality, and the political background of the struggle. In January, 1938, she delivered a radio review of Edgar Snow's landmark *Red Star Over China*, several chapters of which had earlier appeared as essays in *Asia*. Snow was the first Western journalist to reach Mao Tse-tung's Communist headquarters in Yenan (Yan'an), in the remote, mountain fastness of Shensi (Shaanxi) province. His book was based on a long series of interviews with Mao, out of which he distilled a history of Chinese Communism.

Pearl used her review to acknowledge the magnitude of Mao's achievement. In her radio commentary, she located the strength of the Communist movement in this fact: "it is a genuine peasant movement, as no revolution in China has yet been." It is, she added, "incontrovertible that modern Chinese Communism has accomplished something which nothing else has done – it has awakened . . . the common people. It has done this . . . by a complete partisanship for the causes of the common people. The common man has been believed and accepted and his cause, right or wrong, has been championed."[17] Since Pearl continued to loathe Chinese Communism, her grudging concessions to Mao's leadership were an impressive measure of her integrity. Unlike others in the 1930s and 1940s, she refused to replace her political judgment with her personal preferences. Mao was a winner; Chiang Kai-shek was a loser. For saying such things, Pearl would later be harassed by Henry Luce and the China Lobby, who supported Chiang long after the Nationalists had been driven from the mainland.

Though she was not a pacifist, Pearl had a visceral fear of war. For one thing, she knew more about the reality of warfare than most Americans. In both Anhwei and Nanking, she had seen rape and riot and murder, and she had come near death herself. Beyond that, she subscribed to a sentimental sexual division of labor in matters of war and peace. On more than one occasion, she proposed that women should take the chief responsibility for eliminating war. She wrote to Emma White: "I feel so strongly that women can prevent war by refusing by all means to allow men to resort to it."[18]

More generally, she believed that America was a poorer place because of the untapped potential of its millions of women. In the late 1930s, she wrote a series of essays on women that provoked nationwide comment. The first was "America's Medieval Women," which appeared in the August, 1938 issue of *Harper's Magazine*.[19] This is a deftly managed argument in which Pearl defines the position of middle-class women in contemporary America as essentially a condition of comfortable serfdom: thus the essay's title. Women "have privileges but they have no equality." She describes the United States as actually a rather "backward" country, lamed by obsolete traditions, innovative only in its use of machinery. In human relations, including those between women and men, Americans cling to attitudes and beliefs they have inherited from the dark ages. Among other things, they seem depressingly unable to discuss sex except in terms of obscenity.

Anecdotes and invented dialogue are sprinkled across Pearl's pages, all pressing the point that America has imprisoned its middle-class women in well-furnished isolation, denying them access to the larger world of work and risk and opportunity. Pearl tells of men who insist on the intellectual inferiority of their wives, and of talented women who must conceal their intelligence in order to attract men.

Like much of Pearl's polemic writing, "America's Medieval Women" is enlivened by her sense of theatricality. She was less interested in subtle distinctions than in sharp contrasts. In this essay, her adversaries are repeatedly said to sneer and murmur and laugh, even at one point shouting and swearing at her: "You don't know what you're talking about!" Against this noisy if imagined opposition, she patiently argues that women must be given their freedom, and men must accept the idea of equality.

Pearl conducts her argument impersonally, but her own emotional investment repeatedly breaks through. When, for example, she defends Labor Secretary Frances Perkins from detractors, she is obviously speaking for herself as well. If a woman, she writes, "persists in being interested in things beyond her home we insist that she must be neglecting her home. If she still persists and makes a success through incredible dogged persistence we laugh at her."[120] Pearl herself, of course, followed a punishing schedule of writing, lecturing, traveling, fund-raising, and organizing, and she heard nasty whispers that she was inadequate as a "homemaker." As she accurately observed, the charges would never have been raised if she were a man, though only outmoded customs made such distinctions seem natural. The kinship she felt with Perkins, the first woman to hold a cabinet office, encompassed admiration, but a weary frustration as well.

An even more revealing glimpse into Pearl's personal feelings at the time of this article is provided in her attack on masculine "boyishness." American men, she writes, have truly been called adolescents: "kind, delightful, charming adolescents." In Pearl's view, this seemingly harmless commonplace conceals a sinister reality. Saying that a man is "just like a boy" is considered "a compliment to a man in America [but] ought to be an insult." Boyishness in persons who should be adult, according to Pearl, is actually "horrible . . . as dismaying as mental retardation."

Pearl's language here, which might seem at first glance overwrought, suggests the decade of pain that lies under her analogy. Lossing Buck's "boyishness" had of course nothing to do with causing Carol's retardation, which had been the source of the most acute anguish Pearl had ever felt. Nonetheless, his inability to help her cope with the tragedy, his emotional abandonment of both mother and daughter, seemed to Pearl to be childish inadequacy, which became intertwined in her mind with Carol's impairment itself. In some profound sense, Carol's situation became a symbol of her father's failures as a husband and parent. In turn, the anger Pearl felt toward Lossing was generalizing into bitterness against the large number of American men who neglected their adult responsibilities and retreated into the charming but false poses of boyhood.

The article provoked a storm of reaction. The editors of *Harper's* received hundreds of letters supporting and attacking Pearl's position. She wrote jokingly to a friend that she had decided to "get out of town," even to go find a "deserted island" somewhere and escape from her critics.[121]

Pearl was one of the most successful women in America. Nonetheless, she knew that her gender more often hindered her career than helped her. She believed that, in the arts (including literature), "women are not often taken seriously, however serious their work." And her own renown merely proved the rule that while women "often achieve high popular success . . . this counts against them as artists."[122] At the same time, she knew that she was a kind of cultural pioneer, and she usually accepted the tributes that came to her as a woman. In 1938, for example, while Pearl was sadly contemplating the shrunken status of women in America, she was selected as one of the "Outstanding Women" of the year by Durward Howes, editor of *American Woman*. It was the first of many such awards she would gather over the years.[123]

Pearl's next novel, *This Proud Heart,* incorporates one of her most extended meditations on the fate of American women. The story tells of a talented, passionate, self-reliant woman, Susan Gaylord, a sculptor who ultimately chooses the riskiness of art and independence over the security of marriage. *This Proud Heart* reverses the matchmaking plot of traditional romance: the book opens on Susan's wedding day and ends with her decision to live on her own. Over the nearly four hundred pages between those two events, the novel follows its main character with the single-minded purpose of registering her growing commitment to herself and her art.

Susan Gaylord is an improbably splendid woman, coined out of the alloy of Pearl's own achievements and ambitions. Everything from schoolwork to music to poetry comes easily to her. For her wedding, she designs her own dress and bakes her own cake. As several reviewers impatiently pointed out, Susan is actually a little tiresome in her virtues and effortless skill. In fact, she is less a fictional character than an allegorical emblem, a sign of the opportunities and limits women faced in the American 1930s.

Susan learns that she can't have it all. Her husband, Mark, is a dull man, indifferent to her work, and hostile to the idea that she might become a self-supporting professional. Though she briefly considers giving up sculpture to save her marriage, she refuses to extinguish her own identity to buy domestic peace. At a crucial moment she receives encouragement from an established artist, an older man named David Barnes. Among other things, he tells her to attack the marble she is working on as if she were a man: " 'Forget forever that you're a woman. . . . Pound that line deeper, harder . . . it's muscle you want.' "[124]

"David Barnes" is the pseudonym Pearl had used thirteen years earlier when she submitted her Cornell master's thesis. In effect, Pearl has imported her own masculine alter ego into the novel to guide her female hero toward self-fulfillment. David warns Susan that the training she needs will take almost all of her time. When she protests that she has a husband and child to look after, he dismisses the point: " 'Any woman can have husband and children. What have they to do with you?' "

At the same time, David reminds her that " 'it's hopeless for a woman,' " because male artists and critics will not tolerate a female competitor. " 'They won't take you seriously,' " David says, echoing Pearl's own bitterness: " 'And artists are the damnedest, rottenest, selfish lot. . . . A woman hasn't a ghost of a show.' " In spite of such odds, David remains confident in her abilities and urges her to get on with her career.

Conveniently, Susan's husband dies of typhoid while she is deciding whether to defy him by traveling to France for additional study. Shortly after the funeral, she moves to Paris with her son, settles into a small apartment, and enrolls in the studio of a renowned master, never named in the book, who bears a predictable and unmistakable resemblance to Rodin.[125] Like David Barnes, this man sees at a glance that Susan is an artist of exceptional talent. He insists that she work only on marble: "Only the marble was large enough for all her powers." Marble, of course, is sculpture's most difficult medium, and has traditionally been the preserve of male artists.

Halfway through the novel, a new threat to Susan's independence appears in the form of Blake Kinnaird, a modestly gifted painter who seems to appreciate her accomplishments and who also awakens her sexual passion. Susan describes his lovemaking in sculptural terms: "In his detailed love of her body she felt as though she were marble and he were carving her free, as though she were clay and he were giving her shape. His hands, touching her, defined her. She had not seen herself until now." Language like this is Susan's highest sexual compliment. Since Blake is also rich, his offer of marriage proves irresistible. Within a few months, the couple is established in Blake's enormous New York mansion.

In the early months of this second marriage, Susan begins to slip into the comfort of affluent idleness, nearly satisfied in the roles of pampered wife, indulgent mother, and popular society matron. However, her life soon begins to feel claustrophobic. After interminable inner debates over the authentic identity of a modern woman, Susan reclaims her independence. She rents a studio in a shabby East Side neighborhood and returns to work.

Her first teacher, David Barnes, had sculpted a series of famous American men. Significantly, the first statues Susan completes are images of anonymous women, a series that she calls "American Procession." And the first statue in the group is an African-American woman: twelve years before Ralph Ellison published *Invisible Man*, Pearl Buck, through her artist-heroine Susan Gaylord, tried to confer the dignity of visibility on black women.

The public adores Susan's work, and even the critics grudgingly acknowledge its power. These statues of women, sculpted in a style described as "simple" and "elemental," are obviously intended as three-dimensional analogues for Pearl's writing. Susan's egalitarian subject matter ratifies Pearl's sexual and racial politics, and Susan's success serves, in a self-congratulatory way, to validate Pearl's accomplishments as well.[126]

As she becomes more engrossed in her vocation, Susan and Blake drift apart. She has no need of him, and he can't cope with her success. She moves out of his New York mansion, buying a weather-beaten barn in Bucks County that serves her as house and studio. She lives productively alone, sometimes looking back but more often planning her future work. In the novel's final pages, Blake pleads with her to come back to him, promising that she can continue her career on any terms she chooses. Susan turns the offer down. She acknowledges that she will sometimes grieve, "sometimes at night perhaps." However, "in the morning she would get up and go to work, and then she would not grieve. She would forget to grieve."

The ending reverses the conventions that usually governed the lives of women in romance fiction. Instead of collapsing into marital reconciliation, Susan Gaylord pledges herself to a life of work, sculpting the women of her American procession.[127] Pearl's sister, Grace Yaukey, wrote that "Women who read the story of Susan understood and loved her, and men who read it wondered sometimes why she must want to use all her gifts and not be content with husband and family."[128] The distinction had a relevance to much of Pearl's work.

In October, Pearl published a short story called "Ransom" in *Cosmopolitan*. Based vaguely on the kidnapping of the Lindbergh baby in 1936, this little melodrama is chiefly interesting because it elicited a fan letter from J. Edgar Hoover. After commending Pearl for her "keen understanding of human nature," Hoover said that as he read the story he "again lived the horrors of kidnapping."[129] He closed by inviting her to come to FBI headquarters, where he would arrange a special tour. Pearl never accepted the invitation. Nor did she know that a copy of Hoover's pleasant letter was added to a file of observation and surveillance that had begun a year earlier, and would remain active to the end of her life.

Like many other Americans who were disturbed about the drift toward war, Pearl looked forward uneasily to November 11, 1938, the twentieth anniversary of the Armistice that had ended World War I. A variety of anti-war events were planned for that day in New York and elsewhere around the country. As it happened, the date would prove to be of tremendous significance for Pearl for a completely different reason. Early that morning, NBC radio picked up an English-language announcement from Stockholm. It was the first word that Pearl had won the 1938 Nobel Prize for literature.

6

The Prize

W HEN PEARL HEARD that she had won the Nobel Prize, she was aston-ished in two languages. Her first reaction was in Chinese: "wo pu hsiang hsin" ("I don't believe it"). And, she added in English: "That's ridiculous. It should have gone to Dreiser."¹ Both comments were widely reported in the hundreds of news accounts that appeared across the country and around the world.

Just a week later, the *New York Times Magazine* published a flattering profile by S. J. Woolf that offers a description of the new Nobel Prize winner at the time of the award. After describing Pearl's brown hair, high cheek bones, and striking, light blue eyes, Woolf called particular attention to what might be called Pearl's presence: "Although she is not a large woman, there is something sturdy about her – a statuesque quality that one sees in the figures of Rodin and Epstein, a bigness without grossness, a massiveness in miniature." This was a tactful way of remarking on Pearl's weight, which had gone up again. Woolf also found Pearl to be courteous but reserved: "although she is affable, there is a suggestion of remoteness about her. This may be the result of shyness, or of the solemnity of an older nation which has left an indelible impression upon her."²

It is more likely that Pearl was using reticence as a shield. Still hiding Carol's existence, and still slightly nervous about her status as a divorced woman, she was always vexed by her encounters with journalists. She tried to steer all of her conversations away from personal questions. Ever since her return to the United States four years earlier, she had kept a wary distance from the engines of American publicity – except on her own calculated terms.

Furthermore, Pearl was subdued about the prize because she continued to feel like an outsider on the American cultural scene. She realized that her reputation was hostage to a literary establishment that was mostly male and mostly antag-onistic. Though she had received hundreds of good notices in the daily and weekly press for her work, she was routinely ignored or belittled by "the deep thinkers," as John Marquand called them, the highbrow cultural gatekeepers who wrote for the serious quarterlies.[3] Beyond that, however, Pearl was plagued by a self-doubt she could never completely suppress. She harbored the inescapable fear that her critics were essentially right: she did not deserve such extraordinary recognition. In any case, her long years of obscurity in China had made her instinctively skeptical about any stroke of good fortune: she knew enough about failure to understand that her success might prove short-lived.

Pearl was the third American to win the Nobel Prize for literature – and all three of those awards had come in the 1930s. After bypassing U.S. writers for three decades, the Swedish Academy had chosen Americans in rapid succession: Pearl followed Sinclair Lewis, who won the first American prize in 1930, and Eugene O'Neill, whose award was announced in 1936. Among other things, this flurry of recognition demonstrated to Americans that their writing had come of age, and that international opinion was now ready to treat the writers of the United States with the respect previously reserved for Europeans.[4] This had been the gist of Lewis's famous acceptance speech when he received his prize, and most observers on both sides of the Atlantic agreed.

Pearl also commanded special attention, of course, because she was the fourth woman – and the first American woman – to win the literature prize.[5] Her female predecessors were Dr. Selma Lagerlöf of Sweden (1909), Grazia Deledda of Italy (1926), and the Norwegian Sigrid Undset (1928). Lagerlöf had been one of Pearl's principal supporters for the award, an act of sponsorship that the younger woman always acknowledged with gratitude.

At a PEN dinner in New York convened in her honor a week after the announcement, Sinclair Lewis advised her: "Don't let anyone minimize for you the receiving of the Nobel Prize. It is a tremendous event, the greatest of a writer's life. Enjoy every moment of it, for it will be your finest memory."[6] Lewis's camaraderie was noticeably defensive: the salute of one underappreciated Nobel laureate to another.

Pearl later testified that her Nobel Prize provoked massed outrage among the American literati.[7] This was an exaggeration, but not by much. A few critics came to the lively defense of her work. Carl Van Doren, for example, in a summary judgment of the novels Pearl wrote in the 1930s, called the body of her writing "abundant and distinguished."[8] Pearl's old friends and stalwarts, among them Dorothy Canfield Fisher, William Lyon Phelps, Edward Weeks, and Katherine Woods of the *New York Times,* also rallied to her support.

On balance, however, the reaction to Pearl's Nobel Prize was negative, and sometimes fierce. A day after the announcement, for example, critic Norman Holmes Pearson grumbled that "this woman, Pearl Buck, was given the Nobel Prize for literature. Do they intend to make it as hammish [sic] as the Pulitzer award? Thank heavens I have seen no one who has taken it seriously and none of the great congratulatory articles which followed a similar award to O'Neill last winter. Mrs. Buck's only comment seemed to be, 'I was terribly surprised' – nuts to her, say I, I think that was putting it mildly.'"[9]

Pearson's derisory views echoed those of most of the country's leading cultural opinion makers. Pearl's Asian subjects, her prose style, her gender, and her tremendous popularity offended virtually every one of the constituencies that divided up the literary 1930s. Marxists, Agrarians, Chicago formalists, New York intellectuals, literary nationalists, and New Humanists had little enough in common, but they could all agree that Pearl Buck had no place in any of their creeds and canons.[10]

Over the years, Pearl's selection for the Nobel Prize became a shorthand proof of the Swedish Academy's bad judgment. Pearl Buck had won the prize, while Mark Twain, Henry James, and Theodore Dreiser (to name just a few of the Americans who had been passed over) had not. William Faulkner's unkind comments were typical. In 1949, when newspapers were floating speculation about his own award, Faulkner wrote to his friend Joan Williams: "I don't know anything about the Nobel matter. Been hearing rumors for about three years, have been a little fearful. It's not the sort of thing to decline; a gratuitous insult to do so but I don't want it. I had rather be in the same pigeon hole with Dreiser and Sherwood Anderson, than with Sinclair Lewis and Mrs. Chinahand Buck."[11]

In part, such hostility was the price Pearl paid for her outsized success. Malcolm Cowley confessed that many intellectuals were affronted by the sheer scale of her popularity. Her writing, Cowley argued, "didn't succeed in the fashion that critics regard as orthodox. They like to think that a really good novelist is discovered by those younger critics who act as scouts for the rest, and that afterwards his reputation spreads from this center in widening rings until it reaches the general public."

Cowley's examples of writers whose reputations were manufactured in just this way included Faulkner, Ernest Hemingway, and Thomas Wolfe. They "all succeeded by this formula, but Miss Buck turned it inside out: she was discovered by the public at large while the literary scouts were looking the other way. I know that *The Good Earth* was extravagantly praised by pundits like William Lyon Phelps, but the effect in serious literary circles was merely to clinch the case against her."[12]

While her supporters and detractors disagreed about the quality of Pearl's writing, everyone assumed that the Academy had made a political statement in awarding her the prize. The literary events of 1938 took place under the storm clouds of fascism and war. By the fall of that year, Franco's Falange had nearly completed its destruction of the Spanish Republic. Hitler had triumphed diplomatically at Munich and had then annexed the Sudetenland. (British Prime Minister Neville Chamberlain had returned to London from Munich with "a piece of paper," leaving Hitler to ingest central Europe at his leisure.) Mussolini's troops had overrun Ethiopia and had thereby demonstrated the impotence of the League of Nations. And the Japanese, who had invaded Manchuria in 1931 and China proper in 1937, were continuing their apparently irresistible air and infantry campaign against Chinese cities and major production areas.

Pearl had established herself as a powerful voice against the rising tide of international violence and totalitarianism. In her novels, and also in literally scores of essays, reviews, and lectures, she had spoken out on behalf of liberal democracy, self-determination, and ideological and racial tolerance. She had lobbied the U.S. government to provide aid to fascism's victims, and she helped to raise hundreds of thousands of dollars for war relief. In a decade when writers on both the left and right insisted on the social responsibility of the artist, Pearl's exertions seemed exemplary. "The influence of her writing far transcends its importance as literature": this was the opinion of *Time* magazine's anonymous reviewers.[13]

When the Nobel Prize was announced, Pearl received congratulations from family, friends, and a sprinkling of literary and political celebrities, including Sholem Asch, Hermann Hagedorn (a Harvard classmate of Richard Walsh), Ida Tarbell (who told her that she did indeed deserve the prize more than Dreiser), Katherine Cornell and Guthrie McClintic, Sinclair Lewis, Dorothy Canfield Fisher (who had proposed *The Good Earth* to fellow Book-of-the-Month Club jurors seven years earlier), Bruce Bliven, Elmer Carter (managing editor of *Opportunity*, the magazine of the National Urban League), Dr. Hu Shih (the Chinese ambassador to Washington), and Lin Yutang, whose best-selling books were published by the John Day Company.

Most of the hundreds of telegrams and letters were briefly effusive. Even the Presbyterian mission board cabled its best wishes, suggesting that a reconciliation might be in order. A few writers made the political implications of the prize explicit. Poet Arthur Davison Ficke, for example, added a handwritten note to his typed letter: "Oh how sore this is going to make the Japanese!!!"[14] Two telegrams also arrived from Spain. The National Committee of Antifascist Women of Spain cabled its congratulations from Barcelona, and the loyalist Women's Aid Committee wired that the "women of Spain never lose sight [of] the achievements of other democratic women of the world. . . . We received news of the award made upon you with satisfaction."

The most provocative and perceptive letter came from Edna C. McAfee, a former missionary who had known Pearl slightly in China. McAfee wrote from Rochester, Minnesota, where she had gone with her ailing husband, Wallace, a patient at the Mayo Clinic. "I feel that Carol stands by you in your hour of victory," McAfee wrote. "Her life, as it is, has counted for more in the world than most children's, because your living for and thru her has given you a 'something vital' which has won the heart of the world."[15]

McAfee's remark was acute, if not altogether sensitive. By coincidence, Pearl's sister Grace Yaukey checked into a New York hospital to deliver her fourth child on the day that Pearl sailed for Europe for the Nobel ceremonies. Pearl telephoned Grace the day before she left to say that she would rather be having a baby than going to Sweden.[16]

Pearl and Richard, accompanied by Richard's daughter, Betty, made the transatlantic crossing on the elegant French liner, the *Normandie*. Pearl was continuously seasick on the rough voyage across the North Atlantic. She distracted herself by writing comic rhymes that she sent back to Janice, verses that reveal an unexpected, pawky humor:

I think the Aquitania
Has a mania.
And as for the Normandie,
She acted abnormandly.

The only thing 'twixt me and Sweden
Is that the ocean is betweeden.
I think that all the Nobel prizes
Should wait until the ocean dryses.[17]

The family landed in England, then traveled across Western Europe by steamer and train. In Copenhagen, Pearl announced that she had refused an invitation to visit Nazi Germany. The episode was, of course, widely reported, as was Pearl's statement that Chiang Kai-shek had lost the support of the Chinese masses and would not be able to provide the strong central government China needed to survive its war with Japan.

Her visit to Stockholm was a triumph. Because she insisted on returning home for Christmas with her children, she spent only four days in Sweden, but she always recalled them as the happiest of her professional life. At the ceremony, she made a greatly favorable impression with a gallant act of courtesy toward Sweden's aging king, Gustavus V. Custom required that Nobel laureates, after crossing a wide stage to receive their prize from the king, step backward to their seats rather than turning their backs on the monarch. This polite maneuver was easier for men in trousers than for women in long gowns. Nonetheless, though Pearl was wearing a tight sheath dress, she gamely persevered – across what she called "endless acres of deep Oriental rugs."[18] Newsreel footage of the event shows that she stumbled slightly once or twice, but completed the ritual with her dignity intact. The Swedes were delighted.[19]

Despite a durable misconception, Pearl did not receive the Nobel Prize for *The Good Earth*. Like all laureates in literature, she was honored for the body of her work. The Academy's citation referred collectively to Pearl's Chinese novels as pioneering stories, but it specifically identified the biographies of her parents as the finest "literary works of art" she had written. Since she was already be-

23. Pearl and Enrico Fermi during the Nobel Prize ceremonies in Stockholm, December, 1938. (Reproduced with permission of the Pearl S. Buck Foundation.)

coming frustrated by her exclusive identification with *The Good Earth,* she eagerly embraced the Academy's judgment.[20]

For her Nobel lecture, Pearl revised the talk she had given at Nanking several years earlier, "The Chinese Novel." She repeated, before a Western audience, what she had previously said to a few hundred listeners in China: that China's classic fictions were "as great as the novels in any other country in the world."[21] She insisted that a truly educated person had to know such books as *The Dream of the Red Chamber* and *Three Kingdoms.*

Pearl undoubtedly had two quite different purposes in mind when she chose Chinese novels as her subject. First, she was informing European and American readers about a rich and neglected tradition, describing landmarks of Asian literature. Virtually unknown in the West, the novels she surveyed were no less important to world culture than the work of Dickens or Tolstoy.[22]

24. Pearl receiving the Nobel Prize from King Gustavus V in Stockholm, December, 1938. (Reproduced with permission of the Pearl S. Buck Foundation.)

However, Pearl's choice of Chinese fiction for her Nobel lecture had a second, more subterranean motive. Uneasy about her reputation and shaken by the contempt she had already felt, she could hide behind her credentials as an expert on Asia. In effect, "The Chinese Novel" was Pearl's effort to change the subject and to deflect attention from her own problematic status in the canon of English-language literature.

When she returned to the United States with the Nobel Prize, Pearl faced multiplied demands for speeches, articles, reviews, and interviews.[23] She and Richard rationed her schedule to avoid controversy and to capture as much positive publicity as they could from each of her appearances. In particular, they kept New York's literary society at a cautious arm's length.

The first event she attended was a gala reception in her honor at the Cosmopolitan Club on New Year's Day, 1939. The highlight of the evening was the first public reading of Pearl's play, *The Empress*. Cornelia Otis Skinner read the part of the Dowager Empress, while Vincent Price and Joseph Holland took supporting roles. A small Chinese orchestra provided the musical background. The reading, which had provoked an unprecedented demand for tickets, was not a success.[24] Skinner, who had been recruited for the reading by Mary Kennedy, a friend of Lin Yutang's, did her best with the script. She found the whole evening difficult, however, because she thought *The Empress* was "a very bad play."[25]

A couple of weeks later, Pearl presided over a dinner at the Astor Hotel for Dorothy Thompson, the celebrated foreign correspondent for the *New York Herald Tribune* and other papers. Thompson was being honored for the vocal support she had given to refugees from Nazi Germany. Pearl admired Thompson, like herself a woman who had made an international success as a writer. She also felt a bond of loyalty with Thompson's husband, Sinclair Lewis. At the award dinner, Pearl presented Thompson with a book of appreciative letters, including tributes from Eleanor Roosevelt, Albert Einstein, Herbert Hoover, and feminist leader Carrie Chapman Catt. Several thousand dollars were raised through an auction of autographed books, among them Thomas Mann's *Joseph in Egypt,* Thompson's *Refugees,* and Pearl's recently published *This Proud Heart.*[26]

Throughout the early months of 1939, Pearl followed a flexible but regular routine: Tuesdays and Wednesdays (sometimes Mondays or Thursdays, too) in the 43rd Street apartment, and long weekends on the Bucks County farm. Whether in the country or in New York, Pearl carefully protected mornings for her writing. While she was edgy about critical responses to her work, she continued to approach her writing as a daily task to be accomplished, not as a raid on inspiration. She wrote about 2,500 words each day, covering eight to twelve handwritten pages, inserting her relatively few changes along the way. She rarely went back to a text to make a major revision.[27]

Pearl could take her choice among literally dozens of offers she received from magazines for stories and articles. She wrote about what interested her, and also accepted commissions that paid well. She needed the money: nonstop renovations at Green Hills Farm, including a swimming pool and several flower gardens, kept her under pressure to earn every dollar she could. She published her stories profitably in such magazines as *Collier's, Cosmopolitan,* and the *Saturday Evening Post.* She wrote "What Women Can Do For Peace" and "Speaking As a Mother" for *Woman's Day,* and received a high fee for each of them.

In the July issue of *Harper's* she published a more substantial essay, "America's Gunpowder Women," which continued the argument she had made in "America's Medieval Women." American women, Pearl warned, were a privileged but an increasingly frustrated group. Excluded from adult responsibilities, treated as ornamental, and confined to domestic chores, they threatened to become dangerously combustible. Either they would play a larger role in the nation's public life or they would inevitably explode.

Pearl's analysis of gender relations stirred up a bruising debate among her women readers. "America's Medieval Women," she said, "seemed to make women angry enough, but I have not really dared to undertake the correspondence that has followed" the second article ('America's Gunpowder Women')." She said that she intended to write one more article about women; after that, she added, repeating a joke she had made before, "perhaps I shall have to go and live on an island."[28]

At Elmer Carter's request, Pearl wrote a brief article on African-American theater for *Opportunity* magazine. She criticized the way blacks were represented in such plays as Marc Connelly's immensely successful *Green Pastures.* "The white man shaped . . . them," she said of Connelly's black characters. "He took as much of the Negro as he thought would suit the public and no more." Because the Negro "has all his side of American history to tell, which no one has told," Pearl called for plays "written by Negroes, about Negro themes, with settings designed by Negro artists, acted by Negroes." The resulting energy and authenticity would provide "a real infusion of life into the theatre."[29] Pearl's arguments echoed those of such African-American critics as Alain Locke, Sterling Brown, and W. E. B. Du Bois.

Pearl's *Opportunity* essay elicited an admiring letter from Hallie Flanagan, the gifted, combative director of the WPA's Federal Theatre Project. For Pearl's information, Flanagan surveyed the work of the FTP's Negro Unit. Among other things, she pointed out that in 1936 the black actors and directors had themselves decided to debut with Shakespeare rather than a play by an African-American. As Flanagan accurately remarked, the performance that resulted, *Macbeth,* under the direction of John Houseman and Orson Welles, was "a tremendous success."[30]

Pearl continued to serve as literary advisor for the John Day Company, and her editorial contributions were significant. She read a large number of manuscripts, responding to each of them briefly but in some specific detail. She read only novel-length fiction, returning poetry, short stories, plays, and essays unread, usually with a courteous note inviting the author to send a novel. She worked quickly: she wrote to Mrs. Martha Turner, for example, "Your manuscript, *Twilight in Berlin,* met me in my office this morning and I have read it with much interest." (Her interest stopped short of recommending the book for publication.)[31]

In the first half or so of 1939, for which copies of her editorial reports survive, she read at least thirty manuscripts – in itself a rather remarkable accomplishment, given the other demands on her time. She also methodically pursued her own writing, turning out her reviews for *Asia,* producing several stories, and completing a new novel, *The Patriot.* When a friend asked her how she accomplished so much, she said without much exaggeration that she had no social life and no leisure time. She claimed that she avoided most dinner parties because she found them boring. Though she did not confess it, she also felt awkward about her social skills. Forty years in a foreign country had left her permanently nervous about the tribal customs and small talk of New York parties. When she said that she did nothing but work and take care of her family, she was stating a preference as much as a fact.[32]

Aside from documenting her capacity for hard work, Pearl's comments on the manuscripts she read for John Day often disclose her literary tastes and her own preoccupations. When she rejected a novel by one John P. Jones, for example, in which Jones tried to combine fiction with abundant factual material, she advised him to read John Steinbeck's short novel *Of Mice and Men,* "for what seems to me perfection in compact, beautiful writing on a theme about as difficult as yours." The theme Pearl referred to was mentally handicapped children, a subject of fundamental importance for her.

One of her most extended replies elaborated her rejection of Mrs. Sabine Baker's *Barbara Sheldon.* "It seems to me," Pearl wrote, "the theme of a woman doctor is an excellent one, and obviously one which you know something about." Not surprisingly, she welcomed a tale about a woman doctor as a timely and possibly important contribution to the current debate over gender. However, she rejected *Barbara Sheldon,* and her reasons also illuminate something of her own professional commitments and personal conflicts. "I know you want my frank opinion," she wrote,

and it is this: that while many parts of your novel are interesting and thoughtfully written, I do not think that you have truly mastered your theme. It seems to me incidental that Barbara Sheldon is a doctor and that the chief story is a love story. [However,] I think in such a woman's life love could not be the chief story. If she is a real doctor, her work must come first, and the struggle must be between her necessity to work and the hunger for love, too.

25. Pearl in a studio photograph taken shortly after she won the Nobel Prize. (Reproduced with permission of the Pearl S. Buck Foundation.)

The conflicts that Pearl looked for in the fictional life of Barbara Sheldon were precisely those that had defined her own life. Pearl had tried, as a younger woman, to subordinate her needs to those of her husband and her child. From the beginning, her accommodation to the roles imposed on her by convention was ambivalent. She had hoped to find fulfillment as a wife and mother, and had been smothered in disappointment.

Nonetheless, her early commitments had been real, and every hour of her later life was darkened by the failure of her first marriage, her daughter's mental illness, and her sterility. When she ultimately declared her independence and her sense of literary vocation, she knew that she was only drawing a veil over her pain. Her nonstop work relieved the sense of inadequacy that lay like a canker underneath her self-sufficiency. In common with many women in her generation, Pearl Buck was struggling to create a new vocabulary for female identity.

IF PEARL BUCK'S NOBEL PRIZE was intended to honor democracy against fascism, neither she nor anyone else expected that such a symbolic gesture would interrupt the world's headlong rush toward war. In Europe, the year 1939 seemed "like a strange period," as literary historian Samuel Hynes had described it, "a sort of war-year *before* the war":

The Spanish Civil War ended in March 1939, when Madrid surrendered; Czechoslovakia ended in the same month, when German troops entered the country; Chamberlain's appeasement policy ended when Britain and France pledged their support to Poland (also in March); faith in the Soviet Union ended, for many left-thinking persons, when the Russo-German Pact was signed in August.[33]

In Asia, of course, 1939 was not a pre-war year: the catastrophe that loomed over Europe had already engulfed China.

By early 1939, the conflict between China and Japan had reached a critical stage. The Japanese controlled the air, and had established military rule over Peking and the major coastal cities of Shanghai and Canton. Chiang Kai-shek had been driven out of the Nationalist capital of Nanking and had relocated his headquarters to Chungking (Chongqing), in the western province of Szechuen. The Communists were isolated in Yenan in the impoverished northern province of Shensi.

Throughout the 1930s, when Pearl commented on the war between China and Japan in lectures and in essays, she usually spoke and wrote as a partisan of China. She did so again in her new novel *The Patriot*. The first book she published after receiving the Nobel Prize, *The Patriot* covers the years from 1926 to 1938, tracing the political and personal career of its Chinese hero, a young man named Wu I-wan, against the background of Chinese civil conflict and the intensifying war between China and Japan.

The major political and military events in the novel are transcribed more or less verbatim from the period's history. Malcolm Cowley, when he reviewed *The Patriot,* spoke of Pearl's "almost Puritanical respect for facts"; and the *New Yorker* called the book a "documentary."[34] The Japanese invasion of Manchuria and the creation of the client state of Manchukuo; the Communists' legendary

Long March of 1934–1935; the tragic, accidental bombing of Shanghai civilians by the Nationalist air force in August, 1937; the fall of Canton in October of the same year and the Japanese rape of Nanking in December; the construction of the Burma Road: these are some of the historical episodes that Pearl incorporated in her novel.

While most of these subjects have to be reconstructed for late twentieth-century Western readers, they were front-page news in the 1930s, still fresh in the minds of Pearl's audience. She did not include this factual material merely to give her book a realistic texture, nor was she trying to capture the attention of contemporary readers by invoking a cluster of glamorous personalities and exciting events. Rather, she pressed history into the service of one of *The Patriot's* central themes, the irresistible and usually calamitous consequences of political turmoil for ordinary men and women.

In this novel, as in many of her other books, individual human choice is overwhelmed by indifferent combinations of natural, political, and military force. Pearl was right to call herself a naturalist. Her principal characters, whether middle-class or peasant, live inside the narrow limits that circumstance imposes on the human will.

Wu I-wan, a teenager when the novel opens, is the younger of two sons of a rich Shanghai banker and his Westernized wife. Wu I-wan's grandfather was a soldier, trained in Germany, who rose to the rank of general. Although the old man is long retired, he still wears his uniform and medals around the house, and he still occupies the preeminent position in his family. It was he who determined that his son, Wu I-wan's father, would go into banking. The Wu family lives in a large, Western-style brick house, whose other residents include Wu I-wan's grandmother, the general's wife, who is an opium addict; his older brother, I-ko; and a slave girl, Peony. In effect, the family comprises a cross section of the forces oppressing China: economic exploitation, militarism, opium, and slavery.

Reared in affluence, Wu I-wan nonetheless devotes himself more or less wholeheartedly to the cause of revolt. He joins a revolutionary youth group composed mostly of intellectuals and working-class radicals, attaches himself to a cynical but charismatic peasant leader, Liu En-lan, and waits for the approaching armies of Chiang Kai-shek to liberate Shanghai (and all of China) from the rule of the monied and military classes.

The first of the novel's three parts tells the story of Wu I-wan as young revolutionist, goaded by the guilt of privilege into idealistic commitments that are overtaken by events. Chiang arrives in Shanghai, but he immediately makes alliances with the city's bankers, including Wu I-wan's father, renounces revolution, and commences a bloody purge of dissidents, Communist and non-

Communist alike. Ironically, Wu I-wan is saved from execution only by his father's influence with Chiang. The young man is sent into comfortable exile in Japan.

The novel's long second part is set in Japan, mostly in the small and then relatively obscure seaside city of Nagasaki. (Pearl knew Nagasaki from the year she had spent in nearby Unzen following the Nanking Incident in March, 1927.) Wu I-wan has been sent to work for a wealthy merchant, Mr. Maraki, who trades in Chinese handicrafts and antiquities and who, like Wu I-wan's father, believes that a natural partnership ought to link Japan and China. Wu I-wan is welcomed into the Maraki household, becoming a trusted senior manager in the company, and eventually marries Maraki's daughter Tama, a self-described "moga," or modern woman. Through the early and mid-1930s, the happy marriage that Wu I-wan and Tama share is counterpointed by war – rumors at first, then isolated incidents leading to the Japanese annexation of Manchuria and finally the invasion of China proper in 1937. Wu I-wan, who had determined to leave politics behind him in the wreckage of his youthful idealism, is increasingly isolated in Japan, and finally decides that he must leave his wife and two sons to return and fight for China.[35]

The war zones of China, Shanghai, Nanking, and the mountainous north provide the scenes of the novel's third part. Wu I-wan enlists in Chiang's service and is sent to negotiate an alliance with the Communists. When he arrives in the unnamed northern province with Chiang's message, Wu I-wan is taken to the local Communist leader, his onetime revolutionary comrade En-lan, who is accompanied by his wife, the Wu family's former slave, Peony. Though he is still suspicious of the Communists, Wu I-wan reluctantly concludes that they are the only force in China that has forged a genuine alliance with the masses and therefore has a chance to defeat the Japanese. The novel ends in the midst of fierce warfare, with Wu I-wan's future, like China's, in the balance.

The Patriot was the first of a series of novels and stories Pearl would write over the next several years that used the Asian war as their subject and setting. In a sense, the war came to Pearl's rescue as a writer, by authorizing her to return to the Chinese material she knew best. She was still having difficulty shifting her focus to the American scene. Five years after moving back to the United States, she had published only one American novel, and the tepid critical response to *This Proud Heart* had struck another blow to her confidence. Now that a full-scale war was raging in her old homeland, she could defer the question of her artistic national identity by putting her pen honorably at the service of China's beleaguered nationhood. Over the next four years, Pearl would publish four novels, three of them set in China. Duty and preference conveniently coincided.

Because of her loyalty to China and her fears that the Japanese were winning the war, Pearl agreed to join the American foreign policy debate as a spokeswoman for Chinese interests. While Americans had a good deal of sympathy for China in 1939, they had little stomach for participating in an Asian conflict.[36] Public opinion surveys indicated that the majority of Americans were resolutely isolationist; most would remain so through the elections of 1940, and indeed right up to the eve of Pearl Harbor. The reaction against World War I had convinced an entire generation that foreign wars led only to disaster. Americans wanted to avoid entanglements with Europe, despite the ties of kinship that linked millions of families on both sides of the Atlantic. They wanted even more emphatically to stay out of Asia, which seemed utterly remote and irrelevant.

From time to time, Pearl spoke out on events in Europe. In April, 1939, for instance, she sent telegrams to President Roosevelt and Secretary of State Cordell Hull, urging that the United States grant political asylum to hundreds of Spanish intellectuals condemned to death by Franco for their anti-fascism.[37] However, such pronouncements from Pearl on the European crisis were relatively rare. She knew that she was more likely to be heard when she spoke out on Asia. She also believed, quite accurately, that few people in the West would plead the case for China, while there were many who "speak for and win sympathy for Europe."[38]

Furthermore, Pearl's solidarity with China was profound and nearly instinctual. The Japanese armies were marching over cities and villages that she knew intimately. When she reviewed a Japanese memoir about the war in the Yangtze basin, Ashihei Hino's *Wheat and Soldiers,* she responded with a cry of pain: "I suppose I feel this book too keenly," she wrote in the *New Republic.* She confessed:

I know as I know the lines on my own face every foot of the countryside about which it is written. Hangchow was the place where my parents spent their first years in China and where I have been many times. Suchowfu and all the countryside about I know from years of my own life there.

. . . So when I read this book by a Japanese and realize that these things of which he writes took place in the little villages I know, where I have sat and drunk tea and talked in peace and understanding with the people whom I loved, that the country over which he marches, where peasants lie dying, is country where I walked among good and harmless people, living on their land, that upon these well known country roads they now lie, dead and dying, it is too much for me. I cannot fairly review this book.[39]

Pearl's political judgments about the Asian war were obviously shaped by her deep-rooted emotional involvement with China's land and people. In a vexed but real sense, China remained her home.

In April, she agreed to give a radio talk for the American Committee for Non-Participation in Japanese Aggression. Chaired by former diplomat Roger

S. Greene, and boasting such high-profile board members and sponsors as journalist William Allen White, critic Van Wyck Brooks, and theologian Reinhold Niebuhr, the Committee lobbied Congress and tried to shape public opinion to restrict shipments of American oil, steel, and other industrial products to Japan. Corporations such as United States Steel and Standard Oil wanted to continue their profitable (and legal) trade with Japan behind the protective wall of American neutrality. The Committee, abetted by a number of important newspapers and politicians, opposed such trade on moral grounds, arguing that American supplies made the United States a partner in Japanese aggression.

Pearl spoke at a Town Hall meeting that was broadcast over New York's WQXR. She suggested that true neutrality had become impossible because neutrality actually favored Japan. Americans may desire "to do nothing," she said; however, "simply by doing nothing we may inadvertently be taking a stand" on the Japanese side of the conflict. The situation in Asia demonstrated that "to declare peace may be at the same time to declare war." In its zeal for profits, American business had made a corrupt bargain, "helping Japan to kill and to bomb human beings, to seize territories to which she has no right whatever, and to make herself an important part of that whole regressive movement in Europe which we call the totalitarian state."[40]

The bloodstained profiteering of American industrialists obviously weighed heavily on Pearl's conscience. Her protests included a short story, "The Face of Gold," which she wrote for the *Saturday Evening Post*. The story's main character, Timothy Stayne, is the thirty-five-year-old heir to an American arms fortune. For ten years, as a form of dissent from his father's trade, he has lived quietly in exile in a decayed Chinese temple, learning the Chinese language and identifying with the common people. His retirement is shattered by the Japanese invasion. When the Japanese armies march toward his village, Timothy learns that they are using Western guns and tanks, probably bought from the Stayne company. To atone a little for the immoral dealings of arms merchants like his father, Timothy uses his inherited money to buy ten thousand rifles from his father's company, which he turns over to the local Chinese guerrilla leader.[41]

The irony of Timothy's gift is attractive – profits from sales to Japan subsidize weapons for China – but the outcome is more miraculous than plausible. Once again, Pearl was using fiction to indulge a kind of wishful thinking, simply decreeing the justice that was absent from the war's real events. More significantly, the story illuminates Pearl's bedrock beliefs that self-defense is always legitimate and that resistance is preferable to surrender. Neither the peace-loving Timothy Stayne nor the temple's Buddhist monks ever suggest appeasing the Japanese invaders.

Despite Pearl's vision of Chinese–American solidarity, the United States did practically nothing to help China. Month after month, China's casualties mounted inexorably, and its defense efforts faltered because Japan had crippled its manufacturing capacity. Since most Chinese heavy industry was concentrated on the coast and along the Yangtze River, Japan's military domination of those regions meant that nearly three-quarters of China's production was either destroyed or effectively under Japanese control by 1938.

The Chinese responded by launching the *gung ho* (work together) industrial cooperative movement, a network of small factories scattered across the countryside, operating out of peasant huts, army tents, sometimes even caves. Indusco, as the industrial cooperatives were called, eventually played a major part in Chinese resistance by providing a reliable supply of agricultural and military equipment. From three thousand factories in sixteen provinces came a steady stream of bicycles, rifles, hand grenades, blankets, uniforms, plows, textiles, pruning hooks, hammers, and nails. Without these supplies, the war against Japan would almost certainly have been lost. Edgar Snow called Indusco "one of the great human adventures of our time."

Snow and his wife, Nym Wales (Helen Foster Snow), played a part in the cooperative program. However, the chief architect was another foreigner, a forty-year-old New Zealander named Rewi Alley.[42] A veteran of World War I, Alley had been working in China since the late 1920s, including seven years as a reform-minded factory inspector in Shanghai. His leadership of the cooperative movement made him a legendary figure in China; he became an advisor to Mao Tse-tung and lived in Peking until his death in the 1980s.[43]

Edgar and Helen Snow, who had been friends of Pearl's since the early 1930s, persuaded her to propagandize for Rewi Alley's efforts. She responded with her usual energy: a blizzard of articles, speeches, and fund-raising appeals over the next several years. She began with an essay called "Free China Gets to Work," which appeared in the April, 1939 issue of *Asia,* and was reprinted in both American and foreign magazines. In the essay, Pearl explained how the cooperatives worked and argued that Indusco was the key to China's survival. Citing R. H. Tawney's recent influential book, *Land and Labor in China,* Pearl also related the cooperative movement to China's traditions of small-scale craftsmanship and local manufacturing.[44] She agreed with Tawney that China's economic welfare could best be secured through a system of small industries of the sort Rewi Alley was spearheading. In effect, Japanese aggression had done the Chinese a useful service by forcing them to abandon Western-style mass production.[45]

Forgotten today, Rewi Alley was a world figure in the late 1930s, the subject of newspaper and magazine stories around the world. He makes an appearance in almost every Western travel book of the period, including *Journey to a War,* which W. H. Auden and Christopher Isherwood co-authored after spending six months touring behind the lines in China in 1938. *Journey* is an entertaining, lightweight travelogue, combining Isherwood's journalistic prose and Auden's poetry and photographs.

Pearl hated the book. She was still her father's earnest daughter, sternly convinced that serious matters should be treated seriously. She had no ear for Isherwood's gallows humor and no patience with his mild ironies. She didn't even like Auden's poems. She complained that the two Englishmen "somehow manage to make the Chinese-Japanese war look like a modern *Mikado*. . . . [T]he whole book prances to a Gilbert and Sullivan rhythm."[46] Perhaps she was also offended by Isherwood's occasional references to China as "the Bad Earth."

Pearl's criticism is humorless but fair. In their several months in China, Auden and Isherwood actually had little contact either with the war or with the Chinese people: in their book, they simply rehearsed the shopworn ideas and images they had brought with them when they came to China. In Isherwood's prose, the Chinese are consistently reduced to the faceless masses of Orientalist caricature:

What an anonymous country this is! Everywhere the labouring men and women. . . . The naked, lemon-coloured torsos, bent over their unending tasks, have no individuality; they seem folded and reticent as plants. The children are all alike – gaping, bleary-nosed, in their padded jackets, like stuffed, mass-produced dolls.

Elsewhere, Isherwood reaches the mournful conclusion: "Really, the proceedings of the Chinese are so mysterious as to fill one, ultimately, with a kind of despair."[47]

Isherwood's Chinese are anonymous, gaping masses, undifferentiated and mysterious: these were the stereotypes that for generations had made the Chinese invisible behind the screen of Western condescension. Though Pearl didn't bother to point it out, even Isherwood's details were wrong: except for victims of jaundice, there has never been a Chinese man or woman with a "lemon-coloured" torso.

Of course, Isherwood's retrograde attitudes were a sadly accurate sample of what most Westerners believed. A United States senator, visiting Asia in 1940, actually made the zany promise that, "with God's help, we will lift Shanghai up and up till it's just like Kansas City."[48] Pearl spoke out against this sort of nonsense whenever she could. She understood that she would be heard when others, including most Asians themselves, were ignored. She knew a great deal about China, but her opinions mattered mainly because she had become one of the most famous women in the world. Much as she complained about the triumph of image over substance in American culture, she was a beneficiary of the modern star system.

She was frequently called on to represent the "woman's point of view" in panel discussions and articles. In May, 1939, for example, Edmund Dorfman of the American Institute of Motion Pictures wrote to Pearl, asking that she make a short filmed statement on "Peace and Democracy," which would be shown continuously in the Science and Education Building at the New York World's Fair. Dorfman listed the other "outstanding personalities" who had agreed to the project, among them Thomas Mann, Albert Einstein, Cordell Hull, and Harold Ickes. "To this point," Dorfman added, "among the ten personalities selected we have not included a woman. It has been urged that you represent woman-hood in America in making such a statement."[49] Pearl accepted the assignment. While she cringed at the idea of representing all of American womanhood, she never turned down a chance to climb into any secular pulpit and preach on subjects like world peace.

After her appearance at the Fair, Pearl and Richard drove to Vineyard Haven, off the Massachusetts coast, where they had rented a house not far from Katherine Cornell's large compound. They took Janice and their four youngest children, leaving Carol at Vineland. Pearl's letters from that summer are filled with family chat and pleasant gossip. She wrote to Emma White that she spent every after-noon on the beach, "watching the babies dig in the sand and enjoying myself between a perfect blue sky and a perfect blue sea." She added, quite convinc-ingly, that she and Richard were "perfectly happy."[50]

Pearl's idyllic holiday lingered through August. Only a few visitors intruded on the family's privacy, and they were trusted friends. Free from distractions, Pearl was working on a new book, writing her reviews for *Asia* and other mag-azines, and helping Lin Yutang revise his novel *Moment in Peking,* which John Day would publish the following spring. She enjoyed the time she had with her small sons and her younger daughter. Pearl was always more comfortable with babies than with older children. Babies were less demanding emotionally, their problems simpler. Furthermore, since Pearl now had a retinue of domestic help-ers, she could be a mother to her infants more or less on her own schedule. As the children grew, they would need more of Pearl's time and energy than she was prepared to give.

Pearl's domestic happiness was still troubled by an undercurrent of regret. She called her adoptive sons and daughters "an exceptionally nice family . . . a hand-picked family . . . collected . . . by sheer force of obstinacy."[51] Although this was intended as a breezy, contented remark, there is actually something chilling in the self-centered imagery here, an implication that Pearl was reimbursing herself through her adopted children for Carol's defects.

On September 1, the summer's peace was shattered by the news from Europe. Hitler had invaded Poland. The battles that had begun in China years earlier had now reached Europe; World War II was under way. The following day, Richard and Pearl packed up for the trip back to Green Hills Farm.

AS PEARL POINTED OUT in an *Asia* article in November, 1939, the war in Asia involved more people and a larger territory than the conflict in Europe. Nevertheless, Americans remained generally indifferent to events on the other side of the Pacific. American ignorance about Asia was profound. Most people in the United States knew at least a little about the major European countries. But the majority of Americans could not even locate China on an outline map of the world.[52] Quite understandably, Pearl found this sort of revelation shocking. It reminded her of the indifference she had met at Randolph-Macon, almost thirty years earlier, when she had descended on provincial Virginia from a land ten thousand miles away, and no one seemed to notice or care.

Pearl's response to the war was deeply divided. On the one hand, she was vigorously anti-fascist and a frank partisan of democratic forces. At the same time, her first-hand experience of suffering and warfare during her years in China had brought her to the edge of pacifism. In a letter to Roger Greene, she said that she was thinking of joining the Quakers, because she admired their opposition to war.[53]

Early in 1940, Pearl published a new novel, *Other Gods*. The book opens in Asia but moves quickly to the United States, once again recapitulating Pearl's own migration several years earlier. Though the novel is awash in provocative ideas, it received deservedly perfunctory notices. The lackluster critical response, which was matched by anemic sales, warned Pearl that her claims to public attention were dwindling.

Other Gods tells the story of Bert Holm, a handsome young American who suddenly becomes a hero by climbing one of the world's highest mountains. Bert's achievement occurs in the first few pages, and is more or less incidental to the novel's plot; the book's focus is principally on the manufacture of a celebrity in modern America.[54] Handsome, courageous, and plain-spoken, Bert Holm is rapidly converted from an individual into a national symbol. It hardly matters that his limits are even more striking than his strengths, that he is a person of small intelligence, childish appetites, and uncertain morality. He is a triumph of public relations, idolized by crowds of ignorant but adoring, spiritually needy men and women. At first skeptical of the adulation, Bert comes to depend on it as the wellspring of his own identity.

The character of Bert Holm owes something to Pearl's fear of the European dictators who were dragging the world into war, those strutting egomaniacs who dilated murderously in the worship of their hordes of followers. Bert's more local source was Charles Lindbergh, whom Pearl had met in China in 1931, during the terrible Yangtze floods. (For most readers in 1940, Lindbergh was announced immediately in the novel's subtitle, *An American Legend*.)[55] Lindbergh had gone to China mainly for the adventure of the flight. To his credit, once he saw the extent of the calamity, he had helped with relief efforts by flying rescue and

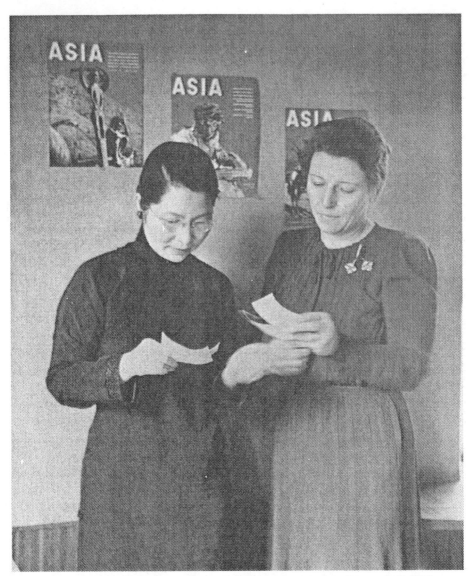

26. Pearl and Mrs. Y. H. Wei, treasurer of the Chinese Women's Relief Association, in the offices of *Asia* magazine, January, 1940. Pearl was receiving the pictures of twelve Chinese war orphans whom she had agreed to support for the year. (Courtesy Harry Ransom Humanities Center, University of Texas.)

reconnaissance missions over the flood-stricken areas.[56] When Pearl met Lindbergh at a Nanking dinner, she had taken an immediate dislike to him. She conceded his extraordinary good looks and his boyish sincerity, but she found him boring and politically naive.[57] Throughout the late 1930s, as if to prove the validity of Pearl's harsh judgment, Lindbergh retreated ever more deeply into political paranoia.[58] He became a clamorous isolationist, associating himself with some of the more unsavory, racist elements in American politics.

In *Other Gods,* for the first time in her career, Pearl deployed satire as a device for cultural comment. Her target was only incidentally the attractive, fumbling Bert Holm, with his "vast unconscious vanity [and] colossal self-centeredness."[59] Pearl was more disturbed by the opportunists who take advantage of Bert's fame, the journalists and professional image makers who fuel the fires of public frenzy, turning mobs into profit. George Gallup had invented modern polling in the mid-1930s, just a few years before the novel was published. The consequences for American politics and culture would prove to be incalculable, and *Other Gods* is Pearl's mordant prophecy. Bert Holm is an early fictional example of a life shaped and guided by the pseudosciences of polling and public relations. In effect, Bert's paltry reality is superseded by a carefully groomed illusion, cynically manipulated to suit the public's shifting moods.

In its turn, the public as Pearl renders it is not a mere collection of dupes. Frightening in their anonymity, America's shouting masses try to drown their own discontent in the blind adoration of celebrities. Bert Holm is merely a convenient, and temporary, instrument of catharsis. Rather like the title character of Nathanael West's *Miss Lonelyhearts* (1933), Bert becomes the vessel into which wounded and desperate people pour their pain. Women plead for advice with their marriages; men demand help in finding a job. A crippled boy writes that Bert's mountain-climbing exploits have given him hope that he might someday walk again.

Especially amid the collective helplessness of the Depression decade, Bert's achievements radiate over his fellow citizens with a gleam of reassurance. To Pearl, on the other hand, the crowds that pursue Bert are a fearful reminder that demagogues and tyrants can arise anywhere, even in the United States. Pearl's friend, Sinclair Lewis, had entertained the same hypothesis several years earlier in his anti-fascist novel, *It Can't Happen Here* (1934). More than most Americans, Pearl had personal experience of mobs aroused to lethal action.

A small portion of the irony in *Other Gods* may have been self-directed. At a minimum, Pearl's interest in the rise and fall of American heroes had unmistakable biographical origins. After all, she had herself been both the beneficiary and the victim of publicity campaigns. Working closely with Richard, she tried to manage every detail of her encounters with the press and public. One small and typical episode will illustrate the effort she put into the cultivation of her image.

In late January, 1940, the same week the novel was published, Pearl agreed to read a short speech at the end of an NBC radio program called "Women of Letters." The broadcast was one episode in a series that ran under the general title "Gallant American Women," produced for NBC by Eva Hansl.

When Hansl sent the Walshes a draft of her proposed introduction, Richard fired back a whole list of corrections that would have to be made if Pearl were to agree to appear. First, Pearl must always be referred to as "Pearl Buck," never as Mrs. Buck or Miss Buck. Second, Richard insisted that Hansl must include the titles of several of Pearl's books in her opening remarks, not just *The Good Earth*. (Richard suggested five others: *Sons, A House Divided, The Mother, The Exile,* and *Fighting Angel.*) Next, Richard objected to Hansl's reference to Pearl as the "second" woman to win the Nobel Prize in literature. He pointed out that she was the third (in fact, she was the fourth), and proposed that Hansl should therefore say that Pearl was the first *American* woman to win. Finally – "and this is most important," Richard emphasized – Sweden's King Gustavus was misquoted in the script, and Pearl would "not take part in any program which would seem to be discourteous to the King and the people of Sweden." In yet another letter, Richard raised an additional objection. Hansl had proposed identifying Pearl as a novelist whose work was set exclusively in Asia. "I must correct your impression that she does not fit into the scheme as one of the women who have described the American scene. Her novel, *This Proud Heart* . . . was wholly American, and her next novel, *Other Gods* . . . is almost entirely American."[60]

All of these elaborate precautions and preparations led to a stunning anticlimax: Pearl produced a flaccid statement of less than three hundred words – under two minutes of air time – in which she commented vaguely on her own ambition to be a writer whose work would accurately reflect whatever culture and country she happened to be living in at any moment.

Pearl's views on fiction were usually less provocative than her observations on society and politics. She was constantly involved in public and private controversy. In the summer of 1940, for example, shortly after she was elected to the National Committee of the American Civil Liberties Union, she was caught up in the notorious case of Elizabeth Gurley Flynn. Flynn was a radical whose credentials stretched back to the early twentieth century – she had been an IWW organizer before World War I and a founder of the ACLU in 1920.[61] Nonetheless, in 1940 the ACLU board voted to expel Flynn because of her membership in the Communist Party. Pearl, voting sheepishly under the name Mrs. Richard J. Walsh, concurred in the decision.[62]

Pearl's anti-Communism had hardened in the late 1930s. She had come to regard Stalin as a monster, and the Soviet system as "one of the greatest tyrannies of history."[63] Nonetheless, personal loyalty sometimes blunted the edge of her ideology. Shortly after she voted against Elizabeth Gurley Flynn, she defended the British radical writer Freda Utley, who had been denied entry into the United States.[64] Pearl sent off a dozen letters and telegrams demanding that the case be reopened. Among other things, Pearl insisted that Utley's onetime membership in the Communist Party was irrelevant: "the use of this as a reason [for refusing Utley's request for a visa] would not be in keeping with the principles of a free democracy."[65]

A few months later, Pearl tried to intervene in the case of a young Thai student, Kumut Chandruang, who had published a couple of essays in *Asia*. In the late summer, Chandruang was abruptly sent back to Thailand when his government decided that his writing was embarrassing to the Thai royal family. As one of Chandruang's mentors, Pearl felt indirectly responsible for his troubles. She wrote to Murray Sheehan, an advisor to the Thai ambassador, objecting to the "absurd" and "illogical" behavior of the government.[66] Her protest was ignored.

The widening war occupied much of Pearl's attention throughout the summer. In June, Pearl returned to the New York World's Fair to give a lecture for the Women's International League for Peace and Freedom. She called her talk "Planning for Peace," choosing the title to rebuke a government policy that was single-mindedly driven by plans for war. Among other things, she insisted that war is always the worst course, and always fails to achieve its objectives. Once again, she argued that "it is women who must end war if it is ever to be ended."[67] At the same time, in a deleted line, she also rejected absolute pacifism as naive. Presumably, she wrote the line to placate her conflicted conscience, and took it out to accommodate her largely pacifist audience.

Pearl also continued to speak out against discrimination and in support of civil rights for African-Americans, and against racism more generally. She gave an enthusiastic review to Ruth Benedict's *Race: Science and Politics*, a book that demonstrated at length that the idea of a pure race was a myth, and that all humanity is, in Pearl's summary phrase, "a creature hopelessly mongrel." Benedict, said Pearl, had successfully assaulted "the fallacious belief that one race can prove itself superior to another on any scientific ground."[68] Among her other accomplishments, in Pearl's view, Benedict had unmasked the racist use of so-called intelligence tests.

In a letter to Lillian Harris, an African-American woman in Philadelphia, Pearl wrote that "a great future is ahead of the Negro American." Harris had written to Pearl, grieving about the inferiority of blacks. Pearl responded by repeating her conviction that "there is no such thing as an inferior race." After reminding Harris that as a white person she had been considered inferior in China, she urged Harris: "Do not be ashamed of your race. Be proud of it. The Negro has many gifts . . . to contribute to the world."[69]

Pearl was especially active in the long, frustrating struggle to pass a federal anti-lynching law. Mary White Ovington, one of the founders of the NAACP, regarded Pearl as a major ally in the organization's struggle. Ovington recalled going to "a dim, quiet room to hear Pearl Buck voice her horror both at the suffering of the hunted Negro, and at the indifference with which white America views it." In Ovington's authoritative opinion, "Pearl Buck has never failed us."[70]

Eugene Kinckle Jones of the National Urban League had a similarly high estimate of Pearl's contribution. Jones heard Pearl speak at an Urban League meeting in upstate New York. He later wrote to congratulate her for her remarks, taking the opportunity to denounce the newly famous Richard Wright in the process. A "magnanimity such as yours," Jones wrote, "is the antidote to the misanthropy and the cynicism of a 'Native Son' who has lost faith, if any he ever had, in the ability of man to devise some solvent to eradicate the invidious distinctions of society."[71]

Though Pearl's subjects ranged widely, the bulk of her published commentary in these months dealt with women. In July, 1940, she published an article, "Women: A Minority Group," in *Opportunity* magazine. She drove home the point that women all over the world, despite their numbers, occupy the inferior status of a minority group. No race is in the minority in every country. For example, "Negroes in one part of the world may consider themselves a minority, in other parts of the world they are not."[72] Women, on the contrary, though they are numerically not a minority at all, have been consigned to a second-class humanity in every society.

Pearl warned of the devastating consequences of relegating women to medieval servitude merely because of their sex. In her indignation, Pearl's rhetoric took on the passionate rhythms of her preacher-father. In 1940, she wrote, a hundred years after the organized battle for women's rights had begun in America,

women are having still to struggle against more than a thousand laws in various states discriminating against them as a sex; they are having to struggle, and without apparent success, for the right to have the Constitution of the United States apply to them in the same way as it applies to men, and must struggle, for a long time to come, against wages lower than men's for the same work, against a fresh tide of prejudice toward married women working, against almost undiminished prejudice toward women in the professions, in business, in government, and to some extent in the arts.[73]

Pearl said that she didn't advocate revolution: "I have seen revolutions in a country more than once [and] I never saw a revolution that did not leave people debased and conditions worse than before." Nonetheless, she demanded change, and her anger had its obvious sources in her own experiences as a daughter, wife, mother, and professional.

In the spring of 1940, Pearl reviewed a book called *Restless Wave*, the autobiography of a Japanese woman. The writer, Haru Matsui, was a frustrated figure who had been educated in the United States and then returned to Japan, where she was entombed in the suffocating demands of a traditional culture. Pearl said that Matsui "is that most solitary of human beings, a woman who cannot conform to the patterns her people have set for a woman. . . . [She was] a girl born with the misfortune of an independent mind."[74]

Pearl's sympathy with Haru Matsui was anchored in painful resemblance: she, too, was a woman with an independent mind, a woman who refused to conform, who found herself living an emotionally solitary life as a consequence. As she said in yet another review, a good mind is "born unhappily in the body of a woman, [for] even in the best parts of this world a first-rate mind is still hampered if it happens to belong to a woman."[75] In 1941, at Pearl's urging, the John Day Company published *My Narrow Isle,* the autobiography of Sumie Seo Mishima. Again, as in her sympathetic response to Haru Matsui's portrait of herself in *Restless Wave*, Pearl was attracted by the points of resemblance between Mishima's life and her own. Both Pearl and Mishima were born in the 1890s; both had spent years in Asia and America and knew the languages and cultures of different societies; both struggled to establish independent careers in societies that abridged their opportunities because they were women.[76]

Pearl's lifelong discontent with the patriarchal status quo, which was growing sharper in her middle age, surfaced repeatedly in her writing. Reviewing a biography of Gertrude Bell, the British expert on the Middle East, Pearl called Bell "a great woman who in some ways accomplished more in Arabia than [T. E.] Lawrence did."[77] Yet, in spite of her achievements, almost no one had heard of Bell, while Lawrence had become a romantic hero. The explanation for Bell's obscurity, Pearl was sure, lay in gender. Women were not eligible for greatness.

Pearl refused to join any of the groups that were promoting women's causes. At the same time, she was vocal in advocating women's rights, and she became friends with a number of activist women, among them Alma Lutz, an important feminist organizer and secretary of the National Woman's Party (NWP). In the late 1930s and early 1940s, Lutz and the NWP had chosen the Equal Rights Amendment as their principal issue. First proposed in the early 1920s, shortly after the Nineteenth Amendment secured for women the right to vote, the ERA – sometimes called the Lucretia Mott amendment – had languished for nearly twenty years. The amendment's opponents included most of the individuals and organizations that had supported votes for women.[78]

The groups that fought the ERA included the National Women's Trade

Union League, the General Federation of Women's Clubs, the League of Women Voters, the National Consumer's League, the National Association for Labor Legislation, the Woman's Christian Temperance Union, the Charity Organization Society, the National Council of Catholic Women, the Council of Jewish Women, the Girl's Friendly Society, the American Association for Organizing Family Social Work, the Parent Teachers' Association, the National Federation of Federal Employees, the YWCA, and the American Association of University Women. According to historian Kathryn Kish Sklar, "only the National Federation of Business and Professional Women's Clubs did not openly oppose the proposed amendment."[79]

These diverse organizations lobbied against the ERA for different reasons, but most shared a concern that the amendment would lead to the abolition of the laws that protected women from economic exploitation.[80] At the same time, the arguments over the amendment within each organization were often strenuous. The American Association of University Women (AAUW), to give one example, debated the ERA for years. It was only at the 1939 convention that opposition to the amendment was made official policy. The AAUW *Journal* that year reported that the convention's members had voted to endorse the following resolution: "The Association supports the principle of equality for women; but opposes the proposed Equal Rights Amendment to the Constitution as a method of obtaining equality."[81] The bland bureaucratic prose of the resolution disguised the more colorful language in which the debate had been conducted. One of the women who spoke against the ERA declared that equal rights was "one of those weasel-like phrases like 'fraternity,' 'equality,' and 'democracy,' into which we all fall so easily."[82] A majority of those attending apparently agreed, and the convention went on record in opposition.

The AAUW's decision indirectly brought Pearl Buck into the debate. Alma Lutz and the other leaders of the National Woman's Party strongly endorsed the amendment. Lutz was outraged by the AAUW's resolution, and recruited Pearl to speak out on the other side. Lutz approached Pearl as a friend and fellow writer. She had first met Pearl and Richard Walsh shortly after John Day had agreed to publish *Created Equal,* her worshipful biography of Elizabeth Cady Stanton.

Lutz had lunch with the Walshes in October, 1939, and then jotted down her impressions. "It was easy to see," she wrote of Pearl and Richard, "that they were very much in love." At the same time, like so many others who met Pearl, Lutz noted "an aloofness about her," which she interpreted "as a wall she had built for self-protection or an oriental aloofness." The conversation that afternoon had touched on Elizabeth Cady Stanton "and women in general and I felt we would have much to talk over in the future."[83]

When she decided to enlist Pearl in support of the ERA, Lutz sent her a

National Woman's Party pamphlet that reviewed the legal subordination of women throughout American history. Pearl said she read the material "with interest and indignation." She agreed to make a statement, adding: "It is my habit, however, to wait until I boil down before I make a decision, so it will be a few days before I do so."[84]

Pearl waited three weeks to "boil down," and then sent Lutz her statement. She put the case for the ERA in terms of both female emancipation and the national interest: a society that aspires to justice will make laws that apply equally to all "its citizens and not [to] male and female" separately. Even rules that seem to discriminate in favor of women are ultimately destructive of democracy. What women need, Pearl argued, is not special treatment, but "an unequivocally equal place with men before the law."[85]

Pearl urged that women's employment opportunities had to be expanded. Few issues were more important than the right to earn a living, yet a 1936 Gallup poll had indicated that over 80 percent of the public opposed work for married women unless their husbands could not support them.[86] If this was the conventional wisdom, Pearl loathed it. In a conversation with critic Robert Van Gelder, she asked, "Why should only the home be the stronghold for women?" She acknowledged that American girls were often brought up as the well-educated equals of boys. However, when they tried to find jobs, they discovered with a shock that they were not regarded as equal – nor even taken seriously.[87] Pearl offered the provocative argument that men were actually afraid of women, and resisted women's rights because they feared female competition.[88]

In such a climate of hostility, Pearl believed that the ERA was indispensable to enlarging women's opportunities. She concluded her statement to Alma Lutz by declaring, "I believe that the Lucretia Mott amendment is the only self-respecting basis for citizenship in a true democracy." Lutz was understandably delighted with Pearl's manifesto, which she reprinted in full and in part repeatedly in NWP pamphlets and letters.

Whenever she spoke on behalf of women's rights, Pearl always identified herself as a mother, and linked her support for the ERA to her maternal obligations. In her mind, the connection was simple. She knew that feminists were divided on the question of women's special responsibilities as mothers. However, she had also concluded that women would, in fact, continue to do most of the nation's childrearing. She intended to educate her own sons and daughters in sexual equality; when they left her home for the world of work, she wanted them to find opportunities that were equitably distributed.

Though Pearl continued to resist the term "feminist" – "I myself am not and have not been a feminist or active in woman's suffrage" – she had in fact become a leading spokesperson for women's equality.[89] She was invited to give the main address at the Tenth Biennial Convention of the National Woman's Party in

Washington, D.C., on December 7, 1940. The day was filled with speeches and panel discussions in which delegates devised strategies to secure ratification of the Equal Rights Amendment by 1943. The evening concluded with what the program called – somewhat optimistically – the "Victory Banquet."

Following the dinner, Pearl gave a talk on "The Place of Woman in Democracy." She repeated the argument she had made in her earlier statement on behalf of the ERA: democracies that deny full partnership to their female citizens have betrayed their promise. In Europe, she said, the rise of fascism has been accompanied by the systematic subjugation of women, their confinement to kitchen and nursery. As a corollary, Americans who call for the domestication of women are, whatever their intentions, tools of a home-grown fascist mentality.[90]

Though Pearl's message was threatening, she told Alma Lutz that she had enjoyed the convention: "The National Woman's Party is a good crowd and I am happy to have made their acquaintance."[91] For the first time in her life, Pearl was searching for women allies. She was deeply troubled by the connections she saw between fascism and the treatment of women. In the fall of 1940, she circulated an anxious letter to several dozen prominent women, among them Margaret Bourke-White, Anne O'Hare McCormick, Margaret Mead, and Eleanor Roosevelt. In the letter, Pearl described herself as "thoroughly alarmed at the number of women who feel the tide of discrimination and reactionary feeling rising against them." She fearfully compared America with Europe and Asia, proposed that "there are tides of fascism in our country . . . which will unless they are checked swell to meet foreign fascism," and concluded by referring darkly to "what has happened to women in fascist countries."[92]

By Pearl's own accounting, two-thirds of the women she wrote to had immediately written back to declare their complete disagreement with her gloomy analysis. Typically, this response did not cause her to back down. On the contrary, as she wrote to Margaret Bourke-White and Helen McAfee in subsequent letters, she simply concluded that successful women were insulated from the recent upsurge of discrimination. She also told McAfee that *Harper's Magazine* and *Atlantic Monthly* had adopted a decidedly reactionary attitude toward women, which was proved by the *Atlantic's* decision to reject an article by Virginia Woolf.[93] McAfee disagreed with Pearl about that, too.

Pearl's fears about the fate of women under fascism collided with her hatred of war. Even as she continued to oppose war in her public statements, she privately confessed that Hitler was "a mad dog" who needed to be caught and killed. Both alternatives, appeasement and war, seemed equally abhorrent to her. She believed that women had a special role to play in preventing war; at the same time, she had also concluded that fascism, whose particular targets included women, could only be halted by war.

Reluctantly, she acknowledged that national and personal honor sometimes demanded military responses. However, she insisted that Western nations, including the United States, have translated sad necessity into a corrupt species of glory, creating a homicidal, militaristic "creed which sends millions of young men to compulsory death in every generation."[94] Pearl told friends that two subjects, war and the condition of women, were keeping her awake at night.[95]

As a prominent opponent of war, Pearl attracted attention around the world, some of it unwelcome. Fascist sympathizers, who were eager to encourage America's continued neutrality, misunderstood and applauded Pearl's anti-war stance. Ezra Pound, for example, sent her a letter declaring that the European conflict had no political or moral stakes worth fighting for. "The war is mainly for money lending and three or four metal monopolies," Pound assured her.[96] Pearl, on the contrary, regarded fascism as a great and real evil, which Americans would eventually have to confront. She didn't bother to answer Pound's letter.

Though she was tormented with ambivalence about America's proper role in the global war, she continued to support China in its struggle against Japanese aggression. She had long been active as a propagandist and fund-raiser, especially for medical relief. In the summer and fall of 1940, she led a campaign called "The Book of Hope," with a target of $100,000 for hospital supplies and equipment. Pearl raised the money by soliciting $100 contributions from one thousand women, each of whom also signed their name in an ornate book. Eleanor Roosevelt presided over a reception at the Chinese embassy at which the book was presented, along with a check for the proceeds, to the Chinese ambassador, Dr. Hu Shih.[97]

The "Book of Hope" campaign, which proved that Pearl could raise a great deal of money in a short time, was a subsidiary of the American Bureau for Medical Aid to China. Encouraged by the results, and restless working for other people, Pearl decided to set up her own organization and to reach for even more ambitious goals. In November, she and Richard announced the new venture, which they called the China Emergency Relief Committee (CERC). The stated purpose was to raise one million dollars in six months – a formidable total. The money would be spent on a long list of humanitarian items: hospitals and medical supplies, food and clothing, the care of orphans. The organization would raise no money for military supplies, nor items such as trucks and jeeps that might be appropriated by the armed forces. In addition, CERC scrupulously avoided engaging in official political activities.

Pearl served as chairman of CERC from its founding, and Eleanor Roosevelt accepted the position of honorary chairman. Richard Walsh was a member of the administrative committee, along with Dr. Co Tui, representing the Chinese government, *Time* publisher Henry Luce, Dorothy Canfield Fisher, Colonel

Theodore Roosevelt, and IBM chief executive Thomas J. Watson. Board meetings were held at the Walshes' New York apartment.

WHETHER PEARL QUITE REALIZED it or not, she was changing the pattern of her life when she set up the China Emergency Relief Committee. She had always juggled half a dozen different tasks, hurrying between her homes and offices as she coped with a lengthening list of domestic and professional obligations. Now, however, she was starting to devote an ever larger share of her daily schedule and her energy to humanitarian activities. For the first time, she was also taking on the encumbrances of administration. She would order her life in this way for the next three decades, creating one organization after another to address such questions as interracial conflict, immigration, transnational and interracial adoption, and foster care.

Her new priorities had several implications. The most striking was that she depended less on her writing to define or justify her identity. Henceforward, she would be an indefatigable humanitarian and philanthropist, a woman who presumed to speak for the conscience of the nation. Consequently, she may have calculated that her books would represent a declining fraction of her productivity or her value to society.

Several explanations suggest themselves for Pearl's reconception of herself and her rearrangement of her commitments. To begin with, she cared, genuinely and deeply, about war and injustice, and she suspected that dealing with such evils directly was simply more important than writing novels. She was still governed by a secular version of the missionary impulse she had inherited from her father. And she harbored the suspicion, also inherited from her father, that fiction was, in the end, slightly frivolous. At some level, she needed to feel that what she did was useful, not merely pleasing or even successful.

Beyond that, however, she may also have been trying to flee from her primary identification as a writer. Ironically, both her reputation and her self-confidence had been damaged beyond remedy by the Nobel Prize. In the years before she won the prize, she was regarded as merely one of a large number of popular writers, a name on a list that would have included Margaret Mitchell, Erskine Caldwell, Hervey Allen, and John O'Hara. While no one had made extravagant claims for Pearl's talents, her early books had been well received by newspaper and magazine critics. Indeed, her first success had been greeted as rather admirable, even charming: a penniless missionary wife living obscurely in distant China, trying valiantly to earn money to support her family.[98]

In the second half of the 1930s, Pearl gradually renegotiated her cultural position. She transformed herself into a wealthy (and divorced) professional, a perennial best-seller and would-be woman of letters who was also an outspoken advocate for the rights of women and American minorities. When the Swedish Academy abruptly elevated her to a supreme literary position, the decision represented a challenge, even an insult, to established highbrow opinion. Pearl's books could no longer be filed quietly on the lower fictional shelf among numberless other popular romances and "women's novels." Instead, because singular honors had been conferred on her, she was treated to a singular punishment. She was transformed into an emblem of unmerited success.

Confronted with adverse judgments of her work, she concealed her growing discomfort behind a surface of counterfeit indifference. She often insisted that she ignored unfriendly critical opinion, yet several of her children recall that she was regularly wounded by bad reviews.[99] As time went on, her feelings of isolation and rejection had become a sad fact of her daily life. "One dies at the hands of critics," she complained to her sister Grace, and added the bitter outburst: "Other professionals pursue their professions without having to support a parasitic group who make their bread and butter off the work done by others."[100]

Yet the critics spoke Pearl's own inmost fears. She thought of herself as a storyteller rather than an artist, and she had always been uncertain about the aesthetic quality of her writing. When she exclaimed that it was "ridiculous" for her to receive the Nobel Prize, she was being sincere, not falsely modest. However, even she did not predict how high an emotional price she would eventually pay for her moment of triumph. "Be careful when you get famous," she said late in her life to journalist Ross Terrill; "you will be attacked."[101] She spoke from decades of bitter experience.

According to her sister, Grace, Pearl was not given to introspection.[102] She left a record of her internal struggles, but it was typically indirect. In the fall of 1940, she wrote an article for the *Saturday Review* on the need writers have for appreciation. Referring to writers in general, she said: "I think on the whole writers are a self-distrustful lot and wilt under lack of recognition more readily than most people. . . ." Pearl was probably right about the sensitivity and thin skins of writers. Beyond that, however, her remark was clearly autobiographical: she was conspicuously self-distrustful and had wilted under the pressure of a hostile critical consensus. She added the defensive comment that "popularity ought not to be despised," since some of our greatest writers "have been in their day extremely popular. . . ."[103] The comment is a measure of her discomfort. Surrounded by critics who sneered at her claims to greatness, Pearl was condemned to mere popularity. There was no place for her in the house of serious fiction.

Pearl's uneasiness about her status may explain her oddly violent attacks on best-seller lists. On one occasion, for example, she told a meeting of the League of American Writers that she would like to see such lists abolished: sales volume should be "kept a secret, even in advertizing." This, she said, would force readers to make their decisions on the basis of merit alone.[104] Since she knew perfectly well that her own merit was at best a subject of dispute, her imperious tone betrayed her insecurity.

The objections to her work expressed an amalgam of aesthetic and political attitudes, some of them explicit, others not. For one thing, at a time when reputations were made and broken by men, she was a woman whose work was cherished by countless women. Furthermore, she had resolutely followed an old-fashioned narrative practice in the face of an ascendant modernism. Here, too, her gender as much as her literary technique counted against her: the modernist pantheon was reserved for male heroes, strong men striving valiantly against a status quo that was often symbolized as effeminate.

In addition, Pearl had already become ideologically homeless. She was rejected by the left because of her anti-communism and her distance from left-wing cultural circles. At the same time, she was abandoned by the right because of her unfashionable proletarian sympathies and her tireless advocacy of civil rights for women and African-Americans. Finally, at a moment of intense American nationalism Pearl quixotically embraced an international point of view. She was a world citizen who always thought in multicultural terms. She had strenuously promoted classical and contemporary Chinese literature, and her own stories had introduced Western readers to Asian characters who were recognizable human beings rather than stereotypes.

These were, in fact, considerable achievements, but they were irrelevant to a generation of academics who were busily manufacturing the new field of "American studies." At Yale, Harvard, the University of Minnesota, and a dozen other institutions, scholars were devising reading lists and courses that would allegedly document "the American character" or "the American mind" or "the American identity." As far as those founding Americanists were concerned, neither Pearl Buck nor Asian culture had any contribution to make to their grand but ultimately myopic enterprise.

Still a best-selling writer, Pearl was rapidly becoming an invisible woman in literary history. Even as she pondered her situation in late 1940, the young, prodigiously gifted Alfred Kazin was drafting the pages that would shortly become *On Native Grounds*. Kazin's pathbreaking and widely influential book was a capacious study of American prose from 1890 to 1940, in which several hundred writers were given longer or briefer notice. Though Pearl was at the height of her fame when Kazin's survey appeared, she was never mentioned.

In public, and even with friends, Pearl acknowledged very little of her self-doubt or discontent. In any case, she had many reasons to be satisfied. On New Year's Day, 1941, she wrote a buoyant letter to her sister, Grace, in which she declared: "I never felt better in my life than I do now."[105] This was partly the pretense of a proud, private woman reassuring a worried loved one that all was well. She was shadowed by critical rejection, by Carol's illness, by her memories of the lost years of her first marriage, and by the encroaching war.

But there was also a good deal of truth in Pearl's contented self-assessment. Along with all her troubles, she had found much happiness. She was pleasurably immersed in the many jobs she was doing vigorously and well; she had earned the money that would ensure her independence for the rest of her life; she enjoyed the considerable influence she wielded over public opinion; and she had found a degree of stimulation and affection in her relationship with Richard and her ever-growing family.

Whatever her inner doubts, she kept busy. A few days after New Year's, Pearl wrote to President Roosevelt to protest the British government's imprisonment of Jawaharlal Nehru. She asked Roosevelt to call for Nehru's release as a proof of the West's commitment to democracy. She also suggested that Roosevelt publicly "demand the equal treatment of the Negro American, especially and at least in matters of defense, where now the most ruthless and shameful discrimination . . . is being carried on." Pearl saw a corrupt link between British colonial policies and American racism, a theme to which she would return repeatedly throughout the war years. She asked the President how a democratic society could authorize imperialism or "ignore the oppression by stupid prejudice of a whole race in our nation?"[106] Roosevelt sent Pearl's letter over to the State Department, where Cordell Hull prepared an excruciatingly noncommittal reply for the president's signature: "I know that you will understand that my inability to act on your suggestion in no way diminishes my real interest in the particular matters which you mention."[107] In fact, Pearl never understood such temporizing.

She continued to speak her own mind both in private and in public. In mid-January, she took part in a symposium called "Woman's Next Step," which was convened by the *New York Times*. Along with Pearl, the discussion included Eleanor Roosevelt, anthropologist Margaret Mead, actress Ethel Barrymore, and eighty-two-year-old feminist leader Carrie Chapman Catt. Roosevelt applauded women who worked outside the home, while Catt called for a national gathering of women to protest inequality. Mead warned women that standards are controlled by men in all societies: "the best cooks may be women but the best chefs are men. In other words, men have always and still do define what is achievement. If men started to do nothing but hunt hummingbirds, that would be accepted by society as the correct and most important thing to do."

Pearl herself made the most uncompromising remarks. She commented that "present programs for women are pathetically inadequate," that American women have "privileges but not equality," and that American society was trapped in the sexual Middle Ages. She prophesied that change would never come from men: "Women might as well realize that if there is going to be any modernization of their medieval position the struggle will have to be carried on largely by themselves."[108] Pearl had been elaborating all of these themes in her essays and lectures over the past two or three years.

At the beginning of 1941, Pearl published a new book, *Today and Forever,* a collection of thirteen stories.[109] The first few selections are sketches of China in the early 1930s, before the Japanese invasion. Most of these stories are slight, offering by turns glimpses of fumbling missionaries, anecdotes about the diversions of Shanghai dance halls, and studies of bewildered, Western-educated Chinese trying to find their way back into the society of their childhood.

The longer and more significant second half of *Today and Forever* gathers stories of war and resistance. Most of them celebrate Chinese patriotism, and almost all of them dramatize the heroism of China's women. The title character of "Golden Flower," for example, is a young woman, the head of a band of guerrillas, who harasses the Japanese for months in a series of brilliant raids. In "Guerrilla Mother," the fifty-year-old Madame Chien exchanges her position as wife and mother in a wealthy Chinese family to lead a company of soldiers in a successful attack on the Japanese army.

Meng-an, the brave female soldier in "A Man's Foes," typifies the thousands of Chinese women who committed themselves to the war. She is valued by her male comrades for her military skill, not her appearance: "She was not beautiful. An earnest face, a square, an unchanging mouth with small full lips, eyes very black and white, short shining black hair, skin as brown as a peasant's and a slim breastless body, carried like the soldier she was. . . ."[110] In "The Old Demon," the final story in the book, old Mrs. Wang opens the dike that holds back a rising river, flooding her own village and drowning the Japanese who have marched into it.

Refusing to submit to the Japanese, these women also defy the conventions of their own culture that have confined them in family tasks and in automatic deference to male authority. They are women warriors, descendants of China's legendary Mu-lan, who had led her dead father's armies to victory hundreds of years earlier. (Mu-lan is explicitly named as a precedent in the story "Golden Flower.")

The anonymous reviewer for the *Times Literary Supplement,* after declaring that the stories in *Today and Forever* carried too many marks of "popular writing" for his (or her) taste, immediately added: "popular or too popular in manner though these stories are, they are at the same time very illuminating in their way. As magazine stories, in fact, they probably evoke something of genuine interest in China and the Chinese in a good many people not easily reached by other means."[111]

Whatever Pearl thought of this backhanded tribute, she was eager to stir up interest in China, and especially to coax Americans into contributing additional dollars for Chinese relief. After four years of war, an estimated two million Chinese had died of wounds, disease, and starvation; most of the casualties were civilians.

Throughout much of 1941, Pearl virtually submerged herself in fund-raising. She pointed with justifiable pride to the two emergency medical training facilities that her China Emergency Relief Committee had built in free China. These schools were especially important because China had so few Western-trained doctors: at the beginning of the war, in 1937, China had fewer than six thousand doctors in a population of nearly 500 million people.[112] (New York City alone, with about 1 percent of China's population, had over twice as many doctors.)

In the spring, Pearl accepted the post of chairman of United China Relief (UCR), an umbrella organization that linked China Emergency Relief with seven other agencies. Eleanor Roosevelt presided as honorary chairman, and the campaign committee included Henry Luce, John D. Rockefeller, 3d, David O. Selznick, and Wendell Willkie, the Republican presidential candidate who had lost the 1940 election to Franklin Roosevelt.

The UCR launched an ambitious $5,000,000 campaign with a Waldorf-Astoria dinner in late March. In brief opening remarks, Pearl described China's resistance to Japanese aggression as pivotal to any hopes the world might have for a democratic future. Wendell Willkie, the featured speaker, lashed out at American isolationists, and predicted that the United States would not be able to remain permanently aloof from the global war against fascism. At the end of the speeches, Ambassador Hu Shih surprised the audience by announcing that the Chinese government had awarded Pearl the Order of Jade, an exceptional mark of recognition.[113]

Under Pearl's general management, UCR met its multimillion-dollar goal. She was gratified, but also disgruntled, because China's suffering had become something of a modish charity among well-to-do New Yorkers. In September she wrote to Grace that "the season has begun in New York with China Relief very fashionable. I groan to think of it. I shall try to withdraw from it gradually, now that others are taking it up."[114] A little like her father, Pearl preferred lonely commitments and causes that were at least slightly unpopular.

ALONG WITH THEIR FUND-RAISING, Pearl and Richard began working on a plan in the spring of 1941 to reorganize *Asia* magazine. They sent a draft of their ideas to Leonard Elmhirst, who remained their chief financial backer. Richard told Elmhirst that he and Pearl intended to expand the magazine, and that they also wanted to create a foundation to improve understanding between Western

27. Pearl and Wendell Willkie, standing in front of a portrait of Mme. Chiang Kai-shek, at the launching of the United China Relief campaign, March, 1941. (Courtesy Harry Ransom Humanities Center, University of Texas.)

and Eastern societies. The two projects, Richard estimated, would cost about $100,000 a year.[115] When Elmhirst decided against the additional investment, the Walshes took on the project themselves. They bought *Asia* outright, and installed Pearl in the new office of president.

Beginning in July, 1941, Richard took a more prominent editorial role in *Asia,* publishing a signed column of news and comment in the front pages of each issue. Compressed but impressively well informed, these essays ranged all across the Asian political world from Turkey to the Philippines, touching by turns on such topics as British policy in the Middle East, the Chinese cooperative movement, the military situation in Mongolia, and fluctuations in the Japanese stock market.

Pearl's role as *Asia*'s president was largely ceremonial, but she did publish an important statement of her editorial views to mark her appointment. "I am a great believer," she wrote, "in people speaking for themselves. . . . Too much is written from the outside looking in, and far from enough is written from the inside looking out. Especially is this true about the peoples of Asia."[116]

This point of view, which Pearl and Richard shared, had long driven their policy of encouraging articles and stories from Asian writers. Over the years, Western reports on the countries and cultures of Asia alternated with essays and sketches produced by Chinese, Japanese, Thai, Indian, Filipino, Korean, and Burmese writers. The Asians who published in the magazine made up a various and distinguished roll call, including Jawaharlal Nehru, Lu Hsün, Mao Tse-tung, Rabindranath Tagore, Soong Ching-ling (Sun Yat-sen's widow), and Chinese ambassador Hu Shih. Though most of the *Asia*'s contributors were less well known, a sampling of their work suggests the diversity of authors and subjects: Radhakamal Mukerjee's "Communities of India," a survey of rural India; Jack Chen's "Why They Go To Yenan," an admiring glimpse of the Communists' northwestern headquarters; Tsuyoshi Matsumoto's comment on Japan's new system of romanization, "Mt. Huzi for Mt. Fuji"; Y. P. Mei's "Stronghold of Muslim China"; Salvador Lopez's "Philippine Youth Defends Democracy"; and T. S. Chen's military profile, "General Pai: Chinese Patriot."

As another mechanism for informing Americans about Asia, Pearl and Richard moved ahead with an idea they had been discussing for months to set up a new organization, with an educational and cultural focus. Tentatively referred to as the Asian-American Foundation in Richard's correspondence, the new project was officially named the East and West Association when it was announced in March. (Pearl may have enjoyed the allusion to *East Wind, West Wind,* the title of her first book.) Pearl served as president, and ran the operation herself for the first few months before she hired Mildred Hughes as director in August. With headquarters at the John Day offices, East and West mounted an ambitious program of lectures, publications, radio broadcasts, translations, and cultural exchange.

Pearl described the purpose of the new association in the sort of populist language she always used when she talked about culture. East and West, she wrote, had been founded "to help ordinary people on one side of the world to know and understand ordinary people on the other side."[17] Along with Richard and Pearl, the board of directors included Ruth Benedict and Margaret Sanger. There was also an advisory board, whose members included novelist Louis Bromfield, artist Miguel Covarrubias, philosophers John Dewey and Ernest Hocking, *Time* publisher Henry Luce, IBM's Thomas Lamont, and Juan Trippe, chairman of Pan American airlines.

Richard and Pearl were now active in almost all of America's non-governmental dealings with China. They were simultaneously managing the new East and West Association, the reorganized *Asia* magazine, the China Emergency Relief Committee, and United China Relief. Along the way, they had created a network of friends and co-workers – journalists, academics, writers, and wealthy patrons – that resembled an interlocking directorate. Their several ventures were designed to intersect and overlap: the educational programs of East and West, for example, were described at length in *Asia*, while many of the magazine's contributors took part in East and West events; full-page advertisements for several China relief agencies regularly appeared in *Asia*, and the writers and editors served on most of the fund-raising boards.

While she was spending most of her waking hours coping with the politics and human costs of the war, Pearl's anxieties about American women continued to rise. She knew that war was a masculine blood sport in which women were reduced to the roles of trophies and victims. Beyond that, she was frightened by the anti-feminist repression that accompanied both war and fascism, and she remained convinced that fascism was stirring in the United States.

Prompted by her fears, Pearl published her most extended statement on the subject of gender in America. *Of Men and Women*, a collection of nine essays, offers a tough-minded survey of relations between the sexes on the eve of American entry into World War II. Pearl's theme was simple: the survival of American democracy ultimately depends on the equality and full freedom of women. While she did "not believe there is any important difference between men and women," she also knew that "no woman has . . . a man's chance."[118] Repeatedly insisting on the need to redefine democracy to include all Americans, she submitted a fierce challenge to the hierarchical status quo: "If the white, Gentile, adult male believes that his nation is a democracy, let him remember that there are others – and perhaps nearer to him than he knows or cares to believe – to whom he appears only as a dictator."

In the home, the workplace, the universities, and the political arena, women need to demand the same opportunities and responsibilities as men. Barred from what Pearl called "the engine rooms" of society, women exhaust their potential in a narrow round of domestic tasks, and often sink into "devastating loneliness." Educating women will prove a bitter fraud unless they can use what they have learned. "A man is educated and turned out to work. But a woman is educated – and turned out to grass." If women are to play no role in the affairs of the world, it would be better for them to take advanced courses in "cosmetics, bridge, sports, how to conduct a club meeting gracefully, how to be an attractive hostess, with or without servants. . . ."

In a chapter called "Women as Angels," Pearl dismantles the specious sentimentality that pretends to sanctify women as higher moral beings in order to deny their ordinary humanity. The myth has engendered a vexing confusion about the value of women's participation in the public sphere. Pearl cites "that laughable business of the female vote, for instance." Women had been assured that they "would purify politics and uplift, by their angelic qualities, the affairs of men . . . merely by their presence." Such a view was not only false, it was actually "degrading." Women have suffered from "a complete confusion between women and angels. . . . They should have demanded their rights as persons and forgotten themselves as angels. Angels have no place in politics or practical life." In a later chapter, Pearl adds: "All that woman has gained from her endeavor to be man's moral teacher has been the lonely task of practicing what she preached."

What women need is neither a separate sphere nor the "poor rag of righteousness" that covers their political nakedness, but equal opportunities to succeed and fail in every calling. A century earlier, the pioneering feminist Margaret Fuller had famously declared: "If you ask what offices [women] may fill, I reply – any. Let them be sea-captains if you will!" Pearl made the same demands, insisting that a woman "may sit upon a throne and rule a nation, she may sit upon the bench and be a judge, she may be the foreman in a mill, she could if she would be a bridge builder or a machinist or anything else." Sadly, however, American women rarely had the chance to test their talents, because they were still hemmed in by the conventional expectations handed down by tradition. "Tradition is the culprit," Pearl wrote, again echoing Fuller. "Break it."

Pearl's inspiriting hopes for women's emancipation were darkened by her suspicion that sexual oppression might actually intensify. Progress in human rights, after all, is always fragile, never more so than in times of war and reaction. If her catalogue of jobs that women might fill recalls the prophecies of Margaret Fuller, her description of life under a more thoroughgoing patriarchy resembles the nightmare world evoked by Margaret Atwood in *The Handmaid's Tale*. Unless women are fully free, Pearl warned, "some day men are going to find that it is cheaper just to keep women in cells and cages or barracks or harems whence they can be summoned when service is wanted or the state needs new recruits. Women have always been relegated whenever men have relapsed into thinking that the sole important functions of women are to service men and to breed children." This fate, which had overtaken women in fascist countries, could easily slide like a noose around the necks of American women as well.

Pearl argued that men and women both shared responsibility for the subordination of one sex to the other. Men have hoarded their power, and will not voluntarily give it up. At the same time, middle-class women have too often embraced their own diminishment, in exchange for security or comfort:

[C]ontent with their so-called spiritual superiority, women have let their souls rot into pettiness and idleness and vacuity and general indifference in a world crying and dying for want of real superiority of spirit and moral worth. . . . If women were really superior to men in righteousness or spirituality, could they sit blind and deaf and dumb, knitting their interminable knitting, crocheting and talking and going to teas and bridge parties and knitting again, and filling the theaters day in and day out, and rolling bandages and knitting again, and exchanging recipes and knitting, and re-arranging their furniture and curling their hair and painting their nails and going to style shows and knitting, knitting, knitting while the world goes down to darkness . . . ?

Reviewing *Of Men and Women* in the *New York Times,* Katherine Woods pointed out the resemblance between Pearl's analysis of gender and Virginia Woolf's.[119] The comparison is fair. Although Pearl's work has inexplicably slipped from sight – dragged down by the collapse of her literary reputation – it speaks with an eloquent and still-relevant voice in the continuing debate over women's place in American society. In one of the book's later essays, Pearl observed that "the truth has never been told about women in history." The insight not only foretold the reconstruction of history that would follow two generations later; it also serves to throw Pearl's own neglected contribution into sharper relief.[120]

Pearl was among the few feminists of the interwar years who coupled gender and race in her egalitarian vision (psychologist Olga Knopf was another).[121] Measuring the pressures that deformed American society, she concluded that racial and sexual inequality had an identical moral weight. Beyond that, she repeatedly objected that the treatment of African-Americans gave the lie to the nation's democratic rhetoric. In her view, there was an unsavory ideological connection between American segregation and European colonialism.

In the March, 1941 issue of *Asia,* she published a brief but powerful political manifesto, "Warning to Free Nations." Around the world, Pearl said, millions of people were being asked to fight in the name of freedoms they did not enjoy. She spoke for the Indians who were pressed into the service of an allegedly democratic government "which has not given them democracy," and has in fact imprisoned one of the foremost leaders of Indian democracy, Jawaharlal Nehru. She spoke as well for the peasants of China, victimized by their own rapacious government.

Finally, she spoke for the "twelve million Negroes in the United States of America, who are oppressed by race prejudice which prevents their taking any active share in the life of the nation." Though they are excluded from the economic and social advantages enjoyed by white Americans, "yet they are being told today to fight for the liberty and equality of democracy. Who can blame them if they ask: 'Whose liberty?' What equality?' "

Unless the democracies acknowledged and remedied these failures of political morality, Pearl said, they would lose the war even if Hitler and the Japanese were ultimately defeated:

To fight with England for Europe's freedom while India is governed by tyranny, is a monstrous contradiction, and yet no more monstrous than that while the United States prepares for a mighty defense of her democracy twelve million Americans should be denied equality in a nation founded upon equal opportunity for all. . . . [122]

The distance between democratic ideals and racial reality gaped like a chasm at the center of American life. Throughout the war years, Pearl would continually return to this subject, lecturing her fellow citizens about the elementary meaning of justice.

In the summer and fall of 1941, most white Americans had other things on their minds than racial discrimination. At home, a lingering economic depression was finally being rolled back by the military production that accompanied America's drift toward war. In Europe, Hitler's invasion of Russia had bogged down in the bloodiest stalemate in military history. National and world news competed for attention with two baseball stories: Joe DiMaggio's fifty-six game hitting streak and Ted Williams's pursuit of a .400 batting average.

Pearl frequently decried the myopia that rendered African-Americans invisible to whites. In the late fall, she confronted the *New York Times* in an exchange that became a celebrated debate. On November 12, the *Times* published an editorial under the heading "The Other Side of Harlem." Commenting on a recent "crime wave," the *Times* assured its readers that "the Harlem situation is not a race problem"; rather, the causes of Harlem's crime could be traced to "poverty, overcrowding, and neglect." Taking what it apparently assumed was an evenhanded position, the paper called both for improved educational and employment opportunities for blacks and for "increased police protection" to combat "an epidemic of violence."

The editorial was only one of several that appeared in the *Times* that morning, and it would probably have vanished quietly except for Pearl Buck's aroused response. In a letter of 2,300 words, which was printed just three days later, Pearl condemned the editorial for fundamentally misunderstanding the reality of black life in Harlem and the rest of America. According to Pearl, the problems of Harlem will not be solved by either jail sentences or the ministrations of social workers. Neither punishments nor well-intentioned palliatives will reach to the racial prejudice that Pearl identified as the "basic cause" of black suffering and of black hostility to white society.

Pearl itemized the long list of injustices to which racial prejudice had condemned African-Americans:

The reason why colored Americans live in ghettos, where they are helpless against high rents and miserable housing, is the segregation to which race prejudice compels them. Race prejudice compels colored people to take what work they can get because there are so many jobs Negroes cannot get. Race prejudice makes and keeps Negroes' wages low because some labor unions will not admit colored labor on the same basis as white labor. Race prejudice and race prejudice alone is the root of the plight of people in greater and lesser Harlems all over our country.

According to Pearl, prejudice turned the hopes of blacks into despair, eroded democracy, and mocked the Constitution: "If the United States is to include subject and ruler peoples, then let us be honest about it and change the Constitution and make it plain that Negroes cannot share the privileges of the white people." This, at least, would relieve white Americans of hypocrisy. Beyond that, Pearl judged America's institutionalized racism to be even more insidious than Hitlerism, which did not disguise itself behind false pretenses of humanity.[123]

Pearl's statement created a national sensation. Walter White, executive secretary of the NAACP, wrote to congratulate her on a "magnificent letter."[124] The NAACP reprinted the text, in full, under the title "Democracy and the Negro," in the December, 1941 issue of *Crisis*. An introductory note told readers that publication was warranted because Pearl Buck had "caught and expressed so completely the problem of the Negro and democracy in America."[125] White sent a copy of Pearl's letter to Eleanor Roosevelt, and received a reply from Roosevelt's secretary, Malvina Thompson: "Mrs. Roosevelt has asked me to thank you for your letter of November 19 and to say that she will be glad to bring Pearl Buck's letter to the attention of the President."[126]

Pearl's letter was also reprinted in the *Congressional Record* at the request of Senator Arthur Capper of Kansas. Both the NAACP and the Urban League circulated thousands of copies of Pearl's letter in this format in their information and fund-raising appeals. The Common Council for American Unity printed yet another version of the statement, under the title "Pearl Buck Speaks for Democracy." Eleanor Roosevelt provided a foreword, which concluded with a challenge to her readers: "If we older people have the courage that Miss Buck has had, perhaps the next generation will have the courage to make this country a real democracy."[127]

Pearl's sensitivity to racial equality and to white discrimination was rooted in the decades she had lived in Asia. Throughout World War II, she would steadfastly argue that Westerners were going to pay a heavy cost for their long history of colonial and racist dealings. She made this point in a long and prescient letter to Eleanor Roosevelt, just a few days after Pearl Harbor. Writing on December 12, Pearl warned Roosevelt of "a very deep sense" shared by Asians that "the white man generally is, or may be, their common enemy." Asians have found the white race to be "historically aggressive against them . . . historically their exploiters." To emphasize her fears, Pearl quoted a striking statement she said had been recently made by a Chinese professor: " 'Although the Japanese are our enemies just now, if it came to the ultimate choice, we would rather be a dependency of Japan than of the United States, because at least the Japanese do not consider us an inferior race.' " Any Asian-American alliance would depend upon a more enlightened white attitude toward peoples of color.

28. Pearl and Senator Arthur Capper. (Reproduced with permission of the Pearl S. Buck Foundation.)

Pearl said that white supremacy had emerged as the paramount moral and political issue of the war, and that nothing could prevent the "solidarity" that was growing throughout the world among non-white nations. The domestic implications were obvious: "Unless we make the country worth fighting for by Negroes, we would have nothing to offer the world at the end of the war."[128] Eleanor Roosevelt passed Pearl's letter on to the president, and was surprised by his sympathetic response. "He told her," biographer Joseph Lash reports, that "he would have to compel the British to give dominion status to India, and that it was essential to enlarge Negro rights in the United States."[129]

By an uncanny coincidence, Pearl had spent much of December 8, the day after Pearl Harbor, with her friend Yasuo Kuniyoshi, a leading Japanese artist. Kuniyoshi came to her New York office, where he sat, speechless, with tears running down his cheeks. "He did not wipe them away, he did not move, he simply sat there gazing at me," Pearl wrote years later, "the tears running down his cheeks and splashing on his coat."[130] The two friends did what they could to console each other, but they both knew that their countries now faced a

future that would be torn by conflict and reddened by bloodshed. That morning
– eleven years after Japan had seized Manchuria, four years after Japanese armies
had invaded China proper, and two years after Hitler had destroyed Poland –
the United States entered World War II.

7

Wartime

IN THE LONG RUN, the Japanese attack on Pearl Harbor proved to be a strategic blunder, because it galvanized anti-Japanese sentiment in the United States and brought America's vast industrial capacity into World War II. Winston Churchill said that on the night of Pearl Harbor he slept soundly for the first time in months, because he knew that the United States would now be joining the Allies as a full partner.

In the short run, however, the surprise attack was almost completely successful. In less than an hour, Japanese fighters, bombers, and torpedo bombers sank or damaged six battleships, three cruisers, and three destroyers. The simultaneous raid on Hickham and Wheeler airfields left over 175 planes burning on the runways. Nearly four thousand American soldiers and sailors were killed or wounded. Only the aircraft carriers escaped; at the time of the attack, they were at sea on routine training exercises.

The raid on Pearl Harbor disabled almost half of the United States Navy, paralyzed America's Pacific forces, and served as prologue to a long succession of Japanese victories throughout Southeast Asia and the Pacific. On December 8, Japanese troops landed in Malaya; two days later, the splendid new British battleship *Prince of Wales* and the battlecruiser *Repulse* were sunk off the Malayan coast. In rapid succession, the Japanese forced the surrender of Guam, Wake Island, and Hong Kong. On February 15, 1942, the 130,000 British troops manning the supposedly impregnable fortress of Singapore surrendered, after one day of mild resistance. "In Britain's long military annals," one historian has written, "there is no more dismal chapter than the fall of Singapore."' By late March, Japanese troops commanded Java and most of Burma, including Rangoon. Japan's imperial navy controlled much of the Indian Ocean.

Following the fall of Manila in early January, 35,000 American troops retreated to the Philippine peninsula of Bataan; they surrendered in April after two months of bloody battle. Thousands of these men died on a sixty-five-mile "death march" to their prison camp. Corregidor, a heavily fortified island at the mouth of Manila Bay, fell on May 6. In June, in one of their more audacious under-takings, Japanese soldiers successfully occupied the outermost Aleutian Islands.

By mid-spring, 1942, through a combination of conquest and intimidation, the Japanese had built up an astonishing strategic position. The imperial perimeter traced a huge circle that stretched thousands of miles, from Burma's Irrawaddy River in the west to the edge of Alaska in the east, from Manchuria and Sakhalin in the north across much of the South Pacific. A dozen unwilling nation-states and colonies were incorporated into the so-called Greater East Asia Co-Prosperity Sphere, a benevolent euphemism that Japan used to describe its sud-denly swollen empire.

The great prize was China, home to one-fifth of the world's people, with an area twenty-five times the size of Japan. The Japanese had long coveted China's millions of acres of arable land and its immense, untapped reserves of coal and iron. In late 1941, after four years of fighting, the Japanese controlled eastern China from Manchuria to Shanghai, all the major ports on the China Sea, and the Yangtze River as far inland as I-ch'ang (Yichang). China was divided into ten separate units, and the nation was threatened with dismemberment.[2]

In December, 1937, Chiang Kai-shek had decamped from Nanking and re-treated to Chungking in remote Szechuen province. Chungking's location and terrain made it a poor staging area for attacks against the Japanese, but this apparently served Chiang's purposes quite well. The Generalissimo, who re-garded the Communists as his greatest enemies, had little appetite for confronting the Japanese. For their part, the Communists had more enthusiasm for fighting the invaders, but they were badly equipped and still concentrated in mountainous Shensi province. A united front reluctantly bound the Kuomintang and Com-munists together for the duration of the war, though it barely survived the sus-picions and hostility on both sides.

By the end of 1941, when America declared war on Japan, upwards of one hundred million Chinese were living as prisoners in their own lands. They faced a brutal military regime that imposed discipline through torture, confiscation, and summary executions. Over the next four years, until the war ended in the summer of 1945, millions of peasants would die of wounds, disease, and starvation as troops marched back and forth across the Chinese countryside.[3]

Dragon Seed is Pearl Buck's fictional response to the calamities that Japanese aggression visited upon China's rural population. Pearl's timing was politically and commercially lucky: the novel was published just a month after the United States entered the war, when Americans were eager for encouraging stories about their new Asian allies.[4] Sales were strong (the Book-of-the-Month Club printed 290,000 copies) and MGM paid a rumored $105,000 for movie rights.[5]

Reviewers greeted the book enthusiastically, though a few complained about the preachiness and the trademark Buck mannerisms – the quasi-biblical style and the one-dimensional characters. However, most readers regarded the novel as an authoritative communiqué from the Chinese front: "vivid and painful," *Time* said, "the first sharp, fictional account of resistance in Occupied China."[6]

Set in a village west of Nanking in the years from 1937 to 1941, *Dragon Seed* tells the story of the farmer Ling Tan and his family, whose quiet, stable lives are demolished by the Japanese invaders. Men and women who have never seen an airplane or a tank suddenly find themselves overwhelmed by bombs and artillery, then reduced to virtual slavery by invaders who steal their crops, livestock, and tools. Fathers and sons are murdered or imprisoned, mothers and daughters raped and then killed.

The novel's twenty chapters describe how China's ordinary people respond to the catastrophe of war and occupation. Some of them collapse into inert despair, and a few, including one of Ling Tan's cousins, even collaborate with the enemy. Most of the villagers, however, do what they can to harass and defy their Japanese oppressors. Inspired by the example of the righteous robbers of the classic novel *Shui Hu Chuan,* the townsfolk risk their lives in daily acts of resistance and sabotage.

Like all of Pearl's stories of wartime China, *Dragon Seed*'s fictional plot closely tracks historical events. In particular, the novel memorializes and condemns the rape of Nanking, one of the most savage atrocities of the entire war. On December 13, 1937, in a mindless orgy of violence, Japanese troops sacked Nanking, burning much of the city to the ground and killing at least 30,000 defeated Chinese soldiers and perhaps 150,000 civilians. They also raped an estimated 20,000 Chinese women, many of whom died of their injuries or were deliberately killed after they were assaulted.[7] It was a "period of terror and destruction that must rank among the worst in the history of modern warfare."[8] Even today, nearly sixty years later, Nanking remains for many Chinese "the prime symbol of Japanese savagery during the war in Asia."[9]

Haunted by these heartbreaking reports, Pearl uses rape as the central motif in *Dragon Seed.* Rapes occur repeatedly throughout the book, beginning with the rapes in the devastated city of Nanking itself. Later, when the attacking Japanese first arrive in Ling Tan's village, they rape and murder an elderly, overweight grandmother, the only woman too fat to escape through a small hole in a garden wall. Soon after, Orchid, the wife of Ling Tan's eldest son, is assaulted by five Japanese soldiers when she leaves a Christian compound where she has been hiding with other women. Orchid dies after the fourth soldier rapes her; the fifth rapes her dead body. Finally, Ling Tan's youngest son, a teenager named Lao San, is raped by a squad of Japanese as they pillage Ling Tan's homestead.

The epidemic of rape creates a universe of degradation. Pearl's preoccupation with rape had its sources in her materials and probably in her gender, but the prevalence of rape precisely served her thematic purposes. Ultimately rape becomes a lurid emblem of Chinese powerlessness and Japanese brutality, a symbol of the continuing violation that Japan's soldiers inflicted on China's people, male and female alike.

But *Dragon Seed* does not merely mourn China's suffering and losses during the long years of Japanese occupation. The novel also celebrates the determination of plain people to resist oppression, often at a terrible cost. Armed with ancient muskets or pitchforks or sometimes only their bare hands and their wits, Ling Tan's family and his neighbors conduct a ceaseless campaign against the Japanese war machine.

Each day, in thousands of villages like Ling Tan's, China was forging heroes in the crucible of resistance. At one point, a woman named Mayli denounces a well-meaning American teacher who requires her young Chinese students to memorize "Paul Revere's Ride." In Mayli's view, the assignment is worse than a waste of time; it diminishes China's history. " 'What trash – what nonsense,' Mayli cried out. ' "Paul Revere's Ride" – when every day our own guerrillas fight like heroes!' "[10] Pearl believed that the Chinese people were creating a new Asian epic in their long struggle against aggression; *Dragon Seed* (from its title on) is her contribution to that collective work.

Courage belongs to men and women alike. The novel's heroes include several of the female characters, among them a woman named Jade, the wife of Lao Er, Ling Tan's second son. Jade combines what Pearl regarded as the best of old and new China. She is free-thinking and independent, and at the same time loyal to her husband and family. She has learned to read and is proud of her achievement, but she takes equal pride in her domestic tasks. She hates war and killing. However, when the opportunity arises, she poisons a whole houseful of Japanese officers. Characters like Jade and Mayli embody Pearl's anxious hopes for female emancipation in China.

Dragon Seed was written in the midst of the Asian war, when defeat for the Chinese seemed at least as likely as victory. Individual acts of heroism and sacrifice were no match for a well-armed, modern army of occupation that numbered over one million men. True to the heavy odds, the book closes on a question. Free China Radio has broadcast one of Winston Churchill's speeches, in which the British prime minister has vowed to aid China and the other conquered people of Asia. Ling Tan and Lao Er are heartened, but they have suffered long enough to know that Churchill's words are no more than a promise.

It was a promise Pearl herself mistrusted; she believed that Churchill's racial attitudes and his unyielding commitment to the colonial ideal made him a bad ally for Asians and Americans alike. His imperialism, which seemed inspirational to some of his countrymen and quaintly Victorian to others, continuously hobbled Britain's Asian campaigns. Native populations had little reason to prefer

Whitehall to Tokyo; what they actually wanted was independence. Paradoxically, Churchill's contempt for persons of color hastened the end of the empire by steeling the resolve of Asian nationalists.[11] A few, such as Subhash Chandra Bose and the Indian National Army, even fought against the British, alongside the Japanese.[12] Many others simply refused to cooperate with their white masters.

Pearl worried that Churchill's well-publicized devotion to Anglo-Saxon supremacy was "as good as battleships to Japan."[13] Throughout the war, she directed much of her polemic energy against the British prime minister. She conceded his rhetorical genius but she believed that he represented a failed world view: in the 1940s colonialism was at once morally bankrupt and politically obsolete.[14]

Her language could be incendiary. On one occasion, in a speech at the Aldine Club in New York, she insisted that America's alliance with the British Empire was tantamount to "fascism," and would "convince three-quarters of the people of the world that we are fascist-minded, that we believe in a dominant race, a dominant State, the domination of color, of empire."[15]

Clifton Fadiman once suggested that Pearl be named ambassador to China, saying that she had earned the job.[16] Certainly her status as America's best-known authority on Asia gave her an influence that few civilian men or women enjoyed. On January 5, for example, just four weeks after Pearl Harbor, she presided over a remarkable gathering of American and Chinese officials who wanted to hear what she had to say about the Japanese and the Asian war. Her audience included Colonel William ("Wild Bill") Donovan, who was organizing the Office of Strategic Services (OSS); Supreme Court Justice William O. Douglas; Chinese ambassador Hu Shih; T. V. Soong, China's foreign minister; and Lowell Mellett, press officer to President Roosevelt. Among other matters, the group discussed Donovan's suggestion that Pearl write a series of radio plays supporting the Chinese–American alliance; these would be broadcast by shortwave directly into China. On at least two occasions, Pearl made the broadcasts herself, reading in Chinese.[17]

Pearl's prominence, and the restless energy that tempted her to invent and publicize a dozen projects at a time, inevitably led to conflict. Her speeches and fund-raising always found their way into the *New York Times* and other newspapers, while less well-known men and women labored in obscurity. She rarely paused to coordinate her initiatives with anyone else.

Her plans for the educational programs of the East and West Association, for example, seemed to duplicate some of the work being done by the venerable Institute for Pacific Relations (IPR). Edward Carter, IPR's director, wrote to Pearl, complaining that she was about "to go full steam ahead in a great many of the fields covered by the IPR." Aside from the "not too healthy competition," as Carter called it, the East and West programs flatly reversed an agreement of some months earlier, which was supposed to keep East and West from poaching on IPR's academic turf. Carter suggested that East and West either desist or become a department of IPR.[18]

Pearl's reply was unrepentant and uncooperative. In effect, she described IPR as an elite organization, with a small constituency of specialists and researchers. East and West, on the contrary, aspired to reach a mass audience, thousands and perhaps even millions of men and women with no interest in IPR's technical publications. IPR could continue to sponsor serious scholarship. Pearl proposed to educate masses of people. To do so, she wanted "to get down into the level of people who don't and won't listen to your programs or read your books." She intended, she repeated with a flourish, "to get down to the level of the comic strip, if I can."

Pearl concluded two pages of populist evangelism by claiming, unconvincingly, that "I do not plead my case for I am not interested in one organization more than another. All I care about is how to get the work done. . . . God knows, I wouldn't do more work if I could help it!"[19] She said that she was forced by circumstance to lead where others would not.

As an exchange like this suggests, disagreement made Pearl impatient and irritable. She distrusted ambiguity, and could barely see shades of moral gray. If she was insecure about the value of her fiction, she was serenely self-confident in debates over political and social issues. She hurried from one public question to another, offering up solutions to a whole list of national and international problems, from Indian independence to civil rights to family planning.

In the early months of the war, Margaret Sanger praised the "magnificent things" Pearl was doing, through the East and West Association and through her writing and lecturing. "You know," Sanger added, "you have the boundless admiration of all who prize integrity and nobility of spirit." Pearl, who regarded Sanger as a heroic figure — "what a life and what a woman!" she wrote to a friend when she reread Sanger's *Autobiography* in 1942 — accepted the kind words with gratitude.[20]

AFTER THE UNITED STATES entered the war, Pearl focused much of her attention on discrimination against African-Americans in the military services and in defense industries. Black Americans were the victims of a fundamental injustice. Once again, as in every war from the Revolution onward, they were compelled to fight to preserve the blessings of a democratic system that did not include them.

Racism infected every inch and ounce of the war effort. Blacks in uniform were consigned to segregated units and subject to apartheid indignity in the towns around Southern bases. They had to agitate for the right to join in combat.

Only a law suit, for example, persuaded the Secretary of War to open training schools for black airmen. The first, at Tuskegee, produced the pilots and crews who manned the planes of the legendary 99th Pursuit Squadron.

Black civilians were denied access to most jobs in war-related manufacturing. The U.S. Employment Service sent a racial inquiry in January, 1942, to several hundred companies holding substantial war contracts. Over half of the executives who replied stated "that they did not and would not" hire black workers.[21] Discrimination was rampant in Northern and Southern industries alike, despite an executive order signed by President Roosevelt in 1941 requiring equal employment opportunities. In Texas, for example, of 17,435 defense jobs, 9,117 were closed to African-Americans; the figure in Michigan was 22,042 of 26,904.[22] Many labor unions also continued the longstanding practice of excluding blacks.

Segregation was enforced with pathological consistency. The Red Cross War Drive refused to accept blood from African-American donors, caving in to pressure from Southern politicians who insisted that wounded white soldiers receive blood and plasma only from other whites. A few days after Pearl Harbor, War Drive director S. Sloan Colt announced, with what sounds like a bizarre sense of accomplishment: "The Red Cross is now able to obtain from white donors enough blood to keep all the processing plants fully occupied so that the total amount of blood plasma available to the armed forces is not lessened by our inability to accept Negro donors."[23] Despite vigorous protests by the NAACP and others, Secretary of War Stimson refused to intervene. Langston Hughes recorded the outrage he and other blacks felt in a short, bitterly ironic poem:

The Angel of Mercy's
Got her wings in the mud,
And all because of
Negro blood.[24]

Pearl Buck quickly emerged as one of the most tenacious white opponents of America's systematic wartime discrimination. At her instigation, the American Civil Liberties Union set up a national Committee Against Racial Discrimination (CARD) in early 1942. Members included William Baldwin, president of the National Urban League, Roy Wilkins of the NAACP, and Pearl's old friend, Elmer Carter, editor of *Opportunity* magazine. Pearl chaired the committee, which lobbied for equal employment opportunity, a federal anti-lynching law, abolition of the poll tax, and the elimination of segregation in the military.[25] Sadly, none of these modest objectives would be achieved until after the war was over. Nonetheless, Pearl's tireless campaigning against racism led Langston Hughes to hail her as "certainly the current Harriet Beecher Stowe to the Race!"[26]

She used every occasion to press her demands for racial equality. In February,

1942, for example, speaking at a literary luncheon, she surprised the 1,700 people in the Astor Hotel ballroom with a sober lesson in politics. She warned her audience that American discrimination against blacks usefully served the purposes of Japanese propaganda. "Prejudice," she said, was obviously "the most vulnerable point in our American democracy." In radio broadcasts and countless pamphlets and posters, the Japanese were repeating a single message: colored races "have no hope of justice and equality from white peoples because of their unalterable racial prejudice. . . ." Every race riot, every lynching, "gives joy to Japan."

Once again, Pearl attacked Churchill, inviting her audience to judge Churchill's rhetoric from an Asian point of view:

There could have been nothing reassuring or comforting to our Asiatic allies in the closing words of Churchill's first speech in Washington, "The British and American peoples will for their own safety and the good of all walk together, side by side, in majesty, justice, and peace." An England, a United States, "walking together in majesty," can only mean to the colored peoples a formidable white imperialism, more dangerous to them than anything even a victorious Japan can threaten.

Pearl concluded bluntly: "If we plan to persist" in discriminating against blacks, "then we are fighting on the wrong side on this war. We belong with Hitler." The speech caused a tremendous reaction. Demand for the text prompted the *New York Herald Tribune* to print Pearl's remarks in full – they took up five columns – a few days after the lunch.[27] Pearl herself published a revised version in the March issue of *Asia,* and again separately as a John Day pamphlet.

The African-American critic Alain Locke wrote a congratulatory letter, telling Pearl of the "thrill" her speech caused him, and of his "complete agreement with it." Above all, Locke thanked Pearl for speaking "so plainly and incisively. Few others could have been so outspoken in the present state of public opinion, yet this is just what is imperatively needed."[28]

Locke's reference to the "present state of public opinion" underscores Pearl's courage in speaking out against bigotry in the early days of the war. Most whites, and a number of blacks as well, regarded her demand for equality as divisive and unpatriotic. "The whole effort now throughout the country," Pearl wrote to Edwin Embree, "is to force the race issue out of sight."[29] Those white Americans who did acknowledge a racial problem tended to prefer the expedient of silence: justice would have to wait until after the war was won. On the contrary, Pearl argued that silence about racism played into the hands of the Axis.

The FBI, which had kept a desultory watch on Pearl for several years, now became more aggressive in its surveillance. Even before J. Edgar Hoover took over as director, the bureau had equated demands for civil rights with subversion.[30] Hoover perfected the agency's paranoia, and made a special target of anyone who challenged the nation's racial status quo.[31] According to one of his biographers, Hoover was governed by "a racial hostility so strong it could overwhelm any sense of fairness or justice."[32]

Hoover also nurtured a peculiar hatred of writers. At one time or another during his half-century tenure as FBI director, a long list of novelists, poets, and journalists was singled out ("indexed," in bureau jargon) for investigation. Most were associated with liberal causes, though a few were right-wing figures, and some had no discernible political attitudes at all; writing itself brought them under suspicion. Hoover was afraid of writers because they were America's least conformable citizens. They made a living by thinking for themselves and saying what they thought.

Hoover actually set up a unit called the Book Review Section. At his direction, the FBI gathered files on Carl Sandburg, William Carlos Williams, Edna St. Vincent Millay, John Dos Passos, Langston Hughes, Robert Lowell, Thomas Wolfe, Kay Boyle, William Faulkner, Theodore Dreiser, Dorothy Parker, Ernest Hemingway, John Steinbeck, Tennessee Williams, Thornton Wilder, T. S. Eliot, Louise Bogan, James Baldwin, Marianne Moore, Sinclair Lewis, John Cheever, F. Scott Fitzgerald, Richard Wright, Robert Frost, and Arthur Miller, among dozens of others. Jack London, Edith Wharton, and William Dean Howells were investigated years after they died. In the FBI's gloomy caverns, Hoover's agents were compiling a perverse literary history of twentieth-century America.

Pearl's file, opened in 1937 when the bureau noted her support for the Spanish Loyalists and the Women's International League for Peace and Freedom, eventually reached over three hundred pages – one of the longer dossiers in the writers' group. As a prominent writer and an outspoken advocate for civil rights, Pearl met two of the main criteria Hoover used to identify suspicious persons. Most of the documents that agents filed on her activities in the early 1940s were connected to her attacks on racial discrimination.[33]

Pearl stepped up her campaign for racial justice in the spring of 1942. In April, along with Paul Robeson and Lillian Hellman, she spoke at a rally sponsored by the New York-based Council on African Affairs. Half of the three thousand people in the Manhattan Center audience were African-American, the other half white. They roared approval when Robeson demanded the right to fight fascism "on an equal basis with the free peoples of every race, color and creed in the world." In her remarks, Pearl labeled racial discrimination as "undemocratic," and warned that it dangerously "disunifie[d]" the forces struggling against fascism in Asia and Europe.[34] She agreed with the African-American writer Chester Himes that "race prejudice is bred of fear," and she pleaded with her fellow citizens to find the courage to embrace equality.[35]

One journalist called Pearl "the spiritual descendant of Tom Paine."[36] Another said she was embarked on a "single-handed crusade for justice."[37] Poet Witter

29. Pearl and Channing Tobias before a Greater New York Inter-Racial Rally
at Lewisohn Stadium, New York, June, 1942. (Courtesy Harry Ransom
Humanities Center, University of Texas.)

Bynner was dazzled by the "resolute and indefatigable campaign" Pearl had
launched in support of human rights. He commented, quite accurately, on "the
uncanny amount of work" she was doing on a dozen projects at once.[38] Her
crowded schedule of lectures and meetings amounted to an inventory of human
rights struggles around the globe: Indian independence, opportunities for
women, Chinese relief, an end to Chinese exclusion from the United States,
even the liberation of Korea, a country about which most Americans knew
absolutely nothing.[39]

In rapid succession, in March and April, Pearl spoke at a convention of the
American Association of University Women and at rallies of the Japanese-
American Committee for Democracy and the Federal Union organization. She
gave the principal address at the celebration of India–China Friendship day in
New York, and spoke to several thousand at an East and West Association
meeting in Boston's Symphony Hall.

In May, in a letter to the *New York Times,* she took a stand on the notorious Odell Waller case. Waller was an African-American sharecropper sentenced to die by a Virginia court for killing his white landlord in an argument over the sale of a crop. Pearl called Waller a "personification of all to whom democracy is denied in our country"; she said that his fate was a test of American justice – a test the nation failed.[40] In June, she published an essay in the *New Republic* attacking the Chinese exclusion policy as an insult to America's main Asian ally.[41] Following the Harlem riots of August, she appeared as a guest on Fiorello LaGuardia's radio program, speaking on "Unity at Home, Victory Abroad."[42] In September, Pearl joined Eleanor Roosevelt in a radio broadcast to the women of Poland, promising an early victory over the Nazis.[43]

Pearl suspected that Americans had only a halfhearted commitment to democracy. "In certain compartments of their mind," she once said, "which they open on holidays, they think everybody should be free."[44] Her self-appointed job was to browbeat her fellow citizens into taking their own holiday rhetoric seriously. Like a schoolteacher drilling a group of slow-witted students, she kept reciting her declaration of faith in America's democratic dogma. Her lectures and essays were repetitive and uncomplicated, a single thesis nailed to the door of the American conscience. She demanded equality: between men and women, black and white Americans, Asians and Westerners.

Pearl's politics had been permanently affected by the thirty years she spent breathing in the air of her mother's homesick patriotism. For the rest of her life, she was not only disappointed, she was continually surprised and embarrassed whenever American behavior fell short of the unsophisticated idealism she had carried in her immigrant's baggage. She made it her job to remind her countrymen of what they ought to know about democracy.

She wrote, at about this time, "It is a fashion just now to think that whatever is simple is 'too simple.' But we are where we are at this tragic moment because we could not act simply and straightly at the critical moments. . . . It takes strength to be simple, and those who do not feel themselves strong find refuge in complexity. . . ."[45] The paragraph ostensibly describes someone else, but Pearl expressed her own values when she wrote it. She inhabited an uncomplicated, well-lit ethical world, in which self-evident principles led to straightforward conclusions about right and wrong. It would be "easy to have a better world," she said to her sister Grace, "if only a few clear things were said and done."

She often said that she was apolitical. What she actually meant was that she had neither the training nor the inclination for substantive political argument. Instead, she tended to appeal directly to broad moral categories and personal virtues. This is certainly unsophisticated. On the other hand, in a century in which abstract ideas and ideologies have engendered so much destruction, Pearl Buck's more primitive humanitarianism has much to commend it. "I am extremely frightened," she once wrote, of "any theorist, political or religious. I have a deep belief in the average person of all countries."[46] She assumed that good will would make practical measures self-evident.

Of course, despite Pearl's (perhaps defensive) opinion, complexity is often a fact of life, not merely the hideout to which moral weaklings retreat. The recalcitrant troubles of the world will not be remedied by a few clear statements and gestures. Pearl's moral rigor, which narrowed the psychological range of her fiction, also reduced the events of the political world to versions of allegory and melodrama. Nevertheless, her defiant simplicity had its uses. It endowed her insights with a bracing clarity: she saw and named the inequity in racial and sexual hierarchies that others took for granted. She used the yardstick of common sense to measure the distance between the soaring egalitarian rhetoric of the Western democracies and the inequalities that diminished the lives of women and people of color. She told her sister Grace that "in the night, or a dozen times a day, I find myself thinking furiously about the peoples of the world, as if they were my personal responsibility."[47]

To extend the reach of her influence (and to help the John Day Company meets its payroll), Pearl collected ten of her recent articles and speeches on civil rights and international politics and published them as a book in the summer of 1942, under the title *American Unity and Asia*. Along with several statements on the status of African-Americans and women, Pearl rather bravely included a speech she had made in April, condemning the internment of Japanese-Americans. With that speech, she joined a small handful of white Americans who opposed one of the most shameful domestic proceedings of World War II.

On February 19, 1942, after much internal debate in his cabinet, President Roosevelt signed Executive Order 9066, which directed the Secretary of War to remove potentially treacherous persons to places of military confinement. Although Japanese and Japanese-Americans were not specifically named in the order, they were the group that Roosevelt and his advisors had in mind. Over the next two years, before the order was rescinded in 1944, several thousand Japanese-Americans were interned in ten isolated concentration camps spread across half a dozen Western states. Entire families, including small children, were imprisoned as enemies of the United States.[48] Congressman Robert Matsui, a baby in 1942, asked years later: "How could I as a six-month-old child born in this country be declared by my own government to be an enemy alien?"[49]

Americans tended to keep quiet about the internment policy. Most probably approved of it; the rest knew that opposition would be unpopular and even dangerous. Characteristically, Pearl launched a vigorous attack. Speaking at a rally of the Japanese-American Committee for Democracy on April 15, just two months after Roosevelt's order, she warned that a democratic country did not send its citizens to concentration camps because of their race. "That is the sort of thing fascism does," she said; it is "blind, stupid, unreasoning."[50] (A few weeks later, Pearl voiced her objections to internment in a letter to Eleanor Roosevelt: "It is not only what is being done to the Japanese but it is the effect upon our own people that is so evil.")[51]

The essays in *American Unity and Asia* stirred up both fierce opposition and fervent support. Several pages were torn out of one copy of the book and sent anonymously to FBI headquarters, with the words "Sabotage" and "Lies" scrawled across the margins. Against that sort of outrage, many of the reviews were favorable, and a few were downright reverential. In the *New York Times,* John Chamberlain called Pearl's essays "magnificent." He reiterated the book's arguments against racial discrimination, and urged the Freedom House foundation to purchase *American Unity* in wholesale lots for wide distribution.[52] Eleanor Roosevelt, in one of her "My Day" columns, declared that "we have needed this book and I hope it will find its way into the hands of the great masses of people in our nation."

As Roosevelt's tribute indicates, Pearl's tireless efforts had made her a recognized authority on the nation's racial politics. Walter White acknowledged Pearl's civil rights leadership in a speech that he delivered at Madison Square Garden in mid-June. He deplored the racism of the American public and military, but said that the greater "tragedy of the situation is that only a few intelligent and brave souls . . . in the white world are wise enough to see the picture as it is." He named just two of those brave souls: Eleanor Roosevelt and Pearl Buck.[53]

Faced with virtually universal discrimination, some blacks expressed little enthusiasm for fighting in a "white man's war." Walter White, general secretary of the NAACP, sadly reported the embittered statement made to him by a college student in 1942: "I hope Hitler wins. The Army Jim Crows us. The Navy lets us serve only as messmen. The Red Cross refuses our blood. Employers and labor unions shut us out. Lynchings continue. We are disenfranchised, Jim Crowed, spat upon. What else could Hitler do?"[54]

Most black leaders, however, including Walter White and W. E. B. Du Bois, believed that the best hope for African-American progress lay in joining the war effort. Blacks conceived of the war as a "Double V" campaign, with the United States as the second front and racial equality as the second victory.[55] An editorial in the *Crisis,* a few weeks after Pearl Harbor, insisted on "the bargaining power of battlefield bravery in the struggle for advancement."[56] The argument recalled the ideas of Frederick Douglass, who believed that black freedom would be secured by the black soldiers who fought in the Civil War.

Pearl also adopted this strategy; she spelled out her position in the commencement address she gave at Howard University in early June. After receiving an honorary Doctor of Laws from the university's president, Dr. Mordecai Johnson, she spoke for nearly an hour under a hot midday sun. She referred to

Howard's graduates as "Americans of old families and not of recent immigration . . . well above the average of all Americans," who nonetheless harbored profound questions about their place in the nation's life. Voicing the inner doubts that most white speakers would have ignored or denied – that many whites would not even have understood – she told her young audience: "You are asking how much you can actually accomplish, even with your unusual equipment, and how relentlessly the barriers of race prejudice in your country will hold you back."

Eradicating bigotry, Pearl warned, would take leadership and even heroism. She praised black heroes of the past, but pointed out that Crispus Attucks and Harriet Tubman were dead: "We hark back too much to the people who are dead," she said, sounding an Emersonian note. "We need living heroes of our people." (A black woman in the audience whispered admiringly, "She said 'we.' ") Suggesting that Howard's graduates find living heroes, Pearl nominated Paul Robeson, Dorothy Maynard, and Marian Anderson.

Pearl asked African-Americans to support the war, but to do so only on the condition that the United States government recognize the aspiration of black Americans for equality. Finally, she urged black Americans to join with the non-white majority of the world in a larger struggle for freedom. Events in India, China, Korea, and Indonesia, she said, would help to shape the racial landscape of the United States.[57] According to her sister Grace, when Pearl finished speaking, the audience "applauded again and again."[58]

Pearl's address at Howard was the first commencement speech she had ever delivered. She accepted the invitation because she stoutly believed that education had the power to eliminate prejudice. If people knew more about each other, she felt, they would treat each other with more tolerance – a doubtful but noble conception. She believed that literature could promote understanding, and in the spring she wrote to several dozen critics, asking them to name the ten books that would "tell an Asiatic reader the most about the American people."[59] She gave her own, slightly eccentric choices as examples: Sinclair Lewis's *Arrowsmith,* journalist Mark Sullivan's six-volume series, *Our Times,* and Ruth Suckow's *The Folks.*[60]

Pearl's approach to cultural comparisons was dependably evenhanded.[61] She planned an East and West lecture series that would "show how we appear in the eyes of nations abroad, and what is now expected of us."[62] She hoped to set up East and West units in China, India, Australia, and Mexico, because she firmly believed, as one journalist put it, that, "as in trade, the balance of culture should not be preponderantly on one side."[63]

Like many people who opposed imperialism and promoted civil rights, Pearl had to strike a delicate balance throughout the war. She despised German and Japanese fascism, but she worried that Western patriotism would be exploited to

30. Pearl and Jesse Jones, U.S. Secretary of Commerce; both received honorary degrees at the St. Lawrence University commencement, June, 1942. (Reproduced with permission of the Pearl S. Buck Foundation.)

buttress the colonial and racial status quo. She told her sister Grace that she "could not head up any organization which would work against this war."[64] At the same time, she worried that victory would be hollow if it reinforced white supremacy. Her views on America's alliance with Great Britain resembled those of W. E. B. Du Bois, who summarized his own ambivalence in a memorable, weary epigraph: "If Hitler triumphs the world is lost; if England triumphs the world is not saved."[65]

Pearl wrote several times to Eleanor Roosevelt, pleading with her to persuade the president that America had to provide moral as well as military leadership if an enduring peace were to be won. At the least, this required the United States to distance itself from Churchill's unyielding claims to continued white rule in India and the rest of the empire. She wanted Franklin Roosevelt to declare his support for Indian independence. Privately, Pearl was skeptical. "There are reasons why the President does not come out as the moral leader for whom we all wait," she confided to Bernhard Knollenberg, Yale University's librarian. For one thing, Roosevelt's affection for Britain and his personal loyalty to Churchill made him reluctant to repudiate the prime minister. Beyond that, Pearl speculated that Roosevelt, like many Western leaders, was troubled by "a genuine fear lest the white man's world will fall."[66]

Pearl's suspicions were justified. Roosevelt did make intermittent requests that Churchill should promise independence to the Indians, but these were mere gestures, no more than "occasional irritants" in the relationship between the two leaders.[67] On one occasion, Roosevelt sent a personal delegate, Louis Johnson, who encouraged Churchill to make concessions to the Indian Congress party. When Churchill explosively rejected the proposal, even threatening to resign, Roosevelt pulled back. He concluded that he needed Churchill more than he needed the Indians.[68]

By the end of 1942, it was Pearl Buck, not Franklin Roosevelt or any politician, who had become the leading American spokesperson for Indian liberation.[69] In late September, she gave the main address at a New York rally sponsored by the India League of America. The agitated report in the *New York Times* tried to capture the scene: "The cry 'India must be free!' rang through Town Hall last night to the accompaniment of the vociferous approval of more than 2,000 persons who jammed the meeting place." Hundreds more who tried to get in were turned away by a special detail of police. Pearl and the other speakers characterized British policy in India as "barbaric," "stupid," "Tory imperialism."[70]

When she went back to her apartment that evening, exhausted, Pearl might have calculated that she had given at least fifty speeches, interviews, and press conferences in the ten months since the war began, most of them on the subject of equal rights. Like her father, she was blessed with an iron constitution and bottomless reserves of stamina. Her energy seemed to grow when she fought in a good cause. Pearl had celebrated her fiftieth birthday in June, taking only a few hours off from her nonstop writing, lecturing, fund-raising, and organizing. Her children sometimes disappeared from her life for days at a time, but that caused her only a little discomfort, especially since Richard was never far from her side. As she took the measure and balance of her life, she decided that she had found the work she was born for.

IN BOTH EUROPE AND ASIA, the tide of war began to turn in the second half of 1942. In May, the Battle of Midway ended Japanese control of the Pacific and initiated MacArthur's methodical advance toward Japan's home islands. In November, Montgomery's victory on the field of El Alamein, along with the Allied invasion of North Africa and the failure of Hitler's invasion of Russia, signaled Germany's inevitable defeat. Millions more would die in the nearly three years of catastrophic suffering that lay ahead, but the eventual outcome had now declared itself.

Throughout the fall, Pearl continued to batter the president and the American public with repeated demands for racial justice at home and overseas. Roosevelt finally moved toward recognizing China's equality by accepting the repeal of the infamous unequal treaties, which had bedeviled relations between the American and Chinese governments for nearly a century. The United States abandoned its extraterritorial privileges and persuaded Britain to make similar concessions (outside of Hong Kong). The president's timing was shrewd; he announced America's decision on the eve of October 10, China's Independence Day.[71]

Pearl worried, as she wrote to Dorothy Thompson, that the war was "fast becoming a tool in the hands of those who want neither freedom nor equality in the world." Roosevelt had taken a progressive step forward in abolishing the unequal treaties, but his failure to speak out on Indian independence signaled the worst: "We *are* headed straight for an Anglo-American hegemony, and a hegemony ruled by reactionaries."[72]

She uttered a similar warning at the annual Nobel anniversary dinner, which took place on December 10, at the end of the first year of American participation in World War II. Over half of the twenty-eight Nobel Prize winners then living in the United States attended, and several, among them Thomas Mann and chemist Harold Urey, were asked to address the theme "The World We Fight For and American Unity."

Pearl's remarks were the most widely reported, perhaps because she refused to issue a simple call to patriotic arms. On the contrary, she warned her distinguished audience that the war had already "ceased to be a fight for freedom": it was now "not even a war to save civilization, but only a war to save European civilization."[73] The people of Asia had learned that they could not trust their Western allies, because the West had no intention of designing a postwar world in which the nations of Asia would be released from colonial subjection. In Pearl's disillusioned view, the governments of Europe and America fought only to preserve their own dominant places in the global order.

Witter Bynner worried that he heard "a note of despair" in the speech. Pearl denied that she was desperate, but Bynner's reading of her unhappy comments seems close to the mark.[74] At the very least, she was growing angry and frustrated about America's democratic double standard; she stood far outside the nation's flag-waving wartime consensus. Wendell Willkie sent her a telegram congratulating her for giving "a great and true talk." She responded with a note of thanks, adding that "I am getting the usual flowers – few – and rotten tomatoes – not so few."[75]

She was pelted again when she published an impassioned article in the *New York Times Magazine* a couple of months later, once more scolding the Allies for failing to include universal human equality among their war aims. Quoting R. H. Tawney, she insisted that "War is either a crusade or it is a crime." Responding a week later, H. I. Brock accused Pearl of confusing her naive humanitarianism with the realistic and limited aims of the war. The objective of the war, said Brock, was survival, and turning the conflict "into a crusade" was dangerous, since it might "sap the common will to win, and thus lose both the war and the crusade."[76]

Despite such criticism, Pearl remained vocal in support of equality. In March, 1943, she published an article defending the Equal Rights Amendment in the *New York Times,* adjacent to an opposition statement by Anna Lord Strauss, president of the New York City League of Women Voters. In the *Times* article, Pearl acknowledged the value of protective legislation but concluded that "no amount of special benefit to women is good enough to offset the basic damage done to human equality." In any case, she insisted that "special benefit for women is a manifestation of that old-fashioned 'chivalry' which has kept women so long upon a pedestal of inferiority to men." The nation must accept its women "not as dear and weaker possessions," but as fully equal human beings.[77]

Pearl was becoming an increasingly controversial figure. She came to the attention of the House Un-American Activities Committee (HUAC) for the first time in the spring of 1943. Joseph Tooru Kanazawa named her, along with Albert Einstein and "this anthropologist at Columbia, Franz Boas," as members of the advisory board of the "pro-Communist" Japanese-American Committee for Democracy.[78] A few months later, one of her East and West programs, "Our Neighbors, East and West," was attacked because it allegedly tilted in favor of "known Communists, Communist fellow-travelers, or sympathizers with and apologists for the policies of the Communist dictatorship in Russia."[79]

In spite of Pearl's notoriety, she and Eleanor Roosevelt remained in fairly regular contact throughout the spring of 1943. (Roosevelt, a frequent target of red-baiters herself, seldom revised her list of friends to suit right-wing hysteria.) Roosevelt asked Pearl to speak at a Washington ceremony in March honoring

Mary McLeod Bethune on her retirement as president of Bethune-Cookman, the black college in Florida. Roosevelt also invited Pearl to stay overnight in the White House. Pearl promptly agreed to give the talk, "because of my interest in the subject and because it is an honor to speak with you," but she declined the overnight invitation.[80]

Eleanor Roosevelt wanted to hear what Pearl had to say about Chiang Kai-shek. Mme. Chiang had recently spent several weeks at the White House, representing her husband and the Nationalists, and behaving, as one historian puts it, "like a petulant princess."[81] She slept on silk sheets she had brought with her, and clapped her hands for service. She had come to the United States in November, 1942, supposedly for medical treatment, but stayed on until May, 1943. Her visit turned into a campaign tour.

On February 18, glamorous in a tight-fitting black Chinese dress and speaking in impeccable English, Mme. Chiang talked for an hour to a joint session of Congress. She affirmed Chinese–American solidarity and pleaded for increased military aid. The speech was a triumph. The senators and representatives, who were "captivated . . . amazed . . . dizzied" by her "grace, charm and intelligence," gave her a standing ovation.[82]

Mme. Chiang traveled around the country, from New York to Boston to Chicago to Los Angeles, pumping up American enthusiasm for Nationalist China at every stop. Thirty thousand people filled the Hollywood Bowl for her last appearance, and gave her another standing ovation. The guest list at the official banquet that followed the speech was a roll call of film celebrities: Robert Taylor, Barbara Stanwyck, Gary Cooper, Bob Hope, Irene Dunne, Loretta Young, Tyrone Power, and dozens of others. Greer Garson and James Cagney offered toasts.[83] Chiang Kai-shek could not have found a more effective ambassador than his elegant, articulate, masterful wife.

Eleanor Roosevelt, probably suppressing an assortment of misgivings, joined in the chorus of applause. She acknowledged "a great feeling of pride" in Mme. Chiang "as a woman" who was also a world figure in her own right.[84] Watching the Chinese First Lady with her husband Franklin, in Congress, and in meetings with the Joint Chiefs of Staff, Eleanor decided that she had rarely seen a more charming and persuasive advocate. Franklin, on the other hand, distrusted Mme. Chiang. By the end of her visit, Treasury Secretary Henry Morgenthau confided that "the President . . . is just crazy to get her out of the country."[85]

Shortly after Mme. Chiang left the White House, Pearl came for dinner with Eleanor Roosevelt. She warned her hostess that neither of the Chiangs was likely to bring democracy to China, except under stiff American pressure. The Kuomintang, over which the Generalissimo and his wife presided, was being swallowed up in its own inefficiency and corruption. Pearl conceded Mme. Chiang's charm — she called the Chinese First Lady "imperious and beautiful and expensive" — but warned that she was fatally distant from her country's common people.

Finally, Pearl complained that Henry Luce, the fervently pro-Chiang publisher of *Time* and *Life,* had been given too much authority in planning Mme. Chiang's tour.[86] Luce, like Pearl the child of Presbyterian missionaries to China, famously forecast in 1941 that "the American Century" had arrived. He had begun to preach a hard, dogmatic chauvinism that Pearl found offensive and dangerous. She was afraid that Luce would ultimately play the role of an American Churchill, an evangelist spreading the good news that the whole world was properly America's postwar sphere of influence. Events would confirm her fears.

In the wake of Mme. Chiang's departure and Pearl's visit, Eleanor Roosevelt proposed to Franklin that she might fly to China as an unofficial U. S. envoy, to demonstrate solidarity with the Nationalist government and also to evaluate conditions for herself. She prepared for the trip by asking Pearl to send her a written summary of her views. In response, Pearl drafted a confidential, twelve-page memorandum on the situation in China.

She traced Chiang Kai-shek's failure to his wife and her family, the wealthy and powerful Soongs. She devoted a good deal of space to Mme. Chiang's regal pretensions, her Westernized alienation from her own culture, and her indifference to democracy. Among China's squabbling factions, Pearl told Roosevelt, only the Communists had embraced the peasants, making the hopes and frustrations of China's masses their own agenda. "I am myself an anti-communist of the deepest dye," Pearl insisted, but she nonetheless found much to admire in the Communists' agrarian reforms, and much to despise in Chiang's murderous purges — which she compared to Stalin's.

Pearl predicted that a bloody civil war would follow the struggle against Japan, and that the people would not support Chiang. Pearl advised Roosevelt, if she wanted to learn something of Chinese Communism firsthand, to include Chou En-lai (Zhou Enlai) somewhere in her schedule. Finally, she urged Roosevelt to make contact with China's ordinary men and women — as an antidote to what Pearl called "the opéra bouffe" misconceptions that Westerners have long cherished about the Chinese. And she warned the First Lady away from missionaries: "good people and nearly always well-meaning persons, but usually rather ignorant of the real people."[87]

Following a debate among his advisors, the president decided to postpone Eleanor's trip to China. Eleanor wrote to Pearl, telling her of this change of plans, thanking her evasively for her memorandum ("I was enormously interested"), and assuring her that the two women would meet before any future Asian journey that Eleanor might undertake.[88]

Pearl knew that her critique of the Chiangs would bring savage reactions from the Generalissimo's well-placed American friends. Since U.S. policy depended on a dependable, democratically inclined Kuomintang, Pearl's views were not welcome in the State Department or in most editorial offices. For some time, she refused to make her opinions public, translating her objections into the code of a disapproving silence.[89]

When she finally decided to speak out, she chose the most visible journal in America: she asked Henry Luce to publish a moderate but critical estimate of Chiang in *Life*. It proved to be one of the most important articles she ever wrote. She told Luce that she was "fearful that certain dark possibilities now looming in China will materialize and cause undue disillusionment and pessimism about China over here. . . . I have endeavored to prepare a background, in this article for whatever comes."[90]

After some considerable hesitation, Luce agreed to publish the article, under the title "A Warning About China." Pearl argued that Chiang was still regarded in China as a great military figure, but that he was losing popular support through his ruthless suppression of liberal voices. His success, indeed his survival, would depend upon reforms within the Kuomintang and within his innermost circle. "In China, this is ceasing to be a people's war," Pearl wrote; but if Chiang would not trust the people, they would not trust him.[91] Pearl called for greater American assistance, but she also placed much of the blame for the failures of Chiang's leadership squarely with Chiang himself.

To Luce's credit, he published Pearl's article in spite of his violent disagreement with it. As he predicted, "A Warning About China" helped to swing American opinion away from Chiang. Looking back on Chinese–American relations in that period, John King Fairbank later wrote: "American disillusionment as to Free China came with a bang in the summer of 1943 through three articles – Pearl Buck in *Life* for May 10, Hanson Baldwin of the *New York Times* in the *Reader's Digest* for August, and T. A. Bisson in *Far Eastern Survey*."[92]

Pearl had another grudge against Chiang and his wife. They had never used their considerable influence to oppose the Chinese exclusion laws, which had stood for two generations as the most durable symbols of American contempt for Asians. The politics of wartime alliance created a favorable framework for repeal, and Congressional hearings opened in May, 1943. Mme. Chiang knew of the hearings, but made no public statement. Her silence served the purposes of those who wanted to leave exclusion intact: a coalition of the American Legion, some labor unions, and Southern politicians who instinctively revolted at the idea of humane treatment for any non-white group, whatever their color.

In the absence of Chinese leadership, Richard and Pearl set up the Citizens Committee to Repeal Chinese Exclusion (CCRCE), with Richard as chairman. CCRCE shared quarters with the John Day Company, the East and West Association, and a dozen other projects Pearl and Richard were involved in. The

Walshes recruited a national committee, but Pearl served as the chief spokesperson. She published several articles attacking exclusion. In May, accompanied by an honor guard of young Chinese, Pearl testified before the House Committee on Immigration and Naturalization. In her prepared remarks, she made the case for repeal on two grounds: simple decency and the war effort. Democracy demanded equal treatment for Chinese with other foreign nationals; and success in the Pacific war depended on China's belief in American solidarity. Pearl told the committee that every man and woman in China knew about America's policy of exclusion, and that the law's very existence posed an "unwarranted test" of Chinese patience.

To her dismay, Pearl was met with a hectoring racism, which ignored her arguments altogether. Representative A. Leonard Allen of Louisiana subjected her to a merciless grilling, asking her over and over to "confess" that she believed "in full social equality among the races." Shaken, Pearl insisted that the question had no relevance. She did indeed believe in "social equality," but she knew that the term had the electric force of a cattle prod in the racial discourse of the period.[93] Allen's spiteful interrogation was further evidence of the paranoid drift of American politics.

Despite such resistance, the repeal legislation, buoyed by wartime enthusiasm, marched toward enactment. Both Eleanor and Franklin Roosevelt eventually lent belated but vital support. Eleanor devoted one of her newspaper columns to the subject, and Franklin informed Congress that he regarded "this legislation as important in the cause of winning the war and of establishing a secure peace."[94] On October 22, 1943, more than sixty years after the first Chinese exclusion law had been passed, the whole discriminatory system was dismantled. Henceforward, Chinese would be eligible to emigrate to the United States on a quota basis and to become citizens.

THE REPEAL OF EXCLUSION was a small but undeniable victory for equality; Pearl celebrated over dinner in New York's Chinatown. At the same time, most of the other battles she was fighting remained at stalemate. Rioting against blacks in Mobile, Beaumont, and Detroit, and anti-Mexican riots in Los Angeles, were "danger signals."[95]

So too was the threat of a postwar alliance between the United States and Britain that would entail American support for the maintenance of the British Empire. In an article called "Postwar China and the United States," published in November, 1943, she wrote that she was "taking it for granted that we will *not* become a part of the British Empire as Churchill invites us to become . . . and that, after the efforts of our forefathers in 1776, we *will* continue to exist as a separate and independent nation." If the United States were to align itself with

31. Pearl and a group of Chinese-American supporters during a break in her testimony before the House Committee on Immigration and Naturalization, May, 1943. (Reproduced with permission of the Pearl S. Buck Foundation.)

Britain, "we should force three fourths of the world's people to believe that we believe in empire – that is, that we believe in the rule of the few over the many, that we believe in the superiority of one race over another. . . ."[96]

Pearl's attacks on colonialism contributed a central theme to her next wartime novel, *The Promise,* which appeared in October. The book tells the tragic story of China's failed collaboration with the British armed forces in the fight against Japan. The central male character, a young commander named Lao San (nick-named Sheng, the third brother in *Dragon Seed*), is sent with his troops to Burma to help retreating British units escape from Japanese encirclement. The "promise" of the title refers to British pledges of desperately needed military equipment, in particular the airplanes that might shield China's civilian populations from in-discriminate Japanese bombing. *Dragon Seed* ended with this "promise."

Sheng and his comrades, themselves the long-suffering victims of British ra-cism and colonialism, cooperate only because the Japanese evil seems larger than the British; the distasteful alliance is dictated by events. When the Chinese troops enter Burma, they meet hatred and opposition from the Burmese people. Ancient ethnic distrust is inflamed because the Chinese are now allies of the white men "who were hated by the people, men who had ruled here for years upon years."[97] Japanese propaganda has quite effectively portrayed the Chinese armies as tools of British imperialism, and rallied Burmese opinion to Asian solidarity. The Anglo-Chinese operation ends in disaster.

In picturing the Burma campaign as a fiasco, Pearl took her fictional cues from historical facts.[98] The British betrayed their Asian allies because they couldn't imagine dealing with them as human beings. Beyond that, Burma simply didn't matter very much to its Western defenders. The few Americans posted there thought of it as the last place on earth; the British considered it only a dispensable buffer defending India. In 1940, in need of time to gather strength for the European war, Churchill had even placated Japan by agreeing to close the Burma Road for three months. The action, which crippled resistance to the Japanese in all of Southeast Asia, was a gross demonstration of British priorities.[99] Pearl's story resonates with the anger she felt at Britain's behavior and attitudes.

Only a few British characters appear in the novel: a few deserters and stragglers who have escaped the systematic annihilation that has followed from Japanese ruthlessness and British stupidity. Stupidity and treachery: in one scene, British units escape across a bridge with Chinese aid and then cut the bridge, leaving the Chinese to certain massacre. That episode is based on an actual event; so too is a sequence in which the British distribute their propaganda pamphlets in English, a language almost no one in Burma could read. For Pearl, this farcical proceeding epitomized the self-destructive arrogance of Western imperialism.

Though the novel does not sentimentalize its Asian characters, they undoubtedly embody most of the novel's fully realized, complex humanity. The British never reach beyond their instinct for domination; even those who are personally decent or brave are possessed by dreams of empire and tainted by an irrepressible assumption of racial superiority. The British can't even tell the difference between Chinese, Burmese, and Japanese; their defeat is history's mocking reply to generations of bigotry.

The Promise presents the Allied experience of World War II from an Asian point of view, a perspective that precisely inverts Churchill's moralizing certitudes. In Pearl's account of it, the British Empire embodies a bankrupt old order that will necessarily be replaced by independent Asian nations. Her revisionist version of events redefines the issues at stake in the war.

Although Pearl's intentions in the novel were polemic, as usual her strongest writing occurs in descriptive and narrative passages. The novel creates a sequence of powerful images: lepers seeking shelter in an air raid tunnel; famished dogs digging up newly buried corpses; ambulances dodging Japanese bombs on the Burma Road; beaten soldiers lost in the dense, pathless jungles of northern Burma. Scenes like these effectively dramatize the strangulation of Southeast Asian freedom.

Even as reviews of *The Promise* appeared, Pearl was embarked on a new project, raising money for relief of a famine in India. Once again, Pearl and Richard gathered a large committee but reserved most decisions for themselves, a habit that quite a few of her co-workers found high-handed and even impertinent. Not surprisingly, a number of the people who joined the boards of her various fund-raising and educational ventures also left fairly rapidly.

When Clark Minor, for example, president of International General Electric, resigned from the East and West Association, a friend speculated that "he has just gotten tired of Pearl Buck. The whole show seems to belong to her and

Mr. Walsh. They have made many broadcasts, she has translated innumerable pamphlets and books, she has participated in discussions on India and so on."[100]

Thomas Lamont's unhappy participation in the East and West Association in the early 1940s provides another example of the reaction Pearl could provoke. At the time, Lamont was a prominent figure in New York financial and social life, the wealthy, Harvard-educated head of J. P. Morgan's New York office – the sort of person Pearl wanted on one or another of the East and West committees. Lamont agreed to join the advisory board, but had only minimal dealings with the association. He apparently attended no meetings and made no contributions. He received, acknowledged, and filed a series of letters and pamphlets from the association. By May of 1943, he had begun to question the association's work, among other things questioning the value of a project to establish "Russian Clubs." In early January, 1944, when Lamont heard of Clark Minor's resignation, he decided that he, too, would probably resign: "Pearl Buck is a fine woman but goes off the deep end now and then in her enthusiasm for good causes."[101]

In her own defense, Pearl would have said that she was pushed off the deep end. Except for Richard, she knew almost no one who shared her commitment to racial and sexual equality – certainly no one among the affluent white men who filled most of the spaces on her various advisory boards and who made most of the donations that she depended on. She felt increasingly desperate about the dry rot of inequality that threatened to topple the entire democratic edifice.

She was impatient "with the word minority, for minorities vary in different parts of the world. Taking the world as a whole, the white people are a minority." She said that in a speech in early 1944 to New York City teachers, and she added an anecdote that summarized America's sadly insular view of the world. She had recently read an essay by a high school student who defended Chinese exclusion because "the Chinese had taken over most of China and what would they do if they ever got to America." This, she said, was not a joke, but an actual story.

The only remedy for confusion on this scale was education, what Pearl called "global education," that would put both cultural difference and common humanity at the curricular center. Such teaching wouldn't inevitably lead to affection between nations and races – it would be "sentimental nonsense" to think so. But it would lead to understanding and the eradication of "sheer ignorant prejudice."[102]

Pearl concluded that the schools could not and would not provide the education Americans would need in the postwar world. To make up the intellectual deficit, she invested a growing fraction of her hopes and her energy in the East and West Association. Throughout 1944, she was involved in a staggering list of association projects and publications: raising funds for the organization (and contributing a good deal of her own money to the work), recruiting new members and patrons, writing pamphlets and news releases, personally managing dozens of activities, chairing committees, and speaking at an endless round of public meetings and press conferences.

Among other programs, East and West sponsored lecture courses all over the country, including films, music, art exhibits, and dramatic readings; weekly Town Hall forums, under the general title "The People's Congress"; radio broadcasts; and workshops and demonstrations for teachers, covering the history and culture of Asian nations. One of Pearl's favorite projects, the Chinese Living Theatre, dispatched young Chinese actors on national tours. Another initiative, "East and West in the Comics," produced color cartoon supplements on Asian life that were distributed by two newspaper syndicates.

Every day, Pearl spent hours designing, supervising, and evaluating all these activities. She had achieved an influence that was unusual by any measure and especially rare for a woman. In one way or another, the programs of East and West reached millions of Americans. Pearl proved to be a gifted organizer, a fine judge of character, and a sharp businesswoman. She delighted in her talents, but she knew that her gender surely had something to do with the resistance she provoked. Her visibility, tenacity, and tireless campaigning seemed unwomanly, unnatural, and automatically repugnant to a large segment of the population.

As a controversial public woman, Pearl found inspiration in other public women, including Margaret Sanger, her slightly older contemporary and the pioneering leader of the American birth control movement. After the two women met in the mid-1930s, their acquaintance soon ripened into an intimate friendship.[103] Pearl had appeared at several major events honoring Sanger. Sanger in turn took an active interest in East and West; by 1944 she had become one of Pearl's principal confidantes and advisors.

In a series of long letters, the two women shared opinions and debated tactics. Sanger volunteered for fund-raising assignments, visiting wealthy men and women who had contributed to the birth control movement ten or twenty years earlier and asking them now to support Pearl's new, internationalist crusade. She sent a letter to a combined list of birth control and East and West sponsors, telling them: "I consider Pearl Buck not only one of America's great women, but one of the great women of the century." Pearl, she said, had "aroused millions of people all over the earth to a new vision."[104]

Sanger and Pearl were world-historical figures, tempered by conflict, and consciously stretching the limits that tradition had drawn around female accomplishment. Each took special pleasure in the other's admiration. Sanger told Pearl that "knowing you has been one of the loveliest experiences of my life, to sit with you and to work with you." Pearl reciprocated, telling Sanger that "your coming to me remains a miracle." She said that she had read Sanger's autobiography yet again, and was overwhelmed by "what you have done, how hard it was, what spirit and courage were yours."[105]

Enveloped in Pearl's admiration, Sanger could criticize and give advice where others kept still. She told Pearl that East and West needed to be run more professionally. Potential donors were discouraged because they felt that "the whole venture was amateurish." Looking back on her own work, Sanger admitted that she had initially run the birth control movement on "a tin-cup basis," but she had quickly learned the virtues of professional accounting. Many people, she said, were "entirely sold on Pearl Buck," but not "altogether sold on EAST-WEST."[106]

Pearl accepted Sanger's comments more or less gracefully, though the idea of pleasing foundations and rich donors rankled. When Philadelphia's Janice Lit, of the Lit Department Store family, offered to help Pearl "arouse interest among the idle rich women," Pearl said that she had "such a low opinion of these ladies who live in the Stork Club and the Colony Club . . . that I doubt my own ability to interest them."[107] A few days later, still bristling, she added: "Quite frankly, dear Margaret, . . . I am not inclined to do any fawning around . . . anybody for money. I consider it an opportunity to be able to give money and time to the sort of thing EAST WEST is doing."[108]

The galling superiority of that last remark often crept into her conversation, alienating potential supporters and even annoying her friends. Her perpetual rectitude could be tiresome. Pearl thought of herself as uncompromising, the plain-talking advocate of causes that ought to command universal allegiance. Understandably, on the other hand, the ordinary souls around her sometimes found her tone sanctimonious and even shrill. The anonymous remarks scribbled in the margins of one of her many fund-raising letters are the work of an obviously exasperated person: "Buck – passes the buck"; "East and West Association: The Bundles-for-Buck Association"; and, at the bottom of the letter, with an audible sigh, "What a trying world it is."[109]

Though Pearl claimed to stand above politics, she constantly found herself embroiled in partisan acrimony. Her critical analysis of Chiang Kai-shek reverberated internationally, mobilizing Chiang's anti-Communist supporters. A Catholic priest, George Barry O'Toole, who had served as rector of the Catholic University in Peking from 1925 to 1933, decided that the best way to defend Chiang was to smear his critics. In the spring of 1944, he published an article "exposing" Chiang's opponents as "Red Snipers . . . eager to potshot the Chungking government and chant the praises of Yenan" [the Communists]. Pearl was named among the "snipers," along with Agnes Smedley, T. A. Bisson, Edgar Snow, and Vincent Sheean.[110] Most of the people on O'Toole's list had published in *Asia* magazine; some, like Smedley, Snow, and Sheean, were regular contributors.''' In the view of her right-wing enemies, Pearl lurked near the center of a sinister pro-Communist conspiracy.

She launched another attack on Chiang in the spring of 1944 by organizing a New York rally to celebrate the anniversary of Sun Yat-sen's death. East and West rented the Metropolitan Opera House and sponsored a mass meeting on March 12. Pearl and half a dozen other speakers paid tribute to China's greatest Republican hero, linking him with Chinese freedom fighters in the seventh year of their war against Japan.

On the same day, Pearl published an advance copy of her speech in the *New York Times Magazine*. While she praised Sun Yat-sen effusively, she never mentioned Chiang. In the circumstances of the moment, Pearl's silence amounted to an oblique but unmistakable rejection of Chiang and the Kuomintang. Chiang had struggled for almost two decades to demonstrate that his authority descended legitimately from Sun's. Pearl's contrary version of history suggests that in 1944, nineteen years after Sun's death, no legitimate successor had appeared.

Pearl doubled her rebuke by yoking Sun closely with his wife, Soong Ching-ling, Mme. Chiang's older sister. The Suns, she said, "made a pair whose match the world has not seen."''² While Sun was dead, his widow continued to embody the ideals of the revolution. Pearl had told Eleanor Roosevelt that Mme. Sun, not Chiang or Mme. Chiang, was the country's moral center and the symbol of its democratic hopes. Unlike Mme. Chiang, who actually despised her own people, Pearl said, Mme. Sun "has made the cause of common Chinese people hers, and they know it."''³ Pearl's preference for Sun Yat-sen and Soong Ching-ling amounted to a humiliating renunciation of Chiang Kai-shek and Soong Mei-ling.

Pearl reserved her sharpest attacks for the men around Chiang, such as Tai Li, the head of the Kuomintang's notorious secret service, the Chen brothers, and the Green Gang thugs who carried on a thriving criminal business under the cover of the national government. In an inflammatory comparison, Pearl suggested that these men resembled Martin Dies, former chairman of the House Un-American Activities Committee, as threats to democracy.''⁴

In late July, after traveling to Ohio to speak at an Antioch College conference, Pearl returned to New York to attend the opening of MGM's screen version of *Dragon Seed*.''⁵ Hoping to duplicate the critical and commercial success of *The Good Earth*, MGM had spent lavishly on sets and costumes, and assembled a first-line corps of actors, headed by Katharine Hepburn in the role of Jade. Though several nationalities were represented in the cast, Chinese was not one of them: the actors included Walter Huston, Agnes Moorhead, Akim Tamiroff, and Turhan Bey.

Since the Office of War Information (OWI) wanted a film that would help the war effort, the script went through months of revisions.[116] OWI bureaucrats were delighted with the final version; the critics were decidedly mixed. The *New York Times,* the *Daily Mirror,* and *PM* printed enthusiastic notices. On the other hand, James Agee announced that *Dragon Seed* was an "unimaginably bad movie," and the *Chicago Tribune* thought the "garbled English" was embarrassing. Interestingly, all the film's critics agreed that the Caucasian actors were a distraction, which suggests that Hollywood's casting conventions were lagging somewhere behind public taste.

The August 1 opening at Radio City Music Hall served as a fund-raiser for East and West. MGM turned over the entire mezzanine for the event, and Pearl persuaded the new Chinese Ambassador, Wei Taoming, to head a glittering guest list. (Eleanor Roosevelt declined, but sent a supportive personal letter.)[117] In private, Pearl complained that the movie was wrong in almost every detail: Katherine Hepburn wore a man's jacket instead of a woman's because she found it more stylish; Hepburn's bangs were inappropriate; the bridge in the opening scenes was architecturally inaccurate.[118] Publicly, Pearl claimed that she was generally pleased with the film, though she said that Luise Rainer had done a better job imitating a Chinese woman than Katharine Hepburn. "But you must remember," she said to a reporter, "this is the first picture in which Miss Hepburn hasn't had to be simply Katharine Hepburn."[119]

The main domestic story in the summer and fall of 1944 was Franklin Roosevelt's campaign for an unprecedented fourth term. Tired, visibly shrunken, the president made few political appearances. He stayed in the White House, running for office by managing the war, and easily defeated his Republican opponent, Thomas Dewey, the jaunty, inexperienced governor of New York.

To Pearl, the election seemed to offer a dreadful choice, "between an old, tired man, already twelve years in the most difficult possible job, and a young, untried, untrained and quite ignorant man." She said she was "frankly terrified" at both alternatives.[120] Despite Allied advances on the battlefield, she had sunk into the gloomy conviction that neither America's leaders nor its people understood the great stakes being contested in the war. There was talk that Pearl might run for Congress herself, as a Democrat, but she quickly scotched the reports.

She wrote a short letter to the *New York Times* in September, commenting on the refusal of Anglo-American diplomats to include an article recognizing racial equality in the new United Nations constitution. She recalled the eerie parallel between this decision and the refusal of the League of Nations to recognize racial equality in 1919. Transatlantic blindness in 1919 had finally "expressed itself in the attack on Pearl Harbor. . . . What, I wonder, will be the fruit" of the same stupidity "say, in twenty years?"[121] Barbarous choices like this, she said in a review of Carey McWilliams's important book on prejudice, along with discrimination against blacks and internment of Japanese-Americans, prove that the United States "is the world's chief offender, next to Nazi Germany, in the matter of racial intolerance."[122]

The charge was overwrought, but it threw Pearl's frustration into sharp relief. She leveled similar accusations against the British government, which remained oblivious to the demands for equality that were echoing across the colonial world. In September, 1944, she accepted yet another assignment, agreeing to become one of two "Honorary Presidents" (with Lin Yutang) of the India League of America. The working president was Sirdar J. J. Singh; the board members included Roger Baldwin of the ACLU, Albert Einstein, Walter White, and journalist William Shirer.

As usual, Pearl and Richard drew up a long and ambitious program, intended to transform the League into a major engine of Indian liberation. The usual flurry of pamphlets, lectures, press conferences, fund-raising, and Washington lobbying followed Pearl's appointment. Millions throughout Asia, she said, "are watching to see if democracy means what it says and if the Four Freedoms are true or false. By what we do about India, democracy will stand or fall."[123] In mid-December and again in January, Pearl hosted dinners to honor Mrs. Vijaya Lakshmi Pandit, Nehru's sister and a major figure in Congress Party politics. Pandit was the first Indian nationalist leader permitted entry into the United States since the beginning of the war.

Upwards of a thousand people attended the dinners. At the second one, held in the Grand Ballroom of New York's Commodore Hotel, Pearl likened India under British authority in World War II to Czarist Russia during World War I. In each case, the masses were tyrannized by undemocratic rulers; they were forced to fight in a war in which they had no part and no choice, and from which they would receive no benefit. In India, she declared, "as in Russia yesterday, a rising anger, born of intolerable agony, is sweeping out of the people."[124]

While she was overseeing Mrs. Pandit's visit, Pearl also finished an article for the *New York Times Magazine,* a year-end review of the current situation in China. She was in the odd situation of trying to revive support for Chiang's government, in the face of the widespread American disappointment that she had done much to create. With that in mind, she focused on the insults China had suffered at the hands of her supposed Western allies, in particular the exclusion of Chinese delegates at the Quebec Conference, where Churchill and Roosevelt alone had planned the course of the war against Japan. Pearl distrusted Chiang – she even began to detect a likeness between Chiang and Churchill – but she harbored a deeper distrust of the racial assumptions that separated Americans from their obligations in Asia.

32. Green Hills Farm. (Reproduced with permission of the Pearl S. Buck Foundation.)

Pearl and Richard spent Christmas week at Green Hills Farm with five of their children. As always, she supervised every detail of the decorating, cooking, singing, skating, and sleigh riding that occupied the family for the entire week. Even during her holiday, she spent hours making phone calls and drafting memos and position papers for East and West, for the ACLU Committee Against Racial Discrimination, which she continued to chair, for the India League, and for the John Day Company.

ON JANUARY 21, 1945, the entire front page of the *New York Times* was taken up with a large map of Europe, labeled "Roads to Berlin." Around the edges of the map, a dozen arrows pointed dramatically at the center of Germany from east, west, and south. The point was clear: the costliest, bloodiest war in human history had reached its final stages. Politicians, scholars, and journalists increasingly shifted their attention toward predicting and planning the postwar world.

Pearl wanted the East and West Association to play an influential part in shaping the new international order. She hoped to expand the organization, and hired Gordon Halstead to fill the new post of executive director. Pearl would continue to design most of the programs and head up the fund-raising effort.

33. Carol Buck in the early 1940s. (Reproduced with permission of the Pearl S. Buck Foundation.)

Above all, she intended to speak out on future relations between Asia and America. Halstead would manage the large staff of paid and volunteer workers, and take responsibility for the association's budget.

Halstead had lived and worked in Asia, and had served in the National Youth Administration and in the United Nations Reconstruction and Relief Agency. Aside from his credentials and experience, he suited Pearl because he would not compete with her for authority or attention. In a letter to Margaret Sanger, Pearl predicted that Halstead would provide "a very fine quiet sort of leadership." She added, "We have enough of the fireworks kind around the office with what I can supply."[125] Her small joke suggests that she had some awareness of her abrasive style, her impatience, and her preference for center stage. Whenever she descended on the East and West offices, the staff braced itself for turmoil. Furthermore, as Halstead would quickly learn, Pearl didn't intend to seek out his advice. "The problem with her was she didn't really *listen*," actress Aline MacMahon said years later.[126]

One of the new ventures Pearl conceived was a series of small books on world affairs, each consisting of an interview that she would conduct with a significant international figure, annotated with a few editorial and narrative comments. The first of these books, *Tell the People,* described the work of James Yen (Yan Yangchu), who had led the Mass Education Movement in China in the 1930s.

A Yale-educated Christian, Yen spent the latter months of World War I on the French front, working on behalf of the thousands of Chinese laborers who had been lured to Europe with the false promise of high wages. The suffering he saw there convinced him that literacy was the key to peasant progress. The link between literacy and emancipation was particularly critical for the Chinese, because of the exceptional difficulty of the written language. The ancient character system took years to master, ensuring that written Chinese was "a ruling class monopoly." Rather than providing China's peasantry with "an open door," through which they could find opportunity, it was "a heavy barrier pressing against any upward advance."[127]

James Yen developed a simplified character system, which he taught to hundreds of illiterate workers. When he returned to China in 1921, he continued the work on an increasingly large scale. He published the landmark *People's 1000 Character Literacy Primer* and founded the National Association of Mass Education Movements in 1923.

The Mass Education Movement (MEM) was the most far-reaching of the many efforts made by non-Communist intellectuals to lift the masses out of illiteracy and poverty. By 1931, MEM had organized more than four hundred People's Schools, which enrolled fifteen thousand students. The People's Library, a series of booklets published by MEM, eventually numbered one thousand titles. The Movement's headquarters in Ting Hsien, in northern China, hosted upwards of five thousand visitors each year – educators, writers, tourists – from all over the world. "The movement had local government support, international acclaim, and village roots."[128] For two decades, Yen was a celebrated international figure.

James Yen's closest American friends, and his most loyal and effective Western supporters, were Pearl Buck and Richard Walsh. Yen was invited several times to lecture to the East and West Association. In addition, Richard headed up MEM's American operation, while Pearl propagandized for the movement and helped Yen raise money. Pearl was attracted to James Yen's combination of pragmatism and egalitarian populism. Yen's devotion to the dispossessed and forgotten people of his country, including the maligned and long-suffering coolies, matched Pearl's own. The Chinese characters for "coolie" literally mean "bitter strength." James Yen was convinced that he could multiply the coolie's strength and relieve his bitterness. Pearl, who revered the power of education to change lives, embraced Yen's ambitious objectives with enthusiasm. She also endorsed his belief in China's village democracy. *Tell the People,* a partisan celebration of James Yen's accomplishments, received a large number of admiring reviews, and gave an impressive boost to Yen's work.

Throughout the spring, as she followed Allied advances in both theaters, Pearl continued to receive sad reports of young relatives and friends who were dead, wounded, or missing. In March, she heard from Dorothy Canfield Fisher, whose only son, Jimmy, had been killed in the Pacific. The news of Jimmy Fisher's death elicited a long, emotional letter from Pearl, two thousand words in which she poured out her grief, frustration, and hatred of war. "I have lived nearly all my life in one form of war or another," Pearl wrote, "I mean the actual danger and violence of war." She had been a frequent eyewitness to the "heartsickening tragedy of innocent people struck down, homes torn to pieces," and young men and women killed. "I have been through too much horror in my life," she wrote; "nobody knows what sights I have seen. I can't put them down."[129] The news of Jimmy Fisher's death touched Pearl more deeply than she had expected; the letter she wrote to Fisher lurches in several different directions under the pressure of the pain she felt. She said that the work of East and West offered her a kind of therapy by permitting her a role in the war, and then ruminated on the efforts of "big business, cartels, etc." to smash the plans of Bretton Woods and Dumbarton Oaks for a functioning United Nations. She complained about the racism and imperial interests of the British. "I didn't mean to keep on writing and writing," Pearl said almost apologetically near the end of this anguished and angry letter. "But my heart is so full this morning. . . ."

Along with Dorothy Fisher's letter, she had also received twenty letters from families who had lost sons and brothers and husbands in Asia. Only one of these people knew Pearl Buck, but all of them felt compelled to write to her in their despair, hoping that she could tell them something about the places where their loved ones died. One woman, a widow in Texas, wrote that she had spent hours "trying to find the place on the map of China where they tell me my dear boy fell. He is my only child. I can't find the place." Bitterly, Pearl explained to Dorothy Fisher that the young man had died in Manchuria, which "of course" was "not on the map of China at all." The Allies, as part of their appeasement of Japan in the 1930s, had permitted the Japanese simply to swallow up Manchuria without a whisper of dissent.

A few days after she wrote this letter, Pearl traveled to Washington at Eleanor Roosevelt's invitation. Roosevelt had asked a hundred dignitaries to attend "An East and West Evening" at the White House. As Pearl described the evening's genesis: "Mrs. Roosevelt, bless her, has recently seen what we are trying to do – desperately singlehanded, without much money or help . . . and she has asked us to give an EAST AND WEST evening." Referring to Franklin Roosevelt, Pearl added that, thanks to Eleanor, "the Big Chief is to be there himself."[130] (An exhausted FDR did attend, briefly; the president had only a month to live.)

The speeches that followed the dinner surveyed the work of East and West. Along with Pearl, the speakers included a Philadelphia school teacher, a New York City librarian, and two association staff members. To be sure, such a roster demonstrated Pearl's egalitarian inclinations. As she wrote a few weeks later to Margaret Sanger: "We could have got famous persons [as speakers] if we wanted, but we are not working for famous persons."[31] At the same time, however, the ordinary citizens with whom she shared the podium catered to her vanity since they enhanced her own visibility.

The centerpiece of the White House evening was a performance by the Chinese Unit of the Living Theatre. The Chinese Unit was a remarkable repertory company, touring the country under Pearl Buck's auspices as part of the Theatre Project of East and West. In the mid-1940s, Asian roles in films and on stage — few enough in any case — were routinely given to white actors. The Chinese Unit consisted of half a dozen Chinese performers who offered plays by Chinese writers; there were no whites in the cast. The group's leader was Wang Ying, widely regarded as one of China's foremost actresses.

Everyone at the East and West event knew that the war in Europe was grinding to an end. At the end of April, as the Berlin garrisons collapsed, Hitler committed suicide; the Germans surrendered a week later. The entire Allied military effort now turned to Asia, where intelligence services predicted two more years of combat, culminating in a lethal invasion of Japan. The atomic bomb would force a Japanese surrender in just three months, but the bomb remained a well-kept secret.

Hollywood's cinematic propaganda helped Americans prepare for a long, bloody struggle. RKO released *China Sky,* based on a serial Pearl had published in *Collier's* several years earlier. Randolph Scott starred as an American doctor working with the guerrillas in northwest China; Anthony Quinn was cast as the guerrilla leader Chen Ta. RKO's writers bleached every trace of ambiguity out of Pearl's text. In the movie version of history, relations between the Chinese and their American partners are productive and mutually trusting, unblemished by the suspicions and recriminations of actual events.

Pearl claimed that she didn't dare to go see the film. She wrote to a friend that she had heard it was "pretty bad. . . . I am getting more and more disgusted, in fact, with what comes out of Hollywood. It doesn't matter what one sends in — what comes out is pretty much the same old stuff."[32] Despite her complaints, Pearl never refused a Hollywood offer. *China Sky* was the third of her novels to be adapted to the screen in eight years, a profitable result of her famous association with Asian subjects.

Pearl's close identification with Asia paid handsome dividends, but it also imposed significant limits on her. She found herself, as she later wrote, "strangely oppressed. I felt suddenly that I was no longer a free individual. I had been cast in a mold. I had written so many books about Chinese people that I had become known as a writer only about China.'"[133] She also believed that her rough treatment at the hands of the literary establishment had something to do with the double bind of her Asian subject matter and her gender. Many critics were not going to take either women writers or stories set in China very seriously.

To resolve the dilemma, Pearl decided on a daring and somewhat risky strategy. In May of 1945, she published a long novel, *The Townsman,* under the pseudonym John Sedges. The pen name gave her a measure of artistic freedom – and the chance to test her talent in the marketplace as an unknown writer. The name itself was the result of Pearl's calculations about the sexual politics of American letters: "I chose the name of John Sedges, a simple one, and masculine because men have fewer handicaps in our society than women have, in writing as well as in other professions."[134]

The Townsman offers an engaging, sometimes a frankly sentimental portrait of American small-town life. Pearl effectively evokes the hardships of pioneer society and the rigor of Kansas weather. The endless sequence of winter snowstorms and crushing summer heat is described in some of the book's strongest paragraphs. In the end, however, Pearl celebrates the pastoral virtues that have long attached themselves to the small town in America's mythology.

Other writers, among them Sherwood Anderson and Pearl's friend Sinclair Lewis, had famously disputed these images of small-town tranquillity and security, exchanging them satirically for sketches of a village life marked by ignorance and repression. Anderson's stultified grotesques and Lewis's boorish hustlers are dull and conformist victims of what Lewis called "the village virus," inhabiting crude outposts of American materialism.

However, Pearl Buck's perspective on American society was dramatically different from that of her contemporaries. In the years immediately following World War I, when such books as *Winesburg, Ohio* (1919) and *Main Street* (1920) appeared, she was still living in China. She had spent several years in the rural north of the country, in villages of such appalling poverty, superstition, and despair that the small towns of America seemed by comparison quite elevated places. The revolt against the village among American writers in the 1920s had essentially expressed the distaste of middle-class intellectuals for standards and behavior they found vulgar. For her part, Pearl Buck had a long, first-hand acquaintance with rural deprivation on a scale that made the question of mere vulgarity seem rather trivial.

Pearl's allegorically named hero, Jonathan Goodliffe, comes to America from his native England as a boy of fifteen, accompanying his parents in their search for New World opportunity. The novel patiently records Jonathan's long and useful life in the town of Median, Kansas. Jonathan's ambitions are at once modest and exalted: to build a functioning, self-sufficient community on the formidable landscape of the Great Plains. He opens the first school in his part of the state, plans the town's growth from a cluster of sod huts to a prosperous county seat of 6,000, and finds his fulfillment in the tasks of settlement and civilization.

As this summary suggests, Pearl didn't simply use literary formulas; she transformed them to serve her thematic purposes. She could rarely resist preaching in her fiction, especially on the subjects of racial and sexual equality. Beneath its frontier trappings, *The Townsman* teaches an extended lesson in civic virtue. To begin with, Jonathan Goodliffe is not the typical hard-riding sheriff (or outlaw) of most Western fables. Instead, as Pearl herself describes him, he is a rather ordinary fellow, "who refuses to ride wild horses, be a cowboy, shoot pistols into the air, kill his enemies, find gold in any hills, destroy Indians, or even get drunk. He is content merely to become the solid founder of a city."

In short, Pearl used her main male character to embody a new notion of (male) American heroism. Jonathan exemplifies productive domesticity rather than flamboyant adventuring, and to that extent he represents the sort of masculinity Pearl had called for in *Of Men and Women,* her spirited inquiry into America's gender roles. Pearl thirsted after a society in which men would behave like adults by abandoning their fascination with violence and their alienation from family responsibilities. To do so, men would have to embrace a cluster of values usually identified with women. A remarkable number of pages in the novel are devoted to Jonathan's work building his house, teaching school, mending his own clothes, and caring for his younger brothers and sisters and for his own children.[135]

The Townsman also addresses America's racial prejudices, which Pearl found even more retrograde and destructive than the nation's obsolete attitudes toward women. Her passion for tolerance emerges in the novel by way of a major subplot involving Median's only black residents, a family named Parry. Pearl apparently believed that she could contribute to racial understanding by creating strong black characters in her fiction; the Parrys are examples. They have come to Kansas as "exodusters" in the years following the Civil War. Despite the racism of the white settlers around them, they prove to be one of the more stable and successful families on the frontier. Jonathan's loyalty to the Parrys, often against the bigoted opposition of Median's leading citizens, is of course a mark of his own integrity, and a signal of Pearl's intentions in the novel.

Beaumont Parry, the family's oldest son, is among Jonathan's students; he proves himself the most brilliant person in the town. Eventually, the unlikely generosity of a white benefactor enables Beaumont to become a rich and successful surgeon. The plot twist is utterly implausible but revealing. Beaumont Parry's fairy-tale triumph expresses something more important than Pearl's failure of narrative imagination. It is a symbolic gesture, a vision of the journey's end, when equality would replace racism. Pearl was being driven to the sad conclusion that the ideal of democracy was itself a dream and a delusion: racial equality would require the same sort of escape from reality as Beaumont's magical success. Like so much of Pearl Buck's writing and lecturing throughout the war, *The Townsman* combined a patriotic call to arms with a jeremiad against American racial attitudes.

PEARL WAS CONVINCED that the Allied nations must choose between two starkly simple alternatives: they must either revolutionize their racial beliefs and practices, abandon imperialism, and embrace equality, or they must prepare for World War III. A return to the racial status quo, which Churchill, Roosevelt, and even De Gaulle seemed to prefer, would not be possible.

At a minimum, Pearl believed that American bigotry was suicidal in the contest for world influence. She made this point emphatically in a combative June speech defending the Fair Employment Practices Commission (FEPC). The commission was under the combined attack of big business and Southern politicians. She called FEPC "one of the most democratic acts ever designed and planned in our nation," a necessary guardian of fairness in employment. "It seems ridiculous," she said, "to have to stand here and say such obvious things as I am saying – that the prejudices in this country are so various and so numerous that there must be some sort of overall protection for those of us who are not white, adult, male Protestant Gentiles." The commission was under siege, she said, because white Americans are "befuddled and crazed by our supreme prejudice against the Negro." White racial hatred not only nurtured a systematic injustice against blacks. Beyond that, American prejudice makes us "absurd in the eyes of the world"; it is "at this very moment handing the peoples of Asia to Russia as a free gift."[36] Pearl Buck seemed to be one of the few Americans who understood the elementary connections between the nation's domestic behavior and its foreign policies.

She accused American leaders of exhibiting a "colonial mentality," as she called it, which linked white nations in a shared contempt for all people of color. She expressed her views repeatedly, nowhere with greater emphasis than in a review she wrote of W. E. B. Du Bois's important polemic, *Color and Democracy: Colonies and Peace*. This book attacked the imperialist and fundamentally racist assumptions underlying the Allied military effort. In seven chapters, Du Bois massively documented his central charge: that the new United Nations charter had affirmed colonialism, suppressed questions of race, and effectively discouraged the expansion of democracy. Characteristically weaving together statistics and passages of lyric outrage, Du Bois exposed the moral confusion of a political order in which the Western "democracies" undemocratically controlled the lives of one-third of the world's inhabitants.[137]

At the time he published *Color and Democracy,* Du Bois was serving as Director of Special Research for the NAACP, and his views were widely interpreted as a quasi-official statement of association policy. In fact, as Arnold Rampersad has argued, Du Bois's book demonstrated that he "was far beyond the NAACP in the scope of his world view and his radicalism."[138]

Color and Democracy received mixed notices. Several reviewers referred somewhat condescendingly to Du Bois's "little book," or complained about the angry tone, while others insisted on the volume's wisdom and importance.[139] Pearl's review was the lead item in the *New York Herald Tribune's Weekly Book Review,* and she used that prominent position to support Du Bois emphatically. "Those gathered at Dumbarton Oaks," she wrote, "had no intention of changing the existing organization of empire." Consequently, the new United Nations will merely "put force behind the existing systems, ignoring the injustice out of which war will come." As a response to the political inequality and economic imbalance that underlies world tensions, the United Nations "is a poultice put on a cancer."

Pearl enclosed her review in a cover letter to Irita Van Doren, the *Tribune's* book editor; the letter is a good deal less restrained than the review. In it, she wrote: "I am sure Du Bois wrote this book out of his disgust at the pussyfooting of the State Department about Dumbarton Oaks. At the meeting of the 96 nations [the initial United Nations conference in San Francisco] . . . people I know who were there told me he put the same frank questions he puts in his book, and was consistently ignored or shut up."[140]

Pearl did not attend the San Francisco conference, but she wrote a speech, "American Imperialism in the Making," which she delivered twice, at East and West meetings that were scheduled to coincide with the United Nations sessions. In front of large crowds, first in New York and then in Boston, she railed against the U.S. decision to line up with Britain in opposing independence for colonial peoples. She warned that the countries of Asia would turn to Russia for leadership in the postwar struggle: "The great thing Russia has contributed to human history is an alternative to empire, empire such as Britain knows it in her colonial system, and empire as we are developing it through our industrial and economic monopolies."[141]

Like many on the left at the time, Pearl overestimated the sincerity of Soviet talk about self-determination. She had become profoundly discouraged by the scorn with which both Britain and America treated the aspirations of non-white colonies. She needed to find an answer to imperialism; if the West refused to provide it, she would look to Russia. She had been more clear-eyed about Stalin's ruthlessness in the late 1930s, in the wake of the purge trials and the

34. Pearl in one of the libraries she added to Green Hills Farm. (Reproduced
with permission of the Pearl S. Buck Foundation.)

Nazi–Soviet non-aggression treaty. As she surveyed the much-changed world of
mid-1945, she revised her estimate.

Pearl's opinions about the Soviet Union were influenced by a Russian woman
named Masha Scott, whom she met in the early 1940s. In May, Pearl published
the first installment of "Talks With Masha" in *Asia and the Americas*. The series,

which reached seven parts, told the story of Magnitogorsk, the new steel-making city that was the most ambitious effort at industrialization in Soviet history.[142]

Like James Yen's Mass Education Movement, Magnitogorsk has now dwindled to a historical footnote; in the mid-1940s, however, both were receiving widespread attention. Around the world, leaders and citizens alike were searching for ideas and models that might give practical shape to the uncertain future. James Yen's remarkable success in bringing literacy to tens of thousands of Chinese peasants and Stalin's mobilization of hundreds of thousands of Soviet citizens in the construction of a huge industrial center beyond the Urals seemed immensely significant. Above all, MEM and Magnitogorsk appeared to offer specific, practical responses to the social and economic chaos that threatened to engulf the postwar societies of Europe and Asia.

Masha Scott had worked in Magnitogorsk in the 1930s, married an American, and emigrated with him to the United States in 1941. Pearl had been introduced to Masha and her husband, John Scott, shortly after their arrival in New York, and had immediately become friends with both of them.[143] She was eager for first-hand reports on life in the Soviet Union; the Scotts brought her their personal experience, along with an unusual Russian-American perspective.

John Scott's own biography was a fairly typical case study in twentieth-century radicalism and reaction; his youthful devotion to the Soviet experiment eventually gave way to militant anti-Communism.[144] Born John Scott Nearing, he was the eldest son of Scott Nearing, one of America's most celebrated left-wing radicals and pacifists. While still in his teens, he changed his name to escape his father's shadow, but he initially embraced a similar ideology. In 1931, in the depths of the Depression, the nineteen-year-old Scott dropped out of the University of Wisconsin, took a course in welding, and sailed for Russia. In his view, he had abandoned the economic and moral bankruptcy of the United States to take his place in the brave new society that was emerging in the Soviet Union. He found himself in Magnitogorsk, where he spent the next five years helping to build the largest steel factory in the world.

By any reckoning, Magnitogorsk was a titanic achievement. Literally built on a mountain of nearly pure iron, it was no more than a blueprint in 1929. By the end of the 1930s the city's population had reached 250,000, and its plants were producing 10 percent of Russia's steel. Located east of the Urals, out of reach of the aircraft of any potential enemy, Magnitogorsk's factories embodied Stalin's strategic foresight. Throughout World War II, steel manufacturing continued without interruption; the steel for half of Russia's tanks was produced in Magnitogorsk.

In the 1930s and 1940s, the whole world had heard about Magnitogorsk, but few foreigners had been there, and fewer still had written about it. John Scott, who had been expelled from the city in 1938, became an editor for *Time* magazine; in 1942, he published a book about his experiences, *Behind the Urals: An American Worker in Russia's City of Steel.*[145] The book gives a richly detailed description of the brutality and immense sacrifice that accompanied Stalin's campaign of forced industrialization. Scott worked alongside peasants, laborers, and convicts, in temperatures that often dropped to thirty degrees below zero; he saw poorly trained, badly equipped workers killed and crippled in daily accidents; he observed corruption, incompetence, and Stalinist purges. Yet he was also convinced that he was a witness to an enterprise of historic proportions: "I had participated in the collective effort of one hundred and seventy-odd million people building a society along collective lines, coordinated and synchronized by a general plan."

Pearl Buck's *Talk About Russia* is the companion piece to *Behind the Urals.* John Scott's book told the story of an outsider who shared the life of the factory floor and of its (almost exclusively male) workers. Pearl's account puts Masha Scott at the center, giving her an extended chance to describe Soviet life from the vantage point of a Russian peasant and a woman. In the long and clamorous debate between Communism and capitalism, Masha Scott represented a vast group of people who had been neglected. As usual, Pearl was eager to give a forum to voices that had not been heard.

The two women first met over dinner in the Scotts' Greenwich Village apartment. Masha immediately impressed herself on Pearl as a "symbol of all we think of as Russian" – by which she meant that the young woman looked the part: angular, high-cheeked face, blond hair drawn up in braids, large capable hands. Indeed, it is difficult to sort out Masha Scott from Pearl's conventionally picturesque sketch of her. As she appears in the pages of *Talk About Russia,* Masha rather closely resembles the gallery of competent, self-sufficient women who fill the pages of Pearl's fiction. In the tacit equation that Pearl often relied on, Masha Scott's political testimony is validated by her appealing personality.

Masha Scott's enthusiasm for the Soviet system was anchored in her childhood experiences. She had been born in 1912 and had grown up in a small, poverty-stricken village in the Kalinin district, two hundred miles north of Moscow. Her father and mother and the family's eight children slept on the floor of their three-room wooden house. The Revolution came to Masha Scott's village in 1919, when she was seven years old. Her recollections marshal themselves into a train of sentimental anecdotes, in which kindly commissars and well-mannered Red soldiers liberated the peasants from their traditional oppression.

Masha Scott either did not know about Communist excesses or, more likely, chose not to report on what she knew. There was, of course, good reason for her partisan attitude. She was loyal to the Revolution because it had actually improved the lives of the peasants, abolishing the hierarchies that had bound them in half-human servitude and providing a modest security in bad economic times, sickness, and old age.

Pearl had witnessed the deprivations of pre-Revolutionary Russia with her own eyes, when she had traveled across the country on the Trans-Siberian railroad in 1910. She never forgot the shock of seeing the "savage hungry people in the country, peasants and villagers clad in skins with the fur turned inside and filthy with crusts of ancient dirt." Worse than the physical conditions she witnessed was the peasants' utter torpor. "Besotted ignorance was on the faces of these poor people, and a terrible despair, as though it was beyond their memory or their imagination that anyone had ever cared for them or ever could care for them, so that all they could think of was a little coarse food to stuff into their empty mouths."[146]

Pearl sympathized with the accomplishments of the Revolution because she believed that it had improved the lives of these suffering men and women. She insisted, naively if typically, that her admiration had nothing to do with politics. As she put it near the end of the book, in a rather oratorical passage that labors to exclude ideology: "The strength of [Soviet] Russia does not lie in her political theory. It lies in the fierce simplicity of her local realism. The people were oppressed and the oppressors were removed. The people were hungry and means were found to feed them. The people were ridden with fear of old age, sickness, unemployment, and those fears were taken away."[147]

Masha Scott shared Pearl's interest in the condition of women, and discussions of women's rights take up a substantial portion of *Talk About Russia*. Under the Czars, women had no legal status whatever. Masha remembered that, before the Revolution, her own father had routinely beaten her mother, who had no recourse of any kind. Under the Soviet constitution, women found themselves quite suddenly lifted out of the Middle Ages and transported into a modern world of rights and citizenship. Education, careers, electoral rights, legal protection, and divorce were now guaranteed to women who, a few years earlier, had been treated as chattel. While the reality of Soviet society lagged well behind the government's promises of equality, the changes for Russian women were real.

Masha Scott's own biography exemplified her arguments. Under the old regime, she would have spent her life as an illiterate peasant, married with or without her consent to a man who would abuse her or not as luck would have it. She would never have left her village, nor seen a doctor. The Revolution offered her a different life. At the time of her conversations with Pearl, she was a college-educated teacher. She had chosen her husband, had frankly told him of her misgivings about him when she married him, and had reminded him how easy it would be for her to get a divorce if she decided to do so. She had gotten pregnant when she decided she was ready, and had borne two children in state-funded hospitals.

It is not difficult to see why such a woman appealed to Pearl. Indeed, her earnest sense of identification with Masha Scott ultimately damages the book, since she consistently retreats from debate, softens her tone, and turns *Talk About Russia* from a potentially exciting story into a one-dimensional tribute. In the end, the book's undeniable value lies not in Pearl's quite meager analysis, but in the opportunity it gave one Russian peasant woman to speak in her own voice on the eve of the Cold War.

On August 6, 1945, forty-four months after Pearl Harbor, the United States dropped an atomic bomb on Hiroshima; a second bomb was dropped on Nagasaki three days later. Within twenty-four hours, the Japanese surrendered. Although the combined death toll exceeded 100,000, the bombs shortened the war, probably by eighteen months, and saved thousands of lives.[148] The alternative, an invasion of the Japanese home islands, would have entailed far greater casualties — some postwar estimates ranged up to 250,000 Allied dead and wounded, and a larger number of Japanese defenders. In addition, the Japanese had made detailed plans to butcher Allied prisoners of war as the invaders approached each prison camp.

The defeat of the Axis, and the uncertain peace that followed, precipitated a fundamental global realignment. Armed struggle would be replaced by decades of threat and counterthreat, massive military spending, and dangerous nuclear brinkmanship.

With the end of the war, Pearl's place in the arenas of American politics and culture was also about to change irrevocably. She would find herself abused and damaged in the fevered debate over national security, the "loss of China," and the Communist conspiracy. At the same time, she would watch herself erased from literary history as the academic canon was defined in the postwar years. She had a gift for fatalism, but nothing could have prepared her for the long, discouraging twilight that lay ahead.

8

Losing Battles

Pᴇᴀʀʟ ʜᴇᴀʀᴅ ᴛʜᴇ ɴᴇᴡꜱ of Japan's surrender on the radio at the summer place she and Richard had rented on the New Jersey shore, where she went every August to escape from Pennsylvania's heat and the hay fever season. She was working steadily on her next two novels: *Portrait of a Marriage,* another American book, which appeared in December, 1945; and *Pavilion of Women,* set in China, which John Day held over to 1946.

By a predictable but frustrating irony, the end of the war brought a financial crisis to the East and West Association and to the Walshes' magazine, *Asia and the Americas.* With the defeat of Japan, Asia was no longer news, and American interest in the region rapidly subsided. Gordon Halstead, hired in January as East and West's executive director, was gone by May, the victim of money troubles and of his disagreements with Pearl. He followed Margaret Valiant, who was deemed unsuitable by Pearl and removed from the Theatre Project. In June, the association's treasurer, Charles Pharis, threatened to resign when Pearl brusquely ignored his advice about dealing with the budget deficit that was threatening to close the organization down.

By August, Pearl's desperation over money and staff problems led her to submit her own resignation. She was surprised and rather humiliated when the board seemed at first inclined to accept; after she made it clear that the gesture had been intended symbolically, she was persuaded to stay on. But she and her few remaining staff members were demoralized.

Pearl attributed her troubles in part to hostility stirred up by the British. "I am afraid," she wrote in August to Margaret Sanger, "my determined stand for freedom of colonial peoples has served the Association very ill. I have tried to keep this separate from the educational activities and have in fact done so, but the British have looked on me as a calamity."' She was also accused of "anti-Americanism," because she continuously denounced U.S. policymakers for letting themselves become entangled in British imperial designs.

In the August issue of *Asia and the Americas,* Pearl published a compendium of her opinions under the title "American Imperialism in the Making."[2] Like W. E. B. Du Bois, she insisted that the Allied victory in the war would be hollow unless it led to the liberation of subject colonial peoples. And like Du Bois, she warned that those subject peoples would not patiently wait for the gradual mobilization of progressive opinion in Europe and the United States. Finally, she warned that the Asian masses would find much to appeal to them in Soviet Communism, and would turn to Russian leadership unless the West offered swift and meaningful change. According to Pearl, millions of Asians were beginning to regard America as the newest imperial power.

In late October, Pearl went on a two-week speaking tour in the Midwest. She returned to host an East and West luncheon on November 10 at the Roosevelt Hotel in honor of Ilhan New, a Korean businessman, then settled in at Green Hills Farm to fight a fairly serious case of the flu.[3] She monitored the publication of her new novel from her sickbed.

Portrait of a Marriage, which Pearl published under her own name, earned lukewarm reviews and modest sales. In the *Saturday Review,* Grace Frank rhapsodized over Pearl's "supreme artistry" and "the exquisite patterns of her prose," but most readers found both the story and its characters mechanical and rather dull.[4] The marriage of the novel's title joins William Barton, a talented painter and son of a wealthy Philadelphia family, with Ruth Harnsbarger, an uneducated but self-reliant farm woman who lives in rural Pennsylvania. Completely unsuited for each other in any ordinary sense, William and Ruth are nonetheless linked indissolubly by the sheer strength of their passion. Pearl never presents this unlikely marriage convincingly. Rather, she simply declares, repeatedly, that love bound her two characters together for fifty years, against all the obvious odds.

The novel's contrived basic premise provides a glimpse into Pearl's state of mind as she wrote. In a letter to Emma White, Pearl talked at length about the satisfactions she had found in marriage, work, and children. She said she had found the reviews of *Talk About Russia* "very funny – very contradictory," some calling the book Communist propaganda, others praising it as the only objective account of contemporary Russia. After telling Emma that she was sending her a copy of *Portrait of a Marriage* – "a very simple tale" – she described the progress of each of her children, in whom, she said, "I find my deepest satisfaction."[5]

A few weeks later, Pearl was once again embroiled in a controversy that resounded across the country. On March 5, 1946, Winston Churchill announced the advent of the Cold War in a famous speech in Fulton, Missouri. "From Stettin in the Baltic," Churchill declared, "to Trieste in the Adriatic, an iron curtain has descended across the Continent." In Churchill's view, Stalin's ruthless domination of Eastern European nations constituted "a growing challenge and peril to Christian civilization," and he called for an Anglo-American alliance to resist the Communist tide.[6]

The Fulton speech would eventually be seen as one of the documents that defined Western policy toward the Soviet Union – the "iron curtain" became the governing metaphor of the next forty years. At the time, however, Churchill's polemic provoked a hostile reaction on both sides of the Atlantic. The *Times* of London lectured its readers that communism and Western democracy had "much to learn from each other," and chided Churchill for the bellicose extremity of his rhetoric. More pungently, the *Chicago Sun* called the speech "poisonous."[7]

Pearl joined in the attack. Her contempt for Churchill, her fear of another war, and her admiration for ordinary Russians – "we can like and understand the people in Russia" – determined her fierce opposition to Churchill's new crusade.[8] By coincidence, she found herself addressing a large audience the day after Churchill's Fulton speech. Standing before a meeting of the People's Congress of the East and West Association, she discarded her prepared remarks and delivered a rebuttal to Churchill. After repeating her opposition to the prime minister's colonial and imperial views, she concluded with a warning: "we are nearer war tonight than we were last night."[9]

Pearl's attack on Churchill catalyzed J. Edgar Hoover's doubts about her loyalty. He ordered his aides to prepare a full-scale report for his personal inspection. On March 21, agent D. M. Ladd submitted a ten-page, single-spaced memorandum, summarizing Pearl's political activities and associations over the previous decade. In this hodgepodge of fact, error, gossip and innuendo, the FBI's operatives catalogued Pearl's involvement in a wide range of civil rights and internationalist projects.[10]

According to the report, she was affiliated with at least four "Communist Front Organizations": the Japanese-American Committee for Democracy, the East and West Association, the American Civil Liberties Union, and the Indian [sic] League of America. The specific charges against her included the allegation that, as chairman of the Committee Against Racial Discrimination of the ACLU, she had launched a campaign "to wipe out all race discrimination in the war effort." This seemed suspicious to the FBI, and so did the fact that "the Abraham Lincoln School, Chicago, Illinois, the policy of which is controlled by the CP [Communist Party], maintains in its library a copy of [Pearl's] pamphlet 'Mass Education in China.' " Guilt by association had already become a routine strategy in the Bureau's repertoire.

Dozens of Pearl's speeches and articles are indexed in the report, along with some of her correspondence with Eleanor Roosevelt. In at least one ironic case, when Pearl had cabled Roosevelt to protest the "wave of mob violence against

Negroes and other minority groups spreading across the country," she had urged the First Lady to join her in calling for an FBI investigation. Even "The Twain Shall Meet," the comic strip published by East and West to promote cross-cultural understanding among children, was transformed into a sinister engine of subversion under the Bureau's baleful scrutiny. "While no information has been received that this comic strip is Communist propaganda," agent Ladd wrote, "it is definitely the type of material the Communist Party would capitalize on and use if possible.""[11]

A cloud of allegations hovered over Pearl. Nevertheless, after sifting and sorting through ten years of her public life, the Bureau conceded: "No information is contained in the Bureau's files which would indicate that Pearl S. Buck is a member of the Communist Party or that her activities are influenced or controlled by Communists. All of her activities tend to indicate that she considers herself a champion of the colored races, and she has campaigned vigorously for racial equality."

In the FBI's bigoted logic, of course, Pearl's commitment to racial justice made her a dangerous character, whether she was a Communist or not: "Although it is not believed from the information available that Miss Buck is a Communist, her active support of all programs advocating racial equality has led her to associate with many known Communists and other individuals of varying shades of political opinions.""[12]

In June, Pearl invited James T. Farrell to a small luncheon she had organized in honor of her friend, the novelist Lao She.[13] Lao She, one of modern China's major literary figures, had recently earned a portion of celebrity in the United States (and a good deal of money) when the Book-of-the-Month Club offered a translation of *Rickshaw Boy* as a main selection in late 1945. *Rickshaw Boy* had the distinction of being one of the few novels about China, other than Pearl's own, to earn major sales in the 1940s. In spite of her misgivings – she told Emma White that Lao She's book was too much of an "intellectual performance" – she befriended Lao She and promoted *Rickshaw Boy* with editors and booksellers.[14]

The novel's main character, Hsiang-tzu, is a ricksha coolie whose dreams of independence and comfort are methodically beaten out of him. Neither his bodily strength nor his cunning can save him from defeat and despair. Rendered without sentimentality, Hsiang-tzu's fate represents the grim triumph of injustice and bad luck over individual aspirations. (The novel, originally published in 1937, was much altered and prettified by its translators. Despite the changes, Lao She's powerful rendering of human life on the edge of the abyss survived more or less intact.)[15]

Pictures of the ricksha were a commonplace of Western tourist brochures in the first half of the century, images of the seductive pleasures available to affluent

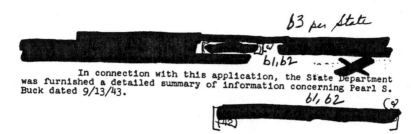

In connection with this application, the State Department was furnished a detailed summary of information concerning Pearl S. Buck dated 9/13/43.

"The Furniture Workers Press," newspaper of the United Furniture Workers of America, CIO ███████, dated September, 1943, contained an article captioned "Sponsors Race Unity Conference". The article revealed that a conference on racial and national unity organized by several outstanding American leaders in various fields, including Pearl Buck, would be held in Chicago during October, 1943.

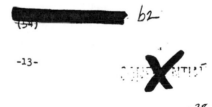

MID advised that Pearl Buck was among those invited to the home of Mrs. Junius S. Morgan, 28 East 36th St, NYC to attend a gathering of representatives of the underground and guerilla movement of the Axis occupied countries. This affair was sponsored by the United Nations Information Center ███████ Pearl Buck did not acknowledge the invitation nor signify her intention of attending this affair.

Pearl S. Buck appeared before the California Senate Fact Finding Committee, Los Angeles, Calif. and opposed discrimination against Japanese on a racial basis stating such action would react against the US in its relationship in the Orient. (Date not given) (Los Angeles Teletype 10/23/43)

The serial indicated the above hearings were held from 10/18 - 21/43.

-13-

35. A page from Pearl Buck's FBI file.

travelers in the exotic, romantic East. In fact, pulling a ricksha was a particularly degrading form of manual labor, in which the ricksha "boy" was reduced from a man to an ox-like animal. Pearl used the ricksha as a symbol of inhumanity in several of her stories. Some of the most memorable scenes in *The Good Earth,* for instance, portray Wang Lung's suffering when he is forced to pull a ricksha in Nanking.

Along with many Asian writers, Pearl also regarded the ricksha as an emblem of Western imperialism. She made this political point most explicitly in her novel

China Flight, a war story serialized in *Collier's* in 1943 and published in book form in 1945, just a few months before Lao She's *Rickshaw Boy.* To punish the novel's hero, Lieutenant Daniel James, a young American prisoner of war, a Japanese officer named Shigo compels him to pull his ricksha. As the humiliation takes hold, Shigo says to James: " 'Did you know that it was an American who first invented the ricksha? Yes, it was in Japan, and he hired Japanese to pull him about in it. . . . Americans so enjoy the ricksha – pulled by Japanese. Now you will doubtless enjoy it also, but between the shafts.' "

The scene serves a vivid anti-colonial tableau, a reminder that Asian xenophobia had some of its sources in Western behavior. Stripped of his humanity, Daniel James is turned into a beast of burden. He is, in short, obliged to act out the fate that has overtaken thousands of Asians at Western hands.[16]

THOUGH PEARL SAID REPEATEDLY that she wanted to remake herself as a writer of American stories, her deepest affinities still tied her to Asian subjects. Beyond that, most of the commercial success she enjoyed depended on her reputation as America's leading fictional interpreter of China. In short, her own inclinations conspired with marketplace pressures to keep her in her familiar place. She knew the likely penalty – her work would drift further and further away from the chief preoccupations of postwar literary taste – but there was nothing she could do to prevent it.

Her next novel, *Pavilion of Women,* published in late 1946, returned to Chinese material. The book did well, selling over 200,000 copies as a Literary Guild selection and briefly attracting Hollywood's interest; Otto Preminger asked Darryl Zanuck to buy the movie rights (Zanuck declined).[17] Pearl had worked on *Pavilion of Women* for several years; she had the idea for the book, and even the title, as far back as early 1943.[18]

The novel's chief character is Madame Wu, a deeply thoughtful woman who presides over a large, prosperous household in a town somewhere west of Nanking. (*Pavilion of Women* was Pearl's first extended portrait of an upper-class Chinese family.)[19] The book's central premise, presented in the opening pages, is simple but dramatic: on her fortieth birthday, Madame Wu announces that she is leaving her husband's bed and moving to separate quarters so that she can finally "live for herself." She declares that she has a brain as well as a body; she has done her duty, having produced several healthy sons, and she intends to spend her remaining years on her own terms. To provide for her husband's sexual needs, she selects a concubine for him.

The rest of the novel traces the implications of Madame Wu's choice over the next several years. Initially, her family, and much of the town as well, is scandalized by behavior they consider eccentric and even unnatural. For her part, Madame Wu only finds the self-sufficiency she seeks after falling under the spell of a renegade Western missionary, an excommunicated Catholic priest named André who preaches a creedless humanitarianism.

André, a man of limitless tolerance and worldly wisdom, embodies yet another rebuke to Pearl's fiercely sectarian father. Conceived more allegorically than as a figure of flesh and blood, his function is to soften the hard edges of Madame Wu's unyielding individualism with his generosity. Beyond that, the friendship between the Chinese woman and the European man is intended to suggest that affection and understanding can leap across borders of ethnic, cultural, and sexual difference. After a provocative beginning, the novel declines into a mystical haze.

As usual in Pearl's fiction, *Pavilion of Women* is strongest in a series of scenes that convincingly re-create the details and rhythms of women's daily lives inside and outside the household. Within the walls of the Wu compound, dinners are cooked and served, clothes are mended, sick children are nursed, account books are balanced, all against a background of changing seasons and the bustle of the city. Pearl describes the elaborate ordering of a feast day, the workings of a brothel, and the horrors of foot-binding. In one fine scene, following André's death, Madame Wu finds herself surrounded by the twenty little orphan girls the priest has adopted. And in the novel's most memorable sequence, Madame Wu attends a woman friend in a long, near-fatal labor that ends in a stillbirth.

The reviews of *Pavilion of Women* marked a further erosion of Pearl's literary reputation. The notices were mainly favorable, but they were at the same time grudging and even patronizing. *Newsweek* captured the critical consensus in the title of its review: "A Woman's Novel." *Pavilion of Women,* in the opinion of the magazine's anonymous reviewer, was "technically excellent" and "beautifully written," a "fine, full, flavorsome novel." Nonetheless, it would only interest women, who would discuss it over afternoon tea, "for this is a woman's novel, by a woman, about a woman all women will understand."

Time's reviewer went a step further. In an essay titled "Woman's World," *Time* predicted that *Pavilion of Women* would be extremely popular, "especially with women." Looking down from its middle-brow heights at the novel and its readers, *Time* concluded that the book's popularity "will not be due to its literary or philosophical qualities but to its precise and colorful descriptions of women's lives and customs."[20]

In short, the magazine simply took for granted a disjunction between literary merit and the representation of women's lives. Here, in primitive but explicit form, is a formula that would govern the codification of the literary canon in the postwar years: male equals universal; female equals ornamental. Pearl was always ready to argue that women's lives were in fact important subjects, but her views would go unheeded and undefended for more than two decades.

She watched as her status inevitably congealed in the emerging consensus. She was a woman who offered "precise and colorful" portraits of women, whose novels spoke to women about women's lives. In the macho culture of postwar America, such a reputation would have done lethal damage to any writer's prestige. The 1940s and 1950s were to be an era in which men wrote for men, about men, when Mailer's *The Naked and the Dead,* Ellison's *Invisible Man,* Salinger's *The Catcher in the Rye,* Kerouac's *On the Road,* and Bellow's *Adventures of Augie March* became the signature pieces of a generation.

Women did respond to *Pavilion of Women,* and not just because it put female experience at the center of the story. More importantly, the entire structure of the book rested on the idea of women's equality with men. Florence Kitchelt, who headed the Connecticut Committee for the Equal Rights Amendment, seized the political significance and wrote Pearl in a rush to tell her that "[a]t almost one sitting, completely absorbed, I have just read the first half of 'Pavilion of Women.' " Kitchelt believed that the novel would give a great boost to the ERA by persuading its readers that women "first . . . are *persons,* and secondly female."[21]

Kitchelt's letter reached Pearl at Green Hills Farm, where she and Richard spent Christmas week. The house was filled with Pearl's extended family; holidays had become an occasion for reunions between Richard's grown children and their families and Pearl and Richard's younger children. At a typical dinner, Pearl had written to Emma White, "we sat down fourteen at table to a twenty-five-pound turkey of our own raising and were thankful for much."[22] She never regarded herself principally as a mother, but she did enjoy presiding as host over these large gatherings, organizing activities and cooking much of the food.

Pearl's Christmas celebrations were tempered by further evidence of her declining fortunes. *Asia and the Americas,* no longer able to meet payroll and production costs, ceased publication with the December, 1946 issue. Pearl had been associated with the magazine for over two decades; some of her first essays and stories had appeared in *Asia* in the mid-1920s. Since the end of the war, advertisers and subscribers had abandoned the magazine in increasing numbers. Although she and Richard mounted a vigorous fund-raising campaign to save their publication, they were defeated by the shifting tides of public opinion in the early days of the Cold War.

Like the East and West Association, *Asia* was victimized by America's postwar return to international indifference. Both the association and the magazine were also damaged by Pearl's notoriety as a cultural and political progressive. She had become a lightning rod for right-wing attacks, and a good many people who had been attracted to her fame and her humane internationalism now hurried to divorce themselves from any connection with her work.

Over the Christmas holiday, Pearl finished another article on racial prejudice, this time for the popular press. "Do You Want Your Children to Be Tolerant?" appeared in the February, 1947 issue of *Better Homes and Gardens*. With a circulation of three million families, the magazine gave Pearl the largest audience she had so far reached for her views on race.[23] She attacked segregation – "All the teaching the school can give a child will not teach him tolerance if colored children are not admitted to the classrooms" – and she bluntly blamed politicians and clergy alike for their failure to provide moral leadership.

Pearl repeated several of the arguments she had been making since the mid-1930s, for example reminding her readers that "the world is full mostly of colored people," and that Africa is a continent "rich in every sort of life and resource, [with] a history, a civilization, languages and arts, yesterday and today." It was strange, she said, "that our western educational emphasis has been placed upon the relatively short life of Greece and Rome, whose peoples were white, rather than upon the far more ancient, and in some ways, the far more important and valuable civilizations of peoples who are dark."

She grieved at the speed with which young boys and girls are initiated into bigotry by their parents and communities. Children, she wrote, are instinctively, even thoughtlessly, egalitarian. In support of her views, Pearl told a bizarre story (cribbed from the *New Yorker*). A group of black and white children decided to play "race riot." However, the white children outnumbered the black, "so in order that the game could be perfectly fair, some of the white boys volunteered to be 'colored.'" A good deal of America's unending racial nightmare is encoded in that sad anecdote.

"Do You Want Your Children to Be Tolerant?" attracted nationwide attention. Pearl's longtime admirer, Walter White of the NAACP, thought the essay was a "a good piece"; he sent a memo to the staff of *Crisis*, advising them to cover the article as a news story in a forthcoming issue.[24]

Pearl poured her anguish about American racism into her next novel, *The Angry Wife*, the second book she published under the name John Sedges. Set in the years just after the Civil War, the story revolves around the conflicts between two brothers, Tom and Pierce Delaney, white men who have fought on opposing sides in the war, and who represent opposing beliefs about race. Though it rarely rises above a plodding symbolism, the novel offers further evidence of Pearl's single-minded commitment to racial justice. She was trying again, as she had in *The Townsman*, to excavate the sources of twentieth-century discrimination in earlier American history.

The Angry Wife was one of three books that Pearl published in 1947. The others were *How It Happens*, a nonfiction account of Germany between World War I and the rise of Hitler, and a collection of stories, *Far and Near*. None of these volumes attracted as much attention as her earlier novels, essays, and anthologies of short fiction.

The subtitle of *How It Happens* describes the subject: *Talk About the German People, 1914–1933*. The book is an annotated, three-hundred-page transcript of a conversation between Pearl and a German woman named Erna von Pustau, who had lived through World War I and Hitler's emergence, then fled with her husband to the United States in the late 1930s. Like *Tell the People* and *Talk About Russia*, her two earlier "talk books," as she called them, *How It Happens* offered its American readers the chance to see world historical events from the point of view of participants.

The book compresses the economic and political turmoil of Weimar Germany into the experience of one woman, translating the abstractions of historical explanation into the desperate struggle of a single family to survive. Erna von Pustau presents a thickly textured description of what it felt like to live inside a nation that spent two decades sliding toward fascism. The calamity of World War I, the humiliating terms of the Versailles Treaty, the years of hyper-inflation and political instability, the rising tides of violence and anti-Semitism, the eventual despair that made Hitler's messianic oratory irresistible: *How It Happens* anchors the tragic chronology in the daily lives of ordinary people.

Reduced to eating turnips and weeds, unable to clothe their children, stripped of hope, the Germans became a people without pity: " 'We had seen and heard of too many suicides, of too much misery and desperation. . . . To lose pity – it is the result of too much misery – you get accustomed, used to too much suffering.' "[25] Hunger, fear, and hatred conspired to transform Germany into a forcing ground for fascism.

Though it is largely forgotten today, *How It Happens* contributed valuable and indeed pioneering insights into the psychology of totalitarianism.[26] Beyond that, Pearl intended the book as a warning to Americans. As the title makes clear, with its verb in the present tense, she did not regard the rise of fascism as a uniquely German phenomenon.[27] She had felt the seismic rumblings of an American fascism throughout the war, and she would do so again in the later 1940s as she measured what she considered America's Cold War drift toward militarism.

She saw the evidence everywhere. She spent part of one Sunday in early July reading Charles Ferguson's *A Little Democracy Is a Dangerous Thing*, in which Ferguson enumerated the weaknesses of democracy in the United States. Pearl immediately wrote to Ferguson to express her fellow feeling. She went further, tracing rising international tensions to America's democratic failures: around the globe, "other peoples . . . expect of us a stand for world democracy which we would not and could not make, because we ourselves did not have the democracy which other peoples thought we had." The consequence is a menacing "disillusion with democracy" itself, in every corner of the world.[28]

Pearl complained bitterly that the American government was basing every judgment – even the allocation of food relief in Europe and Asia – on a Cold War calculus. She had seen starvation on a massive scale in China, and had come to believe that "food is the basic human right." The United States, however, had defined "food as a political weapon in exactly the same sense that Hitler did. . . . The world knows it and starvation lies at our door."[29]

Pearl wanted to combat such attitudes through the work of the East and West Association, but East and West continued to struggle in the face of a flagging membership. Pearl applied to Alger Hiss, then serving as program director at the Carnegie Endowment for International Peace, for a grant, but the application was turned down. She felt a palpable despair in the face of the patriotic freeze that was settling over American political discussion. "I have a very heavy sense of foreboding these days about our own country," she wrote to one of her correspondents, "lest the time come soon when none of us can speak freely any more. We must use these days very carefully while we can."[30] Even the ACLU, she felt, was "in some ways . . . extremely reactionary."[31]

Pearl's ceaseless agitation for liberal causes and ideas had changed her reading habits. Ever since her lonely childhood in China, she had displayed an insatiable appetite for books, with an early preference for fiction: Dickens, in the first place, and the great Chinese novels of the Ming period, then later the modern realists on both sides of the Pacific, Dreiser and Sinclair Lewis, Lu Hsün and Lao She. In the later 1930s and the 1940s, however, pronouncing almost daily on public policy, Pearl immersed herself in the literature of fact: journalism and political analysis and social commentary. The hundred book columns she wrote for *Asia* magazine reflected her commitments rather than her choices.

In the fall of 1947, with *Asia* defunct and the pressure of monthly reviews relieved, Pearl had more time to read fiction. She embarked on a full-scale campaign to master the work of Edith Wharton. She already owned two of Wharton's books, *The Age of Innocence*, which had earned Wharton the Pulitzer Prize in 1920, and *A Backward Glance*, the eloquent if evasive memoir she had published in 1934, the year Pearl returned to the United States. Pearl ordered seven more of Wharton's books from Dutton's book shop in New York (carefully itemizing the price of each): *The Buccaneers, French Ways and Their Meaning, The Gods Arrive, Here and Beyond, Hudson River Bracketed, The Mother's Recompense,* and *Old New York*.[32]

Pearl may have felt some affinity with Wharton, who had been the first woman to win the Pulitzer, and whose novels were undervalued in the late 1940s. Wharton often portrayed the disappointed lives of women who were defeated by some combination of ineffectual or treacherous men and their own scanty moral resources. The pattern of Wharton's exile had reversed Pearl's – she had chosen a life of comfortable French expatriation in her later years, at about the age when Pearl had moved back to the United States – but she had much to teach any woman about female marginality and the vagaries of literary reputation.

PEARL WAS NOT INDIFFERENT to the controversy her opinions aroused. On at least one occasion, she anxiously resigned from an organization, the Japanese-American Committee for Democracy, after the group had been labeled subversive.³³ Nonetheless, she continued to speak out as an advocate of racial tolerance at home and peaceful coexistence abroad. Alarmed at the growing influence of the military on civilian life, she appeared before the Senate's Armed Services Committee, in March, 1948, to testify against a bill directed toward the imposition of universal military training (UMT).

As she prepared her testimony, Pearl consulted with her sister, Grace, about the right-wing effort to portray any opposition to UMT as Communist-inspired. The atmosphere in Washington, Grace said, was "awful," thick with red-baiting and threats.³⁴ In January, the *New York World-Telegram* had run a story, headlined "Anti-UMT Reds Draft Sucker List," which claimed that prominent Americans were being enlisted in the campaign against military training by the Communist Party. Pearl was named in the article.

In spite of the risks, Pearl appeared before the committee and read a long, passionate denunciation of peacetime conscription and universal military training. Only four of the thirteen committee members attended the hearing, and three of them soon left. Pearl found herself facing three high-ranking Army officers – "grimlooking military men in uniform" – who glared at her disapprovingly throughout her testimony.³⁵

She called the proposed legislation "sinister" and wasteful measures, which would create a permanent class of professional soldiers, expose Americans to "the perils of Prussianism," and make the United States "a laughing stock" among civilized nations. Above all, Pearl insisted, UMT would work against democracy: "There is nothing democratic about a military camp, wherever it is. The barking of petty officers, the high and mighty eminence of upper officers, the abject obedience demanded of the young soldier . . . the blind subjection to caste and position rather than deference to human worth – can such things by any stretch of the imagination be called democracy, or can they teach democracy?"³⁶

Over the next several years, the fight against universal military training and the peacetime draft was led by the National Council Against Conscription, which had headquarters in Washington. Pearl joined the Council in 1948, and worked with other members, including Albert Einstein, novelist Louis Bromfield, and labor leader Victor Reuther, on a series of booklets that documented the pervasive spread of military influence across all of American life.

Pearl and her co-authors argued in one of these booklets that the scale of military intrusion into civilian life was unprecedented: "Never before in American history has the military establishment had so much money to spend, so many officers or ex-officers in important civilian government posts, so much influence in the formulation of foreign policy, or such an ambitious publicity department as it does today."[37] The federal budget had been made hostage to military spending, and whole sectors of the nation's collective enterprise, including education, health care, and scientific research, were subordinated to military priorities. Pearl wrote in despair to a friend: "The military power over our government now seems paramount."[38]

Wherever she looked, Pearl detected the lengthening shadows of an engorged, dangerous nationalism. When she canceled all the Book-of-the-Month subscriptions she had bought as gifts for friends, she said that she was fighting a small skirmish in the Cold War. "I have got fed up with them," she wrote to Emma White. "They are too Tory for me. I believe they are choosing books ideologically, especially since Marquand and Fadiman joined the judges."[39]

Pearl's next novel (not a Book-of-the-Month Club choice) was *Peony*, which appeared in May.[40] The book's plot derives from a little-known chapter in Chinese history: for hundreds of years, from perhaps the twelfth century through the twentieth, a large community of Jews lived in the city of K'ai-feng (Kaifeng), the capital of Honan (Henan) province. Though Pearl had known about the Jews all her life, her most detailed information came from an article by Bishop William C. White that she and Richard had published in *Asia* in 1936.[41] By that time, according to White, the disintegration of the Jewish community was complete: "the few remaining Jews have no religious bond, and even their historical relationships are now almost forgotten."[42]

Peony, a memorial to the vanished Jewish families of K'ai-feng, is set in the mid-nineteenth century, when the community was still intact, but when generations of religious integrity and material prosperity had begun to decay into poverty, assimilation, and dispersal.[43] The story is told from the point of view of its main non-Jewish character, Peony, the servant who attends the large Jewish family of Ezra ben Israel. Beyond the details of a busy, melodramatic plot, the novel serves as a vehicle for Pearl's belief in human equality and her resistance to exclusive religions.

Although Pearl said that *Peony* was a tribute to the Jewish victims of the Holocaust, the thematic center of the book is a good deal more argumentative than such a claim would imply. Pearl vigorously opposed anti-Semitism (she had written a strong attack on American prejudice against Jews in 1942), but she had no patience with the providential claims of any group.[44] She believed that Judaism, like Christianity and Islam, rested on a mischievous exceptionalism, which could only lead to disharmony and strife. Pearl's forty years as the daughter of a single-minded zealot had permanently alienated her from any version of other-worldly tribalism.

"All men are brothers": Pearl had adopted the Confucian phrase as her own, using it as the epigraph to her master's thesis in 1925 and again as the title of her translation of *Shui Hu Chuan* in 1932. Rejecting the idea that the Jews, or anyone else, are a "chosen people," one of *Peony*'s non-Jewish characters, a man named Kung Chen, concludes: " 'God – if there is a God – would not choose one man above another or one people above another. Under Heaven we are all one family.' "[45] When *Peony*'s blind and aging rabbi denounces the Chinese as heathens, Kung Chen says that " 'This old teacher is mad.' " He adds, echoing Pearl's estimate of her father: " 'We must pity him. So it often happens when men think too much about gods and fairies and ghosts and all such imaginary beings. Beyond this earth we cannot know.' "

Not surprisingly, given her views of culture as essentially hybrid, Pearl believed that the Jews of China would make their strongest contribution by merging their distinctive qualities into a larger Chinese identity. The novel concludes with a rhapsodic prophecy on the theme that "nothing is lost." The blood of the K'ai-feng Jews, Peony meditates, " 'is lively in whatever frame it flows, and when the frame is gone, its very dust enriches the still kindly soil. Their spirit is born anew in every generation. They are no more and yet they live forever.' "

Peony affirms Pearl's strenuous if vague commitment to universal human solidarity. She displaced her fable of brotherhood onto the Chinese past because the world around her offered small grounds for hope. In mid-1948, the civil war in China raged with unspeakable ferocity, and American politics had become the scene of escalating paranoia.[46] Addressing the members of the American Library Association at their summer convention in Atlantic City, Pearl warned that "a growing censorship of books and other printed matter is endangering intellectual freedom."[47]

Pearl found the summer unusually hot and depressing. Even a private family trip to her parents' old homes brought her to the edge of tears. Both houses had passed out of the family's ownership, and she sent back the ungenerous report that her father's house was covered in "shameful filth . . . occupied by a shiftless tenant farmer and his enormous family."[48] A visit with her old friend Vijaya Lakshmi Pandit brought a rare opportunity for political celebration. Mrs. Pandit was now serving as the head of independent India's delegation to the United Nations.

In the fall, contemplating the presidential elections, Pearl wrote to James Yen, who had returned to China after the Japanese surrender and was headquartered in Nanking. Describing the American atmosphere as "very low," Pearl added: "It is expected that Dewey will become the next president and then we shall have a swing to even deeper reaction." The country had fallen into the hands

36. Pearl and Mrs. Vijaya Lakshmi Pandit, April, 1948. (Courtesy Bettman Archives.)

of "big business," which would hide behind the slogans of anti-Communism while helping the European powers renew their imperialist intrusions into Asia. On the same day, in another letter, she warned that "business is now fairly committed to a war economy." She also said, despairingly: "I doubt if anything can be done."[49]

This mood of angry helplessness, which gripped Pearl throughout the fall of 1948, heavily influenced her next book, *American Argument,* co-authored with Eslanda Robeson. Pearl's connection with Paul and Eslanda Robeson went back to the early 1930s.[50] Both Robesons had admired Pearl's work before they met her. Eslanda said that *The Good Earth* helped to determine her career as a writer: "I thought . . . if some day I can write a book that will introduce readers to my people the way Pearl Buck introduced me to the Chinese people, then Eslanda, my girl, you will have done something!"[51] In the mid-1930s, Paul Robeson and Sergei Eisenstein had considered making a film of one of Pearl's novels. During the war, Eslanda and Pearl had collaborated on a "practical plan" to ensure federal protection for civil rights.[52] And in 1945, on Pearl's recommendation, John Day had published Eslanda's autobiographical *African Journey.*[53]

American Argument is a sprawling, rather shapeless book, recording a conversation between Pearl and Robeson that took place over several days in late 1948. The two women shared opinions on subjects ranging from anthropology to family life to world peace. On some matters, they disagreed sharply; the book's title refers primarily to the clash over Robeson's defense of Soviet repression (which she called necessary to building a new society). Robeson was less squeamish about "liquidating" enemies of the people than Pearl.

On other matters, their agreement was profound. Both believed that the nation's politics were controlled by reactionaries. And both believed that racism was, in Pearl's words, "a center of corruption in our people, a central wrong that hardens our hearts and corrodes our spirits." Eslanda Robeson knew that, in the dark world of American race hatred, even a man as talented and famous as her husband Paul was "just another nigger." If he said in Mississippi the things he said in New York, Eslanda insisted, "He'd be strung up – lynched!"[54]

One passage in *American Argument* proved prophetic. Pearl argued that "the most cruelly treated child" in American society was "the so-called illegitimate child." ("So-called," because Pearl considered the term "illegitimate" an unmerited punishment.)[55] When abandoned by their parents, many of these children were automatically labeled unadoptable and placed in orphanages or foster homes. Mixed-race children, in particular, were treated as outcasts, sometimes consigned to mental institutions because they were regarded as unfit even for orphanages.[56]

Pearl, the mother of five adopted children, became an outspoken advocate for adoption. She conceded that orphanages and foster homes did some good work, but she regarded them primarily as employment schemes for social workers: "twenty children in a boarding home constitutes a job for a social worker." Powerful vested interests, propped up by American prejudice against illegitimacy, had turned orphanages from temporary alternatives of last resort into acceptable and even normal features on the social landscape.

As Pearl's views gained circulation, she began to receive desperate inquiries from people seeking to adopt children, as well as others (usually unwed mothers) who wanted to find homes for their children. Mothers and children alike were the victims of a slow-moving, mindless bureaucracy, which rarely consulted the welfare of children. When the Walsh family gathered for Christmas at Green Hills Farm in late December, 1948, a letter arrived, asking Pearl to help place a fifteen-month-old boy named Robbie, the son of a white woman, an unmarried American missionary daughter, and her Indian lover. The families of both the man and the woman had rejected the child.

Uncertain what to do, Pearl had the boy brought to Green Hills Farm. He arrived, dressed in a red snow suit: "He was sucking his thumb hard and his eyes were huge and tragic with the look that always reveals a child without a home and parents." When the social worker who brought him drove away, "Robbie's eyes did not change. He knew that it did not matter who came or went. He belonged to nobody."[57]

Pearl spent a sleepless night watching the terrified little boy toss and turn in a crib she had retrieved from storage. A few days later, a second baby arrived, this one only a few days old, the child of a Chinese man, a surgeon who had already returned to China, and a white American nurse. Feeling that at fifty-six she was too old to adopt any more infants herself, Pearl called one adoption agency after another, all of whom told her that the children were unadoptable. Her outrage multiplied with each rejection, and finally catalyzed her half-shaped plans to find homes for abandoned children. "I was indignant," she later said, "so I started my own damned agency!"[58]

As a first step, she hired a neighboring couple to take in the children temporarily while she personally recruited permanent parents. Then, over the next several months, she created an administrative infrastructure, raised money (including her own), and legally incorporated a new agency, which she called Welcome House. Her mission was to find families for the children other agencies neglected: mixed-race and minority children to begin with, then handicapped children, older children, and sibling groups.[59]

Pearl coined the term "Amerasian" to describe children of unions between Asians and Americans. In the wake of World War II, thousands of such children were born in Japan, Okinawa, and Korea, usually to American servicemen and Asian women. Such children, condemned alike by American and Asian racism, had no place in either society. The unforgiving patriarchal traditions of Asia meant that a fatherless, mixed-race child was (and is) abused as a pariah, insulted and sometimes beaten, and routinely denied access to any educational or economic opportunity. In Korea, children are registered in their fathers' names; those who were abandoned by their American fathers had no legal existence. Many were killed, and an unknown number of male children were castrated.[60]

Pearl made it her mission to rescue as many of these children as she could, and to evangelize on behalf of a broader conception of humanity. When her Bucks County neighbor, Oscar Hammerstein, II, asked whether homes could be found for "half-caste" children, she snapped back: "We'll no longer use that terribly pejorative term, Oscar; we're all half-castes, one way or another . . . if you go back far enough."[61]

Welcome House exemplified Pearl Buck's restless energy, her reforming impulse, her talent for organization, her generosity, and her courage. The entire project represented Pearl at her best: she had identified a significant social and moral problem, she contrived a solution that was simple, humane, and effective, and then she pushed impatiently past bureaucrats, skeptics, and bigots to find a solution. Pearl conceded that the care of disadvantaged children was "woman's work," but she also insisted that it was the most important work a society could do. She felt that a nation defined itself in the way it treated children, especially children who carried the stigma of illegitimacy, or handicap, or minority status.

At first she worked alone, out of her home. Then she formed an alliance with influential Bucks County residents, among them Hammerstein, Lois Burpee (whose husband owned Burpee Seeds), and James Michener. Pearl, Hammerstein, and Michener became a "kind of triumvirate," in Michener's phrase, but he acknowledged that Pearl "had no help from either Hammerstein or me when she started. She had a lot of help from us later when she had the wheels already moving."[62]

Through sheer force of will, she eventually placed every child who came to her. Her campaign collided with welfare bureaucrats and social workers who were mired in antiquated and often downright reactionary commitments to biological definitions of parenthood and to racial and religious matching.[63] "There is no magic," she insisted, "in blood relationship."[64] Parenthood had to be earned. The "crucial necessity in adoption," she wrote some years later in *Ebony* magazine, "is not similarity of religion or race," but love.[65] She began a public relations blitz to change American attitudes, which led to a long and bitter debate. "I knew Pearl well at that time," Michener has recalled, "and boy, she would take on anybody. She was infinitely more brave than I was. . . . She was a heroic woman."

Her dissident views had made her unwelcome in many quarters. As she said in a letter to Margaret Mead: "Anyone . . . who works for human equality and for the enlightenment of peoples about each other is sure to be called a Communist sometimes."[66] Whittier, California, home town of second-term Congressman Richard M. Nixon, was one of several places where there was talk of banning Pearl's books from the public library. She received fewer speaking invitations from universities, schools, and women's clubs. Membership in the East and West Association continued to decline, at least in part because of Pearl's controversial reputation.

Nonetheless, even a diminished Pearl Buck remained a formidable presence. In January, 1949, she traveled to Alabama, lecturing on relations between America and Asia at both the Birmingham campus of the University of Alabama and at Tuskegee.[67] The following month, at a New York University conference on the United Nations, she accused the American government of weakening international cooperation by treating all problems as military.[68] A couple of weeks later, Pearl accepted the prestigious Children's Book Award of the Child Study Association of America. *The Big Wave,* for which she received the prize, is an unsentimental story of life and death in a Japanese fishing village. Handsomely illustrated with nineteenth-century Japanese woodcuts, it humanized America's recent enemies by insisting on the courage, integrity, and good humor of ordinary Japanese people.[69]

The book prize lifted Pearl's spirits. She received another vote of confidence when her new novel, *Kinfolk,* appeared in April, 1949. Despite her complaints about the rightward tilt of the Book-of-the-Month Club, *Kinfolk* was designated a main selection. Pearl was cheered by the choice (it was the ninth time one of her books had been named either a main or alternate selection), and also by the money. Her expenses, as always, were heavy. She had half a dozen people on her payroll, including a full-time secretary, a housekeeper, a chauffeur to pilot her Cadillac, and a stockman to manage the sixty head of Guernsey cattle she had accumulated. In 1948, she had spent over $20,000 just on renovations to the barn at Green Hills Farm.

Kinfolk's principal character, Dr. Liang, is an expatriate Chinese philosopher who lives in New York and earns a comfortable living by expounding Confucianism and classic Chinese culture in books and lectures. Liang is an elegant fake.[70] He retails a roseate, fairy-tale view of China, a wispy amalgam of ancient texts and stereotype, in which a changeless serenity absorbs all turmoil. Liang's charming fables seduce his American audiences but have no connection to contemporary China, the turbulence of the late 1940s, or the final bitter months of the civil war.

Liang stands for the whole class of Westernized intellectuals with whom Pearl had been disputing ever since she had published *The Good Earth.* When Liang dismisses the Chinese masses as insignificant – " 'It is quality that is meaningful in any nation, the articulate few, the scholars. Surely men like myself represent more perfectly than peasants can the spirit of Chinese civilization' " – he sounds like Kiang Kang-hu and the other intellectuals who attacked Pearl's early work for adopting the point of view of illiterate farmers.[71]

Liang and his wife live in a spacious New York apartment with their four adult children, two sons and two daughters, all of whom have grown up in the United States. Liang's wife, a sturdy, uneducated peasant woman, is terrified of him but also has an unerring sense of his vacancy. "Liang was always pretending," his wife says to herself at one point. "He pretended that Confucius was so big. Confucius was only a man, probably a man like Liang, but his wife could not read or write and so she died unknown. Men were all alike."

Halfway through the novel, the Liang children return to China. Two of them go voluntarily, to put their medical skills at the service of the people; the other two are more or less banished by Dr. Liang to save them from further Western contamination. The professor himself remains behind in the safety of his American affluence.

In a sequence of dramatic scenes set in Peking and the countryside, the children are swept up in China's political and military struggles. The younger daughter, unable to face the hardship, soon returns to New York and marries a white American. The younger son, taking up a revolutionary cause he only half-understands, is shot by the Kuomintang's secret police. The older son and daughter, on the other hand, settle down in their ancestral village, marry local people, and dedicate themselves to improving the lot of the peasants.

Kinfolk is one of Pearl's strongest novels, a splendid combination of achieved satire and shrewd cultural analysis. The book methodically unmasks Dr. Liang and endorses his wife's unschooled wisdom, in the process affirming Pearl's familiar populist commitments. Beyond that, the plight of the four Liang children brings a new theme into Pearl's fiction, the dilemma faced by many Asian-Americans, attempting to craft an identity out of their unusual hybrid experience. It was a motif for which Pearl was uniquely prepared: with the national and ethnic terms reversed, the fate of the Liang children had been her own.

AT THE END OF *Kinfolk,* the outcome of China's civil war remains doubtful. History quickly overtook the novel. Throughout the spring and summer of 1949, the People's Liberation Army overran Nationalist forces throughout the country. Chiang Kai-shek decamped for Formosa (Taiwan), preceded by several tons of gold and trainloads of artistic treasures. Nanking, Pearl's old home and the capital of China since the late 1920s, fell in April. On October 1, Mao Tse-tung proclaimed the new People's Republic from the Gate of Heavenly Peace in Peking.

Events in China reverberated ominously across every corner of American politics. In the opinion of General David Barr, the chief military advisor to Chiang Kai-shek, the Nationalists had lost the civil war because they were saddled by "the world's worst leadership [and] widespread corruption and dishonesty throughout the armed forces."[72]

Most qualified observers, including Pearl Buck, agreed with General Barr and traced the Kuomintang defeat to Chiang's incompetence. The Republican Party, on the other hand, smelled a conspiracy. Smarting from their unexpected defeat in the 1948 presidential election and searching for an exploitable issue, the Republicans laid the Communist victory at the door of the Democratic administration, abetted by fellow-traveling writers and academics. The "loss of China" was added to the Yalta agreement, the Berlin blockade, the Russian atomic bomb: the growing catalogue was invoked as evidence of foreign policy ineptitude that might reach to treason. The Cold War entered a virulent new phase, presided over by the clownish but sinister figure of Senator Joseph McCarthy.

It was a mean time, in David Halberstam's phrase, a time in which an evil fog of recrimination settled over the country. Reputations and careers were ruined by politicians who saw irresistible opportunities in the anti-Communist crusade. International relations were held hostage by men of almost sublime ignorance: in a debate over Southeast Asia, Senator Kenneth Wherry of Nebraska warned darkly of the Communist threat to "Indigo-China."[73]

Pearl was periodically smeared by accusations of disloyalty. In June, 1949, she found herself sharing a front-page story in the *New York Sun* with a long list of other celebrities who had been named as "Red appeasers" by a California state legislator. According to Senator Jack Tenney, Pearl had "conspicuously followed or appeased some of the Communist Party line over a long period of time," and so had Charles Chaplin, Helen Gahagan Douglas, Langston Hughes, Danny Kaye, Gene Kelly, Thomas Mann, Frederic March, Burgess Meredith, Dorothy Parker, Gregory Peck, Vincent Price, Paul Robeson, Edward G. Robinson, Artie Shaw, Frank Sinatra, and Orson Welles, among many others.

Pearl issued a denial, part of which was quoted in the *New York Times*. "I am anti-Communist," she said, "to the last drop of my blood." At the same time, she condemned the California report as undemocratic, and – in sentences the *Times* chose not to quote – she warned that anti-Communist excesses were "making our country a laughing stock for the whole world." To our foreign allies and adversaries alike, we seemed to be "a nation of fools."[74]

Foolishness prevailed everywhere. The Moscow telephone book was classified as secret information.[75] A witch-hunting broadsheet called *Counterattack* listed Pearl, along with Eleanor Roosevelt, among the subversives who had appeared as guests on Mary Margaret McBride's popular radio talk show. McBride was also denounced because one of her sponsors was a company that imported Polish hams.[76]

In a season of hysteria, Pearl tried to restore a measure of balance. In late October, just a few weeks after Mao had installed himself in Peking, she published a long article, "Our Dangerous Myths About China," in the *New York Times Magazine*. Americans, she said, stored "an amazing amount of trash in our mental attics when it comes to the Chinese," including the stereotype, "old and cobwebby indeed," that the Chinese are "mysterious and inscrutable."[77] Displaying considerable courage, she attempted to puncture another myth: the belief that "all those who now proceed under the Communist banner are evil men."

She made a number of predictions about China's probable course under the Communists. History confirmed her judgment that "collective farms go against [the Chinese] grain," and that collectivized farming would fail. On the other hand, she underestimated Mao's demagogic powers. Mao would never hypnotize his people, Pearl said, because "the sort of ecstasy into which the German people seem to have fallen before a man in a uniform, shouting among flags, is impossible to a people as long sane as the Chinese." On the contrary, Mao would soon become the center of the twentieth-century's most hysterical cult of personality, presiding over decades of insanity whose victims would be numbered in the millions.

A couple of months later, in a speech for the Women's International League for Peace and Freedom at Goucher College, Pearl said that the Chinese had only accepted Communism because they "were in desperate need of something to improve their living conditions." The victory of Communism, in other words, should be understood in pragmatic terms, as a purely practical choice that the Chinese people had made when every other alternative had failed. Pearl made three other contentious points: that American fumbling had contributed to the Communist triumph; that the United States would have to learn to coexist with the new Chinese government; and that aid to Chiang Kai-shek would be "more money down the drain."[78]

In the hardening climate of anti-Communist orthodoxy, opinions like these were heresy. Public opinion was being saturated with the charge that the fall of China was an act of betrayal. Chiang's supporters, gathered together in a loose confederation of right-wing politicians, journalists, and businessmen known as the China Lobby, emerged as a powerful, predatory interest group. Anyone who had played a part in America's Asian policymaking since the late 1930s was automatically suspected of pro-Communist machinations. The Institute for Pacific Relations (IPR), with which Pearl had often worked and sometimes competed, was systematically destroyed by a conspiracy between the China Lobby and the FBI.[79]

In late March, 1950, just two months after a New York jury convicted Alger Hiss of perjury, Pearl's longtime colleague Owen Lattimore came under attack. Lattimore, a professor at Johns Hopkins University, had worked on Asia all his life, and was recognized as America's leading expert on Mongolia. During World War II, at President Roosevelt's recommendation, he had served as political advisor to Chiang Kai-shek. Senator McCarthy called Lattimore "the top Russian espionage agent in the United States," identified him as Alger Hiss's boss, and blamed him for collaborating in the Communist victory.[80] Every one of the charges was absurd. Lattimore's real crime was that he had accurately predicted Chiang's defeat. Calling him a spy was "silly on the face of it," according to President Harry Truman, but it took Lattimore years to clear himself of suspicion.[81]

Pearl and Lattimore had been associated for almost two decades. They had met first in Peking, in the early 1930s, when Pearl was gathering illustrations for her translation of *Shui Hu Chuan*. Later, Lattimore had served on the Advisory Board of East and West, along with such people as John Dewey, William Ernest Hocking, and Lin Yutang. In 1942, he spoke at one of Pearl's fund-raising rallies for United China Relief.

Pearl found Lattimore's views congenial. Near the end of World War II, she had reviewed Lattimore's pathbreaking book, *Solution in Asia,* which called for a fundamental shift in American foreign policy assumptions. Lattimore argued that the Communists had to be included in any future Chinese government. He also believed that Russia would compete quite effectively with the West for influence across all of Asia. Pearl had called Lattimore's book brilliant: it "shines like a lighthouse [upon] the confusion and ignorance" of American policymakers.[82] Now, five years later, those confused and ignorant policymakers were seeking revenge.[83]

"I am not worried about Owen Lattimore," Pearl said hopefully in the midst of his inquisition, "for I believe that he is a man of integrity and will come through all right." But his ordeal had made her "terribly ashamed" of the way American politics was conducted.[84] When the Child Study Association asked her to write a children's story about Armistice Day, she wrote back angrily: "It is a task too difficult for me. Armistice Day has become for me almost a farce."[85]

Shaken by the treachery of events, Pearl retreated temporarily from the political arena and turned inward. In May, she published a long article about her retarded daughter Carol, "The Child Who Never Grew," in the *Ladies' Home Journal.*[86] After nearly thirty years of silence, this was the first time Pearl had publicly acknowledged Carol's existence. A moving tribute to her daughter's humanity and a painfully detailed account of her own suffering as the mother of a retarded child, "The Child Who Never Grew" is the most intimate piece of writing Pearl ever published. She said she wrote the article to help other parents, and as a way to give meaning to Carol's life.[87]

The article lifted a veil. It marked the first time that anyone of Pearl's stature had spoken out as the parent of a retarded child, and it gave comfort to thousands of other mothers and fathers. Beyond that, "The Child Who Never Grew" helped to remove the stigma attaching to retardation, the sense of shame that has always been the second heavy price that families with retarded children have paid. Pearl received letters from parents all over the world, including Madame Charles De Gaulle, who said that she had "borne the same cross, the same sorrow."[88] Physicians and public health authorities also wrote, congratulating Pearl for her courage, and telling her that she had permanently changed the terms of public discussion.

She answered every letter personally, often at great length, displaying a compassion and sensitivity that were often less noticeable in her other correspondence. Typically, she also took a leading part in organizing the parents of retarded children as political lobbyists. "Our children," she often said over the next several years, "*had* to have voices because they are silent; they cannot speak for themselves."[89] She had sought the same goal throughout her life as a writer and public figure. From her first story, "A Chinese Woman Speaks," published in 1926, through such books as *Talk About Russia* with Masha Scott, Pearl had struggled to give a voice to the silent and silenced.

The heartwarming response that greeted "The Child Who Never Grew" contrasted sharply with the punishment Pearl was receiving from her literary and political adversaries. More than ever, Pearl had begun to feel like an exile in her own country. Searching for fellow spirits, people who managed to live good lives in bad times, she befriended Helen and Scott Nearing. In the spring of 1950, she and Richard spent a week on the Nearing farm in Vermont. Shortly afterward, the Walshes bought a neighboring property and spent most of their summers there for the next several years.

Pearl had known the Nearings' son, John Scott, and John's Russian wife Masha, since the early 1940s. That relationship cooled in the postwar years, when John joined the editorial staff of *Time* and exchanged his earlier radicalism for Henry Luce's strident anti-Communism. John's parents appealed to her because of their beliefs, their simplicity, and their resilience.

Scott Nearing had championed progressive causes for forty years, first as an academic economist, then as an independent writer. During World War I, in a case that helped to rewrite the history of academic freedom in America, he had been hounded from his teaching position in the economics department at the University of Pennsylvania's Wharton School. He had shaken the walls of academia by propagandizing for modest controls on child labor. A sympathetic colleague called him the Dred Scott of the teaching profession. When he was fired, the *New Republic* assailed Penn's trustees as a collection of "reactionaries" and accused them of "intellectual repression."[90]

By the time Pearl and Richard met him, Nearing and his wife, Helen, had become revered figures on the American left. Living self-sufficiently in Vermont and then in Maine, growing their own food, making most of their own clothes and furniture, they were pioneer environmentalists who would inspire a later generation of radicals. Pearl and Richard enjoyed their company. The Nearings taught the Walsh children how to tap maple trees for sugar and trim logs for timber. Evenings were spent in gossip and political conversation. Four beleaguered, like-minded people found comfort in each other's company outside the glare and noise of the spotlit hearing rooms and tabloid slanders that dominated America's public life.[91]

The summer's calm was shattered by world events. On June 25, 1950, North Korea invaded the South, crossing the 38th parallel and transforming the Cold War into a shooting war. Weeks of "slaughter and heartbreak" followed, in the words of one soldier, as the North deployed larger numbers and superior equipment to overrun the troops of South Korea and their American allies. President Truman decided that a line had to be drawn. He would have intervened unilaterally if necessary, but Secretary of State Dean Acheson managed to secure a

37. Pearl in a portrait photograph taken by Clara Sipprell in the 1940s.
(Courtesy Syracuse University Library.)

United Nations mandate authorizing collective action. The Korean War was fought in a place that most Americans had never heard of, and few could even find on a map. Later, it would be called "the forgotten war" (the term was first used by General Matthew Ridgway).[92] Throughout the second half of 1950, however, it was the center of American attention. McCarthy and his allies seized on the North Korean invasion to justify an intensified search for subversives; once again, Pearl came under scrutiny.

Although J. Edgar Hoover considered Pearl "way to the left, to say the least," she was never called before a Congressional committee.[93] Nevertheless, she had been chastened by the painful experiences of Owen Lattimore and other outspoken critics of American foreign policy – many of them people she had known for years. She fumed to Emma White that Americans "rule[d] out great areas of humanity, depending on our likes and dislikes." The public no longer wanted to hear a single positive word about China; on the other hand, "since we control Japan, we find Japanese 'nice.' "[94]

Returning from another trip through Alabama, she confessed that "every time I go through that black belt I come back profoundly depressed."[95] Yet she knew that her opinions on race relations, or any other subject, were less welcome than they had once been. Her access to the mass media had shrunk; she complained that she had "been trying to get articles and speeches to public attention without too much success."[96] She had written an article, for example, on the terrible discrimination confronting mixed-race children in Japan, but the *Ladies' Home Journal* "was afraid to touch the thing." The *Journal*'s editors worried that America's patriotic vigilantes would be offended by Pearl's account of the sexual behavior of U.S. servicemen.[97] *Look* also turned the article down.

For the moment, she restricted her comments mainly to conversation and correspondence with friends. When she protested against racial segregation in Washington, D.C., for example, she made her case in a series of private letters rather than mounting a public campaign (one of the letters ended up in her FBI file).[98]

On the record, she said little about the Korean War. She did speak out, in December, when the war had reached a critical turning point. General MacArthur's landing at Inchon in September seemed to have brought an early victory within sight. Instead, American advances up the peninsula provoked China to send troops across the Yalu in December to fight alongside the North Koreans. Like millions of her fellow citizens, Pearl was terrified that she was witnessing the opening engagement of World War III. She told a visiting Tokyo journalist that Chinese behavior was predictable and, to some extent, justifiable. Mao and Chou En-lai had both notified Western leaders of their intentions. She also said that U.S. foreign policy was immature, that American leaders were "as fit to handle [the Korean] situation as a fifteen-year-old boy."[99]

The interview, printed in Japan, found its way back to the States where it received wide and mainly negative comment. Once again, Pearl was obliged to defend herself from charges of disloyalty. In January, Dorothy Thompson used her nationally syndicated column to savage Pearl's analysis. Pearl in turn fired off a heated rebuttal, thanking Thompson sarcastically for the "honor" of her interest, and then insisting on her own anti-Communism: "The Communists in Asia know very well how heartily I oppose their creed." At the same time, she refused to back down from the charge that American "wealth and power" could have been deployed more rationally in China – by which she meant that American money and prestige had propped up Chiang and his corrupt cronies in a losing cause. As for Korea, she blamed America's "occupation personnel and policies" for making "Communist aggression possible."[100]

Pearl's comments appeared in newspapers around the country. The next day, officials at Benjamin Cardozo High School in Washington, D.C., announced that her long-scheduled appearance at the black school's mid-year commencement ceremony had been canceled. Hobart Corning, the District's superintendent, explained that he had acted because Pearl's record with the House Un-American Activities Committee was "not clear." Pearl responded instantly, calling Corning's action "outrageous," reminding her fellow citizens that speech was suppressed in Communist countries, not in functioning democracies, and warning that "we cannot use oppression to gain freedom."[101]

The undelivered speech gained tremendous notoriety. The *Washington Post* printed the full text, along with an editorial attacking the school board for its "craven" policies.[102] Richard Walsh told Scott Nearing that "the blow-up in Washington" had one good result: "a strong [movement] to discontinue the practice of having speakers for the public schools 'cleared' by the Un-American Activities Committee." Richard believed that the time had come for "a vigorous organized campaign against the witch hunters." Nearing, somewhat optimistically, countered: "As to the witch hunt, it has passed its zenith."[103]

For her part, Pearl felt that she was trapped in a "frightful time," in which careers and lives were being wrecked by a politics of hate.[104] She spent part of February in bed with a disabling case of flu.[105] Unable to raise money for the East and West Association, she suspended the organization's activities in February. Officially, she took the position that the closing was only temporary. In private, she conceded that East and West would never do business again.[106]

Though she felt abandoned, she still attracted a measure of sympathy and support. Even before the dust settled on the Cardozo High School incident, she was invited to speak at Temple University, and used the occasion to renew her attacks on the Universal Military Training bill. Militarization leads only to war, she insisted, and "war is a confession of weakness, a disease" that always proves fatal. "Don't think I'll be glad to be a gold-star mother," she said, her voice rising in anger. "I'm not going to be brave. They'll take my sons over my dead body."[107]

In the midst of the latest controversy, Mark Van Doren was quietly arranging Pearl's election to the American Academy of Arts and Letters. Five co-sponsors were needed for the nomination; Van Doren recruited Archibald MacLeish, Van

Wyck Brooks, Chauncey Brewster Tinker, and D. S. Freeman. The nominating papers stated that Pearl's "distinction . . . is worldwide and richly deserved."[108] The compliment may have been sincere, and it was certainly defensible. But the list of co-sponsors, including a cross section of prominent literary liberals, also suggests that Pearl was being honored primarily for her progressive opinions and her defense of free speech.

If Pearl had well-connected friends, she also had powerful enemies, none more formidable than Henry Luce. The relationship between the two had begun harmoniously almost twenty years earlier, grounded at first on the similar backgrounds shared by these remarkable and largely self-made individuals. Both had been raised in China, the children of Presbyterian missionaries. Both had translated the missionary impulse into secular terms, and both possessed an unbending sense of personal rectitude. Finally, both had achieved an unexpectedly large success.

They had first met in Nanking in 1932, when Luce came to dinner at Pearl's home on the Nanking University campus. The thirty-four-year-old Luce was proprietor of the spectacularly profitable and influential *Time* magazine; Pearl, six years older, was the suddenly famous author of *The Good Earth*.

For the next decade or so, Luce treated Pearl with respect. He acknowledged her authority on Chinese politics and culture: she had lived much longer in China than he had, and she knew the language, which he did not. The friendship frayed and eventually snapped over the issue of Chiang Kai-shek and the Kuomintang. By the late 1930s, Luce established himself as Chiang's most tenacious supporter and his most effective propagandist. He enforced a pro-Chiang policy in all his publications, and tolerated little dissent. When a talented correspondent like Theodore White reported on popular discontent with the Kuomintang, Luce had the story rewritten and the writer replaced.[109]

He made a few exceptions, occasionally allowing a more balanced appraisal of Chiang to appear in one of his magazines. The most important instance occurred in May of 1943, when he reluctantly but honorably published in *Life* Pearl's article, "A Warning About China," which helped dampen American enthusiasm for the Nationalists. Although he published the essay, from that time forward, Luce regarded Pearl as his adversary: in his view, she was wrong on Chiang, soft on Communism, sentimental about equality, and unreliable on the use of American power.

Young James Michener saw first-hand the reach of Luce's unquenchable spite. Hired to write a piece for *Life* on postwar American novelists, Michener sent a draft to his editor, Mary Lee Weatherbee, who told him that one paragraph would have to come out: "That one where you praise Pearl Buck, about her having won the Nobel Prize and being an object lesson to younger writers who want to write strong novels." When Michener protested that everything he said was true, Weatherbee replied: "True, but not advisable. Henry Luce has given us strict orders. We must never say anything favorable about Pearl Buck."[10]

As always, Luce was obeyed. *Time,* which had often praised Pearl's earlier novels, now sneered at her "soggy prose and stilted pidgin," and the "cliché-ripe ingredients" of her plots.[11] The abusive language had nothing to do with literary judgments. Pearl was now squarely in Henry Luce's gunsights; she would remain there until the day he died, more than fifteen years later.

Embattled and frustrated, she pilloried Luce in her next novel, *God's Men,* which appeared in March, 1951. The book dramatizes the lifelong confrontation between two men, both children of Protestant missionaries in China. One, Clem Miller, dedicates all of his energy and money to humanitarian work. He intends to feed the hungry people of the world. The second man, William Lane, invents an ingenious brand of photojournalism that catapults him to wealth and unprecedented influence. He intends to shape America to his authoritarian, monomaniacal beliefs.

Clem Miller's altruism has some of its genesis in Pearl's idealistic commitments.[12] She had worked on international medical and food projects for two decades; at the time she wrote the novel, she was heading up the India Famine Relief Committee. Miller's second source was a man named Clifford Clinton, a friend of Pearl's and president of the Meals for Millions Foundation. Like Pearl, Clinton was convinced that world peace depended above all on the elimination of world hunger.[13]

Miller's antagonist, William Lane, is an unprincipled self-promoter with a genius for the market, a journalist who uses his newspapers to manipulate rather than inform the public, an opportunist barricading his sense of inferiority behind a wall of bluster. He is, in short, Henry Luce as Pearl and many others saw him, subordinating facts to his version of the truth and tailoring every story to the sole purpose of enlarging his own power.

In one scene, Lane lectures his China correspondent, a man named Lemuel Barnard, in the same terms Luce used to drive Theodore White out of the Time-Life organization. Barnard has filed several reports mildly critical of the Chiangs, and defends himself by telling Lane that " 'I've only told you what Chinese people themselves are saying.' " Without pausing for a moment of self-doubt, Lane replies: " 'I don't care what Chinese people are saying . . . I never care what people say. I am interested in telling them what to say.' "[14]

Lane is Luce, even in the details. Like Luce, Lane attended Chefoo School in China, and despises the English boys who bully him there. (Resentment, Pearl suggests, was Luce's fundamental motive.) Ambivalent about his missionary father, Lane accommodates himself to his Christian heritage by translating the Gospel into a species of Americanism. He divorces his first wife, much to the dismay of his pious family, and marries a glamorous younger woman (though the fictional second wife is English, unlike Clare Boothe Luce). Lane gives a speech celebrating "the hour of American destiny," which imitates Luce's 1941 prophecy of the impending "American Century."[15] Among other proposals, he urges the government to tie food relief to political compliance. Finally, he embraces Chiang Kai-shek and puts the gigantic power of his journalistic empire at the service of the Kuomintang.[16]

The novel's early scenes, set in China during the Boxer Uprising, are its most accomplished. The Boxer episode defines the values and vocations of the two main characters, who are young boys when the violence erupts. Beyond its function in her plot, the Boxer Uprising dramatizes the legitimacy of China's anti-foreign anger, which continued to motivate the nation's leaders. It took courage for Pearl to underscore this historically relevant analogy at a moment when the Chinese Communist People's Liberation Army had come to the aid of North Korea.

The rest of the novel rolls along in the well-traveled ruts of melodrama. Clem's unsinkable goodness is contrasted with William's coarse scheming. Clem dies with his great task unfinished, but resolute in his convictions. Eventually, the governments of the world will realize that hungry people must be fed. William survives and flourishes at the center of his publishing empire. His confidence, however, has been eroded and by the end of the novel he has begun to feel the inward gnawing of something like conscience.

Aside from enacting Pearl's revenge on Henry Luce, *God's Men* condemns a whole journalistic system of rewards and punishments in which editors discount reputations like used clothes in a pawn shop. While the satire undoubtedly gave her a moment of satisfaction, she knew it would have little effect on the world's most powerful opinion maker. Outside her novels, which commanded a small fraction of Luce's audience, Pearl's voice now went almost unheard.

In a time of "terrifying disillusionment," she told Dorothy Thompson, "I write what I can, and get as much published as editors will take. They cut my stuff and change my titles, of course, and refuse outright what I really want to say."[17] Pearl wanted to proselytize for world peace, and disarmament, and food relief, and racial and sexual equality, and cross-cultural appreciation: the same simple, humanitarian message she had been preaching all her life. She was learning the discipline of failure, but she remained unembarrassed by her commitments.

Toward the end of the year, the FBI renewed its interest in Pearl's activities. She circulated a letter attacking the peacetime draft and endorsing the work of the Women's International League for Peace and Freedom, with which she had worked for fifteen years. "Our freedom is threatened at its very source by a permanent military conscription," Pearl warned. "We are in grave danger."

When a copy of the letter reached the Bureau, the headquarters staff contem-

38. Pearl with Welcome House children, parents, and friends at a Chinese restaurant in Philadelphia in the early 1950s. (Reproduced with permission of the Pearl S. Buck Foundation.)

plated an interview with Pearl. The Philadelphia office advised Director Hoover to move cautiously because "an interview of a person of Miss BUCK's prominence might result in repercussions and adverse publicity for the Bureau." The agent reminded Hoover that "Miss BUCK has in the past been outspoken in her beliefs and has not hesitated to lend her support to controversial issues."[118] No interview took place.

IN FACT, THE FBI'S pusillanimous memo was more flattering than accurate. Pearl remained prominent and outspoken, but her prominence had dimmed and the range of issues on which she spoke out had narrowed. *Asia* magazine had expired, and the East and West Association was defunct. Several of the principal causes she had fought for, including repeal of Chinese exclusion and Indian independence, had been won. Others, such as the Equal Rights Amendment and expanded civil rights for African-Americans, had receded into the shadows of postwar reaction.

Pearl felt the strain of two decades of nonstop motion. And she was getting older: she marked her sixtieth birthday in June, 1952, with a private dinner at home. In the opinion of her children, Green Hills Farm had become "pretty darned quiet after fifteen years of lively goings-on."[119] Pearl's schedule was less frantic, less crowded with deadlines, meetings, speeches, and interviews.

Though she was still far busier than most sixty-year-old people, much of her time now was devoted to children's welfare. She had assumed fund-raising responsibilities for the Vineland Training School, and she was engineering the expansion of Welcome House. She launched an occasional thunderbolt on divisive public questions such as the draft and the Korean War (the FBI carefully indexed each one), but her pronouncements came less frequently, and her audiences grew smaller.

Pearl and Richard spent more of their time at Green Hills Farm. They looked after their newest child, a five-year-old girl named Henriette, the daughter of an African-American serviceman and a German mother.[120] Pearl now spent just one day each week in New York, squeezing in trips to the theater between meetings of the Hiroshima Peace Center, the American Academy of Arts and Letters, the Mass Education Movement, and the American Civil Liberties Union.

From the Bucks County house she took day trips: to Vineland, to Howard University, where she sat on the board of trustees, and to Doylestown and Media, where she attended adoption ceremonies for Welcome House children. She did appear once on NBC-TV and once on Mary Margaret McBride's radio show, but her speeches now more often took place before such groups as the Hatboro Rotary Club, the Morrisville Women's Club, the Bucks County Council on Human Relations, and the George School, where her children were enrolled.[121] She frequently stopped by the Welcome House Thrift Shop to thank the volunteers for their efforts, and occasionally invited the women for tea at Green Hills Farm.

Pearl's latest novel, *The Hidden Flower*, appeared a few weeks before her sixtieth birthday. In just over twenty years of writing, she had now published more than forty books: novels, short story collections, children's stories, nonfiction, and her translation of *Shui Hu Chuan*. She had also published hundreds of essays, stories, and reviews.

As usual, Pearl incorporated her most recent preoccupations in her new novel. *The Hidden Flower* tells the unhappy story of marriage between a Japanese woman, Josui Satai, and an American man, Allen Kennedy, an officer in the army of occupation. They marry in spite of opposition from both families, but are ultimately defeated by the prejudice in America and Japan that makes life insupportable for them. At the time the novel was written, about twenty American states still had laws forbidding marriage between whites and non-whites. Pearl was appalled by the anguish these barbaric statutes inflicted, and hoped that her fictional propaganda would encourage a more humane attitude.[122]

The novel's characters are less interesting than its central idea. Instead of representing men and women, Josui Satai and Allen Kennedy and the book's other major and minor figures are reduced to allegorical signposts, moving about mechanically as the needs of the argument require. The victims are virtuous, the bigots are relentlessly wicked, and the plot marches inevitably to a sad but morally uplifting conclusion. When Josui becomes pregnant, she conceals her condition from Allen and chooses to give her baby up. The child is adopted by a good-hearted woman, a physician who is willing to battle American racism.

Elizabeth Janeway reviewed *The Hidden Flower* for the *New York Times Book Review,* and used the occasion to offer a more general assessment of Pearl's place in contemporary American letters. The review shrewdly captures Pearl's problematic status after two decades as a writer and public figure. "Always widely read," Janeway wrote, "and at one time the object of critical study, Pearl Buck is . . . relegated today to some amorphous anteroom of writing halfway – or more – between serious literary effort and best-sellerdom." Criticism, which placed high value on "the private struggle of a human mind with its interior world," had no tolerance for Pearl, who dealt in busy plots and created characters that behave like types. Even more damaging, Pearl's "bias toward morality and toward a belief in order and in generosity" made her seem merely naive in the eyes of what Janeway called the "intellectual critics," who mistrusted love and preferred squalor to transcendence.

Janeway's tone is sympathetic, but defensive and slightly baffled. Although she wants Pearl's work to be taken more seriously, she isn't quite sure how to make the case. In the end, she resorts to a rudimentary feminism, identifying Pearl's importance with her female readership: "[I]t is too bad that Miss Buck's audience is, par excellence, the audience which is ignored by contemporary critics of writing[:] the American middle-class woman who reads novels."

The most striking fact about Janeway's review is that she merely reports the marginal status of women, rather than contesting it. Nearly a generation later, fortified in part by Pearl's own example, Janeway would publish *Man's World, Woman's Place,* a protest against the popular mythologies that demeaned women. When she reviewed Pearl's book, however, such insights lay hidden on the far side of the ideological horizon.

In 1952, women were surrounded by retrograde postwar assumptions that defined them as wives and mothers and directed them to follow their vocations into the kitchen and the nursery: Rosie the Riveter had given way to Betty Crocker. When Janeway concluded that Pearl Buck had been communicating with women for twenty years, and that "[i]t is an excellent thing that she continues to do it so well," the compliment was backhanded: in a man's world, writing for women carried the heavy penalty of irrelevance.[123]

Pearl herself was disheartened by the failure of women's history to move forward. *Of Men and Women,* her pre-war manifesto on behalf of sexual equality, had disappeared from sight, forgotten by women as well as men. In the midst of what W. H. Auden called an "Age of Anxiety," the search for security enforced an ethic of conformity.

Pearl interpreted Dwight Eisenhower's victory in the November, 1952 elections as another dreary indicator of the public's retreat from progressive ideas. She wrote to James Michener, complaining that "[i]t is very difficult to talk sense these days, and not always rewarding, as Governor Stevenson has discovered."[124] She made the same point in a comment to Grace Yaukey's son Ray and his wife Dolores: "I feared [Stevenson] was doomed ... when he said he was going to talk sense to the American people and then talked about civil rights in Florida [and] oil in Texas."[125]

Pearl and Richard spent a quiet Christmas at Green Hills Farm. Just before the holiday, Richard sent a note to their daughter Jean, telling her that Pearl had sat up late one night signing two thousand Welcome House Christmas cards.[126] Pearl and Richard enjoyed whatever time they could find alone. By all accounts, the marriage remained happy. They had accomplished a great deal together, their political views harmonized, and they continued to work closely on Pearl's publications.

Ironically, Richard's unquestioning devotion may have done Pearl some literary damage. He was her publisher and sole editor, but he lacked the temperament to make any demands on her writing. She wrote in a vacuum, without editorial direction or resistance. When she emerged from her study with a new manuscript, she handed the pages to Richard who obediently printed them. The evidence of her surviving manuscripts suggests that she rarely permitted second thoughts to intrude on her rapid progress through a book.

By some measures, the system worked. Pearl's American book sales, though no longer prodigious, remained dependable. More important, her novels continued to be immensely popular overseas; she had become one of the most frequently translated authors of the century, and most of her income now consisted of foreign royalties. She needed money, for her own expenses, her children, and her charitable work, and she had found a reliable way to earn it. In any case, it is not clear that painstaking revisions would have altered her fiction profoundly. Her later novels were simply hastier, more lackluster versions of what she had written twenty years earlier.

One proof of Pearl's slipping market value was the difficulty she now encountered in selling stories to magazines. Between 1935 and 1945, she had published thirty stories, most of them in high-circulation weeklies and monthlies

such as *Cosmopolitan, Collier's, Saturday Evening Post,* and *Ladies' Home Journal.*
In the next ten years, through 1955, she would publish just ten stories in magazines. The John Day Company automatically printed every book-length manuscript she wrote; the mass-market periodicals provided a more tough-minded
appraisal of her appeal.

With a pretense of stoicism, Pearl claimed to understand that "markets change
and times change."[127] She sniffed at the popular taste that preferred action and
adventure novels – what she called "bang-bang-bang stories" – and ignored
fiction that was "only rich and profound and full of meaning, not noise."[128] The
remark sags with an unpleasant self-pity.

Like most writers who are going out of fashion, she wanted to blame someone
else for her troubles. She settled on her agent, David Lloyd, who had represented
her from the beginning of her career. In the early spring of 1953, she wrote a
long, badgering letter to Lloyd's daughter and partner, Andrea, complaining
about the agency's failures to place her stories in the magazines that paid the
highest fees. She also chided both Lloyds for neglecting her: "I am accustomed
to hearing from your father regularly," she told Andrea Lloyd, "and that I hear
nothing from you or from him fills me with questions."

She was understandably worried about her own circumstances. Beyond that,
she thought that the whole nation was "anxious [and] fidgeting."[129] The passions
unleashed by the Cold War reached a climax on June 15, when Julius and Ethel
Rosenberg were put to death as Soviet spies, after months of nationwide protests
and counterprotests. Fidgeting Americans searched for assurance from purveyors
of popularized psychology and morality – the age of therapy had begun. Bishop
Fulton J. Sheen broadcast a friendly brand of Catholicism to millions of viewers
on his weekly television program, and Billy Graham began his long career as a
pioneering video evangelist. Norman Vincent Peale produced one of the year's
best-selling books, *The Power of Positive Thinking,* which confided the secrets of
security and self-esteem to millions of unsettled readers.

Pearl's next book refracted this national hunger for spiritual reassurance
through the prism of her skepticism. *Come, My Beloved,* the first of her novels
set mainly in India, is also (somewhat surprisingly) the only one that employs a
missionary cast of characters. Four generations of the MacArd family pass in
review. Industrialist Thomas founds the family fortune in the 1880s and 1890s,
and plans a great missionary college on the Hudson as a memorial to his dead
wife. His relations with his son David are ruptured when David takes the whole
enterprise too seriously, hears the call, and moves to India. Thomas had other
plans for his only child.

David's missionary exertions are directed toward the upper classes. He builds
a school on an English model and lends his support to the imperial government.
His son, Ted, critical of his father's conservatism, leaves the comfortable com-

pound and moves to a small village where he preaches a non-denominational spirituality, occupies himself with good deeds, and welcomes Gandhi's nationalism. Finally, Ted's daughter Livy falls in love with an Indian man, a surgeon who works in the village, but Ted forbids the marriage.[130]

The satire is drawn with almost schematic clarity. Each generation of MacArd men fails the test of his own Christian declarations. Thomas has no interest in India; his proposed school is mere exhibitionism, a version of the self-serving philanthropy that plutocracy uses to celebrate its own generosity. David moves a step closer to a real commitment, but his service to India takes him no further than collaboration with established wealth and the imperial status quo.

Ted devotes himself more fully to the Indian people. However, his fragile belief in human equality disintegrates when he is faced with his daughter's desire to marry across the great divide of racial difference. Ted's refusal encodes Pearl's unsoftened judgment about the missionary movement – in India, China, and throughout the world. Even at their best, the missionaries remained alien outsiders, condemned to irrelevance. Pearl was still disputing with her father, twenty years after his death. Unlike many of her American contemporaries, she had no patience with preachers and no interest in religious anodynes.

In the summer of 1953, Pearl and Richard made plans to take the four teenagers on an extended trip through the American West. They stopped at motels but ate their meals outdoors, Pearl doing most of the cooking on a Coleman stove. Pearl included Sauk Centre, Minnesota, on the itinerary, calling her journey there a pilgrimage to repay the long friendship of Sinclair Lewis, the fellow Nobel laureate who had died just a couple of years earlier.[131]

On August 17, near Sheridan, Wyoming, Richard suffered a stroke. At first the symptoms were mild; a local doctor thought perhaps Richard was only suffering from fatigue and heat prostration. However, his condition soon began to deteriorate. Within a year, he had become an invalid, gradually falling into a stupor in which he lingered until his death in 1960. Pearl was losing the most important person in her life. As the years of Richard's illness sadly lengthened, she once again found herself alone. At one point, she wrote: "He is sweet and uncomplaining but the old sharing of thought and communion is gone. We sit in the same room and it is so lonely – so much more lonely than it would be if I were physically alone." Yet her sense of loss never reached to the searing pain she had felt over Carol's condition.

After going to visit Carol one afternoon, she came home to find Richard "waiting in the living room, doing nothing, just waiting for me – so different, so different." Then she added the important proviso: "But the heart breaks only once."[132] Pearl's capacity for affection had been permanently maimed in the early 1920s by Carol's impairment and the traumas that accompanied it, the hysterectomy that prevented other birth children, and the failure of her first marriage.

Her grief over Richard's illness, and the prospect of her own loneliness, was genuine, but it was tempered by a history of greater suffering that now reached back over thirty years.

Richard's son, Richard, Jr., now took over the day-to-day management of John Day, and Pearl soon found herself working with a deferential but slightly more independent publisher. His first glance at the company's books convinced the younger Walsh that economies would be required. Among other savings, he proposed a cut in his father's salary. Pearl respected her stepson's judgment, but she resented any reduction in her personal control over the editorial or financial direction of the press. It was another sign, this time within the circle of her own family, of her diminished status.

9

Pearl Sydenstricker

IN THE SPRING OF 1954, almost simultaneously, two events occurred that would shape the domestic and foreign politics of America for the rest of the century. On May 7, the French garrison at Dien Bien Phu surrendered to the Viet Minh, signaling the end of a century of French colonial rule in Indochina. Just ten days later, Chief Justice Earl Warren announced the U.S. Supreme Court's decision in the case of *Brown* v. *Board of Education,* which declared racial segregation in the nation's public schools to be unconstitutional.

The French debacle in Indochina precipitated America's entry into a disastrous war that would leave hundreds of thousands of Asians and Americans dead, and would poison domestic politics for a generation. The unanimous ruling in *Brown,* one of the two or three most important judicial decisions of the twentieth century, fundamentally changed the legal and ethical premises on which American society had proceeded.

Pearl commented on both of these epochal events at some length in a letter to her old friend Emma White. In the wake of the *Brown* decision, Emma had asked Pearl to sympathize with the white South, which found itself suddenly disoriented. Pearl had no patience and no stomach for euphemism, even with an old friend. "The present situation," she wrote, "is a sort of retribution for the long delay in doing anything at all about segregation." The South would eventually learn what modern science had long known, she told Emma, that no race is inherently more intelligent or talented than another. Citing an illustration from her own family, Pearl described her youngest child, "our little Negro daughter, Henriette," as by "far the brightest of all our children."

As for Indochina, Pearl reminded Emma that French rule had too often been marked by brutality. As an example, Haiphong was bombarded by French warships in 1946 over a tax dispute; six thousand men, women, and children were killed. "Most Americans know nothing about these matters," Pearl added bitterly, including politicians and public in her indictment. Though she would have preferred a non-Communist nationalism, the era of colonial control had come to an end: "I have always felt it inevitable that the West would lose Indo-China."[1]

In any case, Pearl added, she had lost some of her earlier passion for engagement in all these affairs. In the letter's most revealing sentence, she wrote, "Either I am getting old, or reaching an advanced philosophical stage, for none of these matters concern me or arouse me as once they did."[2] The date was June 29, just three days after her sixty-second birthday, and almost a year after Richard's stroke.

Her fatigue lifted in the fall, when the publication of her autobiography, *My Several Worlds,* brought an unexpected triumph. A main selection of the Reader's Digest Book Club, the volume earned exceptional sales and uniformly enthusiastic reviews. The Kirkus syndicate, in a pre-publication comment, set the tone, calling *My Several Worlds* "[n]ot only Pearl Buck's most important book, but, on many counts, her best book." The *Saturday Review* agreed, judging Pearl's memoirs "her finest achievement."[3] The *New Yorker's* critic said that Pearl's recollections made up a "rambling, discursive, and thoroughly delightful autobiography, which may well be one of the best books Mrs. Buck has written."[4]

Like all literary self-portraits, *My Several Worlds* conceals as much as it reveals. Except for a fairly candid account of the suffering Pearl had gone through as Carol's mother, the book discloses little of her intimate life. In four hundred pages, neither her parents nor Lossing Buck nor Richard Walsh is ever named. Nor could Pearl's multifarious public life be deduced with any consistency from the book. Instead, in *My Several Worlds* she crafted a thickly textured representation of the Chinese and American societies in which she had lived. With a certain amount of self-awareness, she said that the book was in fact not an autobiography at all, because "an autobiography is written from within, and I've always been much more interested in what was happening around me than in what was happening inside me."[5]

Some of the book's best passages are simply catalogues of the objects and practices that define daily life. So, for example, she recalls the rice and pork and vegetables that she ate as a child, and then itemizes the more elaborate dishes she grew to love as an adult in Nanking and Peking:

the Yellow River fish soup so deliciously cooked in Ching-chow, the steamed shad of West Lake, the cured fish and beef of Chang-sha, the plum flower fragrant salted fish of Chao-chow, the steamed crabs of Soochow, the sweet and sour fish of Peking, and the dried shrimps of Tung-ting Lake. And . . . the Shao-hsing wine of Chekiang, and then the Mao-tai wine of Kweichow and the distilled Fen-chow liquor of Shansi. And of teas the green Lung-ching tea of Chekiang was our favorite, but also the Pu-erh tea of Yunnan . . . and the Chi-men red tea, and the Lin-an green tea of Anking or the jasmine and the Iron Lo-han tea of Foochow and the Hangchow chrysanthemum tea.

. . . We [enjoyed] the oranges of Hsin-hui, in Kwangtung, the pumelos of Sha-tien, in Kiangsi, the taro of Li-pu, the red and white dates of Te-chow in Shangtung, the Chefoo apples and T'ang-shan pears, the watermelons and grapes of Sinkiang, the Shanghai muskmelons and the Peking persimmons, the kumquat oranges of Foochow, and the olives of Kwangtung province, the bamboo shoots and mushrooms of South Hunan, and the Kalgan mushrooms, Ho-p'u lichee nuts and Nanking root.

And so on and on, through "Te-chow smoked chicken, Canton steamed young pigeon, Nanking salted duck, Peking roast duck, Canton's one-chicken-three-tastes, Fuchow hash, King-hua ham, Szechuan's pickled salted greens, arrowroot from West Lake, a Peking summer drink made from sour prunes, mushroom oil from South Hunan, rice flour from Kwei-lin, bean curd and sauce from Anking in Anhwei province."[6]

It is a virtuoso performance, documenting Pearl's lifelong habit of attention and observation, and testifying more eloquently than her pious pronouncements to her cross-cultural commitments. For over half a century, she had immersed herself in the sights and sounds and tastes of two societies; *My Several Worlds* patiently transcribes what she had learned. The book's title, in fact, is slyly precise: not her story, but the story of the worlds in which she had lived.

The success of *My Several Worlds* briefly resuscitated Pearl's reputation. She was the subject of several magazine profiles, and she received invitations to appear on a couple of nationally syndicated television programs. She turned down the "Today" show, because she found Dave Garroway's famous co-star, the chimpanzee J. Fred Muggs, undignified, but she agreed to a long interview that was broadcast on the more literate "Omnibus" hour.[7] She was even approached by veteran producer Louis Heyward with a proposal for a series called "The Pearl Buck Theater," a half-hour weekly show that would feature the work of writers Pearl wanted to promote.[8]

In November, Pearl made plans for a big Thanksgiving dinner in the Green Hills barn for the Welcome House families. It was the sort of event she now preferred, since it gave her a respite from her looming concerns about Richard's health, and also offered a sanctuary from the lethal controversies that continued to dominate national politics.

She still spoke out from time to time on public questions. A few days before Thanksgiving, she sent a letter to the *New York Times,* denouncing the horrific treatment immigrants were facing in New York. Ellis Island had been closed, as an economy measure, and immigrants were now being routinely transferred to prisons while they awaited processing. They were housed with convicted criminals, and children were separated from parents. After she complained about the inhumanity of the arrangements, Pearl also commented that such behavior threatened America with a public relations fiasco.[9]

A dozen items that appeared alongside Pearl's letter in the same November 16 issue of the *Times* offer a convenient snapshot of civic discourse in the mid-

1950s. Cold War paranoia dominated the day's events in one guise or another. Senator McCarthy, resisting censure in the Senate, received the support of a group that styled itself "Ten Million Americans Mobilized for Justice." Senator William Knowland of California, breaking with the Eisenhower administration, charged that coexistence with the Soviets was a "Trojan horse" that would lead to annihilation. Defense Department officials concluded that a Chinese Communist attack on a Nationalist destroyer escort had been a deliberate attempt to provoke the U.S. Seventh Fleet. Secretary of State John Foster Dulles affirmed the willingness of the United States to defend Europe by force. The U.S. Military Academy and the Naval Academy announced that cadets at both institutions would be forbidden from taking part in the year's national collegiate debate, because the topic – "Resolved: that the United States should recognize Communist China" – was deemed too inflammatory. The Supreme Court, in a four-to-four ruling, left standing a lower-court decision that officials in Sioux City, Iowa, had not violated the constitutional rights of Sergeant John Rice, an American Indian who had been killed in the Korean War, when they refused to allow his body to be buried in the town's all-white cemetery. The Court also heard arguments from attorneys representing Southern states that school desegregation should be delayed to avoid stirring up white resistance.

It was a typical day in the 1950s: despite Robert Lowell's famous epigram, the decade was not "tranquilized," but feverish. Stories like these, gleaned from a single issue of the *Times*, were grim reminders of America's fears and retreats and bigotries. Small wonder that Pearl was happier to preside over a Thanksgiving dinner for adopted children and their parents.

With the East and West Association out of business, Pearl took part in several schemes brought to her by others to promote peace and international understanding. In May, she was on hand in New York to greet the so-called "Hiroshima Maidens," two dozen young Japanese women, burned in the atomic bombing of Hiroshima, who had been brought to the United States for plastic surgery. The effort was led by Kiyoshi Tanimoto, a Japanese Christian minister, and Norman Cousins, editor of the *Saturday Review*. Throughout the summer of 1955, as surgeons performed a long series of reconstructive operations in Mount Sinai Hospital, Tanimoto and his family stayed in a guest house at Green Hills Farm.[10]

To Pearl, the disfigured Hiroshima Maidens symbolized the inarguable necessity for nuclear disarmament and world peace. She didn't object to the disturbing fact that all the victims chosen for treatment were women, in part because she continued to believe that women had "a peculiar responsibility for world peace."[11] For that reason, she remained close to the Women's International League for Peace and Freedom, heading up a 1955 fund-raising campaign in honor of founder Emily Greene Balch, and serving as chairman of the League's fortieth-anniversary dinner in October. She accepted a special award, gave a speech on "Peace, Freedom, and Bread," and introduced the keynote speaker, V. K. Krishna Menon, India's chief delegate to the United Nations.[12]

Though she gave her time freely to WILPF, money was much on Pearl's mind. She often pointed out that she was supporting eight people, four of them in college. She was still fretting about the performance of the David Lloyd agency. In December, she wrote again to Andrea Lloyd, itemizing the agency's several failures, and offering the disdainful conclusion that the Lloyd organization was evidently "too small to handle my affairs." Andrea Lloyd flattered Pearl by calling her "a colossus"; Pearl accepted the compliment at face value and drew the regal inference: "I am too much for you." After a quarter-century of association, Pearl now began looking for a new agent.[13]

Aside from bearing all of her family's expenses, Pearl also accepted primary responsibility for funding the operations of Welcome House. At the end of 1955, she was delighted to report that Richard Rodgers had paid off the mortgage on the first Welcome House building as a sixtieth-birthday present for Oscar Hammerstein. It was a fitting gift. Pearl told a friend that *The King and I,* which had opened in the fall to extravagant reviews and standing ovations, had been inspired by "our Welcome House children."[14]

She was justifiably proud of the adoption agency. A couple of weeks after Christmas, she wrote to thank a couple who had sent pictures of their adopted daughter: "It gives me so much comfort and joy to see the children growing up happily in their own homes. It is the greatest pleasure I have in life, I do believe."[15] At the same time, she kept up her campaign against orphanages, places where children are made "prisoners of red tape, prejudice and religious division," and which are kept in business by the "reprehensible . . . lethargy [and] delay of present adoption practices." She even talked about "liberating" children from orphanages.[16]

Pearl's association with Welcome House and the Women's International League for Peace and Freedom, her advocacy on behalf of abandoned children and unwed mothers, her disputes about her market value, her struggles to manage her career and support her large household, and her recent immersion in her own autobiography, had all renewed her interest in her identity as a woman, and more generally in the place of women in American and Chinese societies. She read Simone de Beauvoir's *The Second Sex* at about this time, Sophie Drinker's *Music and Women,* and (in typescript) Mary Milbank Brown on Joan of Arc. She studied Ashley Montagu's *The Natural Superiority of Woman* and invited Montagu to lunch.[17] She told Marjorie White of the Lucy Stone League that she was planning a big book "on Woman."[18]

Almost inevitably, Pearl's mediations on gender, status, and authority led her back to the Empress Dowager, Tz'u-hsi, one of history's most powerful women,

39. Pearl receives an award from Eleanor Roosevelt at a 1956 luncheon of the
New York League for the Association for the Help of Retarded Children.
(Courtesy Harry Ransom Humanities Center, University of Texas.)

who had ruled over China throughout Pearl's first sixteen years. Pearl had never
lost her childhood fascination with Tz'u-hsi. She referred to her from time to
time in her letters and essays, occasionally linking her with Mu-lan, the woman
warrior of Chinese folklore. The Empress Dowager was the main character in
Pearl's first full-length play, and she reappeared as an alluring, half-mythical figure
in *My Several Worlds*. Now, in the spring of 1956, Pearl published *Imperial
Woman,* her longest novel and one of her best, a fictionalized biography of Tz'u-
hsi that follows her from her early years as one of the Emperor Hsien-feng's
lower-ranking concubines to her decades of unchallenged command.

Pearl insisted that her novel was carefully researched and true to its historical
sources.[19] She depended heavily on one book, *China Under the Empress Dowager,*
by J. O. P. Bland and Edmund Backhouse, which had appeared in 1910, just
two years after Tz'u-hsi's death. An amalgam of fact and sensational fantasy,
China Under the Empress Dowager fixed its portrait indelibly in the Western imagination for generations. As Bland and Backhouse presented her, Tz'u-hsi was a
woman of incalculable ambition and cruelty, casually disposing of enemies and

potential rivals, bending the fate of 400 million Chinese to the requirements of her vanity and lust. Long accepted as authoritative, the book actually owes as much to the traditions of Chinese literary misogyny as it does to the documentary record.[20]

Like everyone else who wrote about Tz'u-hsi in the first three-quarters of the century, Pearl was deceived by her main source.[21] Nonetheless, guided by her common sense and her personal recollections of the reverence that China's people had felt for the Empress Dowager, Pearl presented a more balanced, frankly more admiring portrayal. She enjoyed revising the appraisals of earlier writers, almost all of them men, who had described Tz'u-hsi "unfavorably and even vindictively" (the phrase comes from the novel's Foreword). Pearl's Empress is ambitious and capable of cruelty, but she is also courageous and principled, trying to rescue what she can of traditional values from the confusion inflicted on the empire by internal reformers and external invaders.

Imperial Woman retells China's late nineteenth-century history from the inside, chronicling the sequence of events, from the Taiping Rebellion to the Boxer Uprising, that brought the old order to the brink of collapse. The novel offers a sympathetic view of an ancient, beleaguered civilization defeated by alien ideas and its own inertia. Split into jealous factions, the Chinese are humiliated by Western guns, outmaneuvered by Western diplomats, and tormented by Western ideologies. Tz'u-hsi especially resents the missionaries, who deny all gods but their own and dishonor China's heritage. Worse, as Tz'u-hsi observes, where the Christian missionaries went, "traders and warships soon would follow."[22]

The mother of Hsien-feng's heir, Tz'u-hsi assumed control of the throne when the Emperor died and held onto power for forty years. She buttressed her problematic claims to authority by a punctilious observance of court ritual. Costumed like a sacred idol in her splendid jewels and regalia, Tz'u-hsi presided over an endless round of stately processions, formal ceremonials, and grandly choreographed receptions.

In reproducing these scenes, Pearl also masterfully evokes the claustrophobic magnificence of the Forbidden City, where pomp and luxury pursued their own courses, cut off altogether from the lives of the Chinese people outside the walls. As Tz'u-hsi governed the world's largest nation at the moment of its gravest crisis, she was sealed inside her literally fabulous palaces and gardens. Surrounded by thousands of courtiers and servants and attended by a vast army of eunuchs, she was utterly alone. The isolation that enveloped her was the price she paid for her preeminence.

Though it ended in tragedy for herself and her people, the Empress Dowager's life was also a story of female achievement on an unprecedented scale. Seldom had a woman risen so high, against such great odds, and endured so long. She dominated her nation and her times in a way that few women (or men, for that matter) have. Pearl acknowledged Tz'u-hsi's crimes and misdemeanors, but she laid a greater emphasis on her strength and tenacity, her gift for leadership, and her earthy wisdom. Pearl said that decades after Tz'u-hsi's death, in villages in the interior of China, she met people who thought the Dowager Empress was still alive, and were frightened when they heard she was dead. "This," she wrote, "is the final judgment of a ruler."

PEARL PROBABLY FELT a sense of symbolic affiliation with Tz'u-hsi, but she harbored no imperial delusions. She was a working woman, struggling to balance her income against her rising expenses. (She lived a "cash-flow life," in the words of one of her children.[23]) In 1957, she adopted another mixed-race child, an eight-year-old girl named Cheiko, the daughter of a Japanese woman and an African-American soldier.[24] The children gave her "great joy," she wrote Emma, but their care added to her financial obligations, and so did the constant nursing that her husband now required.[25]

Half-paralyzed and nearly blind, Richard could no longer provide the intimate friendship that had centered Pearl's life for a quarter-century. She needed more stimulation than her bedridden husband or her own children could provide, and she found it, as usual, in her work, which now revolved around Welcome House and her writing.

In 1958, she published *Friend to Friend,* a conversation with Carlos P. Romulo, the Foreign Minister of the Philippines, which dealt frankly with conflicts between Americans and Asians. Pearl traced the rising anti-American feelings of many Asian nations to the compromises that postwar U.S. governments had made with colonialism. Americans should have provided leadership against the imperialists: "Instead not only have we supported the colonial policies of old powers, but we compelled the Chinese Communists to depend entirely upon Russian Communists, and thereby lost all opportunity to influence the Chinese mainland."[26]

The book contained some of Pearl's sharpest criticism of U.S. foreign policy. The arrogance of the Voice of America, the ignorance of American diplomats, and America's obsession with military solutions and anti-Communism made Asians cautious of embracing the United States as an ally. And, as television spread across the globe, Asians could see for themselves grotesque images of domestic racism, of white violence against blacks in Little Rock, Arkansas, and Levittown, Pennsylvania. Pearl approvingly quoted Lenin, who had predicted that the ideological struggles of the twentieth century would be decided in Asia. "The way to London and Paris," Lenin had told his followers, "is through Peking and Calcutta." Pearl agreed, and she worried that America seemed badly adapted for world leadership: America's racism crippled its moral authority among the people of the non-white world.

At about the time she published *Friend to Friend,* Pearl made a new acquaintance, a young man named Tad Danielewski who would fill at least some of the vacancy left by Richard's illness. Born in Poland, Tad had emigrated to the United States after the war and gotten a job in the fledgling television industry. He first met Pearl when he directed the "Omnibus" show in which she appeared after the publication of *My Several Worlds.* By his own account, he was awed by the Nobel Prize—winning woman, whose books he had read in Polish translations as a child.[27] Their collaboration on "Omnibus" led to a number of other projects, and eventually to a close partnership that lasted for several years.

Pearl wanted to write plays; Tad encouraged her. They produced two television scripts, *The Big Wave* and *The Enemy,* both adaptations of stories Pearl had written in the 1940s, and both quite successful with New York newspaper critics. (Pearl said that *The Enemy* was the first television play produced in the United States that featured an all-Asian cast.)[28] Tad and Pearl formed a production company, Stratton Films, and made ambitious plans. They worked, dined out, and went to the theater together. They traveled, to Vermont, Hollywood, even as far as Europe in the fall of 1959, and Asia in 1960. Pearl became the subject of gossip; several of her children urged her sister Grace to intervene. Grace wisely decided that Pearl's behavior was her own business.

Pearl's collaboration with Tad coincided with her latest public crusade, nuclear disarmament. She had not objected to the American decision to drop the bomb on Hiroshima and Nagasaki, but she later had second thoughts. "The people of America are always sorrowful because of the atomic bomb," she had written to a Japanese physician in the early 1950s. "It was dropped without their knowledge and they regret it very much."[29]

These odd, revisionist claims about American public opinion were surely inaccurate, and they even overstate Pearl's own ambivalence, probably to comfort a tormented Japanese correspondent. In fact, she tended to agree with physicist Arthur Holly Compton, one of the leaders of the Manhattan Project, that the bombing was morally defensible, given the appalling choices that American policymakers faced in August, 1945.[30] On the other hand, her opposition to continued testing and proliferation was unequivocal. For several years, she was active in test-ban protests. In the spring of 1958, she joined fellow Nobel Prize winners Linus Pauling and Clarence Pickett in a call for peace and disarmament.[31]

Pearl decided to incorporate her nuclear anxieties into a play. She prepared by reading intensively in the scientific and political literature, especially *Atoms in the Family,* Laura Fermi's amiable memoir of her late husband, Enrico, and *Atomic Quest,* by Arthur Holly Compton.[32] After the war, Compton had moved from the University of Chicago to Washington University in St. Louis. With her usual single-mindedness, Pearl drove the thousand miles to talk with Compton, then persuaded him to write letters of introduction to some of the other scientists who had worked on the bomb.[33] Accompanied by Tad, she visited Oak Ridge, the Argonne National Laboratory, and Los Alamos, the isolated New Mexico laboratory where the first bombs were produced.

From a notebook full of personal observations and interviews, Pearl cobbled together a three-act play, *A Desert Incident,* set in an unnamed research complex modeled on Los Alamos. The play is a humanitarian allegory, a plea for brotherhood that exchanges dramatic complexity for preachments about the evil purposes to which scientific discoveries can be put. After a New Haven tryout, *A Desert Incident* ran for just seven Broadway performances in March, 1959. Pearl's sentiments attracted more approval than her craftsmanship. Kenneth Tynan, who called it bad theater, nonetheless added that Pearl had chosen "the most important subject in the world, and though she handled it vaguely and emotionally, she came down on the side of life. [Because of] her commitment, I am prepared to forgive Miss Buck a great deal."[34]

Pearl also used her research on the Manhattan Project in a novel, *Command the Morning,* which appeared in March, 1959, the same month her play opened and closed. Three scientists play the book's leading roles: project director Burton Hall, loosely based on Compton; a younger man named Stephen Coast, who resembles Volney Wilson; and Jane Earl, a brilliant physicist invented by Pearl to provide a feminist perspective. Pearl was sensitive to the widespread sexism among male scientists, including Einstein, who regarded women as inherently inferior in science, and publicly dismissed Marie Curie as a genetic accident.[35] Einstein and Curie are among the two dozen major scientists who make cameo appearances in the novel, along with Neils Bohr, Otto Hahn, Ernest Rutherford, and Lise Meitner. (Jane Earl aspires to be the American Meitner.)

The novel manages to communicate a good deal of technical information, and it captures something of the frantic months of work that led to the creation of the most fearsome weapon in world history. Beyond that, and despite its wooden dialogue and stick-figure characters, *Command the Morning* rather convincingly dramatizes the ghastly ethical dilemma the atomic scientists faced. In the end, Pearl was groping toward a kind of moral complementarity, similar to Bohr's, the somewhat desperate hope that the peacetime uses of nuclear energy might eventually outweigh the undeniable evil of the bomb.[36]

Pearl's opposition to nuclear weapons proved to be her last major political effort. A sequence of valedictory gestures marked the final years of the 1950s decade, as Pearl continued to recede from public consciousness. *Friend to Friend,* the fifth of her "talk books," was also the last. At about the same time, Harold

Isaacs published *Scratches on Our Mind,* a pioneering survey of American attitudes toward the people of Asia that indirectly documented Pearl's decline. Isaacs asked a cross section of Americans where their images and ideas came from, and discovered that "no single book about China has had a greater impact than . . . *The Good Earth.* It can almost be said that for a whole generation of Americans [Pearl Buck] 'created' the Chinese, in the same sense that Dickens 'created' . . . Victorian England."[37]

Even this remarkable declaration, of course, reinforced Pearl's diminishment. *The Good Earth,* the book for which she was best known, was now almost thirty years behind her. Furthermore, whatever the effect of her writing about China had been in the past, she no longer wielded the same influence. The mass media, especially television, would soon take over the job of defining societies for each other. Like every other writer, Pearl would be shouldered aside by television's selective, often misleading, but ubiquitous images.

She remained busy – Tad called her a "workaholic" – even in her late sixties. She was elected to the honorific post of president of the Authors Guild in 1958, and served for the next several years, representing the Guild in debates over postal rates and copyright.[38] She collaborated on one more play that made it to Broadway, *Christine,* a musical, with songs by Sammy Fain and Paul Francis Webster, and starring Maureen O'Hara. Based on a novel by Hilda Wernher, *My Indian Family,* the play is a comedy-melodrama in which an Englishwoman gradually exchanges her racial prejudices for tolerance. The show, Pearl's last attempt at a play, opened and quickly closed in April, 1960.

Later in the month, Pearl drove to Washington to deliver the second annual Gandhi Memorial Lecture at Howard University. She called the talk "Principles of Leadership," and used the occasion to try to explain the secret of Gandhi's extraordinary achievement in guiding the largest colonized nation in the world to independence. The lecture falls into a familiar pattern, exemplifying Pearl's weakness as an analyst and her strength as a storyteller. Gandhi's leadership involved genius, talent, integrity: when Pearl appeals to such immense abstractions, her views are merely flaccid and boring. On the other hand, when she illustrates her admiration by telling some of her favorite stories about Gandhi, she becomes a convincing witness. She uses Gandhi's visit to England in the mid-1930s, for example, when he refused to exchange his homespun cloak for formal Western clothes, as an emblem of his tactical skill as well as his truth. The British press ridiculed the eccentric little man, but the people of India understood that Gandhi had made an eloquent symbolic statement.[39]

A couple of weeks after the Howard University lecture, Pearl and Tad flew to Japan to work on a film of her children's book, *The Big Wave.* At the end of May, she received a call from Green Hills Farm: Richard Walsh had died, nearly seven years after his first stroke. Pearl flew back immediately, carrying a burden of guilt because of her absence from her husband's deathbed. An exceptional thirty-year partnership, in which Richard's advice and affection had helped to make Pearl's prodigious activity possible, had come to an end.

Apparently, Richard's extended illness had drained most of the vitality out of the marriage long before he died. While Pearl publicly insisted that she was devastated by her loss, in private she admitted that she was relieved. Within a few weeks, she returned to Tokyo, and spent most of the fall working with a Japanese cast and crew on *The Big Wave*. (Sessue Hayakawa, one of the few Asian actors with a major reputation in the West, played one of the leading parts.)

During her long sojourn in Japan, Pearl met several times with Miki Sawada, who had founded an orphanage and adoption agency for abandoned half-American children, stigmatized products of the long U.S. military presence. On the day of Pearl's first visit, Sawada told her that 148 children were living in the compound she had built two hours outside Tokyo; eventually, Sawada would find American homes for most of them.[40] Before returning to the States, Pearl also visited Korea, where she saw hundreds of other Amerasian children, almost all of whom were suffering the same discrimination and hardship as those in Japan.

Pearl was still in Asia when the American presidential election took place; she observed John Kennedy's narrow victory from thousands of miles away. Her dislike for Eisenhower had ripened during his eight years in office. "Age has weakened his judgment," she wrote to a longtime friend, Gertrude Sen, in the summer of 1960. (Eisenhower was just two years older than Pearl.) "It is high time that we had a new and younger man."[41] She preferred Kennedy to Nixon, though she would soon become disillusioned with his policies in Asia.

When Pearl landed in California on her return flight, she found a story in the *Los Angeles Times* reporting that the Chinese Communists had attacked her as a leading figure in America's campaign of "cultural aggression" against China. The story, which ran under a three-deck headline, "Pearl Buck Wicked, Say Red Chinese," quoted at length from two articles that had appeared in the monthly magazine *World Literature*. One was "A General Analysis of the Reactionary American Writer Pearl Buck," the other was an attack on her 1957 novel *Letter from Peking*.[42]

After denouncing American imperialism and its assorted "agents and running dogs [and] lackeys," the *World Literature* critics singled out Pearl as "the most vicious and the most wicked" of cultural aggressors. She was accused of distorting peasant lives, slandering the Communist revolution, and supporting Chiang Kai-shek.[43] The attack was witless – a symptom of the anti-intellectual hatreds that would torture Chinese society for the next fifteen years – and Pearl was outraged. She wrote to a friend: "I suppose I have done more than any other person to help the Americans to like the Chinese people, and to continue to like them in spite of the present separation between ourselves and the mainland." She also suggested, darkly and accurately, that her Chinese friends could not speak up for her without endangering themselves and their families.[44]

Just a few weeks later, John F. Kennedy was inaugurated as the nation's thirty-sixth president. Pearl was one of 155 men and women, "the most creative, eminent, and world-renowned in their fields," they were told, who received special invitations to the inaugural events.[45] The other novelists on the list included Ernest Hemingway, William Faulkner, and John Steinbeck. Pearl did not attend, but she received a second invitation to the White House, for a dinner honoring American Nobel Prize winners in the spring of 1962, and this time she accepted.

Prior to the occasion, presidential assistant Richard Goodwin asked the FBI for a report on all fifty-two living American Nobel laureates. (Goodwin may not have known that the Bureau already had files on most of these men and women, gathered on its own misplaced initiative.) As in its earlier internal reports, the Bureau informed Goodwin that Pearl was probably not a Communist, but then it reviewed her longtime association with doubtful groups and causes. By a nice coincidence, a couple of months earlier, Pearl had paid the final $100 installment on her life membership in the NAACP. Roy Wilkins, the Association's executive secretary, wrote to thank her; she responded that she was "happy to be of any use to the NAACP."[46]

The Nobel dinner, which took place on April 30, 1962, proved to be one of the most glittering occasions of the Kennedy presidency. In a famous toast, the president saluted the laureates as "the most extraordinary collection of talent, of human knowledge, that has ever been gathered together at the White House, with the possible exception of when Thomas Jefferson dined alone."[47] Forty-nine prize winners attended, including Linus Pauling, who spent the afternoon marching in an anti-nuclear picket line outside the White House fence before walking up the drive to put on a dinner jacket and join the other laureates.

After a lavish meal, the guests adjourned to the East Room for a reception. Pearl was approached by a shy, elderly woman who told her how happy she was to meet one of her favorite writers. "I enjoyed your book *So Big*," the woman told her. Pearl didn't have the heart to correct her.[48] A more serious misunderstanding occurred a few minutes later, when Pearl and John Kennedy had a brief conversation about Asia. "What shall we do about Korea?" he asked her. Then, without waiting for her reply, he answered his own question: "I think we'll have to get out of there. It's too expensive and we'll have to involve the Japanese to play their part in Korea." Pearl was dumbstruck. Kennedy's proposal revealed an abysmal ignorance about Asian politics and history.[49]

Korea was much on Pearl's mind at that moment. She had traveled there and

40. Pearl and President John F. Kennedy, Jacqueline Kennedy, and Robert Frost, at a White House dinner in April, 1962. (Courtesy John F. Kennedy Library.)

brought back scores of abandoned, mixed-race children for adoption through Welcome House. Korea was also the scene of her latest book, a long historical novel called *The Living Reed,* which was published in the fall of 1963. Following four generations of one family across six decades of Korean history, *The Living Reed* opens in 1883, when Korea signed its first treaty with the United States, and ends at the close of World War II, when the Allies liberated the peninsula from Japanese occupation.

The Kim family, who provide the book's central characters, are members of the aristocratic *yangban* class. The Kims, who dramatize Korea's long, tragic campaign to win its national unity and independence, are fictitious. Almost everyone else in the novel is based on a historical character, and the major events make up a factual chronicle of modern Korea.

Indeed, one of Pearl's chief purposes in writing the book was to educate American readers about a country and culture they did not know. Despite the shared suffering of the Korean War, despite the continued, large U.S. military presence, and despite the thousands of half-Korean, half-American children fathered by U.S. servicemen, Americans remained as uninformed as their leaders about the Korean people and their culture. As she had done so often in the past, Pearl put her fiction at the service of cross-cultural understanding: she was (and remains) one of the small group of Western writers who have attempted to represent Korea's story from a Korean point of view.

In an important sense, the Korean nation is actually the book's main character; the inert characters and their somewhat contrived personal relations merely provide a set of pretexts for information about Korea's tumultuous past. Part travelogue, part ethnographic survey, *The Living Reed* offers lessons in Korean geography, literature, architecture, and work. Marriage and funeral ceremonies are described in detail, along with seasonal festivals and customary household rituals. None of this material is reduced to merely picturesque purposes. Instead, the novel dramatizes the tension between old and new, between the traditional values and practices that had governed Korean society for centuries and the pressures of modern, usually Western, ideas.

Above all, *The Living Reed* is a densely plotted chronology of political history, the story of Korea's abuse and betrayal by its powerful neighbors. For centuries, the Chinese treated Korea as a subject province. In the late nineteenth century, China's self-declared sovereignty was challenged by Japan and Russia. All three of these ancient rivals viewed Korea less as a nation than a territorial opportunity and a sphere of influence.

After years of turmoil, negotiation, and bloodshed, the Japanese successfully annexed Korea and installed themselves as governors in 1910. They imposed a brutal regime, denying elementary civil and judicial rights, suppressing the Korean language, and compelling Korea's puppet rulers to sign extortionate commercial and trading agreements. Koreans mounted a heroic liberation struggle that lasted for thirty-five years. They pursued a hopeless guerrilla war in the countryside, and also pressed their claims diplomatically, at one point sending a delegation to meet with Woodrow Wilson at the Versailles Conference. Late in the novel, Pearl pays tribute to Korea's aspirations by quoting extensively from the Korean Declaration of Independence.[50]

Some of the novel's most memorable scenes reproduce episodes from the endless struggle between Japanese oppression and Korean resistance. In one passage, the Japanese deliberately burn a locked Christian church filled with hundreds of Korean civilians whom they suspect of disloyalty; in another, Korean adults teach their nation's classic literature to children under cover of darkness and at the risk of death; in yet another, a pregnant Korean woman is beaten and raped by Japanese police.

In the words of a recent historical survey, the Japanese imperialists "created a powerful, intrusive state unprecedented in Korean experience," which has "left a bitter legacy to this day."[51] (The comment throws John Kennedy's ill-informed views into sharp relief.) Japan's long years of occupation ended only with its defeat by the Allies at the close of World War II. Even then, the Korean tragedy continued – as it does to this day. Divided at the 38th parallel, the peninsula has been for half a century the site of one of the world's most dangerous Cold War confrontations.

Conforming to the facts of Korean political history, most of the major characters in *The Living Reed* are men. However, Pearl incorporated several women into the story, including a woman named Hanya, one of the most fearless of the revolutionaries. Korea had a reputation among Asian countries for the independence of its women. Korean women, a young wife named Sunia reflects, "were proud and never knelt before their husbands as women in Japan did, or had their feet bound small as Chinese women did, or their waists boxed in, as it was said that western women did."

Hanya and Sunia of *The Living Reed* expanded the gallery of Asian and American women that Pearl had been creating for nearly forty years. The reviews of the book indicated that her popularity remained highest among women readers. Pearl continued to resent the treatment she received from male critics, suggesting that gender had more to do with her reputation than quality. "As every woman writer knows," she complained privately, "women writers do not fare well in our beloved country, where the critics seem all to be men." In surveys of important American writers, she went on, women were either not mentioned or were "included in a group of 'authoresses' – hateful word, as though Nature gave her gift only to men!"[52]

Critics and editors frequently tried to capitalize on Pearl's authority with women readers. Eric Swenson, for example, vice president of W. W. Norton, sent Pearl the bound proofs of a new book about women that he was about to publish, and invited her to comment. "One of our problems," Swenson confided to Pearl, "is that much is being written these days about the plight (or whatever it is) of the educated American woman; therefore, this one will have to fight its way out of a thicket. We think it worth a try."

The book was Betty Friedan's *The Feminine Mystique*. Within two weeks, Pearl had read the proofs and wrote back to Swenson: "I am deeply impressed by this book and I would like to do anything I can for it." She provided a paragraph for the book's jacket, praising Friedan for going "straight to the heart of the problem of the American woman [and exposing] the absurd feminine mystique." Swenson replied instantly, thanking Pearl for her help in "launching a book by an unknown author."[53] As part of the launch, a joint interview was scheduled in Pearl's New York apartment.

Based on impressionistic but extensive survey research, *The Feminine Mystique* revealed a generation of women to themselves. White, educated, middle-class American women in the postwar years had become trapped in their domestic roles: browbeaten by the simpering images of advertising and Hollywood, encased in the comfortable isolation of new suburbs, driven from the workplace by returned veterans, tyrannized by the sexual definitions of Freudian psychology. Many women suffered from inescapable boredom, moving listlessly from one repetitive household chore or charitable activity to another. Women could only find a solution to their malaise in themselves, Friedan insisted. They needed to assert themselves as independent, active, contributing adults, the equal partners of men in the doings of modern society.

The Feminine Mystique, which helped to initiate a new era of feminist activism and theory, had much in common with ideas that Pearl had been espousing for decades. Like Friedan, Pearl had counseled women to seek all the education they could absorb and then urged them to put their training to social use. Like Friedan, Pearl had fought against the blinkered notion that women should define themselves exclusively in their roles as wives and mothers. Although her pioneering essays had been forgotten, Pearl could take a measure of satisfaction from the abundant similarities that linked *The Feminine Mystique* and *Of Men and Women,* published more than twenty years earlier. Pearl's endorsement of Friedan's work acknowledged a generational shift in feminist leadership.

IN THE EARLY 1960S, Pearl renewed her acquaintance with Ernest Hocking, now retired from the Harvard philosophy department. She had met Hocking in 1931, when he was touring China as chairman of the Laymen's Commission investigating the state of overseas missionary work. Pearl and Ernest had been strongly attracted to each other at their first meeting, in Nanking, and her vocal support of the controversial Commission report had cemented their friendship.[54] Over the next thirty years, they saw each other once in a while, and corresponded from time to time, but the demands of their families and careers made regular contact impossible. Ernest, who would turn ninety in 1963 but was still vigorous, was living in New Hampshire, not far from Pearl's summer home. After Richard's death, Ernest sent Pearl a copy of *Thoughts on Death and Life,* which he had written after his wife died. Pearl sought him out again and the relationship flourished.

Pearl was flattered by the attentions of a Harvard philosopher, even one whose major work, *The Meaning of God,* had been written in 1912, and who had long since been erased from philosophical history. She found Ernest personally magnetic, and she was also sympathetic to his idealistic but non-dogmatic views.

41. Harvard philosopher Ernest
Hocking. (Reproduced with
permission of the Pearl S. Buck
Foundation.)

Ernest argued that each person has intuitive access to ultimate reality, and that
feelings and ideas are inextricably bound together.[55] Pearl found all of this quite
congenial. Ernest's unfashionable metaphysical idealism encouraged her own
groping efforts to replace the Christianity she had abandoned with some version
or other of spiritual affirmation.

Pearl and Ernest recorded their feelings in a series of remarkable letters, letters that are by turns tender, admiring, and frankly passionate. When Pearl sent
Ernest a framed picture of herself, he made what he called "a silly suggestion
– but I don't mind being silly with you." The picture, he said, reminded him
of Rembrandt's painting of Aristotle and the bust of Homer: "Aristotle's look
of reverence and pity under which glance blind Homer seemed to be opening
his eyes – I don't know what it is you are looking at, but it, too, will come
alive."

On her side, Pearl addressed Ernest in several letters as "dear love," and "my best beloved." She told him that she had always looked up to him: "And now to the respect and admiration is added — the immeasurable." She said that she loved to listen to him talk, and that his affection made her "deeply happy and grateful." "Nothing can take the place," she said in another letter, "of knowing that one is centrally loved and loves the other in the same way. . . . I love you, my darling, and please remember, day and night, that you are centrally loved." To yet another passionate letter, she added the postscript: "If this sounds like a love letter — *well, it is!*"[56]

On several occasions, Pearl stayed for a week or more in Ernest's home, the two of them alone except for the housekeeper. They sat in front of the fireplace holding hands, talking affectionately through the twilight.[57] And at least once, if her fictional testimony is reliable, they spent the night in bed together. Pearl told one of her secretaries that *The Goddess Abides,* published several years after Ernest's death, was autobiographical. The main character, a woman named Edith, visits an aged philosopher named Edwin in his New England home. After dinner, they lie together through the night, naked in each other's arms.[58]

The love between Pearl and Ernest Hocking came at a critical time in Pearl's life. Richard's long illness and death had been followed by a growing estrangement from Tad Danielewski. Most of Pearl's children had grown up and moved away, and her circle of friends had shrunk. She needed companionship. Ernest broke through Pearl's habitual reserve and wariness. For three years, until his death in the summer of 1966, they shared an uninhibited intimacy.

Another man also entered Pearl's life at this time, nearly sixty years younger than Hocking, and forty years younger than Pearl herself. Theodore Harris was a dance instructor with the Arthur Murray studios in Jenkintown, not too many miles from Green Hills Farm. In the summer of 1963, he made his first trip to Pearl's house, summoned to give dancing lessons to her younger daughters. Within a few weeks, he had become a fixture in the house. Pearl decided that she needed dancing lessons, too, and hired Harris to teach her. (She had the lessons prescribed after the fact by her physician, and deducted the cost when calculating her income tax.)

What began as a casual encounter quickly developed into a troubled but intense and lasting relationship. Ted Harris became Pearl's escort, advisor, employee, collaborator, and co-author. From the day he first came to Green Hills Farm until the day Pearl died ten years later, they spent most of their time together. Eventually, Pearl's attachment to Ted would lead her into the greatest scandal of her life. His behavior damaged her reputation, cost her many of her friends, alienated her family, and rattled the walls of Philadelphia's insular society. In the face of universal criticism, she remained his patron and faithful defender to the end.

Born 1931 in rural South Carolina, Fred Hair, Jr., passed a conspicuously unpromising childhood, dropping out of school and drifting from one dead-end job to another.[59] At thirty, possessed of little more than a new name (Theodore Findley Harris) and the title of "dance director" at Arthur Murray, he had few prospects and no assets beyond his charm and an insatiable appetite to better himself. After shrewdly calculating Pearl's need for attention and reassurance, he devoted himself to the task of cultivating her. Shortly after they met, he wrote to tell her that he had read *My Several Worlds,* which had provided him with "one of the most enjoyable experiences Ive [sic] ever had."[60]

Ted's advent coincided with a new project that Pearl had devised, a scheme named for herself that would provide aid to the thousands of Amerasian children languishing in half a dozen Asian nations. Welcome House was finding homes for some of these boys and girls, but the continued presence of American servicemen meant that the numbers of children were growing. Pearl had appealed to legislators in several states to ease the restrictions on foreign adoptions, always making the same two points: the half-American children were victims of devastating discrimination, and they were an American responsibility.[61]

She had seen the conditions in Korean orphanages, where the bodies and souls of children were crushed by poverty and disease. Children in such places, she told a New York State legislative committee, were often condemned to death.[62] She had also walked through the slums of Seoul and been approached by ragged Korean children, some of them with American faces. "I tried to put [those children] out of my mind," she said; but she could not.[63] They were beautiful boys and girls, some as young as six or seven, condemned by the accident of their mixed parentage, shunned even by the other beggars on the street.

Pearl defended the children by attacking the fundamental premise of racial segregation. Though she had lived her entire life in two societies that valued racial separation and enforced racial hierarchies, Pearl remained committed to integration, intermixture, and equality. "These children of mixed race," she wrote, "are nearly always superior children, better than either side of their ancestry." She employed a homely comparison to make her point: "Hybrid rose, hybrid corn and hybrid fruit should teach us a lesson we are reluctant to learn."[64] In one of her novels, she summoned the authority of Ashley Montagu, finding support for her own views in one of Montagu's best-known books, *Man's Most Dangerous Myth: The Fallacy of Race.* There, arguing by analogy with alloys and hybrid plants, Montagu proposed that mixtures often show more desirable qualities and characters than the so-called pure stock from which they were derived. From this, he concluded, "Surely the varieties which man presents in his various ethnic forms would suggest that something more has been produced out of the mixture of elements than was originally brought into association."[65]

Taking up the cause of these mixed-race children, Pearl tried to mobilize public opinion in a series of articles and in a book, *Children for Adoption,* which she published with Random House. Under her prodding, the regulations governing international adoption were gradually liberalized. But the work was slow and the problem was growing. Furthermore, since most of the Amerasian children were not orphans, they could not be adopted. The only way to help them was to provide money for their health care, education, and job training in their own countries. A second strategy was needed. Pearl would create yet another program, which would raise money in the United States and send it overseas where social workers would spend it on the basic needs of mixed-race children.

She knew that such money would be hard to find. Neither the American government nor veterans' organizations had any interest in acknowledging responsibility for the children. During the occupation of Japan, for example, the military simply refused to admit the existence of thousands of children born to Japanese women and American servicemen. Pearl sent information packets to dozens of veterans' organizations, and received no replies at all.

She did persuade humorist Art Buchwald to write a column in which he announced the formation of a club called "Fathers Anonymous." Veterans who had enjoyed female companionship in Asia were invited to join, by paying dues that were apportioned by rank ($5 for a private, $10 for a non-commissioned officer, $15 for an officer – and free honorary memberships for four-star generals over sixty-five). The column produced $50 in contributions, mostly from veterans' wives.

Pearl did not back down. If governments and veterans groups would not help, she would mobilize the resources and opinion of ordinary citizens. She presented her proposal to the Welcome House board in the fall of 1963, suggesting that Ted would make an ideal administrator for the new project. Though they ordinarily deferred to her, the board's members balked at turning over this sort of responsibility to a man who seemed to have no visible qualifications or experience. Pearl refused to compromise, or even to listen to any criticism of her protégé. Instead, she retreated for a few weeks, and concocted a secret plan to go it alone.

In January, 1964, she received Philadelphia's prestigious Gimbel Award for her humanitarian work, in particular the Welcome House adoption program. In accepting the honor, and the $1,000 check that came with it, Pearl announced that she was creating an entirely new organization, the Pearl S. Buck Foundation, to help Amerasian children. She also said that she was turning over the Gimbel prize money as the first contribution to the new project. The Welcome House board members in the large audience were predictably stunned. And they were insulted, as Pearl presumably intended, that they had not been informed ahead of time about her decision. It was the first round in a long struggle.

The foundation was legally incorporated in Delaware, in February, with just three officers. Ted was to serve as president, Pearl took the post of chairman, and a local lawyer was retained as legal counsel (a man who had worked for the Arthur Murray organization). Executives at Arthur Murray immediately fired Ted, citing an obvious conflict of interest. Pearl would now be solely responsible for his support.

Announcing the new foundation in a letter, Pearl wrote, "After fifteen years in the field of lost and needy children I am convinced that the most needy in the world are the children born in Asia whose mothers are Asian but whose fathers are American." She called on the network of celebrities she had known over the past forty years to build a high-profile board for her new foundation. The members included Dwight D. Eisenhower, Joan Crawford, Art Buchwald, Princess Grace of Monaco, R. Sargent Shriver, Steve Allen, Sophie Tucker, and several others. Robert F. Kennedy joined, reluctantly, after Pearl made a personal visit to his office and wouldn't leave when he refused.[66] In any case, while the list made an impressive letterhead, none of the board members played an active role, and many soon drifted away.

Pearl's first priority was raising money for the new project. She spent over $500,000 in the first year, renting a large townhouse on a fashionable block of Delancey Place in Philadelphia, and furnishing all five floors expensively.[67] She also leased several cars, and put Ted and a number of his friends on the payroll. (The staff included a cook, a houseboy, and a rather dubious character named Jimmy Pauls, with whom Ted had been involved for years.) Pearl paid many of the bills out of her own pocket. Under Ted's supervision, she also made a national tour, appearing in over twenty cities as guest of honor at Pearl S. Buck gala balls. The tour broke even, but months passed before any money was sent to Asia to help Amerasian children.

It had been "a crowded year," Pearl told a friend, Bradford Smith, in mid-1964. "I've taken stock of myself," she wrote, "and set into motion the things I really must accomplish before I die."[68] Ted and the foundation now took up most of her time, and she accepted other obligations reluctantly. After repeated letters and calls from the president of Randolph-Macon, she spoke at the college commencement in June and joined her class for its fiftieth reunion. She also spent a day at the New York World's Fair, where she was honored as one of the "Ten Outstanding American Women." Trips like these had become infrequent; her dedication to the foundation and her new partner left little room for other activities.

Quite systematically, Pearl began to extricate herself from the network of connections and commitments she had acquired over thirty years as a public figure. When she came to the end of her tenure as a Howard University trustee, she refused a new term. Though she found time to nominate Katherine Anne Porter for membership in the American Academy of Arts and Letters, she stopped attending the academy's meetings.

As always, Pearl made an exception in Carol's case by serving for several more years as chairman of the board of the Vineland Training School. However, she resigned as chairman of the Pennsylvania Commission on the Handicapped, and tried to resign as vice chairman of the American Civil Liberties Union (executive director John Pemberton persuaded her to stay on in a purely nominal capacity).[69] She informed the Women's International League for Peace and Freedom that she would no longer sign their fund-raising appeal.[70] A few months later, she resigned as president of the Authors Guild. She gave up her New York apartment, which saved money and also signaled her withdrawal to Bucks County and Philadelphia.[71]

Ted absorbed her attention and affection. She delighted in his company and blossomed in the warm light of his approval. In exchange, she supported him and defended him against the suspicions of her family and friends. They regarded Ted as an opportunist and adventurer, taking advantage of a rich and lonely old woman. Pearl insisted that he was a shrewd businessman and a brilliant companion. Kermit Fischer, a wealthy businessman and former president of Welcome House, was revolted by Ted's "toadying obsequiousness," but Pearl took pleasure in the praise and fawning attention her new companion lavished on her.[72]

Ted thanked her for giving him copies of her books, telling her: "I shall always cherish [them] as my dearest possessions." Pearl thanked him in turn for his "wonderful" work for the foundation: "How right I was when I recognized you!" To please Ted, Pearl spent extravagantly on clothes: $9,000 in 1965, including $3,000 for a fur coat and thousands more for hand-tailored dresses.[73] She wore heavier makeup than she had ever done before, and more elaborate jewelry.

Pearl's new relationship caused her trouble from the start. David Burpee, an old friend, a rich man, and one of the original board members of Welcome House, had grudgingly agreed to join the board of the new foundation. As a favor to Pearl, he temporarily suppressed his distaste for Ted. After a single meeting, however, Burpee resigned, complaining that the organization was "dominated by . . . 'Arthur Murray people,'" and hinting at financial irregularities. He asked Pearl to slow down. "Usually it is best to start in a smaller way," Burpee advised, "to learn to try to crawl before you try to walk or run."

Pearl sent a chilly, uncompromising reply. She accepted Burpee's resignation ("it never pays to urge anyone to change his mind"), sneered at his advice ("I have no time now to crawl"), and defended Ted's integrity, his dedication, and his "astounding success." She simply brushed Burpee's questions aside: "Dear

42. Pearl Buck and Ted Harris. (Courtesy *Fort Worth Star Tele-gram.*)

David, please do not worry about me. I have always done what people said was impossible." In a self-congratulatory final remark, she drew an analogy between the new foundation and her earlier literary triumphs: "Publishers and literary agents once told me that I could never make a success at writing about Chinese people. I thought of that the day I stood before the King of Sweden to receive the Nobel Prize!"[74]

The foundation's initial expenditures reveal an undeniable pattern of (at least) bad judgment: too much money was being spent on Ted and the headquarters building, too little was reaching Korea. Frantic to find additional income, Pearl talked the editors of the *Ladies' Home Journal* into offering her a lucrative bi-monthly column called "My World." The first article in the series, on the plight of Amerasian children, appeared in November, 1964. A few more, containing Pearl's reflections on such subjects as India and the Dalai Lama, were published in the first half of 1965. After a half-dozen of these essays, the project was quietly terminated.

At about the same time, Pearl became embroiled in another dispute, this one a local eruption of racial discrimination. Paul Gibson had been named interim postmaster of Southampton, Pennsylvania, not far from Green Hills Farm. He was the first African-American postmaster in the state's history, and he had applied for the permanent position. A promotion of this sort was ordinarily a mere formality; in Gibson's case, however, the process mysteriously ground to a halt.

Pearl immediately sent a telegram to Pennsylvania Senator Joe Clark. "My friend Mr. Paul Gibson," she told Clark, "is applying for the job of Postmaster in Southampton, Pennsylvania. I wish to recommend him warmly. He is a leader in the community and highly respected. He has had sixteen years of experience in post office work. Since he is a Negro, there seems to be some unusual stoppage in Washington. Please see that he is given a fair chance." A month later, Pearl appealed to Clark again, this time in a long letter. Gibson had been officially named acting postmaster, which, as Pearl commented, "is well enough as far as it goes, but the question is how far does it go?" She complained that the position had been opened to wide competition: "As I understand it, this has never been done before. It is explained to me that applicants will take an examination and that the examination will be open for anyone to take. Again this seems to me a ruse of some sort."[75]

It was the sort of injustice that invariably aroused Pearl's outrage. She had always been alert to the daily indignity that white bureaucracies and individuals inflicted on minority people. Paul Gibson's story had a happier ending than most. Because of Pearl's intervention, he got the job, and served as postmaster until 1980.

Although this episode received no publicity, Pearl's reputation as a humanitarian and civil rights activist was well established. In 1965, in the space of a few months, she received four major awards that honored her work as an advocate for children's welfare and interracial understanding. The Business and Professional Women of Philadelphia gave her their Sojourner Truth Award in May. The same month, she was installed in the Women's Hall of Fame at the New York World's Fair; a few weeks later, the Jewish philanthropic agency, Brith Sholom, chose Pearl as the recipient of its sixtieth-anniversary Humanitarian Award. Then, at the fiftieth-anniversary dinner of the Women's International League for Peace and Freedom, she received a special citation and vote of gratitude. (This in spite of the fact that she was no longer willing to raise funds for WILPF.)

Pearl received a different sort of tribute, in March, 1965, from a group of Howard University trustees. As a gesture of gratitude for her twenty years of service on the Howard board, Dr. Percy Julian persuaded a group of board members to make a donation to the Pearl S. Buck Foundation. Pearl returned from a fund-raising tour to find fifteen checks, adding up to $2,000, along with a cover letter from Julian expressing the "love and admiration" of the contributors. In her letter of thanks, Pearl told Julian that "it is like having Christmas over again, and much more."[76]

For a woman who had achieved fame as a writer and who was now nearing her mid-seventies, these awards and tributes constituted a remarkable testimony. Pearl remained an impressive public figure. A Gallup poll found that she ranked among the ten most admired American women of 1966, and a similar *Good Housekeeping* survey of the same year found that she ranked second only to Rose Kennedy.

IN SPITE OF THE MISMANAGEMENT, the disputes over Ted's motives and abilities, and the indifference of most Americans, the foundation's work went forward. Staff members were hired, foundation offices were opened, children were identified, American sponsors recruited. The Korean office, which opened in 1965, was followed by programs in Okinawa and Taiwan (1967), the Philippines and Thailand (1968), and Vietnam (1970).

Pearl visited all these countries in the late 1960s, and also traveled to India, where she met with Prime Minister Indira Gandhi to discuss the problems of caste and poverty. Pearl urged Gandhi to try to improve relations between China and the United States, whose mutual hostility represented "the greatest danger for the world." She told Gandhi that "[y]ou are the only person who can possibly accomplish" this. Gandhi, fulsome but blandly noncommittal, evaded Pearl's political requests while expressing her admiration. "It was such a delight to meet you again," she wrote Pearl. "There is such a warmth in your personality and, if I may say so, a quality of Mother Earth which exudes a feeling of quietness along with capability and strength."[77]

Such talk left Pearl bemused and frustrated. Although she had access to Gandhi and to powerful politicians on both sides of the Pacific, she found little official sympathy for her arguments. She considered herself an expert on Asia; she was treated as a sentimental female icon – "Mother Earth" – an elderly relic from a past age, standing on the fringes of modern politics.

Pearl wanted China and the United States to find mechanisms for accommodation, but the two nations remained frozen in Cold War belligerence. In the second half of the 1960s, the bad relations between them got worse. Americans were justifiably shocked at the excesses of the Cultural Revolution. At the same time, America's massive intervention in Vietnam and China's support for Communist North Vietnam put even greater strains on Sino-American relations.

By February of 1967, Pearl had declared her opposition to the Vietnam War: "I think we could have prevented the war there. . . . We should not have entered into it."[78] In Pearl's view, the continuing Cold War crusade against Communism was still deforming America's policies in Asia. Fifteen years after the Korean War, China and the United States once again edged perilously close to military conflict. Pearl's opinions were neither sought nor accepted.

Unable to influence the geopolitical strategies of Asian or Western governments, Pearl redoubled her efforts to help the children she had taken as her mission.[79] *Matthew, Mark, Luke and John,* a children's book that she published in 1966, tells the heartbreaking story of four Korean-American boys, all abandoned by their American serviceman fathers and their Korean mothers. They cling to a precarious survival by begging, working at menial odd jobs, and living under a bridge in Seoul.[80]

Pearl used every opportunity she could find to propagandize for the foundation and for the mixed-race children of Asia. In July, she was a main speaker at the annual meeting of the American Library Association in New York. Twelve hundred librarians paid $6.50 apiece to attend a lunch in Pearl's honor – an indication, said the *New York Times,* that women still had plenty of interest in Pearl and in reading.[81] She had been asked to talk about books, and she did, commenting on her own fiction and nonfiction as evidence of her interest in "human beings and their relationships." However, she also included a long digression introducing the assembled librarians to the mixed-race children, "for whom the world is not ready."[82] Pearl had turned a literary occasion into a fundraiser for the foundation.

A few months later, *This Week* magazine, a Sunday supplement with a circulation in the millions, accepted an essay she called "A Cry for the Deserted!" It was a plea for abandoned Amerasian children, and Pearl opened it histrionically: "I am a hunter . . . hunting for anonymous fathers – the fathers of children American servicemen have left behind in six countries of Asia." She used plausible but unverified statistics to buttress her moral argument. "It is estimated," she said, "that approximately one in ten of the young men we send abroad to Korea, Japan, Okinawa, Taiwan, the Philippines and Vietnam becomes the father of a child by an Asian girl."[83]

In Japan, the Amerasians were called *konketsuji* or *ainoko,* which meant "hybrid," "half-breed," "mongrel," or (a variation that came into use after the U.S. occupation) "GI baby." Denied by their American fathers and victimized by Japanese racism, these boys and girls lived in a daily round of deprivation and abuse. They were frequently beaten and told to go "home" to America. As in Korea, a few were killed, and some of the males were sexually mutilated.

The Japanese *konketsuji* were lodged near the bottom of a whole structure of disadvantaged minority groups: the despised Koreans; the Ainu people of Hokkaido; the two million Etas, who were treated like India's Untouchables; and the *hibakusha,* the survivors of the Hiroshima and Nagasaki bombs, who were often ostracized.[84] The mixed-race children, whom Pearl called "the new people," were merely the latest victims of old patterns of discrimination; neither the Japanese nor the U.S. governments would accept responsibility for them. Pearl

43. Pearl and one of the Welcome House children in the late 1960s.
(Reproduced with permission of the Pearl S. Buck Foundation.)

tried to get an appointment with President Lyndon Johnson to plead for these children, with no success: "he was too busy to see me."[85]

In the spring of 1967, as her seventy-fifth birthday approached, Pearl announced that she was bequeathing her entire estate, including Green Hills Farm, to the Pearl S. Buck Foundation. Her new will included small bequests for her children but directed that, after her death, all her royalties should be given to the foundation. She estimated that she was providing $7 million to the foundation and its work.[86]

Aside from the Amerasian children, the principal beneficiary of Pearl's new arrangements was Ted, who was drawing the exceptional salary of $45,000 a year. (Pearl had proposed that Ted receive the salary for the rest of his life, whether he remained with the foundation or not.)[87] In effect, Pearl had redefined her parental obligations: she had displaced her sons and daughters as her heirs. She argued that she wanted her money to assist disadvantaged boys and girls in Asian countries – to give those children the sort of chance she had given her own. Her children, on the other hand, felt that their inheritance had been sabotaged by their mother's executive director and companion, who was manipulating Pearl to serve his own ends.

Immediately after her dramatic financial announcement, Pearl left for another tour of Asia, accompanied by Ted and several other members of the staff. She opened the Pearl S. Buck Opportunity Center in Sosa, Korea. This facility, she told Emma White, would provide "rehabilitation . . . for mothers of Amerasian children, special education to help [the] children . . . and training for jobs."[88] She described the dedication ceremony, which was attended by hundreds of Amerasian children, as the happiest day of her life.[89]

Back in Philadelphia, the rumors that swirled around Ted and his behavior were becoming thicker and more sinister. There was gossip that he had molested several young boys, Amerasians brought to the foundation from Korea.[90] There was talk of financial shenanigans – a car dealer wrote to Pearl complaining that he had leased a Cadillac to the foundation which Ted had then sold.[91] There were even charges that Ted was bringing narcotics into the country in Pearl's luggage.

The drug-smuggling allegations brought the FBI into the case. One of Pearl's employees, perhaps her driver, contacted the Bureau's Philadelphia office in June, while Pearl was in Korea, to lodge a series of accusations against Ted and another man, probably Jimmy Pauls. In the tongue-tied language of the agency's report, Ted was accused of "taking the money collected for the Pearl S. Buck Foundation and spending the money other than what the money was donated for." For example, said the source, on one of Pearl's Western fund-raising tours, Ted had gambled heavily in Las Vegas. The informant suspected that Pearl's prestige could be abused as a cover for smuggling drugs: "Source stated he wondered if it were possible" that Ted and his colleague were "transporting dope from foreign countries into the United States inasmuch as their baggage and person is not checked closely inasmuch as they are traveling under the name of the Pearl S. Buck Foundation."

The FBI shared its report with the State and Treasury Departments, with the Philadelphia Police Department, and with the Philadelphia and Bucks County district attorneys. Almost immediately, the secret document was leaked to the local press. The *Philadelphia Inquirer,* which received a copy from an unidentified source, called Pearl as soon as she returned from Korea to follow up on the story. She denied all the accusations, and phoned the FBI to protest. Her "manner," in agent Roger Rogge's words, was "highly incensed, extremely irritated, and rambling." The Bureau sent what it described (presumably with a straight face) as "two mature agents" to interview Pearl on June 30. In a long and emotional scene, she repeated her denials of each accusation, restated her distress that FBI information had fallen into the hands of a newspaper reporter, and reaffirmed her absolute confidence in Ted.

Director Hoover was more interested in the leak than the substance of the inquiry. In July, he wired the Philadelphia office demanding that his agents "determine who furnished the information" on the foundation to the *Philadelphia Inquirer.* A frantic investigation failed to track down the source, and the case was closed.[92]

This incident, along with the pressures of age and travel and Pearl's constant worries about Ted and the foundation, conspired to diminish her legendary productivity just a little. The only novel she published in 1967, *The Time Is Noon,* was actually a recycled manuscript that she had written in the 1930s and suppressed for three decades. Pearl wrote the book just a few years after her father's death and the end of her first marriage, while she was still suffering from the trauma of institutionalizing Carol. The novel explicitly transcribes her intimate recollections, her feelings of grievance and loss as she assessed the life she had led in the 1920s.

The book's heroine, a sensitive and intellectually curious woman named Joan Richards, is the daughter of a God-driven Christian preacher and his warmhearted but emotionally starved wife. It is a joyless union, in which a religious fanatic destroys the life and spirit of his loyal, self-sacrificing spouse. Joan in turn makes a bad first marriage, to a narrow-minded farmer with the oddly threatening name of Bart Pounder. They have only one child, a retarded daughter, after whose birth Joan refuses further sexual relations with Bart. Eventually, Joan falls in love with a more glamorous figure, an aviator named Roger Bair, while Bart drifts into an affair with a local farm girl.

The book's renderings of Joan's grimly sanctimonious father, her defeated mother, her retarded daughter, and her boorish first husband, painfully rehearse some of Pearl's most harrowing memories. Pearl wrote *The Time Is Noon,* as she said later, to "get rid of all my life until that moment," at a time when "there was no hope ahead."[93] Richard Walsh considered the novel dangerously confessional and advised Pearl to suppress it; for thirty years, she did.

Her decision to publish the book suggests that time had not erased the bitterness she felt about her bleak first marriage. Thirty and forty and even fifty years after the events, she was still angry at her father and her first husband. Under the cover of a thin fictional veil, she was, once again, revenging herself on Absalom Sydenstricker and Lossing Buck. Furthermore, she no longer felt the need to protect Carol's privacy. *The Child Who Never Grew* had appeared seventeen years earlier, and anyone who was interested in the existence of Pearl's retarded daughter already knew.

She also needed the money that *The Time Is Noon* would bring in. Every book Pearl published earned a substantial U.S. income and even larger royalties overseas. By one estimate, three-quarters of her "massive earnings" came from foreign sales.[94] In the late 1960s, a UNESCO survey indicated that Pearl was the most translated American writer: sixty-nine translated editions of her work appeared in a single year. (Hemingway ranked second, with sixty-four translations, followed by Steinbeck, with forty-eight.)[95]

She had become "a money machine," in the words of a bemused friend,[96] and a sample of the dozens of checks she received in 1967 bears that description out: $1,500 from *Boy's Life* for a short story, "The House They Built"; a £2,000 advance from Methuen for rights to the unpublished novel *The New Year;* $2,000 from *Woman's Day* for a story called "Certain Wisdom"; $1,500 for a Slovak reissue of the trilogy *House of Earth;* £1,000 for a British reissue of *China Flight* and two other wartime novels; $250 from the *Philadelphia Bulletin* for excerpts from the unpublished nonfiction book *To My Daughters;* £250 for a reissue of *The Promise* in the United Kingdom.[97]

Pearl spent several weeks in August and September of 1967 in Vermont. Her vacation retreat, which now included four buildings on several hundred acres, had been included in the legacy she intended to leave to the foundation. In Vermont, in Philadelphia, and on tour, Ted was her constant companion. He made her arrangements, negotiated her contracts, screened her calls, ordered her meals, sat next to her in every car and plane. She virtually disappeared inside Ted's omnipresent attendance. She grew remote from her friends, sometimes cutting herself off aggressively. She alienated Lois Burpee with a condescending lecture on the foundation's accomplishments, and drove Miki Sawada away by accusing her of taking financial advantage of the sponsors who had contributed to her Japanese orphanage.[98]

In an especially sad act of estrangement, she even separated herself from Welcome House, the agency she had founded and had proudly led through nearly twenty years. The foundation, she now emphasized, did no adoption work. When children eligible for adoption came to the foundation's attention, she said, "we refer [them] to suitable adoption agencies."[99] In the course of one typical seven-page letter on foster care and adoption she wrote at about this time, Welcome House was not mentioned.

Only her obligation to Carol remained unaltered. Two weeks before Christmas, as she had done every year for over three decades, Pearl wrote to a staff member at the Vineland Training School, including a list of gifts that were to be purchased for Carol. Crayons and coloring books, beads and glazed fruit and candy, doll blankets and a musical top: the sad list didn't change much from year to year.

In March, 1968, Pearl traveled to Korea again, to spend a week at the Opportunity Center in Sosa. She saw a small group of Amerasian children that her foundation was helping: well-fed and well-dressed boys and girls who were attending school, and were receiving job training and regular medical care. The children renewed her energy and confirmed her faith in Ted, and she came home brimming with cheerful news.[100]

In fact, the program's results were quite modest in comparison to its budget. However, even though her own lawyer admitted that only three dollars out of every ten was spent directly on the children, Pearl didn't ask Ted for a rigorous accounting.[101] Instead, her genuine delight in the children served to justify the entire project. As always, her responses were personal, visceral, and, in this case at least, self-deluding. Declaring the Center a complete success, she was content to credit Ted's brilliant executive talents.

As soon as she returned from Asia, she made a speaking tour across the Midwest, appearing mostly in front of college audiences and women's groups, pleading the case for Amerasian children at every stop. In a single week, she visited the University of Toledo, Ohio University, the General Motors Institute, and Central State University. Still in demand in such places, she charged (and received) $2,000 for each appearance.[102]

The only novel Pearl published in 1968, *The New Year,* also revolved around her campaign for the Amerasian children. The book's slender plot follows a predictable philanthropic outline. Chris Winters, an American serviceman, has fathered a son with a Korean woman during the war. After abandoning mother and son, Chris has returned to the States, married a woman named Laura, and made a happy (though childless) marriage and a successful political career. In the mid-1960s, a letter arrives from his Amerasian son, now twelve years old and victimized by poverty, Korean bigotry, and his mother's growing hostility. His conscience stirred, Chris confesses the entire story to Laura. After negotiating a good many complications and obstacles, including their own deep reservations, Chris and Laura adopt the boy, whom they name Christopher.

From its title on, *The New Year* is notable less for its story line than its relentlessly optimistic tone. Though Chris is a candidate for governor and fears any threat to his reputation, he acknowledges his son and watches his popularity miraculously increase. In an equally unlikely turn of events, Laura transcends her initial repugnance and her profound sense of betrayal and welcomes her new child. Christopher's mother is relieved of a burden she cannot manage, and the boy himself looks forward to a happy life in America. Rather than offering a realistic account of the sufferings of Amerasian children and the hazards of adoption, *The New Year* merely celebrates Pearl's dreams of justice and reconciliation. The novel translates its strong and potentially disturbing subjects into an appealing but unconvincing fairy tale. The final scene presents a consoling symbolic tableau: conflicts and prejudices dissolve as the interracial family lovingly embraces, cheered by a crowd of supportive friends.

Published in the year that Martin Luther King, Jr., and Robert F. Kennedy were assassinated, when the war in Vietnam was lethally escalated and the nation's social contract was challenged by violence in the streets, *The New Year* contrived an international and interracial harmony that had little connection to American reality. The novel's gratifying outcome unintentionally confessed the fear that had troubled Pearl since she had returned to her homeland over thirty years earlier: perhaps America could only measure up to its high democratic ideals in her imagination.

IN THE FIRST FEW MONTHS OF 1969, the attacks on Ted and the foundation increased. Philadelphia journalists, alerted to the FBI investigation two years earlier, had been probing more systematically. Since Pearl was a respected national figure and a beloved local institution, she presented an editorial problem. Although most publishers were reluctant to trifle with her reputation, they also knew that they were close to a major sensation.

Pearl's days and nights were troubled by the continual noise of rumors and gossip. She lived with the constant fear that the allegations against Ted would erupt in a scandal. Unexpectedly, the story broke first in Korea. In May, several articles appeared in Seoul's largest English-language newspaper, *Korea Times*. According to these reports, the children at the Sosa Center had called a press conference to protest conditions and to complain about the behavior of the staff. The children claimed that they could produce evidence of embezzlement and theft.

Copies of these stories, along with an anonymous letter laying out even graver charges, soon reached Dr. Richard Wilson, a wealthy Pearl S. Buck Foundation supporter and board member. Among other things, Ted was accused of stealing Christmas gifts sent to the children by their American sponsors, and of spending foundation funds on a large wardrobe of hand-tailored suits.[103]

Pearl reacted swiftly. She issued a flat denial of every allegation, told her

44. Pearl with other honorary degree recipients at Rutgers University, June, 1969. Front row, left to right: Rutgers president Mason Gross, John Archibald Wheeler, Pearl Buck, Henry Lewis, Germaine Bree. Back row: A. Leon Higginbotham, Jr., Phillip Alampi, Leonard Baskin, Norman Mailer. (Reproduced with permission of the Pearl S. Buck Foundation.)

attorney to hire a private investigator, and circulated an impassioned, six-page statement to all her board members. The campaign against Ted, she insisted, was the work of a Korean journalist, "an untrustworthy man, anti-American and leftist," who was motivated by sheer spite. She defended everything Ted had done, even his clothing purchases. As she had done so often before, she called him "brilliant," and "totally dedicated," a man "of the highest integrity" who was being "crucified by malicious persons."[104]

The Korean exposé turned out to be mere prologue. Pearl enjoyed a brief respite in June, during which she traveled to Rutgers University to receive an honorary doctorate. A couple of weeks later, the July issue of *Philadelphia Magazine* appeared on the stands, featuring a long essay called "The Dancing Master" by associate editor Greg Walter. "Famed novelist Pearl S. Buck," the subheading declared, "has been waltzed into a heartbreaking story." In 13,000 words, based on months of research and dozens of interviews, Walter crafted a stunning indictment; he dismantled Ted's career and debunked the claims that Pearl made on his behalf. In Walter's account of her recent history, Pearl was rendered as the virtuous but gullible victim of an unprincipled conspiracy among Ted and his friends.

The article had a devastating effect on Pearl and the foundation. Within a week of the magazine's publication, Ted had stepped down as president and left Philadelphia for a house that Pearl had recently bought in Maryland. (One report said that he made his escape in one of the foundation's leased cars, hidden under a rug on the rear floor, or perhaps in the trunk.)[105] Though Pearl immediately rejected all the charges against Ted as "a bunch of downright lies" and took over as the foundation's chief executive, several board members resigned.[106]

Pearl was besieged by reporters and hounded in local radio broadcasts. *Time* magazine, still in thrall to the dead Henry Luce, joined the attack. In a gleefully malicious article called "Crumbling Foundation," Ted was characterized as mawkish and manipulative, a gigolo and a "Svengali in Bucks County." Pearl was presented as his "silver-haired" and pathetic defender.[107]

Pennsylvania's state welfare department commenced an investigation. Foundation business came to a halt. At an emergency meeting, the Welcome House board distanced itself from Pearl, passing a resolution that emphasized the separation between Welcome House and the Pearl S. Buck Foundation. Just a few days past her seventy-seventh birthday, Pearl feared that a lifetime of humanitarian service would disintegrate in humiliation.

As always, she fought back. She had been attacked throughout her adult life: by the Presbyterians, during the missionary debate; by literary critics, especially after she won the Nobel Prize; by McCarthyites, who smeared her as a subversive; by the Chinese Communists, who labeled her a reactionary; by the social work establishment, for her radical views on interracial adoption. Repeatedly, she had demonstrated that she was a brave woman and a tough, resourceful adversary. Now, in her old age, she did what she could to counter the storm of criticism that Ted's behavior had stirred up.

She wrote countless letters to editors, politicians, and foundation sponsors, in which she used the same phrases over and over again, decrying *Philadelphia Magazine* as "a smut journal." Greg Walter had once taken a writing class from Pearl; now she said that he was vile, that she was ashamed of him.[108] She threatened lawsuits and demanded equal time on radio and television to answer negative reporting. On WIP, a Philadelphia radio station, she spoke emotionally for over half an hour. After she explained the origins of the foundation, she attacked her critics as malcontents and troublemakers, and concluded with a long, reverential defense of Ted's integrity and talents. She portrayed herself as the victim of an inexplicable conspiracy. To the insinuation that she had been used by an unscrupulous man, she responded bitterly: "I am getting old, as our officious reporter kindly reminds me." But, she said, "I am not senile."[109]

Pearl's reputation survived more or less intact. A Gallup poll of 1969 placed her eighth on the list of most admired women. (She and Helen Hayes were, as *Parade* magazine pointed out, the only two among the ten women who "achieved fame through their own efforts." The others were mainly political wives, widows, and mothers, such as Ethel and Rose Kennedy, Jacqueline Onassis, Mamie Eisenhower, and Coretta Scott King.) The foundation also survived and began to reorganize under a new board of directors. Though Pearl held the title of president, she withdrew from the organization's daily work. She joined Ted in Maryland, then took him with her to Vermont in the late summer.

In the sort of irony that often dogged Pearl's footsteps, her latest novel, *The Three Daughters of Madame Liang,* appeared almost on the same day as Greg Walter's scandalous revelations. A Book-of-the-Month Club choice and a Reader's Digest "Condensed Book" selection, *Three Daughters* proved to be Pearl's last novel about China.[110] She had begun her career with a trilogy that traced the lives of Wang Lung and his three sons in the years before and after the Revolution of 1911. Nearly forty years later, she presented the story of three daughters in the China of the 1960s.

Madame Liang is an elegant woman in her fifties, living in un-Communist comfort in Shanghai, where she runs an expensive restaurant that caters to high-ranking party cadres and army officers. The arrangement, with its aroma of Communist hypocrisy, is symptomatic, and discredits the party's pretensions to speak for the masses in building a new world. Instead, at every level, the leaders are mediocre men driven by the age-old motives of resentment, self-interest, and ambition.

Madame Liang has made a separate peace. She lives quietly, accommodates herself to the regime, and consoles herself with thoughts of her three daughters, who have made successful careers in the United States: Grace is a physician, Mercy a musician, Joyce a painter. The novel follows the consequences to all four women when the government recalls the three daughters to China, demanding that they return to help make the revolution and hinting that Madame Liang will be punished if they refuse.

Two of the young women do return, only to discover a nightmare of Communist repression. *The Three Daughters* was written in the early years of the Cultural Revolution, when China plunged into a decade of barbarism and violence. In one scene after another, the novel pictures a society that has lost its political and moral equilibrium, as zeal and ignorance lead the world's largest nation into multiplied disorder. Intellectuals and scientists are purged, families broken up, dissidents beaten and killed, all in the name of Mao Tse-tung, who presides like a bad emperor over the suffering he provokes and sanctions. In the book's final episode, Madame Liang herself is beaten to death by a mob of teenagers, for no apparent reason at all.

Though Pearl had not set foot in China in over thirty years, her fearful portrait was essentially accurate. So was the prophecy she made, late in the novel, about China's future. She speaks through the character John Sung, a Chinese-American physicist who has returned to China voluntarily to contribute his skills. Sung has been sent to the countryside for refusing to join a nuclear weapons project, but he counsels patience: "A deep struggle is emerging in our country," Sung tells his wife. "It will rise to the surface the moment the Chairman dies of old age." There will be a contest "between the ideologists and the experts . . . the old-line revolutionists, the fervent dreamers, the ideologists against the men of practical mind, the realists." China's main problem, Sung concludes, "is wrapped up in one word – production. The theorists do not know how to organize for it. The experts are merely biding their time.""" It is a fair summary of the debate that followed Mao's death in 1976 – the battle of "Red versus expert," as Mao himself called it – which continues to bedevil China's politics in the last years of the century.""

Pearl's bitter critique of the Communist regime's excesses sprang from her abiding loyalty to the Chinese masses. She despised the cult of Mao. Unlike much of the American left, which indulged in countercultural fantasies about a benevolent "Great Helmsman," Pearl understood that the Great Leap Forward and the Cultural Revolution were fatal to the aspirations of ordinary people.

Her own life had reached its final turning point. Forced to choose between Ted and everyone else close to her, she chose Ted. By the end of 1969, she had moved more or less permanently to Vermont, where she installed Ted and several of his friends (all refugees from the foundation) in different rooms in a house she bought in Danby. She kept writing, remained distantly connected with the work of the foundation, and planned new projects. She collaborated with Ted on *Pearl Buck,* a two-volume biography in which a sampling of her published and un-published letters and reminiscences are embellished with Ted's cloying, hero-worshiping commentary.

Pearl set up a new organization, Creativity, Inc., to finance yet another phil-anthropic project. Danby, like other small New England towns, had fallen from nineteenth-century prosperity into a terminal slump. A few ramshackle homes and commercial buildings faced each other across a narrow Main Street. Nearby, a Civil War memorial soldier watched over a disheveled village green and a decaying church.

Pearl decided to rescue Danby, by turning the town into an antique market and a center for arts and crafts. She bought several of the old buildings and drew up plans to renovate them.[113] The initial money came, as always, from her own earnings. Beyond that, she started a fund-raising drive. Using mailing lists recycled from ten and twenty years earlier, she wrote to people who had supported United China Relief, the East and West Association, Welcome House, and the foundation. She also created a "Pearl Buck Book Club," which offered members autographed copies of her own novels and stories.

The Danby project made very little headway over the next three years. Pearl actually knew next to nothing about antiques, arts and crafts, or commercial renovation, and Ted knew less. And, while her own writing had been a fairly large enterprise for several decades, she had no experience running a business. It was a quixotic undertaking, but it dramatized once again Pearl's remarkable energy, her resilience, and her pride. She was determined to turn her foundation defeat into a triumph. She also wanted to prove that she had not been driven out of Philadelphia, but had left by her own choice.

It still took a fair-sized staff to handle Pearl's correspondence and literary affairs. In her first Vermont year, she received over a hundred speaking invitations and several hundred fan letters, many of them from women asking for personal advice.[114] (She turned down almost all the invitations, and painstakingly answered most of the letters.) Royalty checks came in from over one hundred publishers around the world. Richard Walsh, Jr., wrote and called regularly to monitor progress on the several novels Pearl had promised to John Day.

One of those novels, *Mandala,* was published in mid-1970. A long book set in contemporary India, the story is crowded with romantic intrigue and international politics, and bathed in an unconvincing aura of Indian mysticism. A few months earlier, Pearl had published *The Kennedy Women,* an enthusiastic tribute to the "greatness" of the family and the uncommon strength of its women. Promoting the book on the "Today" show, she called the Kennedy assassinations a kind of "magnicide," the destruction of greatness by forces of leveling spite.[115]

An article she wrote for *Modern Maturity,* a monthly journal for retired persons with a circulation of seven million, attracted more response than anything the magazine had published. Pearl's "Essay on Life," as she called it, drew on her conversations with Arthur Compton and Ernest Hocking. The article's success demonstrated that she could still cater to the tastes of large numbers of Americans.[116]

Occasionally, she spoke out on public questions. In an op-ed essay in the *New York Times,* for example, she predicted that China would not wage an aggressive war in the foreseeable future.[117] However, such statements were now rare. She traveled less, spending most of her time in Vermont, attended by Ted and one or two of his associates. Visitors remarked that it was almost impossible to see Pearl except in Ted's company. Yet his continual, hovering presence did not alleviate Pearl's loneliness. One visitor came away convinced that "deep down," Pearl knew that Ted was exploiting her but that she couldn't "afford to give up the one friend she could buy."[118] It was a widely shared opinion.

"The truth is," she said to a biographer at about this time, "I don't think I ever shared anything of my inner self with anyone."[119] Ever since her emotionally stunted childhood, she had been an essentially isolated woman. Her loneliness deepened in old age. "I know what it is," she told James T. Farrell, "to wake in the night and feel utterly alone, even in one's own house, and to wake to grey dawn and hesitate to begin the day."[120] Ross Terrill, who spent two days with Pearl at the end of 1971, said that she still possessed a radiant smile, the expression of a "life-affirming power"; but she smiled only now and then.[121]

By retreating to Vermont and cutting herself off from the people she had lived with for most of her adult life, Pearl shaped her last years into a kind of final exile, completing the pattern of homelessness that she had known since childhood. On a trip to Hillsboro, where she presided over the dedication of her birthplace home as a memorial, she said that she had always felt like a West Virginian. It was a friendly comment, but poignantly untrue. She had spent only a few months in her entire life in West Virginia; it had been merely the first of her many stopping places.

As she approached eighty, she often remarked that she had still lived more years in China than in the United States. Ross Terrill concluded that she had "never really got used to America, still does not feel completely at home here." China had been her first home. While she hated the Communist system that Mao had imposed, her allegiance to the country she had grown up in was ineradicable. She became increasingly absorbed – obsessed, in her sister Grace's opinion – with the idea of returning to China before she died.[122] She knew that she had long been *persona non grata* with the Chinese leadership. However, as relations between the two countries slowly warmed, in 1970 and 1971, her chances seemed to improve.

The new diplomacy took most Americans by surprise, but it followed a long preparation. By 1970, the influence of the China Lobby had nearly disappeared.[123] Geopolitical realism and commercial calculation both dictated that Washington could no longer pretend that Communist China, with one-fifth of the world's population, did not exist. In spite of the continued fighting in Vietnam, the United States moved toward diplomatic recognition. Ironically, the agent of change was President Richard Nixon, a militant Cold Warrior who had built his entire political career on his passionate crusade against Communism. A reliable pillar of the anti-Communist establishment, Nixon could risk an "opening" to China, where liberals could not. The president sent Henry Kissinger on a secret mission to Peking in July, 1971, and allowed the admission of China to the United Nations in October. The following February, Nixon himself flew to

Peking, to join Mao in one of the century's most famous (and consequential) handshakes.[124]

Pearl had hoped to accompany Nixon on this trip, perhaps as a journalist. This was a desperate idea ("hare-brained," in Ross Terrill's phrase): at seventy-nine years old, she was not equipped to spend a week fighting for space in a press plane and scrambling from one interview to another. Nonetheless, the scheme demonstrated how badly she wanted to visit China. She peppered Chou En-lai and other leaders with telegrams. She wrote to everyone she knew who might have influence with the Chinese government to help her secure an invitation and a visa: the list included scholars, journalists, and expatriate Chinese friends. She appealed personally to President Nixon and wrote to several members of the Nixon White House. She even sought out John Service, a China hand purged from the State Department years earlier. Service passed Pearl's request along to Chinese authorities and "had the unhappy task of passing back their unfavorable reply."[125]

Pearl's request for a visa was rejected. In May, 1972, after months of official silence, a Chinese envoy stationed in Canada sent her a terse, brutal message:

Dear Miss Pearl Buck: Your letters have been duly received. In view of the fact that for a long time you have in your works taken an attitude of distortion, smear and vilification towards the people of new China and its leaders, I am authorized to inform you that we cannot accept your request for a visit to China.

Adding to the premeditated insult, the note was signed by a second secretary named H. L. Yuan, a low-ranking member of the Chinese diplomatic staff.

Pearl was outraged by the rejection, and mystified. She thought of herself as China's preeminent American friend, the writer whose books had moved an indifferent or even hostile Western public toward sympathy with the aspirations of the Chinese people. For their part, the Communist leaders took a rather different view. Pearl's recent fiction had included savage denunciations of contemporary China. *The Three Daughters of Madame Liang* condemned China's internal politics, while *Mandala* and a story called "The Commandant and the Commissar" criticized the Chinese for invading and annexing Tibet.

In any case, as the attack on Pearl in the 1960 columns of *World Literature* should have warned her, Chinese Communist discontent with her work was not merely a response to her current attitudes and statements. She had made her anti-Communist position clear in all sorts of fictional and nonfictional publications over the years, including *My Several Worlds* in the mid-1950s. In addition, her preference for Chiang Kai-shek throughout the late 1930s and in the opening years of the war, even though it had been severely qualified and reserved, was unforgivable in Communist eyes.

Pearl had also engaged in a number of minor skirmishes that placed her on the wrong side of the Chinese culture wars. In 1933, for example, she had lavished praise on Nora Waln's autobiographical *House of Exile,* the story of Waln's ten years inside the spacious compound of a Chinese gentry family in Hebei province. Pearl's generous remarks were reprinted for months as the centerpiece of advertisements promoting the book in major American magazines. The Communists, who judged the best-selling *House of Exile* to be utterly reactionary, held Pearl accountable for its success.[126]

A few years later, Pearl's friendship with actress Wang Ying cost her the undying enmity of another actress, Chiang Ch'ing (Jiang Qing), who was later to become Mao's last wife, the formidable chief member of the "Gang of Four." In a competition with Chiang Ch'ing in the late 1930s, Wang Ying had won a leading role in a Shanghai play (*Sai Jinhua,* the dramatized life of a heroic Chinese woman in the Boxer Uprising).[127] Chiang Ch'ing never forgave her rival, and she later transferred her anger to Pearl. In 1972, when Pearl applied for a visa, Chiang Ch'ing's influence was at its apogee. Chou En-lai, who needed to shore up his credibility with Chiang Ch'ing and other radicals, helpfully decreed that Pearl should be categorized as an enemy of the revolution.[128] Some of the Chinese leaders had long memories.

The personal grievances raised against Pearl were anchored in the highest cultural authority: in the 1930s, she had been criticized by the revered writer Lu Hsün, China's greatest twentieth-century literary figure. In a letter of 1933, Lu Hsün dismissed Pearl as "an American woman missionary," whose knowledge of China was "superficial."[129] Lu Hsün's distaste for Pearl's work may have been based on a bad translation of *The Good Earth* (he did not read English). Whatever the reason, even a glancing rebuke by Lu Hsün would explain and legitimize the government's refusal to welcome her back to the People's Republic. Indeed, to this day, Lu Hsün's widely quoted comment has presented a nearly insurmountable obstacle to Pearl's literary rehabilitation in China.

Pearl suffered another defeat in the spring of 1972, less personal but no less profound. In April, the National Association of Black Social Workers, meeting in Nashville for their fourth annual conference, condemned the placement of black children with white parents for both foster care and adoption. Calling transracial adoptions "a growing threat to the preservation of the black family," the conference passed a formal resolution opposing the practice. The association's president, Cenie J. Williams, Jr., went further, insisting that black children should not be placed in white homes even if institutionalization were the only alternative.[130]

Despite the honorable motives that led to its formulation, the resolution was wrongheaded and sadly divisive.[131] In an unnoticed but painful irony, this black rejection of interracial adoption was ratified just two weeks after a federal court struck down a racist Louisiana law prohibiting adoptions between blacks and whites.[132] Almost simultaneously, as if to anticipate and answer the black social workers, Pearl had published one of her last articles, "I am the Better Woman for having my two Black Children." After describing the backgrounds and lives of her adopted daughters Henriette and Cheiko, she drew a simple, unrebuttable moral: a child's "chances are better with love than without."[133] It had been the basis of her own choices for over thirty years.

In June, 1972, Pearl returned to Green Hills Farm for the last time, to celebrate her eightieth birthday with her family. Her sister Grace was there, along with most of her seven children and fourteen grandchildren. It was a subdued occasion, shadowed by the tensions between Ted and Pearl's children. Just a week later, back in Vermont, she was taken to the Rutland hospital for treatment of cancer and pleurisy. Cheered by hundreds of telegrams from friends and readers, including President Nixon, who described himself as a longtime admirer, she was released after three weeks.[134] Her apparent recovery was illusory; she had in fact collapsed into what would prove to be a final ten months of unrelieved illness.

Like her father, Pearl had been remarkably healthy into her old age. Aside from the hysterectomy that followed Carol's birth fifty years earlier, the only medical problem that had regularly troubled Pearl was the allergy to ragweed that sent her to the Jersey shore or Vermont every summer. Now, her ailments multiplied. In September, she was hospitalized again, this time to have her gall-bladder removed. Complications required a second operation and a series of X-ray treatments, and Pearl remained in the hospital for nearly three months.

She kept working. The hospital assigned her a second room to use as an office, and she wrote to Tsuta Walsh that she was making progress on three different novels. Ted and a local woman, Beverly Drake, who had initially joined the staff some months earlier as a secretary, stayed with her. Ted handled her finances, Drake typed her manuscripts and correspondence, and both served as nursing assistants. She was released in time to spend Christmas in her Danby home.[135]

Once, when Pearl was asked about her views on the afterlife, she responded that she had no time for such speculation: "I am so deeply engaged in matters having to do with this present life . . . that I must not undertake the complexities of what is to come hereafter." Then she added: "As Eleanor Roosevelt once said, 'Whatever it is I daresay I shall be able to cope with it.' "[136]

After she came back from the hospital, she rallied periodically, but she never recovered. Her children called her; several of them drove to Vermont to visit, provoking nasty quarrels with Ted over access to the dying woman. Pearl spent most of her time in her upstairs bedroom, dressed in one of her brightly colored Chinese robes. Sitting on a large chair by the window, she could see the Vermont mountains, which she had often said reminded her of the Lu Mountains southwest of Nanking. For the first time in her life, she slept for long periods each day. Her books, her correspondence, and her plans all came to a stop.

Sometime in February, Pearl had made an odd but touching valedictory gesture. Lying in bed, she asked Beverly Drake to spread her old copies of Dickens's novels around her. Her sister Grace said that she "was trying to get back to the source," renewing her commitment to her first literary mentor. She was also making contact with her own past and her fondest memories, holding the books that had given her so much pleasure as a girl and young woman. They had survived the Nanking Incident by the merest chance, had been shipped back to the United States in the 1930s, and had then been carried to every house Pearl had lived in, from New York City to Green Hills Farm to Vermont.

Early in the morning of March 6, 1973, after a quiet night, she died. The cause of death was lung cancer. Newspapers around the world covered Pearl's death as a front-page story. The *New York Times* ran a three-thousand-word obituary by Albin Krebs; an appraisal, under the headline, "A Missionary Heritage," by Thomas Lask; and a flattering editorial. Even Pearl's old adversaries at *Time,* after reassuring their readers that she "was anything but a great novelist," made a few kind noises. President Nixon eulogized her as a "bridge between the civilizations of the East and West."[137]

Pearl's funeral took place, as she had instructed, at Green Hills Farm. It was a private ceremony. Only her adopted children attended; Carol was not brought from Vineland, and Ted stayed away. After a brief, non-religious service, Pearl was buried beneath a large ash tree a few hundred yards from her house. Her tombstone, which she designed, does not record her name in English. Instead, inside a cartouche, the Chinese characters representing the name Pearl Sydenstricker are inscribed. She had chosen to identify herself by the name and in the language of her early years. She had always disliked the name Pearl Buck, and she had never thought of herself as Pearl Walsh. If there happened to be an afterlife, she wanted to meet it under her own name.

The controversy between Ted and the family did not end with Pearl's death. The will she had drafted and signed in 1971 directed that the major share of her assets and property, and most of the royalties from her books, were to be turned over to Creativity, Inc., and to the Pearl S. Buck Trust, both of which were controlled by Ted. The children brought suit in Rutland to contest these arrangements, charging that Ted had used "undue influence" to enrich himself at their expense. Edgar Walsh and several of his brothers and sisters testified; Ted did not appear. After deliberating for just over an hour, the jury found in favor of the family.[138]

Epilogue: Green Hills Farm

B Y AN EDIFYING COINCIDENCE, the National Women's Hall of Fame opened in August, 1973, just a few months after Pearl's death. The site chosen – appropriately – was Seneca Falls, New York, where the founding convention of the struggle for women's rights had taken place in 1848. Twenty women were inducted into the Hall of Fame on its opening day: political leaders Elizabeth Cady Stanton, Susan B. Anthony, and Eleanor Roosevelt; the aviator Amelia Earhart; Senator Margaret Chase Smith; nurse Clara Barton; Jane Addams, Helen Keller, and Harriet Tubman; physicians Elizabeth Blackwell, Helen Brooke Taussig, and Alice Hamilton; Marian Anderson; Helen Hayes; educator Mary McLeod Bethune; Mary Cassatt; Emily Dickinson; medical researcher Florence Sabin; environmentalist Rachel Carson. And Pearl S. Buck.

It is a proud, distinguished company of women. And – as this biography has, I trust, demonstrated in abundant detail – Pearl had fully earned her place in it. Whatever the subsequent vagaries of her reputation, she had compiled a list of accomplishments that makes her eighty years seem brief. She also left a legacy of literary and philanthropic work that continues to change lives around the world.

Today, more than two decades after her death, Green Hills Farm serves as the headquarters of the Pearl S. Buck Foundation. The old stone house in which Pearl lived for most of her American years has been designated a National Landmark. It stands in the middle of sixty-five acres of rolling lawns and fields, and is maintained as a museum and memorial. Upwards of ten thousand people visit each year, guided by wonderfully well-informed volunteers (almost all of them women) through rooms that are crowded with furniture and art work and a hundred mementos of Pearl's private and public lives.

In the course of writing this book, I have spent a good deal of time in the house, reading through boxes of files, writing drafts of chapters, and (do I dare to confess it?) trying to make some sort of contact with the woman who spent so many years here. I usually enter through the kitchen, a large, airy room in which Pearl did a lot of her own cooking and supervised the staff who prepared the more elaborate meals for visiting dignitaries and for the reunions of her large family. Her *Oriental Cookbook,* a collection of her favorite Asian recipes, is prominently on display. A narrow archway connects the kitchen with the dining room, where two full-size tables are surrounded by sideboards and chairs in several miscellaneous styles. One of Pearl's prized possessions, the teapot Carie used in Chinkiang, reposes on top of an antique wooden cupboard.

The living room is large enough for both a Steinway grand piano and an organ, along with a half-dozen well-worn couches and chairs. The walls are decorated with Chinese calligraphy on paper and cloth, a portrait of Pearl herself, and two landscape paintings by Pearl's neighbor, American impressionist Edward Redfield. On the far side of the living room, four steps lead down to the first of the two libraries Pearl added to the house. The furnishings here include "the *Good Earth* desk," as the volunteers call it, on which Pearl wrote her most famous novel, and which she had shipped to Pennsylvania from China in the mid-1930s.

The walls of both libraries are lined with books – five thousand in all – an eclectic, polyglot collection that reflects Pearl's immensely wide interests. Along with the books she bought – novels, histories, travelogues, biographies, anthologies of poetry and plays – the collection also includes the hundreds of volumes she received from authors and publishers, eager for a commercially useful comment. On the second floor, at the top of the main staircase, lies an annex, which the volunteer guides call the "trophy room." Here the gold Nobel Prize medal shares space with the scores of other awards and prizes Pearl earned, including the doctoral robes from a dozen honorary degree ceremonies and the keys to fifty cities around the world.

In the hallway that connects the trophy room to Pearl's large bedroom, several glass cases contain an assortment of Chinese objects: silk robes, jade carvings and porcelain vases, bronze figurines and calligraphy scrolls. The most arresting item is a pair of tiny embroidered shoes, made to adorn the bound, crushed feet of a nineteenth-century Chinese woman. Pearl kept these cruelly beautiful objects near her as a constant reminder of the pain that power routinely inflicts on the weak. In a sense, her whole career as a writer and activist is summed up in those lovely, barbaric shoes.

Across a sunny breezeway from the main house, visitors can walk through a second, smaller stone building containing the two adjoining offices in which Pearl and Richard worked through their years of partnership. Pearl's office, the larger one, commands a handsome view of her property, including her gardens and a large pond at the bottom of a gently sloping hill. Through a door in the back of her office, Pearl could reach the greenhouses she had built to keep her supplied with flowers throughout the year. The office is decorated with a poster-size copy of the commemorative U.S. stamp issued in Pearl's honor in 1985, and several of the plaster sculptures she made – quite competent likenesses of her children.

Green Hills Farm's old barn, just a few paces from the main house, has been renovated and contains the foundation's gift shop; it is filled with Pearl Buck books and souvenirs and an assortment of Asian pottery and silk and lacquerware. The proceeds from the gift shop and from the house tours support the foundation's work with children around the world. The barn, now called the Cultural Center, is also the site for art exhibits, chamber concerts, and ceremonial dinners. Twenty national flags, representing all the countries in which the foundation works – South Korea, the Philippines, Thailand, Vietnam, India, China, the United States, and a dozen others – decorate the main room.

Forty yards from the barn stands the only new building on the property, a two-story cluster of offices that house the foundation's administrative staff and meeting rooms. Several years ago, Welcome House and the Pearl S. Buck Foundation merged, ending a quarter-century of division. (Pearl would have approved; the disputes of the 1960s and 1970s are today only the material of antiquarian gossip.) A combined staff supervises thousands of sponsored foster children and a hundred adoptions each year.

Open any filing cabinet and these sorts of stories tumble from the foundation's archives: Filipino Edward M., abandoned as an infant by his U.S. Air Force father, supported by the foundation for twenty years, and now practicing medicine in Olangapo City; Samantha R., an Indian orphan adopted as a baby into an Ohio family who recently finished her sophomore year of college; Jiyeon D., born in poverty in a Korean rice paddy, sponsored through college by the foundation and today a kindergarten teacher in Seoul; and Rewadee S., a malnourished little girl from the Khorat slums of Bangkok, who flourished under the foundation's care and became a nationally celebrated athlete.

To be sure, the thousands of young people with whom the Pearl S. Buck Foundation has worked make up only a tiny fraction of the world's children in need. The appalling statistics I cited in the preface to this book – World Health Organization data on childhood mortality – indicate that more boys and girls are born into poverty every day than the foundation can reach in a year. Despite the good intentions and good work of hundreds of agencies like the foundation, and despite the sentimental rhetoric of politicians in both hemispheres, children everywhere are hostage to economic and cultural systems that victimize them in all sorts of ways. For the world's poorest children, life has probably gotten worse rather than better over the past two decades.

Ten-year-old girls and boys work on carpets and running shoes in factories in Pakistan, Malaysia, and Kenya, while others are sold as prostitutes in Bangkok and Manila, or die from drugs in Philadelphia and Detroit. Thousands of Brazilian street children have been murdered by police, and sectarian, ethnic, and political violence in former Yugoslavia, Northern Ireland, and Cambodia has killed thousands more. Many experts now regard violence as the most serious health risk that the world's children face.

Pearl Buck tried to improve the odds for these children, as well as for women, racial minorities, the disabled — all of those who are put at risk by conspiracies of circumstance and prejudice. "I am," she once wrote, "a quiet woman by nature, unless oppressed by what I consider injustice. Then I become, I am told, excruciatingly articulate."' "Excruciatingly" is a nice touch: a glance at Pearl's indefatigable agitation for human rights from the exhausted viewpoint of the hundreds of politicians, businessmen, editors, and social workers who took the brunt of her letters, speeches, op-ed essays, and personal visits.

Pearl's fiction, too, was often concerned with inequality, injustice, and the role that chance plays in determining human outcomes. She was repeatedly drawn to the uneven struggle waged by ordinary people against the immense forces of nature and politics that dominate their lives. A participant in some of the most tumultuous upheavals of the century, she staged the results in her novels and stories, tracing the changes that accompanied the contest between tradition and innovation, between the past and the future.

The Good Earth was only the second of over seventy books that Pearl wrote, but the novel's main characters and its thematic design proved to be typical. Wang Lung and O-lan represent the efforts of commonplace men and women to cope with the tasks fate has assigned them, who erect makeshift barriers between themselves and necessity. Dominated by the cultural and political burdens of the past, Pearl's characters are tossed about by war and famine and unpredictable contingency — including an occasional bit of good luck. An uncertain future looms in front of them, by turns menacing and filled with promise.

Pearl's fiction gave voice to those who had not been heard, and succeeded in credibly dramatizing people and places that had been unknown and alien to most of her readers. She had, that is to say, a gift for making the strange seem familiar. The strongest fiction, on the other hand, accepts the more difficult task of making the familiar seem strange, of renovating and revitalizing the scenes and clichés of daily human intercourse. This requires a gift that Pearl did not have. Her mind was more attuned to facts than inventive. As I draw near the end of this book, I am tempted to the concluding judgment that her best work, by and large, was probably her nonfiction: the biographies of her parents, her own memoirs, her lively, argumentative essays on race and war and gender.

In her fiction, she was most comfortable when she was telling documentary and semi-documentary stories. She frequently used her novels as political and educational instruments, exchanging the challenges of novelistic art for the easier satisfactions of melodrama, propaganda, and protest. Her ambitions as a writer were hobbled by her certitude; fiction, in general, thrives better in an atmosphere of doubt than dogmatism. Still, her achievements as a writer remain considerable – surely more notable than her virtually complete neglect by scholars and critics would imply.

WHILE I WAS WRITING these final pages, I came across a remark of John Updike's that is calculated to shrivel the soul of any biographer. Reviewing a recent book on Graham Greene, Updike asked: "In an age increasingly reluctant to read anything but E-mail, why do biographies of literary practitioners pile up? These great scholastic mounds of summarized writings, faded gossip, and reconstructed travel schedules seem monuments in a perfect desert waste. . . ."[2] After I stopped cringing at the phrase "scholastic mounds," I tried to reflect usefully on Updike's question. Why do biographies – literary and otherwise – hold an incontrovertibly high rank in the contemporary imagination, and in the marketplace as well? Surely curiosity is one explanation. All of us want to know more about other selves: those Selves that have endured, triumphantly or perhaps just regressively, amid the detractions of deconstructors and poststructuralists.

Surely another explanation is the universal appeal of stories and storytelling. In every culture that we know about, people from childhood onward exhibit the same uncloyable fascination with the narratives that make up history, myth, fiction, memory, and biography. There are pleasures in hearing the episodes of any life in their sequence, and deeper pleasures in detecting the patterns that shape the incomprehensible welter of daily doings into a coherent, explanatory progress. Those patterns are confessedly fictional: Henry Adams rightly warned that chaos is the law of nature, logic merely the trap of the mind. Nonetheless, human beings thirst for meanings, and biography offers the gratifications of cause and effect.

In the end, I cannot explain Pearl Buck, cannot pierce the veil of mystery and accident that led the daughter of pious missionaries on a journey from obscurity and poverty to world fame and a lifelong campaign for justice. I have invented a couple of fairly simple hypotheses, narrative armatures around which to wrap the events of her long life. I have argued that she was a secular, feminist missionary, who inherited a need for vocation from her father and a yearning for female emancipation from the example of her mother's sad defeats. I have also suggested that her commitment to interracial solidarity can be traced to her experience as a white person in a non-white society. Finally, I have proposed that her anguish over her daughter Carol's disability lies at the center of her emotional development as an adult.

All of these conjectures are modest and unchallenging, plausible and perhaps even correct. But they are precisely conjectures, elaborated to fill the empty space between act and explanation. "Read no history," Disraeli famously said;

"read nothing but biography, for that is life without theory." What a marvelously preposterous statement. Lives may repel theories, but biographies depend on them. My own theory, which renders Pearl as an evangelist for equality, has become the lens through which I have tried to make her visible.

I am motivated by personal ambition; I want nothing less than to force the rewriting of American cultural history to include some acknowledgment of Pearl Buck's life and work. But I also feel indebted to her, and this book represents a partial payment. Another of the stories squirreled away in the Pearl S. Buck Foundation files tells of a two-year-old orphan named Kim Kyung Nim – Jennifer Kyung Conn – who entered my life twenty years ago, malnourished and covered with sores. Jennifer came from an orphanage with a 50 percent mortality rate; the children either found a home or they died. Today, she is a graduate of Smith College, an accomplished cook and writer who works for a foundation in New York City that assists the homeless. This book began with Jennifer, though I did not realize that twenty years ago, and I would never have known her except for that extraordinary woman, Pearl Buck, who brought us together.

Notes

Preface: Rediscovering Pearl Buck

1. Cary Nelson, *Repression and Recovery: Modern American Poetry and the Politics of Cultural Memory, 1910–1945* (Madison: University of Wisconsin Press, 1989), p. 51. Students of other national literatures have, of course, also argued that cultural history ought to incorporate popular books that have lurked outside the traditional canon. Robert Darnton, for example, reconstructing the textual prelude to the French Revolution, has remarked that literary history is "an artificial construct, passed on and reworked from generation to generation. 'Minor' authors and 'major' best-sellers inevitably get lost in the shuffle. We do not expect the best-sellers of our own day to be read two hundred years from now. But do we not think that literary history should take account of the literature that reached the most people?" Darnton, *The Forbidden Best-Sellers of Pre-Revolutionary France* (New York: W. W. Norton, 1994), p. 68.
2. Lawrence W. Levine, *The Unpredictable Past: Explorations in American Cultural History* (New York: Oxford University Press, 1993), p. 299.
3. John Hersey, letter to the present writer (January 20, 1991).
4. Maxine Hong Kingston, comments at Randolph-Macon Woman's College (March 27, 1992). Not everyone will agree with Kingston's high estimate of Pearl Buck's representations of China. Nonetheless, Pearl Buck's stories and essays ought to be evaluated on their own terms, not prejudged by resort to a vulgar essentialism that equates cultural authority with ethnic heritage or surname. Apparently ignoring this elementary protocol, Edmund White declared not long ago: "each of us can attest that . . . Maxine Hong Kingston knows more about China than did Pearl Buck." On the contrary, although Kingston has written brilliantly about her experiences as a Chinese-American, she has published almost nothing about China, a country in which she has never lived, and for which she does not presume to speak. Ironically, in short, while Edmund White scorns Pearl Buck and turns to Maxine Hong Kingston for reliable reports on China, Kingston herself has turned to Pearl Buck. Edmund White, "The Politics of Identity," *New York Times* (December 21, 1993), p. A27.
5. Toni Morrison, speech at the Pearl S. Buck Foundation (September 1, 1994).
6. James Thomson, "Why Doesn't Pearl Buck Get Respect?," *Philadelphia Inquirer* (July 24, 1992), p. A15.
7. James Michener, interview with Donn Rogosin (March, 1991).
8. Liu Haiping, interview with the present writer in Nanjing (May 25, 1993).

Chapter 1: Missionary Childhood

1. Andrew L. March, *The Idea of China: Myth and Theory in Geographic Thought* (New York: Praeger, 1974), p. 23.
2. The starting point for any study of the Protestant mission enterprise in China remains Kenneth Scott Latourette, *A History of Christian Missions in China* (New York: Russell & Russell, 1967); Latourette's book was first published in 1929.
3. John Hersey's *The Call* (New York: Knopf, 1985) is undoubtedly the best fictional account of Protestant missionary work in China. Though Hersey's hero, David Treadup, is a YMCA organizer, not an ordained minister, his lineage, motives, and career are brilliantly typical of the men and women who followed an evangelical vocation.
4. Pearl S. Buck, *Fighting Angel: Portrait of a Soul* (New York: John Day Company, 1936), pp. 12–13. Absalom is called Andrew throughout the book; Carie, on the other hand, remains Carie.
5. She did the same in writing about her husband John Lossing Buck's "Work" of reforming Chinese agriculture.
6. The accounts of Absalom and Carie Sydenstricker presented here are necessarily indebted to the biographies that Pearl wrote of them. This book's reconstruction of Pearl's parents has also been supplemented by an analysis of Absalom's published writing and by conversations with Pearl's younger sister, Grace Yaukey.
7. The foreign mission boards of most Protestant denominations also insisted that male missionaries marry before taking up overseas assignment.
8. Pearl S. Buck, *The Exile* (New York: John Day Company, 1936), p. 47.
9. Buck, *The Exile*, p. 88.
10. Absalom Sydenstricker, *Our Life and Work in China* (Parsons, WV: McClain Printing Company, 1978), p. 7.
11. The missionaries were not very attentive to the events that surrounded them. For most of them, the day-to-day reality of China was less important than their evangelistic mission. This conclusion is substantiated at length in Sidney A. Forsythe, *An American Missionary Community in China, 1895–1905* (Cambridge, MA: Harvard University Press, 1971).
12. Buck, *Fighting Angel*, p. 76.
13. Looking back in 1917 at his early days as a Presbyterian missionary in China, Samuel Woodbridge wrote: "Only those who have lived in places where there is no Christian environment can understand fully the desolation and utter loneliness which come down on the soul like a pall of death, when dwelling alone in a large, unhealthy Chinese city, surrounded by indifferent or suspicious neighbors. . . ." *Fifty Years in China* (Richmond, VA: Presbyterian Committee of Publications, 1917), p. 37.
14. The essential reference guide for using the magazine is Kathleen Lodwick, *The Chinese Recorder Index: A Guide to Christian Missions in China, 1867–1941*, two volumes (Wilmington, DE: Scholarly Resources, Inc., 1986).
15. The quoted phrases come from an interview conducted by Donn Rogosin with Grace Sydenstricker Yaukey (February 26, 1990).
16. Cited in John K. Fairbank, *The United States and China*, fourth edition, enlarged (Cambridge, MA: Harvard University Press, 1983), p. 8.
17. Tu Wei-ming, "Cultural China: The Periphery as the Center," in *The Living Tree: The Changing Meaning of Being Chinese Today*, a special issue of *Daedalus*, issued as Volume 120, Number 2 of the *Proceedings* of the American Academy of Arts and Sciences (Spring, 1991), p. 3.
18. Jerome Ch'en, *China and the West: Society and Culture, 1815–1937* (London: Hutchinson, 1979), p. 26.

19. Warren I. Cohen, *America's Response to China: An Interpretative History of Sino-American Relations,* second edition (New York: John Wiley & Sons, 1980), pp. 2–3.

20. Jonathan Spence, *The Search for Modern China* (New York: W. W. Norton, 1990), p. 157.

21. Spence, *The Search for Modern China,* p. 158.

22. Christian notions of original sin, the afterlife, and the equality of all persons before God were also offensive to the Confucian elite.

23. The passage, from Santayana's *Dominations and Powers,* is cited in Arthur Schlesinger, Jr., "The Missionary Enterprise and Theories of Imperialism," in John K. Fairbank, ed., *The Missionary Enterprise in China and America* (Cambridge, MA: Harvard University Press, 1974), p. 361.

24. Woodbridge, *Fifty Years in China,* p. 38; Latourette, *A History of Christian Missions in China,* p. 470.

25. Ch'en, *China and the West,* p. 142.

26. Stuart Creighton Miller, "Ends and Means: Missionary Justification of Force in Nineteenth Century China," in Fairbank, ed., *The Missionary Enterprise in China and America,* p. 281.

27. Wu T'ing-fang, "China's Relation with the West," AAPSS, *The Foreign Policy of the US,* Addresses . . . at the Annual Meeting (Philadelphia, 1899), cited in Arthur Schlesinger, Jr., "The Missionary Enterprise and Theories of Imperialism," in Fairbank, ed., *The Missionary Enterprise in China and America,* p. 366.

28. John K. Fairbank, *Chinese-American Interactions: A Historical Summary* (New Brunswick, NJ: Rutgers University Press, 1975), p. 24.

29. Cited, from a letter to an unnamed recipient, in Theodore F. Harris with Pearl S. Buck, *Pearl S. Buck: A Biography,* volume two, *Her Philosophy as Expressed in Her Letters* (New York: John Day Company, 1971), p. 266.

30. One scholar has estimated that "by 1949 there were 936,000 baptized [church] members and 2,963 clergy, 68 percent of them Chinese and the rest foreign missionaries." Donald MacInnis, *Religion in China Today: Policy and Practice* (Maryknoll, NY: Orbis Books, 1989), p. 313.

31. The early period of this Social Gospel intervention is discussed in Irwin T. Hyatt, Jr., "Protestant Missions in China, 1877–1890: The Institutionalization of Good Works," in Kwang-Ching Liu, ed., *American Missionaries in China: Papers from Harvard Seminars* (Cambridge, MA: Harvard University Press, 1966), pp. 93–128.

32. Ch'en, *China and the West,* p. 380.

33. John K. Fairbank, "Introduction: The Many Faces of Protestant Missions in China and the United States," in Fairbank, ed., *The Missionary Enterprise in China and America,* p. 2.

34. Hersey, *The Call,* p. 245.

35. These three articles appeared in the March, April, and June, 1887 issues of the *Recorder.*

36. Absalom Sydenstricker, "Romanizing the Official Dialect," *Chinese Recorder,* Vol. XIX (January, 1888), p. 37.

37. Absalom Sydenstricker, review of Mr. John's Mandarin translation of the Gospel, *Chinese Recorder,* Vol. XIX (April, 1888), p. 184.

38. In 1889, Absalom published a small textbook, *An Exposition of the Construction and Idioms of Chinese Sentences as Found in Colloquial Mandarin* (Shanghai: American Presbyterian Press). Divided into nineteen chapters, the book was intended "for the use of learners of the language." A review in the July, 1889 issue of the *Chinese Recorder,* signed by a "Friendly Critic," was generally favorable, including praise of Absalom's "courage and industry."

39. Nora Stirling, *Pearl Buck: A Woman in Conflict* (Piscataway, NJ: New Century Publishers, 1983), p. 11.

40. Buck, *The Exile,* p. 125.
41. Much in Carie's experience was typical of other women who went to China as missionaries or missionary wives. See Jane Hunter, *The Gospel of Gentility: American Women Missionaries in Turn-of-the-Century China* (New Haven, CT: Yale University Press, 1984). Hunter makes several references to Carie throughout her study.
42. Grace Yaukey, interview with the present writer (June 5, 1991).
43. Grace Yaukey, interview with Donn Rogosin (February 26, 1990).
44. Buck, *Fighting Angel* p. 210.
45. Buck, *The Exile,* p. 280.
46. Buck, *The Exile,* p. 283.
47. Latourette, *A History of Christian Missions in China,* p. 64.
48. Buck, *The Exile,* p. 142.
49. Absalom Sydenstricker, letter to the *Chinese Recorder* (July, 1887), p. 286.
50. See Absalom's article in the July, 1889 issue of the *Chinese Recorder,* "Preaching to the Chinese by Similarities and Contrasts."
51. Pearl S. Buck, "Advice to Unborn Novelists," *Saturday Review of Literature* (March 2, 1935), p. 513.
52. Absalom Sydenstricker, "Jesus as a Teacher and Trainer," *Chinese Recorder* (September, 1893), p. 418.
53. See John K. Fairbank, "Introduction: The Many Faces of Protestant Missions in China and the United States," in Fairbank, ed., *The Missionary Enterprise in China and America,* pp. 1–19.
54. Buck, *Fighting Angel,* p. 74.
55. Pearl S. Buck, "The Giants Are Gone," *Asia* (November, 1936), p. 712.
56. Pearl S. Buck, *My Several Worlds: A Personal Record* (New York: John Day Company, 1954), p. 10.
57. W. E. B. Du Bois, *The Souls of Black Folk* (Millwood, NY: Kraus-Thomson Organization, 1973 [1903]), p. 3.
58. This information comes from an article, "Two Little Missionaries," by Pearl's older brother, Edgar, which appeared in the magazine *Children's Missionary* (June, 1896).
59. Richard J. Walsh, "Introduction" to Pearl S. Buck, *The First Wife and Other Stories* (New York: John Day Company, 1933), p. 14.
60. Many years later, Pearl memorialized Tz'u-hsi twice, in a long and admiring sketch in her autobiography, *My Several Worlds* (1954), and then in a full-scale historical account in one of her better novels, *Imperial Woman* (1956). See Chapter 9, pp. 338–41, of this volume.
61. Quoted in Spence, *The Search for Modern China,* p. 232. Spence provides a good brief account of the Boxer Uprising. See also Joseph Esherick, *The Origins of the Boxer Uprising* (Berkeley: University of California Press, 1987).
62. Cited in Barbara Tuchman, *Stilwell and the American Experience in China, 1911–1945* (New York: Macmillan, 1971), p. 33.
63. Buck, *My Several Worlds,* p. 49.
64. Stirling, *Pearl Buck,* p. 12. The story has been confirmed by Grace Yaukey, in an interview with the present writer.
65. For demographic data, see Ronald Takaki, *Strangers from a Different Shore: A History of Asian Americans* (New York: Penguin Books, 1990), p. 65.
66. Robert McClellan, *The Heathen Chinee: A Study of American Attitudes Toward China, 1890–1905* (Columbus: Ohio State University Press, 1971).
67. For a discouraging survey of the history of anti-Chinese bigotry in America, see Cheng-Tsu Wu, ed., *"Chink!" A Documentary History of Anti-Chinese Prejudice in America* (New York: World Publishing Company, 1972).
68. McClellan, *The Heathen Chinee,* p. 46.
69. Elodie Hogan, "Hills and Corners of San Francisco," *Californian,* V (December, 1893),

pp. 63–71. "Slumming parties," as they were called, were a fairly commonplace turn-of-the-century phenomenon. Chinatown was only one of the sights that tourists wanted to see; New York's Bowery, Hester Street, and Little Italy were other favorite destinations. Some of the literary evidence can be found in Edgar Fawcett's *The Evil That Men Do* (1889), H. H. Boyeson's *Social Strugglers* (1893), and James Sullivan's *Tenement Tales of New York* (1895). Reformer Jacob Riis shared the queasiness of his contemporaries when he reported on New York's Chinatown in his landmark exposé, *How the Other Half Lives: Studies Among the Tenements of New York* (1890). Among other things, he noted the network of criminality that held the Chinese ghetto together. According to Riis, "A constant stream of plotting and counter-plotting makes up the round of Chinese social and political existence" (New York: Hill and Wang, 1957 [1890]), p. 74.

70. *The Galaxy*, 1867, vol. 4, p. 1881, cited in Loren Eiseley, *Darwin's Century: Evolution and the Men Who Discovered It* (Garden City, NY: Doubleday, 1961), p. 264.

71. McClellan, *The Heathen Chinee*, pp. 6, 22.

72. Cited in Richard Madsen, *China and the American Dream: A Moral Inquiry* (Berkeley: University of California Press, 1995), p. 30. Apparently, the authors of this Maryknoll prayer were either unaware of Mark Twain's anti-imperialist essay, "To the Person Sitting in Darkness," or had missed the point.

73. Ernest May, *American Imperialism* (New York: Atheneum, 1968), p. 3.

74. H. H. Powers, "The War as a Suggestion of Manifest Destiny," *Annals of the American Academy of Political and Social Science* (September, 1898), p. 173.

75. The "missionary mind" would affect America's China policy for decades. Describing American support for Chiang Kai-shek in the late 1940s, John Melby has suggested that "the missionary movement has had more influence in shaping American attitudes toward China than any other single factor; and it paid handsome dividends to the Kuomintang." John F. Melby, *The Mandate of Heaven* (Toronto: University of Toronto Press, 1968), p. 136.

76. Cited in W. A. Swanberg, *Luce and His Empire* (New York: Charles Scribner's Sons, 1972), p. 20. McKinley's famous remark indicates that he either did not know that the Filipinos had been Roman Catholic for three hundred years or did not consider Catholicism to be authentically Christian.

77. James Reed, *The Missionary Mind and American East Asia Policy, 1911–1915* (Cambridge, MA: Harvard University Press, 1983), p. 100. John King Fairbank said that he wanted to "get the study of missionaries developed to a point where he may be able to see how the categorical imperative to reform others formed part of our China approach." Quoted in Paul M. Evans, *John Fairbank and the American Understanding of Modern China* (New York: Basil Blackwell, 1988), p. 320.

78. Forty years later, Pearl could still complain that "the rich and fascinating history of China has scarcely been touched for western readers and students. It is an absurdity that four thousand years of living by almost a quarter of the human race should in our academic histories be crowded into a few pages which more often than not give no emphasis to matters of real importance in Chinese history. The cause of this situation has, of course, been simple ignorance. Even eminent western historians have been too ignorant to value properly the importance of Chinese history in its relation to all history." Pearl S. Buck, "Asia Book-Shelf," *Asia* (May, 1941), p. 261.

79. Typically, the couple of "facts" about the Great Wall that have been repeated from one schoolbook to another have been fanciful. The wall is not visible from the moon; it was not constructed all at once in the reign of the first Chin emperor some two thousand years ago; it is not in fact and has never been continuous across China. See Arthur Waldron, *The Great Wall of China: From History to Myth* (New York: Cambridge University Press, 1990).

80. Theodore Roosevelt to B. I. Wheeler (June 17, 1905), cited in Howard K. Beale,

Theodore Roosevelt and the Rise of America to World Power (Baltimore: Johns Hopkins University Press, 1956), p. 174.

81. Indeed, until quite recently, many American scholars specializing in Asia continued to be persons with missionary connections of some sort.

82. Ch'en, *China and the West*, pp. 120–121.

83. The term "legendary" is used by John K. Fairbank, in his "Introduction: The Place of Protestant Writings in China's Cultural History," in Suzanne Wilson Barnett and John King Fairbank, eds., *Christianity in China: Early Protestant Missionary Writings* (Cambridge, MA: Harvard University Press, 1985), p. 17.

84. Charles W. Hayford, "Chinese and American Characteristics: Arthur H. Smith and His China Book," in Barnett and Fairbank, eds., *Christianity in China: Early Protestant Missionary Writings*, p. 159.

85. Mark Elvin, "The Inner World of 1830," in *The Living Tree: The Changing Meaning of Being Chinese Today*, a special issue of *Daedalus,* issued as Volume 120, Number 2 of the *Proceedings* of the American Academy of Arts and Sciences (Spring, 1991), p. 50.

86. Hayford, "Chinese and American Characteristics," p. 160.

87. "In considering the present condition of China, which is much what it was three centuries ago, it is well to look upon the changes through which we ourselves have passed, for thus only can we arrive at a just comparison." Arthur H. Smith, *Chinese Characteristics* (New York: Fleming H. Revell, 1894), p. 143.

88. Nearly sixty years ago, Robert Coltman estimated Smith's strengths and weaknesses in an article in *Asia* magazine. After acknowledging that Smith's "powers of observation were incisive and penetrating," Coltman adds that Smith's "racial and spiritual insularity was responsible for some shocking and damaging nonsense." Coltman, "Asia Book-Shelf," *Asia* (July, 1935), p. 448.

89. Hayford, "Chinese and American Characteristics," p. xx; see *Chinese Recorder*, 56: 299–305 (1925).

90. On this important missionary, see Peter Duus, "Science and Salvation in China: The Life and Work of W. A. P. Martin (1827–1916)," in Kwang-Ching Liu, ed., *American Missionaries in China*, pp. 11–41. Martin and Absalom Sydenstricker were among those Christians who saw "the hand of God" in the successive humiliations of China by Western and Japanese forces. The phrase, which occurs in Martin's book *The Awakening of China* (1910), is quoted in Warren I. Cohen, *America's Response to China: An Interpretative History of Sino-American Relations*, second edition (New York: John Wiley & Sons, 1980), p. 28.

91. The Sydenstrickers' departure and return were noted in the *Chinese Recorder*, in the August, 1901, and October, 1902 issues.

92. Buck, *My Several Worlds*, p. 59.

93. Absalom Sydenstricker, "The Importance of the Direct Phase of Mission Work," *Chinese Recorder*, Volume XLI (June, 1910), pp. 387–394.

94. *Chinese Recorder*, Vol XL (January, 1909), p. 56.

95. Grace Yaukey, interview with Donn Rogosin (February, 1990).

96. In the 1920s, the Kuling properties were expropriated from their foreign owners. Subsequently, the entire settlement was used by Chiang Kai-shek as a vacation headquarters.

97. The February, 1912 issue of the *Chinese Recorder* included a summary report on famine relief work in north-central China throughout the 1907–1911 period. Relief funds were administered by a special committee formed in 1907. "With some changes in the personnel, that Committee has continued . . . in its general philanthropic work in China." When the new famine relief work began in 1911, the committee "cooperated heartily with the Central China Famine Relief Committee in the distributions." Absalom Sydenstricker served on this committee, which also built orphanages, twenty-nine by the end of 1911. In his memoir, Absalom made it clear that the main purpose of famine relief was to clear the way for the Gospel message (*Our Life and Work*, p. 20).

98. Grace Yaukey, interview with the present writer (May 10, 1991).
99. Grace Yaukey, interview with Donn Rogosin (February 26, 1990).
100. At this time, the cost of a year at Wellesley, including room and board and tuition fees, would have been about $600; the expense at Randolph-Macon would have been a little more than half that amount. Financial aid was, of course, practically non-existent.
101. Pearl S. Buck, "Asia Book-Shelf," *Asia* (April, 1940), p. 222.
102. The International Settlement and French Concession, as it was more formally known, began on 150 acres of marshy land that had been granted to foreigners in 1843, when Shanghai was opened to commerce following the Opium War.
103. Buck, *My Several Worlds*, pp. 69–70.
104. Patricia Buckley Ebrey, "Introduction," in Rubie S. Watson and Patricia Buckley Ebrey, eds., *Marriage and Inequality in Chinese Society* (Berkeley: University of California Press, 1991), p. 15.
105. James Watson, "Transactions in People: The Chinese Market in Slaves, Servants, and Heirs," in James Watson, ed., *Asian and African Systems of Slavery* (Oxford: Basil Blackwell, 1980), p. 223.
106. Ch'en, *China and the West*, pp. 208–209. Edgar Snow's first wife, Helen Foster Snow, confirmed her late husband's view of Shanghai in an interview with the present writer (November 15, 1991). In the early decades of the century, a library of books was published on the exploitation of women in Shanghai; some had a serious scholarly or reforming purpose, others were mere exercises in prurience.
107. See Gail Hershatter, "Prostitution and the Market in Women in Early Twentieth-Century Shanghai," in Watson and Ebry, eds., *Marriage and Inequality in Chinese Society*, pp. 256–285. Hershatter briefly discusses the Door of Hope. See also F. L. Hawks Pott, *A Short History of Shanghai* (Shanghai: Kelly & Walsh, Ltd., 1928), pp. 191–192.
108. Another important relief agency was the Slave Refuge, founded by Mrs. F. R. Graves, which eventually merged with the Door of Hope.
109. The observation was made by Sidney Gamble in his journalistic book *Peking: A Social History* (1922) and quoted in Sue Gronewold, *Beautiful Merchandise: Prostitution in China, 1860–1936* (New York: Haworth Press, 1982), p. 83.

Chapter 2: New Worlds

1. The data come from Barbara Miller Solomon, *In the Company of Educated Women: A History of Women and Higher Education in America* (New Haven, CT: Yale University Press, 1985), pp. 44, 63, and 64.
2. This finding, by Margaret Rossiter, is cited in Solomon, *In the Company of Educated Women*, pp. 82–83.
3. On the history of women's higher education, see Solomon, *In the Company of Educated Women;* Helen Lefkowitz Horowitz, *Alma Mater: Design and Experience in the Women's Colleges from Their Nineteenth-Century Beginnings to the 1930s* (New York: Knopf, 1984); and *Women's History and Women's Education*, essays by Natalie Zemon Davis and Joan Wallach Scott (Northampton, MA: Smith College, 1985).
4. Mary Caroline Crawford, *The College Girl of America* (Boston: L. C. Page & Company, 1904), pp. 155–156.
5. Cited in Solomon, *In the Company of Educated Women*, p. 49. An abundance of similar declarations can be found in Horowitz, *Alma Mater*.
6. Pearl S. Buck, *Fighting Angel* (New York: John Day Company, 1936), p. 208.
7. Joy Elizabeth Abbot has compiled a useful summary of Pearl Sydenstricker's Randolph-Macon career in her unpublished paper "Years Around the Even Post: Pearl S. Buck and Her Alma Mater."
8. Pearl S. Buck, *My Several Worlds* (New York: John Day Company, 1954), p. 91.

9. Solomon, *In the Company of Educated Women*, p. 112.
10. There were a few Asian students enrolled at Randolph-Macon during its early years, including a Chinese woman who graduated a few years ahead of Pearl. Blacks were excluded until the 1960s.
11. Quoted in Nora Stirling, *Pearl Buck: A Woman in Conflict* (Piscataway, NJ: New Century Publishers, 1983), p. 24.
12. Henry Lee, "Pearl S. Buck: Spiritual Descendant of Tom Paine," *Saturday Review of Literature*, 25 (December 5, 1942), p. 18.
13. Pearl Sydenstricker to Mrs. Edmunds (June 14, 1911), Randolph-Macon Woman's College archives.
14. Buck, *My Several Worlds*, p. 96.
15. Solomon, *In the Company of Educated Women*, p. 123.
16. Grace Yaukey, interview with Nora Stirling (n.d.), Randolph-Macon Woman's College archives.
17. Buck, *My Several Worlds*, p. 99.
18. Frederic Wakeman, *The Fall of Imperial China* (New York: Free Press, 1975), p. 225. On the Revolution of 1911, see also Jack Gray, *Rebellions and Revolutions: China from the 1800s to the 1980s* (New York: Oxford University Press, 1990), pp. 139–151; and John King Fairbank, *The United States and China*, fourth edition (Cambridge, MA: Harvard University Press, 1983), pp. 210–219.
19. Robert A. Scalapino and George T. Yu, *Modern China and Its Revolutionary Process: Recurrent Challenges to the Traditional Order, 1850–1920* (Berkeley: University of California Press, 1985), p. 319.
20. Wuhan was actually a cluster of three linked cities, a "tri-city" made up of Hankow, Hanyang, and Wuchang.
21. At the time he took over the presidency, Yuan expressed his skepticism of democracy: "I doubt whether the people of China are at the present time ripe for a republic. . . . The adoption of a limited monarchy would bring conditions back to normal and would bring stability much more rapidly than that end could be obtained through any experimental form of government, unsuited to the genius of the Chinese people or to the present conditions in China." Quoted in Sih-gung Cheng, *Modern China, a Political Study* (Oxford: Clarendon Press, 1919), p. 16.
22. Jonathan D. Spence, *The Gate of Heavenly Peace: The Chinese and Their Revolution, 1895–1980* (New York: Viking Press, 1981), p. 106.
23. Franz Kafka, a shrewd if eccentric student of the Chinese people, made this point in the story fragment "The Great Wall of China." The narrator comments: if "one should draw the conclusion that in reality we have no Emperor, he would not be far from the truth. Over and over again, it must be repeated: There is perhaps no people more faithful to the Emperor than ours in the south, but the Emperor derives no advantage from our fidelity. True, the sacred dragon stands on the little column at the end of our village, and ever since the beginning of human memory it has breathed out its fiery breath in the direction of Pekin in token of homage – but Pekin itself is far stranger to the people in our village than the next world." Whatever allegorical purposes the story has, it also accurately describes the traditional attitude of China's village masses to the central authority. The translation is from Franz Kafka, *The Great Wall of China and Other Pieces*, translated by Willa and Edwin Muir (London: Secker and Warburg, 1946), pp. 92–93.
24. Quoted in Buck, *My Several Worlds*, p. 122.
25. Biographical information on John Lossing Buck comes in part from the following sources: Buck's unpublished autobiographical memoir, on file in the Cornell University archives; Jim Pugh, "J. Lossing Buck, American Missionary: The Application of Scientific Agriculture in China, 1915–1944," unpublished honors thesis (Swarthmore College, 1973); Randall E. Stross, *The Stubborn Earth: American Agriculturalists on Chinese*

Soil, 1898–1937 (Berkeley: University of California Press, 1986); Stirling, *Pearl Buck: A Woman in Conflict;* John Lossing Buck, *Development of Agricultural Economics at the University of Nanking, Nanking, China, 1920–1946* (Ithaca, NY: Cornell University, 1973); and an interview by the present writer with two of Lossing Buck's children, Paul Buck and Rosalind Buck (May 5, 1991).

26. For a survey of discussions of Lossing Buck's work, see Chapter 3, note 97.
27. The town was called Suchow An on most turn-of-the-century Western maps.
28. Copies of letters from J. Lossing Buck are located in the Nora Stirling papers, Randolph-Macon Woman's College archives.
29. Franklin Hiram King, *Farmers of Forty Centuries: Or Permanent Agriculture in China, Korea and Japan* (Emmaus, PA: Organic Gardening Press reprint, n.d.), p. 16.
30. King, *Farmers of Forty Centuries*, pp. 173–174.
31. Fairbank, *The United States and China*, p. 178; Jonathan Spence, *The Search for Modern China* (New York: W. W. Norton, 1990), p. 313.
32. Cited in Stross, *The Stubborn Earth*, p. 170.
33. Stross, *The Stubborn Earth*, p. 111.
34. J. Lossing Buck, "Agricultural Work of the American Presbyterian Mission at Nanhsuchow, Anhwei, China in 1919," *Chinese Recorder* (June, 1920), p. 414.
35. Pearl Sydenstricker to Emma Edmunds (April 17, 1917), Randolph-Macon Woman's College archives.
36. Stirling, *Pearl Buck: A Woman in Conflict*, p. 41.
37. Pearl S. Buck, *My Several Worlds* (New York: John Day Company, 1954), p. 129. Actually the marriage lasted for eighteen years.
38. The figure of Lossing Buck emerges only dimly from the pages of Pearl's several memoirs. He is never named in the four hundred pages of her most extended autobiography, *My Several Worlds*. Instead, he is identified throughout that book only under the chilly formula "the man in the house," an act of suppression that indicates the depth of Pearl's resentment. (Traditionally, Chinese men have referred to their wives as "the person [or woman] in the house." It is possible that Pearl Buck was adapting this formula as a signal of her discontent.)
39. Buck, *My Several Worlds*, p. 139.
40. When she began writing seriously, in 1920 or so, she claimed that she had "no one" to tell. "This was not secretiveness, for if there had been any one to tell I would surely have told. . . ." Buck, *My Several Worlds*, p. 176.
41. Buck, *My Several Worlds*, p. 323.
42. Pearl S. Buck to Emma Edmunds White (August 29, 1918), Randolph-Macon Woman's College archives.
43. Nora Stirling papers (n.d.), Randolph-Macon Woman's College archives.
44. Pearl S. Buck to Grace and Vincent Buck (March 15, 1919), Randolph-Macon Woman's College archives.
45. Pearl S. Buck to the Buck Family (February 2, 1918), Randolph-Macon Woman's College archives.
46. Pearl S. Buck to Grace and Vincent Buck (March 15, 1919), Randolph-Macon Woman's College archives.
47. Pearl S. Buck to Grace and Vincent Buck (March 15, 1919), Randolph-Macon Woman's College archives.
48. Pearl S. Buck to Mrs. Henry Sloan Coffin (December 12, 1918), Randolph-Macon Woman's College archives.
49. Nora Stirling papers, Randolph-Macon Woman's College archives.
50. Pearl S. Buck to Grace Buck (April 8, 1918), Randolph-Macon Woman's College archives.
51. Pearl S. Buck to Grace and Vincent Buck (October 10, 1918), Randolph-Macon Woman's College archives.

52. Grace Yaukey, interview with the present writer (May 10, 1991).
53. Pearl S. Buck to Grace and Vincent Buck (April 8, 1918), Randolph-Macon Woman's College archives.
54. Buck, *My Several Worlds*, p. 146.
55. John Lossing Buck, "Practical Plans for the Introduction of Agriculture into Our Primary and Middle Schools," *Chinese Recorder* (June, 1920), p. 309. Eventually, Chinese schools would incorporate extensive agricultural coursework. Both the Nationalists and the Communists recognized the practical necessity of improving farm productivity through university research.
56. John Lossing Buck, interview with Dr. G. P. Coleman (September 21, 1962), pp. 10–11; Cornell University archives.
57. When he had lived briefly in Nanjing, in 1915, Lossing had toured the city and written his family that in "certain portions . . . they are packed in like sardines."
58. Buck, *My Several Worlds*, p. 191.
59. Alice Tisdale Hobart, *Within the Walls of Nanking* (New York: Macmillan, n.d. [1928]), p. 86.
60. John Reisner, letter to Walter Clay Lowdermilk, quoted in Stross, *The Stubborn Earth*, pp. 107–108.
61. Stross, *The Stubborn Earth*, p. 162.
62. John Lossing Buck to Grace and Victor Buck (March 28, 1920), Randolph-Macon Woman's College archives.
63. John Lossing Buck to John Reisner (October 16, 1920), Yale Divinity School Archives.
64. Pearl S. Buck to Grace and Victor Buck (November 18, 1920), Randolph-Macon Woman's College archives.
65. Buck, *The Exile*, p. 307.
66. Pearl S. Buck, "The Angel," in *Today and Forever: Stories of China* (New York: John Day Company, 1941), p. 39. The story originally appeared in the April, 1937 issue of *Woman's Home Companion*.
67. Buck, *My Several Worlds*, p. 160.
68. Spence, *The Search for Modern China*, p. 315.
69. James Robert Hightower, *Topics in Chinese Literature*, revised edition (Cambridge, MA: Harvard University Press, 1962), p. 114.
70. Leo Ou-fan Lee, *The Romantic Generation of Modern Chinese Writers* (Cambridge, MA: Harvard University Press, 1973), p. 3.
71. Buck, *My Several Worlds*, p. 124.
72. Chow Tse-tsung, *The May Fourth Movement* (Cambridge, MA: Harvard University Press, 1960), chapter 11; Fairbank, *The United States and China*, pp. 231–235.
73. Among recent studies of this subject, see Vera Schwarcz, *The Chinese Enlightenment: Intellectuals and the Legacy of the May Fourth Movement of 1919* (Berkeley: University of California Press, 1986). See also Bonnie S. McDougall, *The Introduction of Western Literary Theories into Modern China, 1919–1925* (Tokyo: Centre for East Asian Cultural Studies, 1971), pp. 4–5.
74. Vera Schwarcz, "No Solace from Lethe: History, Memory, and Cultural Identity in Twentieth-Century China," in *The Living Tree: The Changing Meaning of Being Chinese Today*, a special issue of *Daedalus*, issued as Volume 120, Number 2 of the *Proceedings of the American Academy of Arts and Sciences* (Spring, 1991), p. 99. In this essay and in her book *The Chinese Enlightenment*, Schwarcz emphasizes the complexity and even the internal contradictions of the May Fourth movement.

Schwarcz is among the many writers who have stressed the significance of May Fourth in China's modern search for a political and cultural identity. The students who occupied Tiananmen Square in the "democracy spring" of 1989, for example, explicitly identified themselves as the descendants of the May Fourth dissidents; they emphasized that their protest marked the seventieth anniversary of those earlier events. See Orville

Schell, *Mandate of Heaven: A New Generation of Entrepreneurs, Dissidents, Bohemians, and Technocrats Lays Claim to China's Future* (New York: Simon & Schuster, 1994), pp. 15–32.

75. Absalom Sydenstricker, *Our Life and Work in China* (Parson, WV: McClain Printing Company, 1978), p. 20.

76. Sydenstricker, *Our Life and Work in China,* p. 53.

77. When the memoir was published in 1978, Absalom's younger daughter, Grace Yaukey, inserted descriptions and events in an effort to add some detail and human texture to her father's generalized religiosity.

78. Emma Edmunds White, "Pearl S. Buck," *Randolph-Macon Woman's College Alumni Bulletin* (February, 1939), pp. 4–12.

79. Grace Yaukey, interview with the present writer (May 10, 1991).

80. Lossing Buck's correspondence with John Reisner, John Williams, and others associated with him at Nanking University is housed in the archives of the Yale Divinity School.

81. Buck, *My Several Worlds,* p. 176.

82. Mrs. Rey Kelsey, quoted in Stirling, *Pearl Buck: A Woman in Conflict,* p. 71.

83. Pearl S. Buck, "The Chinese Student Mind," *Nation,* 119, no. 3092 (October 8, 1924), p. 359.

84. In the annual reports she sent back to the Foreign Mission Board, Pearl continued to identify herself as a "housewife" throughout the 1920s.

85. Joseph P. Lash, *Eleanor and Franklin* (New York: W. W. Norton, 1971), p. 311.

86. Paul Buck and Rosalind Buck, interview with the present writer (May 5, 1991).

87. The essay's notes and bibliography contain references to nearly 150 sources.

88. "David F. Barnes" [Pearl S. Buck], "China and the West" (unpublished thesis, Cornell University, 1925), p. 18.

89. Pearl's attacks on the Christian invasion of China in this essay anticipated her full-scale debate with the Presbyterian missionary establishment seven years later.

90. Pearl S. Buck, "A Chinese Woman Speaks," part one, *Asia,* Volume XXVI, Number 4 (April 26, 1926), p. 305. The tale is illustrated with photographs rather than drawings, giving an odd and factitious documentary flavor to the narrative.

91. One of the most honorable campaigns undertaken by the Christian missionaries in China was their vigorous opposition to foot-binding. For a first-hand account from the period of Pearl's childhood, see Mrs. Archibald Little, "Tour in Behalf of the Anti-foot-binding Society," *Chinese Recorder* (May, June, 1900), pp. 258–261, 313–316. There is not a large secondary literature on this subject. See Howard S. Levy, *The Lotus Lovers: The Complete History of the Curious Erotic Custom of Footbinding in China* (Buffalo, NY: Prometheus Books, 1992 [1966]).

92. The significance of Pearl's choice of a female point of view is suggested by comparison with almost any of the Asian fiction published by Westerners up through the time of her first stories. André Malraux's *Temptation of the West,* to give just one example, was also published in 1926, the year "A Chinese Woman Speaks" appeared. Malraux's book is a densely textured contrast between China and the West in the form of an exchange of letters between a Frenchman named A.D. and a Chinese called Ling. Like most Chinese protagonists contrived by Western writers before Pearl Buck, Ling is male. See Geoffrey H. Hartman, "Cultural Relativism and the Literary Critic," in Hana Wirth-Nesher, ed., *The Sheila Carmel Lectures, 1988–1993* (Tel Aviv: Tel Aviv University Press, 1995), pp. 59–76; and Hartman, *Minor Prophecies: The Role of the Critical Essay in the Culture Wars* (Cambridge, MA: Harvard University Press, 1991), chapter 10. An exception of sorts to this general pattern is John Luther Long's "Madame Butterfly," a short story published in *Century* magazine in 1898. Even in this case, though the point of view is mainly that of a Japanese woman, the dominant attitude is male and Western. Cho-Cho San is a relentlessly stereotypical figure, adoring her English lover and submerging her identity in his. This nearly forgotten work of fiction was adapted for the

London stage in a turn-of-the-century production that inspired Puccini to write his opera.

93. Maxine Hong Kingston, comments at Randolph-Macon Woman's College (March 27, 1992).

94. In *Orientalism* (New York: Pantheon Books, 1978), Edward Said argues rather strenuously that Western writers have never adequately represented Asian peoples and cultures. In fact, though Said's thesis is powerful, the question is much disputed and the issues are rather more complex than he allows. For one thing, while arguing persuasively against the essentialism that has disfigured many Western images of "the Orient," he resorts to a species of essentialism, in which "the West" is hypostatized into an agent with a set of representational designs. Furthermore, the example of Pearl Buck indicates that the transactions between East and West are not solely governed by the "cognitive imperialism" to which Said routinely appeals. For a useful set of comments on this debate, see Warren Cohen, ed., *Reflections on Orientalism* (East Lansing: Michigan State University Press, 1983).

95. Pearl appropriated the description of this Western man's nose rising up like a mountain from his face from her own experience in Nanhsuchou. Similarly, "A Chinese Woman Speaks" includes a version of the suicide she witnessed, in which the still-breathing woman was smothered by having her nose and mouth tightly sealed "to keep in the small remaining spirit."

96. Pearl S. Buck, "A Chinese Woman Speaks," part two, *Asia*, Volume XXVII, Number 5 (April 26, 1926), p. 448.

97. The earliest example of this narrative device, using an Asian point of view to lampoon Western customs, is probably Montesquieu's *Persian Letters* (1721). Interestingly, one of the inspirations for this text was Arcadio Huang, a Chinese scholar resident in Paris in the early eighteenth century, whom Montesquieu interviewed in 1713. See Jonathan Spence, *Chinese Roundabout: Essays in History and Culture* (New York: W. W. Norton, 1992), p. 18.

Chapter 3: Winds of Change

1. On the Shanghai Incident and its aftermath, see Putnam Weale, *Why China Sees Red* (London: Macmillan, 1926); Arthur N. Holcombe, *The Chinese Revolution* (Cambridge, MA: Harvard University Press, 1930); William C. Johnstone, Jr., *The Shanghai Problem* (Palo Alto, CA: Stanford University Press, 1937); Dorothy Borg, *American Policy and the Chinese Revolution, 1925–1928* (New York: Octagon Books, 1968 [1947]); Jonathan Spence, *The Gate of Heavenly Peace: The Chinese and Their Revolution, 1895–1980* (New York: Viking Press, 1981); and Hung-Ting Ku, "Urban Mass Movement: The May Thirtieth Movement in Shanghai," *Modern Asia Studies*, 13, 2 (1979), pp. 197–216.

2. Borg, *American Policy and the Chinese Revolution*, p. 38.

3. A comparison of debates in the British Parliament and the United States Congress suggests that British politicians were generally more resistant to change than their American counterparts.

4. "Set the Missionaries Free!," *Christian Century* (September 10, 1925), p. 114. As early as July, 1923, the editors of the *Chinese Recorder* had also advocated that missionaries voluntarily relinquish their extraterritorial privileges.

5. Eric North to J. Lossing Buck (July 23, 1925), Yale Divinity School archives.

6. In a letter to Lossing's mother that Nora Stirling has dated to September, 1925, just after Pearl and Lossing returned to Nanking, Pearl wrote at length of her continued happiness as wife and mother. If Stirling's date is correct, the letter offers a picture of domestic bliss sharply at odds with Pearl's testimony elsewhere. The most likely explanation is that Pearl was rather generously trying to console an old woman who had

written to complain of her own feelings of abandonment and loneliness. Among other things, Pearl wrote that "Carol is developing so fast now, and is so well. She is full of fun and . . . is such a joy to us always." This was of course patently untrue, and suggests that the rest of the letter is suspect as well. The letter is located in the Randolph-Macon Woman's College archives.

7. Pearl S. Buck, "The Rainy Day," in *The First Wife and Other Stories* (New York: John Day Company, 1933), pp. 183–197.

8. Pearl S. Buck, "Personal Report, 1925–1926" (July 13, 1926), Presbyterian Historical Society archives.

9. The story's byline includes a co-author, Shao Teh-hsing.

10. Anna Louise Strong, "Chang and Feng and Wu," *Asia* (July, 1926), p. 598.

11. For accounts of the Northern Expedition, see Jonathan Spence, *The Search for Modern China* (New York: W. W. Norton, 1990), pp. 341–360; and John King Fairbank, *China: A New History* (Cambridge, MA: Harvard University Press, 1992), pp. 283–286.

12. James C. Thomson, Jr., *While China Faced West: American Reformers in Nationalist China, 1928–1937* (Cambridge, MA: Harvard University Press, 1969), p. 35. See also Paul Varg, *Missionaries, Chinese, and Diplomats: The American Protestant Missionary Movement in China, 1890–1952* (New York: Octagon Books, 1977 [1958]), pp. 180–183.

13. Pearl S. Buck to Emma Edmunds White (March 7, 1927), Randolph-Macon Woman's College archives.

14. Pearl S. Buck to Lewis Gannett (March 27 [20?], 1927), Houghton Library special collections, Harvard University. The main point of this letter is Pearl's request for advice in finding a literary agent. She had apparently begun to think of herself as a professional writer.

15. Pearl S. Buck to Mrs. Clarence H. Hamilton (March 12, 1927), Boston University archives.

16. Cited in Spence, *The Gate of Heavenly Peace: The Chinese and Their Revolution, 1895–1980*, p. 207.

17. Quoted in Nora Stirling, *Pearl Buck: A Woman in Conflict* (Piscataway, NJ: New Century Publishing Company, 1983), p. 77.

18. This was confirmed by Grace Yaukey in an interview with the present writer (May 10, 1991).

19. Pearl was convinced that the violence was the work of the Communists, but that question, like many others about this episode, has never been answered with certainty. The soldiers who attacked Nanking's foreigners and Chinese civilians may have been troops of the Kuomintang, but they also may have been rioting elements of Wu Pei-fu's Northern armies. If the attackers were Kuomintang soldiers, it is not certain that they were Communist detachments who hoped to embarrass Chiang. They may have been nationalists who had simply run amok. In either case, it is not clear that the attacks on foreigners were part of a calculated plan, rather than mere random violence. For Pearl's opinion, see her letter from Unzen, Japan, to the Presbyterian Foreign Mission Board (April 13, 1927); Presbyterian Historical Society. She believed the attacks on foreigners were systematic, which proved that "the Communists were in control of Nanking, and not the Conservative Nationalists as we had hoped."

The Nanking Incident has attracted considerable attention from historians for over a half-century. For a sample of different interpretations of the episode, see John Service, ed., *Golden Inches: The China Memoirs of Grace Service* (Berkeley: University of California Press, 1989), chapter 45, "Tense Times (1927)"; Nym Wales [Helen Foster Snow], *Inside Red China* (New York: Doubleday, Doran & Co., 1939); James C. Thomson, Jr., *While China Faced West: American Reformers in Nationalist China, 1928–1937* (Cambridge, MA: Harvard University Press, 1969); Barbara Tuchman, *Stilwell and the American Experience in China, 1911–1945* (New York: Macmillan, 1971), pp. 103–104; Randall E. Stross, *The Stubborn Earth: American Agriculturalists on Chinese Soil, 1898–1937* (Berkeley:

University of California Press, 1986); Jerome Ch'en, *China and the West: Society and Culture, 1815–1937* (London: Hutchinson, 1979); Spence, *The Gate of Heavenly Peace: The Chinese and Their Revolution, 1895–1980.*

20. The shelling commenced on the instructions of the American consul, John C. Davis, who had fled from his official residence to Socony Hill, the Standard Oil compound and the highest point in Nanking. The fifty-two Western civilians and sailors who had sought refuge in the Standard Oil headquarters on Socony Hill made a perilous escape by ropes down the city's walls. For an eyewitness account of the day's events, see Alice Tisdale Hobart, *Within the Walls of Nanking* (New York: Macmillan, n.d. [1928]), pp. 173–231.

21. Pearl's account of this episode in her autobiography is a good deal more melodramatic. After the shelling stopped, she claims that the soldiers returned, treated the family abusively, and marched the whole group off to the university. See *My Several Worlds* (New York: John Day Company, 1954), pp. 214–215.

22. Stross, *The Stubborn Earth: American Agriculturalists on Chinese Soil, 1898–1937*, p. 155.

23. Consul John Davis's father had been a missionary and a friend of Absalom Sydenstricker.

24. Pearl S. Buck, *The Delights of Learning* (Pittsburgh: University of Pittsburgh Press, 1960), p. 5.

25. Buck, *My Several Worlds*, p. 216.

26. Pearl S. Buck to Lewis Gannett (June 15, 1927), Houghton Library special collections, Harvard University.

27. Buck, *My Several Worlds*, p. 218.

28. Buck, *My Several Worlds*, p. 226.

29. Borg, *American Policy and the Chinese Revolution*, pp. 318f.

30. Pearl S. Buck to Mrs. Clarence H. Hamilton (April 27, 1927), Boston University archives.

31. Pearl S. Buck to Emma Edmunds White (May 19, 1927), Randolph-Macon Woman's College archives.

32. Stirling, *Pearl S. Buck: A Woman in Conflict*, p. 80.

33. Cited in Jim Pugh, "J. Lossing Buck, American Missionary: The Application of Scientific Agriculture in China, 1915–1944" (unpublished honors thesis, Swarthmore College, 1973), p. 41.

34. Pearl S. Buck, *Fighting Angel: Portrait of a Soul* (New York: John Day Company, 1936), p. 291.

35. Buck, *My Several Worlds*, p. 220.

36. Pearl S. Buck to Mrs. Clarence H. Hamilton (June 22, 1927), Boston University archives.

37. A few years later, Pearl memorialized Li Sau-tse in the title figure of her novel, *The Mother.*

38. Pearl S. Buck to Polly Small (August 19, 1927), Randolph-Macon Woman's College archives.

39. Pearl S. Buck to Lewis Gannett (June 15, 1927), Houghton Library special collections, Harvard University.

40. Pearl S. Buck to Mrs. Clarence H. Hamilton (June 30, 1927), Boston University archives.

41. See, among many other accounts, John B. Powell, *My Twenty-Five Years in China* (New York: Macmillan, 1945), pp. 151–155.

42. Fairbank, *China: A New History*, p. 283.

43. For discussions of the conflict between Chiang and the Communists in this period, see John King Fairbank, *The United States and China*, fourth edition (Cambridge, MA: Harvard University Press, 1983), pp. 240–243; Jean Chesneaux, Françoise Le Barbier, and Marie-Claire Bergère, *China from the 1911 Revolution to Liberation*, translated by

Paul Auster and Lydia Davis (New York: Pantheon Books, 1977); Jonathan Spence, *The Search for Modern China* (New York: W. W. Norton, 1990), pp. 348–360.

44. Chamberlain outlined British policy in a speech in the House of Commons on May 9, 1927. The speech is printed under the heading "Nanking Outrages and Hankow Agreement," *Parliamentary Debates,* Fifth Series, Volume 206, fifth volume of the 1927 session.

45. Pearl S. Buck to Lewis Gannett (August 3, 1927), Houghton Library special collections, Harvard University.

46. *Ibid.*

47. Pearl S. Buck, "The Revolutionist," *Asia,* volume XXVIII, number 9 (September, 1928), p. 689.

48. Presumably Wang has stolen a Mexican dollar, which was the most widely used currency in China's foreign community.

49. W. H. Auden and Christopher Isherwood, *Journey to a War* (New York: Random House, 1939), p. 246. Isherwood's account was written in the late 1930s, but he would have found the same conditions in the mills and factories in any year between the wars. For the most detailed description of the way the mills operated, see Emily Honig, *Sisters and Strangers: Women in the Shanghai Cotton Mills, 1919–1949* (Stanford, CA: Stanford University Press, 1986), especially chapters 2, 6, and 7.

50. Pearl S. Buck, "Asia Book-Shelf," *Asia* (April, 1940), p. 222.

51. For a journalistic tour of Shanghai at about the time Pearl lived there, see F. L. Hawks Pott, *A Short History of Shanghai* (Shanghai: Kelly & Walsh, 1928).

52. Pearl S. Buck to Mrs. Clarence H. Hamilton (February 8, 1928), Boston University archives.

53. Pearl S. Buck to Rey Kelsey and Helen Daniels (December 26, 1927), Randolph-Macon Woman's College archives.

54. When she transcribed this letter into her memoirs, Pearl silently rewrote her general accusation against the "moral weakness" of the Chinese people. In the altered version, she blamed China's troubles on "the moral weakness of her upper classes, and in the helplessness of the peasants." See *My Several Worlds,* pp. 230–231.

55. Pearl found David Lloyd's advertisement in *The Writers' and Artists' Year Book* for 1927, which she came across in the bookshop of the English-language Shanghai publisher Kelly & Walsh.

56. Buck, *My Several Worlds,* p. 231.

57. Stirling, *Pearl Buck,* p. 84.

58. Pearl S. Buck to Emma Edmunds White (January 4, 1929), Randolph-Macon Woman's College archives.

59. Pearl S. Buck to Mrs. Clarence H. Hamilton (March 23, 1928), Boston University archives.

60. Grace Yaukey, interview with the present writer (May 10, 1991).

61. *Ibid.*

62. Pearl S. Buck to Marian Craighill (November 11, 1936), typescript copy in the Nora Stirling collection, Randolph-Macon Woman's College archives.

63. Nora Stirling reconstructed the details of Pearl's affair with Hsu, based on interviews with Emma White, a woman she called "Sara Burton," and an unnamed secretary who worked for Pearl some years later. See Stirling, *Pearl Buck: A Woman in Conflict,* pp. 86–89. There is some dispute about whether the affair actually took place or was invented later, either by Pearl herself or by Stirling's informants. In separate conversations with the present writer, Helen Foster Snow refused to credit the story, but Grace Yaukey confirmed it. Apparently, the American journalist Agnes Smedley also had an affair with Hsu. See Janice R. MacKinnon and Stephen R. MacKinnon, *Agnes Smedley: The LIfe and Times of an American Radical* (Berkeley: University of California Press, 1988), p. 254.

64. Hsu was in fact sometimes called "the Chinese Byron" by other writers; the label was a mixture of admiration and satire.

65. Buck, *My Several Worlds*, pp. 178–179.

66. Pearl S. Buck to Mrs. Clarence H. Hamilton (July 17, 1928), Boston University archives.

67. Fairbank, *China: A New History*, p. 289.

68. Spence, *The Search for Modern China*, pp. 388–396.

69. A useful account of the American presence in China during the Nanking Decade can be found in James C. Thomson, Jr., *While China Faced West: American Reformers in Nationalist China, 1928–1937.*

70. Pearl S. Buck to Mrs. Clarence H. Hamilton (November 19, 1928), Boston University archives.

71. Edgar Snow, *Red Star Over China* (New York: Random House, 1938), pp. 140–156.

72. Pearl S. Buck to Mrs. Clarence H. Hamilton (March 23, 1928), Boston University archives.

73. Pearl recalled this incident years later, in an article called "The Plain People of China," *Asia* (July, 1941), p. 352.

74. Pearl S. Buck to Emma Edmunds White (January 14, 1929), Randolph-Macon Woman's College archives.

75. Pearl S. Buck to Mrs. Harold F. LaCroix (May 17, 1970), Pearl S. Buck Family Trust archives.

76. Pearl S. Buck to Emma Edmunds White (January 4, 1929), Randolph-Macon Woman's College archives.

77. Buck, *My Several Worlds*, p. 246.

78. Pearl S. Buck to the Presbyterian Board of Foreign Missions (June 10, 1929), Presbyterian Historical Society archives.

79. Whatever his political and strategic failures, Chiang's personal magnetism was undeniable. A few years after Sun's funeral, the British journalist Peter Fleming had a long meeting with Chiang and reported that in spite of his initial skepticism, he was "abashed" by the Chinese leader. "Here was a man with a presence," Fleming continued, "with that something incalculable in him to which the herd instinctively defers. He was strong and silent by nature, not by artifice. . . ." Fleming, *One's Company: A Journey to China* (London: Cape, 1934), p. 227.

80. Pearl S. Buck to Mrs. Clarence H. Hamilton (November 19, 1928), Boston University archives.

81. A quarter-century later, Pearl commented on the new road and its significance in her memoirs; see *My Several Worlds*, pp. 242–243. In her June 10, 1929 report, the new road is mentioned several times without negative comment. This is perhaps another indication that the report is unreliably biased in Chiang's favor.

82. Pearl S. Buck, "The New Road," in *The First Wife and Other Stories*, p. 262.

83. Pearl S. Buck, *The Child Who Never Grew*, second edition (Rockville, MD: Woodbine House, 1992), p. 67. This book was originally published in 1950.

84. Buck, *The Child Who Never Grew*, p. 71.

85. Pearl S. Buck to Mrs. Clarence H. Hamilton (January 9, 1930), Boston University archives. Twenty years later, Pearl repeated this story, almost verbatim, in *The Child Who Never Grew* (New York: John Day Company, 1950), p. 45–47.

86. Pearl S. Buck to Mrs. Clarence H. Hamilton (October 6, 1929), Boston University archives.

87. Pearl S. Buck to Mrs. Clarence H. Hamilton (January 9, 1930), Boston University archives.

88. Helen Foster Snow, interview with the present writer (November 15, 1991).

89. Richard J. Walsh, in collaboration with Milton S. Salsbury, *The Making of Buffalo Bill: A Study in Heroics* (Indianapolis: Bobbs-Merrill, 1928), p. v.

90. Richard J. Walsh to David Lloyd (September 17, 1929), Pearl S. Buck Family Trust archives.
91. Pearl S. Buck to Richard Walsh ([December, 1929]), Randolph-Macon Woman's College archives.
92. Pearl S. Buck to Dr. Sanderson (July 6, 1930), Cornell University archives.
93. Pearl S. Buck, *East Wind, West Wind* (New York: John Day Company, 1930), pp. 251, 259–260. Women have been largely absent from both Asian and European conceptions of justice, whose abstract notion of "humanity" implicitly favors male experience. Similarly the family is typically ignored by theorists of justice, who regard it as a "natural" institution, beyond the reach of philosophical systems. For an example of the recent work that tries to reexamine these assumptions, see Susan Moller Okin, *Justice, Gender, and the Family* (New York: Basic Books, 1992).
94. Pearl S. Buck to Mrs. Clarence H. Hamilton (January 26, 1930), Boston University archives.
95. The image of Gethsemane comes from a letter Pearl wrote to Polly Small, dated August 19, 1927, Randolph-Macon Woman's College archives.
96. Stross, *The Stubborn Earth*, p. 107.
97. See, for example, the following uses of Lossing's research by more recent scholars. (1) Jurgen Domes, *Socialism in the Chinese Countryside: Rural Societal Policies in the People's Republic of China, 1949–1979*, translated by Margitta Wendling (London: C. Hurst and Company, 1980); Domes uses Lossing's estimates of tenant ownership to support a less exploitative model of Chinese agriculture. (2) Robert C. Hsu, *Food for One Billion: China's Agriculture Since 1949* (Boulder, CO: Westview Press, 1982); Hsu accepts Lossing's data on tenant ownership, but draws diametrically different conclusions from those of Domes (p. 27). (3) Benedict Stavis, *The Politics of Agricultural Mechanization in China* (Ithaca, NY: Cornell University Press, 1978); on the basis of Lossing's statistics, Stavis estimates the number of farm tools in the whole of China in the 1930s as 721 million (p. 39). (4) Kenneth Walker, *Planning in Chinese Agriculture: Socialization and the Private Sector, 1956–1962* (London: Frank Cass & Company, 1965); Walker takes his data for the size of pre-1949 farms from Lossing's publications (p. xiii). (5) Dwight H. Perkins, *Agricultural Development in China, 1368–1968* (Chicago: Aldine Publishing Co., 1969); Perkins incorporates dozens of references to Lossing's work in this major study, disputing his sampling methodology, but more often citing the data as reliable. (6) Loren Brandt, *Commercialization and Agricultural Development: Central and Eastern China, 1870–1937* (New York: Cambridge University Press, 1989); interestingly, Brandt corrects Perkins at several points by reference to Lossing (pp. 56, 58). (7) Nicholas R. Lardy, *Agriculture in China's Modern Economic Development* (Cambridge, England: Cambridge University Press, 1983); Lardy depends on Lossing's estimates of the marketing practices of Chinese farmers (pp. 10–11). (8) Kang Chao, *Agricultural Production in Communist China, 1949–1965* (Madison: University of Wisconsin Press, 1970); Lossing figures prominently in the opening paragraphs of chapter 2, a section called "Land Reform" (pp. 36–37). (9) Keith Buchanan, *The Transformation of the Chinese Earth* (New York: Praeger Publishers, 1970); Buchanan claims that Lossing did "the most outstanding pioneer work" in mapping the agricultural regions of China (p. 171). Finally, (10) Randall E. Stross, *The Stubborn Earth: American Agriculturalists on Chinese Soil, 1898–1937* (Berkeley: University of California Press, 1986); Stross devotes an entire chapter to Lossing's career. Stross is relentlessly critical, attacking Lossing's methods, his benign view of tenancy, and his early removal from the countryside to the university.
98. John K. Fairbank, *Chinese–American Interactions: A Historical Summary* (New Brunswick, NJ: Rutgers University Press, 1975), p. 46.
99. Kung was married to Soong Ai-ling, eldest of the three Soong sisters; the other two sisters were Soong Mei-ling (Mme. Chiang) and Sun Yat-sen's widow, Soong Ching-ling.

100. Pearl S. Buck to Mrs. Clarence H. Hamilton (February 13, 1930), Boston University archives.

101. Pearl S. Buck, "China in the Mirror of Her Fiction." Originally published in the February issue of *Pacific Affairs,* the essay was reprinted in *The Week in China,* Vol. XIII, No. 257 (March 1, 1930), pp. 227–236. References are to this reprint.

102. Lu Xun, "Foreword" to Harold R. Isaacs, *Straw Sandals: Chinese Short Stories, 1918–1933* (Cambridge, MA: MIT Press, 1974), p. ix. For a variety of political and economic reasons, this anthology, which was substantially completed in 1934, was not published for forty years.

103. The extent of cannibalism in China's ancient and more recent history has been the subject of much dispute among both Western and Chinese historians. Recently, the dissident writer Zheng Yi has documented an appalling epidemic of cannibalism during the Cultural Revolution. See Liu Binyan, "An Unnatural Disaster," a review of Zheng's books, *Lishi de yibufen* (*A Part of History*) and the unpublished *Hongse jinianbie* (*Red Memorial*), in the *New York Review of Books* (April 8, 1993), pp. 3–6. Nicholas D. Kristof reports episodes of cannibalism during the Cultural Revolution in Guanxi province in Kristof and Sheryl WuDunn, *China Awakes: The Struggle for the Soul of a Rising Power* (New York: Times Books, 1994), pp. 73–75. For a historical survey of the question, see Key Ray Chong, *Cannibalism in China* (Wakefield, NH: Longwood Academic Press, 1990).

104. The information about Edgar Sydenstricker's visit is contained in Lossing's annual report for 1930 (December 3, 1930), Yale Divinity School archives. The English historian R. H. Tawney also visited Nanking University in 1930, to lecture on European agrarian history.

105. Pearl S. Buck to Mrs. Clarence H. Hamilton (April 12, 1930), Boston University archives.

106. Pearl S. Buck to Mrs. Clarence H. Hamilton (May 8, 1930), Boston University archives.

107. B. A. Garside to John Lossing Buck (June 12, 1930), Yale Divinity School archives.

108. Pearl S. Buck to Mrs. Clarence H. Hamilton (September 22, 1930), Boston University archives.

109. Richard J. Walsh to David Lloyd (July 15, 1930), Pearl S. Buck Family Trust archives.

110. Richard J. Walsh to Pearl S. Buck (July 25, 1930), Pearl S. Buck Family Trust archives.

111. Buck, *Fighting Angel,* pp. 299–302.

Chapter 4: The Good Earth

1. Pearl S. Buck to Emma Edmunds White (January 20, 1931), Randolph-Macon Woman's College archives.

2. "During the first half of the twentieth century, an almost unimaginable chaos engulfed China." The country's long civil war and its invasion by Japan turned it into "the world's greatest battlefield." Michael Schaller, *The U.S. Crusade in China, 1938–1945* (New York: Columbia University Press, 1979), p. 2.

3. Pearl only acknowledged her hope that Carol would die many years later: "I longed for her to die, I prayed that she would die. I still pray that I may not die first." Pearl S. Buck to Bradford Smith (August 29, 1963), University of Vermont Library.

4. Pearl S. Buck to Mrs. Clarence H. Hamilton (January 27, 1931), Boston University archives.

5. Quoted in Prunella Wood, "Pearl S. Buck Thinks in Chinese, Knows America Better than America," *New York World-Telegram* (May 4, 1932), p. 20.

6. The first issue of Henry Luce's *Time* magazine appeared on March 3, 1923, just three years before the Book-of-the-Month Club commenced operations. Luce's weekly bril-

liantly appealed to the same audience as the Club, professionals and business people eager to be informed about world events as quickly and efficiently as possible.

7. The data on the Book-of-the-Month Club are taken from Charles Lee, *The Hidden Public: The Story of the Book-of-the-Month Club* (New York: Doubleday, 1958), pp. 21–43. More recent studies of the Club and its cultural significance include Janice Radway, "The Book-of-the-Month Club and the General Reader: On the Uses of 'Serious Fiction,' " *Critical Inquiry*, 14 (Spring, 1988), pp. 516; Radway, "The Scandal of the Middlebrow: The Book-of-the-Month Club, Class Fracture, and Cultural Authority," *South Atlantic Quarterly*, 89 (Fall, 1990), pp. 703–736; and Joan Shelley Rubin, *The Making of Middlebrow Culture* (Chapel Hill: University of North Carolina Press, 1992).

8. In the years between the Club's founding and the late 1940s, books selected as main choices and alternates made up a substantial proportion of best-sellers. See Lee, *The Hidden Public*, pp. 212–213.

9. Fisher recalled her first reading of *The Good Earth* in a lecture at the New York Public Library nearly twenty years later. Published in the *Bowker Lectures on Book Publishing*, third series (1948), the text is cited in Ida H. Washington, *Dorothy Canfield Fisher: A Biography* (Shelburne, VT: New England Press, 1982), pp. 200–201.

10. "Best Sellers, 1932," *Publishers' Weekly* (January 21, 1933), pp. 190–191. (Pearl's next novel, *Sons*, ranked third in 1932.)

11. Richard J. Walsh to Pearl S. Buck (n.d. [March, 1931]), Pearl S. Buck Family Trust archives.

12. Pearl S. Buck to Emma Edmunds White (March [1931]), Randolph-Macon Woman's College archives.

13. Francis L. K. Hsu is one of many Chinese commentators who have argued that Pearl's view of the relation between Chinese farmers and their land is essentially correct. See Hsu's *Americans and Chinese: Purpose and Fulfillment in Great Civilizations* (Garden City, NY: Natural History Press, 1970), p. 286.

14. Adrienne Rich, *Of Woman Born: Motherhood as Experience and Institution*, tenth anniversary edition (New York: W. W. Norton, 1986), p. 166.

15. Pearl S. Buck, *The Good Earth*, ed. Peter Conn (New York: Washington Square Press, 1994), p. 83.

16. In the hierarchy of Chinese prostitution, the *hsien-sheng*, sing-song girl, occupied the highest position. See Gail Hershatter, "Prostitution and the Market in Women in Early Twentieth-Century Shanghai," in Rubie S. Watson and Patricia Buckley Ebry, eds., *Marriage and Inequality in Chinese Society* (Berkeley: University of California Press, 1991), p. 260.

17. Florence Ayscough, wife of American diplomat Harley Farnsworth MacNair, had lived for many years in China. Her own publications included translations of Chinese poetry and *Chinese Women: Yesterday and To-Day* (Boston: Houghton Mifflin, 1937).

18. The Book-of-the-Month Club "News" announcing *The Good Earth* also emphasized the novel's avoidance of ethnic cliché in its presentation of the Chinese people. "The people in this rather thrilling story are not 'queer' or 'exotic,' " Harry Scherman wrote, "they are as natural as their soil. . . . This is surely as sympathetic and knowledgeable a picture of the Chinese as is possible for a Westerner." Scherman quoted Dorothy Canfield Fisher's letter nominating the book to her fellow panelists: "Most Oriental novels, you know, are for Americans really only curiosities, travel books of the mind." Fisher believed that *The Good Earth* was much more substantial.

19. Younghill Kang, "China Is Different," *New Republic*, 67 (July 1, 1931), pp. 185–186. Somewhat unusually, the magazine's editors attached a note to the end of Kang's review, separating themselves from what they called his unjust attack on *The Good Earth*.

20. Kiang Kang-hu's comments were originally published in the *Chinese Christian Student* and were reprinted in the *New York Times* (1933).

21. For the best brief survey of Chinese responses to *The Good Earth,* and to Pearl Buck's work more generally, see Liu Haiping, "Pearl S. Buck's Reception in China Reconsidered," in Elizabeth J. Lipscomb, Frances E. Webb, and Peter Conn, eds., *The Several Worlds of Pearl Buck* (Westport, CT: Greenwood Publishing Group, 1994), pp. 72–94.
22. Quoted in Nora Stirling, *Pearl Buck: Woman in Conflict* (Piscataway, NJ: World Publishing Company, 1983), p. 109. Helen Foster Snow makes essentially the same point in her own autobiography, *My China Years: A Memoir* (New York: William Morrow and Company, 1984), p. 42. Shortly after she got to China, Foster met Edgar Snow, who would become her husband. Her first question to him was: " 'Don't you realize you're the most famous American writer on the Far East except for that missionary, Pearl Buck?' " Reported in *My China Years,* p. 28.
23. Buck, *The Good Earth,* pp. 126–127.
24. Pearl S. Buck to Emma Edmunds White (May 29, 1931), Randolph-Macon Woman's College archives.
25. Courtenay H. Fenn to Pearl S. Buck (March 23, 1931), Presbyterian Historical Society archives.
26. In fact, book sales are famously difficult to determine with real accuracy. Scholars of such matters generally rank *The Good Earth* second or third in sales in the 1930s, certainly behind Margaret Mitchell's *Gone With the Wind* (1936), and possibly also behind Hervey Allen's *Anthony Adverse* (1932). In the decades since, Mitchell's novel has remained an American favorite, as has *The Good Earth,* while Allen's book has virtually disappeared.
27. The political consequences of Pearl's work began to emerge almost immediately. In the opinion of at least one observer, *The Good Earth* had much to do with the decision of the United States government to grant a substantial wheat loan to China in the summer of 1932. See the article "Pearl Buck Wins Coveted Pulitzer Novel Prize" in *China Weekly Review* (June 11, 1932), p. 41.

    According to Steven Mosher, "no one taught more Americans to appreciate better what Arthur Smith called 'the numerous admirable qualities of the Chinese' than the Nobel Prize-winning author Pearl S. Buck." These new images of the Chinese she created "could not have come at a better time. When a few years later the Japanese escalated their piecemeal attacks to all-out war, it was not the nameless, faceless masses of China who took up arms against the invaders, but Buck's noble Chinese peasants. America's generally favorable view of the Chinese quickly deepened and broadened into an unreserved admiration. . . ." Mosher, *China Misperceived: American Illusions and Chinese Reality* (New York: Basic Books, 1990), pp. 45–46.
28. Chuang Hsin-tsai (Zhuang Xinzai), "Mrs. Buck and Her Works," *Maodun vuekan (Paradox),* 2.1 (1933), p. 82, cited in Liu Haiping, "Pearl S. Buck's Reception in China Reconsidered," in Elizabeth Lipscomb, Frances Webb, and Peter Conn, eds., *The Several Worlds of Pearl Buck,* p. 59.
29. Robert Hughes, *The Culture of Complaint: The Fraying of America* (New York: Oxford University Press, 1993), pp. 83–84.
30. For a useful survey of this theme, see David Shi, *The Simple Life* (New York: Oxford University Press, 1989).
31. In this moral calculus, Wang Lung also fits fairly comfortably inside another well-known American formula, that of the Horatio Alger hero. Alger's hundred or so novels of luck and pluck were published in the last quarter of the nineteenth century but were even more popular in the opening decades of the twentieth. They had a considerable influence on the American imagination for two or three generations. In its emphasis on hard work and determination, *The Good Earth* resembles these earlier stories, as it does in its misgivings about wealth. As several students of Alger have pointed out, it is inaccurate to call his novels tales of "rags to riches"; rags to respectability would be better. Pros-

perity is desirable, but too much wealth, in Alger's stories as in Pearl Buck's, is usually a sign of moral decay.

32. Pearl S. Buck to Polly Small (May 29, 1931), Randolph-Macon Woman's College archives.

33. These meetings are mentioned in Pearl S. Buck, *My Several Worlds* (New York: John Day Company, 1954), pp. 267–268.

34. Lattimore told the story of his harassment by Congress in his book *Ordeal by Slander* (Boston: Little, Brown, 1950).

35. On the flood and its consequences, see O. Edmund Clubb, *Twentieth-Century China* (New York: Columbia University Press, 1964), pp. 194–195; and Jonathan Spence, *The Search for Modern China* (New York: W. W. Norton, 1990), p. 434.

36. According to at least one Chinese observer, the large contributions Americans made to flood relief efforts were stimulated by the impact of *The Good Earth*. Hu Zhongchi made this remark in his "Preface" to a Chinese translation of the novel.

37. Cited in Cornelia Spencer [Grace Yaukey], *The Exile's Daughter: A Biography of Pearl S. Buck* (New York: Coward-McCann, 1944), p. 172.

38. Pearl S. Buck to Mrs. Clarence H. Hamilton (July 31, 1931), Boston University archives.

39. Pearl S. Buck to Emma Edmunds White (July 29, 1931), Randolph-Macon Woman's College archives.

40. Absalom Sydenstricker, "The Changing Missionary Message," *Chinese Recorder*, Vol. LX (June, 1929), p. 393.

41. In October, 1929, the *Recorder* published a list of the fifty senior missionaries in China in years of service. The honor roll begins with Miss Mary E. Andrews, of the American Board Mission, who arrived in 1868. (Twenty-two of the fifty longest-serving Protestant missionaries on this list were women.) Absalom is tenth, with forty-nine years in the field.

42. Buck, *My Several Worlds,* p. 258.

43. Pearl S. Buck, *Fighting Angel* (New York: John Day Company, 1936), p. 192. Pearl wrote a dutiful, edifying obituary for Presbyterian headquarters, a document useful for biographical data on Absalom but completely unreliable as a guide to Pearl's feelings. (The obituary is on file at the Presbyterian Historical Society in Philadelphia.)

44. Buck, *My Several Worlds,* p. 261.

45. John King Fairbank, *The United States and China,* fourth edition (Cambridge, MA: Harvard University Press, 1983), pp. 261–262.

46. Pearl S. Buck to Emma Edmunds White (September 24, 1931), Randolph-Macon Woman's College archives.

47. Cited in Stirling, *Pearl Buck: A Woman in Conflict,* p. 115.

48. Pearl S. Buck, "East and West and the Novel," in the American Association of University Women *Bulletin* (November, 1931), p. 9. Pearl repeated this lecture several months later at the North China Union Language School.

49. Pearl S. Buck, *All Men Are Brothers,* two volumes (New York: John Day Company, 1933). In 1948, the Heritage Press published a large-format, one-volume edition of this translation, with illustrations by Miguel Covarrubias and a preface by Lin Yutang.

Before she took up the formidable task of translating *Shui Hu Chuan*, Pearl had rendered several Chinese short stories into English. One of these translations, "The Clutch of the Ancients," appeared in the August, 1924 issue of the *Chinese Recorder*. In the story, a young boy who yearns for education and a modern career is literally beaten into obedience and conformity by his father.

50. *Shui Hu Chuan* has an extremely complicated composition history and has appeared in several different versions ranging from 70 to 120 chapters. Pearl Buck translated the seventy-chapter edition of the novel, which most of the critics she was familiar with

considered the finest version. Among other things, the longer editions include endings that suggest reconciliation between the bandits and the established authorities. The shorter text, on the other hand, concludes with an undiminished sense of dissent and resistance. See Lu Hsün, *A Brief History of Chinese Fiction,* translated by Yang Hsien-yi and Gladys Yang (Peking: Foreign Languages Press, 1959 [1925]), pp. 183–196; and Ch'en Shou-yi, *Chinese Literature: A Historical Introduction* (New York: Ronald Press, 1961).

51. Liu Wu-chi, *An Introduction to Chinese Literature* (Bloomington: Indiana University Press, 1966), p. 209. See also C. T. Hsia, "Comparative Approaches to *Water Margin,*" *Yearbook of Comparative and General Literature,* XI (Bloomington, 1962), Supplement, Third Conference on Oriental–Western Literary and Cultural Relations, 1962, pp. 121–128.

52. A different reading has been proposed by Andrew H. Plaks, who argues that *Shui Hu Chuan* presents its outlaw material ironically. Plaks insists on the "central role of irony" in the novel. "The idea of an ironic reading of the *Shui-hu chuan* obviously goes against the impression of the book as an essentially positive treatment of the deeds of the Liang-shan band." What we actually have in the novel, Plaks concludes, is "neither a blind approval of the Liang-shan mentality in disregard of its more troubling implications, nor a bitterly cynical denunciation of all that the band stands for, but rather a manifestation of a basic uncertainty." Plaks, *The Four Masterworks of the Ming Novel* (Princeton, NJ: Princeton University Press, 1987), pp. 319–320.

More recently Jing Wang has restated a more traditional view of the novel's significance: "Critics often disagree as to whether the Liang-shan heroes are just bloodthirsty followers of gang morality or faithful instruments of the heroic code prescribed by Heaven. Modern readers often feel repulsed by the ritualistic vengeance carried out by the bandits. . . . Yet however unreasonable the demonic fury of the heroes may appear to the sensitive readers of today, there is little doubt that within the framework of the fictional logic of the *Water Margin,* this particular code of heroism is endorsed by Heaven." Jing Wang, *The Story of Stone: Intertextuality, Ancient Chinese Stone Lore, and the Stone Symbolism in Dream of the Red Chamber, Water Margin, and The Journey to the West* (Durham, NC: Duke University Press, 1992), p. 260.

53. Fairbank, *The United States and China,* p. 284. See also Li Hsi-fan, "A Great Novel of Peasant Revolt," *Chinese Literature,* No. 12 (1959), pp. 62–71. In the press release he distributed in advance of the publication of *All Men Are Brothers,* Richard Walsh called particular attention to the Communist appropriation of the novel (see John Day Company, "News of Books and Authors," July 27, 1933). In fact, as C. T. Hsia has pointed out, while the novel's heroes are bandits, there is very little explicit talk of revolution. C. T. Hsia, *The Classic Chinese Novel: A Critical Introduction* (New York: Columbia University Press, 1968), pp. 106–107.

54. Pearl tried to stay as close as possible to the Chinese original. Her version of the novel is thus methodical and careful, more literal than imaginative, generally reliable but a little dull. Years ago, Richard Gregg Irwin called *All Men* "by far the most conscientious and complete" translation of *Shui Hu.* Irwin, *The Evolution of a Chinese Novel: Shui-hu-chuan* (Cambridge, MA: Harvard University Press, 1953), p. 94.

55. The working titles Pearl had used during her five years of work on the translation included "The Good Robbers" and "The Righteous Robbers." She decided on "All Men Are Brothers" shortly before the book was published. Years later, she repudiated the title, claiming that she had "reluctantly and mistakenly agreed" to the demands of her publisher. Pearl S. Buck, *China: Past and Present* (New York: John Day Company, 1972), pp. 74–74.

56. James Robert Hightower, *Topics in Chinese Literature,* revised edition (Cambridge, MA: Harvard University Press, 1962), p. 104. Hu Shih included *Shui Hu Chuan* among those classic texts that had made a national vernacular literature possible. See Hsia, *The Classic Chinese Novel,* p. 3.

57. Charles Hayford provides evidence of the revolutionary texture of *Shui Hu Chuan*. In the late 1930s, when the Mass Education Movement was suspected of left-wing subversion, "capital tongues wagged to the rumor that the MEM spread a revolutionary ditty which complained of the farmer's harsh life: 'The blazing sun like a fire burning, / Crops in the field to a crisp are turning, / Farmer's blood bubbles like a boiling soup, / Gentlemen at ease for fans are yearning.' This turned out not be a Marxist anthem, but a verse from the *Shui hu chuan* (*All Men Are Brothers*), the sixteenth-century popular novel in which the heroes turn to a life of virtuous rebellion." Charles Hayford, *To the People: James Yen and Village China* (New York: Columbia University Press, 1990), p. 174. In defense of Nationalist paranoia, however, it should be noted that the Communist Party adopted *Shui Hu Chuan* as its own, publishing an edition with revolutionary commentary in the 1930s. Min-chih Chou has concluded that "[r]ebels of different types and ideological persuasions in Chinese history, including Mao Tse-tung, were all fond of *Water Margin*." Chou, *Hu Shih and Intellectual Choice in Modern China* (Ann Arbor: University of Michigan Press, 1984), p. 153. And, according to Stuart Schram, Mao Tse-tung exhorted his fellow students to imitate the bandits of *Shui Hu Chuan* as early as 1917. Schram also remarks on the similarity between Mao's first guerrilla camp in the Kiangsi mountains in 1927 and the mountain fortress of the novel's heroes. Schram, *Mao Tse-tung* (New York: Simon and Schuster, 1967), pp. 43–44. See also Eric Hobsbawm, *The Age of Extremes: A History of the World, 1914–1991* (New York: Pantheon Books, 1994), p. 79.
58. Pearl S. Buck, *The Chinese Novel* (New York: John Day Company, 1938), p. 44.
59. "The reason, of course, why *Sons* seems like *All Men Are Brothers* is because there are phases of China today which *are All Men Are Brothers*." Pearl S. Buck to Richard J. Walsh (September 28, 1932), Pearl S. Buck Family Trust archives.
60. Pearl S. Buck, *Sons* (New York: John Day Company, 1932), pp. 296, 118, 120.
61. Published by the Friendship Press, *The Young Revolutionist* was initially distributed by the Missionary Education Movement along with an elaborate study guide, "Youth and Revolution in China." The guide outlined a six-session course, based closely on Pearl's book, intended to instruct young Americans in contemporary Chinese events. Though the study materials follow a Christian party line, they provide a fairly sophisticated introduction to China in the 1930s.
62. Over the next forty years, when she periodically drew up bibliographies of her writings, Pearl never included *The Young Revolutionist*.
63. In a letter to Lulu Hamilton, Pearl herself called *The Young Revolutionist* "a mission study book for juniors – a very short and mild affair" (May 11, 1932), Boston University archives.
64. By the time Pearl died, no fewer than eight Chinese translations of *The Good Earth* had appeared, none of them with her approval.
65. Pearl S. Buck to Mrs. Clarence H. Hamilton (December 30, 1931), Boston University archives.
66. Pearl S. Buck to Polly Small (January 10, 1932), Randolph-Macon Woman's College archives.
67. Pearl S. Buck to Emma Edmunds White (February 24, 1932), Randolph-Macon Woman's College archives.
68. Parts of this article were lifted from Pearl's 1931 speech "East and West and the Novel."
69. Pearl S. Buck, "China and the Foreign Chinese," *Yale Review*, Vol. XXI, No. 3 (March, 1932), p. 543.
70. In an article in *China Critic*, reprinted in the October, 1932 issue of the *Chinese Christian Student*, C. F. Lo attacked Pearl's essay. He insisted that Chinese culture had been and remained essentially "Confucian."
71. Richard Walsh had nominated *The Good Earth* for the Pulitzer in October, but had not told Pearl he had done so. The committee that selected *The Good Earth* for the

Pulitzer included Robert Morss Lovett, professor of English at the University of Chicago, Jefferson Fletcher, professor of comparative literature at Columbia, and the well-known biographer Albert Bigelow Paine.

72. Pearl's comment to Grace Yaukey is quoted in Stirling, *Pearl Buck*, p. 119; Pearl S. Buck to Mrs. Clarence H. Hamilton (May 11, 1932), Boston University archives.

73. An exchange of correspondence between Richard Walsh and the *St. Louis Post-Dispatch* illustrates the sort of intrusion Pearl was trying to avoid. On July 8, a reporter for the paper wired: "Am informed there is a dramatic human interest story concerning Pearl S. Buck. Is it that she has a daughter like little fool in Good Earth? Understand she put child in institution on promise to turn over profits from first success to pay $5000 costs. Would appreciate return wire and if possible details." In his reply of July 10, Richard said he had no information about Pearl's family circumstances and that in any case he was "under definite instructions from Mrs. Buck" not to encourage personal publicity of any sort. Pearl S. Buck Family Trust archives.

74. A. F. [not identified], "Popularity of 'The Good Earth' Was a Surprise to Pearl S. Buck," *Kansas City Star* (July 22, 1932).

75. Cited in Irvin Block, *The Lives of Pearl Buck: A Tale of China and America* (New York: Thomas Y. Crowell, 1973), p. 99.

76. Alexander Woollcott, "Shouts and Murmurs: The Vanishing Lady," *New Yorker*, Vol. VIII, No. 26 (August 13, 1932), p. 22.

77. Pearl's income tax return for 1932 indicates that she earned just over $100,000 in that calendar year.

78. C. A. Steele, memo to Dr. George T. Scott (August 29, 1932), Presbyterian Historical Society archives.

79. Pearl S. Buck to Dr. George T. Scott (July 16, 1932), written aboard the *Empress of Japan*, Presbyterian Historical Society archives. A few months later, when her royalty income seemed more assured, Pearl did remove herself completely from the Mission Board payroll. The effective date of her financial separation was November 1, 1932, the day before her celebrated speech in New York City attacking the missionary enterprise.

80. Carol Buck spent the rest of her life at Vineland, dying there at the age of seventy-two in September, 1992.

81. Pearl S. Buck to Mrs. Clarence H. Hamilton (November 15, 1932), Boston University archives.

82. Pearl S. Buck to Emma Edmunds White (n.d. [summer, 1932]), Randolph-Macon Woman's College archives.

83. David Lloyd to Pearl S. Buck (December 3, 1931), Pearl S. Buck Family Trust archives.

84. Pearl S. Buck to David Lloyd (January 2, 1932), Pearl S. Buck Family Trust archives.

85. Pearl S. Buck to David Lloyd (May 7, 1932), Pearl S. Buck Family Trust archives.

86. Brooks Atkinson of the *New York Times* called the play "a complete failure." In the *Herald Tribune,* Percy Hammond said that the play was "only a hesitant approximation" of the novel. Burns Mantle of the *Daily News* complained: "To put actors, even the best actors, in make-up of so completely foreign appearance as to be continually distracting, and to give them the language of simple peasants to speak in cultivated voices, is to demand more of the average playgoer's imagination than that eager patron has to give."

87. Richard wrote to Adeline Bucher, who was serving as Pearl's secretary: "The advance sale of *Sons* is phenomenal, nothing like it has happened in the book business for some years. Our advance orders are almost unprecedented. We shall have sold by Monday over 47,000 copies. Second printing goes on the press tomorrow." Richard J. Walsh to Adeline Bucher (September 23, 1932), Pearl S. Buck Family Trust archives. Just two weeks later, Pearl wrote to Emma White that sales had reached 80,000 copies (October 7, 1932), Randolph-Macon Woman's College archives.

88. Pearl S. Buck to Emma Edmunds White (October 7, 1932), Randolph-Macon Woman's College archives.
89. Reviews in the *Boston Herald* and *Philadelphia Inquirer* also declared a preference for *Sons* over *The Good Earth*.
90. The conversation was reported by Adeline Bucher, in a letter to C. Wade (May 9, 1933), Randolph-Macon Woman's College archives.
91. The number of guests and other details come from the *New York Times* account of the luncheon, published on November 3, 1932.
92. Pearl S. Buck, "Is There a Case for Foreign Missions?" (New York: John Day Company, 1932), p. 8.
93. In a letter published a few months earlier in the *Chinese Recorder*, Pearl had anticipated much of the argument she made in the Astor Hotel speech. She said that she had grown up among "narrow, bitter missionaries," and that she had never been in any circle of people where there was "such criticism, harsh and pharisaical . . . such contempt and lack of understanding of the Chinese." She went on to contrast the good work some missionaries were doing in medicine and education with "that arid and sterile preaching of the mere word of the gospel." Pearl S. Buck, "Give China the *Whole* Christ," *Chinese Recorder* (July, 1932), pp. 450–452.
94. The Presbyterian Historical Society has a large file of correspondence and news clippings from around the world relating to this controversy.
95. "To eradicate indigenous values was deemed undesirable; to graft Christianity on to them plainly absurd. The spread of anthropological and psychological knowledge thus dampened the zeal of young people either to save souls or to improve social conditions overseas." Jerome Ch'en, *China and the West: Society and Culture, 1815–1937* (London: Hutchinson, 1979), p. 100. See also Mosher, *China Misperceived: American Illusions and Chinese Reality*, p. 44.
96. Alvyn J. Austin, *Saving China: Canadian Missionaries in the Middle Kingdom, 1888–1959* (Toronto: University of Toronto Press, 1986), p. 229.
97. *Rain* was a United Artists production. Maxwell Anderson wrote the script, adapting Somerset Maugham's story "Sadie Thompson."
98. Sinclair Lewis's *Elmer Gantry* (1927) offered yet another satiric portrait of the preacher as a huckster and sexual predator.
99. The progressive platform outlined in Hocking's report expressed the new liberal orthodoxy of the 1920s and 1930s. "The liberal synthesis deserves to be regarded as the official foreign policy of American Protestantism at the time of the Laymen's Report." William R. Hutchinson, "Modernism and Missions: The Liberal Search for an Exportable Christianity, 1875–1935," in John K. Fairbank, ed., *The Missionary Enterprise in China and America* (Cambridge, MA: Harvard University Press, 1974), pp. 126–127.
100. William Ernest Hocking, ed., *Re-Thinking Missions: A Laymen's Inquiry After One Hundred Years* (New York: Harper & Brothers, 1932), p. 37.
101. John K. Fairbank, "Introduction: The Many Faces of Protestant Missions in China and the United States," in Fairbank, ed., *The Missionary Enterprise in China and America*, p. 9.
102. Sidney Brown of the Foreign Missions Board, in an interview with the *New York Times*, dismissed the Laymen's Inquiry report as an attack on the Christian faith itself. James Reed argues that it may not have been quite the case that the "central idea" of the report "ran to the effect that Christianity was no better than any other religion." Nonetheless, such a conclusion could easily be supported from the Hocking Commission's patient tabulation of missionary failures and its admiration for "universal" religious aspirations. James Reed, *The Missionary Mind and American East Asian Policy, 1911–1915,* (Cambridge, MA: Harvard University Press, 1983), p. 197.
103. Stirling, *Pearl Buck: A Woman in Conflict,* pp. 100–101. Decades later, Pearl's friendship with Ernest Hocking ripened into an autumnal love; see Chapter 9 of this volume.

104. Pearl's supporters included John D. Rockefeller, Jr., who had financed the Hocking commission.

105. Cited in Spencer, *The Exile's Daughter*, p. 178. A few months later, Pearl wrote of her admiration for the Urban League's efforts to achieve "genuine understanding between races." She promised to write two articles each year for *Opportunity*, "as evidence of my interest." Pearl S. Buck to Dr. Jones (June 6, 1933), Pearl S. Buck Family Trust archives.

106. Roy Wilkins, "Talking It Over," *Kansas City Call* (December 23, 1932)..

107. Spencer, *The Exile's Daughter*, p. 179.

108. Cited in Spencer, *The Exile's Daughter*, p. 179.

109. At the Murray Hill, Pearl stayed in adjoining rooms, 128 and 130, for which she paid $63.00 a week rent.

110. *Washington Post* (February 15, 1933).

111. A detailed summary of Pearl's speech was printed in the *Dairymen's League News* (February 28, 1933).

112. Witter Bynner's verse included a translation of Chinese poetry, *The Jade Mountain*, (1929), on which he collaborated with Kiang Kang-hu. Kiang gave *The Good Earth* one of its few negative reviews.

113. Pearl S. Buck to Hendrick Van Loon (March 7, 1933), Cornell University archives.

114. Quoted in Stirling, *Pearl Buck*, p. 138.

115. Rev. James R. Graham, Jr., in a circular memorandum (February 4, 1933), Presbyterian Historical Society archives.

116. Pearl S. Buck, "Easter, 1933," in *Cosmopolitan* (May, 1933), p. 170. The issue went on sale in mid-April.

117. *New York Times* (April 14, 1933), p. 14.

118. For a useful analysis of Machen's opinions, within the context of American Protestant fundamentalism, see D. G. Hart, *Defending the Faith: J. Gresham Machen and the Crisis of Conservative Protestantism in Modern America* (Baltimore: Johns Hopkins University Press, 1994). Hart discusses Pearl's defense of the Hocking Commission report in chapter 6, "The Responsibilities of the Church in the New Age." See also James Alan Patterson, *Robert E. Speer and the Crisis of the American Protestant Missionary Movement, 1920–1937* (Ann Arbor: University of Michigan Press, 1981), pp. 152–154.

119. The comment is part of a caption under a photograph of Pearl that accompanied the story of her resignation. The story itself, which portrays Pearl as the victim of orthodox intolerance, is headlined "Mrs. Pearl S. Buck a Lynch Lesson."

120. Pearl S. Buck, "On the Writing of Novels," Randolph-Macon Woman's College *Alumnae Bulletin* (Summer, 1933).

121. *New York Herald Tribune Books* (June 25, 1933), p. 3; *Times Literary Supplement* (September 14, 1933), p. 608; *Spectator* (September 22, 1933), p. 380.

122. Pearl S. Buck, *My Several Worlds* (New York: John Day Company, 1954), pp. 284–285.

123. Cited in Stirling, *Pearl Buck: A Woman in Conflict*, p. 145.

124. Buck, *My Several Worlds*, p. 291.

125. Pearl S. Buck to Emma Edmunds White (September 17, 1933). These quotations are taken from Nora Stirling's typescript transcription of the letter, in the Randolph-Macon Woman's College archives. The original letter apparently either has been destroyed or is among the material under seal in the college archives.

126. Quoted in Pearl S. Buck, "Friends and Enemies of China," *Asia* (April, 1936), p. 279.

127. Janet Fitch, *Foreign Devils: Reminiscences of a China Missionary Daughter, 1909–1935* ([Republic of China]: Chinese Materials Center, 1981), pp. 435–436.

128. Pearl S. Buck to William Lyon Phelps (November 13, 1933), reprinted in Phelps, *Autobiography With Letters* (New York: Oxford University Press, 1939), p. 913.

129. Buck, *My Several Worlds*, p. 302.

130. Fitch, *Foreign Devils*, p. 433.
131. The trip was reported in the *China Mail* (February 22, 1934).

Chapter 5: An Exile's Return

1. Malcolm Cowley, *Exile's Return: A Narrative of Ideas* (New York: W. W. Norton, 1934), p. 10.
2. Of course, this literary migration was a familiar story. Before and again after the 1920s, a long list of American writers has chosen to live abroad as expatriates, among them Henry James, Edith Wharton, T. S. Eliot, Ezra Pound, Gertrude Stein, Richard Wright, James Baldwin, and Gore Vidal. Typically, these men and women have defined their choice as an act of protest, either against America's supposedly impoverished cultural opportunities, or, in the case of Wright and Baldwin and other black writers, against the burdens of racial inequality.
3. It was also in the mid-1930s that Walter Benjamin published his most famous essay in cultural theory, "Art in the Age of Mechanical Reproduction." Among other signs of twentieth-century unease, Benjamin talks about "exile" as the governing condition of modern life. More concretely, the Office of the United Nations High Commissioner for Refugees recently estimated that the total number of people who have become refugees in the twentieth century, suffering either temporary or permanent displacement, approximates 100 million.
4. Ann Douglas is surely correct when she observes that "America's identity was, and is, at bottom, a theological and religious one." Douglas, *Terrible Honesty: Mongrel Manhattan in the 1920s* (New York: Farrar, Straus, and Giroux, 1995), p. 7.
5. There were exceptions: a number of twentieth-century writers who have turned to Asia for models of art or government. Ezra Pound's work offers one such instance, and the essays of the Southern Agrarians another. Robert Casillo has delineated the "Confucian myth" that formed one of the central tenets of Pound's thought: "Of all intellectual traditions, Pound probably most preferred that of the ruling mandarin bureaucracy of Confucian China, who stand at a far remove from the tradition of Western philosophy as it descends from the Greeks." Robert Casillo, *The Genealogy of Demons: Anti-Semitism, Fascism, and the Myths of Ezra Pound* (Evanston, IL: Northwestern University Press, 1988), p. 341.

   In the Agrarian manifesto, *I'll Take My Stand*, John Gould Fletcher's essay on education has a long quotation from Confucius as epigraph. According to Fletcher, Confucian education placed virtue rather than worldly advancement at its center, and is therefore to be preferred to Western pragmatism. John Gould Fletcher, "Education, Past and Present," in *I'll Take My Stand* (New York: Harper Torchbooks, 1962 [1930]), pp. 92–121.
6. Pearl S. Buck to Mrs. Clarence H. Hamilton (November 15, 1932), Boston University archives.
7. Pearl S. Buck, untitled speech to the National Committee on Federal Legislation for Birth Control (February 12, 1935), p. 5, Smith College archives.
8. Pearl S. Buck, *My Several Worlds* (New York: John Day Company, 1954), p. 274.
9. The folklore that smell is a marker of race had even been enshrined in scientific literature. The ninth and tenth editions of the *Encyclopedia Britannica*, for example, which were current from the 1880s through 1911, contained an article under the heading "Negro," by A. H. Keane. The essay locates Africans at "the lowest position in the evolutionary scale," and summarizes fourteen pseudo-scientific reasons for black inferiority. The twelfth is "cool, soft, and velvety [skin], mostly hairless, and emitting a peculiarly rancid odor, compared by Pruner Bey to that of the buck goat." For a discussion of such racist mumbo jumbo, see Peter Conn, *The Divided Mind: Ideology*

and Imagination in America, 1899–1917 (New York: Cambridge University Press, 1983), pp. 138–142.

10. See Dan T. Carter, *The Scottsboro Boys: A Tragedy of the American South* (Baton Rouge: Louisiana State University, 1969); and James E. Goodman, *Stories of Scottsboro* (New York: Pantheon, 1994).

11. In fact, lynchings increased in 1930, when twenty-one persons were lynched, twenty of them African-American. The outrages led the Commission on Interracial Cooperation to set up the Southern Commission on the Study of Lynching. The study resulted in a book: Arthur F. Raper, *The Tragedy of Lynching* (Chapel Hill: University of North Carolina Press, 1933). For the next five years, 1931–1935, the figures were 13, 8, 28, 15, and 20.

12. In 1933, Pearl wrote that news of American lynchings often reached China, convincing the Chinese that the United States was indeed a nation of barbarians. Cited in Theodore F. Harris, *Pearl S. Buck: A Biography* (New York: John Day Company, 1969), pp. 155–158.

13. For a useful analysis of anti-lynching legislation, see Robert L. Zangrando, *The NAACP Crusade Against Lynching, 1909–1950* (Philadelphia: Temple University Press, 1980).

14. Buck, *My Several Worlds*, p. 256.

15. On the financial condition of the John Day Company, see Nora Stirling, *Pearl Buck: A Woman in Conflict* (Piscataway, NJ: New Century Publishers, 1983), pp. 154–55; and correspondence in the David Lloyd papers, Princeton University archives.

16. Richard J. Walsh to Pearl S. Buck (December 15, 1933), Pearl S. Buck Family Trust archives.

17. On the rescheduling of *The Mother*'s publication, see Richard J. Walsh to David Lloyd (September 10, 1933), Pearl S. Buck Family Trust archives.

18. Adams's review appeared in the January 14, 1934 issue of the *New York Times Book Review*. For a sample of the many moderately to strongly favorable notices that *The Mother* received, see the *New York Herald Tribune Books* (January 14, 1934); the London *Times Literary Supplement* (January 25, 1934); the *Saturday Review of Literature* (January 13, 1934); the *Boston Evening Transcript Book Section* (January 13, 1934); the *Chicago Daily Tribune* (January 13, 1934); *Forum and Century* (March, 1934); the *Yale Review* (Spring, 1934); and the *New Republic* (March 14, 1934). The novel also elicited a few decidedly negative reviews, including those in England's *New Statesman and Nation* (January 27, 1934) and *Spectator* (February 2, 1934).

19. Paul A. Doyle usefully suggests that Pearl's nameless Mother can be compared with two other symbolic maternal figures from the same literary era: Brecht's Mother Courage and Steinbeck's Ma Joad. Doyle, *Pearl S. Buck,* revised edition (Boston: Twayne Publishers, 1980), pp. 64–65.

20. Dorothy Canfield, untitled review of *The Mother*, in "Asia Book-Shelf," *Asia* (February, 1934), p. 123.

21. Pearl S. Buck, *The Mother* (New York: John Day Company, 1934), p. 153.

22. Pearl S. Buck, "Debt to Dickens," *Saturday Review of Literature*, Vol. 13, No. 23 (April 4, 1936), pp. 11, 20, 25.

23. George Orwell [Eric Blair], "Charles Dickens," in *An Age Like This, 1920–1940*, volume one of *The Collected Essays, Journalism and Letters of George Orwell*, Sonia Orwell and Ian Angus, eds. (New York: Harcourt, Brace & World, 1968), p. 417.

24. Buck, *My Several Worlds*, p. 311.

25. The collapse of real estate prices in the Depression brought thousands of small Northeastern farms onto the market at deep discounts. These were the years in which city-based writers, artists, and professionals began to colonize Bucks County, Connecticut's various Cornwalls, Rockland County in New York, and southern Vermont. Some, like radical economist Scott Nearing, were part of the "back-to-the-land" movement of the 1930s; others, like Pearl, were simply looking for open spaces and a small-town am-

bience for their children. See J. C. Furnas, *Stormy Weather: Crosslights on the 1930s: An Informal Social History of the United States, 1929–1941* (New York: G. P. Putnam's Sons, 1977), pp. 311–320.

26. Pearl S. Buck, "Fool's Sacrifice," *Cosmopolitan* (April, 1934), pp. 26–27.

27. *Asia* was founded in 1917 by Willard Straight, with financial support from his wife, Dorothy Whitney Straight. Three years earlier, also with his wife's backing, Straight had begun the *New Republic*. After Willard Straight's death, Dorothy married Leonard K. Elmhirst, who took over as *Asia*'s publisher. For a brief history of the magazine's first two decades, see Louis D. Froelick, "Twenty Years of *Asia*," published as the foreword to a special twentieth-anniversary issue (March, 1937), pp. 148–149.

28. Richard J. Walsh, "Editor's Note," *Asia* (January, 1934), p. 64.

29. Helen Foster Snow to Richard J. Walsh (September 30, 1935), Hoover Institution archives.

30. Anna Louise Strong, "The Last Word in the Far East," *Asia* (October, 1935), p. 595.

31. Pearl S. Buck, "Asia Book-Shelf," *Asia* (September, 1936), p. 614.

32. Nehru's prison letters, addressed to his daughter "on her thirteenth birthday," first appeared in India in 1930. Thirty years later, Indira would follow her father as a prime minister of India.

33. Pearl S. Buck, "Asia Book-Shelf," *Asia* (September, 1937), p. 654.

34. F. M. de Mello, "Birth Control in India," *Asia* (December, 1935), pp. 754–759.

35. Anne Guthrie, "The Traffic in Women," *Asia* (July, 1937), pp. 522–523.

36. See Jacques Gernet, *A History of Chinese Civilization,* translated by J. R. Foster (New York: Cambridge University Press, 1982), pp. 631–634; John King Fairbank, *The United States and China,* fourth edition (Cambridge, MA: Harvard University Press, 1983), pp. 251–252; and Jonathan D. Spence, *The Search for Modern China* (New York: W. W. Norton, 1990), pp. 415–417. For a while at least, many knowledgeable Westerners in China supported the New Life Movement as a genuine reform effort. As the case of Dr. Ruth Hemenway suggests, disillusion set in inevitably but only gradually. Ruth V. Hemenway, M.D., *A Memoir of Revolutionary China, 1924–1941,* edited with an introduction by Fred W. Drake (Amherst: University of Massachusetts Press, 1977).

37. Mark Van Doren, "Abstract Woman," *Nation,* vol. 138, no. 3576 (January 17, 1934), p. 78.

38. Pearl and Richard did maintain a casual friendship with V. F. Calverton (the pen name of George Goetz), one of the principal left-wing critics of the 1930s. In 1932, Calverton published *The Liberation of American Literature,* a pioneering history of American literature from a Marxist point of view.

39. Deming Brown, *Soviet Attitudes Toward American Writing* (Princeton, NJ: Princeton University Press, 1962), p. 48. Soviet esteem for Pearl's writing continued through the 1930s. In 1939, Edward Carter, director of the Institute of Pacific Relations, wrote to Pearl on his return from Moscow. He told her: "Our IPR Bolshevik friends there say that the Soviet public is a very enthusiastic admirer of your writings." Edward C. Carter to Pearl S. Buck (July 20, 1939), Columbia University rare book and manuscript library.

40. Hailed as authoritative by most of its first reviewers, *My Country and My People* has subsequently attracted much criticism for its representation of the Chinese. See, for example, A. C. Scott, *Literature and the Arts in Twentieth-Century China* (Gloucester, MA: Peter Smith, 1968), pp. 177–179.

41. Pearl S. Buck to Emma Edmunds White (n.d. [fall, 1936]), Randolph-Macon Woman's College archives.

42. Cited in Stirling, *Pearl Buck: A Woman in Conflict,* p. 177.

43. Grace Yaukey, interview with the present writer (May 10, 1991).

44. Janice C. Walsh, "Afterword," to Pearl S. Buck, *The Child Who Never Grew* (Rockville, MD: Woodbine House, 1992), pp. 105–106.

45. Helen Foster Snow, interview with the present writer (November 15, 1991).

46. Pearl S. Buck to Emma Edmunds White (n.d. [November/December, 1934]), Randolph-Macon Woman's College archives.
47. Pearl S. Buck, "Advice to Unborn Novelists," *Saturday Review of Literature*, vol. 11, no. 13 (March 2, 1935), pp. 513–514, 520–521.
48. Pearl S. Buck, *A House Divided* (New York: Reynal & Hitchcock / A John Day Book, 1935), p. 248.
49. Malcolm Cowley, "The Good Earthling," *New Republic* (January 23, 1935), p. 309.
50. Lewis Gannett, "Books and Things," *New York Herald Tribune* (January 21, 1935), p. 12.
51. Over the next several years, the literary rediscovery of America would reach its Depression-era fulfillment in the State Guide series. A massive undertaking of the Federal Writers' Project, the Guides included individual volumes on all forty-eight states. These splendid books have been repeatedly and rightly commemorated in memoirs and criticism. See, among many other examples, Jerre Mangione, *The Dream and the Deal: The Federal Writers' Project, 1935–1943*, second paperback edition (Philadelphia: University of Pennsylvania Press, 1983).
52. Pearl S. Buck, "Foreword" to the 1958 Pocket Book reprint of her novel *The Townsman*.
53. In 1935, Pearl made some progress on a novel under the working title "American Woman." However, she abandoned the project and apparently destroyed the manuscript.
54. Pearl S. Buck, untitled speech to the National Committee on Federal Legislation for Birth Control (February 12, 1935), pp. 1, 4, Smith College archives. In the November, 1936 issue of *Asia*, Pearl and Richard printed the transcript of a debate between Margaret Sanger and Gandhi. In the debate, which took place at Gandhi's ashram in Wardha, Gandhi argued that women could prevent pregnancy by refusing sexual relations with their husbands. Sanger dismissed this proposal as unrealistic, and insisted that Indian women needed access to contraception.
55. Pearl S. Buck to Helen Stevens (January 30, 1942, and March 24, 1942), Columbia University archives.
56. Lossing had been hired to advise Morgenthau on a proposal that the United States purchase large quantities of Chinese silver. See John Morton Blum, ed., *From the Morgenthau Diaries*, vol. 1, *Years of Crisis, 1928–1938* (Boston: Houghton Mifflin, 1959), pp. 210–211.
57. Quoted in Stirling, *Pearl Buck: A Woman in Conflict*, p. 163.
58. Buck, *My Several Worlds*, p. 320.
59. Reported in the *New York Times* (June 12, 1935), p. 19. Pearl's success in concealing Carol from the press is indicated by the fact that this story refers to her as the mother of two children, a fifteen-year-old son and a ten-year-old daughter.
60. Pearl S. Buck to Emma Edmunds White (June 9, 1935), Randolph-Macon Woman's College archives.
61. Pearl S. Buck to Margaret Thomson (July 1, 1935), Randolph-Macon Woman's College archives.
62. Janice Walsh, interview with the present writer (January 21, 1992).
63. Pearl S. Buck, "Women at Work," *Horizons* (The Manor Club: Pelham Manor, NY: May, 1935), p. 33.
64. Courtenay Fenn to J. Lossing Buck (June 13, 1935), Presbyterian Historical Society archives. In his few surviving comments, Lossing took a more generous view of Pearl's actions than others in the missionary community. He wrote back to Fenn, from a hotel in Shanghai, thanking him for his kindness, but advising him "not to attach any blame because it is very difficult to know how another feels. No two people are alike and hence how can we judge rightly the action of another. I know Mrs. Buck did what to her seemed the right thing to do and that is all that anyone can ask of any individual."

J. Lossing Buck to Courtenay Fenn (August 11, 1935), Presbyterian Historical Society archives.

65. Clarence A. Barbour to Margaret S. Morriss (April 20, 1935), Brown University archives.

66. See Stirling, *Pearl Buck: A Woman in Conflict,* p. 166.

67. Pearl S. Buck, "Conflict and Cooperation," typescript of a lecture given at the University of Virginia (July 8, 1935), pp. 4–5, University of Virginia archives.

68. Pearl S. Buck, abstract of an untitled lecture at the University of Virginia (July 8, 1935), p. 3, University of Virginia archives.

69. Among many discussions of the scientific racism that dominated social research in the late nineteenth and early twentieth centuries, see Robert C. Bannister, *Social Darwinism: Science and Myth in Anglo-American Social Thought* (Philadelphia: Temple University Press, 1979); George M. Frederickson, *The Black Image in the White Mind: The Debate on Afro-American Character and Destiny, 1817–1914* (New York: Harper & Row, 1971); Jan Breman, ed., *Imperial Monkey Business: Racial Supremacy in Social Darwinist Theory and Colonial Practice* (Amsterdam: VU University Press, 1990); and Carl N. Degler, *In Search of Human Nature: The Decline and Revival of Darwinism in American Social Thought* (New York: Oxford University Press, 1991).

    Most theories of racial superiority on both sides of the Atlantic proposed a hierarchy with white races at the top and black at the bottom. The Asian people were usually ranked somewhere in the middle. Stephen Jay Gould provides a European example from the mid-nineteenth century. In an article called "Dr. Down's Syndrome," Gould asks why the British physician Dr. John Langdon Haydon Down chose (in 1866) to call the condition he had diagnosed "Mongolian idiocy." Down's decision was based on a larger system of classification, in which different sorts of mental defectives were linked analogically with different inferior races, including – moving upward from the lowest – Ethiopian, Malay, American Indian, and (just below Caucasian) the Oriental. A European who suffered from this affliction was, in effect, an Oriental: a degenerated Caucasian. Gould's essay is reprinted in *The Panda's Thumb: More Reflections in Natural History* (New York: W. W. Norton, 1980), pp. 160–168.

70. For an informative account of changing scientific attitudes toward race in the 1920s and 1930s, see Elazar Barkan, *The Retreat of Scientific Racism: Changing Concepts of Race in Britain and the United States Between the World Wars* (New York: Cambridge University Press, 1992).

71. Pearl S. Buck, "Asia Book-Shelf," *Asia* (November, 1937), p. 782.

72. Among the many books and articles that shaped America's changing attitude toward race, two of the most influential were Ruth Benedict's *Race: Science and Politics,* first published in 1940, and Ashley Montagu's landmark study, *Man's Most Dangerous Myth: The Fallacy of Race,* which appeared in 1942.

73. Pearl S. Buck, "Asia Book-Shelf," *Asia* (November, 1939), p. 665. The quoted passages come from Pearl's favorable review of Herbert J. Seligman, *Race Against Man* (New York: G. P. Putnam's Sons, 1939).

74. For information on Pearl's stormy relationship with Henry Luce, see W. A. Swanberg, *Luce and His Empire* (New York: Charles Scribner's Sons, 1972); Patricia Neils, *Chinese Images in the Life and Times of Henry Luce* (Savage, MD: Rowman & Littlefield, 1990); and Chapter 8, pp. 324–326, of this volume.

75. Pearl S. Buck, "Asia Book-Shelf," *Asia* (August, 1935), p. 507.

76. Information and correspondence concerning Pearl's relationship with the Women's International League for Peace and Freedom is located in the WILPF records on deposit at Swarthmore College. Other signers of the Peoples' Mandate included Lillian Wald, Fannie Hurst, John Dewey, Sherwood Anderson, Alice Paul, Alma Lutz, William Allen White, and Robert Sherwood.

77. Pearl S. Buck, "Asia Book-Shelf," *Asia* (April, 1937), p. 310.

78. This information is contained in a letter from Elmer Carter to Pearl (October 24, 1935), Pearl S. Buck Foundation archives.

79. Pearl S. Buck, "Asia Book-Shelf," *Asia* (November, 1936), p. 755.

80. The story was reported, under the headline "Pearl Buck's Book Opens School Inquiry," in the *New York Times* (October 19, 1935), p. 15.

81. Details of Pearl's appearance are contained in the *Pen and Brush Bulletin* (November, 1935). A few years later, Pearl turned down the presidency of Pen and Brush, citing the demands of wartime work. Pearl S. Buck to Katherine Woods (January 11, 1943), Bryn Mawr College Library.

82. In his comments at the award ceremony, Robert Grant pointed out that all three of the Howells Medals had gone to women. He noted, either proudly or defensively, that three of the four members of the selection committee were men.

83. In his irritated reference to the distorted uses of "proletarian," Grant was undoubtedly complaining about the active left-wing campaign for literature in the service of revolution. The most comprehensive gathering of relevant texts had been published just a few months before the Howells Medal was awarded. The anthology *Proletarian Literature in the United States,* edited by a committee that included Granville Hicks and Joseph Freeman, comprised four hundred closely printed pages of fiction, poetry, drama, journalism, and literary criticism. Several dozen writers were represented, among them John Dos Passos, Josephine Herbst, Michael Gold, Malcolm Cowley, Isidore Schneider, James T. Farrell, and Richard Wright. Pearl Buck's work was not included. The only item that dealt with China was Agnes Smedley's "The Fall of Shangpo," a pro-Communist report of a civil war battle.

84. Quoted in Stirling, *Pearl Buck: A Woman in Conflict,* p. 174.

85. Details of the speech were carried in stories in several newspapers in Washington and New York, including the April 12 issue of the *New York Times.*

86. For a discussion of the origin and significance of Du Bois's idea of the "talented tenth," see David Levering Lewis, *W. E. B. Du Bois: Biography of a Race, 1868–1919* (New York: Henry Holt, 1993), especially pp. 165, 206, and 441–442.

87. Pearl S. Buck, "On the Cultivation of a Young Genius," *Opportunity,* Volume XV, Number 1 (January, 1937), p. 7.

88. Only twelve minutes of the footage shot in China survive in the finished film. For the troubles that MGM faced, including opposition from the Kuomintang, see Chapter 4, p. 159, of this volume.

89. Andrew Sarris, *The American Cinema: Directors and Directions, 1929–1968* (New York: E. P. Dutton, 1968), p. 231.

90. Pearl S. Buck to Emma Edmunds White (February 5, 1937), typescript copy in the Nora Stirling papers, Randolph-Macon Woman's College archives.

91. See James L. Hoban, Jr., "Scripting *The Good Earth:* Versions of the Novel for the Screen," in Elizabeth Lipscomb et al., eds., *The Several Worlds of Pearl Buck* (Greenwood, CT: Greenwood Press, 1994), p. 172.

92. Some of the changes in the handling of sexuality in the film were the result of interventions by Joseph Breen of the Hays Office. After reviewing a draft of the script, Breen made several demands. Among other things, he insisted that the birth of Wang Lung's first son be treated in less detail, and that there should be no sexual suggestiveness in Wang Lung's discussion with his father about his future wife. See Hoban, "Scripting *The Good Earth,*" p. 182.

93. Thalberg had tried to hire Arnold Schoenberg to do the musical background for the film. Schoenberg asked for $50,000, and said that he was relieved when Thalberg turned him down. If he had gone to Hollywood, he said, "It would have been the end of me."

94. Theodore F. Harris, *Pearl S. Buck: A Biography* (New York: John Day Company, 1969), p. 148.

95. Years earlier, D. W. Griffith's *Broken Blossoms* (1919) had featured Richard Barthelmess as a saintly Chinese. Barthelmess plays a Chinese working man, living in a tenement in London's Limehouse, who tries to shelter Lillian Gish from her abusive drunken father and is brutally murdered for his interference. Barthelmess's character is likened to the crucified Christ, a Eurocentric but sincere tribute to his virtue.
96. Pearl S. Buck to Emma Edmunds White (February 5, 1937), typescript copy in the Nora Stirling papers, Randolph-Macon Woman's College archives.
97. Pearl's interest in the differences among media was genuine, but she often used the distinctions as a diversion, to avoid offering opinions.
98. One of the most heartbreaking stories concerned the German ship *St. Louis,* which carried nearly a thousand Jewish refugees to Cuba. When their Cuban visas expired, Jewish relief agencies began efforts to have these men, women, and children admitted to the United States. The ship sailed into the waters off Miami Beach – close enough so that the passengers could hear the sound of band music coming from beachfront hotels. But permission to land was denied; the ship returned to Europe, where hundreds of the passengers died in the Holocaust. See Roger Daniels, *Coming to America: A History of Immigration and Ethnicity in American Life* (New York: HarperCollins, 1990), pp. 299–300. See also Arthur D. Morse, *While Six Million Died: A Chronicle of American Apathy* (New York: Random House, 1968); Sheldon Morris Neuringer, *American Jewry and United States Immigration Policy, 1881–1953* (New York: Arno Press, 1980); and Barbara McDonald Stewart, "United States Government Policy on Refugees from Nazism, 1933–1940," unpublished dissertation (Columbia University, 1969).
99. Pearl S. Buck, "On Discovering America," *Survey Graphic,* Vol. XXVI, No. 6 (June, 1937), pp. 313–315, 353, 355.
100. Correspondence and editorial material concerning this article is located in the Pearl S. Buck Foundation archives.
101. In March, 1938, Pearl published another article in *Survey Graphic,* "Security in a Cage." An attack on militarism, the essay consisted mainly in a personal diatribe against Hitler, Goebbels, Mussolini, and Stalin. Pearl described them as inferior men, thugs and bullies who had almost inexplicably been given power over decent but docile populations.
102. Anne Polzer to the Pearl S. Buck Foundation (January 27, 1992), copy in the possession of the present writer. Polzer has appended a series of letters she received from Pearl Buck.
103. An extensive file of correspondence between Pearl Buck and Katherine Cornell is contained in the Randolph-Macon Woman's College archives.
104. Pearl S. Buck to Emma Edmunds White (n.d. [fall, 1937]), Randolph-Macon Woman's College archives.
105. Pearl S. Buck, "Asia Book-Shelf," *Asia* (February, 1937), pp. 132–133.
106. Jonathan Spence, *The Search for Modern China* (New York: W. W. Norton, 1990), p. 445.
107. Michitaka Hiramoto, "Our Little Visits to Nanking," *Asia* (January, 1938), pp. 7–9.
108. Pearl S. Buck to Emma Edmunds White (n.d. [fall, 1937]), Randolph-Macon Woman's College archives.
109. Pearl S. Buck, "Western Weapons in the Hands of the Reckless East," *Asia* (October, 1937), pp. 672–673.
110. Pearl S. Buck, "Asia Book-Shelf," *Asia* (November, 1937), p. 782.
111. The work of F. H. King is discussed briefly in Chapter 2, pp. 56–57, of this volume.
112. Rudolf P. Hommel, *China At Work* (New York: John Day Company, 1937). In his discussion of *tou fu,* bean curd, Hommel suggests that Americans should learn to eat this healthy and inexpensive soy bean product (pp. 108–109). In another place, comparing Asian and Western animal traps, Hommel says that Western technology has "enslaved us to the use of any conceivable mechanical principle" (p. 128). He explains the use of chopsticks, and argues that they make superior eating utensils (p. 158).

113. For the best account of Henry Mercer's career and the significance of his historical thinking, see Steven Conn, "Henry Chapman Mercer and the Search for American History," *Pennsylvania Magazine of History & Biography*, Vol. CXVI, No. 3 (July, 1992), pp. 323–355.
114. Mercer's museum in Doylestown is only a few miles from Green Hills Farm. In her memoirs, Pearl said of the collection: "anyone can see the extraordinary likeness between the tools the early Pennsylvanians used and the tools which the Chinese used and do still use." Buck, *My Several Worlds*, p. 318.
115. Pearl S. Buck, "Thanks to Japan," *Asia* (May, 1938), pp. 279–280.
116. Pearl S. Buck to Florence Lurty (August 10, 1938), Pearl S. Buck Family Trust archives.
117. Pearl made these remarks on a radio broadcast on January 17, 1938. She used substantially the same text as her review of *Red Star Over China* in her "Asia Book-shelf" column in the March issue of *Asia*.
118. Pearl S. Buck to Emma Edmunds White (November 3, 1938), Randolph-Macon Woman's College archives.
119. Pearl S. Buck, "America's Medieval Women," *Harper's Magazine*, Vol. 177 (August, 1938), pp. 225–232. A long excerpt from this article was included in *An American Retrospective*, an anthology of writing published in *Harper's* from 1850 through 1984.
120. A 1937 Gallup survey indicated that 65 percent of those polled said they would not vote for a woman for president even if they were convinced she was qualified for the job. Cited in John Harwood and Geraldine Brooks, "Ms. President," *Wall Street Journal*, Vol. CCXXII, No. 116 (December 14, 1993), p. 1.
121. In an article in the *New York Post* (July 30, 1938), Dorothy Dunbar Bromley accused Pearl of blaming men for the failures of women. On the other hand, Alma Lutz, a leader of the National Women's Party, wrote Pearl congratulating her for the gist of her article, but asking why she refused to identify herself as a "feminist." Perhaps, Lutz suggested, Pearl had "a mistaken idea of feminism. It is not fighting men and setting up a matriarchy. It is working for equal opportunity for women in all fields." Alma Lutz to Pearl S. Buck (August 9, 1938), Vassar College archives.
122. Pearl Buck, "America's Medieval Women," *Harper's Magazine*, 177 (August, 1938), p. 230.
123. The other names on Howes's list provide an interesting context and a cross section of prominent American women in the late 1930s: Judge Florence Allen, of the U.S. Court of Appeals, Sixth Circuit, the "first woman ever mentioned as a candidate for the U.S. Supreme Court"; Dr. Jean Broadhurst, bacteriologist at Teacher's College; Jacqueline Cochran, aviator and businesswoman; Grace Noll Crowell, poet laureate of Texas since 1935, who had been "chosen as 'Typical American Mother' of 1938"; the actress Helen Hayes; tennis champion Alice Marble; the singer Kate Smith; Eleanor Patterson, "the only woman publisher and editor-in-chief of a metropolitan morning daily in the U.S."; and Julia Stimson, president of the American Nurses Association.
124. Pearl S. Buck, *This Proud Heart* (New York: John Day Company, 1938), p. 91.
125. One probable source for the character of Susan Gaylord was Malvina Hoffman (1885–1966), a sculptor whom Pearl had known and admired since the early 1930s. In 1909, Hoffman had moved to Paris and spent four years studying with Rodin. Her most famous project was a 1930 commission from Chicago's Field Museum for a group of one hundred sculptures in a series called "The Living Races of Man." In 1934, Pearl rented Hoffman's Greenwich Village house briefly. A few months later, Pearl presented an American Academy of Arts and Sciences medal to Hoffman at a ceremony covered in the *New York Times*. Hoffman's subjects included a series of Chinese heads that Pearl and Richard had photographed and published, also in 1934, in *Asia*.

    Years later, Pearl read Hoffman's memoirs, *Yesterday Is Tomorrow* (New York: Crown Publishers, 1965), and wrote to congratulate her: "The book is crowded with richness and beauty. It is the life story of an artist – hard work and joy and deserved success."

Pearl S. Buck to Malvina Hoffman (June 28, 1965), Pearl S. Buck Family Trust archives. The following year, when Marianne Moore nominated Hoffman for membership in the American Academy of Arts and Sciences, Pearl agreed to serve as one of the seconders.

Another source for Susan Gaylord was Pearl herself. In her memoirs, Pearl confessed that she had once harbored ambitions to become a sculptor, and that writing *This Proud Heart* thus "fulfilled a dream." See *My Several Worlds*, p. 176. After she moved to Green Hills Farm, she did in fact sculpt several portrait busts, which can still be seen in her studio.

126. Pearl did not conceal the autobiographical strata that lay under *This Proud Heart*. See Doyle, *Pearl S. Buck*, p. 79; and Theodore F. Harris, *Pearl S. Buck: A Biography*, Volume One (New York: John Day, 1969), pp. 210–212.

127. Susan, who expresses Pearl's hard-won beliefs about gender, walks in an American cavalcade of her own, a tradition of strong women who populate the novels of the first few decades of the twentieth century. The memorable list includes Undine Spragg, the efficiently unscrupulous heroine of Edith Wharton's *The Custom of the Country* (1913); the competent Dorinda Oakley, in Ellen Glasgow's *Barren Ground* (1925); Scarlett O'Hara, incorrigible and inexhaustible in Margaret Mitchell's *Gone With the Wind* (1936); and Janey Crawford, the main character in *Their Eyes Were Watching God* (1937) by Zora Neale Hurston. These fictional women – all created by women – were rather exceptional, to be sure, both before and especially after the 1930s. In *The Feminine Mystique* (New York: W. W. Norton, 1963), Betty Friedan contrasted the stories she found in women's magazines of the late 1930s and late 1950s. She observed a significant shift in the representation of female identity, in which an emphasis on female activity and self-reliance was replaced by a highly valued passivity and dependence.

128. Cornelia Spencer [Grace Yaukey], *The Exile's Daughter* (New York: Coward-McCann, 1944), p. 197.

129. J. Edgar Hoover to Pearl S. Buck (September 8, 1938), Federal Bureau of Investigation files.

Chapter 6: The Prize

1. Dreiser agreed. According to Ross Terrill, Dreiser wrote Pearl a fairly rude letter after the Nobel Prize announcement. Quoted in "East Wind, West Wind" (1993), a televised documentary on the life of Pearl Buck.

2. S. J. Woolf, "Pearl Buck Finds that East and West Do Meet," *New York Times Magazine* (November 20, 1938), p. 4.

3. Cited in Stephen Birmingham, *The Late John Marquand: A Biography* (Philadelphia: J. B. Lippincott, 1972), p. 153.

4. The Nobel Prize in literature has generally been managed as a fairly parochial, transatlantic monopoly. In the first several decades of Nobel competition, only one literature prize went to an Asian writer: Rabindranath Tagore of India, in 1913. In 1945, Gabriela Mistral of Chile received the first prize awarded to a South American. Over forty years later, in 1986, Nigerian Wole Soyinka received the first Nobel Prize won by an African writer.

5. In 1993, fifty-five years after Pearl Buck's award, Toni Morrison became the second American woman to win the Nobel Prize in literature.

6. Pearl Buck, *My Several Worlds* (New York: John Day Company, 1954), p. 342.

7. Buck, *My Several Worlds*, p. 342.

8. Carl Van Doren, *The American Novel* (New York: Macmillan, 1940), pp. 350–353. Van Doren also raised the possibility that Pearl's prose style was influenced by the Chinese novels she had been reading from her childhood.

9. Norman Holmes Pearson to John Gould Fletcher (November 12, 1938), special collections, University of Arkansas (Fayetteville). Fletcher replied a couple of weeks later, agreeing that "Pearl Buck certainly didn't deserve the Nobel Prize," but added, "who else *in this country* did?" Pearson responded with the suggestions of Willa Cather and Dos Passos. Fletcher to Pearson (November 23, 1938) and Pearson to Fletcher (December 17, 1938), special collections, University of Arkansas, Fayetteville.

10. At forty-six, Pearl was one of the youngest persons to win the literature prize. This, too, probably fueled the animosity of her critics.

11. Joseph Blotner, ed., *Selected Letters of William Faulkner* (New York: Random House, 1977), p. 299. Faulkner's letter is dated February 22, 1950. Somewhat ironically, Pearl voted in favor of Faulkner's membership in the National Institute of Arts and Letters in March, 1939, just a few months after she won the Nobel Prize. She also voted for the other candidates on the slate that year, among them Charles Beard, Marjorie Kinnan Rawlings, William Beebe, and John Steinbeck. (Pearl S. Buck Foundation archives.)

12. Malcolm Cowley, "Wang Lung's Children," *New Republic* (May 10, 1939), pp. 24–25. Cowley, longtime literary editor of the *New Republic*, was himself a leading shaper of intellectual taste in the 1920s and 1930s. By 1939, although he was identified with an increasingly isolated, doctrinaire left, his pronouncements remained much consulted – as they would be for several more decades. "On reading *The Good Earth* after all these years," he admitted, "I found that Mr. Phelps was right for once, and the high-brow critics mistaken." He concluded that *The Good Earth* was "a masterpiece."

13. "Sino-Japanese Romance," *Time*, 33 (March 6, 1939), 62.

14. Now vanished from literary history, Arthur Davison Ficke was a widely published poet, the author of a dozen volumes of verse, including *An April Elegy* (1917) and *Mountain Against Mountain* (1929). His work was included in several editions of Louis Untermeyer's influential anthology *Modern American Poetry*. Ficke was also a collector and student of Japanese prints.

15. The letters and telegrams cited here are contained in a folder labeled "Nobel Prize" in the Pearl S. Buck Family Trust archives.

16. Grace Yaukey, in an interview with this writer (May 10, 1991).

17. Cited in Theodore F. Harris, *Pearl S. Buck: A Biography* (New York: John Day Company, 1969), pp. 239–240.

18. Cited in Cornelia Spencer [Grace Yaukey], *The Exile's Daughter* (New York: Coward-McCann, 1944), p. 202.

19. The other 1938 Nobel laureates included German Richard Kuhn in chemistry, Corneille Heymans of Belgium in physiology or medicine, and the Nansen International Office for Refugees, in peace. Because of Europe's unsettled conditions, only two winners attended the Stockholm ceremony, Pearl Buck and Enrico Fermi, who won the prize in physics. The two laureates commenced a casual but cordial friendship that lasted until Fermi's death in 1954.

20. Just a few months after she won the Nobel Prize, Pearl had an exchange of correspondence with Clifton Fadiman about a biographical sketch he had written. She told him that she had deleted the phrase "probably her masterpiece to date" from a description of *The Good Earth*. "I know that this represents your personal opinion, to which you are of course entitled, and I know that many other Americans agree with you. In most other countries, however, various books of mine are liked better than *The Good Earth*. . . ." Pearl S. Buck to Clifton Fadiman (March 20, 1939), University of Virginia manuscripts collection. A couple of years later, she made a similar remark in a letter to Mrs. Charles Towne, who had written some kind words about *The Good Earth*. "I have almost forgotten that book," Pearl wrote, disingenuously; "you know how one feels *finished* with a book, so that it ceases to be a part of one's life." Pearl S. Buck to Mrs. Charles H. Towne (August 31, 1942), University of Virginia manuscripts collection.

21. Pearl S. Buck, *The Chinese Novel* (New York: John Day Company, 1939), p. 28.

22. Unfortunately, the Chinese novels Pearl discussed and praised are probably no better known in the West today than they were when she gave her speech over a half-century ago. The multicultural curriculum has not yet made room for the masterpieces of Chinese fiction.

23. One proof of the pressure on Pearl's time in the weeks immediately following the Nobel Prize is that she failed to write her "Asia Book-Shelf" column for *Asia* magazine for three consecutive months, January through March, 1939. Given her usual level of productivity, this was a rare lapse.

24. Cosmopolitan Club program (January, 1939), Beinecke Library, Yale University.

25. Cited in Nora Stirling, *Pearl Buck: A Woman in Conflict* (Piscataway, NJ: New Century Publishers, 1983), p. 196. A decade later, Skinner published a funny account of the reading. Since the original script ran over four hours, the actors cut two-thirds of it, pruning almost every political and historical reference and leaving only the love story intact. "Our one concession to history," Skinner wrote, "was to retain, as first-rate theatre, a scene in which some missionaries were burned during an embassy garden party." Cornelia Otis Skinner, "Actors Will Do Anything," *New Yorker*, 25 (March 19, 1949), p. 77. Pearl, who is not named in Skinner's anecdote, was not amused by the performance, and presumably not amused by Skinner's reminiscences either.

26. Details of this event are contained in a story headlined "Dorothy Thompson Honored at Dinner," *New York Times* (January 25, 1939), p. 7.

27. Robert Van Gelder, "Pearl Buck Talks of Her Work," *New York Times* (March 10, 1940), section VI, p. 22.

28. Pearl S. Buck to Mrs. Kenneth L. Washburn (August 2, 1939), Pearl S. Buck Family Trust archives. The source of Pearl's "gunpowder" figure may have been Ruth Benedict's *Patterns of Culture* (Boston: Houghton Mifflin, 1934), though Benedict uses the metaphor to emphasize the complexity of culture rather than the dangers that follow from discrimination. In a chapter called "The Integration of Culture," Benedict writes that "[g]unpowder is not merely the sum of sulphur and charcoal and saltpeter. . . . Cultures, likewise, are more than the sum of their traits" (p. 47). For a discussion of Benedict's conception of cultural composites, see Judith Schachter Modell, *Ruth Benedict: Patterns of a Life* (Philadelphia: University of Pennsylvania Press, 1983), pp. 197–199. More generally, Pearl found in Benedict's widely influential book scientific confirmation for many of her own views: that customs, not biology, generally govern human behavior; that cultural differences are not the sign of cultural hierarchies; that the idea of racial purity is a delusion.

29. Pearl S. Buck, "Wanted: True Drama of the Negro Race," *Opportunity*, Vol. XVII, No. 4 (April, 1939), pp. 100–101. For a summary of Du Bois's views, see Nathan Iwin Huggins, *Harlem Renaissance* (New York: Oxford University Press, 1971), p. 292.

30. Hallie Flanagan to Pearl S. Buck (April 21, 1939), Pearl S. Buck Foundation archives. For a detailed recollection of the production of the FTP's *Voodoo Macbeth*, see John Houseman, *Run-Through* (New York: Simon and Schuster, 1972), pp. 185–186, 189–205.

31. The file of commentary from which the material in this section is taken is located in the Pearl S. Buck Family Trust archives.

32. Pearl made this remark in a conversation with Alma Lutz, in December, 1939. She went on to say that she found most dinner parties boring; on one occasion, she told Lutz, "Lynn Fontanne sat like a beautiful statue saying nothing," and Alexander Woollcott behaved just like "the man who came to dinner." The notes of this conversation are preserved in the Vassar College archives.

33. Samuel Hynes, *The Auden Generation: Literature and Politics in England in the 1930s* (New York: Viking Press, 1976), p. 340.

34. Cowley, "Wang Lung's Children," *New Republic,* pp. 24, 25; "Ladies Week," *New Yorker,* 15 (March 4, 1939), p. 74.

35. Donald Lammers has argued that *The Patriot* incorporates a sensitive and largely accurate portrait of Japanese family life. See Lammers, "Taking Japan Seriously: Some Western Literary Portrayals of the Japanese During the Climax of Their National Self-Assertion (c. 1905–c. 1945)," in Warren I. Cohen, ed., *Reflections on Orientalism* (East Lansing: Michigan State University, 1983), p. 54.

36. American opinion had been aroused by Japan's invasion of China proper in 1937, in part because Western interests in China were put at risk by the war. The media also focused sympathy on China's plight as the victim of aggression: "Day after day the China war was splashed across the pages of newspapers in America; dramatic newsreel shots of the bombing of Chinese towns were seen by millions of moviegoers." Felix Greene, *A Curtain of Ignorance: How the American Public Has Been Misinformed about China* (Garden City, NY: Doubleday, 1964), p. 13. *Time* magazine named Chiang and Madame Chiang "Man and Woman of the Year" in 1937. Polls showed "only 2 percent of the public pro-Japanese against 74 percent pro-Chinese." However, these sentiments did not lead to any widespread desire for involvement in an Asian war. Barbara Tuchman, *Stilwell and the American Experience in China, 1911–1945* (New York: Macmillan, 1971), p. 189.

37. Pearl S. Buck, typescript copy of telegram to Franklin D. Roosevelt (April 1, 1939), Randolph-Macon Woman's College archives.

38. Pearl S. Buck to Jane Sherman (November 15, 1940), Pennsylvania State University archives. Sherman was an officer of the left-wing League of American Writers.

39. Pearl S. Buck, "A Soldier of Japan," *New Republic,* volume 99 (June 7, 1939), p. 134. "Ashihei Hino" was the pen name of Katsunori Tamai, an established Japanese author and winner of the Akutagawa Prize, who was serving as a corporal in the Japanese Imperial army.

40. Pearl S. Buck, untitled speech at the Stop Arming Japan Rally (April 25, 1939), Pearl S. Buck Family Trust archives.

41. The story was published in the August 24, 1940 issue of the *Saturday Evening Post.*

42. Nym Wales (Helen Foster Snow) published the first book-length account of the industrial cooperative movement, *China Builds for Democracy* (1940). In the "Foreword" he contributed to the book, Edgar Snow claimed that the Indusco idea was "first of all the brain child of Nym Wales. It was she who first interested Rewi Alley in the possibilities of industrial cooperatives." Other historians of the movement have assigned a larger share of the credit to Alley himself, to Edgar Snow, and to Ida Pruitt.

43. Alley was the author of over thirty books, including several volumes of Chinese poetry that he translated into English. He was an influential figure among the so-called Hundred Percenters, the foreign nationals who devoted themselves to the Chinese Communist cause. Other members of the group included Anna Louise Strong and Agnes Smedley. Edgar Snow wrote an admiring profile of Alley that was published in the *Saturday Evening Post* (February 8, 1941). For additional information on Alley, see Lloyd Shearer, "Rewi Alley: Fifty Years in China," *Parade* (November 14, 1976); Willis Airey, *A Learner in China: A Life of Rewi Alley* (Christchurch, New Zealand: The Caxton Press & The Monthly Review Society, 1970); and Rewi Alley, *An Autobiography* (Beijing: New World Press, 1986).

44. Tawney and his wife had stayed with Pearl and Lossing for several months during Tawney's visit to Nanking University in 1930.

45. Pearl S. Buck, "Free China Gets to Work," *Asia* (April, 1939), pp. 199–200.

46. Pearl S. Buck, "Asia Book-Shelf," *Asia* (October, 1939), pp. 604–605. In this review, Pearl contrasted the Auden and Isherwood book with Freda Utley's *China At War.* Utley's study, she said, was far more important and serious. Among other things, Pearl praised Utley for telling the truth about the fate of China's common soldiers, who have

suffered at the hands of their own leaders. Drawn from the lowest classes, Pearl pointed out, such men have "always suffered unspeakably, and without notice from the intellectuals and the wealthy – suffered in civil war and in famine and in disease."

47. W. H. Auden and Christopher Isherwood, *Journey to a War* (New York: Random House, 1939), pp. 74, 91–92. Isherwood's references to "the Bad Earth" occur on pages 82 and 107.

48. Cited in M. Searle Bates, "The Theology of American Missionaries in China, 1900–1950," in John King Fairbank, ed., *The Missionary Enterprise in China and America* (Cambridge, MA: Harvard University Press, 1974), p. 138.

49. Edmund L. Dorfman to Pearl S. Buck (May 5, 1939), Pearl S. Buck Family Trust archives. The film that Pearl and the other celebrities made has not been found among the surviving World's Fair material that is housed in several collections.

50. Pearl S. Buck to Emma Edmunds White (July 18, [1939]), Randolph-Macon Woman's College archives.

51. Spencer, *The Exile's Daughter*, p. 211.

52. A poll conducted by George Gallup in April, 1942, found that 60 percent of a national sample of Americans could not locate either China or India on an outline map. If this was the case several months after Pearl Harbor, presumably the figure would have been even more alarming in 1939. See Harold R. Isaacs, *Scratches on Our Minds: American Images of China and India* (New York: John Day Company, 1958), p. 37.

53. Pearl S. Buck to Roger S. Greene (January 13, 1940), University of Michigan archives.

54. Some of the geographical details in *Other Gods,* and perhaps even the idea for the novel itself, probably came from two books that Pearl was reading in late 1939. *The Throne of the Gods,* by Arnold Heim and August Gansser (New York: Macmillan, 1939), is an account of the first Swiss expedition to the Himalayas. *Five Miles High,* edited by Robert H. Bates (New York: Dodd, Mead & Company, 1939), is the story of an American attempt to climb Mount Godwin Austen, the second-highest mountain in the world. Pearl reviewed both these books in the January, 1940 issue of *Asia*.

55. Somewhat disingenuously, Pearl claimed that Bert was not modeled on Lindbergh, but on a combination of her father and Lossing. She insisted that any similarity between her main character and Lindbergh was merely "a chance resemblance." Pearl S. Buck to Dorothy Canfield Fisher (January 8, 1940), University of Vermont library.

56. For some of the details of Lindbergh's visit to China in 1931, see Joyce Milton, *Loss of Eden: A Biography of Charles and Anne Morrow Lindbergh* (New York: HarperCollins, 1993), pp. 206–207.

57. For Pearl's meeting with Charles and Anne Morrow Lindbergh, see Chapter 4, p. 133, of this volume.

58. Lindbergh's tortured politics were partly the product of his parochial, Midwestern upbringing, and partly the result of his savage treatment by the press when his baby son was kidnapped and murdered in 1932.

59. Pearl S. Buck, *Other Gods: An American Legend* (New York: John Day Company, 1940), p. 370.

60. All of the material quoted and paraphrased in connection with Pearl's January 23, 1940 appearance on the radio show "Women of Letters" is filed in the Sophia Smith archives, Smith College.

61. Flynn was the model for Joe Hill's famous Wobbly ballad, "The Rebel Girl," a song that inadvertently reveals a good deal about American radicalism's ambivalence toward women.

62. For a partisan account of the Flynn case, including an attack on ACLU Director Roger Baldwin for colluding with FBI Director J. Edgar Hoover, see Corliss Lamont, ed., *The Trial of Elizabeth Gurley Flynn by the American Civil Liberties Union* (New York: Horizon Press, 1968). Along with Pearl, twenty-six other members of the National Committee voted to confirm Flynn's expulsion, among them Van Wyck Brooks, A. J. Muste,

Robert Sherwood, and Mary Woolley. Twelve members voted in Flynn's favor, while twelve others abstained.

63. Pearl S. Buck, "Asia Book-Shelf," *Asia* (October, 1940), p. 557.

64. Freda Utley was a regular contributor to *Asia*. Her most recent article, "Auction in the Far East," had appeared in the March, 1940 issue of the magazine. A few months later, John Day published Utley's memoir, *The Dream We Lost,* an account of Utley's early communism, her marriage to a Russian who was arrested and presumably executed by Stalin's secret police, and her revulsion from the party. Never too scrupulous in such matters, Pearl gave a handsome review to the book her company had published, in the October, 1940 issue of *Asia.*

65. Pearl S. Buck to Byron H. Uhl (July 22, 1940), Hoover Institution archives. Pearl sent similar letters and telegrams to the Department of Justice, the office of immigration appeals, Eleanor Roosevelt, and Congressman Jerry Voorhis, among others.

66. Several letters documenting the Kumut Chandruang case are filed in the Pearl S. Buck Family Trust archives.

67. Pearl S. Buck, "Planning for Peace," a speech delivered at the New York World's Fair under the auspices of the Women's International League for Peace and Freedom (June 12, 1940), Swarthmore College archives. Pearl had also been a featured speaker at the opening session of the World Congress of Writers, which was held under the auspices of PEN (Poets, Playwrights, Essayists, Editors and Novelists) at the fair in early May. On that occasion, following a fiery call to arms from Jules Romains, Pearl chose an unpolitical subject, the relation between American diversity and its literature. Both speeches were covered in the *New York Times* (May 9, 1939), p. 18.

68. Pearl S. Buck, "Asia Book-Shelf," *Asia* (November, 1940), p. 613. A few months earlier, Pearl and Richard had commissioned Franz Boas to write on race. Boas's article, "Racial Purity," which patiently dismantled the pseudoscience on which claims for racial hierarchies rested, appeared in the May, 1940 issue of *Asia.*

69. Lillian Harris to Pearl S. Buck (January 11, 1941) and Pearl S. Buck to Lillian Harris (January 17, 1941), Pearl S. Buck Foundation archives. There is an apparent discrepancy between Pearl's attacks on the idea of race as a scientific category and her exhortations to Lillian Harris and other blacks to be proud of their race. The tension is real, but familiar. Some version of the uncertainty can be found in the views of many progressives who have simultaneously resisted the pernicious use of racial identities as an instrument of subordination and supported the struggles of ethnic minorities for equality.

70. Mary White Ovington, *The Walls Came Tumbling Down,* with a new introduction by Charles Flint Kellog (New York: Schocken Books, 1970 [1947]), p. 263.

71. Eugene Kinckle Jones to Pearl S. Buck (October 10, 1940), Randolph-Macon Woman's College archives. Richard Wright's *Native Son* had been published to great acclaim and notoriety just a few months earlier. Wright's best-selling novel was the first by an African-American to be selected by the Book-of-the-Month Club.

72. Pearl S. Buck, "Women: A Minority Group," *Opportunity,* volume XVIII, No. 7 (July, 1940), p. 201.

73. *Ibid.,* pp. 201–202.

74. Pearl's comments are included in her review of Haru Matsui, *Restless Wave: An Auto-biography* (New York: Modern Age Books, 1939), in the "Asia Book-Shelf" column, *Asia* (March, 1940), p. 165.

75. The comment comes from Pearl's October, 1940 review of Freda Utley's memoir, *The Dream We Lost.*

76. Mishima was educated at the famous Tsuda college in Japan, and then came to the United States to attend Wellesley College in the 1920s. She spent, altogether, seven years in America, and returned to Japan with the intention of pursuing an uncompromising, independent course, in defiance of the received opinions that governed ideas

of woman's place in Japanese society. Her book reveals a life shaped toward pathos and tragedy by the competing cross-currents of Western liberalism and traditional Japanese conceptions of gender. Her dream of emancipation quickly collapsed under the weight of old and durable social conventions. As Mishima portrays it, Japanese society in the 1920s and 1930s remained intractably patriarchal, feudal in its codes of personal loyalty, and adamant in its resistance to female opportunity.

When she married at thirty, Mishima was expected to adopt the forms and rituals that signify her own inferiority. For example, she was to serve her husband and step-children warm rice, and eat only the cold, glutinous leftovers. Despite her adulthood, her education, and the several teaching jobs she holds, she was told that she must still address her husband in the terms of vassal to master. Should she need to go shopping, for example, she must ask for permission, and then express her gratitude in the sentence: "Thank you most respectfully for your lordship's great favor in letting your humble wife go out of the house."

Pearl arranged to have Haru Matsui review *My Narrow Isle* in the April, 1941 issue of *Asia*. Among other things, Matsui wrote that Mishima's book expressed "the heart-rending cry of all Japanese women who try to free themselves from the yoke of feudal tradition." The review appeared in "Asia Book-Shelf," *Asia* (April, 1941), p. 206. To give the book more visibility, Pearl wrote personally to women booksellers around the country, pleading with them to help bring *My Narrow Isle* before their readers. See Pearl S. Buck to a Mrs. Webster (February 19, 1941), Pennsylvania State University archives.

77. Pearl S. Buck, "Asia Book-Shelf," *Asia* (January, 1941), p. 53.
78. "The vast majority of suffrage supporters were opposed to the Equal Rights Amendment when it was first proposed in the 1920s." Kathryn Kish Sklar, "Why Were Most Politically Active Women Opposed to the ERA in the 1920s?" in Joan Hoff-Wilson, ed., *Rights of Passage: The Past and Future of the ERA* (Bloomington: Indiana University Press, 1986), p. 25.
79. *Ibid.*, p. 32.
80. For another analysis of female opposition to the Equal Rights Amendment, see J. Stanley Lemons's chapter "Feminists against Feminists" in his book *The Woman Citizen: Social Feminism in the 1920s* (Urbana: University of Illinois Press, 1973).
81. *Journal* of the American Association of University Women, Volume 33, No. 1 (October, 1939), p. 40.
82. Cited in Susan D. Becker, *The Origins of the Equal Rights Amendment: American Feminism between the Wars* (Westport, CT: Greenwood Press, 1981), p. 224.
83. The lunch took place in New York, on October 18, 1939; the notes are filed in the Alma Lutz papers, Vassar College archives.
84. Pearl S. Buck to Alma Lutz (March 2, 1940), Vassar College archives.
85. Pearl S. Buck to Alma Lutz (March 22, 1940), Vassar College archives.
86. Becker, *The Origins of the Equal Rights Amendment*, p. 141.
87. Van Gelder, "Pearl Buck Talks of Her Work," p. 22.
88. Pearl S. Buck, "Woman's Place," in *Equal Rights*, 26 (December, 1940), pp. 37–38.
89. Pearl included the disclaimer about "feminism" in the letter she circulated in October, 1940, warning against the rise of American fascism.
90. An abridged version of Pearl's speech was published as "Women's Place in a Democracy," *Equal Rights* (December, 1940), pp. 37–39. (Pearl's title had actually been "Woman's Place in Democracy.") At the direction of Representative Carl Hinshaw of California, the full text of Pearl's speech was reprinted in an appendix to the *Congressional Record* (January 16, 1941).
91. Pearl S. Buck to Alma Lutz (December 14, 1940), Vassar College archives.
92. Pearl S. Buck to Anne O'Hare McCormick (October 25, 1940), New York Public Library manuscripts collection.

93. Pearl S. Buck to Margaret Bourke-White (October 25, 1940), Syracuse University archives; Pearl S. Buck to Helen McAfee (October 21, 1940, and December 17, 1940), Beinecke Library, Yale University.
94. Pearl S. Buck, "Asia Mail," *Asia* (April, 1940), p. 173.
95. Pearl S. Buck to Emma Edmunds White (June, 1940), Randolph-Macon Woman's College archives.
96. Cited in C. David Heymann, *Ezra Pound: The Last Rower* (New York: Viking Press, 1976), p. 94.
97. The "Book of Hope" campaign was covered intermittently in New York and Washington newspapers. See the *New York Times* (June 19, 1940; July 11, 1940; August 3, 1940).
98. Jane Rabb, interview with Donn Rogosin (1990).
99. Henriette Walsh, interview with Donn Rogosin (1990).
100. Cited in Stirling, *Pearl Buck: A Woman in Conflict*, p. 209.
101. Ross Terrill, interview with Donn Rogosin (1990).
102. Spencer, *The Exile's Daughter*, p. 195. Years later, Pearl made the same observation. To a reader who asked her for information about herself, she replied: "[I] find it very difficult to answer questions about myself. This is not due to modesty so much as lack of interest. I am not an introspective person in [the] sense of finding myself interesting." Pearl S. Buck to Ferrell Roundy (April 12, 1967), Pearl S. Buck Family Trust archives.
103. Pearl S. Buck, "Recognition and the Writer," *Saturday Review of Literature* (May 25, 1940), p. 13. This essay originated as a lecture for the Society for Libraries at New York University.
104. "Pearl Buck Scores Best-Seller Lists," *New York Times* (November 30, 1939), p. 18.
105. Cited in Stirling, *Pearl Buck*, p. 203.
106. Pearl S. Buck to Franklin D. Roosevelt (January 10, 1941), Franklin D. Roosevelt Library.
107. Franklin D. Roosevelt to Pearl S. Buck (January 31, 1941), Franklin D. Roosevelt Library.
108. The symposium was described in an article by moderator Susan B. Anthony, II, under the title, "Woman's Next Step," *New York Times Magazine* (January 12, 1941), pp. 11, 20.
109. All the stories in *Today and Forever* had been published previously, most of them between 1935 and 1940. The list of magazines in which the stories had appeared, including *Collier's Weekly, Cosmopolitan, Ladies Home Journal, Saturday Evening Post,* and *Woman's Home Companion,* was an index to Pearl's continued commercial success. According to the *New York Times* (September 5, 1940), Booth Tarkington was also writing a new book with the working title "Today and Forever," but withdrew his claim to the phrase when he learned of Pearl's collection.
110. Pearl S. Buck, *Today and Forever* (New York: John Day Company, 1941), p. 292. The collection received a large number of favorable reviews, including an enthusiastic front-page notice in the *New York Times Book Review.* Several reviewers, among them Clifton Fadiman and Gladys Graham Bates, commented on the central part played by women in the stories. Fadiman's notice appeared in the *New Yorker* (January 4, 1941), Bates's in the *Saturday Review of Literature* (January 11, 1941).
111. Review of *Today and Forever* in the *Times Literary Supplement* (February 8, 1941), p. 65.
112. These statistics are contained in the "Thanksgiving Day Report" of the Chinese Emergency Relief Committee (November 20, 1941). Charles Hayford has dramatically documented China's tragic lack of doctors at the time of the Japanese invasion. He reviews the work of Dr. C. C. Ch'en (Ch'en Chih-ch'ien), a 1929 graduate of Peking Union Medical College, who also had earned a master's degree in public health from Harvard. Ch'en "made simple, startling calculations: countries in the developed West had as many as one doctor for every 1000 people; for China, on the other hand, to have as many

as one per 10,000, a shortage of 35,000 physicians would have to be overcome within twenty years, well beyond the capacity of existing or future medical schools to produce. Even the few Chinese doctors with scientific training were concentrated in the cities – of the sixteen members in his class at PUMC, Ch'en was the only one not working in a major city by 1937. Those few graduates of medical colleges who made it to the countryside often just gave up; some survived by selling opium and giving heroin injections." Hayford, *To the People: James Yen and Village China* (New York: Columbia University Press, 1990), pp. 135–136.

113. Details of the UCR dinner and the full text of Wendell Willkie's speech were reported in the *New York Times* (March 27, 1941), p. 12. Throughout 1941, Willkie proved himself a tireless fund-raiser and advocate for China. See *New York Times*, March 20, 1941, p. 15; and September 18, 1941, p. 12.

114. Pearl S. Buck to Grace Yaukey (September 9, 1941), Randolph-Macon Woman's College archives.

115. Richard J. Walsh to Leonard Elmhirst (January 25, 1941), Pearl S. Buck Family Trust archives.

116. As part of her campaign to bring Asian voices within the hearing of American audiences, Pearl regularly reviewed Chinese poetry and fiction in the mass media. For an April, 1940, issue of the *New Republic*, for example, she wrote a favorable notice for Bernard Miall's new translation of the novel *Chin P'ing Mei*, a celebrated pornographic text. And she published an enthusiastic review of Chi-chen Wang's translation of Lu Hsün's stories, *Ah Q and Others*, in the *New York Herald Tribune* (June 3, 1941). "Ah Q," Pearl correctly informed her American readers, "more than any other story in modern China has affected both the literary style and thought of Chinese. . . . [A]t a certain period, this story was read everywhere."

117. Pearl S. Buck, unpublished memorandum on the East and West Association (n.d.), Pearl S. Buck Family Trust archives.

118. Pearl S. Buck, *Of Men and Women* (New York: John Day Company, 1941), p. 61.

119. Katherine Woods, "Pearl Buck on Men and Women," *New York Times* (June 22, 1941), p. 5.

120. After reading *Of Men and Women*, Alma Lutz sent Pearl a fervent letter of appreciation: "For a long time I have been wanting to tell you what a great inspiration "Of Men and Women" has been to me, but it has been hard to put all I feel about it into words. The subject of the book is, as you know, one on which I feel very deeply, and it has been a tremendous comfort and satisfaction to have someone like yourself think these thoughts and publish them. It is a book that I should like to have written and with which I agree in every particular." A few days later, Pearl responded with gratitude: "How kind your letter is and how much I appreciate the review of my small book! You know as well as I that such a book makes enough people angry so that it is a great comfort to a writer's heart to have those who feel about it as you do." Alma Lutz to Pearl S. Buck (July 7, 1941) and Pearl S. Buck to Alma Lutz (July 7, 1941), Vassar College archives.

121. Along with Pearl Buck's *Of Men and Women*, see Olga Knopf's *Women on Their Own* (Boston: Little, Brown, 1935). The two writers are discussed in Becker, *The Origins of the Equal Rights Amendment*, pp. 239–240.

122. Pearl S. Buck, "Warning to Free Nations," *Asia* (March, 1941), p. 161.

123. Correspondence between Pearl Buck and Walter Lippmann in the weeks immediately preceding her letter to the *Times* gives some insight into the urgency Pearl felt about the question of racial prejudice in late 1941. Lippmann was one of those Pearl invited to the John Day–*Asia* magazine offices to discuss with selected African-American leaders "the problems which they find facing them now as Americans." After Lippmann evaded her invitation twice, Pearl wrote with some impatience: "I quite understand your being occupied with other things." However, she went on, "this happens to be a strategic

moment in the thinking of colored Americans. The newspapers do not give the facts and most white people have no idea of the psychological situation of colored Americans. ... The strange thing is that there are so many white Americans who are alive to foreign situations and quite oblivious to the same situations here at home." Pearl S. Buck to Walter Lippmann (October 14 and November 8, 1941), Yale University manuscripts department.

124. Walter White to Pearl S. Buck (November 19, 1941). Pearl wrote back to White, thanking him, and adding: "Please be sure that I am determined to do anything I can on this problem of race prejudice in our country" (November 24, 1941). Both letters are filed in the Library of Congress manuscript collections.

125. Pearl S. Buck, "Democracy and the Negro," *Crisis* (December, 1941), p. 376. The introductory note also charged that the "crime wave" was "largely created in the editorial rooms of some New York daily newspapers."

126. Malvina Thompson to Walter White (November 25, 1941), Library of Congress archives.

127. Mrs. Franklin D. Roosevelt, "Foreword," *Pearl Buck Speaks for Democracy* (New York: Common Council for American Unity, n.d. [December, 1941]), unpaged. Pearl used her letter as the text for a radio broadcast in the "Speaking of Liberty" series in late November.

128. Pearl S. Buck to Eleanor Roosevelt (December 12, 1941), Roosevelt papers, Hyde Park, NY. Though Pearl's important letter has been ignored by most historians of World War II, it is cited in Joseph P. Lash, *Eleanor and Franklin* (New York: W. W. Norton, 1971), p. 669, and in John Toland, *The Rising Sun: The Decline and Fall of the Japanese Empire, 1936–1945* (New York: Random House, 1970), volume two, pp. 566–567.

129. Lash, *Eleanor and Franklin*, p. 669.

130. Buck, *My Several Worlds*, p. 226.

Chapter 7: Wartime

1. Peter Young, *World War 1939–45: A Short History* (New York: Thomas Y. Crowell, 1966), p. 176.

2. Jonathan Spence, *The Search for Modern China* (New York: W. W. Norton, 1990), pp. 450–454.

3. Among the many books that describe and analyze the war in China, see Dick Wilson, *When Tigers Fight: The Story of the Sino-Japanese War* (New York: Penguin, 1983); John Boyle, *China and Japan at War, 1937–1945: The Politics of Collaboration* (Stanford, CA: Stanford University Press, 1972); Lloyd E. Eastman, *Seeds of Destruction: Nationalist China in War and Revolution, 1937–1949* (Stanford, CA: Stanford University Press, 1984); and Hsi-sheng Ch'i, *Nationalist China at War: Military Defeat and Political Collapse, 1937–1945* (Ann Arbor: University of Michigan Press, 1982). Lincoln Li, *The Japanese Army in North China, 1937–1941: The Politics of Collaboration* (Tokyo: Oxford University Press, 1975), provides useful background for *Dragon Seed*.

4. *Dragon Seed* was serialized in *Asia* in six installments, beginning with the September, 1941 issue.

5. The MGM deal was handled by the Myron Selznick company. A rhapsodic note in "Of Books and Writers," a house paper published by Selznick's story department, estimated *Dragon Seed*'s commercial prospects. The novel is "tailor-made for the screen," Donald Friede wrote. "We can't deny that it will cost a great deal of money to make, but it should gross a fortune. And we expect to close our deal for it any day."

6. "Books," *Time* (January 26, 1942), p. 80.

7. The Chinese government places the Nanking death toll at 300,000. Gerhard Weinberg,

in his recent history, says that "over 200,000 civilians" were murdered in Nanking. See Weinberg, *A World at Arms: A Global History of World War II* (New York: Cambridge University Press, 1993), p. 322. Jonathan Spence gives a much lower figure, reporting an estimate of 12,000 murdered civilians. See Spence, *The Search for Modern China,* p. 448.

8. Spence, *The Search for Modern China,* p. 448.

9. Ian Buruma, *The Wages of Guilt: Memories of War in Germany and Japan* (New York: Farrar, Straus, and Giroux, 1994), p. 114. In an interview with a man named Azuma Shiro, a Japanese veteran of Nanking, Buruma elicited the remarkable comment that Shiro had read two books during the Chinese campaign: *The Good Earth* and Hitler's *Mein Kampf.* He said that he worshiped Hitler, but had no comment on Pearl Buck.

10. Pearl S. Buck, *Dragon Seed* (New York: John Day Company, 1942), p. 321.

11. Commenting on the Japanese invasion of Manchuria in the early 1930s, Churchill suggested that the Chinese might be better off under Japanese rule. Ironically, he said that Pearl Buck's picture of China's peasant life in *The Good Earth* had encouraged him in this view. See Henry Pelling, *Winston Churchill* (New York: E. P. Dutton, 1974), p. 368.

12. Peter Ward Fay, *The Forgotten Army: India's Armed Struggle of Independence, 1942–1945* (Ann Arbor: University of Michigan Press, 1993).

13. Pearl S. Buck to Dorothy Canfield Fisher (January 12, 1942), University of Vermont Library.

14. In *An American Dilemma,* Gunnar Myrdal's landmark study of race relations in the United States, Pearl is quoted extensively in support of the conclusion that "caste is becoming an expensive luxury of white men." Myrdal, *An American Dilemma: The Negro Problem and Modern Democracy* (New York: Harper & Row, 1962 [1942]), p. 1017.

15. As reported in the *New York Times,* Sept 16, 1943, p. 5.

16. The proposal, Fadiman insisted, was "not as visionary as it may seem. We have a long and dignified tradition of literary ambassadors, and they have surely done as well as the millionaires. Miss Buck is one of our greatest writers and finest citizens. She speaks Chinese and is loved and known by the Chinese people, and to some extent by the Indian and Japanese peoples. Her appointment would be a symbolic promise of our determination to understand and cooperate with the Orient." Fadiman later served with Pearl on the Writers' War Committee.

17. The January 5 meeting in Washington is described in the "rough drafts of minutes" of a January 7 special meeting of the board of directors of the East and West Association, Pearl S. Buck Foundation archives. Later in 1943, Pearl sent Donovan a confidential memo, warning that Japan was making good use of white prejudice "against peoples of color."

    In the course of her fourteen-page appeal to Donovan, Pearl rehearsed a broad assortment of cultural, political, and military arguments. Aware of the depth of Western ignorance about Asia, Pearl patiently instructed Donovan on such matters as Chinese resentment at being called "Yellow" or "Oriental." The "peoples of Asia deserve . . . to be spoken of as nations and not by color or by 'Orientals.' " She predicted, quite accurately, that China's long war of defense "will one day be written down in history as a masterpiece of strategy." Pearl S. Buck, memorandum to William Donovan (n.d. [1943]), Bentley Historical Library, University of Michigan.

18. Edward C. Carter to Pearl S. Buck (January 22, 1942), Columbia University rare book and manuscript division.

19. Pearl S. Buck to Edward C. Carter (February 3, 1942), Columbia University rare book and manuscript division.

20. Margaret Sanger to Pearl S. Buck (June 15, 1942) and Pearl S. Buck to [Florence] Rose (n.d.), Sophia Smith collection, Smith College.

21. Earl Brown and George R. Leighton, *The Negro and the War* (New York: AMS [re-

print], 1972), p. 10. The volume was originally published in 1942 as Public Affairs Pamphlet no. 71. In an early section of the pamphlet, under the heading "Race Equality a War Issue," Brown and Leighton quote extensively from Pearl Buck's November, 1941 letter to the *New York Times*, which had become a prominent weapon in the war against discrimination.

22. Brown and Leighton, *The Negro and the War*, p. 11.

23. "Report of the Secretary" at the February 5, 1942 NAACP board meeting, Library of Congress manuscripts division.

24. Langston Hughes, "Red Cross," in Arnold Rampersad with David Roessel, eds., *The Collected Poems of Langston Hughes* (New York: Knopf, 1994), p. 290. The poem first appeared in Hughes's 1943 collection, *Jim Crow's Last Stand*.

25. Samuel Walker, *In Defense of American Liberties: A History of the ACLU* (New York: Oxford University Press, 1990), p. 163. In April, Alain Locke wrote to Pearl, suggesting cooperation between her ACLU committee and a group he had organized, which included Ralph Bunche and attorney Charles H. Houston. Alain Locke to Pearl S. Buck (April 19, 1942), Howard University archives.

26. Cited in Arnold Rampersad, *The Life of Langston Hughes, volume II, 1941–1967: I Dream a World* (New York: Oxford University Press, 1988), p. 47.

27. In a May 20, 1942 note to Walter White, secretary of the NAACP, *New York Herald Tribune* book editor Irita Van Doren said that Pearl's speech "caused so much discussion that there were a great many demands for us to print it in full, which we did." New York Public Library manuscripts division.

28. Alain Locke to Pearl S. Buck (February 23, 1942), Howard University archives. Locke added that he would be sending Pearl a copy of his book, *When Peoples Meet*. The two writers, whose association went back to the mid-1930s, had by now become something of a mutual admiration society. Pearl wrote back immediately, thanking Locke for his kind words, and telling him that *When Peoples Meet* was "a great piece of work." Pearl S. Buck to Alain Locke (February 26, 1942), Howard University archives. She reviewed the book in March, recommending it to white readers as an introduction to the new world that people of color would make after the war. Pearl S. Buck, "Asia Book-Shelf," *Asia* (March, 1942), p. 139.

29. Pearl S. Buck to Edwin R. Embree (March 20, 1942), Amistad Research Center archives. Embree, an official of the Julius Rosenwald Fund, collaborated with Pearl in the spring of 1942 as he tried to secure the creation of a presidential committee on racial discrimination.

30. Natalie Robins, *Alien Ink: The FBI's War on Freedom of Expression* (New York: William Morrow, 1992), p. 41.

31. David Garrow, among others, traces the FBI's behavior to the "paranoid style" that Richard Hofstadter famously described a half-century ago. In Garrow's view, the bureau's suspicions were aroused by *any* perceived threat to the mainstream status quo. Garrow, *The FBI and Martin Luther King, Jr.* (New York: Penguin Books, 1983 [1981]), pp. 208–214. See also Frank J. Donner, *The Age of Surveillance* (New York: Knopf, 1980).

32. Richard Gid Powers, *Secrecy and Power: The Life of J. Edgar Hoover* (New York: Free Press, 1987), p. 128.

33. Ironically, one of the items carefully preserved in the file is a three-part attack on Pearl that appeared in the Communist *Daily Worker*. In the early 1940s, Hoover's agents actually missed most of her civil rights activities and much of the writing that ought to have interested them. For instance, Pearl's file contains no copy of her review of John Steinbeck's *The Moon Is Down* in the left-wing *New Masses* (March 24, 1942). Indeed, if the evidence in Pearl's file is indicative, the FBI spent less time investigating than simply indexing and storing what came through the mails, usually from anonymous sources.

34. The Council on African Affairs rally is described in *PM* (April 9, 1942).
35. The reference to Chester Himes occurs in a letter, cited in Theodore Harris with Pearl S. Buck, *Pearl S. Buck: A Biography,* volume two, *Her Philosophy as Expressed in Her Letters* (New York: John Day Company, 1971), p. 81.
36. Henry Lee, "Pearl S. Buck: Spiritual Descendant of Tom Paine," *Saturday Review of Literature,* 25 (December 5, 1942), pp. 16–18.
37. Walter Millis, "Pearl Buck's Crusade Against Color Lines," *New York Herald Tribune Books* (July 26, 1942), VIII, p. 1.
38. Witter Bynner to Pearl S. Buck (January 10, 1943), Houghton Library, Harvard University.
39. On May 27, Pearl spoke to a large New York meeting sponsored by the East and West Association to honor the Korean people and Korean independence. Most Americans had not yet heard of Korea, which had been under Japanese military control since 1910. Over the next several years, *Asia* magazine gave editorial support and regular coverage to Korea's aspirations for independence. In April, 1942, for example, the magazine printed George Kent's article, "Korea – Exhibit 'A' in Japan's New Order." In a series of anecdotes, Kent exposed the brutality of Japan's domination of the Korean people, behavior that belied Japanese promises of benevolent partnership with occupied nations. Vincent Sheean's "Korea and the United Nations" appeared in the August issue. In a telegram to Wendell Willkie, inviting him to speak at another rally in early 1944, Pearl said her object was "to let Americans know something about the unknown people of Korea." Pearl S. Buck to Wendell Willkie (January 8, 1944), Lilly Library, Indiana University.
40. Pearl's comments on the Waller case were quoted in a full-page advertisement in the *Washington Star,* which was placed by the Workers Defense League. On May 4, the U.S. Supreme Court declined to review Waller's conviction. The NAACP and the ACLU were both active in protesting the Virginia verdict and the subsequent Supreme Court decision. After Waller's execution, the March on Washington Movement staged a poorly attended demonstration. See August Meier and Elliott Rudwick, "The Origins of Non-Violent Direct Action in Afro-American Protest: A Note on Historical Discontinuities," reprinted in David Garrow, ed., *We Shall Overcome: The Civil Rights Movement in the 1950s and 1960s* (Brooklyn, NY: Carlson Publishing, 1989), volume 3, pp. 833–930.
41. Pearl S. Buck, "Total Victory," *New Republic* (June 1, 1942), pp. 761–762.
42. Dominic J. Capeci, Jr., *The Harlem Riot of 1943* (Philadelphia: Temple University Press, 1977), p. 157.
43. "U. S. Women Cheer Sisters in Poland," *New York Times* (September 24, 1942), p. 12. Dorothy Thompson and Clare Boothe Luce also made brief statements during the broadcast.
44. Henry Lee, "Pearl S. Buck: Spiritual Descendant of Tom Paine," p. 16.
45. Pearl S. Buck, "Asia Book-Shelf," *Asia* (August, 1942), p. 493. In her praise of simplicity, Pearl was describing the political theories of Hans Kohn of Smith College.
46. Pearl S. Buck to Alfred Kohlberg (April 13, 1945), Smith College archives.
47. This and the previous comment are cited in Cornelia Spencer [Grace Yaukey], *The Exile's Daughter: A Biography of Pearl S. Buck* (New York: Coward-McCann, 1944), p. 221.
48. On the internment program, see Audrie Girdner, *The Great Betrayal: The Evacuation of the Japanese-Americans During World War II* (New York: Macmillan, 1969); Michi Weglyn, *Years of Infamy: The Untold Story of America's Concentration Camps* (New York: Morrow, 1976); John Christgau, *"Enemies": World War II Alien Internment* (Ames: Iowa State University Press, 1985); Peter H. Irons, *Justice at War* (New York: Oxford University Press, 1983); Eric Sundquist, "The Japanese-American Internment: A Reappraisal," *American Scholar* (Autumn, 1988), pp. 529–547.

49. Cited in Ronald Takaki, *Strangers from a Different Shore: A History of Asian Americans* (New York: Penguin Books, 1989), p. 392.
50. Pearl S. Buck, "Japanese Americans," in *American Unity and Asia* (New York: John Day Company, 1942), p. 103. In the September, 1942 issue of *Asia* magazine, Pearl and Richard published ACLU director Roger Baldwin's attack on the internment policy, "Japanese-Americans and the Law." Baldwin made the same argument Pearl did, stating bluntly that "Our treatment of our fellow-citizens of Japanese blood is a shameful evidence of our hysterical war-time intolerance based on race alone – for we do not thus treat white Americans of enemy blood."

    Pearl's FBI file contains a memo from a West Coast agent informing headquarters that she appeared in October, 1943, before the California Senate Fact Finding Committee, meeting in Los Angeles, and "opposed discrimination against Japanese on a racial basis stating such action would react against the US in its relationship in the Orient." FBI file, subject Pearl S. Buck, file number 62-101935, variously paginated, Los Angeles teletype (October 23, 1943). Pearl recalled her testimony in her memoirs, still angry at the "row of hard old faces behind the table" who were willing to endorse injustice. Pearl S. Buck, *My Several Worlds* (New York: John Day Company, 1954), p. 228.
51. Pearl S. Buck to Eleanor Roosevelt (May 22, 1942), Franklin D. Roosevelt Library. Pearl enclosed letters she had received from several women on the West Coast, protesting the evacuations and also describing the appalling conditions in the concentration camps. Roosevelt sent Pearl a brief, mealy-mouthed reply: "I regret the need to evacuate, but I recognize it had to be done. I hear high praise for the way in which the Army has handled this evacuation. . . ." Eleanor Roosevelt to Pearl S. Buck (May 29, 1942), Franklin D. Roosevelt Library. Later in the year, Pearl tried to persuade DeWitt Wallace to print an article on the injustice of internment in *Reader's Digest;* she "was told quite flatly that they were not interested." Pearl S. Buck to Bradford Smith (November 27, 1942), University of Vermont Library.
52. John Chamberlain, "Books of the Times," *New York Times* (July 21, 1942), p. 17. Chamberlain's proposal that Freedom House supply Pearl's book to policymakers is discussed in Aaron Levenstein, in collaboration with William Agar, *Freedom's Advocate* (New York: Viking Press, 1965), p. 40. In August, the Council for Democracy announced that it was mailing one copy of *American Unity and Asia* to each U.S. Senator and Representative. See the *New York Herald Tribune* (August 19, 1942).
53. Cited in Joseph P. Lash, *Eleanor and Franklin* (New York: W. W. Norton, 1971), p. 671. Near the end of the war, in the spring of 1945, Walter White traveled across the European theater of operations, from England to North Africa to Italy, gathering stories from black and white servicemen about racial conditions. The book in which he published his findings, *A Rising Wind,* combines a sad catalogue of injustice with an extended warning to white Americans about the likely consequences of discrimination in the post-war world. As he traced the connections between America's domestic attitudes and its international credibility, White quoted extensively from Pearl's writings, a gesture that signals the esteem in which she was held by black leaders at this time. Walter White, *A Rising Wind* (Garden City, NY: Doubleday, Doran and Company, 1945), pp.47–48, 151–153.
54. Walter White, "What the Negro Thinks of the Army," *Annals of the American Academy of Political and Social Science* 223 (September, 1942), p. 67.
55. The Double V emblem first appeared on the front page of the *Pittsburgh Courier* on February 7, 1942.
56. Cited in Lee Finkle, *Forum for Protest: The Black Press During World War II* (Rutherford, NJ: Associated University Presses, 1975), p. 109. Finkle describes the Double V campaign in detail. See also the chapter "The African American Press in Wartime" in Frederick S. Voss, *Reporting the War: The Journalistic Coverage of World War II* (Wash-

ington, DC: Smithsonian Institution Press for the National Portrait Gallery, 1994), pp. 173–184.

57. Pearl S. Buck, typescript entitled "Full Text of Commencement Address . . . at Howard University on June 5, 1942," Library of Congress Manuscript Division. Throughout the war, Pearl encouraged African-Americans to link their civil rights struggles with liberation movements around the world. In February, 1943, for example, when Mohandas Gandhi was weakening from a hunger strike, she joined with the officers of the NAACP in demanding that President Roosevelt intervene. See "Negroes Appeal to Churchill," *New York Times* (February 21, 1943), p. 21.

58. Spencer, *The Exile's Daughter: A Biography of Pearl S. Buck*, p. 215. Pearl was elected to Howard's board of trustees in the mid-1940s, and served for two decades.

59. Pearl S. Buck to Ralph D. Thompson (April 16, 1942), New York Public Library manuscripts collection. In a follow-up letter to Alexander Woollcott, she said: "Probably I need a list of books myself about America. I have been reading voraciously ever since I came back to repair the years which I missed here." Pearl S. Buck to Alexander Woollcott (April 30, 1942), Houghton Library manuscripts collection, Harvard University.

60. After consulting the nominations she received from critics and reviewers around the country, Pearl published her reading list in the October issue of *Asia*. Along with her own three choices, a dozen other titles were included: Mark Twain's *Huckleberry Finn* and *The Adventures of Tom Sawyer*, Carl Sandburg's multi-volume biography of Lincoln, Van Wyck Brooks's *The Flowering of New England*, Walt Whitman's *Leaves of Grass*, Willa Cather's *My Ántonia*, Marjorie Kinnan Rawlings's *The Yearling*, Charles and Mary Beard's *The Rise of American Civilization*, James Truslow Adams's *The Epic of America*, John Steinbeck's *The Grapes of Wrath*, and Louisa May Alcott's *Little Women*.

61. One of the experts Pearl consulted in drawing up plans for the International School was Howard E. Wilson, a professor at Harvard's Graduate School of Education and chairman of the General Education Committee of the East and West Association. In an article that appeared in the November, 1942 issue of *Asia*, Wilson documented the woeful state of American ignorance about China and the other countries of Asia. Among other things, Wilson reported that high school geography books devoted less than 6 percent of their space to Asia, and world history books about half of that. Howard E. Wilson, "Asiatic Studies in American Schools," *Asia* (November, 1942), pp. 654–657.

62. Prospectus, The International School (typescript; no date), p. 6, Pearl S. Buck Family Trust archives.

63. Henry Lee, "Pearl S. Buck: Spiritual Descendant of Tom Paine," p. 16. In November, 1942, Pearl and Richard changed the name of *Asia* magazine to *Asia and the Americas;* they also attached it officially to the East and West Association.

64. Pearl S. Buck to Grace Yaukey (January 23, 1943), Pearl S. Buck Foundation archives. In the early 1940s, Grace embraced the Quaker faith and pacifism. Her new commitments provoked an angry response from Pearl, and the sisters virtually severed relations for several years.

65. The comment, which appeared in New York's *Amsterdam News* (April 19, 1941), is cited in Finkle, *Forum for Protest*, p. 199.

66. Pearl S. Buck to Bernhard Knollenberg (September 25 and October 1, 1942), Beinecke Rare Books and Manuscripts collection, Yale University.

67. Warren Kimball, ed., *Churchill and Roosevelt: The Complete Correspondence*, volume I (Princeton, NJ: Princeton University Press, 1984), p. 8

68. Frank Freidel, *Franklin D. Roosevelt: A Rendezvous with Destiny* (Boston: Little, Brown, 1990), p. 444.

69. Pearl tried to persuade British liberals to join her in demanding Indian independence.

In a letter to Bertrand Russell, she conceded that "Churchill cannot and will not change." In that case, "it would help a great deal if we could see another kind of Englishman and see him in some numbers and hear him speak. As you know, the liberal English opinion has been fairly rigidly censored. Here in America we have not been allowed to hear dissenting voices in England and the sort of official Englishman we have here, and all his propaganda, does little or nothing to mend the rift [with] the common man." Pearl S. Buck to Bertrand Russell (October 23, 1942), cited in *The Autobiography of Bertrand Russell, 1914–1944* (Boston: Little, Brown, 1968), pp. 394–395.

70. "Freedom for India Is Demanded Here," *New York Times* (September 30, 1942), p. 8.
71. Tuchman, *Stilwell and the American Experience in China*, p. 353.
72. Pearl S. Buck to Dorothy Thompson (December 3, 1942), Syracuse University archives.
73. Citations are taken from a copy of the speech in the Library of Congress archives. The dinner was reported in the *New York Times* under the headline "Pearl Buck Holds Real Aim Lost" (December 11, 1942), p. 16.
74. Witter Bynner to Pearl S. Buck (January 10, 1943) and Pearl S. Buck to Witter Bynner (January 19, 1943), Houghton Library, Harvard University.
75. Wendell Willkie (telegram) to Pearl S. Buck (December 11, 1942) and Pearl S. Buck to Wendell Willkie (December 11, 1942), Lilly Library, University of Indiana. Not all the responses to Pearl's speech were negative. The *New Republic* reprinted a substantial excerpt, accompanied by a long, approving comment.
76. Pearl S. Buck, "The Freedom to Be Free," *New York Times Magazine* (February 28, 1943), pp. 4, 37; H. I. Brock, "Freedom from the Axis First," *New York Times Magazine* (March 7, 1943), pp. 18, 38.
77. *New York Times* (March 28, 1943), p. 15.
78. "Investigation of Un-American Propaganda Activities in the United States," Hearings Before a Special Committee on Un-American Activities, House of Representatives, Seventy-Eighth Congress, First Session, Volume 15, p. 9469.
79. Varian Fry to Paul H. Sheats (January 4, 1945), Tamiment Library, NYU.
80. Eleanor Roosevelt to Pearl S. Buck (February 20, 1943) and Pearl S. Buck to Eleanor Roosevelt (February 24, 1943), Franklin D. Roosevelt Library.
81. John King Fairbank, *Chinabound* (New York: Harper & Row, 1982), p. 253.
82. The quotes, from *Life* magazine, are cited in Tuchman, *Stilwell and the American Experience in China*, p. 349.
83. International Business Machines commissioned a privately published book to commemorate Mme. Chiang's tour. *The First Lady of China: The Historic Wartime Visit of Mme. Chiang Kai-shek to the United States in 1943* is a gushing, lavishly illustrated celebration – an elaborate fan magazine, but a valuable source.
84. Cited in Lash, *Eleanor and Franklin*, p. 678.
85. John M. Blum, ed., *From the Morgenthau Diaries* (Boston: Houghton Mifflin, 1959–1967), volume III, p. 106. See also, Brian Crozier, with the collaboration of Eric Chou, *The Man Who Lost China: The First Full Biography of Chiang Kai-shek* (New York: Charles Scribner's Sons, 1976), p. 248.
86. Theodore F. Harris, *Pearl S. Buck: A Biography* (New York: John Day Company, 1960), pp. 292–293; Lash, *Eleanor and Franklin*, p. 678.
87. Pearl S. Buck to Eleanor Roosevelt (March 22, 1943), Franklin D. Roosevelt Library.
88. Eleanor Roosevelt to Pearl S. Buck (April 13, 1943), Franklin D. Roosevelt Library.
89. In mid-1942, Pearl assured Mrs. Clifford Cowin that she was fully informed about the defects of Chiang's regime: "I am well aware of the faults of the present government in China, and have spoken privately to many Chinese about it." However, for almost another year, Pearl thought that it would not be prudent to speak in public. Pearl S. Buck to Mrs. Clifford C. Cowin (July 31, 1942), Oberlin College autograph file.
90. Quoted in Patricia Neils, *China Images in the Life and Times of Henry Luce* (New York:

Rowan & Littlefield, 1990), p. 104. The quote is from a Pearl Buck letter of March 3, 1943, in the *Time* archives.

91. Pearl S. Buck, "A Warning About China," *Life,* XIV (May 10, 1943), p. 54.

92. Fairbank, *Chinabound,* p. 253. Baldwin and Bisson doubted Chiang's skills as a military strategist and tactician. Pearl was more concerned about Chiang's commitment to democracy. The quote from Luce's private memo recommending publishing Pearl's article reveals how influential Pearl was perceived to be. Luce worried that "President Roosevelt can take the Buck analysis as an excuse for his insufficient aid." Cited in Neils, *China Images in the Life and Times of Henry Luce,* p. 105.

    America's ambassador to China, Christian Gauss, on the other hand, believed that criticism of Chiang and the Kuomintang in the American press met with the approval of liberal elements in China. Referring to the same three articles as Fairbank, Gauss concluded that "an article by Pearl Buck (to a great extent) and those by Hanson Baldwin and T. A. Bisson (to a lesser degree) had a salutary effect on the Chinese government." Earl Latham, *The Communist Controversy in Washington: From the New Deal to McCarthy* (Cambridge, MA: Harvard University Press, 1966), p. 251.

93. Pearl's testimony, printed in *Repeal of the Chinese Exclusion Acts, Hearings of the House Committee on Immigration and Naturalization,* May and June, 1943, is cited in Fred W. Riggs, *Pressures on Congress: A Study of the Repeal of Chinese Exclusion* (Westport, CT: Greenwood Press, 1972 [reprint of the 1950 King's Crown Press edition]). See also Renqiu Yu, *To Save China, To Save Ourselves: The Chinese Hand Laundry Alliance of New York* (Philadelphia: Temple University Press, 1992), pp. 130–137.

94. Cited in Riggs, *Pressures on Congress,* p. 131. Eleanor Roosevelt argued for repeal in her "My Day" column on July 7, the date celebrated as the sixth anniversary of China's war against Japan. On the same day, Pearl appeared at a Carnegie Hall rally with Lin Yutang and others.

95. The phrase is taken from a letter Pearl co-signed, calling for an American Conference for Racial and National Unity (September 1, 1943), Special Collections, Southern Illinois University.

96. Pearl S. Buck, "Postwar China and the United States," *Asia and the Americas* (November, 1943), pp. 613–615.

97. Pearl S. Buck, *The Promise* (New York: John Day Company, 1943), p. 103.

98. See Weinberg, *A World at Arms,* pp. 647–652; Tuchman, *Stilwell and the American Experience in China,* pp. 256–300.

99. On the closing of the Burma Road and Churchill's "loss of face" in Asia, see Arthur Young, *China and the Helping Hand, 1937–1945* (Cambridge, MA: Harvard University Press, 1963), pp. 114–115.

100. KM [unidentified], memo to Thomas Lamont (n.d. [1944]), Harvard Business School archives.

101. Thomas Lamont to Clark Minor (January 5, 1944), Harvard Business School archives.

102. Pearl S. Buck, "Education for Life for Our World," in Peter Conn, ed., *Pearl Buck and Education: An Anthology of Her Writings* (Perkasie, PA: Pearl S. Buck Foundation, 1992), pp. 131, 125, 119. The speech was covered in the *New York Times* (January 20, 1944), p. 13.

103. Ellen Chesler, *Woman of Valor: Margaret Sanger and the Birth Control Movement in America* (New York: Simon & Schuster, 1992), p. 368.

104. Margaret Sanger to Thomas Lamont (October 3, 1944), Harvard Business School archives.

105. Margaret Sanger to Pearl S. Buck (October 9, 1944) and Pearl S. Buck to Margaret Sanger (September 24, 1944), Smith College archives.

106. Margaret Sanger to Pearl S. Buck (November 3, November 10, 1944), Smith College archives.

107. Pearl S. Buck to Margaret Sanger (November 13, 1944), Smith College archives.
108. Pearl S. Buck to Margaret Sanger (December 2, 1944), Smith College archives.
109. The penciled annotations appear on a letter from Pearl S. Buck to Edward Lockwood (May 1, 1942), Columbia University rare book and manuscript division.
110. G. Barry O'Toole, "Debunking an 'Imperial' Debunker," *China Monthly*, V (February, 1944), pp. 12–13. In an earlier article, O'Toole attacked Edgar Snow and Ernest Hemingway as "paid partisans of Stalin."
111. On the campaign to discredit Chiang's opponents, see Ross Y. Koen, *The China Lobby in American Politics* (New York: Octagon Books, 1974 [1960]), pp. 117–118; and Kenneth E. Shewmaker, *Americans and Chinese Communists, 1927–1945: A Persuading Encounter* (Ithaca, NY: Cornell University Press, 1971), pp. 270–272.
112. Pearl S. Buck, "The Man Who Showed China the Vision," *New York Times Magazine* (March 12, 1944), p. 9. A typescript copy of the speech itself, with corrections in Pearl's hand, is filed in the Copley Library, California.
113. Pearl S. Buck to Eleanor Roosevelt (March 22, 1943), Franklin D. Roosevelt Library.
114. Pearl S. Buck, "Our Last Chance in China," *Common Sense* (August, 1944), p. 267.
115. The conference, "Conditions for an Enduring Peace," took place over ten days, from July 5 to 15, under the auspices of the American Friends Service Committee. Pearl attended as a favor to her daughter, Janice, who was attending Antioch at the time.
116. Clayton R. Koppes and Gregory D. Black, *Hollywood Goes to War: How Politics, Profits, and Propaganda Shaped World War II Movies* (New York: Free Press, 1987), pp. 241–242. The film's production is described in Charles Higham, *Kate: The Life of Katharine Hepburn* (New York: W. W. Norton, 1975), pp. 123–125.
117. Pearl S. Buck to Eleanor Roosevelt (July 20, 1944) and Eleanor Roosevelt to Pearl S. Buck (July 29, 1944), Franklin D. Roosevelt Library.
118. Pearl S. Buck, *My Several Worlds* (New York: John Day Company, 1954), p. 392.
119. Cited in Paul P. Kennedy, "When East Meets West," *New York Times* (July 16, 1944), section II, p. 7.
120. Pearl S. Buck to Wendell Willkie (April 8, 1944), Lilly Library, Indiana University.
121. Pearl S. Buck to the *New York Times* (September 19, 1944), p. 20.
122. Pearl S. Buck, "Asia Book-Shelf," *Asia and the Americas* (November, 1944), p. 526.
123. India League of America, press release, "Pearl Buck and Other Prominent Americans Join India League" (September 5, 1944), Pearl S. Buck Foundation.
124. A handwritten copy of the speech is filed in the Pearl S. Buck Family Trust archives.
125. Pearl S. Buck to Margaret Sanger (January 29, 1945), Smith College archives.
126. Cited in Nora Stirling, *Pearl Buck: A Woman in Conflict* (Piscataway, NJ: New Century Publishers, 1983), p. 211.
127. John K. Fairbank, *The United States and China,* fourth edition, enlarged (Cambridge, MA: Harvard University Press), p. 43.
128. Charles Hayford, *To the People: James Yen and Village China* (New York: Columbia University Press, 1990), pp. 118, 126. Hayford's study of the Mass Education Movement includes the contention that Mao Tse-tung based his own radical 1,000-character literacy primer on Yen's earlier work.
129. Pearl S. Buck to Dorothy Canfield Fisher (March 9, 1945), University of Vermont archives.
130. *Ibid.*
131. Pearl S. Buck to Margaret Sanger (April 19, 1945), Smith College Archives.
132. Pearl S. Buck, letter to Edward C. Carter (June 4, 1945), Columbia University archives.
133. Pearl S. Buck, "Foreword" to the 1958 Pocket Book reprint of *The Townsman*.
134. Pearl could be relatively satisfied with her experiment in pseudonymity: *The Townsman* was widely and favorably reviewed, it was a Literary Guild selection, and it sold tens of thousands of copies.
135. In the opinion of at least one scholar, *The Townsman*'s focus on ordinary citizenship

rather than bloodthirsty sensation makes it an important document in the history of the Western novel. See Ernest E. Leisy, *The American Historical Novel* (Norman: University of Oklahoma Press, 1950), p. 205.

136. A copy of Pearl's unpublished speech defending the Fair Employment Practices Commission is filed in the Pearl S. Buck Foundation archives.

137. W. E. B. Du Bois, *Color and Democracy: Colonies and Peace* (New York: Harcourt, Brace, 1945), p. 30. This statement summarizes tables of figures itemizing the possessions of all the colonial powers, including the United States (pp. 26–30).

138. Arnold Rampersad, *The Art and Imagination of W. E. B. Du Bois* (Cambridge, MA: Harvard University Press, 1976), p. 247.

139. A sample of negative comments can be found in reviews by Robert Gale Woolbert in the *American Political Science Review*, Volume 39 (October, 1945), p. 1054; George Streator, in *Commonweal* (July 6, 1945), p. 292; and Ralph Bates, in the *Nation* (August 25, 1945), p. 186.

140. Pearl S. Buck to Irita Van Doren (May, 1945), Library of Congress manuscript division.

141. Pearl S. Buck, "American Imperialism in the Making," *Asia and the Americas* (August, 1945), p. 367.

142. The series was published as a book by John Day in December.

143. Pearl tells part of the story behind her friendship with Masha Scott in her memoir, *My Several Worlds*, pp. 84–86.

144. For a brief summary of Scott's ideological career, see Stephen Kotkin, *Steeltown, USSR: Soviet Society in the Gorbachev Era* (Berkeley: University of California Press, 1990), pp. xiii–xv.

145. For a brief biography of John Scott, see Stephen Kotkin, "Introduction" to the reprint edition (Bloomington: Indiana University Press, 1973). Kotkin calls *Beyond the Urals* "the classic firsthand account of the daily life of Stalinism." Scott remained at *Time*, as correspondent, editor, and special assistant to Henry Luce, for thirty years. After retiring from the magazine in 1973, Scott served as vice president of Radio Free Europe until his death in 1976.

146. Buck, *My Several Worlds*, p. 82.

147. Pearl S. Buck, *Talk About Russia, with Masha Scott* (New York: John Day Company, 1945), p. 127.

148. The controversial literature on the American decision to drop the atom bomb on Hiroshima and Nagasaki is huge and rapidly growing, and the bitter debate that erupted over the planned memorial exhibit at the Smithsonian Institution in the spring of 1995 indicates that positions remain polarized. The conclusion stated here, that the bombing was justified under the circumstances as American policymakers understood them at the time, seems a reasonable one.

Chapter 8: Losing Battles

1. Pearl S. Buck to Margaret Sanger (August 23, 1945), Smith College archives.

2. *Asia and the Americas* (August, 1945), pp. 365–368.

3. The luncheon was covered in the *New York Times* (November 10, 1945), p. 34.

4. *Portrait of a Marriage* was initially published in three installments in *Redbook* magazine, under the title "A Man's Daily Bread."

5. Pearl S. Buck to Emma Edmunds White (December, 1945), Randolph-Macon Woman's College archives.

6. Randolph S. Churchill, ed., *The Sinews of Peace: Post-War Speeches by Winston S. Churchill* (London: Cassell, 1948), pp. 93–105.

7. Cited in Martin Gilbert, *Winston S. Churchill*, Volume VIII, *"Never Despair," 1945–1965* (London: Heinemann, 1988), pp. 200–201.

8. Pearl S. Buck, "The Book-Shelf," *Asia and the Americas* (January, 1946), p. 46. The quoted phrase is taken from Pearl's friendly review of Ella Winters's book, *I Saw the Russian People.*

9. Pearl S. Buck, untitled speech to the People's Congress of the East and West Association (March 6, 1946), Pearl S. Buck Family Trust archives.

10. In the 1940s and early 1950s, Pearl was one of the 125,000 individuals and organizations investigated by the Senate Internal Security Subcommittee, chaired by Senator James O. Eastland of Mississippi. Other targets included Helen Hayes, Joan Crawford, Adam Clayton Powell, Jr., and Linus Pauling. See Richard Halloran, "Senate Panel Holds Vast 'Subversives' File Amassed by Ex-Chief of Army Intelligence." *New York Times* (September 7, 1971), p. 35.

11. From the FBI's point of view, even Pearl's explicitly anti-Communist statements were not militant enough. She attacked Stalin's government as "one of the most oppressive that Russia has ever had," but she urged coexistence over confrontation. She also complained that the United States too often aided the wrong anti-Communists: "persons and groups who . . . have oppressed the people in their own way." She had Chiang Kai-shek in mind. Pearl S. Buck, "How to Understand the Russians," *Look* (September 2, 1947), pp. 14–17.

12. Trying to maintain an ironic distance from his own troubles at the hands of the FBI, Howard Fast described his Bureau file as a compendium of "every – or almost every – decent act I had performed in my life. If I were to seek some testament to leave my grandchildren, proving that I had not lived a worthless existence, but had done my best to help and nourish the poor and oppressed, I could not do better than to leave them this FBI report." *Being Red* (Boston: Houghton Mifflin, 1990), pp. 166–167. Pearl Buck could have made the same remark about her own file.

13. Pearl S. Buck to James T. Farrell, telegram (June 5, 1946), University of Pennsylvania Library.

14. Pearl S. Buck to Emma Edmunds White (October, 1945), Randolph-Macon Woman's College. To avoid competition with *Rickshaw Boy,* Pearl held back her new novel, *Pavilion of Women,* for several months. Richard J. Walsh, sales memorandum (May, 1945), Pearl S. Buck Family Trust archives. Several years later, Pearl wrote to her agent, proposing that Lao She might be interested in signing on as a John Day author. Pearl S. Buck to David Lloyd (March 29, 1948), Pearl S. Buck Family Trust archives.

15. In particular, where Lao She's novel ends with the death of its main character, *Rickshaw Boy* substitutes an unconvincing happy ending, rife with romance and reconciliation. See Liu Wu-chi, *An Introduction to Chinese Literature* (Bloomington: Indiana University Press, 1966), p. 275; and Jonathan Spence, *The Gate of Heavenly Peace: The Chinese and Their Revolution, 1895–1980* (New York: Viking Press, 1981), p. 318. Jean M. James has published a more reliable translation of Lao She's novel, under the title *Rickshaw* (Honolulu: University of Hawaii Press, 1979).

16. The degradations inflicted on ricksha coolies were a constant theme of sympathetic observers in Asia. Agnes Smedley, to give one example, records the horror she felt when she realized that her coolie was a human being. She looked down at this man "silently running like a tired horse before me, his heaving breath interrupted by a rotten cough. Suddenly his broad shoulders began to remind me of my father's. I was a dog and the whole lot of us were dogs!" Agnes Smedley, *Battle Hymn of China* (New York: Knopf, 1943), p. 57. A generation earlier, a British traveler estimated that as many as 400,000 ricksha coolies were to be found in Shanghai alone. See Mary Ninde Gamewell, *The Gateway to China: Pictures of Shanghai* (London: Fleming H. Revell, 1916), p. 93.

17. Some years later, Pearl claimed that Hollywood censors opposed filming *Pavilion of Women* because "someone in the Hayes office, or what used to be the Hayes office, was a Catholic and decided that it was immoral for a woman not to want to sleep with

her husband." Pearl S. Buck to Mary Lombard (March 31, 1955), Pearl S. Buck Family Trust archives.

18. *Pavilion of Women* was published in installments in *Woman's Home Companion* in the summer and fall of 1946. According to one of John Day's field representatives, the serialization had the unusual effect of stimulating rather than depressing sales of the book version. Q. Rossi to Richard J. Walsh, interoffice memorandum (November 26, 1946), Pearl S. Buck Family Trust archives. On the title, see Pearl S. Buck to Alice Salem (February 25, 1943), Buffalo and Erie County Public Library.

19. The character of Madame Wu is based in part on one of Pearl's Nanking neighbors, a Madame Hsiung, who managed a large, prosperous household near the Nanking University campus. See Pearl S. Buck, "The Most Unforgettable Character I've Met," *Reader's Digest* (October, 1946), pp. 69–73.

20. "A Woman's Novel," *Newsweek* (December 2, 1946), pp. 112, 114; "Woman's World," *Time* (November 25, 1946), pp. 110, 112.

21. Florence Kitchelt to Pearl S. Buck (January 3, 1947), Schlesinger Library, Radcliffe College.

22. Pearl S. Buck to Emma Edmunds White (December 1, 1946), Randolph-Macon Woman's College archives.

23. The circulation figure is taken from a memo written by Barbara Young of the news bureau of *Better Homes and Gardens* (January 20, 1947), manuscript division, Library of Congress.

24. Walter White to Mr. Harrington (February 4, 1947), manuscript division, Library of Congress.

25. Pearl S. Buck, *How It Happens: Talk About the German People, 1914–1933* (New York: John Day Company, 1947), p. 208.

26. Three excerpts from *How It Happens* are included in Fritz Ringer, *The German Inflation* (New York: Oxford University Press, 1969), pp. 120–146. Introducing the selections, which he calls "interesting and valuable," Ringer observes that "personal recollections, even those of ordinary people, are often more vivid, more charged with emotion – and therefore more fascinating – than other historical sources." Pearl agreed, though she would have objected to the word "even" in Ringer's sentence. See also William Guttmann and Patricia Meehan, *The Great Inflation: Germany, 1919–23* (Westmead, England: Saxon House, 1975), p. 174; and Claudia Koonz, *Mothers in the Fatherland: Women, the Family and Nazi Politics* (New York: St. Martin's Press, 1987), pp. 45, 125.

27. Several of the reviews of *How It Happens* agreed with Pearl's grim warning. In a strongly positive notice in the *Nation* (February 14, 1947), David Bazelon concluded that "only the wilfully blind will fail to see the relevance of the German experience." Markoosha Fischer made the same point in the *New York Herald Tribune Weekly Book Review* (February 16, 1947): *How It Happens*, she said, "ought to be pondered by many, especially by those who say, 'It can't happen here.' "

28. Pearl S. Buck to Charles Ferguson (July 6, 1947), Boston University archives. Pearl read Ferguson's book in typescript; it was published in 1948 by Association Press.

29. Pearl S. Buck to Anne O'Hare McCormick (May 12, 1947), New York Public Library special collections.

30. Pearl S. Buck to Anna Melissa Graves (September 20, 1947), Swarthmore College Library archives.

31. Pearl S. Buck to Florence Kitchelt (July 21, 1947), Schlesinger Library, Radcliffe College.

32. Pearl S. Buck to Katherine Guyon (October 17, 1947), Pearl S. Buck Family Trust archives.

33. Pearl's FBI files include an unsigned letter from the Committee, dated July 19, 1948, assuring her that her name was "not being used in any way" by the organization.

34. Grace S. Yaukey to Pearl S. Buck (n.d. [March, 1948]), Pearl S. Buck Family Trust archives.

35. Pearl S. Buck, *American Argument: With Eslanda Goode Robeson* (New York: John Day Company, 1949), p. 67.

36. Pearl S. Buck, testimony before the U.S. Senate Armed Services Committee (March 29, 1948), printed in "Universal Military Training," Hearings Before the Committee on Armed Services, United States Senate, Eightieth Congress, second session (Washington, DC: United States Government Printing Office, 1948), pp. 451–456. The witness who followed Pearl, Mrs. Leslie B. Wright of the General Federation of Women's Clubs, had heard Pearl's testimony and began her own remarks by attacking Pearl's comments on the anti-democratic nature of military discipline: "I think every mother of an ex-GI will have their blood boil," Mrs. Wright declared, "to know it is said they were corrupted by the last war. . . . I think I should send an answer to Mrs. Buck, because it is not true, not one word she said about our boys." *Ibid.*, p. 456. For her part, Pearl was "horrified" by Mrs. Wright's testimony, as she told Melissa Graves in a letter of the following September.

37. "New Evidence of the Militarization of America," a report issued by Pearl Buck, Louis Bromfield, Albert Einstein, W. J. Millor, S.J., Victor Reuther, Ray Lyman Wilbur, and others. (Washington, DC: National Council Against Conscription, February, 1949), p. 5.

38. Pearl S. Buck to Frank T. Kauffman (December 11, 1950), Houghton Library archives.

39. Pearl S. Buck to Emma Edmunds White (May 27, [1948]), Randolph-Macon Woman's College archives. Whatever the merits of Pearl's complaint, another half-dozen of her own books would be chosen by the Club as main selections or alternates over the next two decades.

40. *Peony* was a reworking of a play, *Flight Into China,* which Pearl had written in the late 1930s. Directed by Lee Strasberg, the play had received only one production, a semi-professional effort at the Paper Mill Playhouse Festival in New Jersey in 1939.

41. Years later, Pearl claimed that "I did a great deal of research for that book [*Peony*] and it is historically sound." Pearl S. Buck to Mrs. James B. Stock, Baltimore (July 19, 1967), Pearl S. Buck Family Trust archives. Her reading probably included W. A. P. Martin, "The Jewish Monument at Kaifungfu," *Journal of the North-China Branch of the Royal Asiatic Society,* volume XXVII (1906), pp. 1–20.

42. William C. White, "Chinese Jews," *Asia* (January, 1936), p. 60. White published a briefer article, "A Chinese-Hebrew Codex," a comment on the only known document to come from the K'ai-feng synagogue, in the August, 1942 issue of *Asia.* As recently as 1991, David Bittner reported that three hundred persons in K'ai-feng still carried passports identifying themselves as "Youtai," the word for "Jew." Bittner, "The Jews of K'aifeng Revisited in Pearl Buck Novel," *South Florida Jewish Weekly* (May 31–June 6, 1991). Bittner's story was prompted by the republication of *Peony* as a joint venture of two Jewish publishing houses, Bloch and Biblio.

43. Shanghai also housed an ancient community of Jews, whose population grew enormously during World War II. The only city in the world that did not require an entry visa, Shanghai provided refuge for upwards of 20,000 Jews fleeing extermination. See James R. Ross, *Escape to Shanghai: A Jewish Community in China* (New York: Free Press, 1994).

44. In September, 1942, in *PM* magazine, Pearl published a stinging reply to an article, "The Facts About Jews in Washington," by W. M. Kiplinger. The gist of Kiplinger's article, which had appeared in *Reader's Digest,* was that Jews, who numbered only 4 percent of the population, were overrepresented in government jobs. Pearl opened her attack by likening anti-Semitism to other forms of bigotry. Then, after she puckishly pursued the logic of Kiplinger's quotas by demanding half of all government jobs for women, she made her concluding accusation. "When anyone here," she wrote, "begins

inquiring into whether a person is a Jew or a Gentile, he is helping Hitler." Pearl S. Buck, "It Does Not Matter to the True American Which He is – Jew or Gentile," *PM* (September 1, 1942). The *Reader's Digest* article was excerpted from Kiplinger's book, *Washington Is Like That*.

45. Pearl S. Buck, *Peony* (New York: John Day Company, 1948), p. 152. Kung Chen's name is a version of Confucius.

46. On the confusion and bloodshed of the 1945–1949 years in China, see Jonathan Spence, *The Search for Modern China* (New York: W. W. Norton, 1990), pp. 484–513. William Hinton's *Fanshen: A Documentary of Revolution in a Chinese Village* (New York: Vintage Books, 1968) is a classic account of the experience of these years in a single community.

47. Pearl's speech to the American Library Association was covered in the *New York Times* (June 15, 1948), p. 29. A reference to the speech is contained in Pearl's FBI file, among the items released to this writer on appeal.

48. Pearl S. Buck to Emma Edmunds White (July 3, 1948), Randolph-Macon Woman's College archives.

49. Pearl S. Buck to James Yen (September 17, 1948), Randolph-Macon Woman's College archives; Pearl S. Buck to Melissa Graves (September 17, 1948), Swarthmore College Library archives.

50. In 1939, when Pearl and Richard bought a new Capehart phonograph for their Bucks Country home, the first record they ordered was an Aeolian Company release of Paul Robeson singing "Deep River" and "I'm Going to Tell God All My Troubles." Pearl S. Buck Family Trust archives.

51. Eslanda Goode Robeson, "Foreword," Buck, *American Argument*, pp. ix–x.

52. Martin Bauml Duberman, *Paul Robeson* (New York: Knopf, 1988), pp. 190, 294.

53. Eslanda Robeson had published a brief essay, "Proud to Be a Negro," in the February, 1945 issue of *Asia and the Americas*. The essay, based on one of Robeson's trips to Uganda in connection with her doctoral work in anthropology, was later incorporated into *African Journey*.

    Pearl and Eslanda Robeson did not know that their friendship was the subject of continuing FBI scrutiny. In February, 1947, a "confidential informant" sent a copy of a speech on racial discrimination that Robeson had given in Pittsburgh on behalf of the East and West Association. According to the informant, Robeson identified herself as "an old friend of PB." Three years later, "<Name deleted>, Postmistress, Enfield, Conn, (protect identity)," advised that "PB corresponded weekly with Eslanda Robeson . . . from Perkasie, Pa., under the name of Mrs. Richard Walsh. She stated that PB had been very friendly with the Robesons for years. . . ."

54. Red-baiting William Henry Chamberlin said that *American Argument* should have been called "Anti-American Argument," but most other reviewers treated the book with respect. In the *New York Times*, R. L. Duffus sadly consented to the major premise, that "we fail to be a true democracy"; and Mary Ross, writing in the *New York Herald Tribune*, praised the book's "range and caliber of emotion." W. T. Hedden concluded a strongly favorable notice in the *Saturday Review of Literature* by recommending the book especially to the "isn't-it-grand-to-be-an-American school" of patriotism.

55. Pearl had rarely treated the subject of adoption in her fiction. One exception was "Virgin Birth," written in the mid-1930s, which was also one of her rare attempts to deal frontally with the Depression. The main character, Marjorie Bair, is a fifth-grade teacher in a small Midwestern town who will lose her job if she marries her sweetheart, a teacher named Philip. (Women who marry are immediately fired.) When Marjorie becomes pregnant, she conceals her condition from everyone, including Philip. She contemplates an abortion; when that proves impossible, she moves to Chicago to have the baby, and then gives it up for adoption. Pearl uses the plot as a vehicle to attack obsolete notions of illegitimacy. Adoption is presented as an imperfect solution to a problem caused mainly by inhumane conventions. Marjorie's suffering when she gives

up her baby is charged with something of the anguish Pearl felt when she left Carol behind at the Vineland Training School: "The birth pains had been nothing – what was the mere rending of flesh? Pain of the flesh was nothing – pain of the spirit, that was the true agony!" Pearl S. Buck, "Virgin Birth," reprinted in *Far and Near* (New York: John Day Company, 1947), pp. 185, 191.

56. Buck, *American Argument,* pp. 75–80.

57. Pearl S. Buck, "Welcome House," *Reader's Digest* (July, 1958), p. 47.

58. Theodore F. Harris, *Pearl S. Buck: A Biography* (New York: John Day Company, 1969), p. 299.

59. On the founding of Welcome House, see Pearl S. Buck, *My Several Worlds* (New York: John Day Company, 1954), pp. 362–366; Nora Stirling, *Pearl Buck: A Woman in Conflict* (Piscataway, NJ: New Century Publishers, 1983), pp. 220–224; Paul A. Doyle, *Pearl S. Buck,* revised edition (Boston: Twayne Publishers, 1980), pp. 134–135.

60. Pearl dramatized Korea's discrimination against mixed-race children in several stories and in her late novel, *The New Year* (1968).

61. Cited in James A. Michener, "Foreword," Pearl S. Buck, *The Child Who Never Grew* (n.p.: Woodbine House, 1992 [reissue]), p. ii.

62. James Michener, interview with Donn Rogosin (1990).

63. For an intelligent survey of recent adoption debates and the current state of the law, see Elizabeth Bartholet, *Family Bonds: Adoption and the Politics of Parenting* (Boston: Houghton Mifflin, 1993).

64. Pearl S. Buck, "The Children Waiting," *Woman's Home Companion* (September, 1955), p. 129.

65. Pearl S. Buck, "Should White Parents Adopt Brown Babies?" *Ebony* (June, 1958), p. 31.

66. Pearl S. Buck to Margaret Mead (April 11, 1949), Pearl S. Buck Family Trust archives.

67. Pearl S. Buck to Hudson Strode (January 18, 1949), University of Alabama special collections.

68. "West Pacts Seen as Peril to Peace," *New York Times* (February 17, 1949), p. 3.

69. Aside from *The Young Revolutionist* (1932), which she always omitted from her lists of writings, *The Big Wave* was Pearl's sixth book for children. Her earlier children's books included *The Chinese Children Next Door* (1942), *The Water-Buffalo Children* (1943), *The Dragon Fish* (1944), and *Yu Lan: Flying Boy of China,* (1945).

70. The character of Dr. Liang was distilled in part out of Pearl's impatience with her onetime friend Lin Yutang. Pearl was disappointed by Lin Yutang's behavior during the war, when he ostentatiously returned to China but then left again after three months. See Stirling, *Pearl Buck: Woman in Conflict,* pp. 206–207. For a sequence of unflattering comments on Lin and his mystified view of China, see Jerome Ch'en, *China and the West: Society and Culture, 1815–1937* (London: Hutchinson, 1979).

71. Pearl S. Buck, *Kinfolk* (New York: John Day Company, 1949), p. 29. A couple of months after the novel was published, Pearl elaborated on her feelings about China's Westernized elite. "My real grief about these intellectuals who have taken degrees in our universities," she wrote, "is that when they go home, they do not go into the interior, the 'backward' places, but they stay in the few seaports. I have seen surgeons, trained at Johns Hopkins, at great expense, stay in Shanghai and teach English rather than go into smaller towns and help their own people." Pearl S. Buck to Dorothy Canfield Fisher (June 29, 1949), University of Vermont library.

72. Quoted in Dean Acheson, *Present at the Creation* (New York: W. W. Norton, 1969), p. 305.

73. David Halberstam, *The Fifties* (New York: Fawcett Columbine, 1993), pp. 9, 57. See also Douglas T. Miller and Marion Nowak, *The Fifties: The Way We Really Were* (Garden City, NY: Doubleday, 1977), pp. 21–42. The level of information that U.S.

Senators bring to their foreign policy discussions has never been especially impressive. Four decades after Senator Wherry's allusion to "Indigo-China," Senator Jesse Helms, the new Republican chairman of the Foreign Relations Committee, would refer to North Korean dictator Kim Jung Il as "Kim Jung the Second."

74. The quoted statement appeared in "Never Were or Would Be Reds," *New York Times* (June 10, 1949), p. 10. The passages not quoted in the *Times* are taken from the unpublished complete text, Pearl S. Buck Family Trust archives.

75. Michael Beschloss, *Mayday* (New York: Harper and Row, 1886), p. 75.

76. Mary Margaret McBride, *Out of the Air* (New York: Doubleday, 1960), pp. 145–146.

77. Pearl S. Buck, "Our Dangerous Myths About China," *New York Times Magazine* (October 23, 1949), pp. 9, 65–71. A copy of this article eventually found its way into Pearl's FBI file.

78. "Russ [*sic*] Seen Losing Hold on China," *Baltimore Evening Sun* (February 11, 1950).

79. See Ross Y. Koen, *The China Lobby in American Politics* (New York: Octagon Books, 1974 [1960]), chapter 6. Pearl had often reviewed IPR's publications, usually favorably, in her *Asia* magazine book column.

80. McCarthy's more specific list of accusations against Lattimore duplicated the charges that were used to bring down the IPR. See Owen Lattimore, *Ordeal by Slander* (Boston: Little, Brown, 1950), p. 32. According to Lattimore, his harassment was orchestrated by Alfred C. Kohlberg, the millionaire editor of *Plain Talk* and a powerful figure in the China Lobby.

81. Truman's remark is cited in David McCullough, *Truman* (New York: Touchstone Books, 1993 [1992]), p. 769.

82. Pearl's review of *Solution in Asia* appeared in the April, 1945 issue of *Asia and the Americas*, p. 213. A couple of months earlier, Edgar Snow gave Lattimore's book an equally enthusiastic notice in the *New York Times Book Review* (February 25, 1945), pp. 3, 29.

83. For an exhaustive account of Lattimore's pursuit by the China Lobby and its several Congressional allies, see Robert P. Newman, *Owen Lattimore and the "Loss" of China* (Berkeley: University of California Press, 1992).

84. Pearl S. Buck to Anna Melissa Graves (April 6, 1950), Swarthmore College Library archives. In another letter, released by the FBI to this writer on appeal, Pearl and Richard wrote: "We are indignant and dismayed at [the] completely false charges against Owen Lattimore.... The false charges are all the more unfortunate for the United States because this country needs the services of a man of his experience and wisdom. We urge immediate investigation of what persons and interests are behind this destructive attack" (date and recipient not disclosed).

85. Pearl S. Buck to Josette Frank (June 21, 1950), University of Minnesota archives.

86. A longer version of the article was published as a book in September. Pearl turned over all royalties from *The Child Who Never Grew* to the Vineland Training School. Pearl had taken on fund-raising responsibilities for the school in the late 1940s.

87. Twenty years later, Pearl said that *The Child Who Never Grew* "was written in a strange way. I did not wish to write it. The School where my child has been for thirty-nine years needed fund-raising and I gave what I thought I was able to give. The fund-raiser, however, whom I particularly disliked as a person, kept urging me to write the story of my child. I constantly refused. Just one way he found my Achilles heel. He said, in effect, that my child's life was absolutely useless unless I made use of it to others. This struck me to the heart and after considerable agonizing I wrote this little book especially for parents of retarded children." Pearl S. Buck to Robert William Beam (March 2, 1970), Pearl S. Buck Family Trust archives.

88. Madame De Gaulle's comments (translated into English) are contained in a memo from Richard Walsh to Pearl (July 2, 1950), Pearl S. Buck Family Trust archives.

89. The quoted sentence is taken from an unpublished speech Pearl gave to a meeting of the Philadelphia County Chapter of the Pennsylvania Association for Retarded Children in June, 1954.

90. Cited in John A. Saltmarsh, *Scott Nearing: An Intellectual Biography* (Philadelphia: Temple University Press, 1991), pp. 98, 95. See also Stephen J. Whitfield, *Scott Nearing: Apostle of American Radicalism* (New York: Columbia University Press, 1974), pp. 25–50.

91. In 1954, the Nearings sold their Vermont property to Pearl and moved to Maine, where they spent the rest of their lives.

92. There is more than a trace of paradox in a conflict that is so well remembered as "the forgotten war." See Rick Kerin, "The Korean War and American Memory" (unpublished dissertation, University of Pennsylvania, 1993).

93. Hoover's comment is written on the margin of a telegram from Pearl (November 17, 1950), in which she asked the Director to call her to discuss "a matter of immediate and possible national and international importance in connection with China." The material was released upon appeal.

94. Pearl S. Buck to Emma Edmunds White (August, 1950), Randolph-Macon Woman's College archives.

95. Pearl S. Buck to Anna Melissa Graves (March 4, 1950), Swarthmore College Library archives.

96. Pearl S. Buck to Frank T. Kauffman (December 11, 1950), Houghton Library archives.

97. Pearl S. Buck to James Michener (November 7, 1952), Library of Congress manuscripts division.

98. Pearl S. Buck to Mrs. Adria Beaver Lynham (August 2, 1950); this letter from Pearl's FBI file was released upon appeal.

99. Pearl S. Buck, interview with Kimpei Shimba of *Nippon Times* (December, 1950), reprinted in Theodore F. Harris, *Pearl S. Buck: A Biography*, volume two, *Her Philosophy as Expressed in Her Letters* (New York: John Day Company, 1971), p. 116.

100. Months later, Thompson wrote to Pearl to apologize for her column and to tell her that she now agreed with Pearl's views. "Drunk, apparently, with power or with fear," Thompson wrote, "we are pursuing a course which cannot fail to alienate all Asia and the Middle East." Pearl responded, somewhat condescendingly: "It encourages me much that you have come to so clear an understanding of the point at which our country stands." Dorothy Thompson to Pearl S. Buck (September 18, 1951) and Pearl S. Buck to Dorothy Thompson (October 1, 1951), Syracuse University Library archives. On Thompson's political opinions at this time, see Peter Kurth, *American Cassandra: The Life of Dorothy Thompson* (Boston: Little, Brown, 1990), pp. 408–411.

101. "Miss Buck Warns on Loss of Liberty," *New York Times* (January 28, 1951), p. 32.

102. Pearl's speech and the *Washington Post* editorial were reprinted and circulated by the Women's International League for Peace and Freedom. In his memoirs, William L. Shirer refers to the Cardozo High School incident as evidence of the spread of intolerance in America, though he misdates the episode to 1949. Shirer, *Twentieth-Century Journey: A Memoir of a Life and the Times*, volume III, *A Native's Return, 1945–1988* (Boston: Little, Brown, 1990), p. 132.

103. Richard J. Walsh to Scott Nearing (February 8, 1951) and Scott Nearing to Richard Walsh (February 12, 1951), Pearl S. Buck Family Trust archives.

104. Pearl S. Buck to Anna Melissa Graves (February 19, 1951), Swarthmore College archives.

105. Pearl S. Buck to Emma Edmunds White (March 5, 1951), Randolph-Macon Woman's College archives.

106. Pearl S. Buck to Florence Rose (February 19, 1951), Smith College archives. Soon, Pearl was using the East and West mailing list to solicit funds for Welcome House. She sent a mailing to supporters of the East and West Association that included the assurance that "You will receive no appeal this year from the East and West Association. Will

you instead give your gift to the Welcome House children?" Pearl S. Buck to Mrs. Overbury (June 15, 1951), Barnard College Library archives.

107. *Temple University News* (February 12, 1951), p. 1.

108. A file of material concerning Pearl's nomination and election to the American Academy of Arts and Letters is contained in the Academy archives. Though the process commenced in February, Pearl's election was not officially announced until November.

109. The fullest account of the relations between Henry Luce and Theodore White is given in Thomas Griffith, *Harry and Teddy: The Turbulent Friendship of Press Lord Henry R. Luce and His Favorite Reporter, Theodore H. White* (New York: Random House, 1995).

110. James A. Michener, *The World Is My Home: A Memoir* (New York: Random House, 1992), p. 343.

111. The phrases are taken from *Time's* anonymous review of *Peony* (May 17, 1948), p. 113.

112. Though she spoke dismissively of the work that Lossing Buck did, Pearl's several years as Lossing's partner in agricultural research had left her with a particular interest in Chinese farming. See Pearl S. Buck, "Food for China," *Survey Graphic,* volume 36 (July, 1947), pp. 377–379.

113. Pearl had met Clifford Clinton on at least one occasion, and had publicly endorsed his work. She published an approving article, "Mr. Clinton Stops Starvation," in the December, 1949 issue of *United Nations World*. Clinton's efforts to develop a "Multipurpose Food" that would be cheap, nourishing, and universally appealing, are repeated by Clem Miller in the novel. Pearl actually ate a prototype of Clinton's food, and fed it to several of the Welcome House children. "We certainly seem to do very well," she reported in a cheerful note. Pearl S. Buck to Florence Rose (October 5, 1950), Smith College archives.

114. Pearl S. Buck, *God's Men* (New York: John Day Company, 1951), p. 337.

115. Luce's "American Century" editorial appeared in the February 17, 1941 issue of *Life*.

116. The most comprehensive account of Luce's career and his manipulative journalistic practices remains W. A. Swanberg, *Luce and His Empire* (New York: Charles Scribner's Sons, 1972).

117. Pearl S. Buck to Dorothy Thompson (October 1, 1951), Syracuse University Library archives.

118. FBI memo from SAC [Special Agent in Charge], Philadelphia, to Director J. Edgar Hoover (February 27, 1952).

119. The comment is taken from the October, 1951 issue of the "Green Hills News," a newsletter published intermittently by the Walsh children.

120. Pearl said that Henriette was more like her than any of her other children. See Warren Sherk, *Pearl S. Buck: Good Earth Mother* ([Philomath, OR]: Drift Creek Press, 1992), p. 156.

121. The details of Pearl's 1952 schedule are taken from a typed log in the Pearl S. Buck Family Trust archives.

122. At the end of World War II, thirty-one states still had anti-miscegenation laws on their books. That number fell to sixteen by 1967: Alabama, Arkansas, Delaware, Florida, Georgia, Kentucky, Louisiana, Mississippi, Missouri, North Carolina, Oklahoma, South Carolina, Tennessee, Texas, Virginia, and West Virginia – mainly the old South and the border states. In that year the U.S. Supreme Court, in *Loving* v. *Virginia,* finally declared such laws unconstitutional. For a state-by-state survey in the early postwar period, see Pauli Murray, ed., *State Laws on Race and Color* (n.p.: The Woman's Division of Christian Service, 1950). See also Robert J. Sickels, *Race, Marriage and the Law* (Albuquerque: University of New Mexico Press, 1972), especially chapter four, "Miscegenation and the Law Before 1967."

123. Elizabeth Janeway, "The Optimistic World of Miss Buck," *New York Times Book Review* (May 25, 1952), p. 4. Making an exception to the general indifference, Van Wyck Brooks included a kind paragraph on *The Good Earth* in his 1953 survey *The Writer in*

America. Brooks was a loyal friend (he had nominated Pearl to the Institute of the American Academy two years earlier), but even his approval was limited to a book published twenty years earlier.

124. Pearl S. Buck to James Michener (November 7, 1952), Library of Congress manuscripts division.
125. Pearl S. Buck to Ray and Dolores Yaukey (November 7, 1952), Pearl S. Buck Family Trust archives.
126. Richard J. Walsh to Jean Walsh (December 12, 1952), Pearl S. Buck Family Trust archives.
127. Pearl S. Buck to Andrea Lloyd (January 2, 1953), Pearl S. Buck Family Trust archives.
128. Pearl S. Buck, "The Atmosphere of Education," *NEA Journal* (May, 1948), p. 282.
129. Pearl offered this characterization in the remarks she wrote to accompany Thornton Wilder's receipt of the American Academy of Arts and Letters Gold Medal for Fiction.
130. Although no child results from Livy's intercourse with her Indian lover, Jatin, Pearl said that the plot of *Come, My Beloved* had its origins in her speculations about the conception of the first Welcome House baby. Theodore Harris, *Pearl S. Buck: A Biography* (New York: John Day Company, 1969), p. 299.
131. Pearl S. Buck, *My Several Worlds* (New York: John Day Company, 1954), p. 79. When she was elected to the Academy, Pearl had been assigned to Lewis's chair.
132. Cited in Harris, *Pearl S. Buck,* p. 313.

Chapter 9: Pearl Sydenstricker

1. In the memoirs she was completing at this time, Pearl wrote that the American people must not "be asked to share the intolerable and ancient burdens of France in Indo-China" if we want "to prove to Asia that we are not as other white men have been." Pearl S. Buck, *My Several Worlds* (New York: John Day Company), p. 49.
2. Pearl S. Buck to Emma Edmunds White (June 24, 1954), Randolph-Macon Woman's College archives.
3. *Saturday Review of Literature* (November 6, 1954), p. 17. There were several front-page reviews, including strongly favorable notices in the *Chicago Tribune* and the *New York Herald-Tribune Book Review.* Erwin D. Canham, in the *Christian Science Monitor* (November 4, 1954), applauded the "incomparable vividness and accuracy" of Pearl's descriptions, and called *My Several Worlds* "a stirring and emotional study in terms of people's lives, of actual experience, of tragedy and of love."
4. *New Yorker* (November 6, 1954), p. 186.
5. Pearl S. Buck, remarks at "Pearl Buck Day," Beckley (West Virginia) College (November 19, 1970).
6. Buck, *My Several Worlds,* pp. 22–23.
7. Pearl S. Buck, memo to Mary Lombard (October 2, 1954), Pearl S. Buck Family Trust archives.
8. A fairly substantial file on the proposed television series is contained in the Pearl Buck Family Trust archives; some of the documents are housed in the Princeton University archives. The show, sometimes referred to as "Pearl Buck Chooses" in correspondence, never reached production.
9. Pearl S. Buck, "Plight of Immigrants," *New York Times* (November 16, 1954), p. 28.
10. On the "Hiroshima Maidens," see Norman Cousins, *Present Tense: An American Editor's Odyssey* (New York: McGraw-Hill, 1967), pp. 324–352; Virginia Naeve, ed., *Friends of the Hibakusha* (Denver: A. Swallow, 1964), pp. 104–151; Rodney Barker, *The Hiroshima Maidens: A Story of Courage, Compassion, and Survival* (New York: Viking, 1985); John Hersey, *Hiroshima* (New York: Vintage Books, 1989 [1985]), pp. 134–149.
11. Pearl made those observations in a letter she wrote on behalf of the Women's Inter-

national League for Peace and Freedom in the spring of 1955. She asked for contributions, and invited the women she wrote to attend the League's fortieth-anniversary dinner in May. A copy of the letter was placed in Pearl's FBI file. The dinner was reported in the *Philadelphia Tribune* (May 10, 1955), p. 6.

12. Pearl published a brief tribute to Emily Greene Balch in the winter, 1956 issue of the Bryn Mawr *Alumnae Bulletin*.

13. Pearl S. Buck to Andrea Lloyd (December 8, 1955), Pearl S. Buck Family Trust archives.

14. Pearl S. Buck to Sarah Rowe (December 21, 1955), Pearl S. Buck Family Trust archives.

15. Pearl S. Buck to Major and Mrs. R. B. Elliott (January 17, 1956), Pearl S. Buck Family Trust archives.

16. Buck, "The Children Waiting," pp. 131–132.

17. Information on Pearl's reading, and the lunch with Ashley Montagu, comes from the Nora Stirling papers, Randolph-Macon Woman's College archives.

18. Pearl S. Buck to Marjorie White (August 30, 1956), Schlesinger Collection, Radcliffe College.

19. See, for example, Pearl S. Buck to Emma Edmunds White (February 22, 1956), Randolph-Macon Woman's College archives.

20. Though doubts about the veracity of *China Under the Empress Dowager* surrounded the book from the day it was published, the gigantic forgeries on which it was based were only finally exposed in a brilliant study by Hugh Trevor-Roper, *Hermit of Peking: The Hidden Life of Sir Edmund Backhouse* (New York: Knopf, 1977).

21. Marina Warner was another of Backhouse's victims, as she acknowledges in the "Foreword" to the 1986 republication of her 1972 biography, *The Dragon Empress*. For a more recent essay in support of Tz'u hsi, written after Trevor-Roper's revelations, see Sue Fawn Chung, "The Much Maligned Empress Dowager: A Revisionist Study of the Empress Dowager Tz'u-hsi (1835–1908)," *Modern Asian Studies*, 13, 2 (1979), pp. 177–196. Sterling Seagrave also comes to Tz'u-hsi's defense in *Dragon Lady* (New York: Vintage Books, 1993), a bouncy, journalistic biography that is marred by a tendency toward overstatement and voyeurism.

22. Pearl S. Buck, *Imperial Woman* (New York: John Day Company, 1956), p. 218.

23. Edgar S. Walsh, interview with the present writer (April 25, 1995).

24. Quoted in "Pearl Buck Will Adopt Negro-Japanese Child," *New York Herald Tribune* (October 29, 1957).

25. Pearl S. Buck to Emma Edmunds White (November 24, 1958), Randolph-Macon Woman's College archives.

26. Pearl S. Buck and Carlos P. Romulo, *Friend to Friend* (New York: John Day Company, 1958), p. 79.

27. Tad Danielewski's comments are taken from an interview with Donn Rogosin (December 1, 1989), and a telephone interview with the present writer (June 15, 1992).

28. Pearl S. Buck to Emma Edmunds White (March 25, 1957), Randolph-Macon Woman's College archives.

29. Pearl S. Buck to Dr. Hiraku Sandaya (February 19, 1951), Pearl S. Buck Family Trust archives.

30. See Pearl S. Buck, "The Bomb – Did We Have to Drop It?," *American Weekly* (March 15, 1959), pp. 10–11, 16. The record of a conversation between Pearl and Arthur Compton, this article offers reluctant support to the decision to drop the atomic bombs on Japan.

31. "Nobel Prize Winners Discuss Survival in Nuclear Age," *Philadelphia Evening Bulletin* (April 24, 1958), p. 3.

32. Laura Fermi, *Atoms in the Family: My Life With Enrico Fermi* (Chicago: University of Chicago Press, 1954); Arthur Holly Compton, *Atomic Quest: A Personal Narrative* (New York: Oxford University Press, 1956). Not surprisingly, Compton's book somewhat enlarges his contribution to the Manhattan Project. For a more disinterested appraisal,

and for a comprehensive history of the bomb's manufacture, see Richard Rhodes, *The Making of the Atomic Bomb* (New York: Simon & Schuster, 1986).

33. Pearl came to regard Compton as a tragic figure. Asked by *Look* magazine in 1961 to write an article on the previous twenty-five years of world history, she produced an essay, "A Quarter Century: Its Human Tragedies," *Look* (September 26, 1961), pp. 95–104. Characteristically, she made her point by telling the stories of four individuals who had been defeated by twentieth-century war and violence: Chiang Kai-shek; a Korean orphan girl surnamed Kim; a refugee from Poland whose family was murdered by the Nazis; and Compton, a humane scientist forced to turn his talent toward destruction.

34. Kenneth Tynan, *Curtains* (New York: Atheneum, 1961), p. 316.

35. Buck, *Friend to Friend*, p. 110.

36. On Bohr's ideas about complementarity, see Rhodes, *The Making of the Atomic Bomb*, especially pp. 131–132, 243, 528–538.

37. Harold R. Isaacs, *Scratches on Our Mind: American Images of China and India* (New York: John Day Company, 1958), p. 155. *The Good Earth* was mentioned by sixty-nine of the people Isaacs interviewed; in second place, but mentioned only twenty-one times, was Edgar Snow's *Red Star Over China*.

38. For example, Pearl opposed an increase in second-class postage because of the burden the new rates would cause for magazine publishers. See "Statement of Pearl S. Buck, President of the Authors Guild of the Authors League of America, Inc.," *Authors Guild Bulletin* (March–April, 1962), pp. 1–2.

39. Pearl S. Buck, "Principles of Leadership" (April 23, 1960), Howard University archives. Fifteen months after the lecture, Howard's vice president, William Stuart Nelson, sent Pearl a copy of her remarks, along with a note congratulating her for her "deep insights" into her subject. William Stuart Nelson to Pearl S. Buck (July 3, 1961), Howard University archives.

40. Pearl S. Buck, *A Bridge for Passing* (New York: John Day Company, 1962), pp. 61–72.

41. Pearl S. Buck to Mrs. Boshi [Gertrude] Sen (June 27, 1960), Pearl S. Buck Foundation archives.

42. See Chapter 3, p. 103, of this volume.

43. "Pearl Buck Wicked, Say Red Chinese," *Los Angeles Times* (December 11, 1960), E24.

44. Pearl S. Buck to Lily Wen (December 29, 1960), Pearl S. Buck Family Trust archives.

45. "Inaugural Bids Sent to 155," *Philadelphia Bulletin* (January 15, 1961), 13.

46. Roy Wilkins to Pearl S. Buck (April 4, 1961) and Pearl S. Buck to Roy Wilkins (April 10, 1961), Pearl S. Buck Family Trust archives.

47. Arthur M. Schlesinger, Jr., *A Thousand Days: John F. Kennedy in the White House* (Boston: Houghton Mifflin, 1965), p. 733.

48. Nora Stirling, *Pearl Buck: A Woman in Conflict* (Piscataway, NJ: New Century Publishers, 1983), p. 279. Edna Ferber (1887–1968), author of *So Big,* was Pearl's best-selling near-contemporary.

49. Ross Terrill generously shared the typescript of his conversation with Pearl Buck (December 26–27, 1971) with the present writer. Pearl did not include this story in her hagiographical book *The Kennedy Women* (1970).

50. Pearl S. Buck, *The Living Reed* (New York: John Day Company, 1963), pp. 344–345.

51. Carter J. Eckert, Ki-baik Lee, Young Ick Lew, Michael Robinson, and Edward W. Wagner, *Korea Old and New: A History* (Seoul: Ilchokak Publishers, 1990 [distributed by Harvard University Press]), p. 254. This detailed survey of Korean history confirms the meticulous accuracy of *The Living Reed*.

52. Pearl S. Buck to G. A. Cevasco (August 12, 1968), Randolph-Macon Woman's College archives.

53. Eric Swenson to Pearl S. Buck (October 10, 1962; October 29, 1962) and Pearl S. Buck to Eric Swenson (October 24, 1962), Pearl S. Buck Family Trust archives.

54. See Chapter 4, pp. 149–50, of this volume.

55. The most useful brief discussion of Hocking's life and work can be found in Bruce Kuklick, *The Rise of American Philosophy* (New Haven: Yale University Press, 1977), pp. 481–495.

56. Selections of the letters between Pearl and Hocking are reprinted in Stirling, *Pearl Buck,* pp. 271–278, and Theodore F. Harris, in consultation with Pearl S. Buck, *Pearl S. Buck: A Biography* (New York: John Day Company, 1969), pp. 352–358.

57. Irvin Block, *The Lives of Pearl Buck: A Tale of China and America* (New York: Thomas Y. Crowell, 1973), p. 158.

58. Pearl S. Buck, *The Goddess Abides* (New York: John Day Company, 1972), pp. 100–102. On the novel as autobiographical, see Beverly Rizzon, *Pearl S. Buck: The Final Chapter* (Palm Springs, CA: ETC Publications, 1989), p. 128.

59. Much of the information on Ted Harris is taken from Greg Walter, "The Dancing Master," *Philadelphia Magazine* (July 1969), pp. 55–59, 112–126. Harris refused to speak with Walter and has refused to speak with the present writer.

60. Theodore F. Harris to Pearl S. Buck (n.d. [August, 1963]), Pearl S. Buck Family Trust archives.

61. Pearl S. Buck to Philip Sterling (August 26, 1959), Pearl S. Buck Family Trust archives. Sterling chaired the Adoption Standards Committee in the Pennsylvania state senate.

62. "Pearl Buck Pleads for Orphans," *New York Herald Tribune* (January 7, 1959). She testified before the Joint Legislative Committee on Marriage and Family Laws.

63. Pearl S. Buck to Mrs. Marina Polvay (April 30, 1968), Pearl S. Buck Family Trust archives.

64. Pearl S. Buck, "American Children: Alien by Birth," *Ladies' Home Journal* (November, 1964), p.39. Pearl undoubtedly derived some of her ideas about the advantages of hybridity from her friend David Burpee, whose Burpee Seed Company introduced hybrid vegetables to the American market in 1945. Their resistance to disease and copious yields made the hybrids instantly successful.

    In the past decade, hybridity has become a subject of increasing interest to writers, anthropologists, and literary critics. For a useful historical survey and analysis, with special reference to American culture, see Gary B. Nash, "The Hidden History of Mestizo America," *The Journal of American History.* vol. 82 no. 3 (December, 1995), pp. 941–962.

65. Quoted in Pearl S. Buck, *The New Year* (New York: John Day Company, 1968), p. 216.

66. Pearl S. Buck, *The Kennedy Women* (New York: Cowles Book Company, 1970), pp. 111–113.

67. Details of the Pearl S. Buck Foundation's expenditures are taken from Walter, "The Dancing Master," and Stirling, *Pearl Buck,* supplemented by interviews with former foundation staff and records in the foundation archives.

68. Pearl S. Buck to Bradford Smith (May 10, 1964), University of Vermont library.

69. John de J. Pemberton, Jr., to Pearl S. Buck (December 30, 1964), Pearl S. Buck Family Trust archives.

70. Pearl S. Buck to Katherine M. Arnett (June 25, 1965), Swarthmore College Peace Collection.

71. Pearl S. Buck to Annie Kate Gilbert (July 8, 1964), Pearl S. Buck Family Trust archives.

72. Kermit Fischer to Pearl S. Buck (September 30, 1960), Pearl S. Buck Family Trust archives.

73. Theodore F. Harris to Pearl S. Buck (n.d. [1964]) and Pearl S. Buck to Theodore F. Harris (August 19, 1964), Pearl S. Buck Family Trust archives. Pearl's expenditures on clothing in 1965 were detailed in a 1968 letter to her attorney in connection with an income tax audit.

74. David Burpee to Pearl S. Buck (March 5, 1965) and Pearl S. Buck to David Burpee (March 8, 1965), Pearl S. Buck Family Trust archives.

75. Pearl S. Buck to Senator Joe Clark (January 14 and February 10, 1965), Pearl S. Buck Family Trust archives.
76. Percy L. Julian to Pearl S. Buck (March 16, 1965) and Pearl S. Buck to Percy L. Julian (March 22, 1965), Pearl S. Buck Family Trust archives.
77. Pearl S. Buck to Indira Gandhi (January 24, 1966) and Indira Gandhi to Pearl S. Buck (April 14, 1966), Pearl S. Buck Family Trust archives.
78. Pearl S. Buck to Grace Mullen (February 21, 1967), Pearl S. Buck Family Trust archives.
79. One scholar has argued that Pearl's involvement in humanitarian activities, including her work on behalf of abandoned, orphaned, and mixed-race children, represented a political strategy. See Robert Shaffer, "Pearl S. Buck, China, and Dissent from the Cold War: A Gendered Perspective on U.S. Policy," unpublished paper presented at the 109th Annual Meeting of the American Historical Association convention (January 5–8, 1995).
80. In the *New York Times Book Review*, Barbara Wersba praised Pearl's story of the abandoned boys as "an eloquent reply to all those who complain that children's books bear no relation to life" (April 16, 1967, p. 22). In a little under three years, from late 1966 through mid-1969, 25,000 copies of the book were sold, in six separate printings.

    A copy of *Matthew, Mark, Luke and John* is preserved in Pearl's FBI files. Apparently, somebody thought the book was subversive, either because of its critical presentation of the American military or because of its provocative use of the Evangelists' names.
81. Harry Gilroy, "Books Outgrown in Library Today," *New York Times* (July 14, 1966), p. 71.
82. Pearl's speech at the American Library Association meeting was subsequently published under the title "Essay on Myself," together with a study of her work by Jason Lindsey. John Day printed one thousand copies of the booklet for distribution "solely to those attending the luncheon." Pearl gave one of the copies to Ted, inscribing it: "For Theodore F. Harris / This book is inscribed / with my love and gratitude, / Pearl S. Buck."
83. Pearl S. Buck, "A Cry for the Deserted!," *This Week* (January 29, 1967), p. 4.
84. For a contemporary journalistic account of discrimination in Japan, see Robert Trumbull, "Amerasians," *New York Times Magazine* (April 30, 1967), pp. 112–114.
85. Pearl S. Buck to Alma Severson (July 17, 1967), Pearl S. Buck Family Trust archives.
86. "Pearl Buck Estate to Aid Children," *New York Times* (May 22, 1967), p. 39.
87. Stirling, *Pearl Buck: A Woman in Conflict*, p. 292.
88. Pearl S. Buck to Emma Edmunds White (July 14, 1967), Randolph-Macon Woman's College archives.
89. Harris, *Pearl S. Buck*, p. 346.
90. Stirling, *Pearl Buck: A Woman in Conflict*, p. 300.
91. T. P. O'Connor to Pearl S. Buck (March 4, 1967), Pearl S. Buck Family Trust archives.
92. The statements in these paragraphs are taken from FBI memoranda and reports (June 19, July 5, July 11, and August 11, 1967) released to this writer under the Freedom of Information Act. The Bureau investigated Pearl at least once again, in 1972, when she applied to the Chinese government for a visa.
93. Pearl S. Buck with Theodore F. Harris, *For Spacious Skies: Journey in Dialogue* (New York: John Day Company, 1966), p. 191.
94. Ross Terrill, quoting Ted Harris, in unpublished notes (December 26–27, 1971).
95. The UNESCO data are cited in Stirling, *Pearl Buck: A Woman in Conflict*, p. 313.
96. Louise White Walker, in a conversation with this writer (September 22, 1994).
97. Records of these checks are housed in miscellaneous financial papers in the Pearl S. Buck Family Trust archives.
98. Pearl S. Buck to Lois Burpee (January 3, 1967) and Pearl S. Buck to Mrs. Bruce McNeil (September 21, 1967), Pearl S. Buck Family Trust archives.
99. Pearl S. Buck to Marina Polvay (April 30, 1968), Pearl S. Buck Family Trust archives.

100. Pearl reported on her trip in a letter to Richard and Tsuta Walsh (March 18, 1968), Pearl S. Buck Family Trust archives.
101. "[D]uring 1968, the support donations were $310,000. The total income of the Foundation was $1,160,000." Charles M. Solomon to [Pennsylvania Attorney General] William C. Sennett (June 18, 1969), Pearl S. Buck Family Trust archives.
102. Information on Pearl's itinerary and speaking fees is located in the Pearl S. Buck Family Trust archives.
103. Anonymous to Richard Wilson (May 16, 1969), Pearl S. Buck Family Trust archives.
104. Pearl S. Buck to Members of the Board of Directors of the Pearl S. Buck Foundation (May 26, 1969), Pearl S. Buck Family Trust archives.
105. Stirling, *Pearl Buck: A Woman in Conflict*, p. 306.
106. "Pearl Buck Aide Quits Under Fire," *New York Times* (July 10, 1969), p. 34, and "Pearl Buck to Head Her Own Foundation," *New York Times* (July 23, 1969), p. 28.
107. "The Press," *Time* (July 25, 1969), p. 60.
108. *Ibid.*
109. Pearl S. Buck, untitled transcript of WIP statement (n.d.), Pearl S. Buck Family Trust archives.
110. The reader's report recommending *The Three Daughters* as a Book-of-the-Month Club choice was written by Gilbert Highet.
111. Pearl S. Buck, *The Three Daughters of Madame Liang* (New York: John Day Company, 1969), pp. 262–262.
112. John King Fairbank, *The United States and China*, fourth edition, enlarged (Cambridge, MA: Harvard University Press, 1983), p. 421.
113. Stirling, *Pearl Buck: A Woman in Conflict*, p. 309.
114. Scores of these invitations and letters are contained in the files of the Pearl S. Buck Family Trust archives.
115. Pearl appeared on the "Today" show on July 14, 1970.
116. Stirling, *Pearl Buck: A Woman in Conflict*, p. 313.
117. Pearl S. Buck, "Topics: The Chinese Way Is Not Aggressive War," *New York Times* (May 30, 1970), p. 22.
118. Sheila Sadowsky, quoted in Stirling, *Pearl Buck: A Woman in Conflict*, p. 324.
119. Irvin Block, *The Lives of Pearl Buck: A Tale of China and America* (New York: Thomas Y. Crowell, 1973), p. 154.
120. Pearl S. Buck to James T. Farrell (April 7, 1969), University of Pennsylvania rare book and manuscript collections.
121. This and the following comments are taken from the notes Terrill made after nine hours of conversation with Pearl (December 26–27, 1971).
122. Grace Yaukey, interview with the present writer (May 10, 1991).
123. See, e.g., " 'China Lobby,' Once Powerful Factor in U. S. Politics, Appears Victim of Lack of Interest," *New York Times* (April 26, 1970), p. 14. According to this article, the decline of the lobby's coalition of politicians and military figures "was directly connected with a gradual shift in public opinion on Communist China." A State Department official was quoted as saying that " 'people today are perfectly willing to consider dealing with Peking, where they weren't willing to even think about it ten or fifteen years ago.' "
124. In a *Good Housekeeping* poll at the end of 1971, Pearl placed third among America's most admired women, behind only Rose Kennedy and Mamie Eisenhower. The result was probably influenced by rising American interest in China.
125. John S. Service to the present writer (February 26, 1992).
126. This suggestion was made by Liu Haiping in a conversation with the present writer (October 10, 1991), and is repeated in his essay "Pearl S. Buck's Reception in China Reconsidered," in Elizabeth Lipscomb, Frances Webb, and Peter Conn, eds., *The Several Worlds of Pearl S. Buck* (Westport, CT: Greenwood Press, 1994), pp. 55–67. In the

quote that was used as a promotional blurb, Pearl said that *House of Exile* was "undoubtedly one of the most delightful books of personal experience that has yet been written about China. Its authenticity is beyond question."

127. For the best account of this incident, see Ross Terrill, *The White-Boned Demon: A Biography of Madame Mao Zedong* (New York: Simon & Schuster, 1984), p. 103.

128. James C. Thomson, Jr., "A Petty Clash Made Pearl Buck an Outcast," *Boston Globe* (August 2, 1992), p. 70.

129. Cited in Liu Haiping, "Pearl S. Buck's Reception in China Reconsidered," pp. 62–63. Lu Hsün's hostility to Pearl's work was encapsulated within a small irony, since she had been among his earliest Western supporters. Among other things, she and Richard Walsh had published Lu Hsün's work in *Asia* in the mid-1930s.

130. For reports of the meetings and discussions of the annual conference of black social workers, see the *New York Times* (April 9, 1972), p. 29, and *New York Times* (April 10, 1972), p. 27. A column of analysis by Judy Klemesrud appeared in the April 12 issue.

131. Rita J. Simon and Howard Altstein have undertaken several longitudinal studies of black children adopted into white families; see Simon and Altstein, *Transracial Adoptees and Their Families: A Study of Identity and Commitment* (New York: Praeger, 1987), and *The Case for Transracial Adoption* (Washington, DC: American University Press, 1994). This research indicates that transracial adoptions are successful. Among other indicators, black adopted children in white families demonstrate the same levels of self-esteem, educational achievement, and career ambitions as their white siblings. In a 1992 article, Simon has written that the "position of the National Association of Black Social Workers (NABSW) that the 'placement of black children in white homes is a hostile act against our community' and 'a blatant form of racial and cultural genocide' is clearly anti-children and certainly inconsistent with the 'best interests of the child' standard." Simon, "Comment on 'Where Do Black Children Belong?'," *Reconstruction*, vol. 1, no. 4 (1992), p. 51.

132. See "Federal Court Voids a Law Prohibiting Biracial Adoptions," *New York Times* (March 25, 1972), p. 33.

133. Pearl S. Buck, "I Am the Better Woman for Having My Two Black Children," *Today's Health* (January, 1972), p. 64.

134. Lawrence Van Gelder, "Notes on People," *New York Times* (July 7, 1972), p. 13.

135. Information on Pearl's hospitalization comes from Stirling, *Pearl Buck: A Woman in Conflict,* pp. 320–330; Rizzon, *Pearl S. Buck: The Final Chapter;* and Grace Yaukey, in an interview with the present writer (May 10, 1991).

136. Pearl S. Buck to Marjorie Ashbrook Temple (May 2, 1967), Pearl S. Buck Foundation archives.

137. Several months later, John Hersey presented a graceful but clear-eyed tribute to Pearl at a meeting of the American Academy of Arts and Letters. He celebrated her humanity, but he distinguished between "the large generous impulse and the artistic limitations of her body of work." John Hersey, "Pearl S. Buck, 1892–1971 [*sic*]," *Proceedings of the American Academy of Arts and Letters and the National Institute of Arts and Letters,* second series, number 24 (New York: 1974), pp. 102–105.

138. Ted and his allies appealed the verdict, and brought new suits of their own. The case carried on in one form or another for seven years before reaching a negotiated, still-secret settlement.

Epilogue: Green Hills Farm

1. Pearl S. Buck, *A Bridge for Passing* (New York: John Day Company, 1961), p. 102.

2. John Updike, "Books: The Man Within," *New Yorker* (June 26 and July 3, 1995), p. 182.

INDEX

AAUW (*see* American Association of University Women)

Abbott, Lyman, 32

Abbott, Ruby (*see* Ruby Walsh)

Abraham Lincoln School (Chicago), 299

Academy Awards, 192

Acheson, Dean, 320

Adams, Henry, 381

Adams, J. Donald, 145, 148, 167

Addams, Jane, 377

The Adventures of Augie March (Saul Bellow), 304

"Advice to Unborn Novelists" (Pearl S. Buck), 178

African Journey (Eslanda Goode Robeson), 311

The Age of Innocence (Edith Wharton), 307

Agee, James, 131, 281

The Akron Times, 190

Alampi, Phillip, 367

Aldine Club (New York City), 252

All Men Are Brothers (Pearl S. Buck), 137–9, 157, 159, 166

Allen, A. Leonard, 274

Allen, Hervey, 238

Allen, Steve, 355

Alley, Rewi, 224

American Academy of Arts and Letters, 187, 323, 328, 356

American Academy of Political Science, 16

American Academy of Political and Social Science, 155

American Argument (Pearl S. Buck and Eslanda Goode Robeson), xvi, 311–12

American Association for Organizing Family Social Work, 234

American Association of University Women (AAUW), 136, 234, 262

American Association of University Women Journal, 234

American Bureau for Medical Aid to China, 237

American Civil Liberties Union, 230, 259, 282, 299, 304, 328, 356

American Committee for Non-Participation in Japanese Aggression, 222

The American Diplomatic Game (Drew Pearson), 181

American Exodus (Dorothea Lange and Paul Taylor), 131, 180

"American Imperialism in the Making" (Pearl S. Buck), 298

American Institute of Motion Pictures, 225

American Jitters (Edmund Wilson), 180

American Legion, 273

American Library Association, 310, 360

American Unity and Asia (Pearl S. Buck), 264–5

American Woman (periodical), 205

American Women's Club (Shanghai), 136

"America's Gunpowder Women" (Pearl S. Buck), 216

"America's Medieval Women" (Pearl S. Buck), 203–4, 216

Amoy (Xiamen), 14

Analects (Confucius), 137

Anderson, Marian, 264, 277

Anderson, Sherwood, 144, 175, 180, 210, 288

"The Angel" (Pearl S. Buck), 72

The Angry Wife (John Sedges [Pearl S. Buck]), 305

Anhwei (Anhui) province, xiv, xix, 56, 124, 139, 203

Anti-lynching bills, 165, 232, 259

Anthony, Susan B., 48, 377

Antioch College, 280

Argonne National Laboratory, 343
Arrowsmith (Sinclair Lewis), 266
Arthur Murray Dance Studios, 352
Asch, Sholem, 211
Asia (periodical), xv, 82, 85, 89, 97, 101, 159–
   60, 171–4, 181, 196, 198–9, 202, 217, 224,
   226–7, 231, 243–6, 260, 279, 292, 297, 304,
   309, 327
Asia and the Americas (see Asia)
"Asia Book-Shelf" (column), 181, 183
Associated Press, 160
Astor Hotel, 148, 215, 260
The Atlantic Monthly, 32, 75, 77, 145, 236
Atomic Quest (Arthur Holly Compton), 342
Atoms in the Family (Laura Fermi), 342
Attucks, Crispus, 266
Atwood, Margaret, 247
Auden, W. H., 224–5, 330
Authors Guild, 344, 356
Autobiography (Margaret Sanger), 258
Ayscough, Florence, 126

Backhouse, Sir Edmund, 339–40
A Backward Glance (Edith Wharton), 307
Baker, Sabine, 217
Balch, Emily Greene, 337–8
Baldwin, Hanson, 273
Baldwin, James, 261
Baldwin, Roger, 282
Baldwin, William, 259
Bamberger, Louis, 197
Barbara Sheldon (Sabine Baker), 217
Barbour, Clarence, 184
Barnard College, 46
"Barnes, David" (pseudonym, Pearl S. Buck),
   80–1, 205
Barnes, Harry Elmer, 145
Barr, David, 316
"Barren Spring" (Pearl S. Buck), 134
Barrymore, Ethel, 241
Barton, Clara, 377
Barzun, Jacques, 185
Baskin, Leonard, 367
Bataan, 253
Battle of Midway, 269
Beard, Charles, 172
"Beauty in China" (Pearl S. Buck), 77–8
*Behind the Urals: An American Worker in
   Russia's City of Steel* (John Scott), 294
Bell, Gertrude, 233
Bellewood Female Seminary, 9
Bellow, Saul, 304
Benchley, Robert, 112

Benedict, Ruth, 231, 245
Benét, William Rose, 145
Bethune-Cookman College, 271
Bethune, Mary McLeod, 271, 377
Better Homes and Gardens, 305
Bey, Turhan, 280
The Big Wave (Pearl S. Buck), 314–15, 342
The Big Wave (film), 344–5
"Birth Control Comes of Age" (Pearl S.
   Buck), 152
"Birth Control in India," 173
Bisson, T. A., 273, 279
Blackwell, Elizabeth, 377
Bland, J. O. P., 339–40
Bliven, Bruce, 145, 211
Blue Shirts, 174
Boas, Franz, 185, 270
Bogan, Louise, 261
Bohr, Neils, 343
The Bokhara (steamship), 22
Bombay, 158
Bonnel, Katherine, 42
"The Book of Hope" (fundraising campaign),
   237
The Book of Martyrs (John Fox), 25–6
Book-of-the-Month Club, xii, 122–3, 141,
   145, 188, 211, 254, 300, 309, 315, 369
Book Review Section (Federal Bureau of
   Investigation), 261
Borg, Dorothy, 86
Bose, Subhash Chandra, 257
Bourke-White, Margaret, 236
Boxer Uprising, xviii, 8, 27–8, 37, 326, 340,
   374
Boyle, Kay, 261
Boy's Life (periodical), 364
Brace, Donald, 145
Brandt, Carl, 101
Bree, Germaine, 369
Brith Sholom, 358
Bretton Woods, 386
Brock, H. I., 270
Bromfield, Louis, 158, 245, 308
Brooks, Van Wyck, 203, 323–4
Broun, Heywood, 122
Brown, John Mason, 147, 187
Brown, Mary Milbank, 338
Brown, Sterling, 216
Brown University, 184
Brown v. Board of Education, 334
Browning, Robert, 26
Bryn Mawr College, 46, 48, 155
The Buccaneers (Edith Wharton), 307

Bucher, Adeline, 160
Buchwald, Art, 354, 355
Buck, Carol, xv, 71, 80, 87, 106–7, 111–12,
    114–16, 121, 123–4, 132, 143, 168, 189–90,
    204, 208, 211–12, 226, 284, 319–20, 332,
    335, 356, 363, 365
Buck, Janice (*see* Janice Walsh)
Buck, John Lossing, xiv, 34, 55–71, 77, 85, 87,
    93, 101–7, 110–11, 114–15, 118, 124, 141,
    144, 147, 153, 156–9, 171, 181–2, 184, 204,
    335, 364
Bucks County Council on Human Relations,
    328
Buddha, 154
Burma, 253–4, 275
Burma Road, 220, 276
Burpee, David, 314, 356
Burpee, Lois, 314, 364
Business and Professional Women of
    Philadelphia, 358
Bynner, Witter, 153, 261–2, 270

Cagney, James, 291
Caldwell, Erskine, 238
Cambridge University, 103
"Can a Missionary Be a Christian?," 149
Canby, Henry Seidel, 122, 145
Canfield, Dorothy (*see* Dorothy Canfield
    Fisher)
Canton (Guangzhou), 14, 89, 90, 121, 219
Capper, Arthur, 250–1
Carnegie Endowment For International Peace,
    307
Carson, Rachel, 377
Carter, Edward, 155, 257
Carter, Elmer, 151, 186, 211, 216, 259
Cassatt, Mary, 377
Catcher in the Rye (J. D. Salinger), 304
Cather, Willa, 187
Catholic Foreign Mission Society (Maryknoll),
    32
The Catholic World (periodical), 128
Catt, Carrie Chapman, 215, 241
CCRCE (*see* Citizens Committee to Repeal
    Chinese Exclusion)
Central State University, 365
Century (periodical), 32
Century Dictionary, 135
Cerf, Bennett, 198
"Certain Wisdom" (Pearl S. Buck), 364
Chalfont, F. H., 34
Chamberlain, Austen, 96
Chamberlain, John, 265

Chamberlain, Neville, 210, 219
Chandruang, Kamut, 231
Chang, H. K., 145
Chang Tso-lin (Zhang Zoulin), 89
Chaplin, Charles, 317
Charity Organization Society, 234
Charlie Chan at the Opera (film), 185
Chase, Mary Ellen, 142
Cheever, John, 261
Chen, Jack, 245
Ch'en, Jerome, 17
Chen, T. S., 245
Ch'en Tu-hsiu (Chen Duxiu), 73–4
Chestnut Theater (Philadelphia), 146
Chiang Ch'ing (Jiang Qing), 374
Chiang Kai-shek (Jiang Jieshi), xviii, 87, 90,
    96, 101, 104–6, 107–8, 121, 141–2, 155,
    173–4, 178, 199, 203, 212, 219, 254, 271–3,
    279–80, 316, 318, 324, 345, 373
The Chicago Defender (newspaper), 154
The Chicago Sun (newspaper), 299
The Chicago Tribune (newspaper), 281
Ch'ien-lung (Qianlong), 13
Child Study Association of America, 314, 319
The Child Who Never Grew (Pearl S. Buck),
    xv, 319, 364
Children for Adoption (Pearl S. Buck), 354
Children's Book Award, 314
"China and the Foreign Chinese" (Pearl S.
    Buck), 142
"China and the West" (Pearl S. Buck), 80–1,
    137
China at Work (Rudolf Hommel), 200–1
"China Bogeyman" (song), 31
China Emergency Relief Committee, 237–8,
    242
China Famine Relief, 202
China Flight (Pearl S. Buck), 302, 364
"China in the Mirror of Her Fiction" (Pearl S.
    Buck), 115–17
China Lobby, 203, 318, 372
China Sky (Pearl S. Buck), 287
China Study Club (Cornell University), 55
China Under the Empress Dowager (J. O. P.
    Bland and Sir Edmund Backhouse), 339–40
Chinatown Charlie (musical), 31
"Chin-Chin Chinaman" (song), 31
'Chinee Soje Man" (song), 31
Chinese Characteristics (Arthur H. Smith), 34–6
The Chinese Christian Student (periodical), 126
Chinese Communists, 54, 85, 87, 90–1, 96, 99,
    101, 105, 118, 121, 127, 139, 142, 174, 178,
    202–3, 254, 272, 317, 341, 345, 368

Chinese Exclusion Acts, xv, 31, 82, 263, 273–4, 327
Chinese Farm Economy (J. Lossing Buck), 55, 114–15
The Chinese Living Theatre, 278
"The Chinese Novel" (Pearl S. Buck), 213–15
The Chinese Recorder (periodical), 11, 18, 19, 22, 38, 39, 55, 68, 89, 101, 128, 134
"The Chinese Student Mind" (Pearl S. Buck), 78–9
Chinese Testament (Tan Shih-hua), 173
"A Chinese Woman Speaks" (Pearl S. Buck), 82–5, 106, 113, 319
Chinese Women's Relief Association, 228
"Chink! Chink!" (song), 31
"Chinky China Charleston" (song), 31
Chinkiang (Zhenjiang), xix, 1, 11, 20–1, 40, 53, 59, 70, 72, 153, 378
Chop Suey One Lung (musical), 31
Chou En-lai (Zhou Enlai), 272, 322, 373, 374
The Christian Century (periodical), 86, 149, 150
The Christian Observer (newspaper), 1
Christine (Pearl S. Buck), 344
Chuang Hsin-tsai (Zhuang Xinzai), 129–30
Chungking (Chongqing), 219, 254
Churchill, Winston, xix, 253, 256–7, 260, 268, 272, 274, 276, 290, 298–9
Citizens Committee to Repeal Chinese Exclusion, 273–4, 282
The City of Tokyo (steamship), 10
Clark, Joe, 358
Clinton, Clifford, 325
Coffin, Henry Sloane, 148
Cohen, Warren, 13–14
Collier's, 112, 216, 287, 302, 331
Color and Democracy (W. E. B. Du Bois), 290–1
Colt, S. Sloan, 259
Columbia University, 74, 155, 185, 270
Columbo, Ceylon, 158
Come, My Beloved (Pearl S. Buck), 331–2
Command the Morning (Pearl S. Buck), 343
"The Commandant and the Commissar" (Pearl S. Buck), 373
Committee on Immigration and Naturalization (U.S. House of Representatives), 274
Commitee Against Racial Discrimination (CARD), 259, 283, 299
Committee on Economic Security, 177
Committee on Un-American Activities (U.S. House of Representatives), 270, 280, 323
Commodore Hotel (New York City), 282

Common Council for American Unity, 250
"Communities of India" (Radhakamal Mukerjee), 245
Company of Revisers of the Mandarin Old Testament, 39
Compton, Arthur Holly, 342–3, 371
"Conflict and Cooperation" (Pearl S. Buck), 184
Confucianism and Modern China (Reginald Johnston), 181
Confucius, 2, 25, 75, 114, 117, 137, 142, 178, 315
Congress Party (India), 173, 268, 282
Congressional Record, 250
Connelly, Marc, 158, 216
Connolly, Walter, 193
Constitution Hall (Washington, DC), 188
Conte Rosso (steamship), 158
Coolidge, Calvin, 96
Cooper, Gary, 271
Cornell, Katherine, 198, 211, 226
Cornell University, 55, 71, 77, 78–82, 136, 152–3, 205
Corning, Hobart, 323
Corregidor, 253
Cosmopolitan (periodical), 141, 167, 170, 207, 216, 331
Cosmopolitan Club (New York City), 215
Co Tui, 237
Council of Jewish Women, 234
Council on African Affairs, 261
Counterattack! (periodical), 217
Cousins, Norman, 337
Covarrubias, Miguel, 245
Cowley, Malcolm, 144, 163, 179, 210, 219
The Cradle (adoption agency), 188
Craighill, Marion, 102
Crawford, Joan, 149, 355
Crawford, Mary Caroline, 46–7
Created Equal (Alma Lutz), 234
"The Creative Spirit in Modern China" (Pearl S. Buck), 173–4
Creativity, Inc., 370, 376
Cressey, G. B., 34
Crisis (periodical), xvi, 250, 265, 305
"A Cry for the Deserted" (Pearl S. Buck), 360
Cultural Revolution, 359, 369
Culture and Crisis, 144
Cummings, E. E., 163
Curie, Marie, 343
Curtis publications, 112
Czolgosz, Leon, 37

Daily Mirror (newspaper), 281
Dalai Lama, 357
"The Dancing Master" (Greg Walter), 367
Danielewski, Tad, 342–4, 352
Daniels, Horton, 71
Davis, Donald, 146
Davis, John, 92
Davis, Owen, 146
Dawson, Margaret Cheney, 157
De Beauvoir, Simone, 338
De Gaulle, Charles, 290
De Gaulle, Mme. Charles, 319
Deladda, Grazia, 209
Demarest, William, 195
"Democracy and the Negro" (Pearl S. Buck), 250
Derr Biggers, Earl, 199
A Desert Incident (Pearl S. Buck), 343
Dewey, John, 74, 95, 245
Dewey, Thomas E., 281, 310, 318
"The Dialect of the River and Grand Canal" (Absalom Sydenstricker), 18
Dickens, Charles, 26, 106, 168–9, 213, 307, 344, 376
Dickenson, Emma, 35
Dickinson, Emily, 377
Dien Bien Phu, 334
Dies, Martin, 280
DiMaggio, Joe, 249
Disraeli, Benjamin, 381
"Do You Want Your Children to Be Tolerant?" (Pearl S. Buck), 305
Donovan, William, 257
The Door of Hope (shelter), 42–4
Dorfman, Edmund, 225
Dos Passos, John, 144, 163, 175, 187, 261
"Double V Campaign," 265
Douglas, Helen Gahagan, 317
Douglas, William O., 257
Douglass, Frederick, 265
Dragon Seed (Pearl S. Buck), xvii, 62, 254–6, 275
Dragon Seed (film), 280–1
Drake, Beverly, 375–6
Dream of the Red Chamber, 213
Dreiser, Theodore, xviii, 144, 175, 180, 208, 210, 211, 261, 307
Drinker, Sophie, 378
Du Bois, W. E. B., xvi, 24, 190, 216, 265, 267–8, 290–1, 298
Du Bose, H. C., 10
Dubs, H. H., 34
The Duchess of Bedford (steamship), 157

Dulles, Foster Rhea, 145
Dulles, John Foster, 337
Dumbarton Oaks, 286, 291
Dunne, Irene, 271
Duranty, Walter, 172

Earhart, Amelia 187, 377
"East and West and the Novel" (Pearl S. Buck), 136–7
East and West Association, xv, 245–6, 257–8, 262, 266, 270, 276–9, 283, 285, 297, 304, 314, 318, 323, 327, 371
"Easter, 1933" (Pearl S. Buck), 154
East Wind, West Wind (Pearl S. Buck), 112–14, 119, 123, 245
East Wind, West Wind (video biography of Pearl S. Buck), xx
Ebony (magazine), 314
Ebry, Patricia Buckley, 42
Edmunds, Emma (*see* Emma Edmunds White)
Einstein, Albert, 153, 215, 226, 270, 282, 308, 343
Eisenhower, Dwight D., 330, 337, 345, 355
Eisenhower, Mamie, 369
Eisenstein, Sergei, 311
Eliot, George (Mary Ann Evans), 40
Eliot, T. S., 261
Ellis Island, 336
Ellison, Ralph, 206, 304
Elmhirst, Leonard, 160, 243
Ely, Richard, 145
Embree, Edwin, 260
Emerson, Gertrude, 145
The Empress (Pearl S. Buck), 193, 215
The Empress of Asia (steamship), 114
The Empress of Russia (steamship), 160
"End Mission Imperialism Now!," 149
"The Enemy" (Pearl S. Buck), 342
Epstein, Jacob, 208
Equal Rights Amendment (ERA), xvi, 48, 233–5, 270, 304, 327
"Essay on Life" (Pearl S. Buck), 371
Ethiopia, 211
Evangelistic Association, 38
Evans, Walker, 131
The Exile (Pearl S. Buck), xvii, 62, 73, 106, 187–8, 230
Exile's Return (Malcolm Cowley), 163
Extraterritoriality, 14, 24, 86, 269

"The Face of Gold" (Pearl S. Buck), 223
Fadiman, Clifton, 257, 309
Fain, Sammy, 344

Fair Employment Practices Commission (FEPC), 290
Fairbank, John King, 17, 81, 96, 115, 273
Far and Near (Pear S. Buck), 305
Far Eastern Survey, 273
Farmers of Forty Centuries (F. H. King), 56
Farrell, James T., xviii, 300, 372
"Fathers and Mothers" (Pearl S. Buck), 134
Faulkner, William, 187, 210, 261, 346
Federal Bureau of Investigation (FBI), xvi, 207, 260–1, 265, 299–300, 318, 322, 326–8, 346, 362–3, 366
Federal Theatre Project, 216
Federal Union, 262
The Feminine Mystique (Betty Friedan), 349–50
Feng Yu-hsiang (Feng Yuxiang), 89
Fenn, Courtenay, 128, 184
Ferguson, Charles, 306
Ferguson, J. C., 34
Fermi, Enrico, 213
Fermi, Laura, 342
Ficke, Arthur Davison, 211
Fighting Angel (Pearl S. Buck), xvii, 188, 230
First Wife and Other Stories (Pearl S. Buck), xvii, 156–7, 197
Fisher, Kermit, 356
Fisher, Dorothy Canfield, 122–3, 167, 180, 209, 211, 237, 286
Fitch, Janet, 159
Fitzgerald, F. Scott, 163, 187, 261
Flanagan, Hallie, 216
Fleming, Victor, 191, 194
The Flesh and the Spirit (Pearl S. Buck), 188
Flynn, Elizabeth Gurley, 230
The Folks (Ruth Suckow), 266
Foochow (Fuzhou), 14
"Fool's Sacrifice" (Pearl S. Buck), 170–1
Formosa (Taiwan), 316
The Forsyte Saga (John Galsworthy), 62
Forum (periodical), 77
Foster, Helen (*see* Helen Foster Snow)
Foster, William Z., 144
Fox, John, 25
Franco, Francisco, 210, 222
Frank, Grace, 298
Franklin, Sidney, 191, 194
"Free China Gets to Work" (Pearl S. Buck), 224
Free China Radio, 256
Freedom House, 265
Freeman, Douglas S., 324
Freeman, Mary Wilkins, 187

French Ways and Their Meaning (Edith Wharton), 307
Freud, Sigmund, 75
Friedan, Betty, 349
Friend to Friend (Pearl S. Buck and Carlos P. Romulo), 341, 343
Frost, Robert, 261, 347
Fryer, John, 33
Fuller, Margaret, 247
Furniture Workers of America, 301

The Galaxy (periodical), 32
"Gallant American Women" (NBC), 230
Gallup, George, 229
Gallup poll, 235, 359, 369
Galsworthy, John, 62
Gandhi, Indira, xix, 173, 359
Gandhi Memorial Lecture (Howard University), 344
Gandhi, Mohandas, 332, 344
"Gang of Four," 374
Gannett, Lewis, 90, 95, 97, 143, 180
Gardner, Marian, 64, 65, 66
Garroway, Dave, 336
Garside, B. A., 118
Garson, Greer, 271
Gate of Heavenly Peace (Peking), 316
The Geary Act, 31
The General Died At Dawn (film), 194
General Federation of Women's Clubs, 234
General Motors Institute, 365
"General Pai: Chinese Patriot" (T. S. Chen), 245
George School, 328
Gibson, Paul, 357–8
Gielgud, John, 158
Gimbel Award, 354
Ginling College for Women, 88
Girls' Friendly Society, 234
The Gods Arrive (Edith Wharton), 307
God's Men (Pearl S. Buck), 325–6
The Goddess Abides (Pearl S. Buck), 352
Goldberg, Rube, 145
"Golden Flower" (Pearl S. Buck), 242
Gone With the Wind (Margaret Mitchell), 131
The Good Earth (Pearl S. Buck), xi, xv, xvii, xix, 62, 68, 119, 122–32, 139, 148, 153, 166, 178, 186, 187, 201, 212–13, 230, 301, 311, 315, 324, 344, 374, 380
The Good Earth (dramatic adaptation), 146–7
The Good Earth (film), 159, 191–6, 280
Good Housekeeping (periodical), 359

Goodwin, Richard, 346
Goucher College, 318
Graham, Billy, 331
Graham, James, 153
Grand Canal, 21
Grant, Robert, 187
The Grapes of Wrath (John Steinbeck), 131
Grapewin, Charley, 194
Great Leap Forward, 370
Great Wall, 34
Greater East Asia Co-Prosperity Sphere, 254
Greater New York Inter-Racial Rally, 262
Green Gang (Shanghai), 104, 280
Green Hills Farm, xv, 169–70, 175, 188, 215,
   226, 283, 304, 312, 315, 328, 358, 375, 377
Green Pastures (Marc Connelly), 216
Greene, Graham, 157, 381
Greene, Roger S., 222–3, 227
Greenstreet, Sydney, 146
Gross, Mason, 367
"Guerrilla Mother" (Pearl S. Buck), 242
Gung ho movement, 224
Gunther, John, 42
Gustavus V, 212, 214, 230

Hagedorn, Hermann, 211
Halberstam, David, 316
Hahn, Otto, 343
Haiphong, 334
Halstead, Gordon, 283–4, 297
Hamilton, Alice, 377
Hamilton, Lulu, 94, 95, 101, 111, 114, 115,
   118, 119, 122, 132, 141, 143, 146
Hammerstein, Oscar, II, xix, 313–14, 338
The Handmaid's Tale (Margaret Atwood), 247
Hangchow (Hangzhou), 10, 222
Hankow (Hankou), 53
Hansl, Eva, 230
Harper's (periodical), 149, 203–4, 216, 236
Harris, Lillian, 231
Harris, Theodore F., 352–7, 359, 362–72, 375–
   6
Hart, B. H. Liddell, 142
Harte, Bret, 2
Harvard *Lampoon*, 112
Harvard University, 240, 350
Hatboro Rotary Club, 328
Hay, John, 32, 34
Hayakawa, Sessue, 345
Hayes, Helen, 369, 377
"The Heathen Chinee" (Bret Harte), 2
Hellman, Lillian, 261

Hemingway, Ernest 163, 175, 187, 210, 261,
   346, 364
Hepburn, Katharine, 280–1
Hepburn, Katharine Houghton, 182
Herbert, Victor, 31
Here and Beyond (Edith Wharton), 307
Hersey, John, xiii, 384
Heyward, Louis, 336
The Hidden Flower (Pearl S. Buck), 328–9
Higginbotham, A. Leon, 367
Hill Crest School, 88, 116
Hill, George, 191
Himes, Chester, 261
Hiramoto, Michitaka, 199
Hiroshima, 296, 342, 360
"Hiroshima Maidens," 337
Hiroshima Peace Center, 328
Hiss, Alger, 307, 318
Hitler, Adolf, 153, 172, 173, 196, 198, 210,
   226, 236, 248, 252, 260, 265, 268, 287
Hocking, William Ernest, 142, 149–50, 245,
   318, 350–2, 371
Holland, Joseph, 215
Holt, Guy, 145
Hommel, Rudolf, 200–1
Honan (Henan) province, 309
Hong Kong, 121, 158, 253, 269
Hoover, Herbert, 112, 144, 215
Hoover, J. Edgar, xvi, 207, 260–1, 299, 322,
   327
Hope, Bob, 271
"The Hour of Worship" (Pearl S. Buck), 50
A House Divided (Pearl S. Buck), 178–80, 230
House of Earth, trilogy (Pearl S. Buck), 180,
   364
House of Exile (Nora Waln), 374
"The House They Built" (Pearl S. Buck), 364
Houseman, John, 216
How It Happens (Pearl S. Buck), 305–6
Howard University, xvi, 265–6, 328, 344, 356,
   358
Howells, William Dean, 187, 261
Howes, Durward, 205
Hsi Yu Chi (novel), 139
Hsu Chih-mo (Xu Zhimo), 103, 113, 159
HUAC (*see* Committee on Un-American
   Activities)
Hu Shih (Hu Shi), xix, 73–4, 211, 237, 243,
   245, 257
Hudson River Bracketed (Edith Wharton), 307
Hughes, Langston, 144, 175, 259, 261, 317
Hughes, Mildred, 245

Hughes, Robert, 131
Hull, Cordell, 222, 226, 241
Hummel, A. W., 34
Hunan province, 90
Hurst, Fannie, 145
Husted, Jennie, 6
Huston, Walter, 149, 280
Hutchins, Robert, 178
Huxley, Julian, 142
Hynes, Samuel, 219

Ibsen, Hendrik 75
IBM (*see* International Business Machine
  Company)
I'ch'ang (Yichang), 254
Ickes, Harold, 226
"I am the Better Woman for having my two
  Black Children" (Pearl S. Buck), 375
I Change Worlds (Anna Louise Strong), 183
"I Don't Want to Christianize the World,"
  149
Immigration Act (1924), 196
Immigration Restriction League, 196–7
Imperial Woman (Pearl S. Buck), 339–41
"The Importance of the Direct Phase of
  Mission Work" (Absalom Sydenstricker), 39
"In China, Too" (Pearl S. Buck), 62, 75–6
India, 160, 262, 266, 268, 276, 310, 331–2,
  338, 344
India-China Friendship Day, 262
India Famine Relief Committee, 325
India League of America, 268, 282, 299
Indian National Army, 257
Indusco (*see* Industrial Cooperative Movement)
Industrial Cooperative Movement (Indusco),
  224–5
Industrial Workers of the World (IWW), 230
Institute for Advanced Study (Princeton), 197
Institute for Pacific Relations (IPR), 155, 257–
  8, 318
Institute of Human Relations (Williams
  College), 186
Institute of Public Affairs (University of
  Virginia), 184
International Broadcast (NBC), 186
International Business Machine Company, 238,
  245
International General Electric, 276
Invisible Man (Ralph Ellison), 206, 304
IPR (*see* Institute for Pacific Relations)
Irrawaddy River, 254
Isaacs, Harold, 343–4
Isherwood, Christopher, xix, 224–5

"Is There a Case for Foreign Missions?" (Pearl
  S. Buck), 148–9
It Can't Happen Here (Sinclair Lewis), 229
IWW (*see* Industrial Workers of the World)

James, Henry, 210
Janeway, Elizabeth, 329
"Japan Loses the War" (Pearl S. Buck), 202
Japanese-American Committee for Democracy,
  262, 264, 270, 299, 308
Japanese internment, 264–5, 282
Jefferson, Thomas, 24, 346
"Jesus as a Teacher and Trainer" (Absalom
  Sydenstricker), 22
John Day Company, 112, 119, 132, 152, 157,
  166, 170, 175, 187, 211, 216, 226, 245, 264,
  283, 311, 331
John Day pamphlets, 149, 260
Johns Hopkins University, 318
Johnson, Louis, 268
Johnson, Lyndon B., 361
Johnson, Mordecai, 265
Johnston, Reginald, 181
Johnstone, Edward, 111
Jones, Eugene Kinckle, 232
Jones, Jesse, 267
Jones, John P., 217
Joseph in Egypt (Thomas Mann), 215
Jou Shih (Zhou Shi) 199
Journey to a War (Christopher Isherwood and
  W. H. Auden), 224–5
Joyce, James, 73
Judge (periodical), 112
Julian, Percy, 358

K'ai-feng (Kaifeng), 309
Kalgan (Zhangjiakon), 18
Kanazawa, Joseph Tooru, 270
Kang, Younghill, 126
Kansas City Call (newspaper), 151
Kansu (Gansu) province, 89
Kappa Delta Sorority, 48
Kaye, Danny, 317
Kazin, Alfred, 240
Keller, Helen, 178, 377
Kellog, Frank, 96
Kelly, Gene, 317
Kelly, Grace, 355
Kennedy, Ethel, 369
Kennedy, John F., xix, 345, 346
Kennedy, Mary, 215
Kennedy, Robert F., 355, 366
Kennedy, Rose, xv, xix, 359, 369

Kennedy, Rosemary, xv
The Kennedy Women (Pearl S. Buck), 371
Kerouac, Jack, 304
Keye Luke, 194, 195
Keynes, John Maynard, 142
Kiang Kang-hu (Jiang Kanghu), 126, 315
Kiangsi (Jiangsi) province, 96, 118
Kiangsu (Jiangsu) province, 36, 38, 139
Kinfolk (Pearl S. Buck), xvii, 315–16
King, Coretta Scott, 369
King, F. H., 56, 61, 201
King, Martin Luther, Jr., 366
The King and I (musical), 338
The King of the Opium Ring (musical), 31
Kingston, Maxine Hong, xiii, 83
Kirkus Syndicate, 335
Kissinger, Henry, 372
Kitchelt, Florence, 304
KMT (*see* Kuomintang)
Knollenberg, Bernhard, 268
Knopf, Olga, 248
Knowland, William, 337
Kobe, Japan, 93
Kolak, Mme., 182
Korea, 93, 262, 345, 346–9, 353, 357, 360
Korea Times (newspaper), 366
Korean War, 320–22, 328, 337, 347
Krebs, Albin, 376
Krishna Menon, V. K., 338
Kuling (Guling), 40, 58, 118, 134
Kung, H. H., 116
Kung, Mr., 25, 40
Kuniyoshi, Yasuo, 251–2
Kuomintang (Guomindang [KMT]), 85, 87,
   89–91, 96, 104, 107, 121, 140, 159, 174,
   254, 271, 280, 316, 324
Kwang Hsu (Guangxu), 27

Ladd, D. M., 299–300
Ladies' Home Journal (periodical), 319, 322, 331,
   357
Lagerlof, Selma, 209
LaGuardia, Fiorello, 263
Lamont, Thomas, 277
Land and Labor in China (R. H. Tawney), 224
Land Utilization in China (J. Lossing Buck), 55
Lane, Gertrude, 153
Lange, Dorothea, 131, 180
Lao She, 300–2, 307
Lao-tse, 117
"Lao Wang, the Farmer" (Pearl S. Buck), 89
Lash, Joseph, 251
Lask, Thomas, 376

Laski, Harold, 142
"The Last Word in the Far East" (Anna
   Louise Strong), 172
Lattimore, Owen, xix, 133, 159, 172, 318–9,
   322
Laura L. Messenger Memorial Prize, 80
Law, William, 193
Lawrence, T. E., 233
Laymen's Inquiry Commission, 149, 350
League for Political Education, 152, 187
League of American Writers, 239
League of Nations, 211, 281
League of Women Voters, 234, 270
Lee, Chingwah, 194
Lenin, 341
Letter from Peking (Pearl S. Buck), 103, 345
Let Us Now Praise Famous Men (James Agee
   and Walker Evans), 131
Levine, Lawrence, xiii
Lewis, Henry, 367
Lewis, Sinclair, xviii, 167, 209, 210, 211, 215,
   229, 261, 266, 288, 307, 332
Lewisohn Stadium (New York City), 262
Liang Chi-ch'ao (Liang Qichao), 91
Life (magazine), 272, 273, 324
Lin Yutang, xviii-xix, 159, 172, 175, 211, 215,
   226, 282, 318
Lindbergh, Anne Morrow, 133
Lindbergh, Charles, xix, 133, 227, 229
Lippmann, Walter, 79
Li Sau-tse, 94, 166
Lit, Janice, 279
Literary Guild, 302
A Little Democracy Is a Dangerous Thing (Charles
   Ferguson), 306
Liu Haiping, xix
Lives (Plutarch), 26
Living China (Edgar Snow), 199
The Living Church (periodical), 128
The Living Reed (Pearl S. Buck), 347–9
Lloyd, Andrea, 331, 338
Lloyd, David, 101, 106, 112, 118, 141, 143,
   331, 338
Loach, Tilly, 194, 196
Locke, Alain, xix, 216, 260
London, Jack, 261
Long March, 220
Look (magazine), 322
Looking Forward (Franklin D. Roosevelt), 157
Lopez, Salvador, 245
Lorre, Peter, 194
Los Alamos, 343
Los Angeles Times (newspaper), 345

Lowdermilk, Mrs. W. C., 190
Lowell, Robert, 261, 337
Lu Hsun (Lu Xun), 116, 199, 245, 307, 374
Luce, Clare Booth, 326
Luce, Henry, xix, 145, 185, 198, 203, 237,
   242, 245, 271, 273, 320, 324–5, 368
"Lucretia Mott Amendment" (Equal Rights
   Amendment), 234, 235
Lucy Stone League, 338
Lung Chi Kwan (Lung Jigan), 66
Lurty, Florence, 202
Lutz, Alma, 233–36

MacArthur, Douglas, 269, 322
Macbeth (William Shakespeare), 216
Machen, J. Gresham, 154
MacLeish, Archibald, 323
MacMahon, Aline, 284
Mme. Chiang Kai-shek (*see* Soong Mei-ling)
Madison, James, 24
Madison Square Garden (New York), 265
Madrid, 219
Magnitogorsk, 293–4
Mailer, Norman, 304, 367
Main Street (Sinclair Lewis), 288
The Making of Buffalo Bill (Richard J. Walsh),
   112
Malinowski, Bronislaw, 157
Malraux, André, 179
Manchester Guardian (newspaper), 160
Manchukuo (Manzhouguo; *see also*
   Manchuria), 104, 135–6, 219
Manchuria, 104, 135–6, 199, 211, 219, 254,
   286
Mandala (Pearl S. Buck), 371, 373
Mandarin New Testament, 39
Manhattan Project, 342
Mann, Thomas, 215, 226, 269, 317
Man's Fate (André Malraux), 179
"A Man's Foes" (Pearl S. Buck), 242
Man's Most Dangerous Myth: The Fallacy of Race
   (Ashley Montagu), 353
Man's World, Woman's Place (Elizabeth
   Janeway), 329
Mao Tse-tung (Mao Zedong), 105, 137–9,
   202–3, 224, 245, 316, 317, 322, 369–70,
   372–3, 374
Mao Tun (Mao Dun), 199
March, Frederic, 317
Marion, Frances, 192
Marquand, John, 208, 309
Martin, W. A. P., 37
Marx, Karl, 75

Mass Education Movement, 118, 285, 293,
   328
Matisse, Henri, 73
Matthew, Mark, Luke and John (Pearl S. Buck),
   360
Matsui, Haru, 233
Matsui, Robert, 264
Matsumoto, Tsuyoshi, 245
May Fourth Movement, xviii, 74–5, 85, 103,
   117
May Thirtieth Incident, 86
Maynard, Dorothy, 266
Mayo Clinic, 79, 211
McAfee, Cleland Boyd, 148, 154
McAfee, Edna C., 211
McAfee, Helen, 236
McAfee, Wallace, 211
McBride, Mary Margaret, 317, 328
McCann, Mrs. E. B., 186
McCarthy, Joseph, 316, 318, 321, 337
McClellan, Robert, 31
McClintic, Guthrie, 198, 211
McCormick, Anne O'Hare, 236
McKinley, William, 33, 37
McWilliams, Carey, 281
Mead, Margaret, xviii, 172, 236, 241, 314
Meals for Millions Foundation, 325
The Meaning of God (William Ernest Hocking),
   350
Mei Lan-fang (Mei Lanfang), 133
Mei, Y. P., 245
Meitner, Lise, 343
Mellett, Lowell, 257
Men of Science, 45
Mencius, 25, 117
Mencken, H. L., 79
Mercer, Henry, 201
Meredith, Burgess, 317
Metro-Goldwyn-Mayer, 141, 159, 191–2, 254,
   280
Metropolitan Opera House, 280
Methuen (publishers), 119, 364
Michener, James, xix, 314, 324–5, 330
A Midsummer Night's Dream (William
   Shakespeare), 158
The Mikado (Gilbert and Sullivan), 225
Milbank Memorial Fund, 118, 152, 176
Millard, Thomas, 28
Millay, Edna St. Vincent, 261
Miller, Arthur, 261
Miller, Stuart Creighton, 15
"The Mind of the Militarist" (Pearl S. Buck),
   200

Minor, Clark, 276–7
Mishima, Sumie Seo, 233
Miss Jewell's School, 41–4
Miss Lonelyhearts (Nathanael West), 229
Mitchell, Margaret, 238
Moby Dick (Herman Melville), 93
Modern Maturity (periodical), 371
Moeller, Philip, 146
Moment in Peking (Lin Yutang), 226
Montagu, Ashley, 338, 353
Montgomery, Bernard, 269
Moore, Marianne, 261
Moorhead, Agnes, 280
Morgan, Mrs. Junius S., 301
Morgenthau, Henry, 181, 271
Morley, Christopher, 122, 143, 145, 153
Morrison, Robert, 80
Morrison, Toni, xii, xiii
Morriss, Margaret, 184
Morrisville (New Jersey) Women's Club, 328
Morrow, Anne (*see* Anne Morrow Lindbergh)
The Mother (Pearl S. Buck), xvii, 166–9, 174, 230
The Mother's Recompense (Edith Wharton), 307
Mount Holyoke Female Seminary, 46
Mount Sinai Hospital, 337
"Mrs. Buck and Her Worlds" (Chuang Hsin-tsai), 129–30
"Mt. Huzi for Mt. Fuji" (Tsuyoshi Matsumoto), 245
Much Ado About Nothing (William Shakespeare), 158
Mukerjee, Radhakamal, 245
Muni, Paul, 194–6
Music and Women (Sophie Drinker), 338
Mussolini, Benito, 172, 210
Must We Fight in Asia? (Nathaniel Peffer), 181
My Country and My People (Lin Yutang), 175
"My Day" (Eleanor Roosevelt), 197, 265
"My Flight from Hawaii to California" (Amelia Earhart), 187
My Indian Family (Hilda Wernher), 344
My Narrow Isle (Sumie Seo Mishima), 233
My Several Worlds (Pearl S. Buck), xvii, 62, 335–6, 339, 342, 353, 373
"My World" (Pearl S. Buck), 357

NAACP (*see* National Association for the Advancement of Colored People)
Nagasaki, 93, 221, 296, 342, 360
The Naked and the Dead (Norman Mailer), 304
Nanhusuchou (Nanxuzhou), xiv, xix, 56–8, 62–8, 139

Nanking (Nanjing), xix, 56, 87, 90–1, 103–4, 106, 114, 133, 139, 199–200, 219, 254, 310, 316, 335
"Nanking Decade," 104
Nanking Incident, 90–1, 93–4, 97, 102, 106, 114, 142, 221
Nanking Theological Seminary, 76, 134
Nanking University, 55, 68, 87, 91, 118, 324
The Nation (periodical), 78–9, 101
National Association for the Advancement of Colored People (NAACP), xvi, 232, 250, 259, 265, 291, 305, 346
National Association for Labor Legislation, 234
National Association of Black Social Workers, 374
National Association of Mass Education Movements, 285
National Committee of Antifascist Women of Spain, 211
National Committee on Federal Legislation for Birth Control, 181
National Conference of Christians and Jews, 186
National Consumers' League, 234
National Council Against Conscription, 308–9
National Council of Catholic Women, 234
National Federation of Business and Professional Women's Clubs, 234
National Federation of Federal Employees, 234
National Institute of Arts and Letters, 187
National Suffrage Association, 48
National University (Nanking), 70
National Urban League, xvi, 151, 186, 211, 232, 250, 259
National Woman's Party, 233, 235–6
National Women's Hall of Fame, 377
National Women's Trade Union League, 233–4
National Youth Administration, 284
Native Son (Richard Wright), 232
The Natural Superiority of Woman (Ashley Montagu), 338
Nazimova, Alla, 146
NBC Radio, 230
NBC-TV, 328
Nearing, Helen, 320
Nearing, John Scott (*see* John Scott)
Nearing, Scott, 320, 323
"The Necessity of Proclaiming the Gospel to the Heathen" (Absalom Sydenstricker), 6
Nehru, Jawaharlal, xix, 173, 241, 245, 248
Nelson, Cary, xii
New, Ilhan, 298

New Life Movement, 174
New Republic (magazine), 145, 222, 263, 320
"The New Road" (Pearl S. Buck), 108–10
Newsom, Earl, 122
New Statesman and Nation (periodical), 126
New Theater (London), 158
The New Year (Pearl S. Buck), 364, 365–6
New York Evening Post (newspaper), 147, 196
New York Herald-Tribune (newspaper), 140,
  157, 179–80, 215, 260, 291
New York League for the Association for the
  Help of Retarded Children, 339
New York Social Register, 122
New York Sun (newspaper), 317
New York Times (newspaper), 126, 145, 148,
  153, 154, 159, 167, 172, 179, 182, 191, 208,
  209, 241, 248, 249–50, 257, 263, 265, 268,
  270, 273, 280, 281, 282, 283, 317, 329, 336–
  7, 360, 371, 376
New York University, 314
New York World's Fair (1939), 226, 231
New York World's Fair (1964), 355, 358
New Yorker (periodical), 145, 191, 219, 305,
  335
New Youth (periodical), 73–4
Newsweek (magazine), 303
Nicholas Nickleby (Charles Dickens), 41
Neibuhr, Reinhold, 223
Ningpo (Ningbo), 14, 18
Nixon, Richard M., 314, 345, 372, 375, 376
Nixon Theater (New York City), 146
Nobel Prize, xi, 172, 207–15, 230, 238, 324,
  332, 342, 346, 357, 368, 376
The Normandie (steamship), 212
Northern Expedition, 90, 96
Northrop, F. S. C., 142
"Now and Forever" (Pearl S. Buck), 180
Nugent, Frank, 191
NWP (*see* National Woman's Party)

Oak Ridge, 343
Oates, Joyce Carol, xx
Of Men and Women (Pearl S. Buck), xvii, 246–
  8, 289, 330, 350
Of Mice and Men (John Steinbeck), 217
Office of Strategic Services (OSS), 257
Office of War Information (OWI), 280
O'Hara, John, 238
O'Hara, Maureen, 344
Ohio University, 365
Oland, Warner, 194
"The Old Demon" (Pearl S. Buck), 242
Old New York (Edith Wharton), 307

"Omnibus" (television show), 336, 342
"On the Cultivation of a Young Genius"
  (Pearl S. Buck), 190–1
"On Discovering America" (Pearl S. Buck),
  197
On Native Grounds (Alfred Kazin), 240
On Our Way (Franklin D. Roosevelt), 175
On the Road (Jack Kerouac), 304
"On the Writing of Novels" (Pearl S. Buck),
  155
Onassis, Jacqueline Kennedy, 347, 369
O'Neill, Eugene, 209
Open Door Policy, 33
Opium Wars, 14, 21
Opportunity (periodical), xvi, 151, 186, 190–1,
  211, 216, 232, 259
Oriental Cookbook (Pearl S. Buck), 378
"Orientalism," 36, 84, 126, 129, 225
Orwell, George (Eric Blair), 168–9
Other Gods (Pearl S. Buck), 227–30
"The Other Side of Harlem" (*New York Times*
  editorial), 249
O'Toole, Barry, 279
"Our Dangerous Myths About China" (Pearl
  S. Buck), 317
Our Life and Work in China (Absalom
  Sydenstricker), 76
"Our Little Visits to Nanking" (Michitaka
  Hiramoto), 199–200
"Our Real Home in Heaven" (Pearl S.
  Buck), 1
Our Times (Mark Sullivan), 266
Outlook (periodical), 32
Ovington, Mary White, 232

Paine, Tom, 261
Pan American Airlines, 245
Pandit, Vijaya Lakshmi, 173, 282, 310
Parade (periodical), 369
Parent Teachers' Association, 234
Parker, Dorothy, 261, 317
The Patriot (Pearl S. Buck), 217, 219–21
"Paul Revere's Ride" (Henry Wadsworth
  Longfellow), 256
Paul Zsolnay Verlag (publishers), 197
Pauling, Linus, 342, 346
Pauls, Jimmy, 355, 362
Pavilion of Women (Pearl S. Buck), xvii, 62,
  297, 302–3
"Peace and Democracy" (Pearl S. Buck), 226
"Peace, Freedom, and Bread" (Pearl S. Buck),
  338
Peale, Norman Vincent, 331

Pearl Buck (Theodore F. Harris and Pearl S. Buck), 370
The Pearl Buck Book Club, 371
"Pearl Buck Speaks for Democracy," 250
"The Pearl Buck Theater," 336
The Pearl S. Buck Foundation, xv, 354–6, 358–68
The Pearl S. Buck Opportunity Center (Korea), 362, 365
Pearl Harbor, 251, 253, 265, 281
Pearson, Drew, 181
Pearson, Norman Holmes, 209
Peck, Gregory, 317
Peffer, Nathaniel, 181
Peiping (*see* Peking)
Peking (Beijing), 28, 96, 133, 142, 160, 199, 224, 279, 316, 318, 335, 372
Peking National Library, 133
Peking Union Medical College (PUMC), 176
Peking University, 73
Pemberton, John, 356
Pembroke College (Brown University), 184
PEN (Poets, Playwrights, Editors, Essayists, Novelists), 143, 209
Pen and Brush Club (New York), 186
Pennsylvania Commission on the Handicapped, 356
Peony (Pearl S. Buck), 309–10
"The People's Congress" (East and West Association), 278, 299
The People's Liberation Army, 316, 326
"The People's Library," 285
"The People's Mandate," 185–6
People's 1000 Character Literacy Primer (James Yen), 285
Perkins, Frances, 204
Pershing, John J., 148
Personal History (Vincent Sheean), 181
Pharis, Charles, 297
Phelps, William Lyon, 148, 156, 160, 209, 210
Phi Beta Kappa, 132
The Philadelphia Bulletin (newspaper), 364
The Philadelphia Inquirer (newspaper), 363
The Philadelphia Ledger (newspaper), 154
Philadelphia Magazine (periodical), 367–8
The Philadelphia Record (newspaper), 148
"Philippine Youth Defends Democracy" (Salvador Lopez), 245
Picasso, Pablo, 73
Pickett, Clarence, 342
"The Place of Woman in Democracy" (Pearl S. Buck), 236
"Planning for Peace" (Pearl S. Buck), 231

Plutarch, 26
PM (magazine), 281
Poems and Translations from the Chinese (Christopher Morley), 153
Polzer, Anne, 197–8
Poor Richard's Almanac (Benjamin Franklin), 11
Porter, Katherine Anne, 356
Porter, R. H., 92
Portrait of a Marriage (Pearl S. Buck), 297–8
"Postwar China and the United States" (Pearl S. Buck), 274
Pound, Ezra, 73, 237
The Power of Positive Thinking (Norman Vincent Peale), 331
Power, Tyrone, 271
Powers, H. H., 33
Preminger, Otto, 302
Presbyterian Board of Foreign Missions, 51, 55, 59, 67, 76, 93–4, 100, 108, 111, 115, 140, 154, 184
Price, Vincent, 215, 317
Prince of Wales (battleship), 253
"Principles of Leadership" (Pearl S. Buck), 344
"Prison Letters to Indira" (Jawaharlal Nehru), 173
"The Proletarian Novel" (Pearl S. Buck), 186–7
The Promise (Pearl S. Buck), 275–6, 364
Pruitt, Ida, 34
Pulitzer Prize, xii, 143, 209, 307
Purple Mountain, 68, 90, 127, 133
P'u-Yi (Puyi), 53, 105, 135
Puzzled America (Sherwood Anderson), 180

Queen of Chinatown (musical), 31
Quinn, Anthony, 287
Quinn, John, 145

Race: A Study in Modern Superstition (Jacques Barzun), 185
Race: Science and Politics (Ruth Benedict), 231
Radcliffe College, 46
Radio City Music Hall (New York City), 281
Rain (film), 149
Rainer, Luise, 192, 194–5, 281
Rains, Claude, 146
"A Rainy Day" (Pearl S. Buck), 88
Rampersad, Arnold, 291
Randolph-Macon Woman's College, xiv, xx, 41, 45–51, 155, 227, 355
Random House (publishers), 354
"Ransom" (Pearl S. Buck), 207
Rape of Nanking, 220, 255

Reader's Digest (periodical), 197
Reader's Digest Book Club, 335
Red Star Over China (Edgar Snow), 202–3
Redbook (periodical), 202
Redfield, Edward, 378
Reed, James, 33
"The Refugees" (Pearl S. Buck), 134
Refugees (Dorothy Thompson), 215
Reisner, John, 55, 68, 70, 71, 101
Repulse (battle cruiser), 253
Restless Wave (Haru Matsui), 234
Re-Thinking Missions (Ernest Hocking), 149–50, 184
Reuther, Victor, 308
Revolution of 1911, xviii, 53–4, 74, 88, 104, 110
Revolutionary Alliance, 54
"The Revolutionist" (Pearl S. Buck), 97–8
Reynal & Hitchcock (publishers), 175, 178
Reynolds, Reginald, 173
Rice, John, 337
Rich, Adrienne, 124
Richard of Bordeaux, 158
Richshaw Boy (Lao She), 300–2
Ridgway, Matthew, 321
Ripley, Robert, 129–30
RKO Studios, 287
Robeson, Eslanda Goode, xvi, 311–12
Robeson, Paul, xvi, 261, 266, 311–12, 317
Robinson, Edward G., 317
Rockefeller Foundation, 110, 114
Rockefeller, John D., 3rd, 243
Rodgers, Richard, 338
Rodin, Auguste, 206, 208
Rogers, Will, xix, 143, 153
Rogge, Roger, 363
Romulo, Carlos P., 341
Roosevelt, Eleanor, xvi, xix, 79, 144, 152–3, 186, 189, 191, 197, 215, 236, 237, 241, 243, 250, 263, 265, 268, 270–2, 274, 280, 281, 286, 299–300, 317, 339, 375, 377
Roosevelt, Franklin D., 144, 157, 165, 175, 222, 241, 243, 257, 259, 264, 268, 269, 272, 274, 281, 286, 290, 318
Roosevelt Hotel (New York City), 298
Roosevelt, Theodore, 32, 34
Roosevelt, Theodore, Jr., 237–8
Rosenberg, Ethel, 331
Rosenberg, Julius, 331
Ross, Harold, 145
"The Rulers of China" (Pearl S. Buck), 181
Russell, Bertrand, 75, 172

Russian Clubs (East and West Association), 277
Rutgers University, 367
Rutherford, Ernest, 343

Sabin, Florence, 377
Sackville-West, Vita, 153
Sai Jinhua (play), 374
Saint Paul, 20
Sakhilin, 254
Salinger, J. D., 394
San Kuo (*Sanguozhi*), 117, 139
Sandburg, Carl, 261
Sanger, Margaret, xvi, xviii, 152, 181–2, 245, 258, 278–9, 284, 287, 297
Santayana, George, 15
Saturday Evening Post (periodical), 170, 216, 223, 331
Saturday Review of Literature (periodical), 126, 239, 298, 335, 337
Sauk Centre (Minnesota), 332
Sawada, Miki, 345, 364
Scherman, Harry, 122, 145
Schuster, Max, 145
Science and Democracy movement, xviii, 57, 73
Scopes Trial, 151
Scott, George, 145
Scott, John, 293–5, 320
Scott, Masha, 292–5, 320
Scott, Randolph, 287
Scott, Walter, 26, 40
Scottsboro case, 165
Scratches on Our Mind (Harold Isaacs), 344
Scribner's (magazine), 32
The Second Sex (Simone de Beauvoir), 338
"Sedges, John" (see Pearl S. Buck), 288, 305
Seelye, L. Clark, 47
Selznick, David O., 243
Sen, Gertrude, 345
Service, John, 373
Shakespeare, William, 158, 216
Shanghai, 10, 11, 14, 29, 41–4, 86, 96, 100–1, 103, 219, 224, 225, 251
Shanghai Incident, 86
"Shanghai Scene" (Pearl S. Buck), 173
Shantung (Shandong) province, 74, 89, 137
Shaw, Anna Howard, 48
Shaw, Artie, 317
Shaw, George Bernard, 144
Sheean, Vincent, 181, 279
Sheehan, Murray, 231

Sheen, Fulton J., 331
Shensi (Shaanxi) province, 202, 219, 254
Sherman, William T., 8
Shirer, William, 282
Shriver, R. Sargent, 355
Shui Hu Chuan (*Shuihuzhuan*), 117, 133, 137–9, 255, 310, 318, 328
Simon, Richard, 145
Sinatra, Frank, 317
Singapore, 158, 253
Singh, J. J., 282
Sipprell, Clara, 321
Skinner, Cornelia Otis, 215
Sklar, Katherine Kish, 234
Small, Polly, 94, 132, 141
Smedley, Agnes, 172, 175, 279
Smith, Arthur H., 34–6
Smith, Bradford, 355
Smith College, 46, 47, 64, 382
Smith, Margaret Chase, 377
Snow, Edgar, xviii, 42, 160, 199, 202, 224, 279
Snow, Helen Foster, xviii, 112, 127, 160, 172, 177, 224
So Big (Edna Ferber), 346
Social Gospel, 18, 81
Social Security Act, 177
Sojourner Truth Award, 358
Solomon, Barbara, 51
Solution in Asia (Owen Lattimore), 319
Sons (Pearl S. Buck), xvii, 139–40, 147–8, 178, 230
Soo Yong, 194
Soochow (Suzhou), 10, 11, 222
Soong Ch'ing-ling (Soong Qingling), 245, 280
Soong Mei-ling (Soong Meiling [Mme. Chiang Kai-shek]), xviii, 116, 244, 271–3, 280
Soong, T. V., 155, 257
The Souls of Black Folks (W. E. B. Du Bois), 24
"Southern Mandarin" (Absalom Sydenstricker), 18
Spanish Civil War, 210, 219, 222, 261
"Speaking as a Mother" (Pearl S. Buck), 216
Spectator (periodical), 157
Spence, Jonathan, 14, 54, 199
Stalin, Josef, 230, 272, 291, 298
Standard Oil Company, 223
Stanton, Elizabeth Cady, 234, 377
Stanwyck, Barbara, 271
Steffens, Lincoln, 144
Steinbeck, John, 217, 261, 346, 364

Stern, Juliet, 148
Stevenson, Adlai, 330
Stimson, Henry, 259
Stowe, Harriet Beecher, 259
Stratton Films, 342
Strauss, Anna Lord, 270
Stravinsky, Igor, 73
Strong, Anna Louise, 89, 172, 183
"Stronghold of Muslim China" (Y. P. Mei), 245
Stulting, Cornelius, 7
Stulting, Hermanus, 6
Stulting, Johann, 6
Suckow, Ruth, 266
Sudetenland, 210
Sullivan, Mark, 266
Sun Yat-sen (Sun Zhongshan), 53–4, 87, 96, 107, 245, 280
Survey Graphic (periodical), 196–7
Swedish Academy, 209, 238
Swenson, Eric, 349
Sydenstricker, Absalom, xiv, 3–11, 16–23, 28–9, 34, 37–44, 47, 51, 59, 61–2, 66, 76–7, 81, 91, 93, 100, 119–20, 134–5, 150–1, 153, 187, 364
Sydenstricker, Alice, 50
Sydenstricker, Arthur, 1, 21
Sydenstricker, Carie Stulting, xiv, 3–4, 6–10, 19–22, 29, 37–44, 47, 51–3, 59, 62, 72–3, 106, 187, 378
Sydenstricker, Clyde, 1, 22
Sydenstricker, Edgar, 1, 10, 21, 23, 29, 50, 82, 87, 118, 152, 176–7
Sydenstricker, Grace (*see* Grace Yaukey)
Sydenstricker, Maud, 1, 19
Symphony Hall (Boston), 262
Sze, Alfred (Shi Zhaoji), 107
Szechuen (Sichuan) province, xix, 219, 254

Tagore, Rabindranath, 172, 245
Tai Li, 280
Taiping Rebellion, 23, 70, 340
Talk About Russia (Pearl S. Buck), 292–5, 298, 306, 320
Tamiroff, Akim, 194, 280
Tan Shih-hua, 173
Tanimoto, Kiyoshi, 337
Tarbell, Ida, 187, 211
Taussig, Helen Brooks, 377
Tawney, R. H., 224, 270
Taylor, Dr., 107
Taylor, Paul, 131, 180

Taylor, Robert, 271
Tell the People (Pearl S. Buck), 285–6, 306
Temple University, 323
"Ten Million Americans for Justice," 337
Tenney, Jack, 317
Tennyson, Alfred, 26
Terrill, Ross, 239, 372–3
Thackeray, William, 26
Thalberg, Irving, 192
Theatre Guild, 146
This Proud Heart (Pearl S. Buck), xvii, 205–7, 215, 221, 230
This Week (periodical), 360
Thomas, Lowell, 172
Thomson, Claude, 93, 101
Thomson, James, xviii, 90
Thomson, Margaret, 93, 183, 188
Thompson, Dorothy, 187, 215, 269, 322–3, 326
Thompson, Malvina, 250
Thoreau, Henry David, 131
Thoughts on Life and Death (William Ernest Hocking), 350
The Three Daughters of Madame Liang (Pearl S. Buck), 369–70, 373
Three Kingdoms, 213
Tibet, 373
Time (periodical), 145, 185, 198, 211, 237, 245, 254, 271, 294, 303, 320, 324–5, 368, 376
The Time Is Noon (Pearl S. Buck), 180, 363
The Times (London), 299
Times Literary Supplement, 157, 242
Timperley, H. J., 160
Tinker, Chauncey Brewster, 324
To My Daughters (Pearl S. Buck), 364
Tobacco Road (Erskine Caldwell), 131
Tobias, Channing, 262
Today and Forever (Pearl S. Buck), 242
"The Today Show" (television), 336, 371
Tokyo, 200, 202, 257, 345
Toler, Sidney, 199
Tolstoy, Leo, 213
Town Hall (New York), 152, 187, 223, 268, 278
The Townsman (John Sedges [Pearl S. Buck]), 288–90, 305
"Toy Monkey" (song), 31
"The Traffic in Women," 173
Tragic America (Theodore Dreiser), 180
Trans-Siberian Railroad, 45, 295
Travers, Henry, 146
Treaty of Nanking, 14

Trippe, Juan, 245
Truman, Harry, 318, 320
Ts'ai Yuan-p'ei (Cai Yuanpei), 73
Tubman, Harriet, 266, 377
Tucker, Sophie, 355
Tugwell, Rexford, 145
Tung Chih (Tongzhi), 27
Turner, Martha, 217
Tuskegee Institute, 259, 314
Twain, Mark (Samuel Clemens), 40, 210
"The Twain Shall Meet" (East and West Association), 300
Twilight in Berlin (Martha Turner), 217
Tynan, Kenneth, 343
Tz'u-hsi (Cixi), 26, 198, 338–41

UCR (see United China Relief)
UMT (see Universal Military Training bill)
Undset, Sigrid, 209
United China Relief (UCR), 243, 318, 371
United Nations, 290–1, 310, 314, 372
United Nations Information Center, 301
United Nations Educational Social and Cultural Organization (UNESCO), 364
United Nations Reconstruction and Relief Agency, 284
United States Department of Agriculture, 56, 71
United States Department of State, 291, 301, 363, 373
United States Employment Service, 258
United States Public Health Service, 176
United States Red Cross, 259, 265
United States Steel Corporation, 223
United States Supreme Court, 334, 337
United States Treasury Department, 178, 181, 363
"Unity at Home, Victory Abroad" (Pearl S. Buck), 262
Universal Military Training bill (UMT), 308, 323
University of Alabama, 314
University of Chicago, 114, 119, 178, 343
University of Minnesota, 240
University of Pennsylvania, 320
University of Toledo, 365
University of Virginia, 184–5
University of Wisconsin, 293
Unzen, Japan, 93–6, 221
Updike, John, 381
Urey, Harold, 269
Utley, Freda, 231

Valiant, Margaret, 297
Van Doren, Carl, 145, 209
Van Doren, Irita, 291
Van Doren, Mark, 174, 323
Van Gelder, Robert, 235
"Variations in the Spoken Language of Northern and Central China" (Absalom Sydenstricker), 18
Vassar College, 46
Verdun military cemetery, 158
Vernon, Mabel, 185
Versailles Conference, 81, 348
Versailles Treaty, 74, 172, 306
Vineland Training School, 111, 115, 121, 146, 178, 188–90, 328, 356, 365
Vineyard Haven (Massachusetts), 226
Voice of America, 341
Von Pustau, Erna, 306

Wakeman, Frederic, 53
Waldorf-Astoria Hotel (New York city), 145, 243
"Wales, Nym" (see Helen Foster Snow)
Waln, Nora, 374
Walsh, Cheiko, 341, 375
Walsh, Edgar, 188, 198, 376
Walsh, Elizabeth, 212
Walsh, Henriette, 328, 334, 375
Walsh, Janice, 80, 87, 88, 116, 121, 133, 146, 164, 171, 177, 183, 198, 226
Walsh, Jean, 188, 198, 330
Walsh, John Stulting, 188, 198
Walsh, Richard, xv, 112–13, 119, 122–3, 132, 143, 153, 156–61, 166, 170–5, 177, 181, 188, 202, 211, 215, 226, 229–30, 234, 237, 243–5, 268, 273, 276, 282, 285, 297, 304, 309, 320, 323, 328, 330, 332–3, 334, 363, 378
Walsh, Richard, Jr., 333, 371
Walsh, Richard Stulting, 188, 198
Walsh, Ruby, 112, 156, 182
Walsh, Tsuta, 375
Walter, Greg, 367–8
Wang amah, 23
"Wang Lung" (working title of *The Good Earth*), 106, 118, 119
Wang Ying, 287, 374
"A Warning About China" (Pearl S. Buck), 273, 324
"Warning to Free Nations" (Pearl S. Buck), 248
Warren, Earl, 334
Warren, Stanley, 57

Washington and Lee College, 5
Washington, George, 24
The Washington Post (newspaper), 323
Washington University, 343
Watson, Thomas J., 238, 245
Weatherbee, Mary Lee, 324
Webb, Beatrice, 157
Webb, Sidney, 157
Webster, Paul Francis, 344
Weeks, Edward, 145, 209
Wei Taoming, 281
Wei, Mrs. Y. H., 328
Weimar Germany, 306
Welcome House (adoption agency), xi, 313–4, 327, 328, 330, 336, 338, 341, 353–4, 356, 364, 368, 371
Welles, Orson, 216, 317
Wellesley College, 41, 46, 105
Wernher, Hilda, 344
West, Nathanael, 229
"Western Weapons in the Hands of the Reckless East" (Pearl S. Buck), 200
Westminster Theological Seminary (Philadelphia), 154
Weybright, Victor, 196
"What Women Can Do For Peace" (Pearl S. Buck), 216
Wharton, Edith, 157, 261, 307–8
Wharton School, 320
Wheat and Soldiers (Ashihei Hino), 222
Wheeler, John Archibald, 367
Wherry, Kenneth S., 317
White, Emma Edmunds, 48, 50, 58, 63, 77, 90, 94, 102, 106, 115, 123, 128, 133, 141, 158–9, 175, 181, 184, 196, 198, 200, 203, 226, 298, 300, 309, 322, 334, 341, 362
White, Locke, 63, 77
White, Marjorie, 338
The White Sahibs in India (Reginald Reynolds), 173
White, Theodore, 324–5
White, Walter, xvi, 250, 265, 282, 305
White, William Allen, 122, 223
White, William C., 309
"Why They Go to Yenan" (Jack Chen), 245
"The Widening Interests of the Family" (Eleanor Roosevelt), 152
Wilder, Thornton, 143, 261
Wilkins, Roy, 151, 259, 347
William Dean Howells Medal, xii, 187
Williams, Cenie J., Jr., 374
Williams College, 186

Williams, Joan, 210
Williams, John, 91
Williams, Ted, 249
Williams Tennessee, 261
Williams, William Carlos, 261
Willkie, Wendell, 243, 244, 270
WILPF (see Women's International League for Peace and Freedom)
Wilson, Edmund, 144, 153, 180
Wilson, Richard, 366
Wilson, Volney, 343
Wilson, Woodrow, 348
Wiltsie, Van, 64
"Winds of Heaven" (working title of *East Wind, West Wind*), 106, 112
Winesburg, Ohio (Sherwood Anderson), 288
WIP Radio, 368
The Wizard of Oz (film), 194
Wolfe, Thomas, 187, 210, 261
Woman in the Nineteenth Century (Margaret Fuller), 247
Woman's Christian Temperance Union, 234
Woman's Day (periodical), 364
Woman's Home Companion (periodical), 112, 153, 170, 180
"Woman's Next Step" (*New York Times* symposium), 241–2
"A Woman's Novel" (*Newsweek*), 303
"Woman's World" (*Time*), 303
"Women: A Minority Group" (Pearl S. Buck), 232
"Women and International Relations" (Pearl S. Buck), 155
"Women in China Today" (Pearl S. Buck), 152
"Women of Letters" (NBC), 230
Women's Aid Committee, 211
Women's Hall of Fame (1964 New York World's Fair), 358
Women's International League for Peace and Freedom (WILPF), 185, 231, 261, 318, 326, 337–8, 356, 358
Woods, Katherine, 209, 248
Woollcott, Alexander, 145
Woolf, S. J., 208

Woolf, Virginia, 236, 248
Work of Art (Sinclair Lewis), 167
Works Progress Administration (WPA), 216
World Health Organization (WHO), xv, xvi, 379
World Literature (periodical), 345, 373
World War I, 74, 79, 112, 149, 207, 222, 285, 306, 320
World War II, 105, 133, 135, 186, 219–21, 226–7, 250–96
WPA (see Works Progress Administration)
WQXR (radio), 223
Wright, Frank Lloyd, 73
Wright, Richard, 232, 261
Wu Pei-fu (Wu Peifu), 89
Wu T'ing-fang (Wu Tingfang), 16
Wuhan, 53, 90, 133
W. W. Norton (publisher), 349

Yale-in-China, 156
Yale Review (periodical), 142
Yale University, 178, 240, 268
Yangtze River (Jinsha Jiang), 21, 68, 89, 91, 133–4, 141, 222, 224, 227, 254
Yaukey, Anne, 176
Yaukey, Grace, xix, 20, 29, 39–41, 50, 51, 67, 90, 100, 102, 134, 143, 152, 175–6, 207, 212, 239, 243, 263, 264, 266, 267, 308, 342, 372, 375
Yaukey, Jesse, 90, 176
Yaukey, Raymond, 90, 330
Yeats, William Butler, 93
Yen, James (Yan Yangchu), xix, 118, 285–6, 293, 310
Yenan (Yan'an), 202, 219
Young, Loretta, 271
The Young Revolutionist (Pearl S. Buck), 140–1
Young Women's Christian Association (YWCA), 234
Yoyang (Yueyang), 160
Yuan, H. L., 373
Yüan Shih-k'ai (Yuan Shikai), 54, 57

Zanuck, Darryl, 302

Printed in the United States
43841LVS00003B/40